Short Notes
on
FOOD SAFETY OFFICER EXAMINATION

(Main subject: A Subjective Approach)

By

SURESH CHANDRA

Ph.D. (Agri. Process and Food Engineering)
Assistant Professor (Agri. Process and Food Engg.)
Department of Agricultural Engineering and Food Technology
Sardar Vallabhbhai Patel University of Agriculture and Technology, Meerut (UP)

&

DURVESH KUMARI

M.Sc. (Food Science and Technology)
Manager Gr.-III (Quality Assurance)
Parag Dairy (GDUSS), Meerut (UP)

2023

JAIN BROTHERS (New Delhi)

16/873, East Park Road, Near Dr. N. C. Joshi Hospital,
Karol Bagh, New Delhi - 110 005
Phones : 011-23618426, 45097398
E-mail : jain_bros@hotmail.com
Website : www.thejainbrothers.com

Published by :

Shri Sunil Kumar Jain
for
Jain Brothers (New Delhi)
16/873, East Park Road, Karol Bagh, New Delhi-110 005
Phones : 011-23618426, 45097398

Branch Office at :

1. **M/s Sunil Book Service**
   Fatima Nagar, Opp. Andhra Bank,
   KAZIPET-506004 (A.P.)
   Ph. : 0870-2459617, Mob. : 9390115435
   E-mail : kpkulshrestha@yahoo.com
2. **M/s Jain Brothers**
   Vidya Vihar, Pilani (Rajasthan)
   Phone : 01596-242144

First edition : 2014
Second edition : 2016
Third edition : 2017
Fourth edition : 2018
Reprint : 2019
Fifth edition : Sept., 2019
Sixth edition : Jan., 2020
Reprinted : March, 2020
Reprinted with additions : Oct, 2021
Reprinted with additions : Aug., 2022
Seventh edition : Nov., 2022
Eighth edition : Oct., 2023

Price : ₹ **425.00**

ISBN: 978-81-8360-214-3

Laser Typesetting by :

Niyati *Graphics*
754/23, Khajoor Road,
Karol Bagh, New Delhi

Printed by : Balaji Offset Printers, Dayabasti, Delhi-35

SOCIETY FOR WORLD ENVIRONMENT, FOOD AND TECHNOLOGY (SWEFT), I-18, JIA SARAI, NEW DELHI-110016

DR. B. P. NILARATNA, IAS (Rtd.)
B.Sc., LL.B., M.A., M.Sc. P.G.D.M.
Ph.D. (Leeds), D. Litt.
President
(Former Managing Director,
Pradeshik Cooperative Dairy
Federation (PCDF), Govt. of U.P

Foreword

Agriculture is the backbone of Indian farmers. About 70 percent of Indian population depends on agriculture and its related sectors for livelihood. Agriculture provides about 95 percent of the world's food requirement. Food products are tailored made to meet specific requirements in terms of functionality, nutrition requirement and therapeutic aspects. Consumers clearly believe in the concept of both 'convenience and better for you attitudes'. They are interested in those food products which boost the immune system, reduce the risk of disease and enhance health. Consumers prescribe these food products for themselves and their families. Consumers are increasingly demanding new and different taste experiences from food products that are also competitive for prices.

Food processing in India is growing with an annual growth rate of 17 percent. These processes consist of all operations that modify chemically and/or physically the characteristics of raw products with the aim to extend its shelf life or to convert it into a form that is better suited for marketing and consumption. Assurance of food quality microbiologically is a great cause of concern today among the consumers. The application of rapid microbial monitoring and adulteration is hindered due to the lack of knowledge of hazards caused by different types of microbes in different food products. Various food products in the market for domestic use can cause serious problems when they are contaminated with harmful microorganisms due to lack of proper sanitary conditions, hygienic practices, proper storage and mishandling.

I hope the efforts put up by the authors of the Book "**Short notes on Food Safety Officer Examination**" will be of immense use in understanding overall content for the examination. This Book will be very helpful to students who have the eligibility in the field of Food Technology / Dairy Technology / Biotechnology / Oil Technology / Agriculture Science / Veterinary Science / Biochemistry / Microbiology / Chemistry / Medicine.

I wish and acknowledge this benevolent endeavour of the authors a grand success.

Dr. B. P. Nilaratn

New Delhi

Dated: 30.09.2014

Preface

The processing of food is no longer as simple or straightforward as in the past. It is now moving from an art to a highly interdisciplinary science. A number of new preservation techniques are being developed to satisfy current demands of economic preservation and consumer satisfaction in nutritional and sensory aspects, convenience, absence of preservatives, low demand of energy, and environmental safety. Better understanding and manipulation of these conventional and sophisticated preservation methods could help to develop high-quality, safe products by better control of the processes and efficient selection of ingredients. The overall goal of the food processing industry is to convert raw materials into high valued finished products at the lowest cost. Due to significant variations in raw material properties, the main challenge of the food process engineer/food technologist is to produce a final product of consistent quality. It is extremely important that the food engineer be aware of the latest scientific advances that would allow for the production of the highest quality products.

Innovative technology in preservation is being developed in the food industry that can extend shelf life; minimize risk; is environment friendly; or can improve functional, sensory, and nutritional properties. The large and ever-increasing number of food products and new preservation techniques available today creates a great demand for an up-to-date handbook of food preservation methods. Food processing needs to use preservation techniques ranging from simple to sophisticated; thus, any food process must acquire requisite knowledge about the methods, the technology, and the science of mode of action. Keeping this in mind, this book has been developed to discuss the fundamental and practical aspects of most of the food preservation methods important to practicing industrial and academic food scientists, technologists, and engineers as well as Food Safety Officer.

This book contains a huge accumulation of subjective material as per syllabus. It is very much hoped that the subject matter will create a confidence among the candidates and the books will help them like an ideal teach.

Though the book is sure to make more useful to the readers it is earnestly hoped that suggestions to improve the book shall be forthcoming from the readers. Great acknowledges are assured. In last, authors are thanks to Mr. S.K. Jain for The Jain Brothers, New Delhi; give us an opportunity to publish this important book in the favor of student's keen interest.

SURESH CHANDRA
DURVESH KUMARI

Food Safety Officer, Food and Drug Administration, Group-B (Maharashtra)

अन्न सुरक्षा अधिकारी, अन्न व औषध प्रशासन, गट-ब

परीक्षेचे टप्पे: 1) लेखी परीक्षा- 200 गुण 2) मुलाखत- 50 गुण

-: परीक्षा योजना :-

विषय व सांकेतांक	माध्यम	गुण	प्रश्नसंख्या	कालावधी	दर्जा	प्रश्नपत्रिकेचे स्वरुप
सामान्य ज्ञान, बुद्धिमापन चाचणी- आणि विषयांशी/विभागाशी संबंधीत घटक-916	इंग्रजी	200	100	एक तास	पदवी	वस्तुनिष्ठ बहुपर्यायी

अंतीम गुणवत्ता यादी ही वस्तुनिष्ठ परीक्षेतील व मुलाखतीतील एकत्रित गुणांवर आधारीत राहील

: अभ्यासक्रम :

सामान्य ज्ञान, बुद्धीमापन चाचणी आणि विषयांशी/विभागाशी संबंधीत कटक यामध्ये खालील घटक व उपघटकांचा समावेश असेल।

अनु.क्र. घटक व उप घटक

(1) सामान्य ज्ञान

i. माहिती अधिकारी कायदा- 2005
ii. भारतीय राज्यघटना
iii. सगणक व माहिती तंत्रज्ञान
iv. मानवी हक्क व जाबाबदान्या
v. जागतिक तसेच भारतातील चालू घडामोडी-राजकीय, आद्योगिक, आर्थिक, सामाजिक, शैक्षणिक, भौगोलिक, खलोगशास्त्रीय, सांस्कृतिक, वैज्ञानिक, इ.
vi. बुद्धिमापन विषयक प्रश्न- उमेदवार किती लवकर व अचूकपणे विचार करु शकतील याचा अंदाज घेण्याच्या दृष्टिने सदर प्रश्न विचारण्यात येतील,

(2) विषयांशी/विभागाशी संबंधीत घटक

I. CHEMISRTY

i. Periodic Table/ Concepts of Qualitative Analysis.
ii. Bonding & structure of organic compound and their nomenclature.
iii. Mechanism of organic Reactions Alkanels and Cycloalkanes.
iv. Chemical calculations -Introduction to Molecular Spectroscopy.
v. Chemical Thermodynamics.
vi. Industrial Organic Chemistry.
vii. Aromatic Hydrocarbons -Haloarenes, Phenols, Ether and Epoxides.
viii. Source of Organic Compounds Chemical Industry

II INTRODUCTION TO FOOD

i. Carbohydrates, Proteins, Fats, Fibers, Vitamins, Minerals, ME etc
ii. Effect of Food Processing on Food Nutrition.
iii. Basics of Food Safety.
iv. Food Contaminants (Microbial, Chemical, Physical)
v. Food Adulteration (Common Adulterants, Simple Tests for Detection of Adulteration).
vi. Food Additives (Classification, Functional Role, Safety issues)

vii. Food Packaging & Labelling (Packaging types, Understanding labelling rules and Regulations, Nutritional labelling, Labeling requirements for pre-packaged food as per CODEX)

(3) INTRODUCTION OF FOOD PROCESSING AND TECHNOLOGY.

i. F&VP, Milk, Meat, Oil, Grain milling, Tea-Coffee, Spices and Condiments processing.
ii. Food Processing Techniques (Minimal processing technologies, Photochemical processes, Pulsed electric field, Hurdle technology).
iii. Food Preservation Techniques (Pickling, Drying, Smoking, Curing, Canning, Bottling, Jellying, Modified atmosphere, Pasteurization etc.)

(4) CODEX ALIMENTARIUS COMMISSION (CODEX)

i. Introduction.
ii. Standards. Codex of practice, Guidelines and Recommendations.
iii. Applying Codex Standards.
iv. Codex India – Role of Codex Contact point, National Codex Contact Point (NCCP)
v. Core functions of NCCP-India.
vi. National Codex Committee of India-TOR (Terms of Reference), Functions, Shadow Committees etc

(5) EMERGING ISSUES IN FOOD PROCESSING

i. Organic food.
ii. Identifying Organic Foods, Advantages, The Organic Certification Process, Organic food labeling.
iii. GM food.
iv. Why are GM food produced. Main issues of concern for Human Health, How are GM Food regulated Internationally, Regulation in India.
v. Role of WHO to improve evaluation of GM food.
vi. Benefits and Controversies.
vii. Irradiated Food
viii. How is food Irradiated, Sources of radiations used.
ix. Potential uses of Food Irradiation.
x. Labelling of Irradiated Food.
xi. Freeze dried food
xii. Definition, Principle of Freeze-drying, Process.
xiii. The benefits of Freeze-Drying.
xiv. Functional Foods and Nutraceuticals.
xv. Functional foods from plant sources, Animal sources.
xvi. Nutraceuticals, Dietary supplements, Regulation.
xvii. Nano-tech in food processing.
xviii. What is Nanotechnology, use in food products and processing.
xix. Food Fortification and Modification.

(6) FSSAI Act 2006

i. Food Safety and Standards Act, 2006
ii. Major aspects of the act.

(7) ADVANCES IN FOOD SAFETY & QUALITY MANAGEMENT

i. Pre-requisite Programme – Good Hygienic Practices (GHP)
ii. Objective, Scope & Use, Key aspects of Hygiene Control Systems etc.
iii. Pre-requisite Programme – Good Manufacturing Practices (GMP)
iv. What is GMP, GMP in Food Industry etc.
v. Food Safety Management Systems – HACCP
vi. HACCP seven Principles, HACCP Applications
vii. HACCP based SOPs by USDA
viii. Food Safety Management Systems – ISO 22000
ix. Key elements of ISO 22000
x. What does ISO 22000 bring to the HACCP Method
xi. Why to use ISO 22000
xii. Quality Management Systems – ISO 9001
xiii. Introduction, Clauses of ISO9001:2000
xiv. Documentation Structure of ISO 9001 : 2000
xv. Quality Manual, Mandatory Procedures, SOP's, Formats and Records etc.

(8) OTHER RELATED ACTS.

i. B.I.S
ii. C.R.P.C / I.P.C.
iii. EC (Essential Commodities Act)
iv. Consumer Protection Act.

FOOD SAFETY OFFICER EXAMINATION
SYLLABUS
(Uttar Pradesh)

The competitive examination comprises two successive stages viz:-

Paper-I General Studies	**75 Questions**	**150 Marks**	**01 Hour**	**9.30A.M. to 10.30A.M.**
Paper-II Main Subject	**125 Questions**	**250 Marks**	**02 Hours**	**2.30 P.M. to 4.30 P.M.**

Personality Test will be of 50 marks.

This test will relate to the matter of General Interest keeping in view of general awareness, intelligence, character, personality, expression power and general suitability for the service.

The paper of General Studies will include questions on the following topics:-

1. General Science
2. Current Events of National and International Importance
3. History of India
4. Indian National Movement
5. Indian Polity and Economy
6. World Geography and Population.

Question on **General Science** will cover general appreciation and understanding of Science, including matters of everyday observation and experience, as may be expected of a well educated person who has not made a special study of any scientific discipline.

In History of India emphasis should be on broad understanding of economic, Social, Cultural and Political aspects of Indian History. In Indian National Movement, the candidates are expected to have a synoptic view of the nature and character of the Indian freedom movement, growth of nationalism and attainment of Independence. In Indian Polity and Economy questions will test knowledge of the candidate pertaining to Indian Polity including the Indian Constitution, Panchayati Raj and community Development, broad features of Indian economy and planning. In world geography and population, only General understanding of the subject will be expected with emphasis on physical/ecological, economic and socio-demographic aspects of Geography of India.

Candidates are expected to have general awareness about the above topics with special reference to Uttar Pradesh.

The paper of **main subject** will include questions on the following topics:-

Desirable and Potentially undesirable food constituents and their importance. Water, Carbohydrates, Lipids, Proteins, Vitamins, Minerals: Classes, Nomenclature, structure and their chemistry.

Enzymes: Nomenclature, Classification and specificity of enzymes, enzyme Kinetics, enzymes and their role in modification of foods. Single cell protein (SCP). Metabolic Pathways: Carbohydrates, proteins and fats, catabolism and anabolism, Digestion and absorption, Assimilation and Transport of nutrients in human beings.

General characteristics of microorganism: Classification, morphology, physiology, growth, nutrition and reproduction; Pure culture techniques and maintenance of cultures, control of microorganism. Sources of contamination. Microbiological standards of foods. Food poisoning and food borne infections, Food toxins, food plant sanitation, inspection and control, personnel hygiene, beneficial microorganisms and their utilization in food fermentation.

Balance diet, Recommended Dietary Allowances (RDA), Dietary utilization and disturbances, Functions and energy values of foods, Basal energy metabolism: BV, NPU, BMR, PER calculations, Protein quality as reference protein. Dietary allowances and standards for different age groups, Techniques for assessment of human nutritional status, Causes and preventions of malnutrition. Biochemical, clinical manifestation & preventive measures due to vitamins deficiency. Diseases caused due to food adulteration.

Basic knowledge of major Indian crops, their total production, losses in storage, storage of perishable and non-perishable foods, Storage requirements: Storage environment and its interaction with stored product; temperature and moisture migration. Storage practices (including fumigation and aeration of stored product). Storage structures for Perishable and non perishables: bulk storage structures (bins and silos) Modified and Controlled atmosphere storage systems.

Technology of fruits and vegetable products: Juices, pulp, Puree, Paste, Ketchup, Sauce, soup, concentrates and powders, Squashes and cordials. Beverage: Still and carbonated. James, Jellies and Marmalades. Preserves, candies and crystallized fruits.

Processing of oilseeds Pretreatments of oilseeds, oil milling, solvent extraction, impurities present in oils and fats. Vegetable oil refining, hydrogenation, enter esterification, processing of de-oiled cake into protein products, textured protein. Peanut butter, Margarine and Spread. Different quality parameters: Peroxide value, Saponification value, Iodine value, acid value, RM value, Polanski value, Adulteration and its detection in oils and fats. Rancidity, auto oxidation and anti-oxidants.

Fluid Milk: Physico-chemical properties, Production and collection, cooling and transportation of milk. Clarification and filtration of milk, pasteurized and homogenized milk.: Whole, Standardized, Toned, Double toned, skim and special milks, Test for milk quality and detection of dairy adulterant. Milk products: cream, butter, Butter oil/Ghee, Cheese, Curd and Yoghurt, Sweet meat, Ice cream. Evaporated and Condensed milk, milk powders. Indian Dairy Products, Manufacture of casein, and Lactose. Causes and prevention of defects in dairy products.

Scientific slaughtering, Tendering and curing of meat, Beef Mutton, Pork Sausages and other meat products. Fish and poultry processing. Physical, Chemical Nutritional and Functional characteristics of Egg. Processing of Egg and egg products.

Principle underlying spoilage and preservation of foods: Low and high temperature, drying and dehydration, chemical, salt and sugar, Radiation, HHP, hurdle technology,

Parboiling and Milling of paddy, Quality characteristics, Curing and aging of rice, Processed rice products. Wheat milling into flour and semolina, Flour grades and their suitability for baking purposes, Flour quality, Macaroni products, Baked products: Bread, Biscuits and cakes, Breakfast cereals. Dry and Wet milling of corn, Starches and its conversion products, Malting of barely, beer, wine, cider, vinegar, Milling of legume-pulses.

Spices: Composition, Structure and characteristics. Preservation and processing of spices, Processing of Tea and coffee, cocoa processing, chocolate and confectionary products.

Concept of food packaging, polymeric, glass, metal packaging materials, Aseptic Packaging. Newer trends, Package printing, Packaging Laws and Regulations, Evaluation of food packaging materials and package performance.

Quality Control/Quality Assurance, Legislation for food safety: National and International criteria, sampling, records, risk analysis and management. Microbial contamination, Nutritional imbalance. Pesticide residues, permitted food additives. Relevant Foods laws: PFA, FPO. SWMA, MPO, Ag Mark, and BIS Standards. Food Safety and Standard Act (FSSA). Testing food for its safety. The HACCP system and food Safety management systems used in Controlling microbiological hazards. Food standards and Specifications, NABL and ISO certification requirements.

RAJASTHAN PUBLIC SERVICE COMMISSION

SYLLABUS FOR SCREENING TEST FOR THE POST OF

FOOD SAFETY OFFICER

MEDICAL AND HEALTH SERVICES DEPARTMENT

Exam Pattern : *The exam pattern is as follows:*

- The Exam Will Be **Objective Type.**
- The Exam Will Be Screening Type (Online/Offline).
- Maximum Marks : 150
- Number of Questions : 150
- Duration of Paper : Three Hours
- All Questions carry equal marks.
- There will be Negative Marking
- Detailed Exam Pattern Will be Provided Separately on the Official Website of RPSC.

Exam Syllabus : The Exam Syllabus is as follows:

UNIT-I: Chemical bonds and forces, concept of pH and buffer, thermo chemistry, chemical equilibrium, chemical kinetics. Aliphatic and Aromatic hydrocarbons-concept of aromaticity, methods of preparation and chemical properties of alcohols, phenols, aldehydes, ketones, carboxylic acids, nitro compounds and amines. Different methods of purification, qualitative and quantitative analysis. Solutions-concentration terms, liquid-properties, surface tension, viscosity and its applications. Surface chemistry-adsorption, homogeneous and heterogeneous catalysis, colloids and suspension.

UNIT-II: Types of micro organism associated with food,their morphology and structure, factors affecting their growth, microbiological standards, sources of micro organism in food, some important food spoilage micro organisms, fermentation-definition and types, micro organisms used in food fermentation, dairy fermentation, fermented foods-types, methods of manufacture for vinegar, sauerkraut, soya sauce, beer, wine and traditional Indian foods.

UNIT-III: Bio molecules-carbohydrates, proteins, lipids and nucleic acids,their classification. structure, bio synthesis, metabolism and calorific value. Enzymes-classification, kinetics, factors controlling enzyme activities, enzymes used during food processing, modification of food by endogenous enzymes. Vitamins and their types. Minerals-important minerals and their functions in human body. Plant alkaloids and their uses. Animal and plant toxins. Toxic substances and their metabolism-pesticides, metals, food additives etc.

UNIT-IV: Classification-five kingdom system upto phylum, plants and animal products used as food by human. Culture of animals used as food. Eukaryotic and Prokaryotic cells. Types of cells, animal tissues and organs. Human physiology-Nutrition and Digestion. Respiration-respiratory pigment, transport and gaseous exchange. Excretion-structure of kidney and urine formation. Circulatory system-Heart, Blood vascular system, blood and its components.Nervous system-conduction of impulses. muscular system-types of muscles and muscle contraction. Reproductive system. Endocrine system-hormones and their role. Immune system-types of immunity, antigen-antibody reaction. Diseases-deficiency diseases, communicable diseases and diseases caused by animals (protozoans, helminthes, arthropodans).

UNIT–V: Genetically modified plants and animals, plant and animal tissue culture and its application, importance of GM-crops and their products, environmental bio technology-pollutants, Bio magnification and microbial bioremediation. Statistical analysis-mean, median, mode, standard deviation, regression and co-relation, T-test, variance, chi-square test.

UNIT-VI: Salient features of agriculture with special reference to Rajasthan. Soil Fertility and Management of Problematic Soils in Rajasthan. Introduction to Dry land Farming and Agro-forestry. Introductory knowledge about Production Techniques of important field crops (Wheat,Mustard, Groundnut, Pulses, Bajra, Maize). Horticultural crops (Citrus, Mango,Guava, Ber, Onion, Tomato, Cucurbits, Chilli, Rose etc.)Spices and Medicinal crops (Cumin, Fenugreek, Fennel, Coriander, Isabgol, Aloevera, etc.) Important diseases and Pests of major Crops and their Management.Importance of agriculture marketing. General awareness about Seed science and Crop Physiology.

UNIT-VII: Importance of Livestock in Economy of Rajasthan. Fundamentals of Livestock and Poultry Production. Artificial insemination and Pregnant animal management. Laboratory diagnostics, Important diseases of livestock and their management. Present status of Milk and Milk products. Milk production and quality of milk. Milk processing and packaging. Dairy equipments and utilities. Introduction to livestock products.

UNIT-VIII: Present status of Food Technology in India and Rajasthan. General methods of food preservation and food processing. Importance of Post harvest technology of fruits and vegetables. Technology for processed products like Squash, Jelly, Sauce, Pickles etc.Post harvest Physiology and handling of fruits and vegetables. Types and functions of Packaging materials used in fresh and processed food. Food laws -brief review of regulatory status in India (FPO, Prevention of Food adulteration Act, Food Safety and Standard Act, Testing Food for its Safety, AGMARK). Hygiene and Sanitation (HACCP, Good Manufacturing Practices, Good Laboratory Practices etc.)

UNIT-IX: Pre & Early history of Rajasthan. Age of Rajput: Major dynasties of Rajasthan and the achievements of prominent rulers.Emergence of Modern Rajasthan: factors of Socio-Political awakening of 19th century; Peasants and tribal movements of 20thcentury; Political struggle of 20th century and the integration of Rajasthan.

UNIT-X: Visual Art of Rajasthan-Architecture of forts and temples of Rajasthan; Sculpture traditions of Rajasthan and various schools of painting of Rajasthan.Performing Art of Rajasthan -Folk music and musical instruments of Rajasthan; folk dance and folk drama of Rajasthan.

UNIT-XI: Various religious cults, saints and folk deities of Rajasthan.Various dialects and its distribution in Rajasthan; literature of Rajasthani language.

UNIT-XII: Broad physical features-Mountains, Plateaus, Plains & Desert; Major rivers and lakes; Climate and Agro-climatic regions; Major soil types and distribution; Major forest types and distribution; Demographic characteristics; Desertification, Droughts & Floods, Deforestation, Environmental Pollution and Ecological Concerns.

UNIT-XIII: Major Minerals-Metallic & Non-Metallic; Power Resources-Renewable and Non Renewable; Major agro based industries-Textile, Sugar, Paper & Vegetable oil; Poverty and Unemployment; Agro food parks

UNIT-XIII: Major Minerals-Metallic & Non-Metallic; Power Resources-Renewable and Non Renewable; Major agro based industries-Textile, Sugar, Paper & Vegetable oil; Poverty and Unemployment; Agro food parks.

UNIT-XIV: Important Persons, Places and Current events of the State.National and International events of importance. National and International Organisations-(BIS, ICMR, ICAR, Council for Social Welfare, APEDA, Export inspection Council, FAO,WHO, ISO, WTO).

Contents

CHAPTER 1

FOOD CHEMISTRY

1.1 DESIRABLE AND POTENTIALLY UNDESIRABLE FOOD CONSTITUENTS AND THEIR IMPORTANCE

Nutrients are the compounds in food that provide us with energy that facilitate growth and repair of tissues and helps to carryout different life processes. An individual food may contain only a few nutrients, or it may supply many, but no single food provides all nutrients in amounts and proportions necessary for adequate health. However, if the total diet supply all essential nutrients, the cells and body organs can synthesize many thousands of additional metabolically important substances. Carbohydrates, fats, proteins, vitamins and minerals comprise the general class of desired nutrients. The first three classes serve as major source of fuel.

In addition, proteins also supply essential amino acids and serve as a source of utilizable nitrogen for cell and tissue protein synthesis. Amino acids may also serve as precursor for metabolically active compounds. *Example*: tryptophan and tyrosine for neurotransmitter; tryptophan for niacin; tyrosine for iodothyronines; lysine for carnitine formation. These uses of the amino acids may be of little quantitative importance, in terms of total daily intake, but they have considerable physiological significance.

Dietary carbohydrates are important source of energy intake. The nutritionally important carbohydrates are:- (*a*) the monosaccharides (glucose or fructose), (*b*) disaccharides (sucrose, lactose), (*c*) polysaccharides (starch, glycogen). In human nutrition the celluloses and other plant polysaccharides are not used for energy because they are not hydrolyzed by secretions of the human digestive tract. However, they contribute to dietary fibre intake (unavailable carbohydrates and lignin, a phenyl-propane derivative), which appears to play an important role in the maintenance of normal gastrointestinal function, metabolism and health. Available carbohydrates such as sucrose, lactose and starch are not specifically required for human health as far as is known. However, they contribute about 40% of energy intake.

Fats are concentrated source of dietary energy also serve as carriers of the fat soluble vitamins. Lipids play essential roles in many enzyme reactions and in the maintenance of cell membrane structure and function. Dietary fats are also source of essential fatty acids, such as linoleic (18:2n-6) $C_{18}H_{32}O_2$, linolenic $C_{18}H_{30}O_2$ (18:3n-3), and arachidonic (20:4n-6) $C_{20}H_{32}O_2$ acids which are involved in the maintenance of normal membrane structure and function. In addition, they are precursors of class of "local" hormone, the prostaglandins involving secretion, blood platelets, smooth muscle metabolism and modulation of nervous system activity. Thus it has recently has been shown that an increase in dietary linoleic acids can influence prostaglandins biosynthesis, decrease the thrombotic tendency of blood platelets and improve heart function. Although dietary fats are important in the maintenance of normal metabolism and health, excessive intake can promote disease. It is found from epidemiological studies that excessive intake of saturated fats is one of the risk factor associated with the development of coronary heart disease (CHD) and possible with various types of cancer in human body.

Vitamins and minerals comprise the remaining two classes of essential nutrients. Both vitamins and minerals appear in foods in a variety of forms, the chemical nature of which may have considerable nutritional importance, since it determines whether the nutrient is made available to the body during the process of digestion and absorption. Thus, a measure of the total amount of various nutrients in a food may not be useful information for the nutritionist; it is important to know the fraction of total nutrient content available to the body.

There are 13 vitamins necessary for normal growth, reproduction, and maintenance of health. Their metabolic functions are diverse for example thiamine, pyridoxine, riboflavin, and niacin act as coenzyme, and a low dietary intake of these vitamins causes reduced activities of enzymes associated with energy transfer and utilization in amino acid metabolism.

The mineral elements constitute the final class of nutrients to be discussed. The so-called macro-inognanic elements (sodium, potassium, chlorine, calcium, magnesium, phosphorous) are present in the body in the significant quantities, their combined mass being about 3 kg in adult men. The micro-nutrients or trace minerals are required only in small amounts usually less than 30 mg per day. Their body content is about 30g only.

The major minerals elements such as sodium, potassium, calcium, magnesium and chloride, fulfill electrochemical functions. Calcium, potassium, magnesium, copper and zinc participate as catalysts in enzyme systems, and calcium, phosphorous, and fluorine play a role in maintaining the structure of hard tissues, bones and teeth. Other essential mineral element include iodine for formation of thyroid hormones (tri- and tetraiodothyronine), and iron as constituents of heme as well as enzymes concerned with oxidation-reduction reactions. Dietary iron inadequacy leads to low blood levels of hemoglobin, which is characterized clinically by weakness and reduced capacity to carry out hard physical labour.

1.1.1 Anti-nutrients

They are natural and synthetic compounds that interfere with the absorption of nutrients.

The three board classes of antinutrients are antiproteins, antiminerals, and antivitamins.

Antiproteins: They are substances that interfere with the digestion, absorption, or utilization of proteins. Antiproteins occur in many plants and some animals. Various protease inhibitors inhibit proteolytic enzymes of the gut, usually by binding to the enzyme's active site. Lectins are antiproteins that have binding sites for cell receptors similar to what antibodies have. Consequently, lectins, also called hemaggulutinins, can agglutinate red blood cells. Ovomucoids and ovoinhibitors are found in eggs and inhibit proteolytic enzymes. Egg whites contain chymotrypsin inhibitors. Many are sensitive to heat treatment and are inactivated at boiling temperatures for 15 min. Trypsin and chymotrypsin inhibitors are found in legumes, vegetables, milk, wheat, and potatoes. The trypsin inhibitor found in milk is only destroyed after heating to 85 °C for at least 1 h. Soybean has pancreatic enzyme inhibitors that have been shown in rodents to reduce growth. Elastase inhibitors have been isolated from soybeans, beans, and potatoes. Lectins have been isolated from the legumes soybean, peanut, lima beans, kidney beans, fava beans, lentils, and pea, and potatoes, banana, mango, and wheat germ. These compounds bind avidly to intestinal mucosal cells and interfere with amino acids, thyroxine, and fat absorption; therefore, such lectins are goitrogenic. Ricin is a toxic lectin isolated from castor bean, and is notorious for causing deaths of children who eat raw castor beans as well for being a substance of concern as an instrument of bioterrorism. Ricin's mode of action is through intestinal cell necrosis. Most lectins are inactivated by moist heat; hence, steaming is an effective processing technique used to inactivate ricin in castor oil. However, dry heat is largely ineffective to deactivate lectins.

Antiminerals: Antiminerals are substances that interfere with absorption or metabolic utilization of minerals. Some examples are phytic acid, oxalic acid, glucosinolates, dietary fiber, and gossypol. Phytic acid's negative effect on iron absorption has been known for decades. Phytic acid is found in bran and germ of many plant seeds and in grains, legumes, nuts and species. In addition, phytic acid can compromise the absorption of magnesium, zinc, copper, and manganese, usually forming precipitates. Formation of soybean protein–phytate complexes during processing has been associated with a reduction in bioavailability of minerals such as Ca, Zn, Fe and Mg. On the other hand, fermentation and other processing techniques are useful in reducing phytate levels. Oxalic acid, like phytic acid, reduces the availability of bivalent cations. Sources of oxalate include rhubarb, spinach, beets, potatoes, tea, coffee, and cocoa. Tea drinking was associated with concerns for Ca deficits via complexes, which apparently can be counterbalanced by using milk with tea drinking. Glucosinolates are goitrogenic and inhibit iodine uptake into the thyroid. Rutabaga, turnips, cabbage, peaches and strawberries are good sources for glucosinolates. Decreases in plasma thyroxin for glucosinolate intakes are found at the 15% dietary level in rodent studies. Dietary fiber, even without phytate, can affect calcium, magnesium, zinc and phosphorus absorption. Collectively, dietary fiber refers to food components in plants cell walls that are not digested. Dietary fiber can act like ion exchangers and bind minerals. Gossypol is a phenolic compound isolated from the cotton plant and is capable of chelating iron and binding up amino acids. This major toxic compound makes up 1% of the seed's dry weight. In the 1930s and 40s, outbreaks of infertility in some areas of China were traced to gossypol in cottonseed oil used as a cooking oil. Various processing techniques to isolate the protein can remove 90% of the gossypol. Gossypol also exerts genotoxic effects in mammalian cell cultures, possibly through production of superoxide anions and singlet oxygen induced strand breakage in DNA. It is not known whether any of these adverse effects of gossypol are related to effects on iron metabolism.

Antivitamins: Antivitamins are substances that inactivate or destroy vitamins or inhibit the activity of a vitamin in a metabolic reaction and increase an individual's need for vitamins. Again, the collection of compounds involved as antinutrients is diverse and does not lend itself to simple characterization. For example, ascorbic acid oxidase, an enzyme found in fruits and vegetables, can oxidize ascorbic acid. Hence, in addition to aerobic conditions, fresh juices lose 50% of the vitamin within less than 1 h. Raw fish contains thiaminase, which has antivitamin properties and splits the thiamin at the methylene linkage into two rings. Also, it is known that tannins found in plants destroy thiamin. Mushrooms contain vitamin B6 antagonists, and linatine found in linseed oil is an antipyridoxine factor. Finally, avidin, a heat-sensitive compound found in egg white, forms a complex with biotin.

1.2 WATER

Water can universally be found in the solid, gaseous, and liquid states. Saltwater oceans contain about 96.5% of our global water supply. Ice, the solid form of water, is the most abundant form of freshwater and most of it, nearly 68.7%, is currently trapped in the polar ice caps and glaciers. About 30% of the freshwater sources are present in aquifers as groundwater. The remaining freshwater is surface water in lakes and rivers, soils, wetlands, biota, and atmospheric water vapor. Water is the most abundant and surely the most frequently overlooked component in foods. It is estimated that over 35% of our total water intake comes from the moisture in the foods we consume. The other contributors to our water intake are beverages and metabolic water, which is produced through chemical reactions in the body. The water content of foods can very to large extent. It may be as low as 0% in vegetable oils and as high as 99% in some vegetables and fruit. Water by itself is free of calories and pure water does not contain nutritive substances, but it may be an ingredient itself in foods. Foods are described as dry or low-moisture foods if they have very low water content. These are most often solid food systems. Liquid food systems and tissue foods where water is the dominating constituent of the solution are high-moisture foods. Foods that contain moderate levels of water are *intermediate-moisture foods* (IMFs). These foods contain 15-50 % moisture and water activity between 6 - 9%. IMF can be eaten without rehydration and are microbiologically stable.

For the food industry, water is essential for processing, as a heating or a cooling medium. It may be employed in processes in the form of liquid water or in the other states of water such as ice or steam. Almost all food-processing techniques involve the use or the modification of water in food. Freezing, drying, concentration, and emulsification processes all involve changes in the water content of the food. Without the presence of water, it would not be possible to achieve the physicochemical changes that occur during cooking such as the gelatinization of starch. Water is important as a solvent for dissolving small molecules to form solutions and as a dispersing medium for dispersing larger molecules to form colloidal solutions. The control of *water activity* in foods is an important tool for extending shelf life. It is responsible for the quality of foods affected by microbiological, chemical, and physical changes. The physical properties, quantity, and quality of water within the food have a strong impact on food effectiveness, quality attributes, shelf life, textural properties, and processing.

Food-preservation processes have a common goal of extending the shelf life of foods to allow for storage and convenient distribution. The activity of microorganisms is the first and most dangerous limitation of shelf life. Water is essential for microorganisms that may cause food spoilage if they are present in a food that offers them favorable conditions for growth. Hence, many food preservation techniques were developed to reduce the availability or activity of water in order to eliminate the danger of microbial spoilage. The presence or activity of water in foods may also enhance the rate at which deteriorative chemical reactions occur. Some products may become rancid through free radical oxidation even at low humidities and thus become unacceptable. Labile nutrients such as vitamins and natural color compounds are oxidized more rapidly when stored at low moisture levels. Enzyme-mediated hydrolytic reactions may reduce the quality of the food product. Other reactions such as the Maillard type of non-enzymatic browning may be enhanced by the presence of higher levels of water. On the other hand, water content is crucial for the textural characteristics and the sensory perception of foods. A food may be found unacceptable by consumers simply because it does not satisfy their textural (sensory) anticipation. Some physical properties of water are presented in Table 1.

Table 1: Some physical properties of water (H_2O)

Property	Value
Freezing temperature at 101.3 kPa (1 atm)	0°C
Boiling temperature at 101.3 kPa (1 atm)	100°C
Heat of fusion at 0°C and 1 atm	6.01 kJ/mol
Heat of vaporization at 100°C and 1 atm	40.66 kJ/mol
Heat capacity of water at 20°C	75.33 J/mol K
Heat capacity of ice at 0°C	37.85 J/mol K
Density of water at 20°C	0.998 g/mL
Density of ice at 0°C	0.917 g/mL
Dielectric constant of water at 20°C	80.4

The state and availability of water in food is just as important as the content of water. As a measurable quantity, water activity, expressed as a_w is used to express the availability of water in a food product. It is defined as the partial lowering in partial pressure created by the food and is the ratio of the partial pressure of water in the food to the partial pressure of pure water at the same temperature. Water activity is also equal to the *equilibrium relative humidity* (ERH) divided by 100. Water activity of pure water is 1.0 and microorganisms can not grow in pure water. Water activity in all foods is always a value below 1.0 because water is associated with the surfaces and solutes in the food. Differences among water activities of food components, food domains, and the external environment outside the food induces a driving force of water transport from high a_w to low a_w until a common equilibrium value for the food system is reached.

Moisture sorption isotherm is a graphical representation of the variation in water activity or % ERH with change in moisture content of a sample at a specified temperature. Sorption isotherms of foods are generally nonlinear and very often sigmoid in shape. The difference in the equilibrium water content between the adsorption and desorption curves is called *hysteresis.* The hysteresis phenomenon is observed in highly *hygroscopic materials*. The curve is divided into three regions. In the first region, the water in the food consists of water that is tightly bound to the product. In the second region, there is more water available and it is less tightly bound and present in small capillaries. In the third region, where the food contains higher levels of water and has a high aw, there is plenty of water that is free or loosely held in capillaries. A detailed knowledge of water sorption isotherms is essential in food technology applications such as concentration, dehydration, and drying of foods, as well as in determining the quality, stability, and shelf life of foods.

1.3 CARBOHYDRATES

Carbohydrates are ubiquitous. Every organism contains some carbohydrate. Carbohydrates can range from a simple monosaccharide to a large complex polysaccharide. Polysaccharides in combination with proteins, lipids, and nucleic acids play an important role in many plant and animal metabolic systems. Carbohydrates have many roles in food systems, where they function to provide flavor, structure, and texture to food and nutritional benefits to the consumer. Carbohydrates have general formula $C_x(H_2O)_y$. Carbohydrates are primarily composed of the elements carbon, hydrogen and oxygen. Some of the carbohydrates possess the empirical formula $(C.H_2O)_n$, where $n \geq 3$, satisfying that these carbohydrates are in fact carbon hydrates. Carbohydrates may be defined as optically active polyhydroxy-aldehydes or ketones or compounds which produce them on hydrolysis. They are the most abundant dietary source of energy (4 Calorie per gram) for all organisms. They are ultimate source of most of our food. We cloth ourselves with cellulose in form of cotton, lines and rayon. We build furniture and houses from cellulose in form of wood. Thus carbohydrates provide us with basic necessities of life, food, clothing and shelter. Carbohydrates are often referred to as saccharides. They are broadly classified into three groups – (*i*) monosaccharides, (*ii*) oligosaccharides, and (*iii*) polysaccharides. Mono and oligosaccharides are sweet to taste, crystalline and soluble in water, hence they are commonly known as sugar.

(A) Monosaccharides: Monosaccharides, which represent the most basic carbohydrate elements, are polyhydroxy aldehydes and ketones commonly referred to as aldoses and ketoses, respectively.

These can not be hydrolised to simpler compounds, depending upon total number of carbon atoms in monosaccharides and aldehyde or ketone functional group present. The term used for their classification are given below.

Different types of monosaccharides

Carbon atoms	General term	Aldehydes	Ketones
3	Triose	Aldotriose	Ketotriose
4	Tertose	Aldotetrose	Ketotetrose
5	Pentose	Aldopentose	Ketopentose
6	Hexose	Aldohexose	Ketohexose
7	Heptose	Aldoheptose	Ketoheptose

The most common pentose sugars are D-xylose and L-arabinose, which are both aldoses. The most common hexose sugars are D-glucose, D-galactose, D-mannose, and D-fructose. D-Glucose, D-galactose, and D-mannose are aldoses. When D and L stands for dextrox and laevo.

All carbohydrates are either monosaccharides or get converted to monosaccharides on hydrolysis.

Glucose and fructose are specific example of an aldohexose and ketohexose respectively.

The most common monosaccharides in the human diet are:

1. Glucose, 2. Fructose, 3. Galactose

Glucose **(Dextrose, Grape sugar):** Glucose occurs in nature in free as well as combined form. It is present in sweet fruits and honey. Ripe grapes contain ~ 20 % of glucose. Its molecular formua is $C_6H_{12}O_6$ and sturctural formula is.

$$H-\overset{\overset{O}{\|}}{C}-(HCOH)_4-CH_2OH$$

(*i*) Glucose can be prepared from sucrose (cane sugar) and starch or cellulose.

Glucose has been assigned a straight chain structure. The fischer projections for D-(dextro/ towards right +ve) and L-(laevo rotary/towards left/ –ve) glucose are shown below.

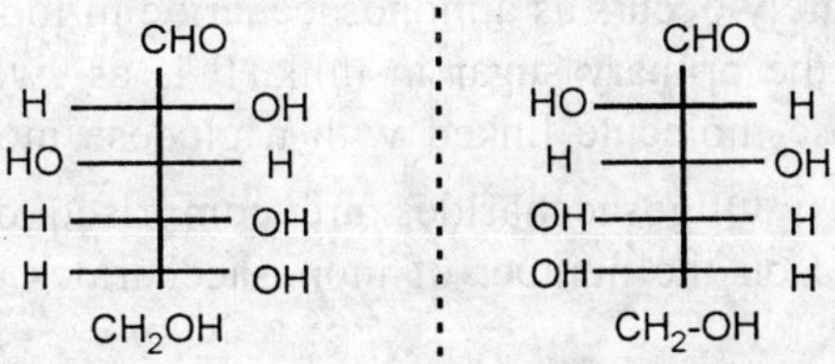

D-Glucose L-Glucose

The monosaccharide glucose is the most abundant simple carbohydrate unit in nature. Also referred to as dextrose, glucose plays a key role in both foods and the body. Glucose gives food a mildly sweet flavor. It doesn't usually exist as a monosaccharide in food but is instead joined to other sugars to form disaccharides, starch, or dietary fiber. Glucose makes up at least one of the two sugar molecules in every disaccharide. Glucose is mainly made by plants and most algae during photosynthesis from water and carbon

In the body, glucose supplies energy to cells. The body closely regulates blood glucose (blood sugar) levels to assure a constant fuel source for vital body functions. Glucose is virtually the only fuel used by the brain, except during prolonged starvation when the glucose supply is low.

Fructose: Also called levulose or fruit sugar, *fructose tastes the sweetest of all the sugars*– it is what commonly sweetens colas and other soft drinks. It is naturally in fruits and vegetables. Although the sugar in honey is about half fructose and half glucose, fructose is the primary source of the sweet taste. Food manufacturers use high-fructose corn syrup as an additive to sweeten many foods, including soft drinks, desserts, candies, jellies, and jams.

Fructose ($C_6H_{12}O_6$) is an isomer of glucose.

Its structure is

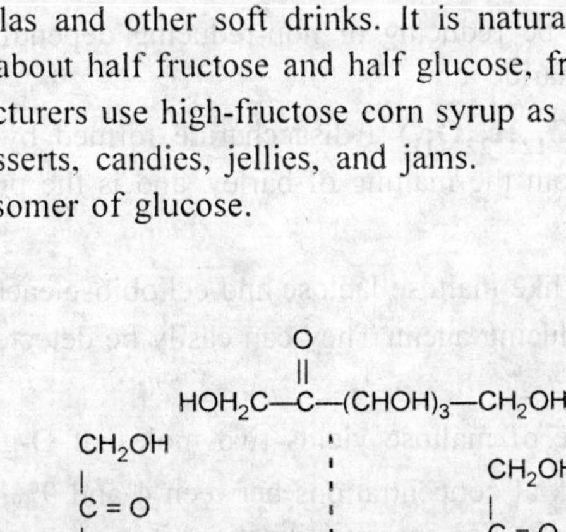

D-Fructose D-Fructose

In many reactions glucose and fructose are formed. For example:- when sucrose (cane sugar) is boiled with dilute H_2SO_4, in alcoholic solution, glucose and fructose are obtained in equal amount.

$$\underset{\text{(sucrose)}}{C_{12}H_{22}O_{11}} + H_2O \xrightarrow{H^+} \underset{\text{Glucose}}{C_6H_{12}O_{11}} + \underset{\text{Fructuse}}{C_6H_{12}O_6}$$

Galactose: Galactose rarely occurs as a monosaccharide in food. It usually is chemically bonded to glucose to form lactose, the primary sugar in milk. It is as sweet as glucose and about 65% as sweet as sucrose. A galactose molecule linked with a glucose molecule forms a lactose molecule.

(B) Oligosaccharides: Oligosaccharides are comprised of 2 to 20 glycosidically-linked monosaccharide units. Based on the number of monosaccharides unit present, the oligosaccharides are further subdivided.

A trisaccharide like raffinose on hydrolysis gives glucose fructose and galactose. Galactose ($C_6H_{12}O_6$) is also isomer of glucose

(*i*) **Disaccharides:** Disaccharides are composed of two monosaccharide units joined by a glycosidic bond. Disaccharides can either be reducing (*e.g.*, maltose and lactose) or non-reducing (*e.g.*, sucrose), depending on whether one or both anomeric carbon atoms are involved in the disaccharide glycosidic bond. Disaccharides on hydrolysis produce two molecules of the same or different monosccarides.

Disaccharides commonly simple sugars soluble in water.

Maltose → glucose + glucose

Sucrose → glucose + fructose

Lactose → glucose + galactose

The disaccharides may be reducing or non-reducing depending upon the position of linkage between the two monosaccharide units.

Maltose (Malt sugar $C_{12}H_{22}O_{11}$) a disaccharide formed by enzymatic hydrolysis of starch, is produced commercially from the malting of barley, and is the primary fermentable sugar used in the production of beer.

Reducing disaccharides like maltose lactose and cellobiose each with one hemiacetal unit which prevents it from acting as reducing agent. They can easily be detected by the Woehlk test or Fearon's test on methylamine.

On hydrolysis one mole of maltose yields two moles of D-glucose. It is a reducing sugar.

Lactose is found in milk at concentrations between 4 and 9%, and is the primary carbohydrate source for developing mammals. For energy utilization, it is necessary that lactose be hydrolyzed by the enzyme lactase (β-galactosidase) to D-galactose and D-glucose in the small intestine to facilitate absorption into the bloodstream. In some individuals, lactose is not (or is only partially) hydrolyzed (lactase deficiency), which condition is clinically termed lactose intolerance, and results in the bacterial, anaerobic fermentation of lactose in the large intestine to lactic acid and gaseous products.

Sucrose, (Cane sugar/$C_{12}H_{22}O_{11}$) a disaccharide, is composed of α-D-glucose and β-D-fructose units that are linked (1→2) through their reducing ends. Thus, sucrose is a nonreducing sugar. Sucrose is made in the cytoplasm of cells in photosynthetically active tissue and is translocated via phloem to metabolically active sites, where it is usually cleaved into glucose and fructose and used as intermediates in various metabolic pathways. In plants such as sugar beet (*Beta vulgaris*) and sugarcane (*Saccharum* spp.), sucrose is a storage carbohydrate. In sugarcane, sucrose accumulates in the vacuoles of cells located in the internodal region of the stem, while in sugar beet; sucrose accumulates in the vacuoles of cells located in root tissue. Sucrose affects colligative properties of water in food systems by depressing freezing point and elevating boiling point and can delay starch gelatinization. Sucrose can interact with ingredients to enhance the retention of aroma and flavor of foods. Its antioxidant properties have been used to prevent the deterioration of flavor in canned fruit. Its humectants properties have been used to prevent moisture loss from baked products. Sucrose can provide a yellow-brown color to food products, through thermal degradation, alkaline degradation, and Maillard products. Sucrose is rapidly degraded into glucose and fructose, which are readily absorbed into the bloodstream in the small intestine. Sucrose provides a quick source of energy for the human body. However, overconsumption of sucrose can cause adverse health problems. It can contribute to obesity, dental caries, and can be problematic to people suffering from defects in glucose metabolism, *e.g.*, hypoglycemia.

Sucrose is dextrorotatory but after hydrolysis gives dextrorotatory glucose and laevorotatory fructose. Thus hydrolysis of sucrose brings about a change in the sign of rotation from dextro (+) to laevo (–) and such a change is known as **inversion** and the mixture is known as **invert sugar**.

Sucrose solution is fermented by yeast when the enzyme invertase hydrolyses sucrose to glucose and fructose, enzyme, zymase converts these monosaccharides to ethyl alcohol.

$$\underset{\text{(sucrose)}}{C_{12}H_{22}O_{11}} + H_2O \xrightarrow{\textit{Invertase}} \underset{\text{(Glucose)}}{C_6H_{12}O_6} + \underset{\text{(fructose)}}{C_6H_{12}O_6}$$

$$\underset{\text{Glucose or fructose}}{C_{12}H_{22}O_6} \xrightarrow{\textit{Zymase}} \underset{\text{Ethanol}}{2C_2H_5OH} + \underset{\text{Carbon dioxide}}{2CO_2}$$

The other important oligosaccharides include tri-, tetra-, or penta-saccharides, respectively, containing 3, 4, or 5 monosaccharides of plant origin.

Raffinose (trisaccharide) → Fructose + Galactose + Glucose

Stachyose (tetrasaccharides) → 2 Galactose + Glucose + Fructose

Verbascose (Pentasaccharides) → 3 Galactose + Glucose + Fructose

(C) Polysaccharides: Polysaccharides are high molecular mass carbohydrates which yields many molecules of monosaccharides on hydrolysis. Common example are starch and cellulose both having general formula $(C_6H_{10}O_5)_n$.

$$\underset{\text{Starch or cellulose}}{(C_6H_{10}O_5)_n} + nH_2O \xrightarrow{H^+} \underset{\text{Glucose}}{nC_6H_{12}O_6}$$

In general monosaccharides and oligosaccharides are crystal line solids, soluble in water and sweet in taste. These are collectively known as *sugars*. The polysaccharides, on the other hand are amorphous, insoluble in water and tasteless and are known as *non-sugars*.

The carbohydrates may also be classified as either **reducing** or **non-reducing** sugars. All those carbohydrates which contain free aldehydic or ketonic group and reduce Fehling's solution and Tollen's reagent are referred to as *reducing sugars*. All monosaccharides whether aldose or ketose are reducing sugars.

In disaccharides if the reducing group of monosaccharides *i.e.*, aldehydic or ketonic group are bonded, these are **non reducing sugars**, *e.g* sucrose while others in which these functional groups are free are reducing sugars *e.g.*, maltose and lactose.

Polysaccharides are composed of more than 20 monosaccharide units. Polysaccharides often are classified as being starch or non-starch. Polysaccharides are the most abudant carbohydrates found in food. Starch polysaccharides represent a source of energy in human beings while non-starch polysaccharides generally are non-digestible and are important in maintaining intestinal health. Polysaccharides are a very diverse set of compounds. They can consist of one type of sugar (homoglycans) or several types of sugars (heteroglycans). They can be branched or non-branched and can vary in type of linkage. The three dimensional structure or conformation of polysaccharide chains is determined by the monosaccharide units and position and type of glycosidic linkages. For example, polysaccharides with α-(1-4)-D-glucosyl linkages or ß-(1-3)-D-glucosyl linkages form hollow helixes while those with ß-(1-4)-D-glucosyl linkages form ribbon-like conformations. The ribbon-like and hollow helix conformations are the two basic chain conformations.

Homoglycans (homopolysaccharides): they yield only single types of monosaccharides when hydrolysis takes place. They are based on the nature of the monosaccharides units. Thus, glucans are polymers of glucose whereas fructosans are polymers of fructose.

Starch or **amylum** $(C_6H_{10}O_5)_n$ is a polymeric carbohydrate consisting of a large number of glucose units joined by glycosidic bonds. This polysaccharide is produced by most green plants particularly in seeds as energy storage. It is the most common carbohydrate in human diets and is contained in large amounts in staple foods like potatoes, wheat, maize (corn), rice, and cassava. Starch is composed of two polysaccharides: amylose (15-20%) and amylopectin (80-85%). Amylose and amylopectin are both polymolecular [contain α-(1-4) and α-(1-6)-D-glucosyl linkages] and polydisperse (vary in degree of polymerization). Amylopectin is a large, highly branched molecule with a degree of polymerization of 10^4–10^7 with 4%–5% of the linkages involved with branch points. Amylopectin branches are categorized as A-chains, B-chains, and C-chains. Starch isolation from cereal grains involves steeping, coarse milling, degerming, fine milling, screening, centrifugal separation, and drying.

Starch occurs in the form of granules which vary in size and shape depending on their plant source. Starch is a white amorphous powder, insoluble in cold water. Its solution in water gives a blue colour with iodine solution. The blue colour disappears on heating and reappears on cooling. On hydrolysis with dilute acids or enzyme, starch breaks down to molecules of variable complexity ($n > n'$), maltose and finally D-glucose.

$$\underset{\text{Starch}}{(C_6H_{10}O_5)_n} \rightarrow (C_6H_{10}O_5)_{n'} \rightarrow \underset{\text{Maltose}}{C_{12}H_{22}O_{11}} \downarrow \underset{\text{D-glucose}}{C_6H_{12}O6}$$

Starch does not reduce Fehling's solution or tollen's reagent and does not form an osazone, indicating that all hemiacetal hydroxyl group of glucose units are linked with glycosidic linkages.

Starch functionality in food systems is primarily related to its gelatinization, retrogradation, and pasting properties. Starch and/or starch derivatives are nearly ubiquitous in food systems. Starch affects the sensory and textural properties of food. Starch is used to stabilize structure by acting as a bulking agent. Starch can function as a thickening agent for sauces and pie fillings and as a colloidal stabilizer for salad dressings. Starch is used as coating, glazing, and gel-forming agents for gum confectionery. High temperature and shear makes native starch granules fragile and susceptible to rupture during processing. Thus, native starches have limited use in the food industry. Starches are often modified to improve the desired properties. Starch suitability depends on the processing temperature, length of time at temperature, shear forces, and pH. Cross-linked starches are more tolerant to harsh food processing conditions. In general, increased cross-linking results in more tolerance to acidic condition and less breakdown of starch.

Cellulose ($C_6H_{10}O_5$)$_n$ is the key structural constituent of plant primary cell walls. It consists of long, linear chains composed solely of (1→4)-linked ß-D-glucopyranosyl units. The nature of the cellulose glycosidic linkage, its regular monosaccharide sequence, and its linear backbone causes cellulose molecules to adopt flat, rigid, ribbon-like secondary structures that readily aggregate to form crystalline, water insoluble superstructures. Thus, in the native state, while cellulose represents a good source of dietary fiber in indigenous whole foods or in isolated form (referred to as powdered cellulose), it generally requires further processing or derivatization to enhance functionality for broader food use.

Some species of bacteria secrete it to form biofilms.

Cellulose is the most abundant organic polymer on Earth.

Cellulose is often added to sauces for both its thickening and emulsifying actions.

Wood contains 45-50 % while cotton contains 90-95 % cellulose, it is a colourless amorphous solid which decomposes on heating. It is largely linear and its individual strands align with each other through multiple hydrogen bonds. Thus lends rigidity to its structure. It is thus used effectively as a cell wall materials. Cellulose does not reduce Tollen's reagent or Fehling's solution. It does not form osazone and is not fermented by yeast.

It does not hydrolysed as easily as starch but on heating with dilute sulphuric acid under pressure yields D-glucose.

Large population of cellulolytic bacteria present in the stomach (rumen) of ruminant mammals (cattle, sheep etc) breaks down cellulose with the help of enzyme cellulase. It is then digested and converted into glucose. Human stomach is different and does not have enzymes capable of breaking cellulose molecules.

Dextrins are the breakdown products of starch by enzyme amylase or dilute acids. Starch is sequentially hydrolyzed through different dextrins and, finally to maltose and glucose. The various intermediates (identified by iodine colouration) are soluble starch (blue), amylopectin (violet) erythrodextrin (red) and achrodextrin (no colour).

Pectin is a high molecular weight complex class of plant cell wall polysaccharides, composed of galacturonans and rhamnogalacturonans. Pectin has a backbone of α-(1-4)-d-galacturonic acid with α-(1-2)-L-rhamnose units interspersed. The galacturonic acid units are partially acetylated and methylated, and the L-rhamnose units contain side chains containing arabinose and/or galactose. Pectins are water soluble and adopt a random coil conformation in solution. There are two major types of pectin. High methoxy pectins (HM-pectin) have >50% methylation, are soluble in water, and form gels in low pH and in the presence of a high concentration of sugar. Low methoxy pectins (LM-pectin) swell and hydrate in cold water and form gels in the presence of calcium. LM-pectin does not need sugar to form a gel. Pectins are used as gelling agents either through the use of calcium cross-linking in the case of LM-pectins or sugar-induced dehydration with HM-pectin. Pectins are used as thickeners and stabilizers in jams, jelly, and fruit products. Pectin can act as a protein dispersion stabilizer in acidified dairy products like yogurt and milk-based fruit drinks. Pectin is a soluble dietary fiber and exerts physiological effects on the gastrointestinal tract such as delayed gastric emptying, reduced glucose absorption, and reduced serum cholesterol, all of which probably relate to its gel-forming and water-holding capacity.

Glycogen is the carbohydrate reserve in animal, hence often referred to as animal starch. It is present in high concentration in lever, followed by muscle, brain etc. Glycogen is also found in plants that do not possess chlorophyll (*e.g.* yeast, fungi). The structure of glycogen is similar to that of amylopectin with more number of branches. Glucose is the repeating unit in glycogen joined together by a (1→4) glycosidic bonds at branching points. The molecular weight (upto 1×10^8) and the number of glucose units (upto 25,000) vary in glycogen depending on the source of glycogen is obtained (Formula $(C_6H_{10}O_5)_n$. Glycogen forms an energy source that can be quickly mobilized to meet sudden demand.

1.4 PROTEINS AND AMINO ACIDS

Proteins are among the fundamental molecules of biology. Proteins are high molecular mass complex biopolymers of amino acids present in all living cells. They are common to all life, are present in every cell on Earth, and are responsible for most of the complex functions that make life possible. There are an estimated 100,000 different proteins in the human body alone. In plants, an inventory of more than 13,000 plant proteins has been cataloged.

The Protoplasm of plant or animals cells contains 10-20% proteins. As enzymes these catalyse biochemical reactions, as hormones they regulate metabolic processes and as antibodies, they protect the body against toxic substances. All proteins contain the elements carbon hydrogen, oxygen, nitrogen and sulphur. Some of these may also contain phosphorus, iodine and traces of metal like iron, copper, zinc and manganese.

Amino acids are a group of organic compounds containing two functional groups- amino and carboxyl. The amino group ($-NH_2$) is basic while the carboxyl group (-COOH) is acidic in nature. Amino acids are grouped according to the characteristics of the side chains:

- Aliphatic—alanine, glycine, isoleucine, leucine, proline, and valine.
- Aromatic—phenylalanine, tryptophan, and tyrosine.
- Acidic—aspartic acid, and glutamic acid.
- Basic—arginine, histidine, and lysine.
- Hydroxylic—serine and threonine.
- Sulfur-containing—cysteine and methionine.
- Amidic (containing the amide group)—asparagine and glutamine.

Every ***amino acid*** contains a central carbon atom to which is attached a carboxyl group (–COOH), an amino group ($-NH_2$), a hydrogen atom, and another group or side chain R specific to the particular amino acid. The general formula for an amino acid is $R-CH(NH_2)-COOH$. Glycine is the simplest amino acid, with the R group being a hydrogen atom (NH_2-CH_2-COOH) There are more than 20 different amino acids in proteins. Their properties depend on the nature of their side chains or R groups.

All proteins on partial hydrolysis give peptides of varying molecular masses which on complete hydrolysis give aminoacids. Depending upon the relative position of two functional groups in the alkyl chain, the amino acids can be classified as α, β, γ, δ and so on. Only α-amino acids are obtained on hydrolysis of protein.

All α-amino acids have trivial names even those for which IUPAC names are not cumbersome. *e.g* H_2NCH_2COOH is better known as glycine rather than α-amino acetic acid. Amino acids or α-amino ethanoic acid. Amino acids are generally represented by a three letter symbol, some times, one letter symbol is also used.

Example	Three letter symbol	One letter symbol
1. Glycine	Gly	G
2. Alanine	Ala	A
3. Lysine	Lys	K
4. Glutamine	Glu	E
5. Serine	Ser	S
6. Methionine	Met	M
7. Triptofan	Trp	W
8. Tyrosine	Tyr	Y

Amino acids are usually colourless, crystalline solids. These are water soluble, high melting solids behave like salts rather than simple amines or carboxylic acid. Except glycine all other naturally occurring α-amino acids are optically active, since the α-carbon atom is asymmetric. These exit both in 'D' and 'L' forms. Most naturally occurring amino acids have L-configuration.

Amino acids are classified as **acidic, basic** or **neutral** depending upon the relative number of amino and carboxylic groups in their molecules. Equal number of amino and carboxyl group makes it basic and more carbonyl as compared to amino make it acidic.

The amino acids which can be synthesized in the body are known as *non-essential amino* acids and those which cannot be synthesized in the body but must be obtained through diet are called *essential amino acids*

Examples

Non essential amino acids:- glycine, alanine, glutamine, cysteine

Essential amino acids:- Valine, phenylalanine, methionine, etc

Proteins are considered to be biopolymers containing a large number of amino acids joined to each other by peptide linkage having three dimensional structure. Protein structure and shape can be studied at different levels.

Primary structure:- Each polypeptide in a protein has amino acids linked with each other in a specific sequence and it is this sequence of amino acids that is said to be the primary structure of that protein. Any change in this primary structure *i.e.*, sequence of amino acids creates a different protein. A protein containing a total of 100 amino acid, residues is a very small protein, yet 20 different amino acids can be combined at one time in $(20)^{100}$ different ways.

Secondary Structure of a protein refers to the shape in which long polypeptide chain can exist.

Tertiary Structure of proteins represents overall folding of the polypeptide chain *i.e.*, further folding of secondary structure.

In acidic solution, an amino acid exists as a positive ion and migrate toward the cathode in an electric field while in alkaline solution it exist as a negative ion and migrates towards anode. At certain hydrogen ion concentration (pH) the bipolar ion exist as a neutral ion and does not migrate to either electrode. This pH is known as **isoelectric point** of amino acid. The isoelectric point depends on other functional groups in the amino acid, and neutral amino acids have isoelectric point in the range of pH 5.5 to 6.3. At isoelectric point the amino acids have least solubility in water and this property is exploited in the separation of different amino acids and obtained from the hydrolysis of proteins.

Proteins consist of polymers of amino acids (AA) that are characterized by the following general chemical structure:

$$R\text{–}CH\ (NH_2)\ COOH$$

Two hydrogen and a nitrogen comprise the amino group, $–NH_2$, and the acid entity is the carboxyl group, –COOH. Amino acids link to each other when the carboxyl group of one molecule reacts with the amino group of another molecule, creating a peptide bond –C(=O)NH– and releasing a molecule of water (H_2O). Amino acids (AA) are the basic building blocks of enzymes, hormones, proteins, and body tissues. *Peptides* consist of two or more amino acids, *oligopeptides* (2–10 amino acids), *polypeptides* (10–50 amino acids or more), and proteins both contain 10 or more amino acids. The polypeptides consisting of more than 50 amino acids are classified as proteins. *A protein is a complex, high molecular weight organic compound that consists of amino acids joined by peptide bonds.*

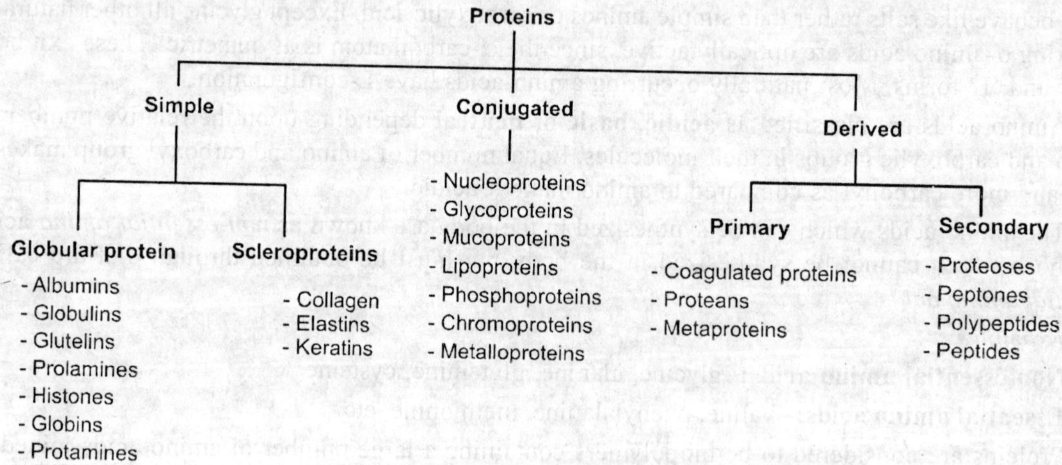

Summary of classification of proteins

Proteins perform various functions in processed foods. The functional properties of proteins, such as foaming, emulsifying, gelling, thickening, texturizing, dough forming, whipping, curdling, water binding, flavor binding, and fat binding properties, are important for imparting desirable sensory attributes in a variety of food products. These various functional properties of proteins emanate from two molecular attributes of proteins, namely hydrodynamic properties and physicochemical attributes of the protein's surface. While the hydrodynamic properties relate to the size and shape of the molecule, the properties of a protein's surface relate to its topology and to the pattern of distribution of polar and non-polar patches. Although these molecular attributes of proteins in their native state can be determined fairly precisely from their crystallographic structure, it has been difficult to predict their functionality in a complex food milieu. This is principally due to denaturation of proteins that inevitably occurs during food processing, which might alter both their hydrodynamic attributes (shape and size) and surface characteristics. In the denatured state, the intensity of intermolecular interactions between proteins, or between proteins and other constituents in the food milieu would dramatically alter the proteins' functionality.

Table 2: Important functional properties of proteins in several food systems

Functional Property	Food System(s)
Solubility	Infant formulas, protein beverages, beer, yogurt drinks
Water-holding ability (capacity)	Tumbled hams, deli meats, frankfurters, poultry products, yogurt
Gelation	Frankfurters, custards, gelatin, comminuted meat and poultry products
Emulsification	Ice cream, liquid coffee creamers, salad dressings, milk, mayonnaise, gravies
Foaming	Angel and sponge cakes, meringues, soufflés, marshmallows, whipped cream and toppings

Denaturation of proteins

Protein found in a biological system with definite configuration and biological activity is called a **native protein**. If a native protein is subjected to physical or chemical treatment which may disrupt its higher structures (conformation) without affecting its primary structure the protein is said to be **denatured** and it loses its biological activity. The denaturation may be reversible or irreversible. The coagulation of egg white on boiling of egg protein is an example of irreversible protein denaturation. However in some cases it is found that if the disruptive agent is removed the protein recovers its original physical and chemical properties and biological activity. The reverse of denaturation is known as **renaturation**.

The extent of denaturation of proteins in a food milieu depends on the susceptibility of intra-molecular interactions that hold the compact native protein structure to temperature, pressure (shear), pH, ionic strength, types of ions, and specific and non-specific interactions with other food components such as sugars, polysaccharides, lipids, and other additives. It should be recognized, however, that from a food application standpoint, protein denaturation during processing is not always undesirable. In fact, in some cases it is highly desirable. For instance, partial denaturation of proteins at the air-water and oil-water interfaces improve their foaming and emulsifying properties, whereas excessive thermal denaturation of soy proteins diminishes their foaming and emulsifying properties. In protein beverages, where high solubility and dispersibility of proteins is a necessity, even partial denaturation of protein during processing may cause flocculation and precipitation during storage and thus may adversely affect the sensory attributes of the product. Thus, to develop appropriate processing strategies, a basic understanding of the environmental and other factors that affect structural stability of proteins in food systems is imperative.

Coagulation refers to a semi-solid viscous precipitate of protein, irreversible denaturation results in coagulation. Coagulation is optimum and requires lowest temperature at isoelectric pH. Albumins and globulins (to a lesser extent) are coagulable protein. Heat coagulation test is commonly used to detect the presence of albumin in urine.

Flocculation is the process of protein precipitation at isoelectric pH. The precipitate is referred to as flocculum. Casein (milk protein) can be easily precipitated when adjusted to isoelectric pH (4.6) by dilute acetic acid. Flocculation is reversible. On application of heat, flocculation can be converted into an irreversible mass, coagulum.

The ***isoelectric point*** of a protein is the pH at which the protein is electrically neutral (it is denoted by $pH^{(I)}$ or pI). At this pH, the global or overall charge on the protein is zero. This does not mean that the protein contains no charged groups. It means that the number of positive charges on the protein is equal to the number of negative charges. At the isoelectric point, the protein molecules usually precipitate because they do not carry a net charge. (Molecules that carry a like charge repel each other, and thus form a stable dispersion in water. Removal of the charge removes the repulsive force and allows the molecules to interact with each other and precipitate, in most cases.) The isoelectric point is important in food processing. For example, cottage cheese is made by adding lactic acid to milk to bring the pH to the isoelectric point of the major milk proteins (the caseins). The proteins precipitate at this pH, forming curds. These are separated from the rest of the milk and may be pressed and/or mildly salted before being packaged as cottage cheese. Good sources of protein include high-quality protein foods, such as meat, poultry, fish, milk, egg, and cheese, as well as prevalent low-quality protein foods, such as fresh vegetables and fruits, except *legumes* (*e.g.*, navy beans, pinto beans, chick peas, soybeans, and split peas), which are high in protein. Cereals are also a good source of proteins.

Maillard browning (Non-enzymatic) is the reaction that is responsible for the brown color of baked products. A free carbonyl group of a reducing sugar reacts with a free amino group on a protein when heated and the result is a brown color. The reaction is highly complex and has a significant effect on the flavor of foods as well as the color. It is known as non-enzymatic browning, because the reaction is not catalyzed by an enzyme (Maillard browning must be distinguished from enzymatic browning, which is the discoloration of damaged fruits or vegetables and is catalyzed by an enzyme such as **phenol oxidase**. The Maillard reaction is favored by the following:

- High sugar content
- High protein concentration
- High temperatures
- High pH
- Low water content

Maillard browning is responsible for the discoloration of food products such as powdered milk and powdered egg. Before drying, eggs usually are "desugared" enzymatically to remove glucose and prevent Maillard browning. The reaction causes loss of the amino acids lysine, arginine, tryptophan, and histidine, as these are the amino acids with free amino groups that are able to react with reducing sugars. With the exception of arginine, these are essential amino acids. (The body cannot make them, and so they must be included in the diet.) Therefore, it is important to retard the Maillard reaction, particularly in susceptible food products in which the nutritional quality of the protein is very important.

Enzymic browing: When the cells of apples, potatoes and some other fruits and vegetables are cut and exposed to the air, enzymes present in the cells bring about an oxidation reaction; colourless compounds are converted into brown-coloured compounds. Browning does not occur in cooked fruits and vegetables since the enzymes are destroyed by heat. Fruits such as apples, pears, bananas, peaches and avocado are prone to discolouration.

Nucleic Acid:- Every living cell contains nucleoproteins, substance made up of proteins combined with biopolymers of another kind, the nucleic acids. These are mainly of two types, the **deoxyribonucleic acid (DNA)** and **ribonucleic acids (RNA)**. Nucleic acids are long chain polymers (polynucleotides) of nucleotides. While proteins have a polyamide chain. Nucleic acids contain polyphosphate ester chain.

In higher cells, DNA is localized mainly in the nucleus, within the chromosome, a small amount of DNA is present in the cytoplasm also where it is contained in mitochondria and chloroplast. RNA is also present in nucleus as well as cytoplasm. DNA is the major source of genetic information, which is copied into RNA molecules **(transcription)**. The sequence of nucleotides contains the code for specific amino acid sequences. Proteins are then synthesized in a process involving translation of RNA. Complete hydrolysis of DNA (or RNA) yields a pentose sugar (ribose in RNA and deoxyribose in DNA), two types of heterocyclic nitrogenous bases viz, purines and pyrimidines along with phosphoric acid. DNA contains the purine bases, adenine (A) and guanine (G), and pyrimidine bases, thymine (T) and cytosine (C) while RNA has uracil (U) in place of thymine (T). There are two main structural difference between DNA and RNA;

(1) DNA has deoxyribose while RNA has ribose sugar,

(2) DNA contains thymine while RNA has uracil.

Nucleosides:- The N-glucosides of purine or pyrimidine bases with pentose sugars are known as nucleosides.

Base + Sugar = Nucleoside

Base	Abbreviation	Nucleoside
adenine	A	adenosine
guanine	G	guanosine
cytosine	C	cytidine
thymine	T	thymidine
uracil	U	uridine

Nucleotides:- A nucleotide is a phosphate ester of nucleoside and consist of purine or pyrimidine base, the 5-carbon sugar and one or more phosphate group.

Base + Sugar + phosphate = Nucleotide

The nucleotides are abbreviated by three capital letters, preceded by d - in case of deoxy series, *e.g.*

AMP = adenosine monophosphate

αAMP = deoxyadenosine monophosphate

ATP = adenosine triphosphate

UDP = Uridine triphosphate etc.

Nucleic acids control heredity at molecular level. The double helix of DNA is the store house of the hereditary information of the organism. Since DNA has only four different bases, the genetic massage can be compared to a language which has only four letters A, C, G and T. DNA must preserve this information and also use it in the following manner.

1. **Replication:-** DNA molecule can duplicate themselves.
2. **Transcription:-** A single strand of DNA can act as a template on which a molecule of RNA is synthesized in specific manner.
3. **Translation:-** The RNA molecule in turn detects the synthesis of specific proteins which are characteristic of each organism.

$$\text{DNA} \xrightarrow{\text{Replication}} \text{DNA} \underset{\text{Reverse Transcription}}{\overset{\text{Transcription}}{\rightleftarrows}} \text{RNA} \xrightarrow{\text{Translation}} \text{Protein}$$

1.5 LIPIDS (FATS AND OILS)

Lipids are naturally occurring compounds related to fatty acids and includes fats, oils, waxes and other related compounds. The lipids are important constituents of diet. In the body the fats serve as an efficient source of energy. These are hydrophobic in nature and dissolve in organic solvents. Phospholipids (lipids containing phosphorus) are important constituents of cell membrane.

Lipids are among the major components of food of plant and animal origin. There is no precise definition available for the term *lipid*; however, it usually includes a broad category of compounds that have some common properties and compositional similarities.

Christie defines lipids as "*a wide variety of natural products including fatty acids and their derivatives, steroids, terpenes, carotenoids and bile acids, which have in common a ready solubility in organic solvents such as diethyl ether, hexane, benzene, chloroform or methanol.*"

Kates says that lipids are "*those substances which are (a) insoluble in water; (b) soluble in organic solvents such as chloroform, ether or benzene; (c) contain long-chain hydrocarbon groups in their molecules; and (d) are present in or derived form in living organisms.*"

Gurr and James pointed out that the standard definition includes "*a chemically heterogeneous group of substances, having in common the property of insolubility in water, but solubility in non-polar solvents such as chloroform, hydrocarbons or alcohols.*"

Sometimes 'lipid' used as synonym for fats. Fats are a subgroup of lipids called *triglycerides.*

A. Simple lipids (homolipids):- Simple lipids are alcohol esters of fatty acids which include.

1. **Neutral fats (glycerides):-** Also known as triglycerides, these are triesters of fatty acids and glycerol.
2. **Waxes:-** These are esters of fatty acids with long chain monohydroxy alcohols. These have higher melting points than neutral fats.

B. Compound lipids (heterolipids):- Lipids with additional group are called compound lipids. These include

1. **Phospholipids (phosphatides):-** These contain additional groups, *e.g.*, a phosphoric acid, nitrogen containing bases and other substituents.
2. **Glycolipids:-** These are esters of fatty acids with carbohydrate, and may contain nitrogen but no phosphorus.

C. Derived lipids: These are the substanced derived from simple and compound lipids by hydrolysis. These include fatty acids, fatty alcohols, mono and diglycerides. These are sometimes present as waste products of metabolism. Glycerides and cholesterol esters are also called neutral lipids since these do not carry any charge.

Fatty acids are long hydrocarbon chains with a methyl group (CH_3) at one end of the chain and a carboxylic acid group (COOH) at the other. Most natural fatty acids contain from 4 to 24 carbon atoms and most contain an even number of carbon atoms in the chain. For example, butyric acid is the smallest fatty acid, having four carbon atoms, and it is found in butter; lard and tallow contain longer fatty acids. Fatty acids may be saturated, in which case they contain only single carbon-to-carbon bonds and have the general formula $CH_3\_CH_2\_nCOOH$. They have a linear shape, as shown in Fig.

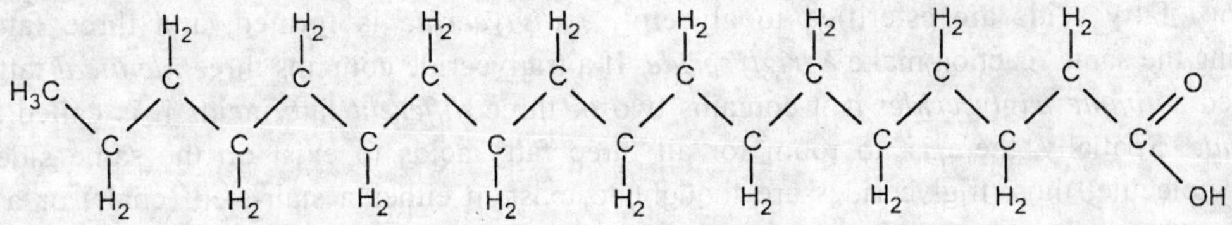

Example of a fatty acid.

Fatty acids always have an even number of carbons and may be saturated *e.g.*, palmitic acid ($C_{17}H_{35}COOH$) or unsaturated *e.g.*, oleic acid ($C_{17}H_{33}COOH$) and linolenic acid ($C_{17}H_{29}COOH$).

Monounsaturated fatty acids (MUFA) such as oleic acid contain only one double bond; polyunsaturated fatty acids (PUFA), such as linoleic and linolenic acids, contain two or more double bonds. Generally, ***unsaturated*** fats are liquid at room temperature and have low melting points.

trans*-Fatty acids** include any unsaturated fatty acid that contains double-bond geometry in the E (*trans*) configuration. Nomenclature differs only from normal ***cis-fatty acids in the configuration of the double bonds. The three main origins of *trans* fatty acids in our diet are bacteria, deodorized oils, and partially hydrogenated oils. Hydrogenation is used to stabilize and improve oxidative stability of oils and to create plastic fats from oils.

Essential fatty acids: the fatty acids that cannot be synthesized by the human body, and therefore, should be supplied in the diet are known as essential fatty acids (EFAs). Chemically, they are polyunsaturated fatty acids, namely linoleic acid ($C_{18}H_{32}O_2$) and linolenic acid ($C_{18}H_{30}O_2$). Arachidonic acid ($C_{20}H_{24}O_2$) become essential, if its precursor linoleic acid is not provided in the diet sufficient amounts.

Glycerides include *monoglycerides, diglycerides*, and *triglycerides*. The first two act as emulsifiers in foods, while the most abundant fatty substance in food—more than 95%—is the *triglycerides*. Triglycerides are insoluble in water and may be either liquid or solid at room temperature, with *liquid* forms generally referred to as *oils* and *solid* forms as fats. Structurally, glycerides contain a glycerol molecule backbone joined to *one* or more fatty acid molecules. A *monoglyceride* contains glycerol esterified to one fatty acid molecule and the equation for that reaction is given in Fig. (The general formula for a fatty acid is used where R represents the hydrocarbon chain).

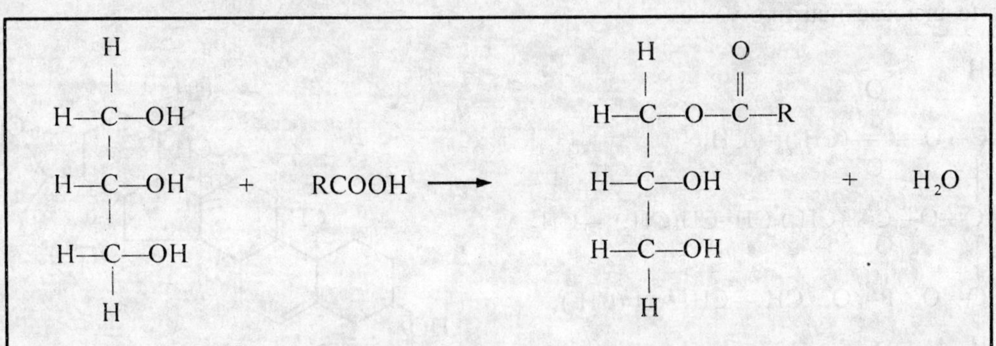

If *two* fatty acids are esterified to glycerol, a *diglyceride* is formed, and three fatty acids undergoing the same reaction make a *triglyceride.* If a triglyceride contains three *identical* fatty acids, it is called a *simple triglyceride*; if it contains two or three *different* fatty acids it is called a *mixed triglyceride*. Spatially, there is no room for all three fatty acids to exist on the same side of the glycerol molecule; thus, triglycerides are thought to exist in either a stair-step (chair) or a tuning-fork arrangement. The arrangement and specific type of fatty acids on the glycerol determine the chemical and physical properties of a fat.

In addition to glycerides and free fatty acids, lipids may contain small amounts of phospholipids, sterols, tocopherols, fat-soluble pigments, and vitamin.

Phospholipids are similar to triglycerides but contain only *two* fatty acids esterified to glycerol. In place of the third fatty acid, there is a polar group containing phosphoric acid and a nitrogen-containing group, the most common is known as ***lecithin***. Lecithin is found in nearly every living cell. The word is derived from the Greek *lekithos*, which means "yolk of an egg," and lecithin is in egg yolk. However, the primary *commercial* source of lecithin is the soybean. The two fatty acids of a phospholipid are attracted to fat, whereas the phosphorus and nitrogen portions are attracted to water. Therefore, a phospholipid forms a bridge between fat and water, two ordinarily *immiscible* substances, and emulsification is observed. "Refined" lecithins are modified to provide important surface active properties to a variety of foods such as instant drink mixes, infant formulas, meat sauces and gravies, dispersible oleoresins, pan releases, chewing gum, and fat-replacer systems. ***Sterols*** contain a common steroid nucleus, an 8–10 carbon side chain and an alcohol group. The chemists view of sterols is *unlike* triglycerides or phospholipids—sterols are round in shape. *Cholesterol* is the primary *animal sterol* although *plant sterols*, or stanols, also exist; the most common ones are sitosterol and stigmasterol. Other plant sterols are found in "margarine"- type products, including those marketed under the trade name Benecol®. ***Tocopherols*** are important minor constituents of most *vegetable oils*; *animal fats* contain *little or no* tocopherols. Tocopherols are fat soluble antioxidants, helping to prevent oxidative rancidity and also are sources of vitamin E. They are *partially removed* by the heat of processing and may be *added* after processing to improve oxidative stability of oils. If vitamin E is added to oil, for example, the oil frequently is marketed as a source of vitamin E or as an antioxidant-containing oil. Fats are *not* good sources of vitamins, apart from vitamin E; however, fat soluble vitamins A and D may be added to foods such as margarine and milk in order to increase nutritive value.

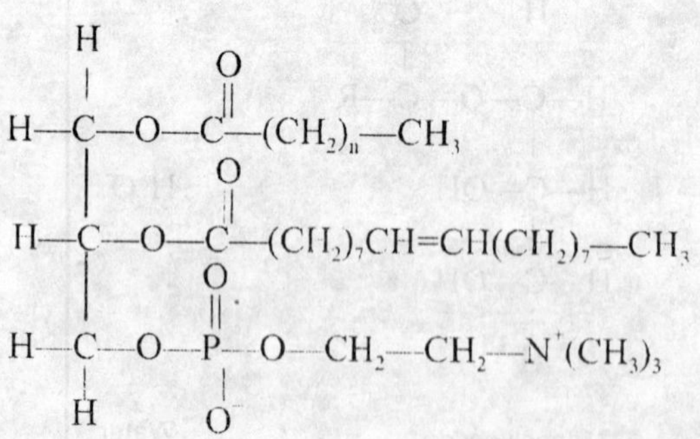

Lecithin

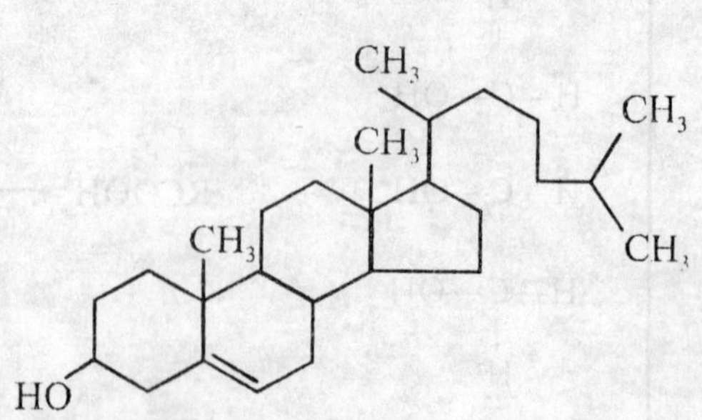

Cholesterol

Fat must be present in the diet for, among other reasons, the absorption of fat-soluble vitamins. Pigments such as carotenoids and chlorophylls may be present in fats, and these may impart a distinct color to a fat. Such colors normally are removed by bleaching during processing.

Waxes:- These are esters of long chain saturated and unsaturated fatty acids with chain monohydroxy alcohols. The fatty acids range between C_{14} and C_{36} and the alcohols range from C_{16} to C_{36}. Most of the waxes are mixtures of wax esters, free fatty acids, free fatty alchols and hydrocarbons.

Fats are important reserves of animal and plant cells. We can extract animals and vegetable fats and oils from natural resources. While we synthesize fat in our own bodies, we also consume fats synthesized by plants and other animals, Phospholipids are indispensable structural components of cell membranes and are also used as detergent to emulsify fat for transport within the body. These are never stored in large amounts. Cholesterol is the principal sterol of higher animals, abundant in nerve tissues and gallstones. Cholesterol is not present in plant fat.

Some of the functions of fat in food preparation are as follows:

- Add or modify flavor, texture
- Aerate (leaven) batters and doughs
- Contribute flakiness
- Contribute tenderness
- Emulsify
- Transfer heat, such as in frying
- Prevent sticking
- Provide satiety

1.6 VITAMINS

Vitamins can be defined as essential dietary factors required by organism in minute quantities and their absence cause specific deficiency diseases. Man's supply of vitamins is obtained from a varied diet of vegetables, cereals, fruits and meats and the quantities of vitamins that are present in the dietary sources can be affected significantly by the processing and storage of the food.

Vitamins are essential for life and a steady supply of these is required in food, since the organism cannot synthesize many of these compounds. Plants can synthesis almost all vitamins whereas only a few are synthesized in animals. Vitamins are widely distributed in nature both in plants and animals. All cells in the body can store vitamins to some extent. However most of the vitamins have been synthesized and are available commercially. These are effective when taken orally. Vitamins have varied chemical structures and are designated by Alphabets A, B, C, D, E etc. in order of their discovery. Further any subgroup of individual vitamins is designated by the number of subscript *e.g.*, A_1, A_2, B_1, B_2, B_6, B_{12}, D_1, D_2 etc. Vitamin D may be supplied through food or may be produced in the skin by irradiation of sterols with sunlight (ultraviolet light). Human body can synthesize vitamin A from carotene and some members of vitamin B complex and vitamin K are synthesized by microorganisms present in intestinal tract.

"Vitamins are a group of bio-molecules other than carbohydrates, protein and fats, which are required in small quantity for the normal metabolic process and for the life, growth and health of human being and animals." Vitamins are divided into two categories, the fat-soluble vitamins and the water-soluble vitamins.

Fat soluble vitamins: these include vitamins A, D, E and K. These vitamins are fat or oil soluble substances.

Water soluble vitamins: these include vitamin B complex (B_1, B_2, B_5 or nicotinic acid, B_6, B_{12}, pantothenic acid, biotin or vitamin H and folic acid) and vitamin C.

Vitamins and some commonly used synonyms are given Table 3.

Table 3: Vitamins and some commonly used synonyms

Vitamin	Synonyms
Fat-soluble	
Vitamin A	Retinol
Vitamin D_2	Ergocalciferol
Vitamin D_3	Cholecalciferol
Vitamin E	Alpha, beta and gamma tocopherols and alpha tocotrienol
Vitamin K_1	Phylloquinone, phytomenadione
Vitamin K_2	Farnoquinone, menaquinone
Vitamin K_3	Menadione
Water-soluble	
Vitamin B_1	Thiamin
Vitamin B_2	Riboflavin
Vitamin B_6	Pyridoxal, pyridoxine, pyridoxamine
Vitamin B_{12}	Cobalamins, cyanocobalamin, hydroxocobalamin
Niacin	Nicotinic acid (vitamin PP), Niacinamide, Nicotinamide (vitamin PP)
Pantothenic acid	–
Folic acid/folates	Folacin, (vitamin M)
Biotin	Vitamin H
Vitamin C	Ascorbic acid

Table 4: Some important vitamins and their (characteristics, sources and deficiency)

Vitamins	Characteristics	Dietary Sources	Deficiency diseases	Excess
Fat soluble vitamins (A, D, E & K)				
Vitamin A or Retinol (Bright eye vitamin)	Pro-vitamin A (beta carotene), constituents of rhodopsin (visual pigments), Soluble in oil and fats but insoluble in water, stable to heat. Promotes growth and vision. It also increases resistance to diseases, role in muco-polysacchrides synthesis	Milk, fish and fish oil (cod lever oil), butter, cheese, green vegetables, fortified margarine. It can also be synthesized in the body from carotenoids present in carrot, tomato, ripe mangoes etc. Carotenoids are the precursor of vitamin A.	Night blindness, permanent blindness, colour blindness, stunted growth, *xerosis* (drying of skin), *xerophthalmia* (keratinization of ocular tissues)	Headache, vomiting, peeling of skin, anorexia, swelling of long bones
Vitamin D or Ergocalciferol (a mixture of vitamins D_2 and D_3)	Promotes growth and mineralization of bones, increases absorption of calcium, stable to heat and resistant to oxidation.	Cod liver oil, eggs, dairy products, fortified milk margarines. Vitamin D_2 is produced by plants from ergosterol when exposed to light. Vitamin D_3 is produced in skin on exposure to sunlight.	Rickets (bone and teeth deformation) in children. Osteomalacia in adults.	Vomiting, diarrhea, loss of weight, kidney damage
Vitamin E (tocopherol)	It is a mixture of 4 vitamins called α, β, γ, and δ-tocopherol. Stable to heat, light and oxidation. Function as antioxidant to prevent cell-membrane damage.	Seeds, green leafy vegetables, margarines, shortening, eggs, milk, fish, wheat germ oil, cotton seed oil peanut oil etc.	Possibly anemia. Antioxidant, Needed for beautiful glowing skin, prevents destruction of RBC.	Relatively nontoxic
Vitamin K (Phylloquinone)	A mixture of two vitamins called K_1 and K_2. Sensitive to light. Important in blood clotting (involved in formation of active prothrombin).	Green leafy vegetables. Small amounts in cereals, fruits (cabbage, spinach, carrot and alfa-alfa). Vitamin K_2 occurs mainly in intestine of bacteria.	Severe bleeding, fault in blood clotting. Internal hemorrhages. It restores normal clotting.	Relatively nontoxic. Synthetic forms at high doses may cause jaundice.
Water soluble vitamins (B & C)				
Vitamin B_1 (Thiamine)	Destroyed by heat above 310 K. Coenzyme (thiamin pyrophosphate) in reactions involving the removal of CO_2	Pork, organ meats, whole grains, egg yolk, legumes, milk, green vegetables and fruits.	Beri-beri (peripheral nerve changes, edema, heart failure, paralysis of legs and general weak-ness) and corner of the mouth.	None reported
Vitamin B_2 (Riboflavin)	Sensitive to light but stable to heat. Essential for growth and general health. Constituents of two flavin nucleotide coenzyme involved in energy metabolism (FAD and FMN)	Widely distributed in foods. Milk, yeast, green vegetables, meat, liver, kidney etc.	Causes pellagra (shriveled skin) and anaemia (blood-lessness) in man. Effects central nervous system. Causes general weakness, insomnia and irritability, lesions of eye, cheilosis.	None reported

Vitamins	Characteristics	Dietary Sources	Deficiency diseases	Excess
Niacin	Constituents of two coenzyme involved in oxidation-reduction reactions (NAD and NADP)	Liver, lean meats, grains, legumes (can be formed from tryptophan)	Pellagra (skin and gastrointestinal lesions, nervous mental disorders)	Flushing, burning and tingling, around neck, face and hands.
Vitamins B_6 or pyridoxine	It is a mixture of three substances - pyridoxine, pyridoxal and pyridoxamine. Coenzyme (pyridoxal phosphate involved in amino acid metabolism).	Rice bran, yeast, meat, fish, whole cereals, vegetables.	Pernious anaemia, inflammation of tongue and mouth, irritability, conv-ulsions, muscular twitching, derma-titis near eye, kidney stones	None reported
Pantothenic acid	Constituents of coenzyme A, which plays a central role in energy metabolism.	Widely distributed in foods	Fatigue, sleep disturbance, impaired coor-dination, nausea	None reported
Folacin	Coenzyme (reduced form) involved in transfer of single carbon units in nucleic acid metabolism.	Legume, green vegetables, whole wheat products.	Anemia, gastrointestinal disturbances, diarrhea, red tongue.	None reported
Vitamin B_{12} or cyanocobalamin	It contains cobalt. Coenzyme involved in transfer of single carbon units in nucleic acid metabolism	Muscle meats, eggs, dairy products, (not present in plant foods).	Pernicious anemia, neurological disorders.	None reported
Biotin vitamin H	Coenzyme required for fat synthesis, amino acid metabolism glycogen (animal starch) formation.	Whole milk egg yolk's Legumes, vegetables, meats.	Fatigue, depression, dermatitis, muscular pains and eye disorders.	Not reported
Vitamin C or Ascorbic Acid	Destroyed by cooking or prolonged exposure to air. It increases resistance of the body against diseases. Maintain intercellular matrix of cartilage, bones, skin and dentine. Helps in healing of cuts and abrasions, important in collagen synthesis.	Citrus fruits (oranges, lemon, grape fruit, lime), aonla, cabbage, guava, green peppers, salad greens.	Scurvy (degene-ration of skin, teeth, blood vessels, epithelial hemorrhages), pyorrhea (loosening of teeth and bleeding of gums).	Relatively nontoxic. Possibility of kidney stones.

1.7 MINERALS IN FOOD

All foods contain varying amounts of minerals. Minerals may be present as inorganic or organic salt or may be in combined form as phosphorus is combined with phosphoproteins and metals are combined with enzymes. More than 60 elements may be present in foods. We may divide these elements into two groups:

1. **Major salt components** like, potassium, sodium, calcium, magnesium, chloride, sulfate, phosphate and bicarbonates.
2. Trace element can be divided into 3 groups

(*i*) *Essential nutrient* element, which include elements Fe, Cu, I, Co, Mn, Zn, Cr, Ni, Si, F, Mo and Se.

(*ii*) *Non-nutritive nontoxic* elements, Al, B and Sn

(*iii*) Non-nutritive toxic elements including, Hg, Pb, As Cd and Sb.

Some of the major mineral constituent especially monovalent species are present in foods are soluble salts and mostly in oxidized form. For examples cations sodium and potassium and the anions chloride and sulfate. Some of the polyvalent ions, however are usually present in the form of an equilibrium between ionic, dissolved nonionic and colloidal species. Such equilibria is often present in milk and meat. Metals are often present in form of *chelates*:

CO-ORDINATION COMPOUNDS AND CHELATES

Co-ordination compounds: The addition compounds that results from the combination of two or more simple stable salts and retain their identity in the solid as well as in dissolved state are called complex compounds. *e.g.*

$$K_4SO_4.(CN)_6] \longrightarrow 4K^+ + [Fe(CN)_6]^{4-}$$

A complex compound contains a simple cation and a complex anion or a complex cation and a simple anion or a complex cation and a complex anion or a neutral molecule. Examples are $K_4[Fe(CN)_6]$, $[Cu(NH_3)_4]SO_4$,$[Co(NH_3)_6]$ $[Cr(CN)_6]$ respectively. Thus, a complex ion is defined as "an electrically charged radical, which consists of a central metal atom or ion surrounded by a group of ionic or neutral species.

Ligands: The neutral molecules or ions (usually anions) which are linked directly with the central metal atom/ion are called ligands. In most of the complexes, ligands act as donor of one or more lone pairs to the central metal atom/ion. It should be noted that in metallic carbonyls, the ligand, CO, acts as both donor and acceptor (M $\rightleftharpoons$ CO).

The ligands may be monodentate (having only donor atom, viz F^-, Cl–, H_2O, NO_2 etc.), biodentate (having two donor atoms, viz. $\ddot{N}H_2-(CH_2)_2-\ddot{N}H_2$ ethylene diamine), tridentate (viz. Diethyentriamine) or polydentate (two or more donor atom).

CHELATES: The name chelate is derived from the claw like manner is which the metal is held by co-ordinate covalent bonds of ligands. Metals are often present in the form of chelates. The characteristic property of polydentate ligands is chelation. When coordination of more than one donor atm from a ligand to the same central atom/ion takes place, it is called chelation and the ligand a chelating ligand. The close ring compound thus formed is called *chelate* (a metal chelate). In the formation of chelate, the ligand function as Lewis base and metal ion acts as Lewis acid.

The stability constant of a chelate is influenced by number of factors. The chelate is more stable when ligand is relatively more basic. The chelate's stability depends on nature of metal ion and is related to electronegative character of the metal. The stability of a chelate normally decreases with decreasing pH. Many transition metal can form complex compounds by accepting pair of electrons in empty orbitals. Some example of four-and five membered rings of chelates are shown below:

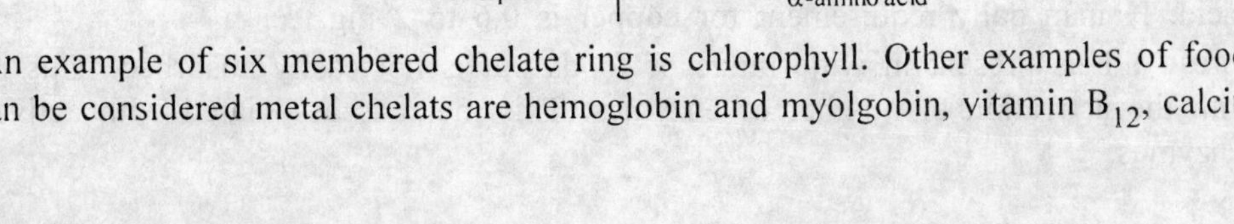

An example of six membered chelate ring is chlorophyll. Other examples of food compounds that can be considered metal chelats are hemoglobin and myolgobin, vitamin B_{12}, calcium caseinate.

Some important characteristic of chelates:

(*a*) **Chelating effect:** Chelating ligands form more stable complexes than the monodentate analogs. The complex ion/compound have such ligands does not dissociate easily.

(*b*) **Forming of rings:** Chelating ligands which do not contain double bonds, *e.g.* ethylenediamine, form five membered stable rings. The chelating ligands such as acetylacetone form six membered stable complexes.

(*c*) **Steric hindrance:** Ligands with large groups form unstable rings than the ligands with smaller groups due to steric hindrance

Importance of Coordination Compounds

Chelation is useful in applications such as providing nutritional supplement. Chelated minerals are meant to boost absorption. They are bound to chelating agent. Which are typically organic compound or amino acids that help prevent the minerals from interacting with other compounds. Because chelated minerals are bound to an amino or organic acid, they do not require as much as stomach acid to be efficiently digested. A mineral is chelated state allow easy passage through the intestinal wall into the blood resulting in increased metabolism of that mineral.

Chelates in animal feed is Jargon for metallo organic compounds added to animal feed. The compounds provide sources of various metals that improve the health of animal. Typical metals salts are derived from cobalt, copper, iron, manganese, and zinc. The objective of supplementation with trace minerals is to avoid a variety of deficiency diseases.

Coordination compounds are of great importance in biological systems. Familiar examples beings-chlorophylls (the green pigments in plants, central to photosynthesis) hemoglobin (the red pigment of blood, which acts as oxygen carrier) along with myoglobin (which stores oxygen and is a regulator of respiration). Vitamin B_{12}, cyanocobalammin, the anti-pernicious anaemia factor. All of these, respectively, are the coordination compound of magnesium iron and cobalt with the macrocyclic porphyrin and corrin ligands. Among the other compounds of biological importance with coordinated metal ions are the enzyme like, carboxypeptidase A and carbonic anhydrase (catalyst of biological system).

TRACE ELEMENT: Trace element are found in all the foods we eat. Trace element may be present in the food as a result of uptake from soils of feed or from contamination during processing or subsequent process of foods. For example level of some trace element is milk depends on the level of element in the feed. Contanination of food products with metal can occur as a result of pickup of metals from equipment for packaging materials. Specially from tin can, The nickel found in milk comes almost from stainless steel in processing equipment, Nine of the trace elements that are essential to humans are cobalt, copper, fluorine, iodine, iron, manganese, molybdenum, zinc and selenium. Recently three more are added to list are: chromium silicon and nickel

Some of the trace element are not essential and show toxicity such as lead, mercury and cadmium. These are known as *contaminants*.

Cobalt is an integral part of the only metal containing vitamin B12. The level of cobalt in food varies widely from as little to 0.01 ppm in corn and cereals to 1 ppm in some legumes. Human requirement is very small and deficiencies does not occur.

Copper is present in food as part of several copper containing enzymes, including polyphenolases. Copper in a very powerful prooxidant and catalyzes the oxidation of unsaturated fats and oils as well as ascorbic acid. Human daily requirement for copper is 0.6 to 2 mg.

Manganese : It is present in wide range of foods but is not easily absorbed. This metal is associated with the activation of number of enzymes. This metal is associated with activation of number of enzymes.

Iron: Iron is a component of the heme pigments and of some enzymes. In spite of the fact that some foods have high iron levels, much of the population has frequently been found to be deficient in this element. Animal food products may have high levels that are well absorbed.; liver may contain several thousands ppm or iron.

Zinc: Zinc is the second most important of the essential trace elements for humans. It is a constituent of some enzymes, such as carbonic anhydrase. The levels of zinc in cereal grains is 30-40 ppm. When acid foods such as fruit juices stored in galvanized containers sufficient zinc may be dissolved to cause zinc poisoning.

Molybdenum: Molybdenum plays a role in several enzyme reactions. Some of the molybdenum-containing enzymes are aldehyde oxidase sulfite oxidase, xanthine dehydrogenase, and xanthine oxidase. This metal is found in cereal grains and legumes; leafy vegetables, especially those rich in chlorophyll; animal organs; and in relatively small amounts, less than 0.1 ppm,in fruits. Recommend RDA is 45 μg/day.

Selenium: Selenium has recently been found to protect against liver necrosis. It usually occurs bound to organic molecules. Different selenium compounds have greater or lesser protective effect. Many selenium compounds are volatile and can be lost by cooking or processing. It is found about a 5% loss of selenium as a result of drying of skim milk. Most fruits and vegetables contain less than 0.01 μg/g. Grain products range from 0.025 to 0.66 μg/g, dried skim milk from 0.095 to 0.24 μg/g, meat from 0.1 to 1.9 μg/g, and seafood from 0.4 to 0.7μg/g.

RDA of selenium - 55μg/day. For Lactating women - 60-70 μg/day.

Fluorine: Fluorine is a constituent of skeletal bone and helps reduce the incidence of dental caries. The fluorine content of drinking water is usually below 0.2 mg/L but in some locations may be as high as 5 mg/L. The optimal concentration for dental health is 1 mg/L. The fluoride content of vegetables is low, with the exception of spinach, which contains 280 μg/100 g. Milk contains 20μg/100 g and beef about 100 μg/100 g. Fish foods may contain up to 700 μg/100 g and tea about 100 μg/g.

Iodine: Iodine is not present is sufficient amounts in the diet in several areas of the world; an iodine deficiency result in goiter. The addition of iodine to table salt has been extremely effective in reducing the incidence of goiter. Fish and shellfish have higher levels. Saltwater fish have levels of about 50 to 150 mg/100 g and shellfish may have levels as high as 400 mg/100 g.

Nickel: Foods with a relatively high nickel content include nuts, legumes cocoa products, shellfish, and hydrogenated fats. Animal products are generally low in nickel, plant products high. Dietary nickel intake has been estimated to be in the range of 150 to 70 μg/day and the suggested dietary nickel requirement is about 35 μg/day.

Chromium: In general dietary intake of chromium is in the order of 50 μg/day.

Chromium is useful to control blood sugar levels. It is also used for high cholestorol, athletic performance, bipolar disorder and many other purposes. Chromium is present in many tools including, meats, grain products, fruits, vegetables, nuts, spices, beer and wine. Daily value of chromium requirement is 35 μg. In general eating whole wheat products may add chromium to the diet. Refining and processing of foods may lead to loss of chromium. Use of stainless steel equipments in food processing results in leaching of chromium in food products.

Silicon : Silicon is ubiquitous in the environment and present in many foods. Foods of animal origin are relatively low in silicon; foods of plant origin are relatively high. Good plant sources are unrefined grains, cereal products, and root crops. RDA- 5μg/day.

Table 5: A summary of the dietary source, function and effects of deficiency or excess intakes of the individual essential minerals

Mineral	Dietary Sources	Major body functions	Deficiency diseases	Excess
Calcium 1000-2000 mg/day	Milk, cheese, dark green vegetables, dried legumes	Bone and tooth formation, blood clotting, nerve transmission.	Stunted growth rickets, osteoporosis convulsions	Can cause nausea constipation or kidney diseases hypercalcemia
Phosphorous 2.5-4.5 mg/day	Milk, cheese, meat, poultry, grains	Bone and tooth formation, acid base balance	Weakness, demineralization of bone, loss of calcium,	Erosion of jaw (phossy jaw) hyperphosphatemia
Sulfur	Sulfur amino acids (methionine and cystine) in dietary protein	Constituents of active tissue compounds, cartilage and tendon	Arthritis, acne, brittle nails and hair convulsions, depression, Eczema, Itchy skin or scalp, Migraine	Excess sulfur amino acid intake leads to burning sensations or Diarrhea
Potassium 3.6-5.2 mmol/L	Meats, milk, many fruits	Acid-base balance, body water balance, nerve function	Muscular weak-ness, paralysis	Muscular weak-ness, tiredness, nausea death (Hyperkalemia)
Chlorine EPA-4 ppm in drinking water	Common salts or drinking water	Formation of gastric juice, acid base balance	Muscle cramps, mental apathy, reduce appetite	Vomiting, Airway irritation
Sodium less than 2300 mg/day	Common salts	Acid base balance, body water balance, nerve function	Muscle cramps, mental apathy, reduce appetite	High blood pressure stroke and heart failure
Magnesium 310-470 mg per day	Whole grains, green leafy vegetables	Activates enzyme, involved in protein synthesis	Growth failure, behavioral disturbances, weakness, spasms	Diarrhea, Nausea vomitting
Iron 45 mg per day	Eggs, lean meats, legumes, whole grains, green leafy vegetables	Constituents of hemoglobin and enzymes involved in energy metabolism.	Iron-deficiency anemia (weakness, reduced resistance to infection)	Siderosis, Cirrhosis of liver.
Flourine 0.7 ppm in water	Drinking water, tea, seafood	May be important in maintenance of tooth decay	Higher frequency of tooth decay	Mottling of teeth (fluorosis) increased bone density neurological distur-bances
Zinc 11 mg/d man 8 mg/d women	Widely distributed in foods	Constituents of enzymes involved in digestion	Growth failure, small sex glands, skin lesions	Fever, nausea, vomiting, diarrhea
Copper	Meats, drinking water	Constituents of enzymes associated with iron metabolism	Anemia, bone changes (rare in man)	Rare metabolic condition (Wilson's disease)
Silicon Vanadium Tin Nickel	Widely distributed in foods	Silicon- Nails, hair, and skin and overall collagen synthesis Vanadium- Essential for some animals Tin- Cellular immune system Nickel- Proper functioning of human body	Not reported in man	Industrial exposures Silicon-silicosis Vanadium – lung irritation Tin – vomiting Nickel- acute pneumonitis

Selenium 55 mcg/day max. 400 mcg/d	Sea foods, meal, grains	Functions in close association with vitamin E	Anemia (rare)	Gastrointestinal disorders, lung irritation
Manganese Upper limit 11 mg/day	Widely distributed in foods	Constituents of enzymes involved in fat synthesis	In animal: poor growth, disturbance of nervous system, reproductive abnormalities	Poisoning in manganese mines: generalized disease in nervous system or anemia
Iodine Max. range 1,100 mcg/d	Marine fish and shellfish, dairy products, many vegetables	Constituents of thyroid hormones	Goiter (enlarged thyroid)	Very high intake depress thyroid activity
Molybdenum 2 mg/day	Legumes, cereals, organ meats	Constituents of some enzyme	Not reported in man	Inhibition of enzymes
Chromium 1000 mcg/d (UL)	Fats, vegetables oils, meats	Involved in glucose and energy metabolism	Impaired ability to metabolizing glucose	Occupational exposures, skin and kidney damage
Cobalt > 1 μg/l	Organ and muscle meats, milk	Constituents of vitamin B_{12}	Not reported in man	Industrial exposure: dermatitis and disease of red blood cells
Water (9-13) cups per/day	Solid foods, liquids, drinking water.	Transport of nutrients, temperature regulation, participates in metabolic reactions.	Thirst, dehydration	Headaches, nausea, edema, high blood pressures. hyponatremia due to low sodium level

1.8 ENZYMES

Enzymes are naturally occurring simple or conjugate proteins acting as specific catalysts in cell process. Some enzymes can be non proteins also some enzyme facilitates a biochemical reaction by providing alternative lower activation energy pathways there by increasing the rate of reactions. Enzymes being proteins have colloidal nature and often get activated during reaction and have to be constantly received by synthesis in the body. At present about 3000 enzymes have been recognized by the international union of biochemistry. However only about 300 (~10 %) are commercially available.

Historical background

French chemist **Anselme Payen** was first to discover enzyme diastase in 1833.

Berzelius in 1836 coined the term 'catalysis' (Greek: To dissolve). In 1878, **Kuhne** used the word 'Enzyme' (Greek: in yeast) to indicate the catalysis taking place in the biological systems.

In 1897 **Edward Buchner** found that sugar was fermented by yeast extract even when there was no living yeast cells in the mixture.

- 2000 BC. The Egyptians and Sumerians developed various and specific fermentations for use in brewing, bread making, and cheese making.
- 800 BC. Calves' stomachs and the enzyme chymosin were used for cheese making.
- 1878. The components of yeast cells, which cause fermentation, were identified and the term "enzyme" was coined. The word itself means "in yeast" and is derived from the Greek *en* meaning "in" and *zyme* meaning "yeast" or "leaven."

- 1926. Enzymes were first known to be proteins.
- 1980s. Enzyme preparations were developed to improve the digestibility and nutrient availability of certain animal feeds.
- 1982. The first food application of a product of gene technology, *i.e.*, α-amylase, took place.
- 1988. Recombinant chymosin was approved and introduced in Switzerland, marking an early approval of a product of gene technology for food application.
- 1990s. Two food processing aids obtained using gene technology were applied, *i.e.*, an enzyme for use in cheese making (United States), and a yeast for use in baking (United Kingdom).
- 2000s. Advances with enzymes (*e.g.*, immobilized enzymes) are taking place with many applications to food industry (flavors, aromas, etc.)

Enzyme may be defined as a protein that catalyses a biochemical and metabolic reaction. Enzymes are specific for both the compounds acted on (the substrates) and the reactions carried out. Because of this, enzymes extracted from plant or animal sources, micro-organisms or those produced by genetic modification are widely used in the chemical, pharmaceutical and food industries (*e.g.* chymosin in cheese-making, maltase in beer production, synthesis of vitamin C and citric acid), as well as in washing powders. Because they are proteins, enzymes are permanently inactivated by heat, strong acid or alkali and other conditions that cause denaturation of proteins. Many enzymes contain non-protein components which are essential for their function. These are known as ***prosthetic groups, coenzymes or cofactors*** and may be metal ions, metal ions in organic complexes (*e.g.* haem in haemoglobin and cytochromes) or a variety of organic compounds, many of which are derived from vitamins. The (inactive) protein without its prosthetic group is known as the ***apo-enzyme***, and the active assembly of protein plus prosthetic group is called the ***holo-enzyme***.

All enzymes are proteins except few are catalytic RNA molecules. Enzymes are important in foods, because they catalyze various reactions that affect color, flavor, or texture, and hence quality of foods. Some of these reactions may be desirable, whereas others are undesirable and produce unwanted discoloration or off-flavors in foods. Each enzyme has a unique structure or conformation, which enables it to attach to its specific substrate and catalyze the reaction. When the reaction is complete, the enzyme is released to act as a catalyst again. All enzymes have an optimal temperature and pH range, within which the reaction will proceed most rapidly. Heat or changes in pH denature the enzymes, making it difficult or impossible for them to attach to their respective substrates, thus inactivating them.

In case of enzymatic reaction the enzyme is so built that it binds to the substrate in a specific manner. The enzymatic reaction may be processed through the following four states.

(*i*) The formation of complex between enzyme and substrate (ES),

(*ii*) The conversion of this complex to an enzyme intermediate complex (EI)

(*iii*) Further conversion to a complex between enzyme and product EP

(*iv*) The dissociation of enzyme product complex, leaving the enzyme unchanged.

Table 6 gives the summary of the some important enzymatic reactions.

Table 6 : Some enzymatic reactions

Enzyme	Source	Reactions
Invertase	Yeast	Sucrose → Glucose and fructose
Zymase	Yeast	Glucose → Ethyl alcohol and carbon dioxide
Diastase	Malt	Starch → Maltose
Maltase	Yeast	Maltose → Glucose
Urease	Soyabeam	Urea → Ammonia and carbon dioxide
Pepsin	Stomach	Proteins → Amino acids.

Characteristics of enzyme catalysis

The following characteristics are exhibited by enzyme catalysts:

(*i*) *Most highly efficient*: One molecule of an enzyme may transform one million molecules of the reactant per minute.

(*ii*) *Highly specific nature*: Each enzyme is specific for a given reaction *i.e.*, one catalyst cannot catalyse more than one reaction. For example, the enzyme urease catalyses the hydrolysis of urea only.

(*iii*) *Highly active under optimum temperature*: The rate of an enzyme reaction becomes maximum at a definite temperature, called the *optimum temperature*. On either side of the optimum temperature, the enzyme activity decreases. The optimum temperature range for enzymatic activity is 298-310 K. Human body temperature being 310 K is suited for enzyme-catalysed reactions.

(*iv*) *Highly active under optimum pH*: The rate of an enzyme-catalysed reaction is maximum at a particular pH and optimum pH, which is between pH value 5-7.

(*v*) *Increasing activity in presence of activators and co-enzymes*: The enzymaic activity is increased in the presence of certain substances, known as co-enzymes. It has been observed that when a small non-protein (vitamin) is present along with an enzyme, the catalytic activity is enhanced considerably.

Activators are generally metal ions such as Na^+, Mn^{2+}, Co^{2+}, Cu^- etc. These metal ions, when weakly bonded to enzyme molecules increase their catalytic activity. Amylase in presence of sodium chloride *i.e.*, Na^+ ions are catalytically very active.

(*vi*) *Influence or inhibitors and poisons*: Like ordinary catalysts, enzymes are also inhibited or poisoned by the presence of certain substances. The inhibitors or poisons interact with the active functional growth on the enzyme surface and often reduce or completely destroy catalytic activity of the enzymes. The use of many drugs is related to their action as enzyme inhibitors in the body.

If an enzymatic reaction is required in food processing, it is important to ensure that the optimal pH and temperature range for that enzyme is achieved. Outside the optimal range, the reaction will proceed more slowly, if at all. Heat treatment therefore must be avoided. If this is not possible, the enzyme must be added after heat treatment and subsequent cooling of the food. On the other hand, if enzyme action is undesirable, the enzymes must be inactivated. This usually is achieved by heat treatment, but also may be accomplished by adding acid to change the pH.

Examples of desirable enzymatic reactions include the clotting of milk by *rennet*, which is the first step in making cheese. Ripening of cheese during storage also is due to enzyme activity.

of meat by proteolytic enzymes such as *papain*, *bromelain*, and *ficin*. These enzymes catalyze hydrolysis of peptide bonds in proteins. They are added to the meat and allowed to work for a period of time. The reaction must be controlled to prevent too much breakdown of the proteins. The optimum temperature for these enzymes occurs during the early cooking stages. (Hydrolysis proceeds very slowly at refrigeration temperatures.) As meat is cooked, the enzymes promote hydrolysis. However, as the internal temperature continues to rise, the enzymes are inactivated and the reaction is stopped.

Although useful as meat tenderizers, proteolytic enzymes may be undesirable in other circumstances. For example, if a gelatin salad is made with raw pineapple, the jelly may not set, due to action of *bromelain*, which is contained in pineapple. This can be prevented by heating the pineapple to inactivate the enzyme before making the gelatin salad. Other examples of unwanted enzymatic reactions include enzymatic browning, which occurs when fruits and vegetables are damaged, due to the action of *polyphenol oxidase*, and produces undesirable discoloration. Development of off-flavors in fats and fat-containing foods also may be a problem in some circumstances, and this may be caused by *lipase* or *lipoxygenase*. Enzymes are inactivated in fruits and vegetables prior to freezing by a mild heat process known as blanching. The fruits or vegetables are placed in boiling water for a short time, in order to inactivate the enzymes that would cause discoloration or development of off-flavors during frozen storage.

Table 7: Applications of enzymes in the food industry

Food Processing	Enzyme	Application
Alcohol production	Amylases	Starch liquefaction
Analytical testing	Cellulase, pectinase, amylases	Testing for dietary fibers, sugars
Baking	Fungal proteases	Dough conditioning, flour bleaching, malting; and antistaling
Brewing	Microbial proteases, papain, pectinase	Low-calorie beer, chill proofing, barley, alternative adjunct liquefaction, and saccharification
Confectionaries	Invertase	Cream candy centers
Coffee processing	Pectinases, cellulase	Removal of burnt flavor in UHT (ultra-heat-treated) milk Separation of bean, viscosity control of extracts
Dairy	Rennins, lactase, lipase	Cheese making, accelerated cheese ripening, natural cheese flavor concentrations, whey utilization, lactase intolerance
Fats and oils	Lipase, phospholipase	Cocoa-butter substitutes, flavor-ester synthesis
Flavors	Protease, lipase	Synthesis of savory flavors, natural flavor esters
Fruits and vegetables	Cellulase	Breakdown of cellulose structure
Fruit juice and wine	Pectinases	Mash treatment, depectinization, starch/araban haze removal, citrus pulp wash viscosity reduction, natural cloud production
Protein	Bromelin, papain, pepsin, pancreatin	Rendering, soy milk production, egg white replacement, emulsifier production, functional hydrolysates
Sugar processing	Amylases, cellulase	Removal of undesirable starches and polysaccharides in the processing of cane sugar
Starch conversion	Glucose isomerase	High fructose corn syrup. maltose, and dextrin syrups
Waste treatment	Proteases, cellulases, lipase and other solid waste material	Breakdown of cellulose, lignins, oil residues
Others	Proteases	Meat tenderizing, coffee soluble-extract viscosity reduction

1.8.1 Nomenclature and classification of enzymes

General principles

- ***First principle:*** Names purporting to be names of enzymes, especially those ending in -*ase* should be used only for single enzymes, that is, single catalytic entities. They should not be applied to systems containing more than one enzyme.
- ***Second principle*:** Enzymes are classified and named according to the reaction they catalyze.
- ***Third principle:*** Enzymes are divided into groups on the basis of the type of reactions catalyzed, and this, together with the name(s) of the substrate(s), provides a basis for determining the systematic name and EC number for naming individual enzymes.

Common and systematic names

- The common name (recommended, trivial, or working name) follows immediately after the EC number.
- While the common name is normally that used in the literature, the systematic name, which is formed in accordance with definite rules, is more precise chemically. It should be possible to determine the reaction catalyzed from the systematic name alone.

Scheme of classification and numbering of enzymes

The first Enzyme Commission, in its report in 1961, devised a system for the classification of enzymes that also serves as a basis for assigning EC numbers to them. These code numbers (prefixed by EC), which are now widely in use, containing four elements separated by periods (*e.g.*, 1.1.1.1), with the following meaning:

- The first number shows to which of the six divisions (*classes*) the enzyme belongs,
- The second figure indicates the *subclass*,
- The third figure gives the *sub-subclass*, and
- The fourth figure is the serial number of the enzyme in its sub-subclass.

The main classes are

- *Class 1.* Oxidoreductases (dehydrogenases, reductases, or oxidases),
- *Class 2.* Transferases,
- *Class 3.* Hydrolases,
- *Class 4.* Lyases,
- *Class 5.* Isomerases (racemases, epimerases, cis-trans-isomerases, isomerases, tautomerases, mutases, cycloisomerases), and
- *Class 6.* Ligases (synthases).

***Class 1 Oxidoreductases*:** Enzymes catalyzing oxidoreductions belong to this class. The reactions are of the form $AH_2 + B = A + BH_2$ or $AH_2 + B^+ = A + BH + H^+$. The substrate oxidized is regarded as the hydrogen or electron donor. The classification is based on the order "donor : acceptor oxidoreductase." Examples are *Peroxidase, Catalase, Polyphenol oxidase, Lipoxygenase, Ascorbic acid oxidase, Glucose oxidase, Alcohol dehydrogenase*

***Class 2 Transferases*:** Transferases are enzymes transferring a group (*e.g.*, the methyl group or a glycosyl group), from one compound (generally regarded as donor) to another compound (generally regarded as acceptor) *i.e.* $A - X + B = A + B - X$. They are. *Amylosucrase, Dextransucrase, Transglutaminase.*

Class 3 Hydrolases: These enzymes catalyze the hydrolysis of various bonds. Some of these enzymes pose problems be- cause they have a very wide specificity. While the systematic name always includes "hydrolase,". The common name is, in most cases, formed by the name of the substrate with the suffix *-ase*. It is understood that the name of this substrate with the suffix means a hydrolytic enzyme. The peptidases, subclass 3.4, are classified in a different manner from other enzymes in this class. Examples are *Invertase, Chlorophyllase, Amylase, Cellulase, Polygalacturonase, Lipase, Galactosidase, Thermolysin.*

Class 4 Lyases: Lyases are enzymes cleaving C–C, C–O, C–N, and other bonds by means other than hydrolysis or oxidation. They differ from other enzymes in that two substrates are involved in one reaction direction, but only one in the other direction. When acting on the single substrate, a molecule is eliminated, leaving an unsaturated residue. The systematic name is formed according to "substrate group-lyase." In common names, expressions like decarboxylase, aldolase, and so on are used. "Dehydratase" is used for those enzymes eliminating water. In cases where the reverse reaction is more important, or the only one to be demonstrated, "synthase" may be used in the name. They are *Pectin lyase, Phenylalanine ammonia lyase, Cysteine sulfoxide lyase, Hydroperoxide lyase.*

Class 5 Isomerase: These enzymes catalyze changes within one molecule. They catalyze isomerization reactions, for example, racemization, epimerization, *cis-trans*-isomerization, tautomerization. Examples are *Glucose isomerase, Carotenoid isomerase.*

Class 6 Ligases: Ligases are enzymes catalyzing the joining of two molecules with concomitant hydrolysis of the diphosphate bond in ATP or a similar triphosphate. The bonds formed are often high-energy bonds. "Ligase" is commonly used for the common name, but in a few cases, "synthase" or "carboxylase" is used. Use of the term "synthetase" is discouraged. Example is *Hydroxycinnamate CoA ligase.*

1.8.2 Specificity of enzymes: Some of the characteristics of enzymes are the following:

- ***High activity***: Enzymes can increase the rate of a reaction millions of times by lowering the activation energy of the reaction like conventional chemical catalysts. The maximum rate of conversion of a substrate to a product by a molecule of an enzyme is known as the "turnover number" (*K*cat). For example, the *K*cat for catalase, which catalyzes the conversion of hydrogen peroxide to O_2 and H_2O, is approximately 600,000 molecules per second per molecule of enzyme.
- ***Selectivity:*** The catalytic active site of an enzyme, which is the result of folding of the polypeptide chain, fits only to a small (specific) number of substrates for the conversion to products. Since an enzyme acts only on one compound of a complex mixture, it can control a reaction independently of many others occurring in the complex. Minor changes, like increasing the temperature, in the structure of the substrate may cause the enzyme to be unable to recognize the substrate and convert it to corresponding products.
- ***Regiospecificity***: An enzyme can detect differences in the spatial arrangement of atoms in a compound. For example, monoxygenase enzymes oxidize methyl cyclohexane, but different enzymes are found to oxidize either the methyl substitute or the methylene ring group. This has potential application in the production of synthetic fragrances and flavors.
- ***Stereospecificity***: Enzymes are highly stereospecific in the choice of substrate or in the formed product. Their selectivity for the substrate usually extends to discernment between different forms (chiral) of the substrate molecule (d or l forms). For example, bacterial glucose oxidase will use only d-glucose.

- ***Controllability***: The catalysis of reactions by enzymes can be controlled by the amount of substrate and by other factors (temperature, pH, etc.). An enzyme is active (switched on) in the presence of a correct amount of the substrate and inactive (turned off) when the substrate is not available. For example, the response of certain bacteria to the presence of lactose induces the formation of â-galactosidase (lactase), which hydrolyses lactose to glucose and galactose used as food by organisms.
- ***Environmental factors***: Reactions catalyzed by enzymes (biocatalysts with high specificity) are less environmentally polluting due to the lower by-product produced. The synthesized products can be classified as "natural" when substrates are naturally derived, and they are valuable to the food industry as they are not chemically manufactured.

Enzyme kinetic: The study of the rate at which an enzyme works is called enzyme kinetics. Following that, enzyme kinetics will be examined as a function of the concentration of the substrate available to the enzyme. Like a chemical catalyst, an enzyme acts by lowering the activation energy of a reaction, thereby inducing the formation of the products from the substrates. Enzymes are regulated by a multitude of mechanisms (*e.g.* phosphorylation, product inhibition) or by localisation. The rate of an enzyme-catalysed reaction depends on multiple factors. These include:

a) ***Temperature of the reaction:*** This increase in heat increases the collision frequency between the reactants. However, beyond a particular temperature, the protein enzyme also tends to denature, thereby making it inactive.

b) ***Substrate concentration***: Increase in substrate concentration favours the reaction, as this increases the collision between the enzyme molecule and the substrates.

c) ***pH of the reaction:*** The protein's active site needs a particular charge inducing a favourable microenvironment for the reaction to occur. This microenvironment varies as the charge of the amino acids also changes with the change in pH.

When the amount of substrate is in substantial excess to the amount of enzyme, the rate we observe is the initial velocity of ***Vi***. By plotting ***Vi*** as a function of [S], the following is observed (Fig. 1).

- At low values of [S], the initial velocity, *Vi*, rises almost linearly with increasing [S].
- But as [S] increases, the gains in *Vi* level off (forming a rectangular hyperbola).
- The asymptote represents the maximum velocity of the reaction, designated *V*max.
- The substrate concentration that produces a *Vi* that is one-half of *V*max is designated the Michaelis–Menten constant, *K*m.

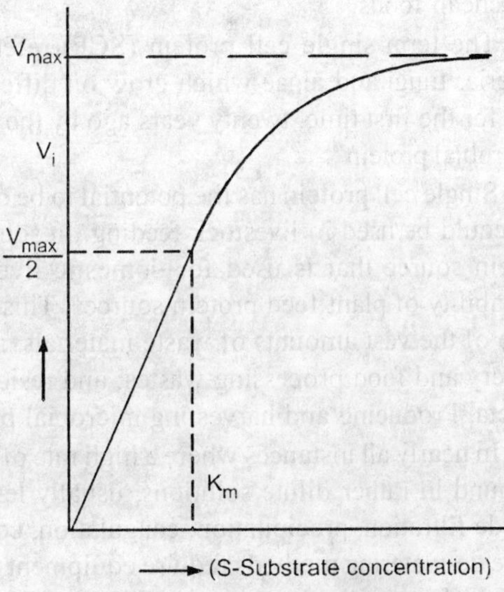

Fig. 1: Initial velocity, V_i (moles/time), as function of substrate concentration, [S] (molar).

*K*m is an inverse measure of the affinity or strength of binding between the enzyme and its substrate. The lower the *K*m, the greater the affinity (so the lower the concentration of substrate needed to achieve a given rate).

In order to understand the mechanisms of the enzymatic process and also predict the reaction characteristics, one needs to understand the kinetics of the reaction. The important factor that effects the enzyme reaction is the availability and concentration of the substrates. An important model that gives a mathematical relationship is the Michaelis–Menten and Hill equation. The equation is denoted as

$$V_i = \frac{V_{max} + [S]}{K_m + [S]} \quad (1)$$

where V_i is the initial velocity, S is the substrate concentration, V_{max} is the maximal velocity, and K_m is the Michaelis constant which is the substrate concentration at which the velocity is half of V_{max}. K_m denotes the affinity of the substrate to the enzyme; a low K_m value indicates that the enzyme binds to the substrate tightly.

In biochemistry, Michaelis–Menten kinetics is one of the best-known models of enzyme kinetics.

The **one gene, one enzyme** hypothesis is the idea that each gene encodes a single enzyme. Today, we know that this idea is generally (but not exactly) correct.

Sir Archibald Garrod, a British medical doctor, was the first to suggest that genes were connected to enzymes. Beadle and Tatum confirmed Garrod's hypothesis using genetic and biochemical studies of the bread mold *Neurospora.* Beadle and Tatum identified bread mold mutants that were unable to make specific amino acids. In each one, a mutation had "broken" an enzyme needed to build a certain amino acid

1.9 SINGLE CELL PROTEIN

Microorganisms have high protein content and contain useful quantities of vitamins. Their rate of growth is very rapid, and the rate of protein synthesis in microorganisms has been compared favorably with that of animals. A 500 kg bullock produces an extra 500 g protein per day, whereas 500 kg yeast grown in suitable conditions can produce 50 tonnes protein a day. It can be seen that micro-organism are potentially a very valuable source of protein, especially if they can be produced economically by the use of a cheap foods.

The term single cell protein (SCP) refers to dead, dry cells of micro-organisms such as yeast, bacteria, fungi and algae which grow on different carbon sources. The name "single cell protein" was used for the first time, twenty years ago by the M.I.T. Professor Carol Wilson to give a better image than "microbial protein".

Single cell protein has the potential to be developed into a very large source of supplemental protein that could be used in livestock feeding. In some regions single cell protein could become the principal protein source that is used for domestic livestock, depending upon the population growth and the availability of plant feed protein sources. This could develop because microbes can be used to ferment some of the vast amounts of waste materials, such as straws; wood and wood processing wastes; food, cannery and food processing wastes; and residues from alcohol production or from human and animal excreta. Producing and harvesting microbial proteins is not without costs, unfortunately.

In nearly all instances where a high rate of production would be achieved, the single cell protein will be found in rather dilute solutions, usually less than 5 % solids. Methods available for concentrating include filtration, precipitation, coagulation, centrifugation, and the use of semi-permeable membranes. These de-watering methods require equipment that is quite expensive and would not be suitable for most small-scale operations. Removal of the amount of water necessary to stabilize the material for storage, in most instances, is not currently economical. Single cell protein must be dried to about 10 % moisture, or condensed and acidified to prevent spoilage from occurring, or fed shortly after being produced. Single cell protein can be produced on a number of different substrates, often this is done to reduce the *Biological Oxidation Demand* of the effluent streams leaving various types of agricultural processing plants. Microbial protein has high nucleic acid content, so levels need to be limited in the diets of monogastric animals. Some organisms can also produce mycotoxins.

Single cell proteins like *Scenedesmug obliques, Chlorella pyrennodosa*, a type algae, and many more yeast cells help in producing more protein from industrial waste like spent grains, rot vegetables, fruits, bagasses of sugarcane, molasses, washed water, unwanted meat and poultry waste from fish and shrimp waste. These single cell proteins increase the protein by 50-60% and enhance the sugars for alcohol conversion, the minerals and vitamins, bioavailability also increases.

Sources

Following are the chief sources of protein production that can be utilized for SCP technology.

- Alga
- Yeast
- Bacteria

Alga: A simple, nonflowering, and typically aquatic plant of large group that includes the seaweeds and many single celled forms. Since ancient times, Spirulina was cultivated by people near Lake Chad in Africa and the Aztecs near Lake Texcoco in Mexico. They used it as food after drying it. Spirulina is the most widely used alga, even astronauts bring it to space during their space travel. Similarly, biomass obtained from **Chlorella** and **Scenedesmus** is harvested and used as source of food by tribal communities in certain parts of the world. Alga is used as a food in many different ways and its advantages include simple cultivation, effective utilization of solar energy, faster growth and rich in protein content.

Yeast: As fungi, yeasts are eukaryotic organisms. They typically are about 0.075 mm in diameter and have many forms, from spherical to egg shaped to filamentous. Most yeasts reproduces a sexually by budding a small bump produces from a parent cell, enlarge, matures and latches. Many fungal species are used as a source of protein rich food. Among these, most popular are yeast species *Candida, Hansenula, Pitchia, Torulopsis and Saccharomyces.* Many other filamentous species are also used as source of single cell protein. In 1973, in Second International Conference convened at MIT, it was reported that *actinomycetes* and filamentous fungi were reported to produce protein from various substrates. During the World War II, trials were made to utilize the cultures of *Fusarium* and *Rhizopus* grown in fermentation as a source of protein food. The inoculum of *Aspergillus oryzae* or *Rhizopus arrhizus* is selected because of their non-toxic nature. Saprophytic fungi grow on complex organic compounds and convert them into simple structures. High amount of fungal biomass is produced as a result of growth. Mycelial yield vary greatly which depends upon organisms and substrates. There are some species of moulds, for example, *Aspergillus niger, A. fumigatus, Fusarium graminearum* which are very dangerous to human, therefore, such fungi must not be used or toxicological evaluations should be done before recommending their use as SCP. Very recently, SCP technology is using fungal species for bioconversion of lignocellulosic wastes.

Bacteria: Bacteria are single cell microorganisms that come in various shapes. They can be spheres rods, or spirals. There are bacteria that are bad, that we call pathogenic, and they cause diseases, but there is also good bacteria. Among bacterial species, Cellulomas and Alcaligenes are the most frequently used bacterial species as a single cell proteins source. Potential phototrophic bacterial trains are recommended for Single Cell Protein production. Some researchers also suggest use of methanotrophic and other bacterial species for single cell protein production. Generation time of *Methylophilus methylotrophus* is about 2 hours and this bacteria is used in animal feed; in general produce a more favorable protein composition than yeast or fungi. Therefore the large quantities of Single Cell Protein animal feed can be produced using bacteria. Characteristics that make bacteria suitable for this application include rapid growth of bacteria, short generation times of bacteria almost can double their cell mass in 20 minutes to 2 hours, they are also capable of growing on a variety of raw materials that range from carbohydrates such as starch and sugars to gaseous and liquid hydrocarbons which include methane and petroleum fractions, to petrochemicals such as methanol and ethanol, nitrogen sources which are useful for bacterial growth include ammonia, ammonium salts, urea, nitrates, and the organic nitrogen in wastes, also it is suggested to add mineral nutrient supplement to the bacterial culture medium to fulfill deficiency of nutrients that may be absent in natural waters in concentrations sufficient to support growth.

Nutritional Benefits of Single Cell Protein: To assess nutritional value of Single Cell Protein, many factors must be considered which include nutrient composition, amino acid profile, vitamin and Na content as well as allergies and gastrointestinal effects. To assess toxicological and carcinogenic affects, long term feeding trails are also required, also processes of drying, harvesting and processing has an effect on the nutritive values of the finished products. Single Cell Protein is basically composed of proteins, fats, carbohydrates, ash ingredients, water and other elements such as potassium and phosphorus. The composition of SCP depends on the nature of substrate and also on organism used, protein not only provide nutritional value but also perform number of other functions. Single Cell Protein from yeast and fungi has up to 50-55% protein it has high protein-carbohydrate ratio than forages. It contains more lysine less amount of methionine and cysteine. It also has good balance of amino acids and it has high B-complex vitamins and more suitable as poultry feed. Single Cell Proteins produced by using bacteria contain more than 80% protein although they have small amount of sulphur containing amono acids and high in nucleic acid content. Some yeast strains with probiotic properties such as *Saccharomyces cerisiae* and *Debaryomyces hansenii* improve larval survival either by colonizing gut of fish larvae, which triggers the early maturation of the pancreas. But many yeast supplements are lacking sulfate amino acids particularly methionine which restricts their extensive use as sole protein source.

Table 8: The nutritional status of SCP obtained from certain microorganisms

Nutrients (% dry weight)	Fungi	Algae	Yeast	Bacteria
Protein	30-45	40-60	45-55	50-65
Fat	2-8	7-20	2-6	1.5-3.0
Ash	9-14	8-10	5-9.5	3-7
Nucleic acid	7-10	3-8	6-12	8-12

Aside from the nutritional benefits of Single Cell Protein, another benefit of Single Cell Protein is its through-out the year production. Also it plays its role in waste management as waste materials are used as substrate. Small area of land is required and SCP is made in less time. Some organisms synthesize useful by-products such as organic acids and fats.

Advantages of Single Cell Protein

The SCP processes and products offer several advantages as listed below:

(*a*) The SCP is rich in high quality protein and is rated poor in fats, which is rather desirable.

(*b*) They can be produced all the year round and are not dependent of the climate (except the algal processes).

(*c*) The microbes are very fast growing and produce large quantities of SCP from relatively very small area of land.

(*d*) They use low cost substrates and, in some cases, such as substrates which are being wasted and causing pollution to the environment.

(*e*) When the substrate used for SCP process is a source of pollution, SCP production helps reduce pollution.

(*f*) Strains having high biomass yields and a desirable amino acid composition can be easily selected or produced by genetic engineering.

(*g*) Some SCPs are good source of vitamins, particularly B-group of vitamins, as well as *e.g.*, yeasts and mushrooms.

(*h*) Mushrooms are considered as delicacy in the human diet.

(*i*) At present, SCP appears to be the only feasible approach to bridge the gap between requirement and supply of proteins.

Disadvantages of single cell proteins

1. SCP ingestion may be detrimental to humans due to the limited capacity of decomposing nucleic acid.
2. SCP can potentially produce allergic reactions in people who have a delicate digestive system or whose bodies fail to recognize the biomass.
3. A high nucleic acid concentration might also cause an increase in uric acid levels in the blood.
4. Regular Consumption of SCP can result in gout and kidney stones.
5. Due to the need for high end machinery, the production cost may be higher.

Table 9: Some important micro-organisms used for SCP production

Microorganisms	Substrate	Used as	Used commercially
Algal			
Chlorella sp.	CO_2 + sunlight	Feed	Yes (Japan & Taiwan)
Scenedesmus acutus	CO_2 + sunlight	-	-
Spirulina maxima	CO_2 + sunlight	Feed	Yes (Mexico)
Yeasts			
Candida utilis	1. Confectionery effluents	-	Yes (U.K.)m Symba process
(Torula yeast)	2. Ethanol	Food	Yes (USA)
	3. Sulphite liquor	-	Yes (Europe, USA, Russia)
C. intermedia	Whey	-	Yes; Vienna process
C. kruswi (+Lactobacillus bulgaricus)	Whey	-	Yes; Kiel process
C. lipolytica	n-alkanes (C_{10} – C_{23}) + ammonia	-	Yes (Russia)
Kluyveromyces fragilis	whey	-	Yes (France); Le Bel process
Saccharomyces cerevisiae (Baker's yeast)	Molasses	(Food)*	Yes
Fungi			
Chaetomium cellulolyticum	Cellulosic waste	-	promising
Fusarium graminearum	Starch hydrolysate	Food	Yes (U.K.)
Paecilomyces varioti	Sulphite liquor	Feed	Yes (Finland); Pekilo process
Bacteria			
Brevibacterium sp.	C_1–C_4 hydrocarbons	-	Process developed
Methylophilus methylotrophus	methanol	food	Yes (U.K.)

1.10 METABOLIC PATHWAYS

Metabolism is a series of interconnected chemical reaction occurring within a cell and the chemical compounds involved in this process are known as metabolites. The entire spectrum of ***chemical reactions occurring in the living system, are collectively referred as metabolism.*** It consists of a hundred of enzymatic reactions organized into discrete pathways. A **metabolic pathway** (or metabolic map) constitutes a series of enzymatic reactions to produce specific products. The term metabolite is applied to a substrate or an intermediate or a product in the metabolic reactions. Metabolic pathway can be linear (such as glycolysis); cyclic (such as citric acid cycle) or spiral (like biosynthesis of fatty acids). Metabolism serves two fundamentally different purposes: generation of energy to drive vital functions and the synthesis of biological molecules. To achieve these metabolic pathways fall into two categories: Anabolic and catabolic pathways (Fig. 2).

1. **Anabolic pathways (Anabolism)** are involved in the biosynthesis reactions involving the formation of complex molecules from simple precursors and endergonic in nature. Building glucose from carbodioxide is example.
2. **Catabolic pathways (catabolism)** are involved in the oxidative breakdown of complex molecules to simpler ones with a concomitant release of energy and exergonic in nature. Energy bonds stored is complex molecules such as glucose and fats is released in catabolic pathways.

Some pathways are can be either anabolic or catabolic depending on the energy condition in the cell. There are referred to as amphibolic pathways.

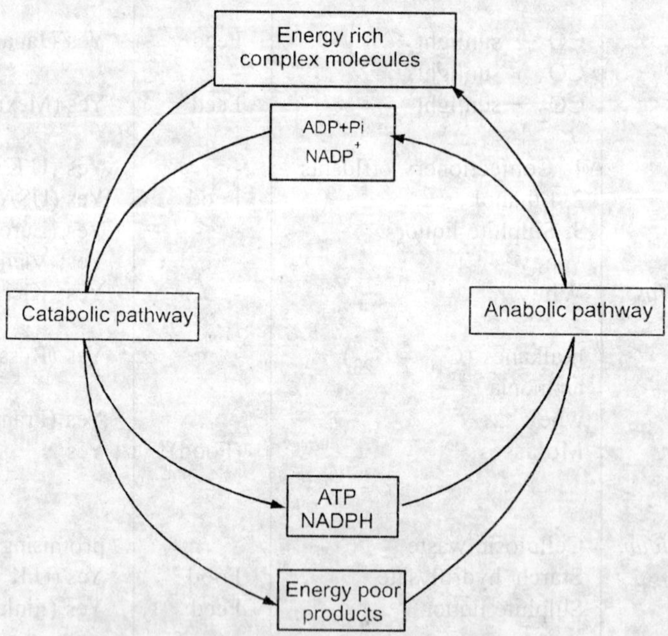

Fig. 2: An outline of catabolic and anabolic pathways

Catabolism: The very purpose of catabolism is to trap the energy of biomolecules in the form of ATP and to generate the substances (precursors) required for the synthesis of complex molecules. Catabolism occurs in three stages.

ATP is specially called an energy currency because it has easily breakable bond between 20% of its phosphate groups. There are several other triphophate molecules present in cells like GTP and CTP that plays various roles, but ATP is main energy trading molecule.

Final but important note is that the chemical reactions in metabolic pathways don't take place automatically, without guidance. Instead, each step in pathway is facilitated, or catalyzed, by a protein called an enzyme.

(*a*) **Conversion of complex molecules into their building blocks:** Polysaccharides break down to monosaccharides, lipids to free fatty acids and glycerol, protein to amino acids.

(*b*) **Formation of simple intermediates:** the building blocks produced in stage (1) are degraded to simple intermediates such as pyruvate and acetyl CoA. These intermediate are not readily identifiable as carbohydrates, lipids or protein. A small quantity of energy (as ATP) is captured in stage 2.

(*c*) **Final oxidation of acetyl CoA:** Acetyl CoA is completely oxidized to carbon dioxide, liberating NADH and $FADH_2$ that finally get oxidized to release large quantity of energy (as ATP). Kreb's cycle (or citric acid cycle) is the common metabolic pathway involved in the final oxidation of all energy-rich molecules. This pathway accepts the carbon compounds (pyruvate, succinate etc.) derived from carbohydrates, lipids or proteins.

Anabolism: These syntheses the large variety of complex compound from relatively few quantity of starting materials. These include pyruvate, acetyl CoA and the intermediates of citric acid cycle. Besides the availability of precursors, the anabolic reactions are dependent on the supply of energy (as ATP or GTP) and reducing equivalents as (NADPH + H^+).

The anabolic and catabolic pathways are not reversible and operate independently. As such, the metabolic pathways occur in specific cellular locations (mitochondria, microsomes etc.) and are controlled by different regulatory signals.

The term 'intermediary metabolism' and 'energy metabolism' are also in use. ***Intermediary metabolism*** refers to the entire range of catabolic and anabolic reactions, not involving nucleic acids. **Energy metabolism** deals with the metabolic pathways concerned with the storage and liberation of energy.

The biochemical reactions are mainly of four types *i.e.*

a) Oxidation-reduction

b) Group transfer

c) Rearrangement and isomerization

d) Make and break of carbon-carbon bonds

These reactions are catalyzed by specific enzymes more than 2000 known so far.

1.10.1 Carbohydrates metabolism

GLYCOLYSIS: Glycolysis is a series of reactions that takes place in the cytoplasm of all prokaryotes and eukaryotes. It converts one molecule of glucose into two molecule of pyruvate [which is then converted to acetyl coenzyme A (CoA) ready for entry into the citric acid cycle]. Two ATP molecules are needed for early reactions in the glycolytic pathway but four ATPs are generated later, giving a net yield of two ATPs per molecule of glucose degraded. Overall, glycolysis has dual role. The first is to generate ATP. Although only two ATPs per glucose are made directly from the reactions of the glycolytic pathway, it also feeds substrate into the citric acid cycle and oxidative phosphorylation, where most ATP is made. The second role is to produce intermediates that act as precursor for a number of biosynthesis pathways. Thus acetyl CoA for example is the precursor for fatty acids synthesis.

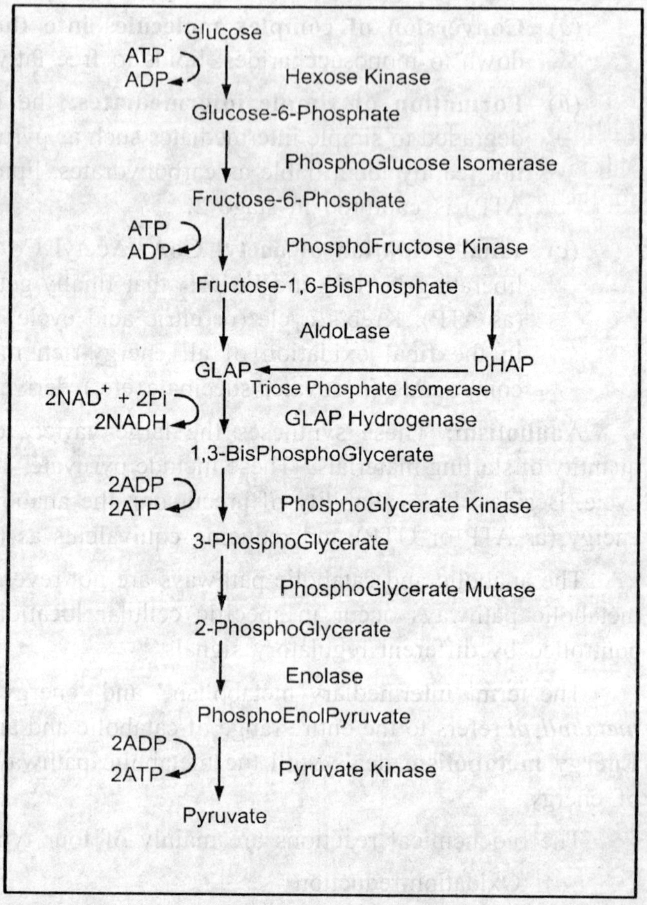

Fig. 3

The main and individual steps of glycolysis are described below.

1. Glucose is phosphorylated by ATP to form glucose 6-phosphate and ADP. The reaction is catalyzed by the enzyme **hexokinase**.
2. Glucose 6-phosphate is converted to fructose by enzyme **phosphoglucoisomerase**. The isomerization involves the conversion of an aldose to a ketose, a conversion that is better seen by viewing the open chain representations of these molecules.
3. Fructose 6-phosphate is phosphorylated by ATP to form fructose 1, 6-bisphosphate and ADP. The enzyme catalyzing this step is phosphofructokinase (PFK).
4. Aldose splits fructose 1, 6-bisphosphate (a six carbon molecule) into two three carbon molecules, glyceraldehyde 3-phosphate and dihydroxyacetone phosphate.
5. Glyceraldehydes 3-phosphate is the only molecule that can be used for the rest of glycolysis. However, the dihydroxyacetone phosphate formed in the previous step can rapidly be converted to glyceraldehydes 3-phospate by **triose phosphate isomerase**.
6. Glyceraldehydes 3-phospate is converted to 1, 3-bisphosphoglycerate. The reaction is catalyzed by **glyceraldehyde 3-phosphate dehydragenase** and uses inorganic phosphate and NAD$^+$. The other product is NADH. The energy for creating this new high energy phosphate bond comes from the oxidation of the aldehyde group of the glyceraldehydes 3-phosphate.
7. The newly created high energy phosphate bond of 1, 3-bisphosphoglycerate is now used to synthesis ATP. **Phosphoglycerate kinase** catalyzes the transfer of the phosphoryl group from the 1, 3-bisphosphoglycerate to ADP, generating ATP and 3-phosphoglycerate.

8. 3-phosphoglycerate is converted to 2-phosphoglycerate by **phosphoglycerate mutase**. Thus the reaction is a movement of the phosphate group to a different carbon atom within the same molecule.
9. **Enolase** catalyzes the dehydration of 2-phosphoglycerate to form phosphoenolpyruvate (PEP). This reaction converts the low energy phosphate ester bond of 2-phosphoglycerate into the high energy phosphate bond of PEP.
10. In the last reaction, **pyruvate kinase** catalyzes the physiologically irreversible transfer of the phosphoryl group from PEP to ADP to form ATP and pyruvate.

Fructose metabolism: Fructose is an abundant sugar in the human diet; sucrose (table sugar) is a disaccharide which when hydrolyzed yields fructose and glucose and fructose is also a major sugar in fruits and honey. There are two pathways for the metabolism of fructose; one occurs in muscle and adipose tissues, the other in liver.

1. In muscle and adipose tissues, fructose can be phosphorylated by hexokinase (which is capable of phosphorylating both glucose and fructose) to form fructose 6-phosphate which then enters glycolysis.
2. In liver, the cells contain mainly glucokinase instead of hexokinase and this enzyme phosphorylates only glucose. Thus in liver, fructose is metabolized instead by the **fructose 1-phosphate pathway**.

- Fructose is converted to fructose 1-phosphate by fructokinase.
- Fructose 1-phosphate is then split into glyceraldehyde and dihydroxyacetone phosphate by fructose 1-aldolase. The dihydroxyacetone feeds into glycolysis at the triose phosphate isomerase step.
- The glyceraldehydes is phosphorylated by triose kinase to glyceraldehydes 3-phosphate and so also enters glycolysis.

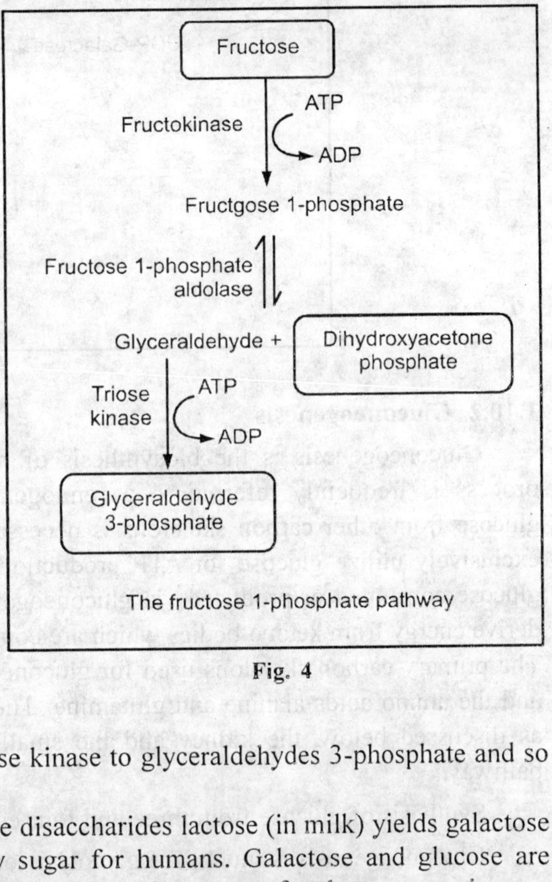

Fig. 4

Metabolism of Galactose: The hydrolysis of the disaccharides lactose (in milk) yields galactose and glucose. Thus galactose is also a major dietary sugar for humans. Galactose and glucose are epimers that differ in their configuration at C-4 (Fig.). Thus the entry of galactose requires an epimerization reaction. This occurs via four step pathway called galactose-glucose inter-conversion pathway.

1. Galactose is phosphorylated by **galactokinase** to give galactose 1-phosphate.
2. **Galactose 1-phosphate uridylyl transferase** catalyzes the transfer of a uridyl group from UDP-glucose to galactose 1-phosphate to form UDP-galactose and glucose 1-phosphate.
3. The UDP-galactose is converted back to UDP-glucose by **UDP-galactose 4-epimerase**. Thus, overall, UDP-glucose is not consumed in the reaction pathway.
4. Finally, the glucose 1-phosphate is converted to glucose 6-phosphate by **phosphoglucomutase**. The glucose 6-phosphate then enters glycolysis.

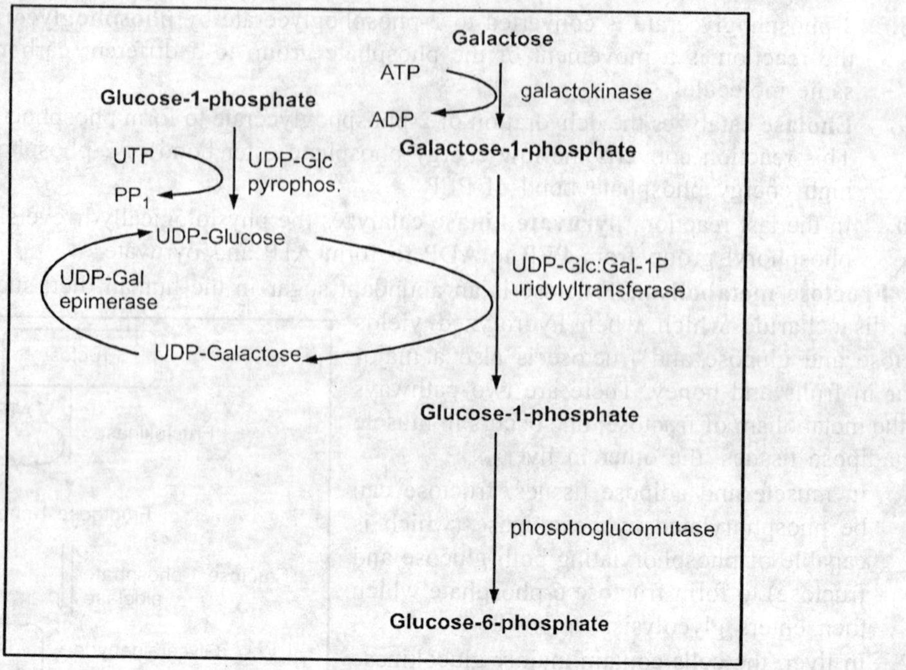

Fig. 5

1.10.2 Gluconeogenesis

Gluconeogenesis is the biosynthesis of new glucose, (*i.e.* not glucose from glycogen). This process is frequently referred to as endogenous glucose production (EGP). The production of glucose from other carbon skeletons is necessary since the testes, erythrocytes and kidney medulla exclusively utilize glucose for ATP production. The brain also utilizes large amounts of the daily glucose consumed or produced via gluconeogenesis. However, in addition to glucose, the brain can derive energy from ketone bodies which are converted to acetyl-CoA and shunted into the TCA cycle. The primary carbon skeletons used for gluconeogenesis are derived from pyruvate, lactate, glycerol, and the amino acids alanine and glutamine. The liver is the major site of gluconeogenesis, however, as discussed below, the kidney and the small intestine also have important roles to play in this pathway.

Synthesis of glucose from three and four carbon precursors is essentially a reversal of glycolysis.

Gluconeogenesis is much like glycolysis only the process occurs in reverse. However, there are exceptions. In glycolysis there are three highly exergonic steps (steps 1,3,10). These are also regulatory steps which include the enzymes hexokinase, phosphofructokinase, and pyruvate kinase. Biological reactions can occur in both the forward and reverse direction. If the reaction occurs in the reverse direction the energy normally released in that reaction is now required. If gluconeogenesis were to simply occur in reverse the reaction would require too much energy to be profitable to that particular organism. In order to overcome this problem, nature has evolved three other enzymes to replace the glycolysis enzymes hexokinase, phosphofructokinase, and pyruvate kinase when going through the process of gluconeogenesis:

1. The first step in gluconeogenesis is the conversion of pyruvate to phosphoenolpyruvic acid (PEP). In order to convert pyruvate to PEP there are several steps and several

enzymes required. Pyruvate carboxylase, PEP carboxykinase and malate dehydrogenase are the three enzymes responsible for this conversion. Pyruvate carboxylase is found on the mitochondria and converts pyruvate into oxaloacetate. Because oxaloacetate cannot pass through the mitochondria membranes it must be first converted into malate by malate dehydrogenase. Malate can then cross the mitochondria membrane into the cytoplasm where it is then converted back into oxaloacetate with another malate dehydrogenase. Lastly, oxaloacetate is converted into PEP via PEP carboxykinase. The next several steps are exactly the same as glycolysis only the process is in reverse.

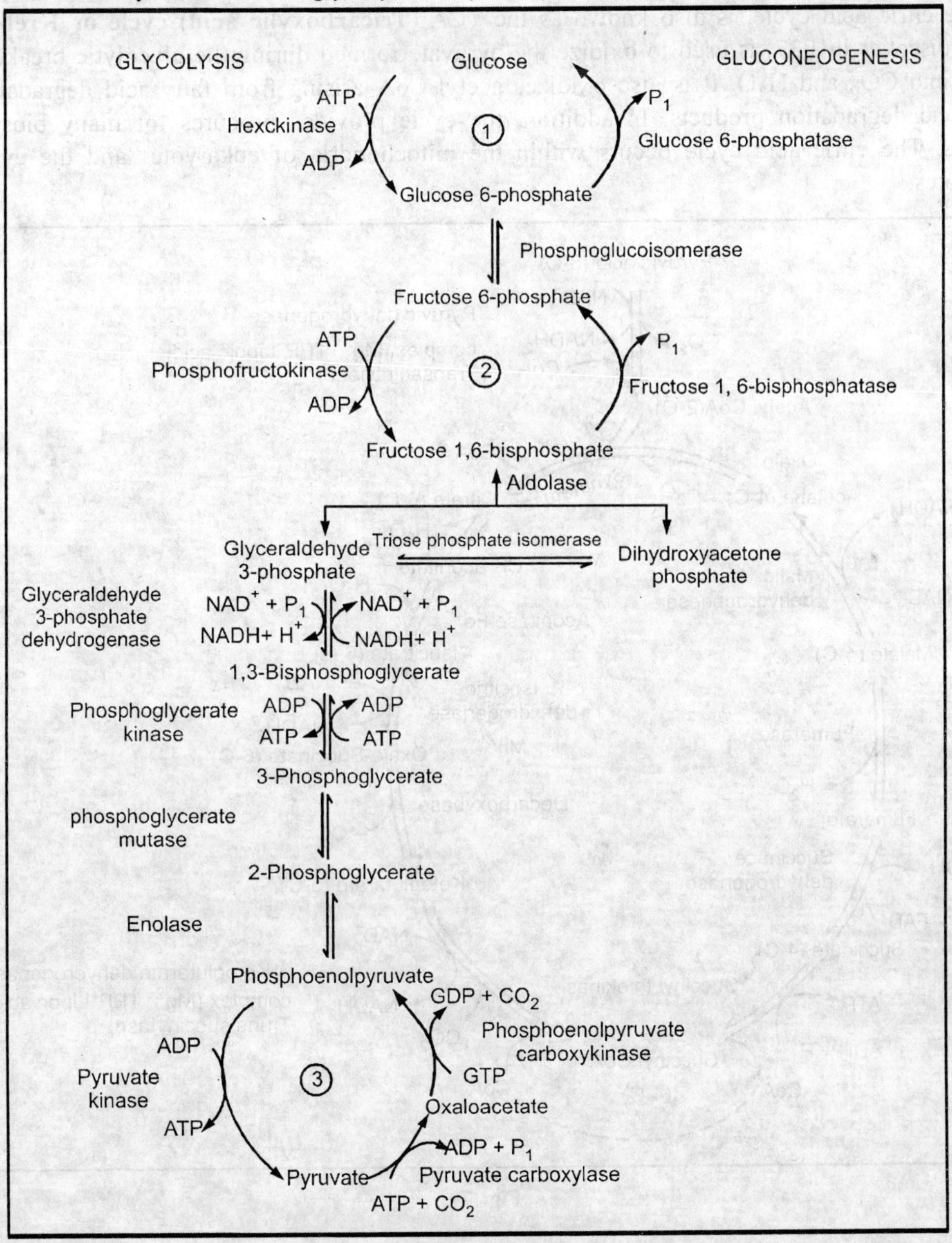

Fig. 6

2. The second step that differs from glycolysis is the conversion of fructose-1,6-bP to fructose-6-P with the use of the enzyme fructose-1,6-phosphatase. The conversion of fructose-6-P to glucose-6-P uses the same enzyme as glycolysis, phosphoglucoisomerase.
3. The last step that differs from glycolysis is the conversion of glucose-6-P to glucose with the enzyme glucose-6-phosphatase. This enzyme is located in the endoplasmic reticulum.

The relevant features of the pathway of gluconeogenesis are diagrammed in Fig. 6

1.10.3 Cirtic acid Cycles or Kreb's Cycles

The citric acid cycle, is also known as the TCA **(Tricarboxylic acid) cycle or Kreb's cycle** (after it discover in1937) is used to oxidize the pyruvate formed during the glycolytic breakdown of glucose into CO_2 and H_2O. It is also oxidizes acetyl CoA arising from fatty acid degradation and amino acid degradation products. In addition, the cycle provides procures for many biosynthesis pathways. The citric acid cycle occurs within the mitochondria of eukaryotes and the cytosol of prokaryotes.

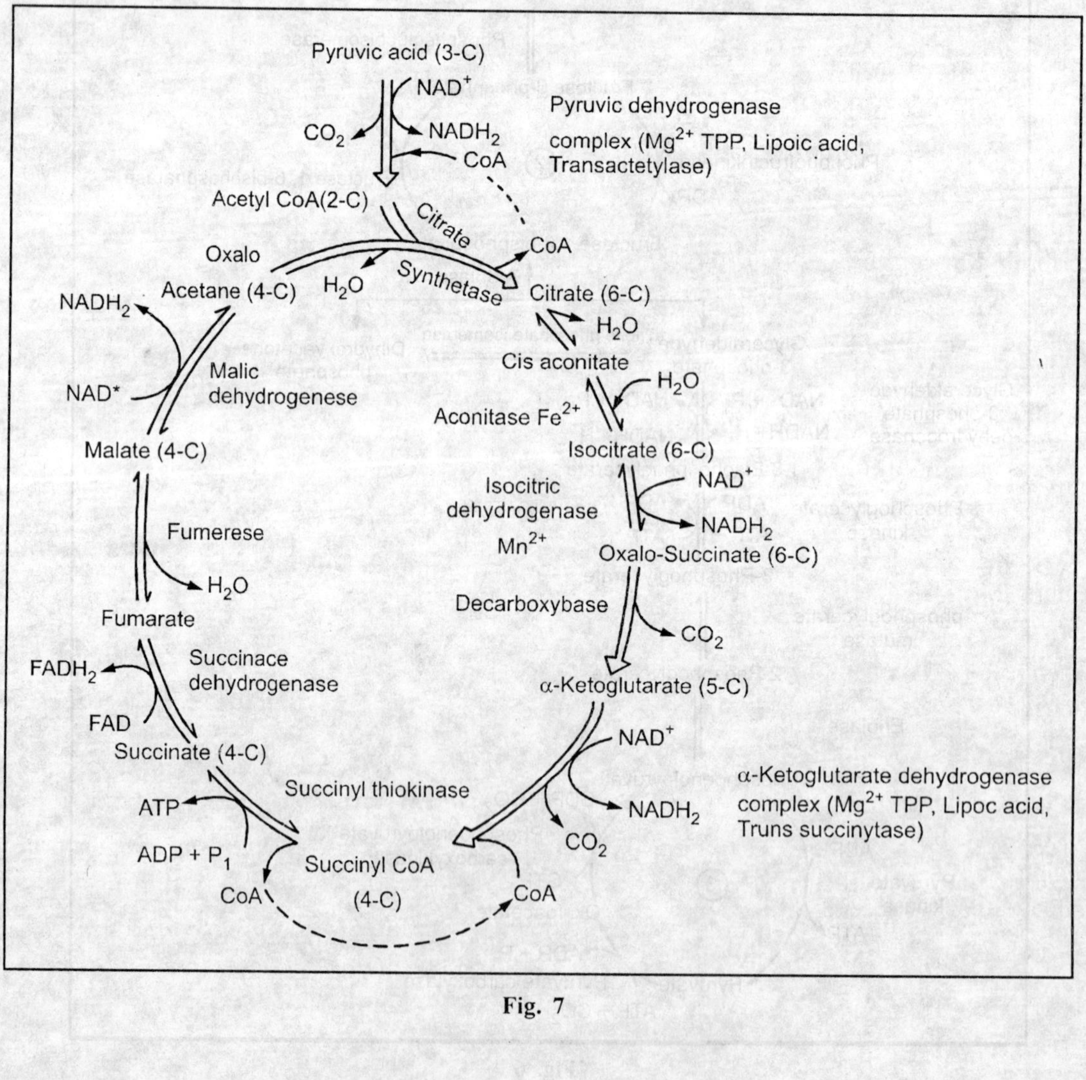

Fig. 7

Step 1. The first step is a condensation step, combining the two-carbon acetyl group (from acetyl CoA) with a four-carbon oxaloacetate molecule to form a six-carbon molecule of citrate. CoA is bound to a sulfhydryl group (-SH) and diffuses away to eventually combine with another acetyl group. This step is irreversible because it is highly exergonic. The rate of this reaction is controlled by negative feedback and the amount of ATP available. If ATP levels increase, the rate of this reaction decreases. If ATP is in short supply, the rate increases.

Step 2. Citrate loses one water molecule and gains another as citrate is converted into its isomer, isocitrate.

Steps 3 and 4. In step three, isocitrate is oxidized, producing a five-carbon molecule, α-ketoglutarate, together with a molecule of CO_2 and two electrons, which reduce NAD+ to NADH. This step is also regulated by negative feedback from ATP and NADH and by a positive effect of ADP. Steps three and four are both oxidation and decarboxylation steps, which release electrons that reduce NAD^+ to NADH and release carboxyl groups that form CO_2 molecules. α-Ketoglutarate is the product of step three, and a succinyl group is the product of step four. CoA binds the succinyl group to form succinyl CoA. The enzyme that catalyzes step four is regulated by feedback inhibition of ATP, succinyl CoA, and NADH.

Step 5. A phosphate group is substituted for coenzyme A, and a high-energy bond is formed. This energy is used in substrate-level phosphorylation (during the conversion of the succinyl group to succinate) to form either guanine triphosphate (GTP) or ATP. There are two forms of the enzyme, called isoenzymes, for this step, depending upon the type of animal tissue in which they are found. One form is found in tissues that use large amounts of ATP, such as heart and skeletal muscle. This form produces ATP. The second form of the enzyme is found in tissues that have a high number of anabolic pathways, such as liver. This form produces GTP. GTP is energetically equivalent to ATP; however, its use is more restricted. In particular, protein synthesis primarily uses GTP.

Step 6. Step six is a dehydration process that converts succinate into fumarate. Two hydrogen atoms are transferred to FAD, producing $FADH_2$. The energy contained in the electrons of these atoms is insufficient to reduce NAD^+ but adequate to reduce FAD. Unlike NADH, this carrier remains attached to the enzyme and transfers the electrons to the electron transport chain directly. This process is made possible by the localization of the enzyme catalyzing this step inside the inner membrane of the mitochondrion.

Step 7. Water is added to fumarate during step seven, and malate is produced. The last step in the citric acid cycle regenerates oxaloacetate by oxidizing malate. Another molecule of NADH is produced.

1.10.4 Lipid Metabolism

Lipid metabolism involves the synthesis of the structural and functional lipids (such as phospholipids, glycolipids, sphingolipids, cholesterol, prostaglandins, etc.) that are characteristic of individual tissues and the degradation of lipids to satisfy the metabolic needs of the body (*e.g.*, energy production).

The first step in lipid metabolism is the hydrolysis of the lipid in the cytoplasm to produce glycerol and fatty acids.

Since glycerol is a three carbon alcohol, it is metabolized quite readily into an intermediate in glycolysis, dihydroxyacetone phosphate. The last reaction is readily reversible if glycerol is needed for the synthesis of a lipid.

The hydroxyacetone, obtained from glycerol is metabolized into one of two possible compounds. Dihydroxyacetone may be converted into pyruvic acid through the **glycolysis** pathway to make energy.

In addition, the dihydroxyacetone may also be used in **gluconeogenesis** to make glucose-6-phosphate for glucose to the blood or glycogen depending upon what is required at that time.

Fatty acids are oxidized to acetyl CoA in the mitochondria using the fatty acid spiral. The acetyl CoA is then ultimately converted into ATP, CO_2, and H_2O using the citric acid cycle and the electron transport chain.

Fatty acids are synthesized from carbohydrates and occasionally from proteins. Actually, the carbohydrates and proteins have first been catabolized into acetyl CoA. Depending upon the energy requirements, the acetyl CoA enters the citric acid cycle or is used to synthesize fatty acids in a process known as LIPOGENESIS.

1.10.5 Protein Metabolism

- Protein metabolism is a key physiological process in all forms of life.
- Proteins are converted to amino acids and then catabolised.
- The complete hydrolysis of a polypeptide requires mixture of peptidases because individual peptidases do not cleave all peptide bonds.
- Both exopeptidases and endopeptidases are required for complete conversion of protein to amino acids.

Amino acid metabolism

- The amino acids not only function as energy metabolites but also used as precursors of many physiologically important compounds such as heme, bioactive amines, small peptides, nucleotides and nucleotide coenzymes.
- In normal human beings about 90% of the energy requirement is met by oxidation of carbohydrates and fats. The remaining 10% comes from oxidation of the carbon skeleton of amino acids.
- Since the 20 common protein amino acids are distinctive in terms of their carbon skeletons, amino acids require unique degradative pathway.
- The degradation of the carbon skeletons of 20 amino acids converges to just seven metabolic intermediates namely.

  a. Pyruvate

  b. Acetyl CoA

  c. Acetoacetyl CoA

  d. α-Ketoglutarate

  e. Succinyl CoA

f. Fumarate

g. Oxaloacetate

- Pyruvate, α-ketoglutarate, succinyl CoA, fumarate and oxaloacetate can serve as precursors for glucose synthesis through gluconeogenesis.Amino acids giving rise to these intermediates are termed as glucogenic.
- Those amino acids degraded to yield acetyl CoA or acetoacetate are termed ketogenic since these compounds are used to synthesize ketone bodies.
- Some amino acids are both glucogenic and ketogenic (For example, phenylalanine, tyrosine, tryptophan and threonine.

Catabolism of amino acids

The **important reaction** commonly employed in the breakdown of an amino acid is always the **removal of its α-amino group**. The product **ammonia** is excreted after conversion to **urea** or other products and the carbon skeleton is degraded to CO_2 releasing energy. The important reaction involved in the deamination of amino acids is.

(*i*) Transamination

(*ii*) Oxidative deamination

(*iii*) Non oxidative deamination

Transamination: A chemical reaction that transfers an amino group to a ketoacid to form new amino acids.

- Most amino acids are deaminated by transamination reaction catalysed by **aminotransferases or transaminases.**
- The α-**amino group** present in an amino acid is transferred to an á-keto acid to yield a new amino acid and the α-keto acid of the original amino acid.
- The predominant amino group acceptor is **α-keto glutarate**. Glutamate's amino group is then transferred to oxaloacetate in a second transamination reaction yielding aspartate.

$$\text{Glutamate} + \text{oxaloacetate} \xrightarrow[\text{pyridoxal phosphate}]{} \alpha\text{-ketoglutarate} + \text{aspartate}$$

- **Pyridoxal phosphate**, the coenzyme of pyridoxine (vitamin B6) plays an important role in these reactions.
- Amino transferase reactions occur in two stages.

✧ Pyridoxal phosphate is covalently attached to the amino transferases via a **Schiff's base linkage** formed between the aldehyde group of pyridoxal phosphate and the **epsilon amino group of lysine** residue of the enzyme. Pyridoxal phosphate is converted to pyridoxamine phosphate.

✧ In the second stage, the amino group attached to pyridoxamine phosphate is transferred to a different keto acid to yield a new amino acid and releases pyridoxal phosphate

Oxidative deamination

- Transamination does not result in net deamination, since one amino acid is replaced by another amino acid.
- The function of transamination is to funnel the amino nitrogen into one or a few amino acids.
- For glutamate to play a role in the net conversion of amino groups to ammonia, a mechanism for glutamate deamination is needed so that á-ketoglutarate can be regenerated for further transamination.
- The generation is accomplished by the oxidative deamination of glutamate by glutamate dehydrogenase.
- Glutamate is oxidatively deaminated in the mitochondrion by glutamate dehydrogenase. NAD^+ or $NADP^+$ functions as the coenzyme.
- Oxidation is thought to occur with the transfer of a hydride ion from glutamate's α-carbon to NAD(P)+ to form á-iminoglutarate, which is then hydrolyzed to α-ketoglutarate and ammonia.
- The ammonia produced is then converted to urea in mammal's two non-specific amino acid oxidases namely, L-amino acid and D-amino acid oxidases catalyse the oxidation of L and D-amino acids utilizing FAD as their coenzymes.

$$\text{Amino acid} + \text{FAD} + H_2O \longrightarrow \alpha\text{-Keto acid} + NH_3 + FADH_2$$

Non-oxidative deamination

- Amino acids such as serine and histidine are deaminated non-oxidatively The other reactions involved in the catabolism of amino acids are decarboxylation, transulfuration, desulfuration, dehydration etc.

Decarboxylation

- The decarboxylation process is important since the products of decarboxylation reactions give rise to physiologically active amines.
- The enzymes, **amino acid decarboxylases** are **pyridoxal phosphatedependent enzymes.**
- Pyridoxal phosphate forms a Schiff's base with the amino acid so as to stabilize the α-carbanion formed by the cleavage of bond between carboxyl and α-carbon atom.
- The physiologically active amines epinephrine, **nor-epinephrine, dopamine, serotonin, α-amino butyrate and histamine** are formed through decarboxylation of the corresponding precursor amino acids.

Amino acid's skeleton metabolism

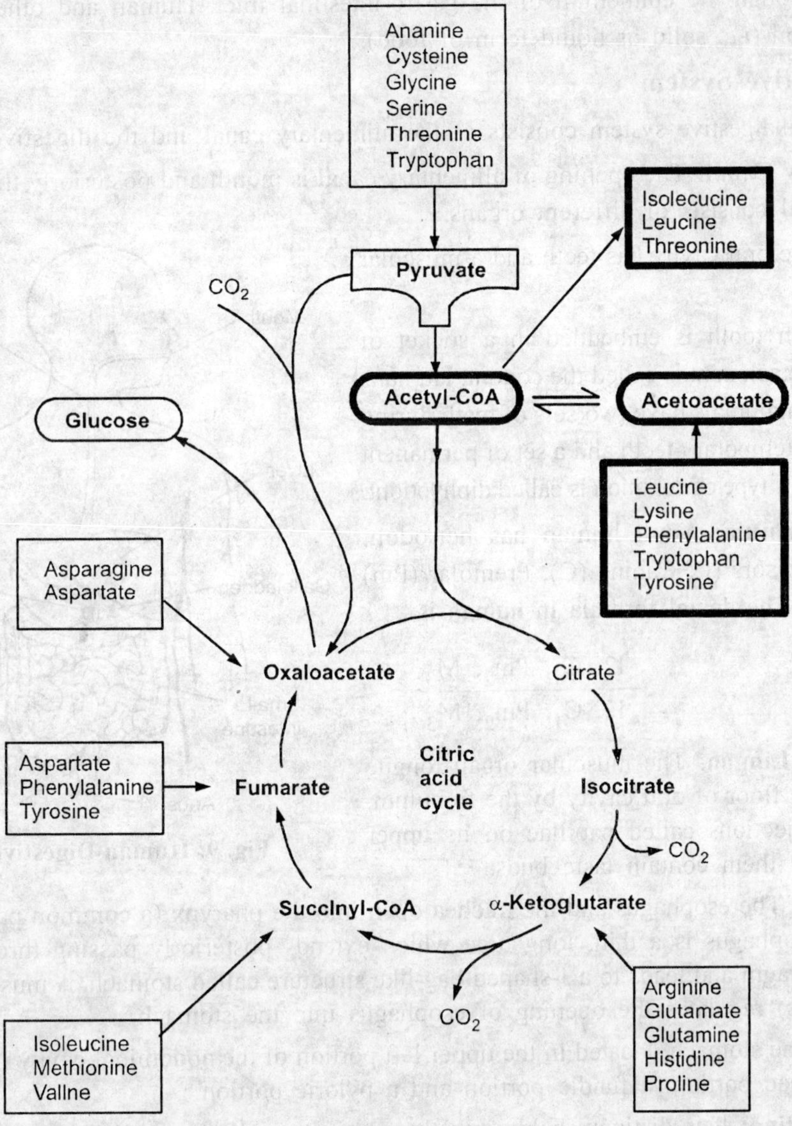

Amino acids are degraded to one of seven common metabolic intermediates. Glucogenic and ketogenic degradations are indicated in thin and thick, respectively.

Fig. 8

1.11 DIGESTION AND ABSORPTION

Digestion: It involves splitting of food molecules by hydrolysis into smaller molecules that can be absorbed through the epithelium of the gastro-intestinal tract. Human and other animals have holozoic nutrition (*i.e.* solid or liquid form of food).

Human Digestive System

The human digestive system consists of the alimentary canal and the digestive glands.

Alimentary Canal: The opening of alimentary canal is mouth and posteriorly through the anus. Alimentary canal consists of different organs.

Mouth: The oral cavity has teeth and a muscular tongue.

Teeth: Each tooth is embedded in a socket of jaw bone. This attachment is called the codont. Humans and majority of mammals have two sets of teeth during their life a set of temporary teeth and a set of permanent adult teeth 32. This type of dentition is called diphyodont.

Dental Formula: Adult human has hetrodont dentition, *i.e.* Incisors (I), Canine (C), Premolar (Pm) and Molar (M). The dental formula in human is

$$\frac{I2,\ C_1,\ Pm_2,\ M_3}{I2,\ C_1,\ Pm_2,\ M_3}$$

Tongue or Lingua: The muscular organ tongue is attached to the floor of oral cavity by the frenulum. It has small projections called papillae on its upper surface, some of them contain taste buds.

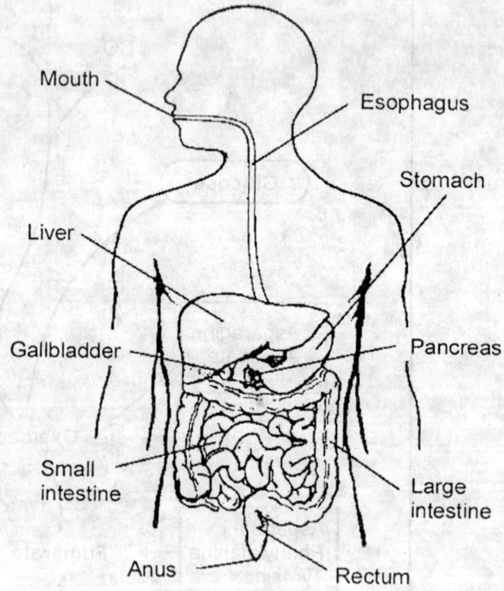

Fig. 9: Human Digestive System

Esophagus: The esophagus and the trachea open into the pharynx (a common passage for food and air). The esophagus is a thin, long tube which extends posteriorly passing through the neck, throax and diaphragm and leads to a J-shaped bag-like structure called stomach. A muscular sphincter (gastro-esophagus) regulates the opening of esophagus into the stomach.

Stomach: The stomach, located in the upper left portion of the abdominal cavity has three major parts, *i.e.* a cardiac portion, a fundic portion and a pyloric portion.

Small Intestine: It is distinguishable into three regions, a U-shaped duodenum, a long coiled middle portion jejunum and a highly coiled ileum. It is the widest, shortest and most flexed part of small intestine.

Ileum opens into the large intestine. It consists of following parts caecum, colon and rectum.

a) **Caecum** hosts some symbiotic microorganisms.

b) **Colon** is divided into three parts, *i.e.* an ascending, a transverse and a descending part.

c) **Rectum** The wall of alimentary canal from oesophagus to rectum possesses four layers, *i.e.* serosa, muscularis, sub-mucosa and mucosa.

Table 10: Functions of Primary and Accessory Organs of Digestion

Organ	Secretion	Main function
Mouth	…………	Mechanically breaks down food
Salivary Glands	Water	Moistens food
Accessory organs	Mucous	Lubricates and binds food into bolus
	Salivary amylase (ptyalin)	Starts breakdown of starch and glycogen
	Bicarbonate	Buffering action neutralizes acidic food in mouth
Stomach	………..	Stores, mixes, dissolves food; regulates emptying of chyme into small intestine
Secretory cells in stomach mucosa	Hydrochloric acid	Dissolves food particles kills many microorganisms.
	Pepsinogens	Activated forms (pepsins) split apart peptide bonds in protein chains
	Mucus	Lubricates and protects stomach lining
	Gastrin	Stimulates hydrochloric acid secretion
Small Intestine	-	Digestion and absorption of most nutrients; mixes and propels chyme forward.
	Gastric-inhibitory peptide	Inhibits stomach acid secretion and motility
Secretory cells in stomach mucosa	Assorted enzymes	Breakdown major food molecules
Intestinal mucosa	Mucus	Lubricates chyme
	Secretin	Stimulates pancreatic bicarbonate secretion, inhibits gastric acid secretion.
	Cholecystokinin	Stimulates gall bladder contraction, pancreatic enzyme secretion; inhibits stomach emptying
	Gastric-inhibitory peptide	Inhibits stomach acid secretion and motility
Pancreas (accessory-organ)	Assorted enzymes (*e.g.* lipase)	Breakdown major food molecules
	Bicarbonate	Buffering action neutralises hydrochloric acid entering small intestine from stomach.
Gall bladder (accessory organ)	-	Stores and concentrates bile from liver.
Large intestine (colon)	-	Stores, concentrates undigested matter by absorbing water and salts; mixes and propels materials forward.
Secretory cells in intestinal mucosa	Mucus	Lubricates undigested residues.
Rectum	-	Distension triggers defecation reflex that rids body of undigested and unabsorbed residues.

The innermost layer lining the lumen of the alimentary canal is the mucosa. This layer forms irregular folds in the stomach and small finger-like folding called villi in the small intestine. The cells lining the villi produce numerous microscopic projections called microvilli giving a brush border appearance.

Mucosa also forms glands in the stomach and crypts in between the bases of villi in the intestine (crypts of Lieberkuhn).

Digestive Glands: The digestive glands are salivary glands, liver and pancreas.

The salivary glands are of three pairs, i.e. the prarotids (cheek), the sub-maxillary/sub-mandibular (lower jaw) and the sub-lingual (below the tongue).

Liver is the largest gland of the body weighting about 1.2 – 1.5 kg in an adult human.

The hepatic lobules are the structural and functional units of liver containing hepatic cells arranged in the form of cords. Each lobule is covered by a thin connective tissue sheath called the Glisson's capsule.

The bile secreted by the hepatic cells passes through the hepatic ducts and stored in gall bladder.

The bile duct and the pancreatic duct open together in to the duodenum as the common hepato-pancreatic duct which is guarded by a sphincter called sphincter of Odii.

The pancreas is a compound organ (both exocrine and endocrine) situated between the U-shaped duodenum. The exocrine part secretes an alkaline pancreatic juice containing enzymes and the endocrine portion secretes hormones, insulin and glucagon.

Process of Digestion

It takes place in following steps

1. Ingestion of food
2. Digestion of food
3. Absorption and assimilation of digested food
4. Egestion of unwanted food

1. Ingestion of Food: Food is taken through mouth cavity. It is masticated by teeth and swallowed. Ingestion takes place in buccal cavity. Salivary glands lubricate the food and bind the food particles together to form bolus. Salivary glands have starch splitting enzyme ptyalin.

2. Digestion of Food: Process of converting complex, insoluble, food particles into simple, soluble and absorbable form is called digestion.

(*i*) **Digestion in Buccal Cavity:** In buccal cavity, salivary amylase acts on starch.

Starch (complex form) $\xrightarrow{\text{Ptyaline}}$ Maltose (simple form)

(*ii*) **Digestion in Stomach:** The food passes down through the esophagus into stomach. Now food is mixed with gastric juice and hydrochloric acid, which disinfect the food and create acidic medium. Pepsin digests proteins and converts them into peptones. Renin converts milk to curd. Digested food now is called **chime.**

(*iii*) **Digestion in Small Intestine:** Chyme moves to duodenum. Food is mixed with bile (liver) to breakdown fats into smaller globules. Trypsin acts upon proteins and breaks them into peptides. Amylase converts starch into simple sugar. Lypase converts fats into fatty acids and glycerol. Food passes into ileum and mixes with intestinal juice. Maltase converts maltose into glucose. Lactase convert lactose into glucose and galactose. Sucrase converts sucrose into glucose and fructose. Trypsin digests and peptides into amino acids. Food now is called **chyle**.

3. Absorption and Assimilation of Digested Food: Ileum's internal surface has finger-like folds called villi. There is a dense network of blood capillaries and lymph capillaries in each villi. It helps in absorption of food.

Absorption

It is the process by which the end products of digestion pass through the intestinal mucosa into the blood or lymph. It is carried out by passive, active or facilitated transport mechanisms.

Transport of water depends upon the osmotic gradient. Active transport occurs against the concentration gradient and requires energy. Nutrients like amino acids, monosaccharide's like glucose, electrolytes like Na^+ are absorbed into the blood by this mechanism.

Fatty acids and glycerol being insoluble cannot be absorbed into the blood. They are re-formed into very small protein coated fat globules called the **chylomicrons,** which are transported into the lymph vessels (lacteals) in the villi. The absorbed substances finally reach the tissues, which utilize them for their activities. This process is called **assimilation.**

Table 11: Summary of Absorption in Different parts of Digestive System

Mouth	Certain drugs coming in contact with the mucosa of mouth and lower side of the tongue are absorbed into the blood capillaries lining them.
Stomach	Absorption of water, simple sugars and alcohol, etc. takes place.
Small Intestine	Principal organ for absorption of nutrients. The digestion is completed here and the final products of digestion such as glucose, fructose, fatty acids, glycerol and amino acids are absorbed through the mucosa into the blood stream and lymph.
Large Intestine	Absorption of water, some minerals and drugs takes place

4. Egestion of Undigested Food: Undigested food passes into large intestine. Large intestine cannot absorb food but absorbs much of the water. The remaining semi-solid waste is called feces and is passed into rectum. The digested wastes, solidified into coherent faeces in the rectum initiate a neural reflex causing an urge or desire for its removal. It is expelled out through the anus.

Role of Digestive Enzymes

1. **In Carbohydrates:** Carbohydrates in the chime are hydrolyzed by pancreatic amylase into disaccharides.

$$\text{Polysaccharides (starch)} \xrightarrow{\text{Amylase}} \text{Disaccharides}$$

2. **In fats:** Fats are broken down by lipases with the help of bile into di and monoglycerides.

$$\text{Fats} \xrightarrow{\text{Lipases}} \text{Diglycerides} \longrightarrow \text{Monoglycerides}$$

3. **In Proteins:** Proteins, proteoses and peptones (partially hydrolysed proteins) in the chime reaching the intestine are acted upon by the proteolytic enzymes of pancreatic juice.

Proteins

Peptones $\xrightarrow{\text{Trypsin/Chymotrypsin}}$ Dipeptides

Proteoses Carboxypeptidase

4. **In Nucleic Acids:** Nucleic acids in the pancreatic juice acts on nucleic acids to form nucleotides and nucleosides.

$$\text{Nucleic acids} \xrightarrow{\text{Nuclease}} \text{Nucleotides} \longrightarrow \text{Nucleosides}$$

The enzymes in the succus entericus (intestinal juice) act on the above products to form following simple absorbable forms.

$$\text{Di and monoglycerides} \xrightarrow{\text{Lipases}} \text{Fatty acids} + \text{Glycerol}$$

$$\text{Dipeptides} \xrightarrow{\text{Dipeptidase}} \text{Amino acids}$$

$$\text{Maltose} \xrightarrow{\text{Maltase}} \text{Glucose} + \text{Glucose}$$

$$\text{Lactose} \xrightarrow{\text{Lactase}} \text{Glucose} + \text{Galactose}$$

$$\text{Sucrose} \xrightarrow{\text{Sucrose}} \text{Glucose} + \text{Fructose}$$

$$\text{Nucleotides} \xrightarrow{\text{Nucleotidases}} \text{Nucleosides} \xrightarrow{\text{Nucleosidases}} \text{Sugars} + \text{Bases}$$

Table 11: Major Enzymes Involved in Digestion of Carbohydrates, Proteins, Fats and Nucleic Acids

Enzyme	Source	Where Active	Substrate	Main Breakdown Product
		For Carbohydrate Digestion		
Salivary amylase	Salivary glands	Mouth	Polysaccharides	Disaccharides
Pancreatic amylase	Pancreas	Small Intestine	Polysaccharides	Disaccharides
Disaccharidases	Small Intestine	Small Intestine	Disaccharides	Monosaccharides (*e.g.* glucose)
		For Protein Digestion		
Pepsin	Stomach Mucosa	Stomach	Protein	Peptide fragments
Trypsin and Chymotrypsin	Pancreas	Small Intestine	Protein and polypeptides	Peptide fragments
Carboxypeptidase	Pancreas	Small Intestine	Peptide fragments	Amino acids
Amino peptidase	Intestinal mucosa	Small Intestine	Peptide fragments	Amino acids
		For Fat Digestion		
Lipase	Pancreas	Small Intestine	Triglycerides	Free fatty acids and monoglycerides
		For Nucleic Acid Digestion		
Pancreatic nucleases	Pancreas	Small Intestine	DNA and RNA	Nucleotides
Intestinal nucleases	Intestinal mucosa	Small Intestine	Nucleotides	Nucleotides bases and monosaccharides

Gastrointestinal Hormones Related to Digestion

The endocrine cells present in different parts of gastrointestinal tract secrete following hormones. All these hormones are proteinaceous in nature.

- **Gastrin** It acts on gastric glands and stimulates the secretion of hydrochloric acid and pepsinogen.
- **Secretin** It acts on exocrine pancreas and stimulates secretion of water and bicarbonate ions.
- **Cholecystokinin** (CCK) It stimulates the secretion of pancreatic enzymes and bile juice.
- **Pancreozymin** It stimulates pancreas to secrete enzymes.
- **Duocrinin** It is an intestinal hormone. It stimulates the secretion of mucus and HCO_3 from Brunner's glands.
- **Enterogastrone** It inhibits the secretion of gastric juice.

Calorific Fuel Value: It is the amount of energy liberated during complete combustion of 1g of substances in bomb calorimeter. For carbohydrates, gross energy of per gram calorific value is 4.7 kcal. For fat, calorific value is 9.45 kcal. For proteins, gross energy or per gram calorific value is 4.64 kcal. According to these calorific values of different nutrients, *fats have the highest calorific fuel value.*

Nutritional and Digestive Disorders: The alimentary canal may be injected with the various infectious agents like bacteria, virus, tapeworm, roundworm, hookworm, etc. These infections and other malnutrition may lead to many common digestive disorders.

Some important ones are given here

Protein Energy Malnutrition (PEM): The common PEM disorders are kwashiorkor and marasmus.

(*i*) **Kwashiorkor:** It commonly affects the infants and children between 1-3 years of age. The common symptoms are underweight, stunted growth, loss of appetite, anemia, bulging eyes. Its main causes are protein deficient diet, diarrhoes, measles, respiratory infections.

(*ii*) **Marasmus:** It is caused by the deficiency of proteins and total food calorific value that is deficient in all nutrients. Ribs become prominent, limbs become thin and skin becomes dry, thin and wrinkled.

Digestive Disorders

- **Indigestion:** It occurs due to overeating or due to some non-easily digestible foods. It can also be due to smoking, drinking alcohol or certain stomach problems. It can be prevented by avoiding fatty, greasy foods, eating too much citrus fruits, etc.
- **Constipation:** It is the condition of difficult egestion of faeces. It can be treated by taking sufficient water and roughage in diet.
- **Vomiting:** It is the ejection of stomach contents through the mouth. This reflex action is controlled by the vomit centre in the medulla.
- **Diarrhoea:** The abnormal frequency of bowl movement and increased liquidity of the faecal matter is called diarrhea. It reduces the absorption of food.
- **Jaundice:** It is the yellowness of the skin, mucosa membranes and eyes due to excessive secretion of bilirubin and deposition of bile pigments. The main reason is the inability of the liver dispose of the bilirubin provided by the circulatory system.

1.12 COLOUR

Colour is important to many foods both those that are unprocessed and those that are manufactured. Together with flavor and texture, colour plays an important role in food acceptability. In addition, color may provide an indication of chemical changes in a food, such as browning and caramelization. For a few clear liquid foods, such as oils and beverages, color is mainly a matter of transmission of light. Other foods are opaque-they derive their color mostly from reflection.

There are several systems of colour classification: the most important is the CIE system (Commission International de l'Eclairage–International Commission on Illumination). Other systems used to describe food colour are the Munsell, Hunter, and Lovibond systems.

Gloss: In addition to colour, there is another important aspect of appearance, namely gloss. Gloss can be characterized as the reflecting property of a material.

Food colourants: The colors of foods are the result of natural pigments or of added colourants. The natural pigments are a group of substances present in animal and vegetable products. The added colorants are regulated as food additives, but some of the synthetic colours, especially carotenoids, are considered "nature identical" and therefore are not subject to stringent toxicological evaluation as are other additives.

The naturally occurring pigments embrace those already present in foods as well as those that are formed on heating, storage, or processing. With few exceptions, these pigments can be divided into the following four groups:

1. *Tetrapyrrole compounds*: chlorophylls, hemes, and bilins.
2. *Isoprenoid derivatives*: carotenoids
3. *Benzopyran derivatives*: anthocyanins and flavonoids.
4. *Artefacts*: melanoidins, caramels.

• The chlorophylls are characteristics of green vegetables and leaves. • The heme pigments are found in meat and fish. • The carotenoids are a large group of compounds that are widely distributed in animal and vegetable products; they are found in fish and crustaceans, vegetables and fruits, eggs, dairy products, and cereals. • Anthocyanins and flavonoids are found in root vegetables and fruits such as berries and grapes. • Caramels and melanoidins are found in syrups and cereal products, especially if these products have been subjected to heat treatment.

Tetrapyrrole Pigments: The basic unit from which the tetrapyrrole pigments are derived is pyrrole.

The basic structure of the heme pigments consists of four pyrrole units joined together into a porphyrin ring. In the heme pigments, the nitrogen atoms are linked to a central iron atom. The color of meat is the result of the presence of two pigments, myoglobin and hemoglobin.

In fresh meat and in the presence of oxygen, there is a dynamic system of three pigments, oxymyoglobin, myoclobin, and metmyoglobin. The reversible reaction with oxygen is

$$\text{Mb} + \text{O}_2 \rightleftharpoons \text{MbO}_2$$

In both pigments, the iron is in the ferrous form; upon oxidation to the ferric state, the compound becomes metmyoglobin. The bright red color of fresh meat is due to the preence of oxymyoglobin; discoloration to brown occurs in two stages as follows:

$$\underset{\text{Red}}{\text{MbO}_2} \rightleftharpoons \underset{\text{Purplish red}}{\text{Mb}} \rightleftharpoons \underset{\text{Brownish}}{\text{MetMb}}$$

Carotenoids: The naturally occurring carotenoids, with the exception of crocetin and bixin, are tetraterpenoids. They have a basic structure of eight isoprenoid residues arranged as if two 20-carbon units, formed by head-to-tail condensation of four isoprenoid units, had joined tail to tail.

The carotenoids take their name from the major pigments of carrot (*Daucus carota*). The color is the result of the presence of a system of conjugated double bounds. The greater the number of conjugated double bonds present in the molecule, the further the major absorption bands will be shifted to the region of longer wavelength; as a result, the hue will become more red.

Chemically carotenoids are the four compounds α, γ, γ-carotene and lycopene-polyene hydrocarbons of overall composition $C_{40}H_{56}$. The prefix apo- is used to designate a carotenoid that is derived from another one by lose of structural element through degradation. These smaller carotenoid molecules are formed in the nature by oxidative degradation of C_{40} carotenoid. Best example of this is the formation of retinin and vitamin A from β-carotene. Another obvious relationship is that of lycopene and bixin. Bixin is a colour additive obtained from the seed coat of the fruit of a tropical brush, *Bixa orellana*. A pigment named crocin has been isolated from saffron. Also obtained from saffron is the bitter compound *picrocrocin*. It is a glycoside and after removal of the glucose, *yields saffronal*. A combination of two molecules of picrocrocin and one of crocin, would yield *protocrocin*. Protocrocin, which is directly related to zeaxanthin has been found in saffron.

Carotenoids may occur in foods as relatively simple mixtures of only a few compounds or as very large mixtures of large numbers of carotenoids. The simplest mixtures usually exist in animal products because the animal organism has a limited ability to absorb and deposit carotenoids. Some of the most complex mixtures are found in citrus fruits.

Beta carotene as determined in fruits and vegetables is used as a measure of the provitamin A content of the food. Provitamin A value of some fruits and vegetables are given in Table-13 on page 454. Usually carotene content of foods does not exceed 0.1% of dry weight basis. In ripening fruits, carotenoid increase at the same time chlorophylls decrease. The ratio of carotenes to xanthophylls also increases. Common carotenoids in fruits arc α and γ-carotene and lycopene. The relative amounts of different carotenoids are related to the characteristics colour of some fruits. In the sequence of peach apricot and tomato there is in increasing proportion of lycopene and redness.

Several of the carotenoids are now commercially synthesized and used as food colours. Beta-ionone is obtained from lemon grass oil and converted into a C14 aldehyde. The C14 aldehyde is changed to a C16 aldehyde, then to a C19 aldehyde. Two moles of the C19 aldehyde are condensed with acetylene dimagnesium bromide and, after a series of reactions, yield β-carotene.

Three synthetically produced carotenoids are used as food colorants, β-carotene, β-apo-8′ carotenal (apocarotenal), and canthaxanthin. Because of their high tinctorial power, they are used at levels of 1 to 25 ppm in food. They are unstable in light but otherwise exhibit good stability in food applications. Although they are fat soluble, water-dispersible forms have been developed for use in a variety of foods. Beta-carotene imparts a light yellow to orange color, aprocarotenal a light orange to reddish-orange, and canthaxanthin, orange-red to red. The application of these compounds in a variety of foods has been described. Natural carotenoid food colors are annatto, oleoresin of paprika and unrefined palm oil.

Anthocyanins and Flavonoids: The anthocyanin pigments are present in the sap of plant cells; they take the form of glycosides and are responsible for the red, blue, and violet colors of many fruits and vegetables.

Anthocynanin pigments can easily be destroyed when fruits and vegetables are processed.

Tannins: Tannins are polyphenolic compounds present in many fruits. They are important as color compounds and also for their effect on taste as a factor in astringency. Tannins can be divided into two classes – hydrolyzable tannins and nonhydrolyzable or condensed tannins. The tannis are characterized by the presence of a large number of hydroxyl groups, which provide the ability to form reversible bonds with other macromolecules, polysaccharides, and proteins, as well as other substances such as alkaloids. This bond formation may occur during the development of the fruit or during the mechanical damage that takes place during processing.

Tannins are present in the skins of red grapes and play an important part in the flavor profile of red wine. Tannins in grapes are usually estimated in terms of the content of gallic acid. This can take place during the growth of fruits (*e.g.* in dates) or during mechanical damage in processing.

Caramel: Caramel colour can be produced from a variety of carbohydrate sources, but usually corn syrup is used.

1.13 FLAVOUR

Flavour is the sensation produced by a material taken in the mouth, perceived principally by the senses of taste and smell, and also by the general pain, tactile and temperature receptors in the mouth. Flavour also denotes the sum of the characteristics of the material which produce that sensation.

This definition makes clear that flavor is a property of a material (a food) as well as of the receptor mechanism of the person ingesting the food. The study of flavour includes the composition of food compounds having taste or smell, as well as the interaction of these compounds with the receptors in the taste and smell sensory organs. Following an interaction, the organs produce signals that are carried to the central nervous system, thus creating what we understand as flovor.

Food safety agencies regulate flavor categories based on specific ingredient compositions and the creation process.

Spices are primarily aromatic vegetables or plants that can be found in many forms, such as dried and ground, broken, or whole. Spices include ingredients such as pepper, rosemary, basil, and more. These ingredients are typically considered GRAS ingredients as they've been used safely for many years.

Natural flavors are processed ingredients derived from plants, essential oils, proteins, yeasts, and more. These ingredients can be classified as a GRAS ingredient or as a food additive as defined by the FDA depending on the ingredient composition (1,2). Natural flavors can include vanilla, lavender, orange, and many more.

Artificial flavors are chemically composed ingredients and are usually regulated as a food additive (1,2). Food additives require additional rigorous safety assessments before being available on the market. While most artificial ingredients are considered additives, there are some artificial flavors are that are classified as GRAS ingredients. Artificial flavors include many different commonly found flavors such as strawberry, cinnamon, vanilla, and many more.

CHAPTER 2

FOOD MICROBIOLOGY

Microbiology is the study of living organisms that are so small that they can only be observed with the aid of a powerful microscope. Bacteria are single-celled microorganisms found in nearly all environments. Bacterial cells are often classified by their outward appearance, including their size, shape, and arrangement. Some bacteria have the ability to form spores. Spores can typically withstand adverse environmental conditions better than the vegetative form of the bacteria. For example, spores can be highly resistant to boiling water or chemical sanitizers. Bacterial spores are not a means of reproduction. Fungi include organisms as small as a single cell or as large as a mushroom. True fungi produce large masses of filamentous hyphae that form a mycelium. Yeasts, along with bacteria, reproduce by fission. Other fungi typically reproduce by spores carried on fruiting structures. Viruses are extremely small parasites. They require living cells of plants, animals, or bacteria for growth. The virus is mainly a packet of genetic material which must be reproduced by the host cells. Protozoa are single-celled organisms that can cause disease in humans and animals. Their cell structure is more complex than that of bacteria.

Beneficial aspects of microbes to the food industry

The actions of microbes can transform foods. Fermentation is the breakdown of substances in food by microbes. Fermentation occurs in a variety of foods and environments, and is essential in the production of some foods. It can give foods unique and wonderful tastes. For example, bread rises through the fermentation action of yeasts, sausages and cheeses are fermented with a mixture of moulds and lactic acid bacteria, and grape juice is transformed into wine through the fermentation of sugars by malo-lactic bacteria and specific types of yeast. Fermented foods also last longer. Without fermentation, people in some countries with short growing seasons would not be able to preserve their fruits, vegetables, grains, milks, or meats. Fermentation gives us sauerkraut from cabbage, miso soup from soy beans, salami from meats, beer from barley, and tastier, longer-lasting olives. Microbes also have other indirect benefits to the food industry. Microbes can be used as vehicles to produce and synthesize various ingredients and food additives, such as enzymes, vitamins, amino acids, and even bio-fuels, that would be otherwise more difficult and expensive to manufacture.

Harmful aspects of microbes to the food industry:

Food spoilage and foodborne illness are the two major harms of microbes to food businesses. Food-safety microbiologists may worry most about pathogenic microbes causing foodborne illness. However, another big concern is that of spoilage microbes, which do not cause illness but when not properly controlled may cause huge, costly problems for the food industry. Note that some types of food spoilage are non-microbial: for example, freezer burn occurs when foods are poorly wrapped;

evaporation and oxidation destroy the quality and flavor. Spoilage microbes (sometimes referred to in the industry as objectionable bacteria) are casually called "stinkies" or "slimies." Spoilage microbes cause undesirable deterioration of food quality that may affect the appearance (colour), odour, and/or taste of the final food product. Rotten-egg smells may arise from putrefaction and breakdown of proteins in foods by specific bacteria that produce sulfurous compounds and odours. Other microbes can produce a surface slime on aging foods, or excessive gas that will cause bulging cans or exploding packets of ketchup. Foods that are drier, acidic, salted or stored under refrigeration tend to be less susceptible to spoilage.

Traditional methods of identifying microbes: Microbes are often identified by specific traits or characteristics. These traits may include:

- Colour (*e.g.*, blue-green or brown algae)
- Size and shape (*e.g.*, bread yeasts are oval and up to 10 μm in diameter)
- How they appear when mixed with dyes (*e.g.*, bacterial Gram staining)
- Whether they can move (motility)
- How they move (*e.g.*, swimming straight or tumbling about)
- Whether they can form spores (tough, environmentally resistant forms of a microbe)
- Whether they can produce toxins (chemical poisons), and
- What they consume (*e.g.*, the types of sugars and other nutrients)

Naming Conventions

Microbiologists would have trouble distinguishing all the different bacteria if they did not give them names. As we may notice, these names are often difficult to spell and to pronounce. Take Escherichia coli for example. This bacteria was named after the German-Austrian pediatrician who discovered E. coli in 1857— Theodor Escherich. The first part of the name, Escherichia, refers to the genus, and the second part, coli, refers to the species. These binomial (two-part) labels are written in italics and the genus is capitalized. The same system is used for classifying plants and animals. For example, the scientific name for the wolf is *Canis lupus*, for the coyote it is *Canis latrans*.

At times, the first name (the genus name) may be abbreviated. Thus, we know Escherichia coli as E. coli . Another naming convention involves extra letters, numbers, and/or names following the name of the bacteria, such as E. coli O157:H7 or Salmonella Newport. These designations are used to describe the specific strain or variant within the bacterial species. This further description refines the group within a particular genus and species. Referring back to the genus of Canis, this is similar to how you will find Rottweilers, Dachshunds, and many other breeds within the population of domestic dogs (*i.e.*, species of Canis domesticus). You may also sometimes see the species name left out; for example, some reports refer to Salmonella Enteritidis, a pathogenic bacteria in the Salmonella genus. However, the full scientific name for Salmonella Enteritidis is Salmonella enterica var. Enteritidis, where the "var." stands for variant. If we were to apply this same naming convention to Dachshunds, we might write Canis domesticus var. Dachshund or just Canis Dachshund.

2.1 GENERAL CHARACTERISTICS OF MICROORGANISMS

1. Bacteria

Morphological characteristics: One of the first steps in the identification of bacteria in a food is microscopic examination to ascertain the shape, size, aggregation, structure, and staining reactions of the bacteria present. The following characteristics may be of special significance.

Encapsulation: The presence of capsules or slime may account for sliminess or ropiness of a food. In addition, capsules serve to increase the resistance of bacteria to adverse conditions, such as heat or chemicals. To the organism they may serve as a source of reserved nutrients. Most capsules are polysaccharides of dextrin, dextran, or levan.

Formation of Endospores: Bacteria of the genera *Bacillus*, *Clostridium*, *Desulfotomaculum*, *Sporolactobacillus* (rods), and *Sporosarcina* (cocci) share the ability to form endospores. *Bacillus* - aerobic and some facultative anaerobic and *Clostridium* - anaerobic. Endospores are formed at an intracellular site, are very refractile, and are resistant to heat, ultraviolet light, and desiccation.

Formation of Cell Aggregates: It is characteristic of some bacteria to form long chains and of others to clump under certain conditions. It is more difficult to kill all bacteria in intertwined chains or sizable clumps than to destroy separate cells.

Cultural characteristic's importance in food bacteriology: Bacterial growth in and on foods often is extensive. Pigmented bacteria cause discolorations on the surfaces of foods; films may cover the surfaces of liquids; growth may make surfaces slimy; or growth throughout the liquids may result in undesirable cloudiness or sediment.

Physiological characteristic's importance in food bacteriology: These changes include hydrolysis of complex carbohydrates to simple ones; hydrolysis of proteins to polypeptides, amino acids, and ammonia or amines; and hydrolysis of fats to glycerol and fatty acids. O-R reactions, which are utilized by the bacteria to obtain energy from foods (carbohydrates, other carbon compounds, simple nitrogen-carbon compounds, etc.), yield such products as organic acids, alcohols, aldehydes, ketones, and gases.

2.1.1 Factors Affecting Microbial Growth

Intrinsic factors:

Factors intrinsic refer to aspects of the composition of the food itself. They incude:

- Nutrients are available to microbes, including sugars, carbohydrates, proteins, and others
- Acidity/alkalinity or pH of the food
- The amount of water available in the food for microbes (water activity or a_w)
- Whether the food contains natural antimicrobial chemicals or features that limit growth
- How much natural oxygen is in the food (redox potential)

Extrinsic factors: Factors extrinsic to the food are essentially the environmental surroundings of the food. They include

- *The temperature of the food during preparation and storage.* Most microbes prefer warm conditions. If temperature is not managed and controlled, microbes can grow
- The time available for microbes present in food to grow, from the time of manufacture to the time of consumption. This includes shelf life considerations for the food as well.
- The atmosphere for the food during preparation and storage. Food packaging that changes the normal atmospheric conditions of oxygen, nitrogen, and carbon dioxide is called "reduced oxygen packaging". Some bacteria survive best in normal aerobic conditions, while others, such as C. botulinum, prefer an anaerobic environment.
- Relative humidity. This is the level of moisture around the food—is it dry or wet?

Processing factors:

Food processing is often overlooked when foods are evaluated, but it is essential to understanding risk. Activities during processing can increase risk. For example, the act of slicing a tomato increases the risk of Salmonella growth. When a fruit is cut, such as a tomato or a melon, the outer skin and protective covering of the fruit is damaged. If the interior flesh of the fruit can support bacterial growth, when its outer skin (tomato) or rind (melon) is damaged, there is a risk that bacteria can enter the fruit and grow. This may occur if the skin is soiled (containing dirt and bacteria), or if the knife or utensil used to cut into the fruit is soiled. Processing can also decrease risk, such as when raw milk is pasteurized, which kills microbes during the heating step. Microbe factors Foods—especially fresh foods—rarely have only one microbe present. A good example of this is fresh cabbage, which has likely hundreds of microbe varieties attached to the outer surface of the leaves, stalk, and roots. When fresh cabbage is submersed in a salty fluid and fermented, fast-growing populations of lactic acid bacteria change the environment to a more acidic, friendly one in which they can grow rapidly.

2.1.2 Genera of bacteria important in food bacteriology

The classification given in Bergey's Manual of Systematic Bacteriology, vols. I and II, 1984 and 1986, are as followed:

Genus *Acetobacter*: These bacteria oxidize ethyl alcohol to acetic acid. They are rod-shaped and motile and are found on fruits, vegetables, souring fruits, and alcoholic beverages. They are a definite spoilage problem in alcoholic beverages.

Genus *Aeromonas*: These are gram-negative rods with an optimum temperature for growth of 22 to 28 C. They are facultative anaerobes and can be psychrophilic. They are frequently isolated from aquatic environments. A. hydrophila can be a human pathogen; it is also pathogenic to fish, frogs, and other mammals.

Genus *Alcaligenes*: As the name suggests, an alkaline reaction usually is produced in the medium of growth. A. viscolactis. causes ropiness in milk, and A. metalcaligenes gives a limy growth on cottage cheese. These organisms come from manure, feeds, soil, water, and dust. This genus also contains organisms which were formerly classified in the genus Achromobacter.

Genus *Alteromonas:* Several former species of Pseudomonas are now classified as Alteromonas. They are marine organisms that are potentially important in sea foods.

Genus *Arthrobacter:* A predominant soil organism, it is inert in most foods. However, some species can grow at 50 C and would be considered psychrotrophs.

Genus *Bacillus:* The endospores of species of this aerobic to facultative genus usually do not swell the rods in which they are formed. Different species may be mesophilic or thermophilic, actively proteolytic, moderately proteolytic, or non proteolytic, gas-forming or not, and lipolytic or not. In general the spores of the mesophiles, *e.g.*, B. subtilis, are less heat-resistant than spores of the thermophiles. Spores of the obligate thermophiles, *e.g.*, B. stearothermophilus, are more resistant than those of facultative thermophiles, *e.g.*, B. coagulans. The actively proteolytic species usually may also sweet-curdle milk; B. cereus is such a species. The two chief acid- and gas-forming species, B. polymyxa and B. macerans, sometimes are termed "aerobacilli." Many of the mesophiles can form acid from glucose or other sugar but usually form only a small amount that often is neutralized by ammonia produced from the nitrogenous food. The thermophilic flat sour bacteria that spoil canned vegetables can produce considerable amounts of lactic acid from sugar, and such a culture, *e.g.*, B. coagulans, may be employed for the manufacture of lactic acid. The soil is an important source of Bacillus species.

Genus *Brevibacterium:* *Brevibacterium* have 35 species according to approved list of bacteria names. These are of interest to the food industry as these produce amino acids such as glutamic acid. *B. linens* may be important in the surface smear of certain cheeses, *e.g.*, brick or Limburger, where the culture produces an orange red pigmentation and helps ripening.

Genus Brochotrix: These are gram-positive rods which can form long filamentous like chains that may fold into knotted masses. The optimum temperature for growth is 20 to 25 °C, but growth can occur over a temperature range of 0 to 45°C depending on the strain. They can spoil a wide variety of meats and meat products when they are stored aerobically or vacuum packed and held refrigerated. B. thermosphacta is the only species listed.

Genus *Campylobacter:* These bacteria were originally classified in the genus vibrio. Several strains of C. fetus subsp. jejuni have been associated with gastroenteritis in humans.

Genus *Clostridium:* The endospores of species of this genus of anaerobic to microaerophilic bacteria usually swell the end or middle of the rods in which they are formed. Different species may be mesophilic or thermophilic and proteolytic or non-proteolytic. Clostridium thermosaccharoolyticum is an example of a saccharolytic obligate thermophile; this organism causes gaseous spoilage of canned vegetables. Putrefaction of foods often is caused by mesophilic, proteolytic species, such as *C. lentoputrescens* and *C. putrefaciens*. The violent disruption of the curd in milk by *C. perfringens* or similar species results in a "stormy fermentation" of milk, and the lactate fermenting *C. butyricum* is a cause of late gas in cured cheese. The soil is the primary source of Clostridium spp., although they also may come from bad silage, feeds, and manure.

Genus *Corynebacterium:* The diphtheria organism, *C. diptheriae*, may be transported by foods. C. bovis, with the slender, barred, or clubbed rods characteristic of the genus, is commensal on the cow's udder, can be found in aseptically drawn milk, and may be a cause of bovine mastitis.

Genus *Dessulfotomaculum*: A gram, negative rod which swells when an endospore forms. They are common inhabitants of the soil, fresh water, and the rumen. Sulfur compounds can serve as the terminal electron acceptor in respiration and thereby be reduced to hydrogen sulfide. Clostridium nigrificans, which is responsible for sulfide stinker spoilage in canned foods, is now called *D. nigrificans.*

Genus *Enterobacter:* Some were formerly classified as Aerobacter. They are widely distributed in nature; a member of the coliform group.

Genus *Erwinia:* The species of this genus are plant pathogens that cause necrosis, galls, wilts, or soft rots in plants and therefore damage the plants and vegetable and fruit products from them. E. carotovora is associated with the market disease called "bacterial soft rot." *E. carotovora* subsp. carotovora causes rotting in a large number of plants. *E. carotovora* subsp. atroseptica produces a black rot in potatoes. *E. carotovora* subsp. *betavasculorum* causes soft rot in sugar beets.

Genus *Escherichia*: Found in feces, a predominant gram-negative rod isolated from the intestinal tract of warm-blooded animals and widely distributed in nature. One of the "coliform group," the genus is divided into many biotypes and serotypes, some of which can be pathogenic to humans.

Genus *Flavobacterium:* The yellow to orange-pigmented species of this genus may cause discolorations on the surface of meats and be involved in the spoilage of shellfish, poultry, eggs, butter, and milk. Some of the organisms are psychrotrophic and have been found growing on thawing vegetables.

Genus *Gluconobacter* (Formerly Acetomonas): Species can oxidize ethanol to acetic acid. *G. oxydans* causes ropiness in beer following viscous growth in beer or wort.

Genus *Halobacterium:* Bacteria of this genus, *e.g., H. salinarium,* are obligate halophiles and are usually chromogenic. They may grow and cause discolorations on foods high in salt, such as salted fish.

Genus Klebsiella: Many are capsulated. Commonly associated with the respiratory and intestinal tracts of humans. *K. pneumoniae* is the causative organism for a bacterial pneumonia in humans.

Family Lactobacillaceae

Genus *Lactobacillus:* The lactobacilli are rods, usually long and slender, that form chains in most species. They are microaerophilic, (some strict anaerobes are known), are catalase-negative and gram-positive, and ferment sugars to yield lactic acid as the main product.

Homofermentation: They ferment sugar chiefly to lactic acid if they are homo-fermentative, with small amounts of acetic acid, carbon dioxide, and trace products. The homo-fermentative lactobacilli with optimal temperatures of 37 °C or above include *L. bulgaricus**, *L. helveticus*, *L. lactis**, *L. acidophilus*, *L. thermophilus*. The homo-fermentative lactobacilli with lower optimal temperatures include *L. casei*, *L. plantarum*, and *L. leichmannii.*

Heterofermentation: If they are hetero-fermentative, they produce appreciable amounts of volatile products, including alcohol, in addition to lactic acid. *L. delbrueckii. L. fermentum* is the chief example of a hetero-fermentative lactobacillus growing well at higher temperatures. Hetero-fermentative species grow at lower temperatures are *L. brevis*, *L. buchneri*, *L. pastorianus**, *L. hilgardii*, and *L. trichodes**.

All the above species except *L. delbrueckii*, *L. leichmannii, L. hilgardii, L. trichodes**, and some strains of *L. brevis* ferment lactose with the production of lactic acid and therefore may be of importance in the dairy industries. Chief sources of the lacto-bacilli are plant surfaces, manure, and dairy products.

Characteristics that make the lactobacilli important in foods are

(1) their ability to ferment sugars with the production of considerable amounts of lactic acid, making it possible to use them in the production of fermented plant and dairy products or the manufacture of industrial lactic acid but resulting in the deterioration of some products, *e.g.*, wine or beer,

(2) Production of gas and other volatile products by hetero fermentative species, sometimes with damage to the quality of food, as with L. fermentum growing in Swiss cheese or L. hilgardii or L. trichodes* in wines.

(3) Their inability to synthesize most of the vitamins they require, making them unable to grow well in foods poor in vitamins but useful in assays for the vitamin content of foods.

(4) The heat resistance, or thermoduric properties, of most of the high-temperature lactobacilli, enabling them to survive pasteurization or other heating processes, such as that given the curd in the manufacture of Swiss and similar cheeses.

In food microbiology, the *lactobacilli* are useful but also cause spoilage. Some lactobacilli form slime and spoil sugar cane. Others cause green discolorations of sausage products. Vacuum-packaged meat becomes sour due to lactobacilli. Even in fermented vegetables, they may be a problem, causing pink sauerkraut or bloater formation in fermented cucumbers. The lactobacilli can cause spoilage of vinegar-preserved products, such as *catsup* and *mayonnaise.*

Species of Lactobacillus different from the ones already mentioned have been found growing in refrigerated meats, but only a few names for these lactobacilli have been suggested, *e.g.*, *L. viridescens* for one causing greening of sausage and *L. salinmandus** for one growing in sausage. These lactobacilli are exceptional because of their ability to grow at low temperatures.

Genus *Leuconostoc*: This genus, called Betacoccus by Orla-Jensen, contains the heterofermetative lactic streptococci, which ferment sugar to lactic acid plus considerable amounts of acetic acid, ethyl alcohol and carbon dioxide. The ability of L. dextranicum* and L. cremoris* to ferment citric acid of milk and produce the desirable flavouring substance diacetyl (the more reduced acetoin and 2, 3-butanediol also produced) and to stimulate the lactic streptococci has led to their inclusion in the so-called "lactic starter" for buttermilk, butter and cheese.

Some of the characteristics of Leuconostoc species that make them important in foods are

(1) Production of diacetyl and other flavoring products,

(2) Tolerance of salt concentrations, *e.g.*, in sauerkraut and dill-pickle fermentations, permitting L. mesenteroides to carry on the first part of the lactic fermentation,

(3) Ability to initiate fermentation in vegetable products more rapidly than other lactics or other competing bacteria and to produce enough acid to inhibit nonlactics,

(4) Tolerance of high sugar concentrations (up to 55 to 60 percent for L. mesenteroides), permitting the organism to grow in sirups, liquid cake and ice-cream mixes, etc.,

(5) Production of considerable amounts of carbon dioxide gas from sugars, leading to undesirable "openness" in some cheeses, spoilage of foods high in sugars (sirups, mixes, etc.), and leavening in some breads,

(6) Heavy slime production in media containing sucrose. This is a desirable characteristic for the production of dextran but a hazard in materials high in sucrose, as in the production of sucrose from sugarcane or beets.

Genus *Listeria:* These bacteria are gram-positive, non-spore-forming rods with tumbling motility. *L. monocytogenes* can cause food-borne disease outbreaks.

Genus *Microbacterium:* Bacteria of this genus are important because of their resistance to adverse conditions and their use in production of vitamins. They are small, nonmotile, grampositive, asporogenous, catalase-positive, aerobic, homo-fermentative, lactic acid-producing rods, which sometimes produce palisade arrangements. *M. tacticum* is the species usually encountered. Microbacteria are very resistant to heat for non-spore-forming bacteria, surviving pasteurization of milk readily and even temperatures of 80 to 85^{0}C for 10 min. They therefore are among the thermodurics.

Genus *Micrococcus:* Most of the species prominent in foods are gram-positive, aerobic, and catalase-positive. The following characteristics make various groups of micrococci important in foods:

(1) Some species can utilize ammonium salts or other simple nitrogenous compounds as a sole source of nitrogen,

(2) Most species can ferment sugars with the production of moderate amounts of acid,

(3) Some are acid-proteolytic (*M. freudenreichii**),

(4) Some are very salt tolerant and hence able to grow at relatively low levels of available moisture; these grow in meat-curing brines, brine tanks, etc.,

(5) Many are thermoduric, *i.e.*, survives the pasteurization treatment given market milk (*M.varians*),

(6) Some are pigmented and discolor the surfaces of foods on which they grow; *M. lute* us is yellow, for example, and *M. roseus* is pink, and

(7) Some of the micrococci can grow fairly well at temperatures around 10C or below. Micrococci are widespread in nature but have been isolated most often from dust and water.

They often are found on inadequately cleaned and sanitized food utensils and equipment.

Genus *Mycobacterium:* The tubercle bacilli that cause tuberculosis, *M. tuberculosis*, has been spread by foods, especially raw milk from infected cows

Genus *Pediococcus:* The cocci occur singly, in pairs or short chains, or in tetrads (division in two planes) and are gram-positive, catalase-negative, and microaerophilic. They are homofermentative. The characteristics that make the organism important in foods have been mentioned: salt tolerance, acid production, and temperature range, especially the ability to grow at cool temperatures. Pediococci have been found growing during the fermentation of brined vegetables and have been found responsible for the spoilage of alcoholic beverages, e.g., beer, where their production of diacetyl is undesirable. *P. damnosus* can spoil beer. *P. cerevisiae* has been used as starter culture in fermented sausages.

Genus *Photobacterium:* The genus includes coccobacilli and occasional rods which can be luminescent. They are not widespread; however, *P. phosphoreum* has been known to cause phosphorescence of meats and fish.

Genus *Propionibacterium:* Members of this genus may be found in foods. In Swiss cheese certain species (e.g., *Propionibacterium freudenreichii*) ferment the lactates to produce the gas that helps form the holes or eyes, and also contribute to the flavor. Pigmented propionic bacteria can cause color defects in cheese.

Genus *Proteus:* Bacteria of this genus have been involved in the spoilage of meats, seafood, and eggs. The presence of these bacteria in large numbers in non refrigerated foods has made themsuspect as a cause of food poisoning.

Genus *Pseudomonas:* A number of species of Pseudomonas can cause food spoilage. These bacteria are gram-negative, usually motile, asporogenous rods.

Characteristics of some of the Pseudomonas species that make them important in foods are

(1) Their ability to utilize a large variety of non carbohydrate carbon compounds for energy and their inability to use most carbohydrates.

(2) Their ability to 'produce a variety of products that affect flavor deleteriously,

(3) Their ability to use simple nitrogenous foods.

(4) Their ability to synthesize their own growth factors or vitamins.

(5) The proteolytic and lipolytic activity of I, some species.

(6) Their aerobic tendencies, enabling them to grow rapidly and produce oxidized products and slime at the surfaces of foods, where heavy contamination is most likely.

(7) Their ability to grow well at low (refrigeration) temperatures.

(8) Pigment production by some species, *e.g.*, the greenish fluorescence by pyoverdin of *Pseudomonas fluorescens* and white, cream-colored, reddish, brown, or even black (*P. nigrifaciens**) colors of other species.

(9) Their resistance to many disinfectants and sanitizers used in the food industry. On the other hand, the pseudomonads are limited by a fairly high aw (0.97 to 0.98), are readily killed by heat, grow poorly if oxygen is not readily available, are not especially resistant' to drying, and grow poorly or not at all above 43°C.

Genus *Salmonella:* Species of these enteric pathogens may grow in foods and cause food infections.

Genus *Serratia:* Many species produce a pink or magenta pigment and may cause red discolorations on the surface of foods. *S. marcescens* is the most common species.

Genus *Shigella:* Species of *Shigella*, causing bacillary dysenteries, may be transported by foods.

Genus *Sporolactobacillus:* *Lactobacillus inulinus* has been classified as *S. inulinus* because of its ability to font endospores. It resembles as Lactobacillus in many characteristics.

Genus *Sporosarcina:* A gram-positive coccus that forms endospores. *S. ureae* and *S. halophila* are the two species listed.

Genus *Staphylococcus:* The gram-positive staphylococci grow singly, in pairs, in tetrads, or in irregular, grapelike clusters. The most important species, *S. aureus*, usually gives yellow to orange growth, although it may be white on occasion. Many of the beta-hemolytic, coagulasepositive strains are pathogenic, and some produce an enterotoxin which causes food poisoning.

Genus *Streptococcus:* Streptococcus is a genus of coccus gram positive bacteria. The cocci in this genus are characteristically in pairs, in short chains, or in long chains, depending on the species and the conditions of growth, and all is homofermentative. The streptococci importance in foods are divided in food four groups: the pyogenic, viridans, lactic, and, enterococcus groups. The pyogenic (pus-producing) group pathogenic streptococci, of which *S. agalactiae*, a cause of mastitis in cows, and *S. pyogenes*, a cause of human septic sore throat, scarlet fever, and other diseases are representatives that have been found in raw milk. The pyogenic streptococci cannot grow at 10 or 45°C.

The *viridans* groups includes *S. thermophilus*, a coccus important in cheese making at at high temperatures and yogurt, and *S. bovis* is like *S. thermophilus* and it is thermoduric and therefore counted in the plating of pasteurized milk. These species can grow at 45°C but not at 10°C.

The lactic group contains the important dairy bacteria, *S. lactis* and *S. cremoris*, grow at 10°C but not at 45°C. These bacteria are used as starters for cheese, cultured buttermilk, and some types of butter, along with *Leuconostoc spp.*, and *S. lactis* often is concerned in the souring of raw milk.

The enterococcus group consists of *S. faecalis* and *S. faecium*, and some related subspecies. *S.faecalis* is usually the more heat-resistant and comes more from human sources, whereas *S. faecium* has been reported to be more from plant sources. *S. faecalis* subsp. *liquefaciens* is an acid proteolytic variety of *S. faecalis*, and *S. faecalis subsp. zymogenes** is a beta-hemolytic variety. Bacteria of this group can grow at both 10 and 45°C. The *enterococci* have several characteristics in common that make them unusual streptococci:

(1) They are thermoduric, readily surviving the pasteurization treatment of milk or even more heating.

(2) They can tolerate 6.5 percent and more of salt.

(3) They can grow at the alkaline pH of 9.6.

(4) They can grow over a wide range of temperatures, some multiplying at as low as 5 to 8°C and most of them at as high as 48 to 50°C.

The term "fecal streptococci" is often used in the food industry to describe those enterococci which are used as indicator organisms.

Genus *Streptomyces:* Members of this genus can cause undesirable flavors and appearance when growing on foods; musty or earthy odors and tastes from these organisms may be absorbed by nearby foods when growth of the Streptomyces is near at hand.

Genus *Vibrio:* Bacteria in this genus are widely distributed in fresh and salt water, in soil, and in the alimentary canal of humans and animals. Some are moderately halophilic. Some species are pathogenic to humans.

Genus *Yersinia:* The genus *yersinia* includes 11 species among them the plague causing *Y. pestis* can be found in the soil. *Y. pestis* is the causative-organism of plague in humans and in rats and other rodents. Some strains of *Y. enterocolitica* are also pathogenic and causative agents of food-borne disease outbreaks.

2.1.3 Groups of Bacteria important in food Bacteriology

1. Lactic acid–forming bacteria or lactics: These bacteria ferment sugars to lactic acid. This may be desirable in making products such as sauerkraut and cheese. But undesirable in terms of spoilage of wines because they usually form acid rapidly. Ex: *Leuconostoc, Lacto bacillus, Streptococcus and Pediococcus.*

2. Acetic acid forming bacteria or acetics: Most of the acetic acid belong to two genera *Acetobacter* and *Gluconobacter*. Both oxidize ethyl alcohol to acetic acid, but *Acetobacter* is capable of oxidizing acetic acid further to CO_2. Characteristics that make acetic acid bacteria important are

(1) Their ability to oxidize ethanol to acetic acid.

(2) Their strong oxidising power, result in oxidation of desired product like acetic acid, by desirable sps or undesirable sps under favourable conditions.

(3) Excessive sliminese of some species

Ex: *Acetobacter acetic sub sp. suboxydans*. This bacteria clog vinegar generators.

3. Butyric acid forming bacteria or butyrics: Most bacteria of this group are spore forming anaerobes of the genus clostridium.

4. Propionic acid – forming bacteria or propionics: Ex: Propionic bacterium

5. Proteolytic bacteria: They produce extracellular proteinases proteolytic bacteria may be aerobic, facultative, spore forming, anaerobic and spore forming.

Bacillus cereus – Aerobic, spore forming

Pseudomonas fluorescens – Non spore forming and aerobic to facultative.

Clostridum sporogenes – Spore forming and anaerobic other examples are clostridium, bacillus, proteus. Acid proteolytic bacteria carry on an acid fermentation and proteolysis simultaneously.

Ex: *Streptococcus faecalis var. liquefaciens, Micrococcus caseolyticus* are acid proteolytic.

Some bacteria are putrefactive *i.e.*, they decompose proteins anaerobically to produce foul smelling compounds such as H_2S, mercaptans, amines, indole and fatty acids.

Ex: *Clostridium*, *Proteus, Pseudomonas.*

6. Lipolytic Bacteria: These bacteria produce lipases which catalyze the hydrolysis of fats to fatty acids and glycerol. Many of the aerobic, actively proteolytic bacteria also are lipolytic.

Pseudomonas fluorescens – Strongly lipolytic

Pseudomonas, *Alcaligenes*, *Staphylococcus*, *Serratia* and *Micrococcus* are genera that contain lipolytic bacteria.

7. Saccharolytic bacteria: These bacteria hydrolyze disaccharides or polysaccharides to simpler sugars. Amylolytic bacteria possess amylase to bring about the hydrolysis of starch outside the cell. Amylolytic bacteria are *Bacillus subtilis* and *Clostridium butyricum*

8. Pectinolytic Bacteria: Pectins are complex carbohydrates that are responsible for cell wall rigidity in vegetables and fruits pectic substances derived from citrus fruits can be used in commercial products as gelling agents.

Ex: *Erwinia, Bacillus, Clostridum, Achromobacter, Aeromonas, Arthrobacter, Flavobacterium.*

9. Thermophilic Bacteria or Thermophiles: Optimum temperature required for these bacteria 45°C - 55°C. *Bacillus stearothermophilus* – thermophilic flat sour spoilage of low acid canned foods.

10. Thermoduric Bacteria: Thermoduric bacteria are usually defined as those which can survive a heat treatment such as pasteurization. Ex: *Bacillus* sps, Micrococci, Enterococci can survive pasteurization of liquid eggs. Fungi like *Byssochlamys fulva*, *Aspergillus* and *Penicillium* are thermoduric. Some thermoduric bacteria like Bacillus and enterococci can also be psychrotrophic.

11. Psychrotrophic Bacteria or psychrotrophs: These bacteria are able to grow at commercial refrigeration temperatures. Unlike psychrophiles, psychrotrophs do not have their optimal temperature for growth at refrigeration temperature and their optimum between 25°C and 30°C.

Ex: *Pseudomonas, Flavobacterium, Achromobacter and Alcaligenes, Micrococcus, Lactobacillus* etc.

12. Halophilic Bacteria or Halophiles: Halophilic Bacteria require certain minimal concentrations of dissolved sodium chloride for growth. Ex: *Pseudomonas, Moraxella, Acinetobacter, Flavobacterium, Vibrio* sps which grow best in media with 0.5 – 3.0 percent salt. These micro organisms are isolated from fish shell fish. These are slightly halophilic. Moderate halophiles are grown in the media. Containing 3.0 – 15% salt salted fish, brined fish, brined meats and some salted vegetables. Extreme halophiles grow in the heavily brined foods 15 – 30% salt. Ex: *Halobacterium, Halococcus.*

Other bacteria are salt tolerant i.e., halotolerant bacteria can grow with or without salt. Usually they are capable of growing in foods containing 5.0% salt or more. Ex: *Bacillus, Micrococcus, Corynebacterium, Streptococcus and Clostridium sps., Sarcina, pediococcus, Alcaligenes.*

13. Osmophilic or Saccharophilic Bacteria: Osmophilic bacteria are those which grow in high concentrations of sugar. Ex: *Leuconostoc.*

14. Pigmented Bacteria: Colors produced by pigmented bacteria growing on or in foods. *Flavobacterium* – Yellow to orange; *Serratia* – Red; *Halobacterium* – Pink

15. Slime or rope forming bacteria: *Alcaligenes viscolactis*, *Enterobacter aerogenes* & *Klebsiella oxytoca* causes ropiness of milk and *Leuconostoc* spp., producing slime in sucrose solutions and slimy surface growth of various bacteria occurring on foods. *Streptococcus* & *Lactobacillus* make milk slimy or ropy. *Micrococcus* makes curing solutions for meats ropy. *Lactobacillus plantarum* and Lactobacilli may cause ropiness in various fruit, vegetable and grain products e.g. in cider, sauerkraut and beer.

16. Gas forming Bacteria: Many kinds of bacteria produce small amounts of gas and yield it slowly. Ex: *Leuconostoc, Lactobacillus* (heterofermentative), Propionic bacterium, *Escherichia, Enterobacter, Proteus, Bacillus* and *Clostridium. Leuconostoc, Lactobacillus, Propionibacterium*, produces only CO_2. Other genera produce both CO_2 and H_2.

17. Coliform and Fecal coliform group: Coliforms are short rods that are defined as aerobic and facultative anaerobic, gram negative, non spore forming bacteria. Ex: *Escherichia coli, Enterobacter aerogenes*. Fecal coliform group includes coliforms capable of growing at 44 - 45°C. *Geotrichum candidum* is the machinery mold and as an indicator of plant sanitation and contaminated equipment. Some of the characteristics that make the coliform bacteria important in food spoilage are

1. Their ability to grow well in a variety of substrates and synthesis most of the necessary vitamins.
2. Their ability of the group to grow well over a fairly wide range of temperatures from below 10°C to about 46°C.
3. Their ability to produce considerable amounts of acid and gas from sugars.
4. Their ability to cause off – flavours often described as unclean or barny.
5. Their ability of *E. aerogenes* to cause sliminess or ropiness of foods.

Bacterial growth

Bacteria typically reproduce by a process known as binary fission: splitting in two. This is a type of asexual reproduction and produces two bacterial cells that are genetically identical. During binary fission, the cell's DNA molecule replicates and attaches to the cell membrane. The cell membrane then begins to grow between the two DNA molecules, and then a cell wall forms to give complete separation, resulting in two bacteria cells. The two cells become four and the four cells become eight and so on, the number of cells continuing to grow exponentially until the environment can no longer sustain them. Because there is a limited supply of food and habitable space, bacterial growth does not go on forever. Once all the food is gone, required resources are depleted, and the environment is full of waste products, life is no longer sustainable

Phases of bacterial growth There are four distinct phases to growth of bacteria: lag phase, log phase, stationary phase, and death phase

Lag Phase

The first phase of bacterial growth is called the lag phase. This phase occurs when bacteria first enter a nutrient-rich environment. During this phase, the growth rate is quite slow, as bacteria begin adapting to their new environment. While in the lag phase, bacteria produce the enzymes they will need to break down the substrate or food source. Provided the environment is nutrient-rich and conditions are favourable, the lag phase tends to be quite short. However, the length of the lag phase is the most variable of the four phases and the one most susceptible to intervention. For example, the lag phase can be prolonged if the temperature isn't ideal for bacterial growth. Other environmental factors that can impact the length of the lag phase include pH, water activity, and competition with other microbial species for nutrients.

Log Phase

Log phase As bacteria begin to multiply more quickly, they enter the growth phase known as the log phase, in which the bacteria experience very fast growth characterized by doubling of the population after each generation. Doubling means, for example, that eight bacteria divide into sixteen bacteria, sixteen bacteria into thirty-two bacteria, and so on. Logarithmic values (log values) are used to count the rapidly increasing numbers of bacteria in the log phase.

During the log phase, bacterial numbers increase dramatically. If it takes twenty minutes for the population to double, after twenty-four hours there will be hundreds of billions of bacteria. The length and rapidity of bacterial growth during the log phase depends on a variety of factors, including nutrient availability, the build-up of bacterial waste products, and temperature. In optimal conditions, most bacteria can double in only ten to thirty minutes. This time period for binary fission to complete is called the generation phase. While bacteria may continue to grow under refrigeration, the rate of growth will generally be slower than at temperatures in the danger zone (between 4°C and 60°C). The log phase comes to an end when resources are exhausted

2.1.4 Stationary Phase

As growth slows, the bacteria enter the stationary phase. During this period, the bacteria are still alive, but the environment will not support more growth and the rate of bacterial growth is the same as the rate of bacterial death. A steady state has been reached between the availability of nutrients and the increase in bacterial waste products. As food becomes scarce and waste products build up, the environment will become toxic for the remaining bacteria. It is during this phase that bacteria may produce chemicals such as antibiotics or toxins to inhibit other types of bacteria from growing. ome types of bacteria may begin what is known as the endospore phase, during which they change their shape to form spores for longer term survival. This form of the bacteria is tougher and more resistant to heat and ultraviolet radiation

Death phase:

Once nutrients are exhausted, bacteria will enter the death phase and begin to die off in large numbers. Some bacteria enter into a viable but non-culturable form. This is important to the food microbiologist, because it means that bacteria may not grow in the laboratory, but are still alive. It is unlikely that 100 % of the bacteria die during the death phase. The bacteria that do survive, however, are adaptable and able to begin growing again once more favourable conditions occur.

2.2 MOLDS

Molds are the most typical form of fungus found on earth, comprising about 25% of the earth's biomass.

Mold grow on foods, with its fuzzy or cottony appearance, sometimes colored, is familiar to everyone, and usually food with a moldy or "mildewed" food is considered unfit to eat. Special molds are useful in the manufacture of certain foods or ingredients of foods. Thus, some kinds of cheese are mold-ripened, *e.g.*, blue, Roquefort, Camembert, Brie, Gammelost, etc., and molds are used in making Oriental foods, *e.g.*, soy sauce, miso, sonti, and other discussed later. Molds have been grown as food or feed and are employed to produce products used in foods, such as amylase for bread making or citric acid used in soft chinks. Some molds do produce various toxic metabolites (mycotoxins).

Althouth molds associated with foods are not considered to be pathogenic, some produce mycotoxins.

Mycotoxins are natural organic compounds the are capable of initiating a toxin response in vegetables. These toxic substances pose a potential health hazards to humans.

General characteristics of molds:

The term "mold" is a common name applied to certain multicellular filamentous fungi whose growth on foods usually is readily recognized by its fuzzy or cottony appearance. Colored spores are typical of mature mold of some kinds and give color to part or all of the growth. The thallus, or vegetative body, is characteristic of thallophytes, which lack true roots, stems, and leaves.

Morphological Characteristics:

Hyphae and Mycelium: The mold thallus consists of a mass of branching, intertwined filaments called hyphae (singular hypha), and the whole mass of these hyphae is known as the mycelium. The hyphae may be submerged, or growing within the food, or aerial, or growing into the air above the food. Molds are divided into two groups: septate, *i.e.*, with cross walls dividing the hypha into cells; and noncoenocytic, septate with the hyphae apparently consisting of cylinders without cross walls. The non-septate hyphae have nuclei scattered throughout their length and are considered multicellular. Special, mycelial structures or parts aid in the identification of molds. Examples are the rhizoids, or "holdfasts," of *Rhizopus and Absidia*, the foot cell in *Aspergillus*, and the dichotomous, or Y-shaped, branching in *Geotrichum*.

Reproductive Parts or Structures:

Molds can grow from a transplanted piece of mycelium. Reproduction of molds is chiefly by means of asexual spores. Some molds also *form* sexual spores. Such molds are termed "perfect" and are classified as either *Oomycetes* or *Zygomycetes* if nonseptate, or *Asco-mycetes* or *Basidiomycetes* if septate, in contrast to "imperfect" molds, the Fungi Imperfecti (typically septate), which have only asexual spores.

Asexual Spores: The asexual spores of molds are produced in large numbers and are small, light, and resistant to drying. They are readily spread through the air to alight and start new mold thallus where conditions are favorable. The three principal types of asexual spores are (1) conidia (singular conidium), (2) arthrospores or oidia (singular oidium), and (3) sporan- giospores. Conidia are cut off, or bud, from special fertile hyphae called conidiophores and usually are in the open, *i.e.*, not enclosed in any container, in contrast to the sporangiospores, which are in sporangium (plural sporangia), or sac, at the tip of a fertile hypha, the sporangiophore. Arthrospores are formed by fragmentation of a hypha, so that the cells of the hypha become arthrospores. Examples of these three kinds of spores will be given in the discussion of important genera of molds. A fourth kind of asexual spore, the chlamydospore, is formed by many species of molds when a cell here and there in the mycelium stores up reserve food, swell, and forms a thicker wall than that of surrounding cells. This chlamydospore, or resting cell, can withstand unfavourable conditions better than ordinary mold mycelium can and later, under favorable conditions, can grow into a new mold.

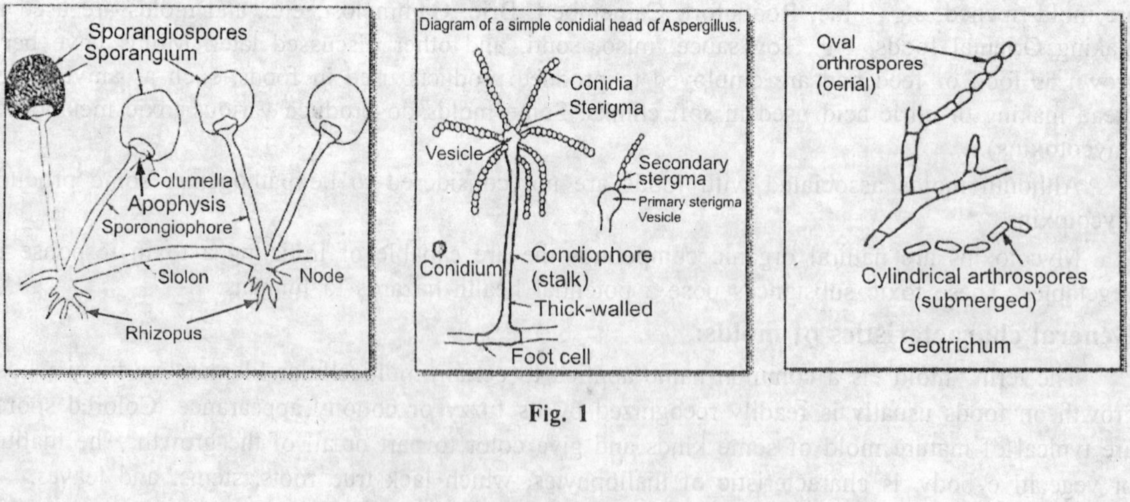

Fig. 1

Sexual Spores: The molds which can produce sexual spores are classified on the basis of the manner of formation of these spores and the type produced. The non septate molds (*Phycomycetes*) that produce.

1. **Oospores** are termed *Oomycetes*. These molds are mostly aquatic; however, included in this group are several important plant pathogens. The oospores are formed by the union of a small male gamete and a large female gamete.
2. **Zygospores:** These fungi produce asexual spores (sporangiospores, arthrospores and conidiospores) or sexual spores (zygospores). The hyphae contain no septa, but older hyphae may have septa. *Zygomycetes* form zygospores by the union of the tips of two hyphae which often appear similar and which may come from the same mycelium or from different mycelia. Both Oospores and zygospores are covered by a tough wall and can survive drying for long periods.
3. **Ascospores:** The *Ascomycetes* (septate) form sexual spores known as ascopores, which are formed after the union of two cells from the same mycelium or from two separate mycelia. The ascospores, resulting from cell division after conjugation, are in an ascus, or sac, with usual eight spores per ascus. There are between 1,900 and 2,000 genera in Ascomycetes. Only few are of importance in foods.
4. **Basidiospores:** The *Basidiomycetes*, which include most mushrooms, plant rusts, smuts, etc., form a fourth type of sexual spore, the basidiospore.

Cultural Characteristics

Some molds are loose and fluffy; others are compact. Some look velvety on the upper surface, some dry and powdery, and others wet or gelatinous. Definite zones of growth in the thallus distinguish some molds, *e.g.*, *Aspergillus niger*. Pigments in the mycelium-red, purple, yellow, brown, gray, black, etc - are characteristic, as are the pigments of masses of asexual spores; green, blue-green, yellow, orange, pink, lavender, brown, gray, black, etc. The appearance of the reverse side of a mold on an agar plate may be striking, like the opalescent blue-black or greenish-black color of the underside of *Cladosporium*.

Physiological characteristics:

The physiological characteristics of molds is discussed briefly as

Moisture Requirements: In general most molds require less available moisture than do most yeasts and bacteria. Approximate limiting total moisture content of a given food for mold growth can be estimated, and therefore it has been claimed that below 14 to 15 percent total moisture in flour or some dried fruits will prevent or greatly delay mold growth.

Temperature Requirements: Most molds would be considered mesophilic *i.e.*, able to grow well at ordinary temperatures. The optimal temperature for most molds is around 25 to 30°C, but some grow well at 35 to 37°C or above, *e.g.*, *Aspergillus spp.*, and some at still higher temperatures. A number of molds are psychrotrophic; *i.e.*, they grow fairly well at temperatures of refrigeration, and some can grow slowly at temoeratures below freezing. Growth has been reported at as low as – 5 to – 10°C. A few are thermophilic; *i.e.*, they have a high optimal temperature.

Oxygen and pH Requirements: Molds are aerobic; *i.e.*, they require oxygen for growth; this is true at least for the molds growing on foods. Most molds can grow over a wide range of hydrogen-ion concentration (pH 2 to 8.5), but the majority are favored by an acid pH.

Food Requirements: Molds in general can utilize many kinds of foods, ranging from simple to complex. Most of the common molds possess a variety of hydrolytic enzymes, and some are grown for their amylases, pectinases, proteinases, and lipases.

Inhibitors: Compounds inhibitory to other organisms are produced by some molds, such as *penicillin* from *Penicillium chrysogenum* and clavacin from *Aspergillus clavatus*. Certain chemical compounds are mycostatic, inhibiting the growth of molds (sorbic acid, propionates, and acetates are examples), or are specifically fungicidal, killing molds.

Mold inhibitors such as *Amonex* are synergistic blends of organic acids and their salts and are formulated in a way to provide immediate and long lasting protection against molds.

Classification and identification of molds

Molds are plants of the kingdom Myceteae. They have no roots, stems, or leaves and are devoid of chlorophyll. They belong to the Eumycetes, or true fungi, and are subdivided further to subdivisions, classes, orders, families, and genera. The following criteria are used chiefly for differentiation and identification of molds:

1. Hyphae septate or non-septate
2. Mycelium clear or dark (smoky)
3. Mycelium colored or colorless
4. Whether sexual spores are produced and the type: oospores, zygospores, or ascospores
6. Characteristics of the spore head
   a) Sporangia: size, color, shape, and location
   b) Spore heads bearing conidia: single conidia, chains, budding conidia, or masses; shape and arrangement of sterigmata or phialides; gumming together of conidia
7. Appearance of sporangiophores or conidiophores: simple or branched, and if branched the type of branching; size and shape of columella at tip of sporangiophore; whether conidiophores are single or in bundles
8. Microscopic appearances of the asexual spores, especially of conidia: shape, size, color; smooth or rough; one-, two-, or many-celled
9. Presence of special structures (or spores): stolons, rhizoids, foot cells, apo-physis, chlamydospores, sclerotia, etc.

Molds of Industrial Importance

Mucor: Mucor species can develop as either individual spherical cells that multiply by budding as (yeasts) or they form typical mycelia of coenocytic hyphae. *Mucor* are involved in the spoilage of some foods and the manufacture of others. A widely distributed species is *M. racemosus*; *M. rouxii* is used in the "Amylo" process for the saccharification of starch, and mucors help ripen some cheese, (*e.g.*, Gammelost) and are used in making certain Oriental foods. *M. pusillus* produces an extra cellular protease that has milk clotting activity (Fig.2).

Zygorrhynchus These soil molds are similar to *Mucor* except that the zygo-spore suspensors are markedly unequal in size. (Fig. 3).

Rhizopus *Rhizopus stolonifer*, the so-called bread mold, is very common and is involved in the spoilage of many foods: berries, fruits, vegetables, bread, etc. (Fig. 4).

Absidia: Similar to *Rhizopus*, except that sporangia are small and pear-shaped. (Fig. 5).

Thamnidium: *Thamnidium elegans* is found on meat in chilling storage, causing "whiskers" on the meat. (Fig. 5).

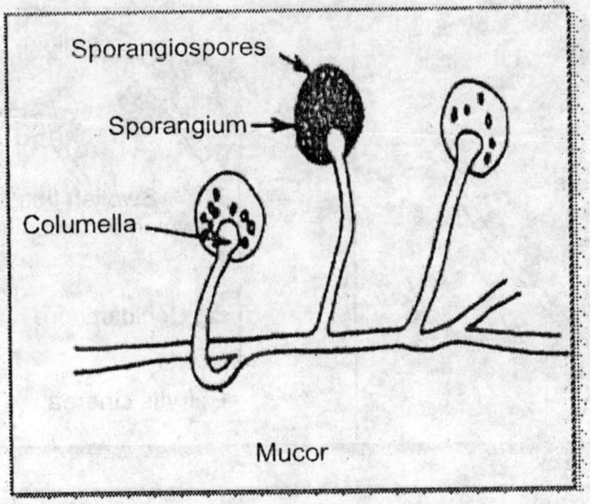

Fig. 2

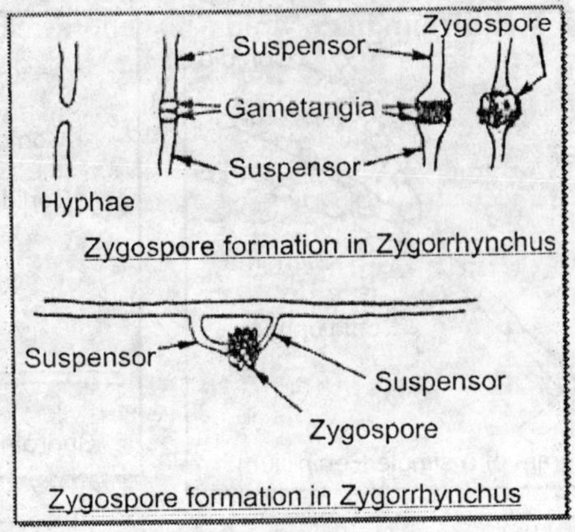

Fig. 3

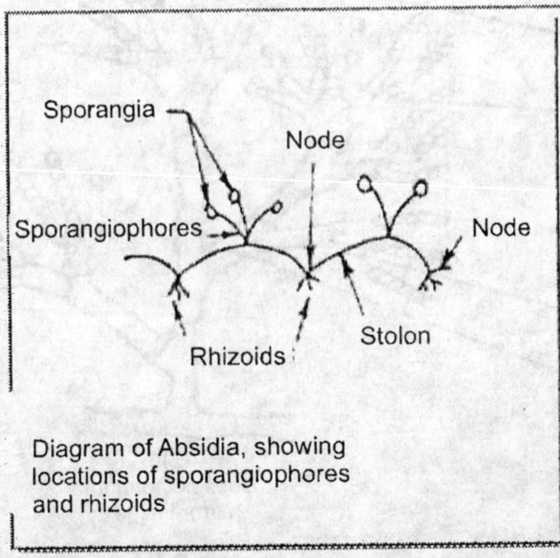

Fig. 4

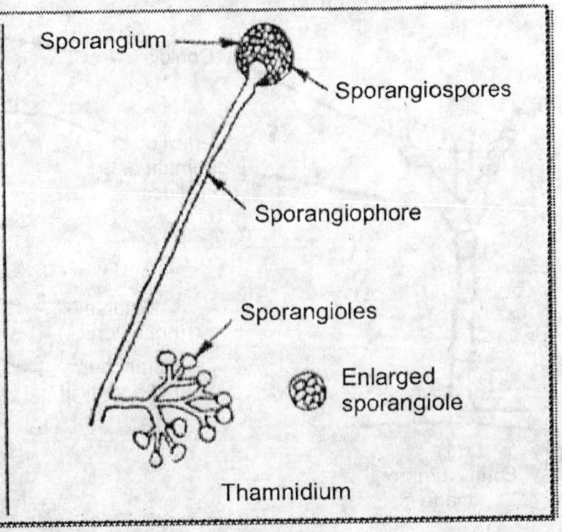

Fig. 5

Aspergillus: These are more than 100 species with genus. The aspergilli are very widespread. Many are involved in the spoilage of foods, and some are useful in the preparation of certain foods. The molds grow well in high concentrations of sugar and salt and hence in many foods of low moisture content. Conidia of this group are some shade of green. *Eurotium*, a name reserved for members having a perfect (sexual) stage. The *A. niger* group, with *A. niger* as a leading species, is widespread and may be important in foods. The spore-bearing heads are large, tightly packed, and globular and may be black, brownish-black, or purple-brown.

The *A. flavus-oryzae* group includes molds important in the making of some Oriental foods and the production of enzymes. Conidia give various yellow to green shades to the spore heads, and dark sclerotia may be formed.

Penicillium: This is another genus that is widespread in occurrence and important in foods. The genus is divided into groups and subgroups, and there are numerous species. The genus is divided into large groups on the basis of the branching of the spore-bearing heads, or penicillin (little brushes). These heads, or verticillata, are a whorl or cluster of three or more elements: sterigmata, metulae (subbranches), and branches. (Fig. 6).

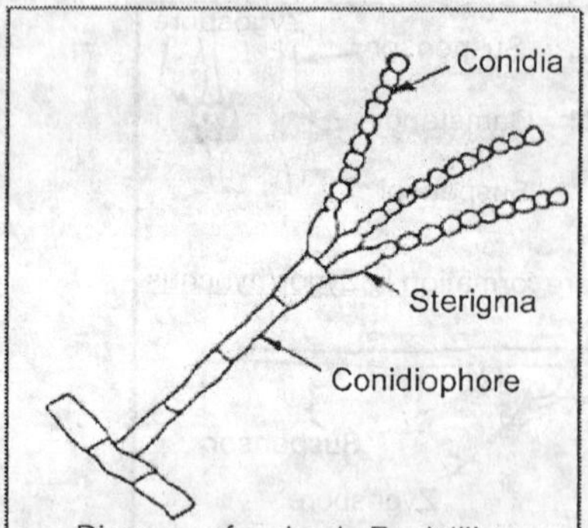

Diagram of a simple Penicillium.

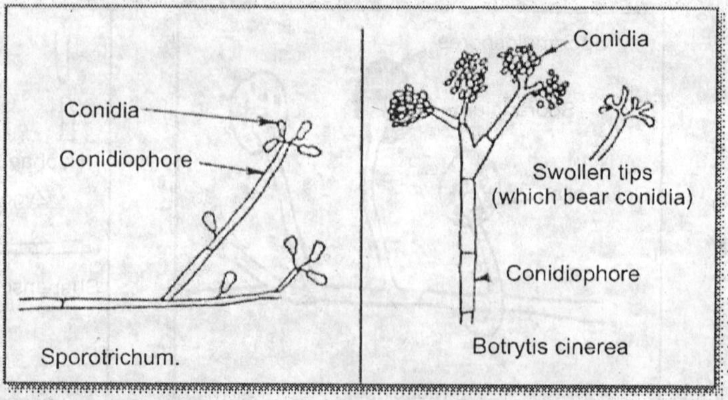

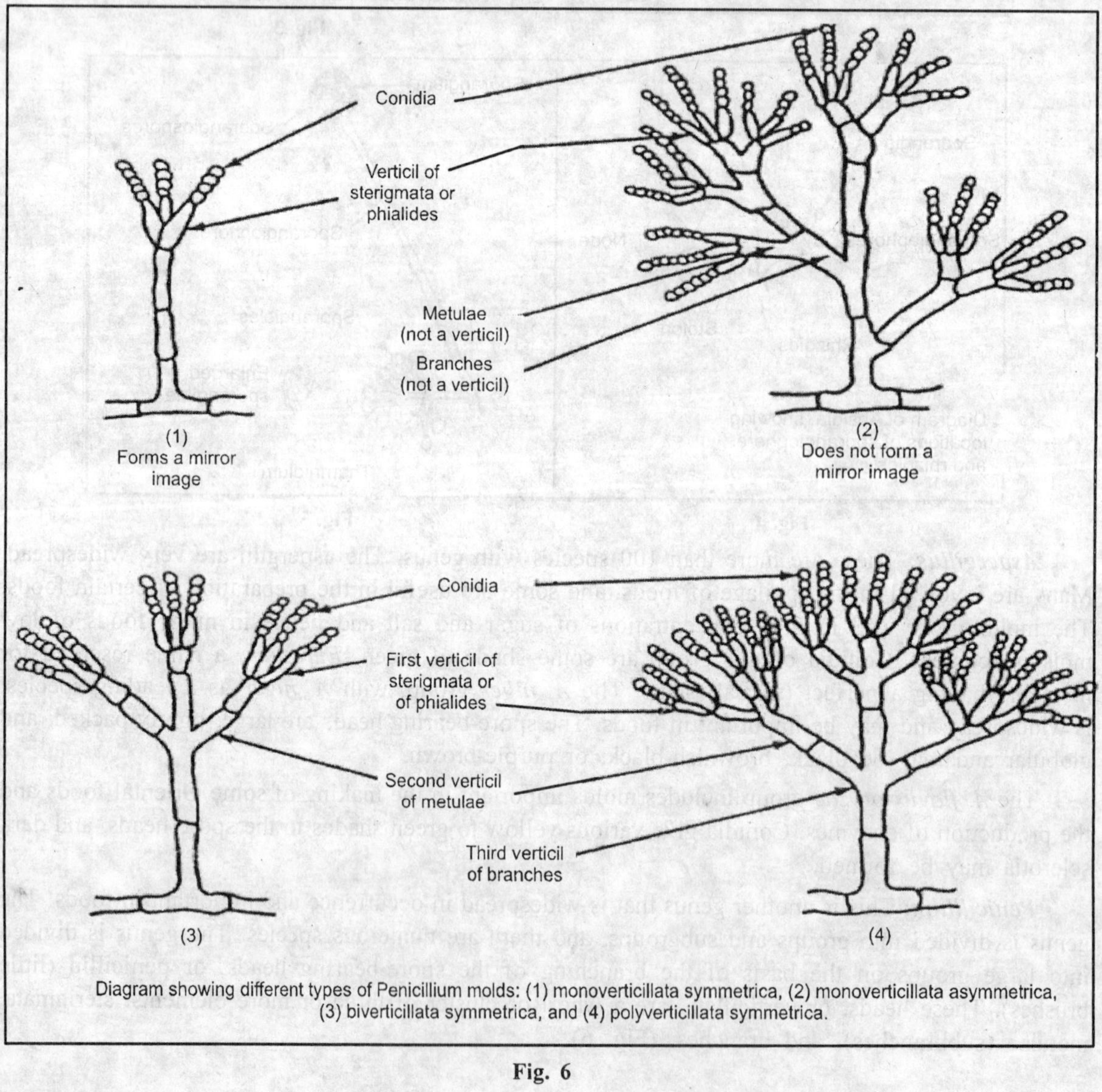

Diagram showing different types of Penicillium molds: (1) monoverticillata symmetrica, (2) monoverticillata asymmetrica, (3) biverticillata symmetrica, and (4) polyverticillata symmetrica.

Fig. 6

P. expansum, the blue-green-spored mold, causes soft rots of fruits. Other important species are *P. digitatum*, with olive, or yellowish-green conidia, causing a soft rot of citrus fruits; *P. italicum*, called the "blue contact mold" with blue green conidia, also rotting citrus fruit; *P.camemberti*, with grayish conidia, useful in the ripening of Camembert cheese; and *P. roqueforti*, with bluish-green conidia, aiding in the ripening of blue cheeses, *e.g.*, *Roquefort*.

Trichothecium: The common species, *T. roseum* is a pink mold which grows on wood, paper, fruits such as apples and peaches, and vegetables such as cucumbers and cantaloupes.

Geotrichum (Oospora or Oidium): This genus is included with the yeast like fungi by some writers and with the molds by others. Species may be white, yellowish, orange, or red, with the growth appearing first as a firm, felt like mass that later becomes soft and creamy. *Geotrichumcandidum* (Oospora lactis), often called the "dairy mold," gives white to cream-colored growth.

Red crumb in bread is caused by *Oidium Geotrichum.*

Neurospora (Monilia): This genus has been described under various names because of the confusion concerning its classification. It is classed among the perfect molds (producing sexual spores) and calls the genus *Neurospora*. *Neurospora (Monilia) sitophila*, the most important species in foods, sometimes is termed the "red bread mold" because its pink, loose-textured growth often occurs on bread.

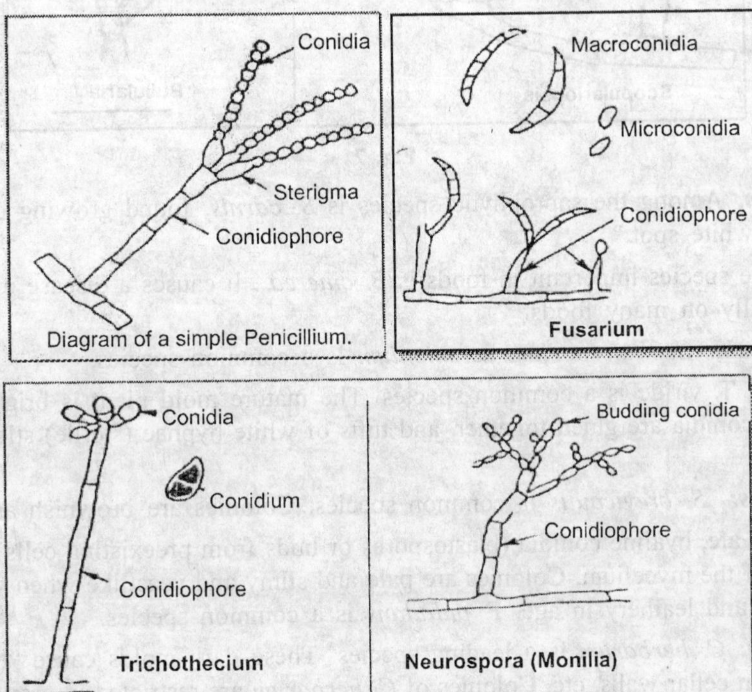

Diagram of a simple Penicillium.

Fusarium

Trichothecium

Neurospora (Monilia)

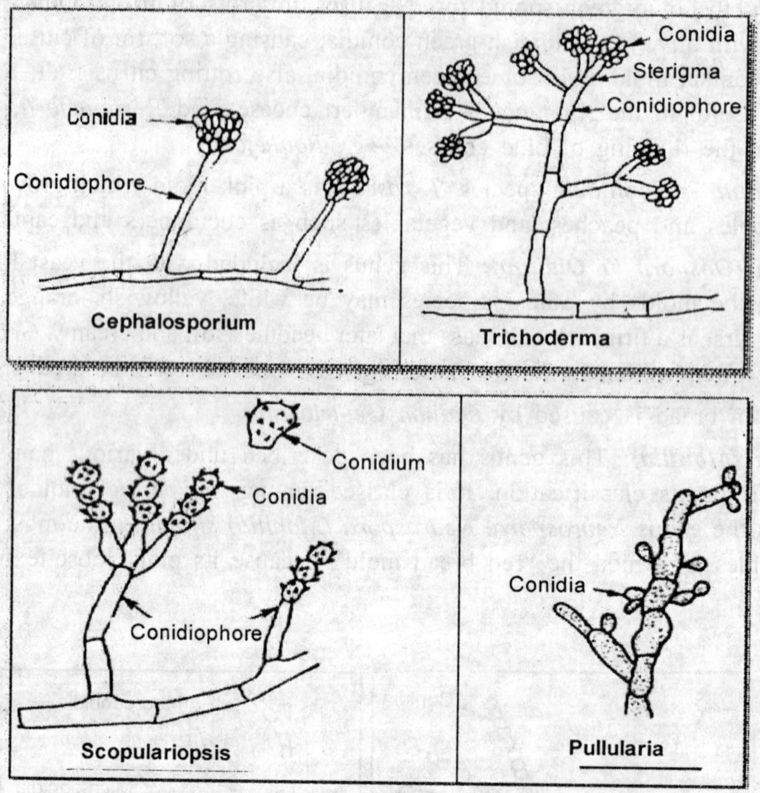

Fig. 7

Sporotrichum: Among the saprophytic species is *S. carnis*, found growing on chilled meats, where it causes "white spot."

Botrytis: One species important in foods is *B. cinerea* . It causes a disease of grapes but may grow saprophytically on many foods.

Cephalosporium: *Cephalosporium acremonium* is a common species.

Trichoderma: T. viride is a common species. The mature mold plant is bright green because the balls of green conidia are glued together, and tufts of white hyphae (sterile) stick up well above the conidiophores.

Scopulariopsis: *S. brevicaulis* is common species. Colonies are brownish and cottony.

Pullularia: Ovate, hyaline conidia (blastospores or buds from preexisting cells) borne as lateral buds on all parts of the mycelium. Colonies are pale and slimy and yeastlike when young, becoming mycelial and dark and leathery in age. *P. pullulans* is a common species.

Cladosporium: *C. herbarum* is a leading species. These dark molds cause "black spot" on a number of foods, on cellar walls, etc. Colonies of *C. herbarum* are restricted in growth and are thick, velvety, and olive - to gray-green; the reverse side of the plant is a striking opalescent blue-black to greenish-black.

Helminthosporium: Species of this genus are for the most part plant pathogens but may grow saprophytically on vegetable materials

Alternaria: These organisms are characterized by muriform, dark coloured spores. The aerial mycelia are describned as wooly, gray, brown, and olive-green. Molds of this genus are common causes of the spoilage of foods. *A. citri* (rotting citrus fruits), *A. tenuis*, and *A. brassicae* common species.

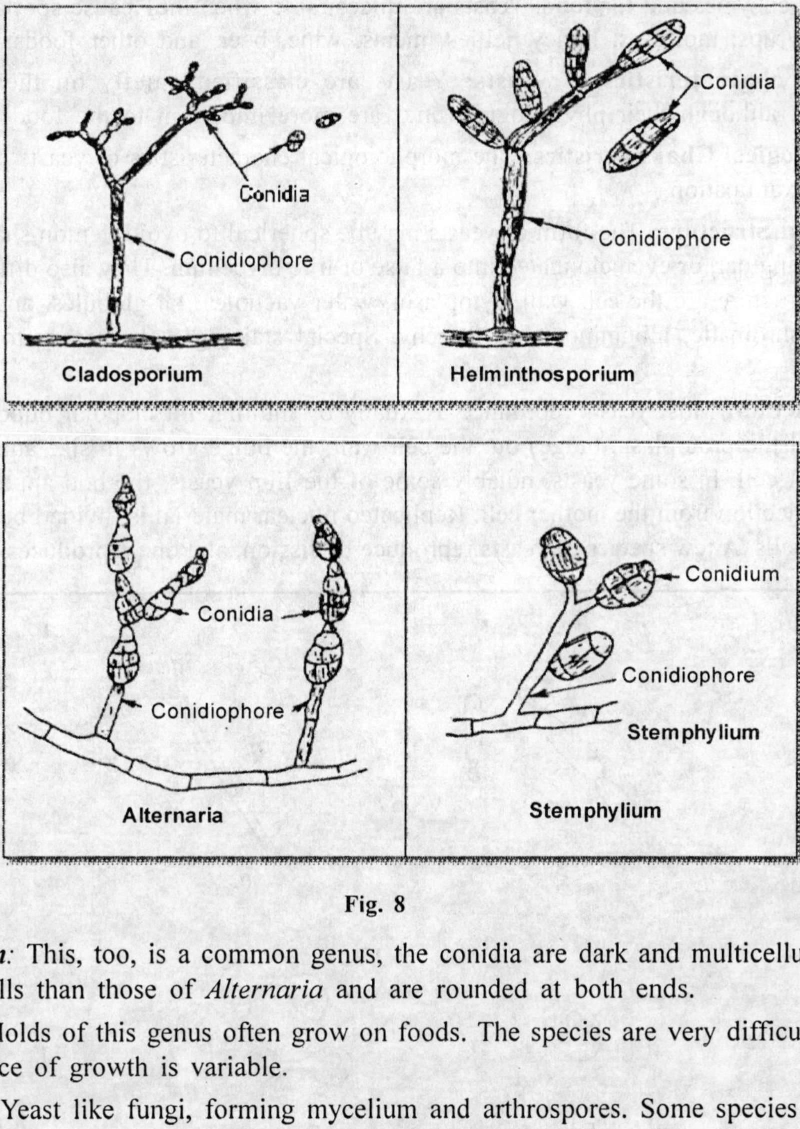

Fig. 8

Stemphylium: This, too, is a common genus, the conidia are dark and multicellular but have, fewer cross - walls than those of *Alternaria* and are rounded at both ends.

Fusarium Molds of this genus often grow on foods. The species are very difficult to identify, and the appearance of growth is variable.

Endomyces Yeast like fungi, forming mycelium and arthrospores. Some species rot fruits.

Monascus Colonies of M. purpureus are thin and spreading and reddish or purple in color. Found on dairy products and on Chinese red rice (ang -khak).

Sclerotinia Some species cause rots of vegetables and fruits, where they are present in the conidial stage. The lemon-shaped conidia are in chains, with a "plug" separating conidia.

2.3 YEASTS AND YEAST LIKE FUNGI

Like mold, the term "yeast" is commonly used but hard to define. It refers to those fungi which are generally not filamentous but unicellular and ovoid or spheroid end which reproduce by budding or fission. Yeasts may be useful or harmful in foods. Yeast fermentations are involved in the manufacture of foods such as bread, beer, wines, vinegar, and surface ripened cheese, and yeasts are grown for enzymes and for food. Yeasts are undesirable when they cause spoilage of sauerkraut, fruit juices, syrups; molasses, honey, jellies, meats, wine, beer, and other foods.

General characteristics of yeasts: Yeasts are classified chiefly on their morphological characteristics, although their physiological ones are more important to the food microbiologist.

Morphological Characteristics: The morphological characteristics of yeasts are determined by microscopic examination.

Form and Structure: The form of yeasts may be spherical to ovoid, lemon shaped, pearshaped, cylindrical, triangular, or even elongated into a false or true mycelium. They also differ in size. Visible parts of the structure are the cell wall, cytoplasm, water vacuoles, fat globules, and granules, which may be metachromatic, albuminous, or Starchy. Special staining is necessary to demonstrate the nucleus.

Reproduction: Most yeasts reproduce asexually by multilateral or polar budding, a process in which some of the protoplasm bulges out the cell wall; the bulge grows in size and finally walls off as a new yeast cell. In some yeasts, notably some of the film yeasts, the bud appears to grow from a tube like projection from the mother cell. Replicated nuclear material is divided between the mother and daughter cells. A few species of yeasts reproduce by fission, and one reproduces by a combination

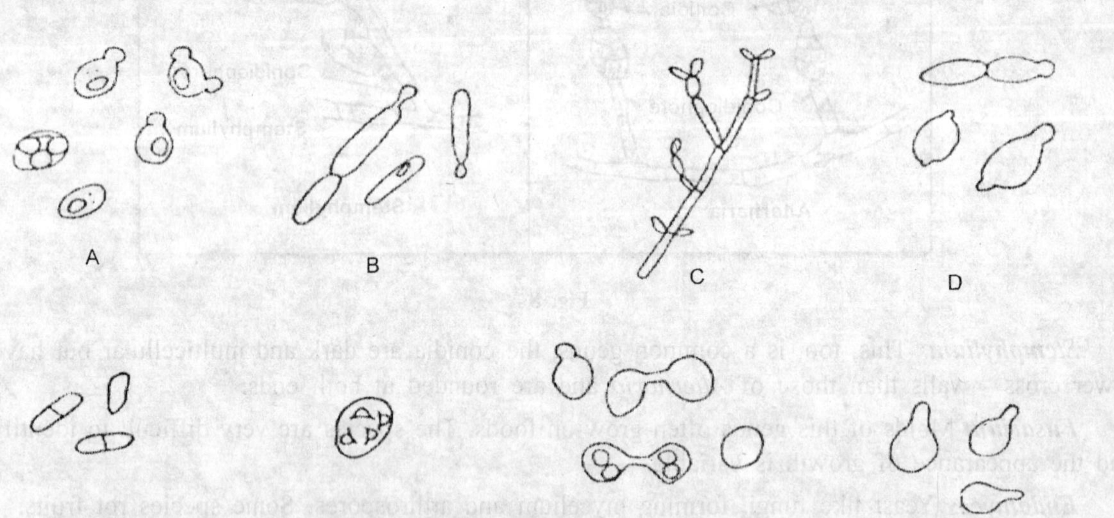

Yeasts of different shapes : (A) Saccharomyces cerevisiae, with budding cells and one ascus with four ascospores, (B) Candida yeast, with elongated cells, (C) Candida, showing pseudomycelium, (D) Apiculate (lemon-shaped) yeast, (E) Schizosaccharomyces, multiplying by fission, (F) Hansenula, with ascospores shaped like derby hats, (G) Zygosacharmyces, showing conjugation with ascus and four ascospores, (H) flask-shaped yeasts.

Fig. 9

of fission and budding. Sexual reproduction of "true" yeasts (*Ascomycotina*) results in the production of ascospores, the yeast cell serving as the ascus. The formation of ascospores follows conjugation of two cells in most species of true yeasts, but some may producc ascospores without conjugation, followed by conjugation of ascospores or small daughter cells. The usual number of spores per ascus and the appearance of the ascospores are characteristic of the kind of yeast. The ascospores may differ in color, in smoothness or roughness of their walls, and in their shape (round, oval, reniform, bean- or sickle-shaped, Saturn- or hat~ shaped, hemispherical, angular, fusiform, or needle-shaped). "False" yeasts, which produce no ascospores or other sexual spores, belong to the *Fungi Imperfecti*. Cells of some yeasts become chlamydospores by formation of a thick wall about the cell, for example, *Candida*, *Rhodotorula*, and *Cryptococcus*.

Cultural Characteristics

Growth as a film on the surface of liquid media suggests an oxidative or film yeast, and production of a carotenoid pigment indicates the genus *Rhodotorula*. The appearance of the growth is important when it causes colored spots on foods. It is difficult to tell yeast colonies from bacterial ones on agar plates; the only certain way is by means of microscopic examination of the organisms. Most young yeast colonies are moist and somewhat slimy but may appear mealy; most colonies are whitish, but some are cream-colored or pink. Some colonies change little with age, but others become dry and wrinkled.

Yeasts are oxidative, fermentative, or both. The oxidative yeasts may grow as a film, pellicle, or scum on the surface of a liquid and then are termed film yeasts. Fermentative yeasts usually grow throughout the liquid and produce carbon dioxide.

Physiological Characteristics

Most common yeasts grow best with a plentiful supply of available moisture. But many types of yeast grow in the presence of greater concentrations of solutes (such as sugar or salt) than most bacteria. Most yeast requires more moisture than molds, however. on the basis of water activity or aw, yeasts may be classified as ordinary if they do not grow in high concentrations of solutes, *i.e.*, in a low aw, and as osmophilic if they do. Lower limits of aw for ordinary yeasts range from 0.88 to 0.94. Osmophilic yeasts have been found growing slowly in media with aw as low as 0.62 to 0.65 in syrups, although some osmophilic yeasts are stopped at about 0.78 in both salt brine and sugar syrup. The aw values will vary with the nutritive properties of the substrate, pH, temperature, availability of oxygen, and presence or absence of inhibitory substances.

The range of temperature for growth of most yeast is 25 to 30°C and the maximum about 35 to 47 °C. Some kinds can grow at 0°C or less. The growth of most yeast is favored by an acid reaction in the vicinity of pH 4 to 4.5, and they will not grow well in an alkaline medium unless adapted to it. Yeasts grow best under aerobic conditions, but the fermentative types can grow anaerobically, although slowly.

In general, sugars are the best source of energy for yeasts, although oxidative yeasts, *e.g.*, the film yeasts oxidize organic acids and alcohol. Carbon dioxide produced by bread yeasts accomplishes the leavening of bread, and alcohol made by the fermentative yeasts is the main product in the manufacture of wines, beer, industrial alcohol, and other products. The yeasts also aid in the production of flavors or "bouquet" in wines.

Nitrogenous foods utilized vary from simple compounds such as ammonia and urea to amino acids and polypeptides. In addition, yeasts require accessory growth factors. Yeasts may change in their physiological characteristics, especially the true, or ascospore-forming, yeasts, which have a sexual method of reproduction. These yeasts can be bred for certain characteristics or may mutate to new forms. Most yeast can be adapted to conditions which previously would not support good growth. Illustrative of different characteristics within a species is the large number of strains of *Saccharomyces cerevisiae* suited to different uses, e.g., bread strains, beer strains, wine strains, and high-alcohol-producing strains or varieties.

Classification and identification of yeasts

The true yeasts are in the subdivision *Ascomycotina*, and the false, or asporogennous, yeasts are in the subdivision *Fungi Imperfecti* or *Deuteromycotina*. Certain yeasts are actually represented in two different genera based on whether they reproduce sexually. The principal bases for the identification and classification of genera of yeasts are as follows:

1. Whether ascospores are formed.
2. If they are spore-forming:

   a) The method of production of ascospores:

(1) Produced without conjugation of yeast, cells (parthenogenetically). Spore formation may be followed by

(*a*) Conjugation of ascospores. (*b*) Conjugation of small daughter cells.

(2) Produced after isogamic conjugation (conjugating cells appear similar).

(3) Produced by heterogamic conjugation (conjugating cells differ in appearance).

b) Appearance of ascospores: shape, size, and color. Most spores are spheroidal or ovoid, but some have odd shapes, *e.g.*, most species of *Hansenula*, which look like derby hats

c) The usual number of ascospores per ascus: one, two, four, or eight. 3 Appearance of vegetative cells: shape, size, color, inclusions.

(4) Method of asexual reproduction:

a. Budding. *b.* Fission. *c.* Combined budding and fission. *d.* Arthrospores (oidia).

5. Production of a mycelium, pseudo mycelium, or no mycelium.
6. Growth as a film over surface of a liquid (film yeasts) or growth throughout medium.
7. Color of macroscopic growth.
8. Physiological characteristics (used primarily to differentiate species or strains within a species):

   a. Nitrogen and carbon sources. *b.* Vitamin requirements. *c.* Oxidative or fermentative: film yeasts are oxidative; other yeasts may be fermentative or fermentative and oxidative. *d.* Lipolysis; urease activity, acid production, or formation of starch like compounds.

Yeasts of industrial importance

Most yeast used industrially is in the genus *Saccharomyces*. The term "wild yeast" is applied to any yeast other than the one being used or encouraged. Thus yeast employed in one process could be wild yeast in another. Most of the troublesome wild yeasts are asporogenous, or false, yeasts.

Genus Schizosaccharomyces: These yeasts, which reproduce asexually by fission and form four or eight ascospores per ascus after isogamic conjugation, have been found in tropical fruits, molasses, soil, honey, and elsewhere. A common species is *S. pombe*.

Genus Saccharomyces: Cells of these yeasts may be round, ovate, or elongated and may form a pseudo-mycelium. Reproduction is by multipolar budding or by ascospore formation. The ascospores, one to four per ascus, are usually round or ovate. The leading species, *S. cerevisiae*, is employed in many food industries, with special strains used for the leavening of bread, as top yeasts for ale, for wines, and for the production of alcohol, glycerol, and invertase.

Top yeasts are very active fermenters and grow rapidly at 20°C. The clumping of the cells and the rapid evolution of CO_2 sweep the cells to the surface, hence the term top yeast.

Bottom yeast do not clump, grow more slowly, and are best fermenters at lower temperatures (10 to 15 °C). The absence of clumping and the slower growth and evolution of CO_2 permit the yeast to settle to the bottom, hence the term bottom yeast. These characteristics of brewers' yeast are observations and do not explain why some yeast clump, or flocculate.

S. cerevisiae var. ellipsoideus is a high-alcohol-yielding variety used to produce industrial alcohol, wines, and distilled liquors. *S. uvarum*, a bottom yeast, is used in making beer. *S.fragilis* and *S. Lactis*, because of their ability to ferment lactose, may be important in milk or milk products. *S. rouxii* and *S. mellis* are osmophilic.

Many of the Saccharomyces have been reclassified. For example, *S. uvarum* is now considered a variant of *S. cerevisiae*, *S. fragilis* is now *Kluyveromyces marxianus*, and *S. lactis* is now *K. marxianus var. lactis*. S. *rouxii*, *S. mellis*, and *S. nussbaumeri* are now *Zygosaccharomyces rouxii*. *Debaryomyces kloeckeri* is now *D. hansenii*.

Genus *Kluyveromyces:* These yeasts reproduce by multilateral budding, and ascopores are liberated upon maturity.

Genus *Zygosaccharomyces:* These yeasts are notable for their ability to grow in high concentrations of sugar (hence they are termed osmophilic) and are involved in the spoilage of honey, sirups, and molasses and in the fermentation of soy sauce and some wines. *Zygosaccharomyces nussbaumeri* grows in honey.

Genus *Pichia:* These oval to cylindrical yeasts may form pseudomycelia. Ascospores are round or hat-shaped, and there are one to four per ascus. A pellicle is formed on liquids; *e.g.*, *P. membranaefaciens* grows a pellicle on beers or wines.

Genus *Hansenula* These yeasts resemble *Pichia* in appearance but are usuually more fermentative, although some species form pellicles. Ascospores are hat- or Saturn-shaped.

Genus *Debaryomyces* These round or oval yeasts form pellicles on meat brines. Ascospores have a warty surface. *D. kloeckeri* grows on cheese and sausage.

Genus *Hanseniaspora* These lemon-shaped (apiculate) yeasts grow in fruit juices. *Nadsonia* yeasts are large and lemon-shaped.

False Yeasts (Fungi Imperfect)

Genus *Torulopsis:* These round to oval fermentative yeasts with multilateral budding cause trouble in breweries and spoil various foods. *T. sphaerica* ferments lactose and may spoil milk products. Other species can spoil sweetened condensed milk, fruit-juice concentrates, and acid foods.

Genus *Candida:* These yeasts form pseudohyphae or true hyphae, with abundant budding cells or blastospores, and may form chlamydospores. Many form films and can spoil foods high in acid and salt. *C. utilis* is grown for food and feed. *C. krusei* has been grown with dairy starter cultures to maintain the activity and increase the longevity of the lactic acid bacteria. Lipolytic *C. lipolytica* can spoil butter and oleomargarine.

Genus *Brettanomyces:* These ogive - or arch-shaped yeasts produce high amounts of acid and are involved in the late fermentation of Belgian lambic beer and English beers. They also are found in French wines. *B. bruxellansis* and *B. lambicus* are typical species.

Genus *Kloeckera:* These are imperfect apiculate or lemon-shaped yeasts. *K. apiculata* is common on fruits and flowers and in the soil.

Genus *Trichosporon:* These yeasts bud and form arthrospores. They grow best at low temperatures and are found in breweries and on chilled beef. *T. pullulans* is a common species.

Genus *Rhodotorula:* These red, pink, or yellow yeasts may cause discolorations on foods, *e.g.*, colored spots on meats or pink areas in sauerkraut.

Groups of Yeasts

Film yeasts, in the genera *Pichia, Hansenula, Debaryomyces, Candida,* and *Trichosporon,* grow on the surface of acid products such as sauerkraut and pickles, oxidize the organic acids, and enable less acid-tolerant organisms to continue the spoilage. *Hansenula* and *Pichia* tolerate high levels of alcohol and may oxidize it in alcoholic beverages. *Pichia* species are encouraged to grow on Jerez and Arbois wine, to which they are supposed to impart distinctive flavors and esters. *Debaryomyces* is very salt tolerant and can grow on cheese brines with as much as 24 percent salt. The film yeasts produce little or no alcohol from sugars.

Apiculate or lemon-shaped yeasts, *in Saccharomycodes, Hanseniaspora, Nadsonia,* and *Kloeckera*, are considered objectionable in wine fermentations because they give off-flavors, low yields of alcohol, and highly volatile acid.

Osmophilic yeasts (*Saccharomyces rouxii* and *S. mellis*) grow well in an environment of high osmotic pressure, *i.e.*, in high concentrations of sugars, salts, or other solutes, causing spoilage of dry fruits, concentrated fruit juices, honey, maple sirup, and other high-sugar solutions.

Salt-tolerant yeasts grow in curing brines, salted meats and fish, soy sauce, miso paste, and tamari sauce. The most salt-tolerant of the film yeasts are species of *Debaryomyces*, which grow on curing brines and on meats and cucumbers in them, as does *Saccharomyces rouxii*, which can grow as a film on brine. Yeasts in various other genera (*Torulopsis, Brettanomyces*, and others) also grow in brines. Yeasts grow in soy sauce with its high content of salt (about 18 percent). *Saccharomyces rouxii* is considered of great importance in the production of alcohol and flavor, but species of *Torulopsis*, *Pichia*, *Candida*, and *Trichosporon* also may grow. Film-forming *S. rouxii* and *Pichia* are sometimes involved in the spoilage of soy sauce. Similar yeasts are involved in miso production, but kinds will vary as the salt concentration is varied between 7 and 20 percent.

2.4 PURE CULTURE TECHNIQUES

A pure culture is a population of cells or multicellular organisms growing in the absence of other species or types. Pure culture (in microbiology) is a laboratory culture containing a single species of organism. A pure culture is usually derived from a mixed culture (one containing many species) by transferring a small sample into new, sterile growth medium in such a manner as to disperse the individual cells across the medium surface or by thinning the sample manifold before inoculating the new medium. Both methods separate the individual cells so that, when they multiply, each will form a discrete colony, which may then be used to inoculate more medium, with the assurance that only one type of organism will be present. Isolation of a pure culture may be enhanced by providing a mixed inoculum with a medium favouring the growth of one organism to the exclusion of others.

- A pure culture may originate from a single cell or single organism, in which case the cells are genetic clones of one another.
- Microbial cultures are foundational and basic diagnostic methods used extensively as a research tool in molecular biology.
- The most common form of microbial cultures are liquid or solid (agar).

Microbial cultures are foundational and basic diagnostic methods used extensively as a research tool in molecular biology. It is often essential to isolate a pure culture of microorganisms. A pure (or axenic) culture is a population of cells or multicellular organisms growing in the absence of other species or types. A pure culture may originate from a single cell or single organism, in which case the cells are genetic clones of one another. For the purpose of gelling the microbial culture, the medium of agarose gel (agar) is used. Agar is a gelatinous substance derived from seaweed. A cheap substitute for agar is guar gum, which can be used for the isolation and maintenance of thermophiles .

Microbiological cultures can be grown in petri dishes of differing sizes that have a thin layer of agar-based growth medium. Once the growth medium in the petri dish is inoculated with the desired bacteria, the plates are incubated at the best temperature for the growing of the selected bacteria (for example, usually at 37 degrees Celsius for cultures from humans or animals or lower for environmental cultures). Another method of bacterial culture is liquid culture, in which the desired bacteria are suspended in liquid broth, a nutrient medium. These are ideal for preparation of an antimicrobial assay. The experimenter would inoculate liquid broth with bacteria and let it grow overnight (they may use a shaker for uniform growth). Then they would take aliquots of the sample to test for the antimicrobial activity of a specific drug or protein (antimicrobial peptides). As an alternative, the microbiologist may decide to use static liquid cultures. These cultures are not shaken and they provide the microbes with an oxygen gradient.

2.4.1 Methods of pure culture isolation

Pure culture of microorganisms that form discrete colonies on solid media, e.g., yeasts, most bacteria, many other micro-fungi, and unicellular microalgae, may be most commonly obtained by plating methods such as streak plate method, pour plate method and spread plate method. But, the microbes that have not yet been successfully cultivated on solid media and are cultivable only in liquid media are generally isolated by serial dilution method.

(1) Aseptic technique

Trying to study this mixed population is often difficult and in the tradition of the scientific method; researchers dissect a system and study each piece in isolation. For microorganisms this means separating the organisms and getting them into pure culture. A pure culture is defined as a growth of microorganisms (a culture) that contains one cell type. It is essential in microbiology to be able to obtain and preserve pure cultures. Over 100 years ago, Robert Koch devised methods to achieve this goal and the methods he developed are essentially still used today. The protocols used to maintain pure cultures are a major part of aseptic technique and are the subject of this chapter.

The goals of aseptic technique are two-fold. The first objective is to obtain pure cultures and secondly to prevent cross-contamination. Microorganisms in culture must not escape into the environment, and microbes in the environment must not get into the cultures we are studying. It is essential that aseptic technique be understood and practiced correctly. Contaminated cultures are worthless for diagnosis or for doing research on, because it is unclear what microbe is performing any action that is being observed.

Aseptic methods commonly used are flame sterilization, tube transfer, streak plates, spread plates and pour plates. Flame sterilization is an easy method to insure sterile transfer of a culture from a source to a growth medium. Tube transfer is useful for moving inocula from one tube to another. Mechanical dilution by making streak plates is the preferred method for obtaining a pure culture of a microorganism. Finally, spread plates and pour plates are common methods for enumerating microorganisms and are sometimes useful for obtaining isolated colonies.

(2) Streak method

The streak plate method is a rapid and simple technique of mechanically diluting a relatively large concentration of microorganisms to a small, scattered population of cells. The goal is to obtain isolated ***colonies*** on a large part of the agar surface, so that desired species can then be brought into pure culture. Proper streaking of plates is an indispensable tool in microbiology. In most cases a closed inoculating loop is used for streaking plates. The wire loop should not be badly oxidized or pitted or it will fail to dilute the inoculum and will scratch the surface of the agar. Streak plates can be made from a broth culture, an agar slant or from an agar plate. It is sometimes convenient to suspend a bit of growth from a solid surface in sterile saline and use this as a source of inoculum. Resuspension of colonies or cultures grown on solid surfaces dilutes the culture and makes streak plating easier. A loopful of inoculum is transferred from the source and put on the agar surface. When using a large inoculum (a turbid culture or growth from a solid surface), a small spot is spread during the initial transfer. If the inoculum is from a lightly turbid suspension, the first phase of the streaking pattern is begun. The three-phase streaking pattern is recommended for beginners because it is most likely to give satisfactory results with suspensions having a wide range of microbial density

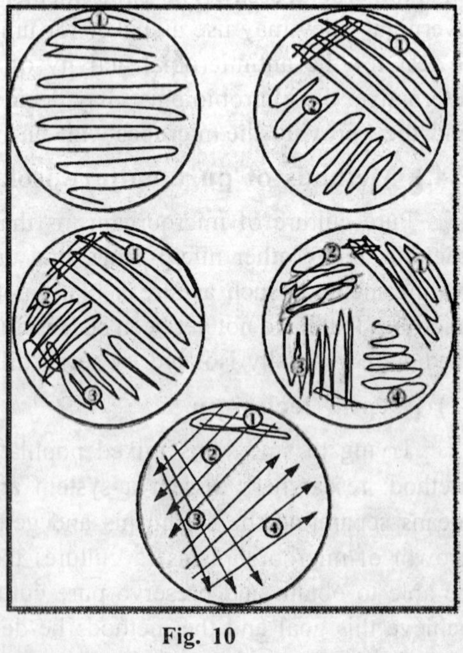

Fig. 10

(3) Pour Plate Method

This method involves plating of diluted samples mixed with melted agar medium. The main principle is to dilute the inoculum in successive tubes containing liquefied agar medium so as to permit a thorough distribution of bacterial cells within the medium. Here, the mixed culture of bacteria is diluted directly in tubes containing melted agar medium maintained in the liquid state at a temperature of 42-45°C (agar solidifies below 42°C).

The bacteria and the melted medium are mixed well. The contents of each tube are poured into separate Petri plates, allowed to solidify, and then incubated. When bacterial colonies develop, one finds that isolated colonies develop both within the agar medium (subsurface colonies) and on the medium (surface colonies). These isolated colonies are then picked up by inoculation loop and streaked onto another Petri plate to insure purity.

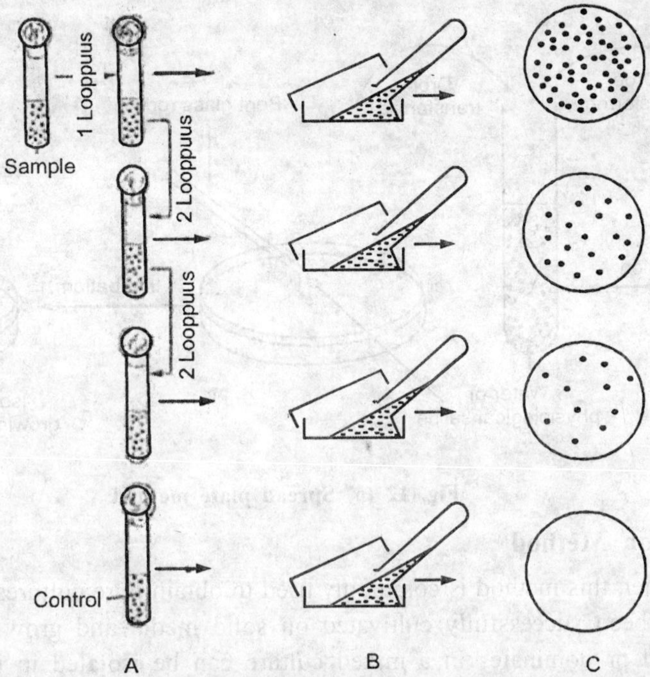

Fig. 11

Pour plate method has certain disadvantages as follows: (*i*) the picking up of subsurface colonies needs digging them out of the agar medium thus interfering with other colonies, and (*ii*) the microbes being isolated must be able to withstand temporary exposure to the 42-45° temperature of the liquid agar medium; therefore this technique proves unsuitable for the isolation of psychrophilic microorganisms.

However, the pour plate method, in addition to its use in isolating pure cultures, is also used for determining the number of viable bacterial cells present in a culture.

A. Media/dilution

B. Pouring of the plate; and

C. Colony development after incubation. Control consists of the sterilized plating medium alone

The isolated colonies are picked up and transferred onto fresh medium to ensure purity. In contrast to pour plate method, only surface colonies develop in this method and the microorganisms are not required to withstand the temperature of the melted agar medium.

(4) Spread Plate Method

In this method the mixed culture of microorganisms is not diluted in the melted agar medium (unlike the pour plate method); it is rather diluted in a series of tubes containing sterile liquid, usually, water or physiological saline. A drop of so diluted liquid from each tube is placed on the centre of an agar plate and spread evenly over the surface by means of a sterilized bent-glass--rod.

The medium is now incubated. When the colonies develop on the agar medium plates, it is found that there are some plates in which well-isolated colonies grow. This happens as a result of separation of individual microorganisms by spreading over the drop of diluted liquid on the medium of the plate.

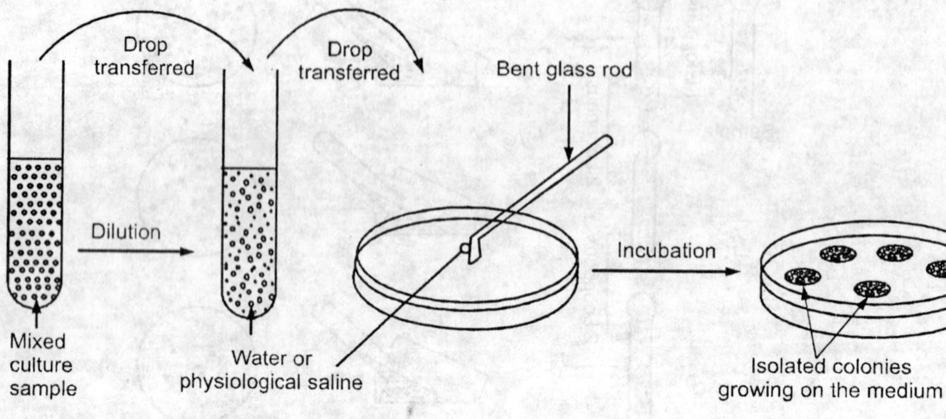

Fig. 12 (a) Spread plate method

(5) Serial Dilution Method

As stated earlier, this method is commonly used to obtain pure cultures of those microorganisms that have not yet been successfully cultivated on solid media and grow only in liquid media. A microorganism that pr dominates in a mixed culture can be isolated in pure form by a series of dilutions.

The inoculum is subjected to serial dilution in a sterile liquid medium, and a large number of tubes of sterile liquid medium are inoculated with aliquots of each successive dilution. The aim of this dilution is to inoculate a series of tubes with a microbial suspension so dilute that there are some tubes showing growth of only one individual microbe. For convenience, suppose we have a culture containing 10 ml of liquid medium, containing 1,000 microorganisms *i.e.*, 100 microorganisms/ml of the liquid medium.

Serial dilution method [Fig. 12 (b)]

Serial dilution is a stepwise series of dillutions that one performed to reduce concentration of a substance in a solution to a more usable concentration.

If we take out 1 ml of any medium and mix it with 9 ml of fresh sterile liquid medium, we would then have 100 microorganisms in 10 ml or 10 microorganisms/ ml. If we add 1 ml of this suspension to another 9 ml. of fresh sterile liquid medium, each ml would now contain a single microorganism. If this tube shows any microbial growth, there is a very high probability that this growth has resulted from the introduction of a single microorganism in the medium and represents the pure culture of that microorganism.

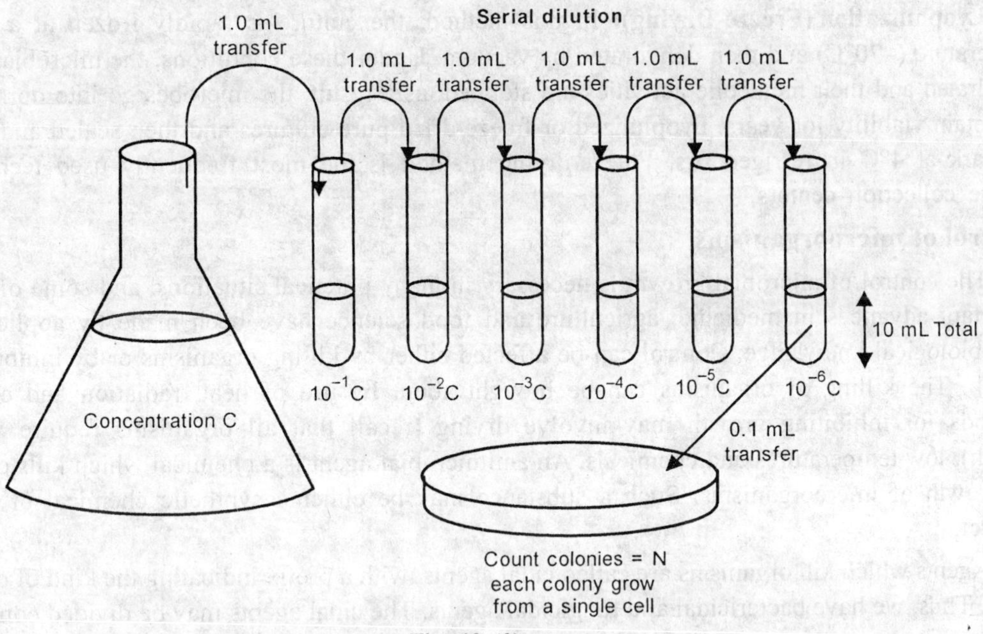

Fig. 12 (*b*)

2.4.2 Maintenance and Preservation of Pure Cultures

Once a microorganism has been isolated and grown in pure culture, it becomes necessary to maintain the viability and purity of the microorganism by keeping the pure cultures free from contamination. Normally in laboratories, the pure cultures are transferred periodically onto or into a fresh medium (subculturing) to allow continuous growth and viability of microorganisms. The transfer is always subject to aseptic conditions to avoid contamination. Since repeated sub culturing is time consuming, it becomes difficult to maintain a large number of pure cultures successfully for a long time. In addition, there is a risk of genetic changes as well as contamination. Therefore, it is now being replaced by some modern methods that do not need frequent subculturing. These methods include refrigeration, paraffin method, cryopreservation, and lyophilization (freeze drying).

Refrigeration: Pure cultures can be successfully stored at 0-4°C either in refrigerators or in cold-rooms. This method is applied for short duration (2-3 weeks for bacteria and 3-4 months for fungi) because the metabolic activities of the microorganisms are greatly slowed down but not stopped. Thus their growth continues slowly, nutrients are utilized and waste products released in medium. This results in, finally, the death of the microbes after sometime.

Paraffin Method: This is a simple and most economical method of maintaining pure cultures of bacteria and fungi. In this method, sterile liquid paraffin in poured over the slant (slope) of culture and stored upright at room temperature. The layer of paraffin ensures anaerobic conditions and prevents dehydration of the medium. This condition helps microorganisms or pure culture to remain in a dormant state and, therefore, the culture is preserved for several years.

Cryopreservation: Cryopreservation (*i.e.*, freezing in liquid nitrogen at –196°C) helps survival of pure cultures for long storage times. In this method, the microorganisms of culture are rapidly frozen in liquid nitrogen at –196°C in the presence of stabilizing agents such as glycerol (Dimethyl sulfoxide) and DMSO that prevent the formation of ice crystals and promote cell survival.

Lyophilization (Freeze-Drying): In this method, the culture is rapidly frozen at a very low temperature (–70°C) and then dehydrated by vacuum. Under these conditions, the microbial cells are dehydrated and their metabolic activities are stopped; as a result, the microbes go into dormant state and retain viability for years. Lyophilized or freeze-dried pure cultures and then sealed and stored in the dark at 4°C in refrigerators. Freeze-drying method is the most frequently used technique by culture collection centers.

Control of microorganisms

The control of microbial growth is necessary in many practical situations, and some of the most important advances in medicine, agriculture and food science have been made by applications of microbiological knowledge. Control can be affected either by killing organisms or by inhibiting their growth. The killing of organisms can be brought about by use of heat, radiation and chemicals. Methods for inhibiting growth may involve drying (recall that all organisms require water for growth), low temperatures and chemicals. An antimicrobial agent is a chemical which kills or inhibits the growth of microorganisms. Such a substance may be either a synthetic chemical or a natural product.

Agents which kill organisms are called cidal agents, with a prefix indicating the kind of organisms killed. Thus, we have bactericidal and fungicidal agents. The cidal agents may be divided conveniently into two groups: antiseptics and disinfectants. An antiseptic is sufficiently harmless so that it can be applied to the skin or mucous membranes, although it is not necessarily safe enough to be taken internally. A disinfectant is an agent that kills microorganisms (but not necessarily their spores) and is distinguishable from an antiseptic by the fact that it is not safe for application to living tissue. Disinfectants are restricted to inanimate objects such as tables, floors and dishes.

Chemicals which do not kill but only inhibit growth are called static agents, and they may be bacteriostatic and/orfungistatic. The distinction between cidal and static is somewhat arbitrary, since an agent that is cidal at high concentrations may be only static at low concentrations. To be effective, a static agent must be present continuously with the product, and if it is removed or its activity neutralized, the organisms present in the product will initiate growth. Static agents are often used as food preservatives, and since they must be present continuously to be effective, they remain in the food when eaten and hence must be nontoxic. Many drugs used in the treatment of microbial infections are static agents and must be kept present for a period of time long enough for body defenses to destroy the infecting agent. Such drugs obviously must be nontoxic to the body.

Thousands of antibiotics, another class of control compounds, have been discovered, but relatively few have become valuable in medicine. These few have found widespread and revolutionary use in the treatment of many infectiousdiseases. Many antibiotics commercially available come from various species of the genus *Streptomyces*. Examples include streptomycin, tetracycline, erythromycin and chloramphenicol. A few species of *Bacillus* produce antibiotics, *e.g.*, polymyxin from *B. polymyxa*. The first commercially-available antibiotic, penicillin, comes from the mold, *Penicillium chrysogenum*.

Organisms sensitive (susceptible) to an antibiotic or similar compound are affected by the agent at a target site, a specific structure or essential biochemical reaction in the cell. As an example, you learned that *Staphylococcus epidermidis* is sensitive to streptomycin which inhibits cells at the ribosomes, stopping translation (protein synthesis).Mutant cells may arise in the population which have resistant ribosomes, and such a cell is then resistant to streptomycin. Indeed, many species of bacteria are naturally resistant to streptomycin and would never be affected by it. Target sites hit by other agents include cell membrane synthesis (polymyxin), cell wall synthesis (penicillin) and DNAreplication (nalidixic acid). Sulfadiazine, like other sulfonamides, can substitute for a reactant in the synthesis of tetrahydrofolate, an essential biochemical process, and thus growth of the organism can be halted after several generations.

Gram-positive bacteria are usually more sensitive to antibiotics than are gram-negative bacteria, although, conversely, some antibiotics act only on gram-negative cells. An antibiotic which acts upon a wide variety of gram-positive and negative bacteria is called a broad-spectrum antibiotic. In general, such an antibiotic will find wider medical usage than one which is narrow-spectrum, although the latter may be quite valuable for the control of specific disease-causing organisms. The physician needs and utilizes a wide variety of antibiotics and must select carefully the one that is needed for a particular patient with a particular kind of infection.

Unfortunately, the use of some antibiotics has allowed for the enrichment of antibiotic-resistant mutant bacteria in the human population. An antibiotic must always be tested on the infectious agent in such a way that it can be found to be truly inhibitory at the target site of that organism. Any indication that resistant mutants will arise will necessitate the consideration of another antibiotic!

2.4.3 Sources of Contamination

Contamination of cell cultures is easily the most common problem encountered in cell culture laboratories, sometimes with very serious consequences. Cell culture contaminants can be divided into two main categories, chemical contaminants such as impurities in media, sera, and water, endotoxins, plasticizers, and detergents, and biological contaminants such as bacteria, molds, yeasts, viruses, mycoplasma, as well as cross contamination by other cell lines.

Micro organisms from various natural sources act as source of contamination.

- From green plants and fruits
- From animals
- From sewage
- From soil
- From water
- From air
- During handling and processing.

1. From green plants and fruits : Natural surface flora of plants varies with the plant but usually includes species of Pseudomonas, Alcaligenes, Flavobacterium, Micrococcus, coliforms and lactic acid bacteria. The no. of bacteria will depend on the plant and its environment and may range from a few hundred or thousand per square centimeter of surface to millions. Ex: Surface of well washed tomato contains 400-700 micro organisms per square centimeter. Outer tissue of unwashed cabbage contains 1 million to 2 million micro organisms. Inner tissues of cabbage contain fewer micro organisms. Exposed surface of plants become contaminated from soil, water, sewage, air and animals, so that micro organisms from these sources are added to the natural flora. Whenever conditions for growth of natural flora and contaminants are present, special kinds of micro organisms may increase. Some fruits have been found to contain viable micro organisms in their interior.

2. From animals: Sources of micro organisms from animals include the surface flora, the flora of the respiratory tract, and the flora of the gastro intestinal tract. Hides, hooves, and hair contain microorganisms from soil, manure, feed and water but contain spoilage organisms. Feathers, feet of poultry carry heavy contamination of micro organisms. Skin of many meat animals may contain micrococci, Staphylococci and beta haemolytic streptococci. Pig or beef carcasses may be contaminated with salmonellae. Salmonellosis associated with eggs has been reduced because of the pasteurization of egg products. Meat from slaughter houses is not frequently associated with human salmonellosis. Many of these diseases have been reduced or eliminated by improvement in animal husbandry, but animal disease causing infections from foods include Mycobacterium, Coxiella, Listeria, Salmonella and entropathogenic E.Coli and viruses. Insects and birds cause mechanical damage to fruits and vegetables, introduce microorganisms and open the way for microbial spoilage.

3. From sewage: When untreated domestic sewage is used to fertilize plant crops, there is a chance that raw plant foods will be contaminated with human pathogens especially those causing gastrointestinal diseases. The use of "night soil" as a fertilizer still persists in some parts of the world. In addition to the pathogens, coliform bacteria, anaerobes, enterococci, other intestinal bacteria and viruses can contaminate the foods from this source. Natural water contaminated with sewage contributes their micro organisms to shell fish, fish, and other seafood.

4. From soil: Soil contains greatest variety of micro organisms. They are ready to contaminate the surfaces of plants growing on or in them and the surfaces of animals roaming over the land. Soil dust is whipped up by air currents and soil particles are carried by running water to get into or onto foods. Soil is an important source of heat resistant spore forming bacteria.

5. From water: Natural water contains not only their natural flora but also microorganisms from soil and possibly from animals or sewage. Surface waters in streams or pools and stored waters have low microbial content because self purification of quiet lakes and ponds or of running water. Ground waters from springs or wells have passed through layers of rock and soil to a definite level hence most of the bacteria, suspended material have been removed. Kinds of bacteria in natural waters are chiefly of in Pseudomonas, Chromobacterium, Proteus, Micrococcus, Bacillus, Streptococcus, Enterobacter and Escherichia coli. Two aspects of water bacteriology are Pùblic health aspects and Economic aspects.

Public health aspects	Economic aspects
Public health aspects include safe to drink, free from pathogens, water should be tested for coliforms, enterobacter before consumption.	Water is used for processing of fruits & vegetables.

The water commonly is chlorinated but there have been presence of chlorine resistant flora. Efficient filtration greatly reduces the microbial content.

6. From Air: Air does not contain a natural flora of micro organisms, but accidentally they are present on suspended solid material or in moisture droplets. Micro organisms get into air on dust or lint, dry soil, spray from stream, lakes or oceans, droplets of moisture from coughing, sneezing or talking and growth of sporulating molds on floors, etc. Micro organisms in air have no opportunity for growth but merely persist there and 'he organisms resistant to dessications will live longer. Mold spores because of their small size,

resistance to drying and large numbers of per mold plant are usually present in air. Cocci are more numerous than rod shaped bacteria. Yeasts especially asporogenous chromogenic ones are found in most samples of air. Number of microorganisms in air at any given time depend on factors like amount of movement, sunshine, humidity, location and the amount of suspended dust or spray. No. of micro organisms vary from mountains to dusty air. Less on mountains and more in dusty air. Direct rays from the sun kill micro organisms suspended in air and hence reduce numbers. Dry air contains more organisms than moist air. Rain or snow removes organisms from the air. Number of micro organisms in air may be reduced under natural conditions by sedimentation, sunshine and washing by rain or snow. Filters in ventilating or air conditioning systems prevent the spread of organisms from one part of a plant to another.

7. During handling and processing: Additional contamination may come from equipment coming in contact with foods, from packaging materials and from personnel.

2.5 FOOD CONTAMINATION

Food contamination refers to the presence of harmful chemicals and microorganisms in food which can cause consumer illness. A **food contaminant** has been defined as any substance not intentionally added to food, which is present in such food as a result of the production, manufacture, processing, preparation, treatment, packing, transport or storage of such food as a result of environmental contamination. It is important to protect food from risk of contamination to prevent food poisoning and the entry of foreign objects. There are three main ways in which food can become contaminated: (*i*) Microbial Contamination; (*ii*) Physical Contamination; (*iii*) Chemical Contamination.

(*i*) Microbial Contamination

If food is consumed that has been contaminated by certain, harmful bacteria (pathogenic bacteria) or their toxins (poisons produced by some of these bacteria), food poisoning may result. Bacteria are responsible for most food poisoning cases. Symptoms of food poisoning may include vomiting, diarrhoea, fever and abdominal pain. The symptoms may take some time to occur depending on the type of bacteria (incubation period). In general, the bacteria must grow in the food to produce sufficient numbers to infect the body, multiply within the intestine and cause illness. Alternatively, toxins may be produced in the foodstuff or within the intestine, to produce symptoms very soon after ingestion. It is important to remember that foods contaminated with pathogenic bacteria will look, taste and smell perfectly normal. Steps must therefore be taken to prevent pathogenic bacteria getting onto food and multiplying to levels that will cause food poisoning. Food poisoning /food- intoxication due to microbes is very common; some of the foods borne diseases are given below-

S. No.	Causal organism	Disease
1.	*Staphylococcus aureus*	Gastroenteritis
2.	*Clostridium botulinum*	Botulism
3.	*Bacellus cereus*	Diarrhea
4.	*Salmonella typhi*	Enteric fever typhoid, food borne salmonellosis
5.	*Escherichia coli*	Gastroenteritis, diarrhea

Controls

- Prevent cross-contamination. Cross-contamination occurs when bacteria are transferred onto food either directly (*e.g.* when raw and cooked food come into direct contact, sneezing or coughing onto food) or indirectly (*e.g.* via a vehicle such as from dirty utensils, pests, hands etc.)

- Prepared and cooked foods should be stored separate to raw foods and unprepared vegetables to reduce the risk of cross-contamination. If this is not possible, raw food and unprepared vegetables should always be stored at the base of the réfrigerator.
- Keep stored foods covered.
- Prevent animals and insects entering the food room.
- Keep food preparation areas and utensils clean.
- Wash hands frequently, particularly after using the toilet, handling raw foods, handling refuse, blowing your nose, combing your hair and after smoking.
- Keep cuts, boils etc., covered with a waterproof dressing (preferably coloured).
- Do not handle food if suffering from symptoms of diarrhoea or vomiting and notify your supervisor immediately.
- To multiply, bacteria require food, warmth, moisture and time. By removing one or more of these criteria the growth of bacteria can be slowed or even stopped. Therefore store foods at safe temperatures (either cold below 8°C or hot above 63°C); cook food thoroughly; do not prepare food too far in advance; avoid keeping food at room temperature for any longer than necessary, if food has to be reheated, heat thoroughly and stir contents during heating; cool cooked food within 1½ hours and refrigerate; prevent dry foods becoming moist.

Food can also be contaminated with fungus which includes:

(*i*) **Mycotoxin:** Toxic substances produced by moulds or fungi are called as Mycotoxin.some mycotoxins are mutagenic and carcinogenic in nature. Of these mycotoxins, Aflatoxin is of most common occurrence in the agricultural produce/ food. **Aflatoxins** are produced by a fungus – *Aspergillus flavus* and *Aspergillus parasiticus*. At least 18 closely related toxins are known. Of these aflatoxin B1, B2, M1, M2, G1, G2 are most commonly occurring in the farm produce/food. Most susceptible food grains are Maize, Paddy/Rice, Jowar, Ground nut ,Wheat ,Barley ,Soybean, and their products. These toxins are heat labile, so there toxicity remains unaffected even after cooking at high temperature. Other important mycotoxins are Citrinin, Ochratoxin, Patulin etc which are produced by *Penicillium s*pecies. In general, **maximum** tolerance limit of mycotoxins including aflatoxin in stored food grains has been recommended at **30 micrograms per Kg** (this limit is considered by CWC/SWC/FCI). **Ergot :Ergotin** is another mycotoxin produced by fungi Claviceps purpurea on rye/bajra, where this fungus causes **Ergot** disease. Mycotoxins are produced at high moisture content and in temperature range of 12°C to 40°C. Therefore, the best way of coming over this food hazard is to dry the farm produce properly and moisture level should be always within the prescribed range.

(*ii*) Physical Contamination

Physical contamination can occur at any stage of the food chain and therefore all reasonable precautions must be taken to prevent this type of contamination. While harvesting, farm produce comes into contact with variety of external material called as physical contaminant. Physical contamination consists of two major groups viz., organic matter and inorganic matter. The former includes plant parts, debris, weed seeds, poisonous seeds of Dhatura and Akra, other food grains, dead insects, excreta, damaged grains, broken, fragments, nooks, rodent hair, uric acid etc, while the latter consists of lump of earth, pebbles, stones, dust etc. The proportion of these contaminants in the sample determines the quality of the produce and also the shelf life. However, the produce must be cleaned, graded and packed in suitable gunny bags/ packing material free from any infestation before storing or marketing the same. **Examples** of physical contamination include:-

- Pieces of machinery which can fall into food during manufacture. Most manufacturers protect against this type of contamination by installing metal detectors on the production lines which reject food if anything metallic is present.
- Stones, pips, bones, twigs, pieces of shell.
- Foreign objects can enter food during handling so care must be taken to adhere to good food handling practices (*e.g.* do not wear jewellery or smoke in a food room).

(*iii*) Chemical Contamination

Contamination may occur through environmental pollution of the air, water and soil, such as the case with toxic metals, PCBs and dioxins, or through the intentional use of various chemicals, such as pesticides, animal drugs and other agrochemicals. Chemicals, including pesticides, bleach and other cleaning materials can contaminate food if not used carefully. For example, store cleaning fluids separate to foods to prevent tainting and contamination if there is a spillage. The impact of chemical contaminants on consumer health and well-being is often apparent only after many years of prolonged exposure at low levels (*e.g.* cancer). Chemical contaminants present in foods are often unaffected by thermal processing (unlike most microbiological agents). Chemical contaminants can be classified according to the source of contamination and the mechanism by which they enter the food product.

Agrochemicals are chemicals used in agricultural practices and animal husbandry with the intent to increase crop yields and reduce costs. Such agents include pesticides (*e.g.* insecticides, herbicides, rodenticides), plant growth regulators, veterinary drugs (*e.g.* nitrofuran, fluoroquinolones, malachite green, chloramphenicol), and bovine somatotropin (rBST).

Environmental contaminants are chemicals that are present in the environment in which the food is grown, harvested, transported, stored, packaged, processed, and consumed. The physical contact of the food with its environment results in its contamination. Possible sources of contamination are:

- **Air**: radionuclides (Caesium-137, Strontium-90), polycyclic aromatic hydrocarbons (PAH).
- **Water**: arsenic, mercury.
- **Soil**: cadmium, nitrates, perchlorates.
- **Polychlorinated biphenyls** (PCB), dioxins, and **polybrominated diphenyl ethers** (PBDE) are ubiquitous chemicals, which are present in air, water, soil, and the entire biosphere.
- **Packaging materials**: antimony, tin, lead, perfluorooctanoic acid (PFOA), semicarbazide, benzophenone, isopropylthioxanthone (ITX), bisphenol A.
- **Processing/cooking equipment**: copper, or other metal chips, lubricants, cleaning and sanitizing agents.
- **Naturally occurring toxins**: mycotoxins, phytohaemagglutinin, pyrrolizidine alkaloids, grayanotoxin, mushroom toxins, scombrotoxin (histamine), ciguatera, shellfish toxins (see shellfish poisoning), tetrodotoxin, among many others.

Processing contaminants are generated during the processing of foods (e.g. heating, fermentation). They are absent in the raw materials, and are formed by chemical reactions between natural and/ or added food constituents during processing. **Examples** are: nitrosamines, polycyclic aromatic hydrocarbons (PAH), heterocyclic amines, histamine, acrylamide, furan, benzene, *trans*-fat, monochloropropanediol (MCPD), semicarbazide, 4-hydroxynonenal (4-HNE), and ethyl carbamate.

Restricted pesticides (India):

1. Aluminium phosphide 2. Ethylene dibromide 3. BHC/Lindane 4. Methyl bromide 5. Captafol 6. Phenyl mercuric acetate 7. DDT 8. Dieldrin

Emerging contaminants (ECs) are chemical compounds that have various structures, are potentially harmful, and whose risk to the environment and to humans is not fully understood. They were either previously unknown or not detected, and were consequently not monitored. Examples of ECs include organics such as antiretroviral drugs, additives, natural and synthetic hormones, pharmaceuticals and personal care products (PPCPs), illicit drugs, fire retardants, solvents, inorganics such as rare earth elements (REEs), and microplastics. Each of these has unique physicochemical characteristics that may impact environment and human health.

The transfer pathways for ECs from the sources to humans are through inhalation, dermal contact, or ingestion of contaminated media. Generally, ECs are concerning because they potentially cause reproductive and neurological disorders amongst other health problems.

Once in the soil, ECs can be uptaken by plants, some of which are edible and, therefore, can go up the food chain to humans. In some cases, ECs can be taken up by soil organisms, resulting in the disruption of the soil ecosystem and threatening food security.

Table 1: Food contaminants rendering food unsafe for human consumption

Physical	Chemical		Biological
	Inorganic	**Organic**	
Foreign matter: Lumps of earth, pebbles Stones, dust, plant parts, Stem, chaff etc	Heavy metals: Lead, Mercury, Arsenic, Cadmium, Sulfur	Pesticide residue, water	
Unhygienic Packaging Material		Uric acid, excreta, rodent hair	Insect and rodents
Unhygienic processing			
Moisture		Mycotoxins *e.g.*, Aflatoxin, ergot, and alkaloids form Karnal Bunt, Smut affected grains	fungus
Unhygienic handling			Bacteria Human being suffering from contagious disease
	•	B-Oxalyl Amino Acid (BOAA), produced by Lathyrus sativus (Khesari Dal) and Alkaloids in the oil from Argemone mexicana	
		Non food grade Colour and preservatives	

Safety and regulations: Acceptable Daily Intake (ADI) levels and tolerable concentrations of contaminants in individual foods are determined on the basis of the "No Observed Adverse Effect Level" (NOAEL) in animal experiments, by using a safety factor (usually 100). The maximum concentrations of contaminants allowed by legislation are often well below toxicological tolerance levels, because such levels can often be reasonably achieved by using good agricultural and manufacturing practices.

The best way to combat the food borne problems is to maintain good hygienic conditions around the storage, packing, processing and marketing places. Precautions should be taken in handling the produce so that there is no damage to the containers and contents remain intact & unexposed to the atmosphere. In case of, agricultural products high sanitary conditions are prerequisite for quality &shelf life. Besides this, sterilization of the packaging material and pasteurization of the product / vacuum packing are other suitable methods to prevent the food from the microbial attack.

Indicators for food quality and food safety

Testing for pathogens (food safety), spoilage organisms (food quality), and toxins of concern (food safety and food quality) in food can be expensive. Therefore, indicator tests are often used for guidance on whether there is a risk that foods have these microbes or toxins present or have the potential to support the growth of these microbes. Indicators used for testing are often microbes themselves. For example, it is much faster and less costly to check whether a processed food has any fecal coliforms (E. coli) than to check specifically for only vertoxigenic E. coli O157:H7. The presence of fecal coliforms in a sample indicates the potential presence of sewage or that unsanitary handling occurred

Indicator organisms:

- Reflect the microbiological quality of foods.
- Shelf life or their safety.
- In general, indicators are most often used to assess food safety/sanitation

Indicator organisms should meet the following criteria:

1. present and detectable in all given foods to be evaluated.
2. their growth and numbers should have a direct negative correlation with product quality.
3. should be easily detected and enumerated and be clearly distinguishable from other organisms.
4. should be enumerable in a short period of time, ideally within a working day.
5. Their growth should not be affected adversely by other components of the food microbiota

There are several items to consider when choosing an indicator to measure the quality and safety of a specific food. Ideally, indicators can be quantified and easily detected. The indicator should be present in greater numbers and persist longer than the microbe of interest, and its presence should only be evident if there is an issue with the process or if spoilage has occurred. Indicators may be used to assess the following:

- The hygiene of an ingredient
- The standards of process control

Whether human or fecal contamination has occurred

- The effectiveness of post-processing contamination
- Whether a product or process meets a regulatory requirement
- Whether potential pathogens survived after thermal treatment
- The time before spoilage, or the shelf life of a product

Common microbial indicators include:

- Aerobic plate count (APC, also referred to as standard, total, or heterotrophic plate count, SPC, TPC, or HPC)
- Coliforms
- Enterobacteriaceae
- E. coli
- Yeasts
- Moulds Not all indicators are microbial. Indicators may also test for chemical parameters, based on enzymes or energy chemicals. A phosphatase test is used to determine if complete pasteurization of raw milk has occurred. Phosphatase is an enzyme found in live cells. It is denatured (rendered inactive) when pasteurization temperatures are achieved. Testing for the enzyme is a fast and inexpensive way to verify that proper heating of raw milk (pasteurization) has occurred. Normally, pasteurization is verified by keeping a paper record of the temperatures in the vat pasteurizer (the equipment used to heat the milk).

2.6 FOOD POISONING AND FOOD BORNE INFECTION

Food Poisoning: Illness caused both by the ingestion of toxins as well as organism resulting from the infection through the intestinal tract.

Intoxication: Illness caused by the consumption of a bacterial toxin formed in the food. Ex: *Clostridium botulinum, Staphylococcus aureus*

Infection: Illness caused by the entrance of the bacteria into the body through ingestion of contaminated food and reaction of the body to their presence or to their metabolites.

Classification of Toxins:

1. Based on their production

a. **Endotoxin:** These are soluble proteins found in cell extracts or in the growth medium called as endotoxins or endogenous toxins. Ex Lipopolysaccharide components of the outer membranes of Gram –ve bacteria.

b. **Exotoxins:** These are soluble proteins secreted outside the bacteria through their cell wall and these substances are heat labile, being inactivated by boiling.

2. Based on site of action

A. Enterotoxin: These toxins stimulate cells of gastrointestinal tract in an abnormal way. Ex:

Cholera toxin – *Vibrio cholerae*

Heat labile enterotoxin(LT) — *Escherichia coli*

Heat stable enterotoxin (St) — *Escherichia coli*

Shiga toxin — *Shigella dysentriae*

B. Neurotoxins: These toxins interfere with normal transmission of nerve impulses.

Ex: Botulinum toxin *Clostridium botulinum*

Tetanus toxin *Clostridium tetani*

C. **Cytotoxins:** These toxins affect the host cells by enzymatic attack. Ex: Diptheria toxin — *Corynebacterium diptheriae,*
Streptolysin O and Streptolysin S — *Streptococcus pyogenes*

2.7 BACTERIAL TOXINS

BOTULISM

Botulism is a disease caused by the ingestion of food containing the neurotoxin produced by the *Clostridium botulinum. Clostridium botulinum* is an anaerobic Gram positive spore forming and rod shaped bacterium. It is widely distributed in soils, fresh water and marine sediments. It produces neurotoxin (BoNT Botulism Neuro Toxin). Other sps of of Clostridium producing neurotoxins are *Clostridium butyricum* and *Clostridium baratii.* Incidence of Botulism: Incidence of Botulism occurred between 1970-1973, 1899-1949. Based on their serological properties, BoNTs are classified into 6 types.

A, B, E, & F types cause disease to humans.

Human pathogenic strains are divided into three groups.

Group I – Proteolytic and Mesophilic. Include Type A, B, F

Group II – Non proteolytic and Psychrotrophic. Include Type E and non proteolytic of strains of B & F.

Group III: Includes types C & D; they are non proteolytic and share a common metabolic pattern.

Common forms of Human Botulism:

1. **Classical food borne botulism:** It is being an intoxication following ingestion of BoNT performed in food. Consumption of improperly processed foods.
2. **Infant Botulism:** It is an infection resulting from Clostridium botulinum spores germinating, growing and producing toxins in child's intestine. It results in floppy baby syndromes.
3. **Wound botulism:** It is rare and occurs when spore germination take place and subsequent growth and toxin formation in deep wounds.
4. **Adult infectious botulism**: A condition equal to infant botulism that may follow heavy antibiotic treatments or abdominal surgery.
5. **Inhalation botulism:** It is rare and does not occur naturally. For example, it is associated with accidental or international events (such as bioterrorism) which results in release of toxins in aerosols. The median lethal dose for humans has been estimated at 2 nano-grames of botulinum toxins per kilogram of human weight.
6. **Iatrogenic botulism:** Use of botulinum toxin as a therapeutic agent.

Effect of Toxin On humans: Initial symptoms of ingestion of toxic food occur between 12-10 days of longer. Early symptoms are generally nausea, vomiting, followed by neurological symptoms such as double vision and fixed dilated pupils, speech impediment and difficulty in swallowing. Ingestion of botulinal toxins results in muscle paralysis by blockade of the release of neuromuscular synapse.

Prevention of Out Break:

1. Use of approved heat processes for canned foods.
2. Rejection of all gassy (swollen) or otherwise spoiled canned foods.

3. Refused even to taste a doubtful food.
4. Avoidance of foods that have been cooked held and not well reheated.
5. Boiling of a suspected food for at least 15 min.

2.8 STAPHYLOCOCCAL GASTROENTERITIS

Staphylococcal gastroenteritis is caused by the ingestion of food that contains one or more enterotoxins. The bacterium responsible for this gastroenteritis is *Staphylococcus aureus*. Staphylococcus aureus is a Gram-positive coccus forming spherical to ovoid cells about 1 µm in diameter. These are facultative anaerobes. It is a typical mesophile with a growth temperature between 7 and 48°C and an optimum temperature is 37°C. Growth occurs at pH 6-7. *Staphylococcus* occurring in masses like clusters or groups or in pairs and short chains. Growth on solid media usually is golden or yellow but may be unpigmented in some strains. *Staphylococcus aureus* produces 6 serologically distinct enterotoxins (A, B, C1, C2, d and E).

- A is most poisoning.
- Enterotoxin producing species are *S. aureus, S. intermedius, S.hyicus, S.delphini, S.caprae, S.cochnii, s.epidermidis, S. haemolyticus, S.warneri*
- The staphylococcal sps are host adapted inhabiting humans solely (*S.cochnii sub sp cochnii*) or humans or other animals (*S. aureus*).

Enterotoxins: Staphylococcal enterotoxins are simple proteins with molecular weights 26000-30,000. Single polypeptide chains are crosslinked by a disulfide bridge to form a characteristic cystine loop. Of the several types of enterotoxins A & D are more often associated with food poisoning outbreaks. More toxin production present at 15.6 - 462.1°C. Enterotoxins are heat stable.

Disease: Symptoms are salivation, nausea, vomiting, retching, abdominal crampings, diarrhea. Blood & mucus may be found in stools and vomiting in severe cases. Head ache, muscular cramping, sweating, chills, prostration, Weak pulse, shock and shallow respiration may occur.

Conditions necessary for outbreak: The following conditions are necessary for an outbreak of Staphylococcus food poisoning:

1. The food must contain enterotoxin – producing staphylococci
2. The food must be a good culture medium for growth and toxin production by the staphylococci
3. The temperature must be favourable to growth of the cocci, and enough time must be allowed for production of enterotoxin, and
4. The enterotoxin-bearing food must be ingested.

Prevention of Outbreaks: The means of prevention of outbreaks of staphylococcus food poisoning include

1. Prevention of contamination of the food with the staphylococci,
2. Prevention of the growth of the staphylococci, and
3. Killing staphylococci in foods. Contamination of foods can be reduced by general methods of sanitation, by using ingredients free from the cocci, *e.g.*, pasteurized rather than raw milk, and by keeping employees away from foods when these workers have

staphylococcal infections in the form of colds, boils, carbuncles, etc. growth of the cocci can be prevented by adequate refrigeration of foods and, in some instances, by adjustment to a more acid pH. Also the addition of a bacteriostatic substance, such as serine or an antibiotic, has been suggested. Some foods may be pasteurized to kill the staphylococci before exposure of the foods to ordinary temperatures, *e.g.*, pasteurization of custard filled puffs and éclairs for 30 min at 190.6 to 218.3°C oven temperature.

Clostridium perfringens

First reported in U.S. in 1945. It causes serious wound infection. It causes gas gangrene. It is a gram positive, rod shaped anaerobe, which forms oval subterminal spores. Optimum temperature is 43 to 47°C. Optimum ph is 6.0-7.5. It produces six major toxins, alpha toxin (CPA), beta toxin (CPB), epsilon toxin (ETX), iota toxin (ITX), enterotoxin (CPE) necrotic enteritis B-like toxin (NetB). Foods involved are meats that have been cooked and allowed for cooling before consumption. Enterotoxin is released in the gut during sporulation of cells and results in excessive fluid accumulation in the intestinal lumen. Food poisoning is generally characterized by nausea, abdominal pain, diarrhoea and vomiting. Prevention of out break: 1. Adequate and rapid cooling of cooked foods. 2. Holding hot foods above 60°C. 3. Reheating of leftover foods. 4. Good personal hygiene.

VIBRIOSIS

Vibriosis caused by *V. parahaemolyticus*. It is curved rod-shaped gram negative bacterium and causes gastroenteritis. Mainly contamination from sea food products. Natural habitat of *Vibrio* sps is sea. *Vibrio parahaemolyticus* is known to cause extra intestinal infections in humans. *Vibrio* consists of 28 species. 3 species are always associated in aquatic environments and seafood are *V. vulnificus, V. alginolyticus* and *V. cholera. Vibrio parahaemolyticus* is common in oceanic and coastal waters. Its detection is related to water temperatures; detected at 19-20°C of water. It cannot tolerate the hydrostatic pressures of ocean depths.

V.parahaemolyticus can grow in the presence of 1-8%NaCl, best growth at 2-4% range. It dies off in distilled water. It does not grow at 4°C, but growth between 5-9°C at pH 7.2-7.3 is observed in food products at higher concentrations of NaCl (3-7%). optimum temperature is 30-35 °C and Optimum pH 7.6-8.6.

Symptoms: Symptoms appear after ingestion of 3-76 hours. Diarrhea, Cramps, weakness, nausea, chills, headache and vomiting. Vehicle foods or carrier foods are oysters, shrimps, crabs, lobsters, clams and shellfish.

- *Vibrio cholera*: Vibrio cholera is best known as the cause of human cholera. Strains that cause epidemic/pandemic cholera belonged to serovar O group 1.
- *Vibrio vulnificus*: It is found in sea water and some foods. It is isolated more often from oysters and clams.
- *Vibrio alginolyticus*: It is also found in sea water and causes soft tissue and ear infections in humans. It can cause serious seafood-poisoning or fatal extra-intestinal infections in humans, such as necrotizing soft-tissue infections, bacteremia, septic shock, and multipled organ failures.
- *Vibrio hollisae* also produces enterotoxin and causes cholera.

Escherichia coli (E. Coli)

Escherichia coli was established as a food borne pathogen in 1971 when imported cheeses were contaminated with an entero invasive strain. *E.coli* is used as **an indicator for fecal contamination of water.** Based on disease syndromes and characteristics and also on their effect on certain cell cultures and serological groupings, five virulence groups of E. coli are recognized:

- Entero aggregative *E.coli* or Facultative entero pathogenic *E.coli*
- Entero hemorrhagic *E.coli* (EHEC)
- Entero invasive *E.coli* (EIEL)
- Entero pathogenic *E. coli* (EPEC)
- Entero toxigenic *E. coli* (ETEC)

This organism was first isolated and described by German bacteriologist Theodor Escherich from children's faeces in 1885. He called it *Bacterium coli commune* as it is found in colon.

Worst outbreak of E.Coli food poisoning occured in Wishaw, Scotland in the year 1996 killing 20 people.

E. coli is an almost universal inhabitant of the gut of humans and other warm blooded animals where it is the predominant facultative anaerobe through only a minor component of the total micro flora.

E. coli sero type 0157:H7 (which is predominantly a bovine origin and some related strains) has been recognized as the cause of a number of out breaks of haemorrhagic colitis and haemolytic uraemic syndrome. E.coli is a catalase positive, oxidage negative, fermentative, short Gram negative, non spore forming rod. Genetically *E. coli* is closely related to the genus Shigella, although characteristically it ferments the sugar lactose and is otherwise far more active biochemically than *Shigella* sps. IMVIC test is used to differentiate from other members of the Enterobacteriaceae.

E.coli is a typical mesophile growing from 7-10°C up to 50°C (opt temp 37°C) It produces both gas and acid on carbohydrate. It causes off flavor, gassiness, off odor described as" barny".

Bacillus cereus

Bacillus cereus is an faculative anaerobic, spore forming rod normally present in soil, dust and water so that it regularly occurs in foods at low levels and often at higher levels in particular foods such as spice, rice, milk and dairy products. It has been associated with food poisoning in Europe since at least 1906. Plazikowski first reported this syndrome. First documented outbreak in the United States occurred in 1969 and also in Great Britain in 1971. Other *sps* of *Bacillus* producing enterotoxins are *Bacillus circulans, Bacillus lentus, B.polymyxa, B. carotanem, B. pastecurii, B. mycoides. B. mycoides* strains from milk have been shown to produce diarrheagenic enterotoxin. *B. thuringiensis* has been isolated from foods and it produces Vero-cell active toxin. This bacterium has a minimum growth temperature around 4-5°C with a maximum around 48-50°C. Growth observed at pH range 4.9-9.3. It produces a wide variety of extra cellular toxins, enzymes, including lecithinase, preoteases, ß -lactamase, sphingomyelinase, cereloysin and hemolysin BL. Cerolysin is a thiol activated toxin analogous to perfringolysin O and causes food borne gastroenteritis. *Bacillus cereus* virulence factor is a hemolytic enterotoxin complex designated HBL and it exhibits hemolysis, dermonerosis and vascular permeability properties.

Diarrheal syndrome is rather mild with symptoms developing within 8-16 hours, more commonly within 12-13 hours. Symptoms consist of nausea, cramp like abdominal pains, tenesmus and watery stools.

Emetic syndrome is also called as Chinese restaurant syndrome because its association with starchy products likes rice and dishes. This form of *Bacillus cereus* food poisoning is more severe and acute than the diarrheal syndrome. It forms similar to Staphylococcal food poisoning syndrome.

It is often associated with fried or boiled rice dishes, pasteurized cream, spaghetti, mashed potatoes etc. The emetic toxin has been determined to be cereulide, an ionophoric water insoluble peptide that is closely related to the peptide antibiotic valinomycin.

Listeriosis

Listeriosis caused by *Listeria monocytogenes*. Listeriae are Gram positive, non spore forming and non acid fast rods. Primary pathogenic species *Listeria monocytogenes, Listeria innocua, Listeria seeligeri.* They grow well in many common media such as brain heart infusion, trypticase soy and tryptose broths. Opt pH 6.0-8.0. Generally Listeriae are widely distributed in nature and in soils, animal feces, sewage, silage and water. Fresh food product of animal or plant origin may harbor varying numbers of *L.monocytogenes*. In general the organism has been found in raw milk, soft cheeses, fresh and frozen meat, poultry and sea food products. Listeriolysin O is produced during exponential grown phase. Listeriolysin is produced by *L. monocytogenes*, *L.welshiiimeri* or *L.grayi*. Ivanolysin O is produced by *Listeria ivanovii* and *L. seeligeri*. It is not identical to Listeriolysin.

Symptoms: Incubation period for the disease have varied from one day to 90 days. Pregnant women are more susceptible to non pregnant humans. In pregnant women symptoms include mild flu like illness to meningitis and meningoencephalitis, fever, headache, occasional gastro intestinal symptoms but there may be an associated transplacental foetal infection which can result in abortion, still birth or premature labour. Listeriosis in the new born babies observed and infection occurs from *in utero*, possibly through the aspiration of infected amniotic fluid and characterized by pneumonia, septicemia and widely disseminated granulomas (abscesses). Meningitis is rare. Listeriosis in non pregnant adults is usually characterized by septicaemia, Meningitis and meningoencephalitis, but can also include endocarditis. First outbreak of Listeriosis occurred in Maritime Provinces of Canada in 1981. *Listeria* can grow at cold temperatures, so refrigeration is inadequate as a control. *Listeria monocytogenes* isolated from a sample of Cole slaw (type of salad) in a patient's refrigerator. Raw vegetables, dairy foods, beet, meat, cheese act as the source of contamination.

European community (EC) directive on milk and milk based products specifies zero tolerance for soft cheeses, and absence of the organism in 1g of other guide lines for ready to eat foods establishes four quality groups based on numbers of *L.monocytogenes*.

1. Satisfactory – Not detected in 25g sample.
2. 102/25g sample – fairly satisfactory
3. 102-103/25g sample – unsatisfactory
4. > 103/25g sample – unacceptable.

International Commission on Microbiological Specification for foods (ICMSF) has concluded that if this organism does not exceed 100/g of food at point of consumption. The food is considered acceptable for individuals.

Salmonellosis

Salmonellosis caused by *Salmonella* sps. Salmonellae are small, Gram negative, non sporing rods. They are widely distributed in nature, with humans and animals being their primary reservoirs.

Salmonella have placed in two species: *Salmonella enterica* and *Salmonella bongori.* **Widal test** is used to detect the *Salmonella.* For epidemiological purposes, the Salmonella can be placed into three groups.

1. Those infect humans only - *S.typhi, S. paratyphia, S. paratyphic.* It includes the agents of typhoid and the paratyphoid fevers, which are the most severe of all diseases caused by salmonella.
2. The host adapted serovars. Ex: *S.enterica Gallinarum* (poultry), *S. enterica Dublin* (cattle), *S. abortus-equi* (Horses), *S. enteric, Abortus-* ovis (sheep), *S.enterica choleraesuis* (swine).
3. Unadapted serovars (no host preference):These are pathogenic for humans and other animals. They include most food borne serovars.

Primary habitat of *Salmonella* sps is the intestinal tract of animals such as birds, reptiles, farm animals, humans and occasionally insects. Also occurs in animal feeds, commercially prepared and packaged foods.

Growth and Destruction of Salmonella: Temp - 37°C; pH - 4.0-9.0. With respect to destruction, pasteurization temperature is enough to kill salmonellae. Ionizing radiation with does of 5-7.5 KGy being sufficient to kill salmonellae.

Kauffman – White serotyping scheme has proved the most useful technique for differentiating with the genus salmonella. This describes organisms on the basis of their somatic (O) and flagellar (H) antigens and by Capsular (vi) antigens possessed by *Salmonella typhi, Salmonella Dublin, Salmonella paratyphi C.* Serotyping is a subtyping test based on differences in microbial (*e.g.,* viral or bacterial) surfaces

Salmonellae Food poisoning Syndrome: This syndrome is caused by the ingestion of foods that contain significant numbers of non host specific or sero types of the genus Salmonella. Symptoms usually develop in 12-14 hours. Symptoms consist of nausea, vomiting, abdominal pain, headache, chills, diarrhea. These symptoms are usually accompanied by prostration, muscular weakness, faintness, moderate fever, restlessness and drowsiness. Among the different sps of *S.enterica choleraesuis* has been reported to produce the highest mortality rate. *S. enterica Enteritidis* –common in eggs (More than 1 million cases in India annually).

Salmonella produce cytotoxin that may play a role in the manifestation of various species. Salmonella strain elaborate one or more enterotoxin like substance which may stimulate interstitial secretion

Prevention:

a) Raw or Undercooked eggs should be avoided.

b) When eggs are not properly cooked, pasteurized egg products should be used.

c) Eggs should be cooked at $\geq$ 145°F (67°C) for 15 seconds.

d) Raw eggs should be stored at $\leq$ 45°F (7.2°C)

e) Avoid eating raw or undercooked beef, pork or poultry and sea foods.

In addition to salmonella food poisoning syndrome, two other disease syndrome can occur by the consumption of salmonella in humans, *i.e.* typhoid fever from salmonella typhi and paratyphoid from *Salmonella enteritidis.*

Shigellosis

Shigellosis caused by *Shigella* sps *(S. dysenteria, S. flexneri, S.boydii and S. sonnei)* and belongs to the family Enterobacteriaceae. The genus *Shigella* was discovered as the cause of bacillary by the Japanese microbiologist Kiyoshi Shiga in 1898. They are non motile, no spore forming, Gram negative, and facultative anaerobes. Temperature required for growth 10-45°C. They grow best in the pH range 6-8.

Shigella produces lipopolysaccharide endotoxin that causes dysentery in humans and other higher primates. Incubation period is 7 hours to 7 periods. Symptoms are of abdominal pain, vomiting and fever accompanying a diarrhea which can range from a classic dysenteric syndrome of bloody stools containing mucus and pus. Source of contamination is sewage, human faeces, sea foods, salads, chickens etc. Globally 80 million cases of Shigellosis and results in about 700,000 deaths per year.

Yersiniosis

Yersinia pestis causes plague. *Yersinia enterocolitica* –commonly found in foods. First isolated in New York State in 1933 by Coleman. It is Gram negative rod and psychotropic.

Growth of *Y. enterocolitica* has been observed over the temperature range of 2°C to 45°C, pH 4.0-5.0. It is distributed in the terrestrial environment lake, well, stream waters. *Y. enterocolitica, Y.intermedia, Yersinia freder jksenii Y. Kristensenii* are associated with fish, fresh waters and foods.

Syndrome: It produces gasteroenteritis. The organism has been recovered from urine, blood, cerebrospinal fluid and eyes of infected individuals. Symptoms include fever, diarrhea, severe abdominal pain, vomiting, headache. Undercooked Meat specially (pork) and Milk are common vehicle foods.

Campylobacter

The syndrome caused by *Campylobacter* is campylobacteriosis caused by *C. JeJuni sub sp. Jejuni*. It is referred to as *C. Jejuni. C. Jejuni* sub sp *Jejuni*. It is resistant to cephalothin. Campylobacters were known primarily to cause abortions in cattle and sheep. *C.Jejuni* is a slender, spirally curved rod that possesses a single polar flagellum at one or both ends of the cell. It is micro-aerophilic, requiring small amounts of oxygen (3-6%) for growth. Temperature required is 30-45°C. It grows in the pH range of 5.5-8.30. It is not an environmental organism but associated with warm blooded animals. A large percentage of all major meat animals have been shown to contain these organisms in their feces. *C. Jejuni* produces a heat labile enterotoxin (CJT). Enteritis syndrome caused by *C. Jejuni* and includes symptoms like abdominal cramps, diarrhea, malaise, headache and fever. It is gram negative bacteria.

In severe cases of campylobacteriosis there may be bloody diarrhea. Among the sequelae to infection are *Guillain-Barre's Syndrome* and *Reiter syndrome*.

Prevention:

1. They are destroyed by pasteurization temperatures.
2. Drinking water should be properly treated.
3. Avoid eating of under cooked or unpasteurized foods of animal origin like milk and chicken.

Aeromonas

Currently, *Aeromonas* has the status of a food borne pathogen of emerging importance. It has the ability to grow at low temperatures. *Aeromonas hydrophila, Aeromonas sobria; Aeromonas caviae.Aeromonas salmonicida* is not a human pathogen but causes diseases of fresh water fish. *Aeromonas* may also cause "travelers diarrhea".

Aeromonas are Gram negative, catalase positive, oxidase positive rods. They are motile by a single polar flagellum. Optimum temperature is 28°C. Aeromonas causes gasteroenteritis in children under five years old. Symptoms include watery diarrhea, dysenteric stools. *Aeromonas hydrophila* and *Aeromonas sobria* produces aerolysin. Aerolysin is heat labile, β-haemolytic, cytotoxic entero toxin.

Mycotoxins: Molds and fungus can infect some foods with mycotoxins while the crop is growing or being stored.

Mycotoxins are mold produced toxins, many of which are of public health importance. Mycotoxins are produced as secondary metabolities of fungi. Some Mycotoxins are mutagenic and carcinogenic. At least 14 Mycotoxins are known to be carcinogens. Secondary metabolities are formed during end of the exponential growth phase. Different types of Mycotoxins are

1. Aflatoxins, 2. Penicillic acid, 3. Patulin, 4. Mush room toxins, 5. Citrinin, 6. Ochratoxin 7. Alternaria toxins, 8. Sterigmatocystin, 9. Fumonisins, 10. Ambutoxin, 11. Zearalenone, 12. Patulin

Aflatoxins

Aflatoxins are most widely studied mycotoxins. The major sources of aflatoxins are fungi such as A. flavus, A. parasiticus, and A. nomius, although they are also produced by other species of Aspergillus as well as by Emericella spp. (Reiter et al., 2009). There are more than 20 known aflatoxins, but the four main ones are aflatoxin B1 (AFB1), aflatoxin B2 (AFB2), aflatoxin G1 (AFG1), and aflatoxin G2, while aflatoxin M1 (AFM1) and M2 (AFM2) are the hydroxylated metabolites of AFB1 and AFB2

In 1974, a major outbreak of hepatitis due to aflatoxin was reported in the states of Gujrat and Rajasthan in India, resulting in an estimated 106 deaths. The outbreak lasted for 2 months and was confined to tribal people whose main staple food, maize, was later confirmed to contain aflatoxin.

The Aspergillus species are an industrially important group of microorganisms distributed worldwide. A. niger has been given Generally Recognized as Safe (GRAS) status by the USFDA. However, some species have negative impacts and cause diseases in grape, onion, garlic, peanut, maize, coffee, and other fruits and vegetables. Moreover, Aspergillus section nigri produces mycotoxins such as ochratoxins and fumonisins in peanut, maize, and grape

Toxin: Toxin produced by *Aspergillus* is Aflatoxin (A- Fla –toxin). These compounds are highly substituted coumarins.

- AF M1 is a hydroxylated product of AFB1 and it appears in milk, urine and feces as a metabolic product.
- AFL, AFLH1, AFQ1 and AFP1 are all derived from AFB1.
- AFB2 is the 2, 3 – di hydro form of AFB1.
- AFG2 is the 2, 3 – di hydro form of AFG1.

The toxicity of the six most potent aflatoxins decreases in the following order:

B1 > M1 > G1> B2 > M2 ≠ G2.

G1 When viewed under ultra violet light, toxins fluorescent as noted:

- B1 and B2 – blue
- G1 – green
- G2 – green – blue
- M1 – Blue – violet
- M2 – Violet.

According to FAO, 30 ppb is permissible limit of aflatoxin. M1 and M2 are present in milk. *They are polyketide secondary metabolities.*

Growth and toxin production occurs at 33°C when pH is about 5.0. Optimum temperature for toxin production is 24-28°C. Growth and formation of Aflatoxin occur mostly during the curing of peanuts after removal from soil.

The U.S. Food and Drug Administration (FDA) have established allowable level of aflatoxins as follows: 20 ppb for food, feeds, Brazil nuts, peanuts pistachio nuts; 0.5 ppb for milk.

> Codex Alimentarius Commission recommended the following maximum levels of mycotoxins in specific foods.
>
> 15 µg/kg – Peanuts; 0.05 µg/kg M1 aflatoxin - Milk
>
> 5 µg/kg – Cereal and cereal products –ochratoxin.
>
> According to W. H. O and F. A. O –30 µg/kg in foods for human consumption.
>
> In India all foods Peanut meal B_1 30 ppb and B_2 120 ppb

Toxicity and Mode of Action: Aflaxtoxins are carcinogenic to humans. EFDV syndrome of Thailand, Reye's syndrome of Thailand, acute hepatoma condition in Ugandan child are related to aflatoxins. LD_{50} values of Aflatoxin B1 0.35 and 0.5mg/Kg body weight of day old buckling and dog. For rat W.H.O and F.A.O –30µg/ Kg body weight.

Degradation of Toxins: AFB1 and AFB2 can be reduced in corn by *bisulfite*. Heating of food product for 1 hr at 45-65°C affects 68% reduction. U.V radiations affect 45% reduction.

Patulin

Patulin (Clavicin or expansin) is produced by a large number of fungi including *Penicillium claviforme*, *Penicillium expansum Penicillium patulum Aspergillus clavatus*, *Aspergillus terreus*, *Byssochlamys nivea* and *Byssochlamys fulva.* Its biological properties are similar to those of Penicillic acid.

This mycotoxin has been found in moldy bread, sausage, fruits, apple juice, cider and other products. LD_{50} for Patulin in rats by the subcutaneous route is 15-20 mg/kg. To inhibit production of patulin, SO_2 was found more effective than Potassium sorbate or sodium benzoate. Patulin in the pure state is a white crystal with a melting point of 110.5°C and molecular weight of 154 KD. It is an unsaturated lactone with the chemical name of 4 –hydroxy -4H -furo (3, 2) puran -2(6H) –one. The Codex maximum limit for patulin in apple juice is 50 µg/litre.

Penicillic Acid

This mycotoxin has biological properties similar to Patulin produced by *Penicillium puberulum*, *Penicillium cyclopium*. It has been found in corn, beans and other field crops and has been produced experimentally on Swiss cheese. LD_{50} in mice by subcutaneous route is 100-300 mg/kg. T

Ochratoxin (Naturally occurring food borne mycotoxin)

Ochratoxin is a potent nephrotoxin was first isolated from *Aspergillus ochraceus* in South Africa. It is commonly contaminant of cereals, barley, infected with *Penicillium verrucosum*. *A.ochraceus, A. alliaceus, A. ostianus, A. mellus, A. niger and A. carbonarius*. Among *Penicillium viridicatum*, *Penicillum lyclopium*, *P. variable*. Ochratoxin A is structurally a chlorinated isocoumarin derivative with an amide bond to phenyl alanine.

Ochratoxin A fluoresces green under U.V light. Ochratoxin B flouresces blue under U. V light. Ochratoxin A is heat stable and could not be destroyed by normal cooking producers.

BEN (Balkan endemic nephropathy) and chronic interstitial nephropathy (CIN) as well as other renal diseases are linked to OTA. (Ochratoxin A). OTA is a chemically stable compound; hence, ordinary food processing measures fail to substantially reduce its presence in foods and beverages.

Ochra Test is a quantitative method for the detection of ochratoxin A in a variety of commodities using a fluorometer or HPLC.

Citrinin

Citrinin mycotoxin is produced by *Penicillium citrinum*, *Penicillium viridicatum*. It has been recovered from polished rice, moldy bread, country – curved hams, wheat, oats, Nye and other similar products. Under long wave U.V light, it fluoresces leman yellow. It is a known carcinogen. **Ciguatera poisoning** is caused by eating fish contaminated by tiny algae found around coral reefs. It is caused by microalgae called *Gambierdiscus toxicus.*

Alternaria Toxin

Alternaria citri, A alternate A.solani and *Alternaria tenuissima* produces toxins found in apples,tomatoes, blue berries, grains and other foods. The toxins produced include alternariol, alternariol monomethyl ether, altenuene, tenuazoic acid and alter toxin-I.

2.9 VIRUSES

Diseases caused by foodborne viruses may be grouped as viral gastroenteritis or viral hepatitis. The majority of viral gastroenteritis outbreaks are caused by small round structured viruses (SRSV). To a lesser extent, astroviruses or caliciviruses may be involved. Other enteric viruses, such as adenovirus and groups A and B rotaviruses have not been fully demonstrated to be foodborne. Viral hepatitis caused by hepatitis A virus may also be carried by foods. Illness caused by a *Norwalk/Norwalk-like virus* has an onset time of 1–2 days and duration of 1–6 days. Symptoms include severe nausea and vomiting. Secondary symptoms may be diarrhea, abdominal pain, headache, and low grade fever. Stools do not contain blood, mucus, or white cells. The infectious dose is 10–100 virus particles. Norwalk/Norwalk-like viruses are unaffected by low pH (ca. 3) and heat at 60°C for 30 min. They are completely inactivated by free residual chlorine at 10 mg/L. At 3.75 mg/L chlorine, the virus was only partially inactivated. *Calicivirus* infection is characterized by diarrhea and vomiting following a 1–3 day incubation period. Respiratory symptoms sometimes are evident. Infants and young children are most commonly infected. Duration is ca. 4 days. Astrovirus infection has an onset of 3–4 days. Primary symptoms include fever, diarrhea, headache, nausea, and malaise. Neither calicivirus nor astrovirus is inactivated by low pH, but both are inactivated by 10 mg/L free residual chlorine.

Hepatitis A (infectious hepatitis) is characterized by a sudden onset of fever, nausea, anorexia, and abdominal discomfort and is followed by jaundice. The onset is 1–7 weeks with an average of 30 days. The illness is transmissible until 1 week after the appearance of jaundice. The duration is 1–2 weeks up to months. All populations are susceptible but the illness is more common in adults. Hepatitis is spread by infected food handlers or fecal contamination of foods or food contact surfaces (fecal–oral route). Foods involved in hepatitis A outbreaks include those that require significant handling, often in food service situations, and those contaminated by polluted water. In 1997, an outbreak of hepatitis A in Michigan was linked to consumption of strawberries imported from Mexico. The strawberries were thought to have been contaminated in the field. Other foods involved in outbreaks are shellfish, salads, and deli foods. Hepatitis A virus is not inactivated by low pH (ca. 3). At 60°C in buffer, the virus was reduced by 0.3 log (infective units) after 10 min, while at 80°C the reduction was 4.3 log. It is inactivated by 70% ethanol and 10 mg/L free residual chlorine. The virus showed a 90% decrease in viability in mineral water at 4°C and room temperature after 519 days and 89 days, respectively.

2.10 PROTOZOA

Cryptosporidium parvum causes an illness known as *cryptosporidiosis*, which is transmitted via fecal contamination of water or food. Onset time is 1–2 weeks and the duration is 2 days to 4 weeks. The microorganism forms oocysts that are resistant to chlorine and persist for long periods in the environment. Oocysts are susceptible to freezing, dehydration, high temperatures, and certain chemical sanitizers such as hydrogen peroxide, ozone, and chlorine dioxide. They may be removed from municipal drinking water supplies by filtration. Symptoms include severe watery diarrhea, abdominal pain, and anorexia. Surveillance for cases of cryptosporidiosis began in 1997 via the Food Net surveillance system of the CDC.

Cyclosporiasis is caused by *Cyclospora cayetanensis*, a coccidian parasite that occurs in tropical waters. The illness is characterized by watery diarrhea, abdominal cramps, anorexia, weight loss, nausea, and vomiting. It has an onset of 1–11 days and lasts for up to several weeks. The microorganism is carried by contaminated water and food borne outbreaks have been associated with raspberries, basil, and lettuce.

Giardia lamblia, the causative agent of giardiasis, is one of the most common protozoal infections of humans worldwide. Several animal hosts may serve as reservoirs for human infections. Human illnesses result from consumption of *Giardia* cysts through poor hygiene (fecal–oral route), drinking contaminated water, or from infected food handlers contaminating foods. High risk groups are infants, young children, and immunosup-pressed individuals. Symptoms include diarrhea, cramps, and bloating. The onset is 5 to 24 days and the illness may last from several weeks to years.

Toxoplasma gondii is a protozoa that is the causative agent of toxoplasmosis. The primary host for the microorganism is the cat. Humans may become infected by consuming infected meat or water or contacting cat feces. Meat from lambs, poultry, and wild game animals may serve as a source for the microorganism. In humans, the illness resembles mononucleosis. Most infected newborns do not exhibit clinical symptoms, but mental retardation may occur later in life. Toxoplasmosis is sometimes seen in AIDS patients. Temperatures of 61°C or higher for 3.6 min or freezing at –13°C will inactivate oocysts and cysts in meat.

2.11 NEMATODES (ROUNDWORMS)

Trichinella spiralis is the organism that causes trichinosis. The illness is transmitted to humans by consumption of infected meats of carnivores, including pork and wild game such as bear and cougar. Dogs may also be infected. The majority of individuals infected by *Trichinella* are asymptomatic. Symptomatic illness begins with gastroenteritis symptoms including nausea, vomiting, diarrhea, and fever. Onset is 72 hr and the infection may last 2 weeks. Following initial symptoms, edema, muscle weakness, and pain occur as the larvae migrate and encyst in the muscles. Respiratory and neurological manifestations may also occur. Without treatment, trichinosis may cause death. Prevention is achieved by preventing contamination of meat or destroying the trichinae (encysted larvae) in meat by cooking to 71°C, freezing meat less than 15 cm thick for 6 (–29°C) to 20 (–15°C) days, or applying irradiation.

2.12 NATURAL FOOD TOXINS

Food contains natural chemicals, including carbohydrates, sugars, proteins and vitamins. But some foods contain potentially harmful natural toxins. Sometimes a toxin is present as a naturally occurring pesticide to ward off insect attack or to protect the plant from spoilage when damaged by weather, handling, UV light or microbes.

Toxic compounds are produced by a variety of plants and animals. Natural toxins may be present serving specific function in the plant and animal or evolved as chemical defense against predators, insects or microorganisms. These chemicals have diverse chemical structures and are vastly different in nature and toxicity.

2.12.1 Natural Toxins Present in Food of Plant Origin

Of over 300 000 different plant species in the world, at least 2 000 species are considered to be poisonous. Cases of poisoning are often reported when wild species of mushrooms, berries or other plants are ingested. Globally, only hundreds of plant species are commonly eaten, yet many of them can become toxic to the body if they are taken in excess or if they are not properly treated before consumption. Depending on the species, the edible parts of plants vary, which may include foliage, buds, stems, roots, fruits and tubers, and so are their poisonous parts.

Plants from the same genera may exhibit similar or vastly different toxicities. The amount and the distribution of the toxins present in a plant vary according to the species as well as the geographical conditions where it is grown.

In general, plant organs that are important for survival and reproduction, such as flowers and seeds, will concentrate defense compounds. These compounds may be more rapidly synthesised or stored at certain stages of critical growth, *i.e.* in buds, young tissue or seedlings as in the case of potato sprouts.

Common examples of natural toxins in food plants include glycoalkaloids in potatoes, cyanide-generating compounds in bitter apricot seeds, *Hypoglycin A* in Ackee fruit, *Microcystins* in Blue-green algae, *Grayanotoxins* in Honey, *Amygdalin* is Stone fruits such as practes or apricots, Mushroom toxins, and bamboo shoots, enzyme inhibitors and lectins in soya beans, green beans and other legumes.

Thujone, a monoterpene ketone, is the primary constituent of essential oils derived from a variety of plants, including sage (*Salvia officinalis*), clary (*Salvia sclarea*), tansy (*Tanacetum vulgare*), wormwood (*Artemisia* spp. and white cedar (*Thuja occidentalis* L.). Essential oils from these plants are used in herbal medicines, as flavorings in alcoholic drinks and fragrances throughout the world. Thujone is potentially toxic and the presence of alpha- or beta-thujone in food and beverages is regulated by law in several countries.

Prussic acid (also known as hydrocyanic acid, hydrogen cyanide, or cyanide) is formed when cyanogenic glycosides found in leaves, cherry, apple and peach pits, oak moss and other plant tissues are damaged and come into contact with *beta*-glycosidase or emulsion enzymes. The enzymes release the cyanide from the glycoside, and the cyanide prevents the body's cells from utilizing oxygen, resulting in cellular necrosis and tissue damage. Clinical signs of prussic acid poisoning include rapid breathing, trembling, incoordination and in extreme cases, respiratory and/or cardiac arrest.

Goitrogens (glucosinolates) in Brassica spp. Or Certain raw foods have been found to contain substances that suppress the function of the thyroid gland by interfering with the uptake of iodine, an essential nutrient in growth, cognitive function, and hormonal balance. A lack of functional iodine is known to result in cognitive deficiencies (*e.g.*, Cretinism). The decrease in iodine uptake causes the thyroid gland to enlarge, forming a goiter. Foods that have been identified as goitrogenic include spinach, cassava, peanuts, soybeans, strawberries, sweet potatoes, peaches, pears, and vegetables in the *Brassica* genus, which include broccoli, brussels sprouts, cabbage, canola, cauliflower, mustard greens, radishes, and rapeseed. Goiter has also been attributed to the consumption of large quantities of uncooked kale or cabbage. High temperatures (*i.e.*, cooking) inactivate the goitrogenic substances, collectively termed glucosinolates. Cassava (*Manihot esculenta*) is an essential dietary source of energy in the tropics, but contains high levels of linamarin, a glucosinolate. Cassava must be properly processed-dried, soaked in water or baked to effectively reduce the linamarin content

Furocoumarins represent a family of natural food constituents with phototoxic and photomutagenic properties. They are found mainly in plants belonging to the *Rutaceae* (*e.g.*, citrus fruits) and *Umbelliferae* (*e.g.*, parsnip, parsley, celery, carrots) families. Furocoumarins are produced in response to stress, to aid plants in defense against viruses, bacteria, fungi, insects and animals, and are regarded as natural pesticides.

α-amylase inhibitors are naturally occurring in aqueous extracts of wheat, rye and kidney beans. However, since α-amylase inhibitors have been shown to be inactivated by gastric acid, pepsin or pancreatic proteinases, their potential as "starch blockers" is limited. α-Amylase inhibitors were once added to foods as "starch blockers" to limit carbohydrate absorption for the purpose of weight loss; however, the FDA later determined that at least this use of á-amylase inhibitors was as drug, and they were consequently taken off the market. á-Amylase inhibitor protein is a major allergen (referred to as Asp o 2) that has been implicated in the development of occupational toxicity known as "baker's asthma disease"

Lectins are a group of glycoproteins that are present in high levels in legumes (*e.g.*, black beans, soybeans, lima beans, kidney beans and lentils) and grain products. Lectins can reversibly bind to carbohydrates without altering their covalent structure. The ability of lectins to bind to and agglutinate red blood cells is well known and used for blood typing—hence the lectins are commonly called hemagglutinins. Lectins also can bind avidly to mucosal cells and interfere with nutrient absorption from the intestine. Because the ability of the lectins to cause intestinal malabsorption is dependent on the presence of enteric bacteria, it has been hypothesized that lectins may also produce toxicity by facilitating bacterial growth in the GI tract.

Phytohaemagglutinin (PHA) is a lectin found in significant quantities (as much as 2.4–5% of total protein) in legumes such as red or white kidney beans, green beans and fava beans. PHA has a number of different properties, including the ability to induce mitosis, affect membrane transport and permeability to proteins, and agglutinate red blood cells.

Anti-thiamine compounds are commonly referred that the substance act on availability of vitamins. These include materials that can cause a deficiency of vitamins by competing with vitamins in various metabolic reactions as the result of similar chemical structure or destroying or decreasing the effects of a vitamin by modifying the molecular conformation or by forming a complex.

Oxalic acid (oxalate) is generally found in rhubarb (0.2–1.3%), tea (0.3–2.0%), spinach (0.3–1.3%), parsley (1.7%) and purslane (1.3%), but may also be found in asparagus, broccoli, Brussels sprouts, collards, lettuce, celery, cabbage, cauliflower, turnips, beets, peas, coffee, cocoa, beans, potatoes, berries, and carrots. Oxalic acid is an organic acid that can bind calcium and other minerals, making them insoluble and decreasing their bioavailability. Ingestion of foods containing high concentrations of oxalates may cause decreased bone growth, kidney stones, renal toxicity, vomiting, diarrhea, convulsions, coma and impaired blood clotting. The significant role oxalate plays in kidney stone development is exemplified by the fact that approximately 65% of kidney stones consist of calcium oxalate.

Phytic acid (also referred to as phytate) is found in bran and germ of many plant seeds and in grains, legumes and nuts. Phytic acid is a simple sugar (myo-inositol) containing six phosphate sidechains, and as such, is a dietary source of phosphorus and an effective chelator of divalent cations such as zinc, copper, iron, magnesium and calcium. Studies indicate that phytate-mineral complexes are insoluble in the intestinal tract, reducing mineral bioavailability. Phytate also has been shown to inhibit digestive enzymes such as trypsin, pepsin, á-amylase and ß-glucosidase. Therefore, ingestion of foods containing high amounts of phytate could theoretically cause mineral deficiencies or decreased protein and starch digestibility. Vegetarians that consume large amounts of tofu and bean curd are particularly at risk of mineral deficiencies due to phytate consumption. Phytate is fairly heat stable, but can be removed by soaking or fermentation. The soybean has one of the highest phytate levels of any grain or legume, and requires a long period of fermentation for reduction. In people who consume large amounts of soy products, mineral deficiencies can be prevented by consumption of meat or dairy products or use of supplemental vitamins. There are no FDA regulations or guidelines restricting the presence of phytates in food.

Safrole (1-allyl-3, 4-methylenedioxybenzene) is found in aromatic oils of nutmeg (*Myristica fragrans*), cinnamon (*Cinnamomum verum*) and camphor (*Cinnamomum camphora*) and is a major constjtuent of oil of sassafras (*Sassafras albidum*)

Myristicin is a naturally occurring insecticide and acaracide that is found in nutmeg and mace (*Myristica* spp.) at concentrations of 1.3% and 2.7%, respectively. It is also present in black pepper, carrot, celery parsley and dill. When ingested, myristicin may produce hallucinogenic effects, and can be converted to MMDMA in controlled chemical synthesis. Myristicin is listed in the Hazardous Substances Data Bank.. It is estimated that the average total intake of myristicin from dietary sources is "in the order of a few mg per person per day"

Tomatine is toxic to a number of different fungi, thereby acting as a natural fungicide. The leaves, stems and unripe fruit of the tomato plant contain á-tomatine, a steroidal alkaloid containing D-xylose, D-galactose, and two molecules of D-glucose. It has been hypothesized that the toxic effects of tomatine on fungi are due to the ability of tomatine to complex with membrane sterols, causing membrane disruption. There are no reports of acute toxicity in humans due to ingestion of green tomatoes and there are no FDA regulations or guidelines specific to the presence of tomatine in food. Ingestion of a rare variety of ripe tomato (*Lycopersicon esculentum* var. cerasiforme) that contains up to 5 mg tomatine/g of dry weight has no adverse effects on natives who commonly ingest them.

The **glycoalkaloids α-solanine and α-chaconine** are natural pesticides that are produced in potatoes. α-Solanine is also found in eggplant, apples, bell peppers, cherries, sugar beets and tomatoes. The only difference between α-solanine and α-chaconine is the sugars in the trisaccharide potion of the molecule, *i.e.*, glucose with two rhamnoses for α-solanine and a glucose, galactose and a rhamnose for α-chaconine.

Acrylamide is found in a number of starch-based foods that are fried or baked at temperatures greater than 120 °C (248 °F), including bread, bakery products, breakfast cereal, and potato products (*e.g.*, chips, french fries). It is also found in cocoa-based products and coffee. Acrylamide is formed via a Maillard reaction, a reaction between the carbonyl group of a reducing sugar and the nucleophilic group of an amino acid. Although a number of carbohydrates can be used as the source of the carbonyl group, the amino acid required for the formation of acrylamide is asparagine. (Also refer short notes for more details)

Chloropropanols are formed in hydrolyzed vegetable proteins (HVP) produced by hydrochloric acid (HCl) hydrolysis of proteinaceous by-products from edible oil extraction, such as soybean meal, rapeseed meal and maize gluten The chloropropanol most commonly found in food is 3-MCPD (3-monochloropropane-1,2-diol), although others may also be present, including 2-MCPD (2-monochloropropane-1,3-diol), 1,3-DCP (1,3-dichloro-2-propanol), and 2,3-DCP (2,3-dichloro-1-propanol).

Furan is a by-product of high-energy and thermal treatment of carbohydrate. Meat and vegetable containing foods that are heat processed in cans and jars (such as soups, pastas, sauces, gravy and baby food) and brewed coffee, typically contain the highest concentrations. Concentrations of furan present in food and coffee range from undetectable to approximately 175 µg/kg. Coffee powders may contain up to 5000 µg/kg on a dry weight basis. Although the mechanism of formation of furan in food is not completely understood, it can be synthesized from vitamin C, amino acids, reducing sugars, organic acids, carotenes and polyunsaturated fatty acids in the presence of heat.

The presence of furan in food is a potential concern because of indications of liver toxicity, including carcinogenicity.

It may be noted that chemical 'furan' is different from *furans*. 'Furans' is an abbreviation of chlorinated dibenzofurans and are chemically related to a group of chemicals called dioxins. Dioxins and furans are environmental contaminants, not processing, induced food contaminants, and have distinctly different chemical structures and behaviours than furan.

Nitrosamines are formed from the interaction of nitrites or other nitrosating agents with amines in food (or *in vivo*), under acidic conditions. Nitrites may be directly added to food or can be formed from bacterial reduction of nitrate. Nitrites and nitrates may occur naturally in water or foods such as leafy vegetables due to the use of fertilizer, or may be added to foods to prevent growth of *Clostridium botulinum*, or to add color or flavor. Nitrosamines have been found in a variety of different foods such as cheese, soybean oil, canned fruit, meat products, cured or smoked meats, fish and fish products, spices used for meat curing, and beer and other alcoholic beverages. Beer, meat products and fish are considered the main sources of exposure. Drying, kilning, salting, smoking or curing promotes formation of nitrosamines.

Natural Toxins Present in Food of Animal Origin

Natural toxin of animal origin may be a product of metabolism or a chemical that is passed along the food chain. While poisoning after eating terrestrial animals is relatively uncommon, poisoning due to marine toxins occurs in many parts of the world. Marine toxins produced by toxic microalgae are accumulated in shellfish, crustacean and finfish following their consumption. Tetrodotoxin, a potent marine neurotoxin, is thought to be produced by certain bacteria. It is found in over 90 species of puffer fish and may cause lethality after ingested even a small amount. Seafood poisoning commonly reported in coral reef fish is due to the presence of ciguatoxin that may be found in more than 300 species of fish. Histamine produced by bacterial spoilage of scombroid fish causes another kind of seafood poisoning.

There are approximately 1200 species of poisonous and venomous animals in the world. While most of them are not used as food, care must be taken to avoid the poisonous glands or tissue containing the toxins when these animals are used as food. Glands of some animals that are not considered poisonous or venomous when ingested can also cause food poisoning such as gall-bladder of grass carp which contains the cyprinol related chemicals.

Consumption of seafood contaminated with algal toxins results in five different syndromes, paralytic, neurotoxic, amnesic, or diarrhetic shellfish poisoning and ciguatera fish poisoning

Prions are misfolded proteins with the ability to transmit their misfolded shape onto normal variants of the same protein. They characterize several fatal and transmissible neurodegenerative diseases in humans and many other animals. It is not known what causes the normal protein to misfold, but the abnormal three-dimensional structure is suspected of conferring infectious properties, collapsing nearby protein molecules into the same shape. The word prion derives from "proteinaceous infectious particle". The hypothesized role of a protein as an infectious agent stands in contrast to all other known infectious agents such as viruses, bacteria, fungi and parasites, all of which contain nucleic acids (DNA, RNA or both). Microscopic "holes" are characteristic in prion-affected tissue sections, causing the tissue to develop a "spongy" architecture. This causes deterioration of that "spongy" tissue in the brain.

Term prion was coined by Stanley Prusiner for a proteinaceous infectious particle. Proteinaceous + Infectious = PRION.

2.13 FOOD PLANT SANITATION

Cleaning a food processing plant is one way to make sure that there is no contamination from the raw ingredients to a final product. To implement the cleaning process, the good manufacture practice (GMP) regulations issued by the U.S. Food and Drug Administration (FDA) serve as a frame of reference. (For details refer to Chapter 13 'Food Standard and Legislations').

Definition of Terms

Three definitions are germane to our discussion:

Cleaning: A process which will remove soil and prevent accumulation of food residues which may decompose or support the growth of disease-causing organisms or the production of toxins.

Sanitizing: A process which destroys disease causing organisms which may be present on equipment and utensils after cleaning. Chemical sanitizer used shall meet the requirements of 21 CFR 178.1010.

Soil: Soil has been appropriately defined as "matter out of place"; grease on a gear, for example, is a lubricant, but that same grease on a table top becomes soil.

Overall sanitation of the plant should be under the supervision of one or more competent individuals assigned responsibility for this function. All reasonable precautions should be taken to ensure that the entire process, from raw ingredients to a finished product, does not contribute contamination from any source, including chemical, microbial, or extraneous material. Basic mechanical manufacturing steps include, among others, washing, peeling, trimming, cutting, sorting and inspecting, mashing, dewatering, cooling, shredding, extruding, drying, whipping, defatting, and forming.

Note the following principles:

- Assure that all operations in the receiving, inspecting, transporting, segregating, preparing, manufacturing, packaging, and storing of food will comply with basic sanitation and cleaning principles.
- Provide adequate physical protection of food from contaminants that may drip, drain, or be drawn into the food. Protection may be provided by adequate cleaning and sanitizing of all food-contact surfaces, and by using time and temperature controls at and between each manufacturing step. If applicable, clean and remove any contaminants.
- Require that all holding, conveying, and manufacturing systems, including gravimetric, pneumatic, closed, and automated systems, are of a design and construction that enables them to be maintained in an appropriate sanitary condition.

- Treat compressed air or other gases mechanically introduced into food or used to clean food-contact surfaces or equipment in such a way that food is not contaminated with unlawful indirect food additives.

Desirable Properties of Good Cleaners

The following lists the most desirable properties of a good cleaner for a food processing plant:

- Quick and complete solubility
- Good wetting or penetrating action
- Dissolving action on food solids
- Emulsifying action on fat
- Deflocculating, dispersing, or suspending action
- Good rinsing properties
- Complete water softening power
- Noncorrosive on metal surfaces
- Germicidal action
- Economy in use

Cleaning Methods:

There are many methods of subjecting the surfaces of equipment to cleaning compounds and solutions. Effectiveness and the economy of the method generally dictate its use:

Soaking: Small equipment or fittings or valves may be immersed in cleaning solutions in a sink, while larger vessels such as vats and tanks may be partially filled with a pre-dissolved cleaning solution. The cleaning solution should be hot (125°F; 52°C) and the equipment permitted to soak for 15–30 min before being manually or mechanically scrubbed. One relatively recent approach is the ultrasonic cleaning tanks in which equipment is immersed in a cleaning solution and cleaned by the scrubbing action of microscopic bubbles caused by high frequency vibrations (20,000–40,000 cycles per second).

Spray methods: Cleaning solutions may be sprayed on equipment surfaces by use of either fixed or portable spraying units using either hot water or steam. These methods are extensively used in the food industry.

Clean in place systems: This method is an automated cleaning system generally used in conjunction with permanent-welded pipeline systems. In CIP cleaning, fluid turbulence in pipelines is considered to be the major source of energy required for soil removal.

Abrasive cleaning: Abrasive-type powders and pastes are still available and used for removing difficult soil. Complete rinsing is necessary and care should be taken to avoid scratching stainless steel surfaces. Scouring pads should not be used on food-contact surfaces because small metal pieces from the pads may serve as focal points for corrosion or may be picked up in the food.

Cleaning compounds and sanitizing agents used in cleaning and sanitizing procedures should be free from undesirable microorganisms and should be safe and appropriate for the intended objectives, *i.e.*, used in cleanings. Identify, hold, and store toxic cleaning compounds, sanitizing agents, and pesticide chemicals to protect food-contact surfaces and food-packaging materials.

2.14 SANITIZATION

The primary reason for the application of effective sanitizing procedures is to destroy those disease organisms which may be present on equipment or utensils after cleaning, and thus prevent the transfer of such organisms to the ultimate consumer. In addition, sanitizing procedures may prevent spoilage of foods or prevent the interference of microorganisms in various industrial processes which depend on pure cultures. The FDA has provided a list of those agents it has approved for sanitizing equipment (178 CFR 1010). There are a wide variety of known chemicals whose properties destroy or inhibit the growth of microorganisms. Many of these chemicals, however, are not suitable for use on food-contact surfaces because they may corrode, stain, or leave a film on the surface. Others may be highly toxic or too expensive for practical use. Therefore, the discussion on chemical sanitizing agents will be restricted to those agents in common use in the food industry.

CHLORINE: Chlorine and its compounds combine indiscriminately with any and all protein and protoplasms. The mode of bactericidal action is thought to be the reaction of chlorine with certain oxidizable groups in vital enzyme systems.

a. ***Inorganic Chlorine Products:*** Types in common use include

- Calcium hypochlorite—generally in powder form of 70% available chlorine
- Sodium hypochlorites—generally in aqueous solution of 2–15% available chlorine

Characteristics and limitations are as follows:

- Effective sanitizer if high enough residual used
- Organic matter may cause a substantial reduction in bactericidal effectiveness.
- Temperature and pH may exert marked influence upon the bactericidal effectiveness.
- Relatively unaffected by water hardness.
- No film left on surface but may leave odor or taste.
- Bactericidal activity if (is?) good against a wide variety of microorganisms.

b. ***Organic Chlorine Products:*** Types include

- Chloramine-T—in powdered form of 25% available chlorine
- Dichlorocyanuric and trichlorocyanuric acids—in powdered form of 70–90% available chlorine

Characteristics and limitations include

- Slower bactericidal action than hypochlorites.
- Factors affecting hypochlorites similarly affect organic chlorine compounds.
- Relatively nonirritating to skin.

IODOPHORS: Iodophors are soluble complexes of iodine combined usually with nonionic surface-active agents, loosely bound. Characteristics and limitations are as follows:

- Rapid bactericidal action in acid pH range in cold or hard water
- Less affected by organic matter than hypochlorites
- Nontoxic in ordinary concentration
- Noncorrosive, nonirritating to skin
- Yellow or amber color of solution is proportional to concentration
- Less effective against bacterial spores than hypochlorites
- Does not stain; only minimal taste and odor

Table : Chemical sanitizer and their minimum concentration

S. No.	Chemical agent	Minimum concentration (ppm)
1.	Hypochlorites	50
2.	Chloramine-T	200
3.	Iodophors	12.5
4.	QACs	200

QUATERNARY AMMONIUM COMPOUNDS: Quaternary ammonium compounds (QACs) compounds are synthetic surface-action agents. The most common ones are the cationic detergents, which are poor detergents but excellent germicides. In these compounds, the organic radical is the cation, and the anion is usually chlorine. The mechanism of germicidal action is not completely understood, but is associated with enzyme inhibition and leakage of cell constituents.

Types of compounds include

- Alkyl dimethyl benzyl ammonium chloride; alkyl dimethyl ethylbenzyl ammonium chloride. These compounds are effective in water ranging from 500 to 1100 ppm hardness without added sequestering agents.
- Diisobutyl phenoxy ethoxy ethyl dimethyl benzyl ammonium chloride; methyl dodecyl benzyl trimethyl ammonium chloride. These compounds require sodium tripolyphosphate to raise hard water levels to a minimum of 500 ppm.

Characteristics and limitations are as follows:

- Require high dilution for germicidal or bacteriostatic action
- Very selective in destruction or inhibition of various types of organisms
- Form bacteriostatic film on surface after treatment
- Noncorrosive and nonirritating to skin
- No taste or odor in used dilutions
- More stable in presence of organic matter than some other chemical sanitizers
- Incompatible with soap, anionic detergents, and inorganic polyphosphate
- Difficult to accurately measure residual

2.15 INSPECTION AND CONTROLS

Food manufacturing plants continue to increase in complexity, and the potential for issues to develop that adversely affect the consumer increase accordingly. To avoid being in a negative spotlight, food plants have developed numerous programs and policies designed to meet their challenges. Good manufacturing practice (GMP) policies, hazard analysis and critical control point (HACCP) programs, plant policies and practices, production parameters, preventive maintenance programs, and sanitation/hygiene programs, along with others, assist facilities in meeting their obligations. One critical program that must be in place to verify that all objectives are being met on a consistent basis includes plant inspections.

Plant inspections are used by several different entities to achieve the same goal. Regulatory agencies utilize plant inspections for the enforcement of food laws. A company's customers utilize inspections to determine the risks of doing business with a particular firm, using either their own resources or a third-party professional organization, to conduct the inspection. Perhaps the most important aspect of the inspection program, however, is the self-inspection program undertaken by a facility's own personnel to monitor the conditions in the plant. Personnel must identify potential food safety risks and take actions to correct deficiencies that develop.

The internal inspection process should be conducted by a well-organized committee dedicated to ensuring a high level of compliance with all the plant's internal policies and all external requirements (those of business partners, federal and state regulatory agencies, etc.). The committee usually consists of management personnel from production, plant sanitation and maintenance, as well as from the quality control and human resources departments. More and more often, the committee includes hourly employees, who have an equal commitment to the success of the plant. The mix of these various personnel offers the committee the opportunity to view the plant from different perspectives and to evaluate the programs using a more comprehensive approach. Often the plant manager will participate in the process to lend a higher visibility to the program as well as to accelerate the corrective actions needed.

Once the committee members have been selected, their responsibility becomes one of assessing what has been neglected and also compiling a report detailing solutions to the food safety risks identified. Generally, these risks are beyond the capability or authority of the individual responsible for the area of concern. This report, called a Corrective Action Report, requires a specific action to be taken within a designated time frame. It also allows for follow-up actions since the issue remains open until it has been corrected.

Inspecting the Plant: Though individual inspectors would appear to have their own unique techniques for inspecting a food plant, close observation of their work will reveal that most of them pursue a logical path, following the production process either from start to finish or vice versa. Doing so can often make it easier for those reading the final report to better visualize the flow the inspection took and improve their understanding of the issues noted.

Raw Material Receiving: The raw material receiving area of the facility requires a thorough review of the materials stored there and also close observation of the procedures followed to allow materials to be accepted into the food plant. Each ingredient or material arriving from outside the plant must be treated as suspect and treated as though each offers the potential for the introduction of a problem. The inspection of raw materials in the storage warehouse provides an excellent opportunity to further identify issues with suppliers and must be paid the appropriate attention. By its design, this area of the plant houses all of the materials acquired from countless "unknown" sources. No other area of the plant provides a higher risk for hazards to impact the plant.

Production Areas: The production areas of factories offer a variety of challenges and opportunities. Often congested with equipment and in a state of haste, extra caution is required by the individual inspecting these areas. Even the most knowledgeable employees have been known to make simple errors of judgment that have caused serious injury. Always be aware of and concerned about the effect your actions may have while working in busy areas of the facility. A primary objective of the inspection conducted in processing areas is often to establish that all of the policies and procedures in place are in fact being followed. Personnel given this responsibility need to recognize that their greatest asset is their ability to observe and then to correlate the observations with the sum total of the processing operations.

Production Periods: Inspections conducted in production areas during production periods offer an opportunity to observe personnel practices and the operational methods employed, as well as the overall state of repair of the facility, systems integrity, and policy compliance. Since personnel are often a source of concern, time spent on the production floor during these periods is extremely valuable. However, recognize the limitations you will encounter if your objective is to inspect the condition of the production equipment; access to critical elements of the system will probably not be available for inspection except during production downtime.

Packaging Areas: Special attention is required when inspecting the packaging area of any facility. This area is the last point in the process where you have the opportunity to remove those products not conforming to established specifications. Your inspection should focus on the ability of the systems used to identify failures (magnets, metal detectors, sieves, etc.) and the level of compliance by area personnel in the proper monitoring of these systems. The inspection process should provide for a very thorough review to identify any and all possible defects that might pass through the system and to ensure that they are detected and corrected. It should be standard practice to test the metal detection equipment and verify its effective operation by using the appropriate test blanks.

Exterior Areas: Failure to inspect the exterior areas of a food plant could lead to serious consequences. Often, infestation issues can be traced directly to conditions that exist in these areas or to a system failure. For example, a ventilation system that is in need of repair and no longer provides the barrier protection it was designed for is a system failure. Ignoring these areas can lead to serious food safety issues. The inspection of the exterior should include the grounds along the immediate building exterior. Also inspect the grounds as far out from the building as necessary to identify unwanted conditions such as water sources, habitats conducive to pest activity, or undesirable practices by personnel.

2.16 BENEFICIAL MICROORGANISMS IN FOOD

Mold Genera

Molds are important in food because they can grow even in conditions in which many bacteria cannot grow, such as low pH, low water activity (*Aw*), and high osmotic pressure. Many types of molds are found in foods. They are important spoilage microorganisms. Many strains also produce mycotoxins and have been implicated in foodborne intoxication. Many are used in food bioprocessing. Finally, many are used to produce food additives and enzymes.

Aspergillus is widely distributed and contains many species important in food. Members have septate hyphae and produce black-colored asexual spores on conidia. Many are xerophilic (able to grow in low *Aw*) and can grow in grains, causing spoilage. They are also involved in spoilage of foods such as jams, cured ham, nuts, and fruits and vegetables (rot). Some species or strains produce mycotoxins (*e.g., Aspergillus flavus* produces aflatoxin). Many species or strains are also used in food and food additive processing. *Asp. oryzae* is used to hydrolyze starch by á-amylase in the production of sake. *Asp. niger* is used to process citric acid from sucrose and to produce enzymes such as α-galactosidase.

Alternaria. Members are septate and form dark-colored spores on conidia. They cause rot in tomatoes and rancid flavor in dairy products. Some species or strains produce mycotoxins. Species: *Alternaria tenuis*.

Fusarium. Many types are associated with rot in citrus fruits, potatoes, and grains. They form cottony growth and produce septate, sickle-shaped conidia. Species:*Fusarium solani*.

Geotrichum. Members are septate and form rectangular arthrospores. They grow, forming a yeastlike cottony, creamy colony. They establish easily in equipment and often grow on dairy products (dairy mold). Species: *Geotrichum candidum*.

Mucor. It is widely distributed. Members have nonseptate hyphae and produce sporangiophores. They produce cottony colonies. Some species are used in food fermentation and as a source of enzymes. They cause spoilage of vegetables. Species: *Mucor rouxii*.

Penicillium. It is widely distributed and contains many species. Members have septate hyphae and form conidiophores on a blue-green, brushlike conidia head. Some species are used in food production, such as *Penicillium roquefortii* and *Pen. camembertii* in cheese. Many species cause fungal rot in fruits and vegetables. They also cause spoilage of grains, breads, and meat. Some strains produce mycotoxins (*e.g.*, Ochratoxin A).

Rhizopus. Hyphae are aseptate and form sporangiophores in sporangium. They cause spoilage of many fruits and vegetables. *Rhizopus stolonifer* is the common black bread mold.

Yeast Genera

Yeasts are important in food because of their ability to cause spoilage. Many are also used in food bio-processing. Some are used to produce food additives. Several important genera are briefly described next.

Saccharomyces. Cells are round, oval, or elongated. It is the most important genus and contains heterogenous groups. *Saccharomyces cerevisiae* variants are used in baking for leavening bread and in alcoholic fermentation. They also cause spoilage of food, producing alcohol and CO_2.

Pichia. Cells are oval to cylindrical and form pellicles in beer, wine, and brine to cause spoilage. Some are also used in oriental food fermentation. Species: *Pichia membranaefaciens*.

Rhodotorula. They are pigment-forming yeasts and can cause discoloration of foods such as meat, fish, and sauerkraut. Species: *Rhodotorula glutinis*.

Torulopsis. Cells are spherical to oval. They cause spoilage of milk because they can ferment lactose (*e.g.*, *Torulopsis versatilis*). They also spoil fruit juice concentrates and acid foods.

Candida. Many species spoil foods with high acid, salt, and sugar and form pellicles on the surface of liquids. Some can cause rancidity in butter and dairy products (*e.g.*, *Candida lipolyticum*).

Zygosaccharomyces. Cause spoilage of high-acid foods, such as sauces, ketchups, pickles, mustards, mayonnaise, salad dressings, especially those with less acid and less salt and sugar (*e.g.*, *Zygosaccharomyces bailii*).

Viruses

Beneficial viral infections

Viruses are mostly known for their aggressive and infectious nature.

But they're not all bad. Some viruses can actually kill bacteria, while others can fight against more dangerous viruses. So like protective bacteria (probiotics), we have several protective viruses in our body.

Protective 'phages'

Bacteriophages (or "phages") are viruses that infect and destroy specific bacteria. They're found in the mucus membrane lining in the digestive, respiratory and reproductive tracts.

Mucus is a thick, jelly-like material that provides a physical barrier against invading bacteria and protects the underlying cells from being infected. Phages have actually been used to treat dysentery, sepsis caused by Staphylococcus aureus, salmonella infections and skin infections for nearly a century. Early sources of phages for therapy included local water bodies, dirt, air, sewage and even body fluids from infected patients. The viruses were isolated from these sources, purified, and then used for treatment.

Viral infections at a young age are important to ensure the proper development of our immune systems. In addition, the immune system is continuously stimulated by systemic viruses at low levels sufficient to develop resistance to other infections.

Some viruses we come across protect humans against infection by other pathogenic viruses.

For example, latent (non-symptomatic) herpes viruses can help human natural killer cells (a specific type of white blood cell) identify cancer cells and cells infected by other pathogenic viruses. They arm the natural killer cells with antigens (a foreign substance that can cause an immune response in the body) that will enable them to identify tumour cells.

This is both a survival tactic by the viruses to last longer within their host, and to get rid of competitive viruses to prevent them from damaging the host. In the future, modified versions of viruses like these could potentially be used to target cancer cells.

Pegivirus C or GBV-C is a virus that does not cause clinical symptoms. Multiple studies have shown HIV patients infected with GBV-C live longer in comparison to patients without it.

The virus slows disease progression by blocking the host receptors required for viral entry into the cell, and promotes the release of virus-detecting interferons and cytokines (proteins produced by white blood cells that activate inflammation and removal of infected cells or pathogens).

Antimicrobials : Many foods have naturally occurring compounds that suppress the growth of microbes, called antimicrobials. Vegetables, fruits, and spices contain chemicals that prevent and suppress fungal and bacterial growth as a protective mechanism to plant injury. Plant injury can occur when insects or weather cause bruising or cutting of plant stems, roots, or leaves. Naturally occurring antimicrobials help to prevent infection by spoilage and pathogenic microbes. Many plants we use as spices contain antimicrobials, such as cloves(eugenol), oregano (carvacrol and thymol), thyme (thymol), garlic (allicin), and ginger (olioresin), along with many others. These compounds are used in the modern food industry during food production and food packaging to limit growth of undesirable microbes. Another example of naturally occurring antimicrobials may be found in eggs. Egg whites (albumen) contain several protein compounds, including the antimicrobial enzyme lysozyme. This enzyme makes up 3.5 % of the albumen contents and protects the egg whites from bacterial growth by damaging the outer cell walls of bacteria. Other compounds in eggs raise the pH of the egg white to a more inhospitable alkaline pH that makes bacterial growth more difficult.

D. Important Bacterial Genera for Manufacturing Foods

Bacteria are used to make a wide range of food products. The most important bacteria in food manufacturing are Lactobacillus species, also referred to as lactic bacteria.

Dairy industry: It would be impossible to make **cheese** without a starter culture. As the culture grows in the milk, it converts the sugar lactose into lactic acid, which ensures the correct level of acidity and gives the cheese its moisture. As the cheese ripens, the culture gives it a balanced aroma, taste, texture. It is also responsible for the 'holes' in cheeses such as Emmenthal. Choosing the right mixture of culture is essential for a high-quality cheese.

In **yoghurt** and other fermented milk products, the culture is responsible for the taste and texture of the final product. Depending on the acidity, the product will have either a mild or strong taste, and the viscosity depends on the quantity of polysaccharides – chains of sugar molecules – that are produced.

In recent years, **probiotic cultures** have become popular in dairy products because of their health benefits. These cultures are all very carefully selected strains, and there is good evidence that they help improve digestion, safeguard the immune system, and keep the body's intestinal flora in balance

Meat industry: Meat starter cultures are used to make dried, fermented products such as salami, pepperoni, chorizo and dried ham. Lactic bacteria develop the flavour and colour of the products. In addition, a wide variety of moulds are use to ripen the surface of sausages, preserving the natural quality of the product and controlling the development of flavour.

Wine industry: Yeasts are responsible for the fermentation process which produces alcohol in wine. However, lactic bacteria also play an important role, as they convert the unstable malic acid that is naturally present in wine into the stable lactic acid. This conversion gives the stability that is characteristic of high-quality wines that improve on storage.

Food industry: Lactic bacteria are used in many different tablets and capsules sold as supplements in the health food industry. Our hectic modern lifestyles often lead to an imbalance in the intestinal flora; travel and medical treatment are two of the major culprits. By taking supplements containing lactic bacteria, this balance can be restored, improving the quality of life.

Food Fermentation

Fermentation in food processing is the conversion of carbohydrates to alcohols and carbon dioxide or organic acids using yeasts, bacteria, or a combination thereof, under anaerobic conditions. Fermentation usually implies that the action of microorganisms is desirable. The science of fermentation is also known as zymology or zymurgy. French chemist Louis Pasteur was the first known *zymologist*, when in 1856 he connected yeast to fermentation. Pasteur originally defined fermentation as "respiration without air".

The term "fermentation" is sometimes used to specifically refer to the chemical conversion of sugars into ethanol, a process which is used to produce alcoholic beverages such as wine, beer, and cider. Fermentation is also employed in the leavening of bread (CO_2 produced by yeast activity); in preservation techniques to produce lactic acid in sour foods such as sauerkraut, dry sausages, kimchi, and yogurt; and in pickling of foods with vinegar (acetic acid). The primary benefit of fermentation is the conversion of sugars and other carbohydrates into preservative organic acids, *e.g.* converting juice into wine, grains into beer, carbohydrates into carbon dioxide to leaven bread, and sugars in vegetables. Food fermentation has been said to serve five main purposes:

- Enrichment of the diet through development of a diversity of flavors, aromas, and textures in food substrates
- Preservation of substantial amounts of food through lactic acid, alcohol, acetic acid, and alkaline fermentations
- Biological enrichment of food substrates with protein, essential amino acids, and vitamins
- Elimination of anti-nutrients
- A decrease in cooking time and fuel requirement.

Fermentation is the process of controlling microbes (bacteria, yeast, and moulds) to modify food, producing a desired product.

Often we talk about the negative issues caused by microorganisms in food such as food spoilage. But they can be used as efficient live factories to produce health beneficial food. Without some microorganisms, production of certain food items may not be possible or may be costly. Microbes are cheap resources that consist of numerous enzymes which can convert complex chemical structures into simple digestible molecules with a high efficiency. These microorganisms use the nutrients in the food as the substrate to produce energy and other required precursors for their growth in which a fermented food results. There are numerous examples for fermented food.

Fish sauce: In production of fish sauce, uneviscerated fish is mixed with salt and placed in fermented tanks to allow liquefaction for about six months. The collected liquid is further ripened for few more months. Halophillic microbes are involved in this fermentation process. *Streptococcus, Micrococcus* and *Bacillus* species predominate. This product is dark coloured with a distinct aroma.

Sauerkraut: This refers to fermented cabbage. Normal microflora in cabbage is involved in the fermentation process under anaerobic conditions. *Leuconostoc mesenteroides* and *Lactobacillus plantarum* is involved. Temperature is a crucial factor in the control of fermentation. If the temperature is below 21 degrees Celcius, Lactobacilli outgrow. L. *mesenteroides* require a lower temperature below 21°C. Acidity created by *Lactobacilli* prevents the growth of L. *mesenteroides.*

Pickels: Pickels consist of vegetables like cucumber, onions, chilies etc. Lactic acid bacteria such as *Leuconostoc mesenteroides*, *P. cerevisiae, L. brevis, L. plantarum* are involved in the fermentation process These bacteria also take part in fermentation of olives.

Soy sauce: In production of soy sauce, a mixture of soybean and wheat flour is inoculated with *Aspergillus oryzae* and *Aspergillus soyae*. These fungi digest complex starch and produce sugars which facilitate the growth of bacteria. Anaerobic bacteria carry out fermentation to produce soy sauce.

Beer and Ale: Malted beverages are produced by brewing. Mainly the yeasts are involved in the process. Yeasts convert fermentable sugars to ethanol and carbon dioxide. As yeasts do not produce enough amylases to hydrolyze starch in barley grains, they are germinated prior to brewing. Hops which are added for bitterness have an inhibitory effect on gram positive bacteria. *Saccharomyces carlsbergensis* is the principle organism used. This species is subjected to various genetic modifications to increase the efficiency of the fermentation. In addition to ethanol and carbon dioxide, yeasts produce a small amount of glycerol, acetic acid and aromatic esters. Ale is a top fermented beverage with *Saccharomyces cerevisiae.*

Wine: Wine is made from grape juice in large scale. Yeasts; *Saccharomyces cerevisiae var. ellipsoideus* is the culture used in wine fermentation. High temperature is not suitable for this fermentation as yeasts die while low temperature allows the growth of lactic acid bacteria.

Environmental factors such as acidity, pH, oxygen level, moisture level, temperature, sugar content are important for this fermentation processes. In most food commodities, acidity is developed by microorganisms. This developed acidity is important for preserving the food. Proteolytic action may bring down the pH to a higher value. Some yeasts produce alkaline by products such as ammonia in their regular metabolism which is encouraged in the production of limburger cheese.

Alcohol: Alcohol, which is a byproduct of many fermentation pathways also have a preservative action. Alcohol content produced will depend on the sugar content, type of yeast involved in fermentation, temperature and the oxygen level. Most yeast can't tolerate high alcohol levels. Temperature has a direct effect on microbial fermentation which in turn affects the final quality of the product. Sauerkraut production is an ideal example to show the importance of temperature in fermentation process.

Microorganisms have different oxygen requirements for their growth and fermentation. In wine production, yeasts grow best under aerobic conditions. In baking, anaerobic conditions favour the quality of the final product. Vinegar production involves anaerobic as well as aerobic fermentation.

Idli: A fermented, thick suspension made of a blend of rice (Oryza sativum) and dehulled black gram (Phaseolus mungo) is used in several traditional foods in Southeast Asian countries. Among them, idli and dosa are very popular in India and Sri Lanka. Traditionally, for idli preparation the rice and black gram are soaked separately. After draining the water, rice and black gram are grinded independently, with occasional addition of water during the process. The rice is coarsely ground and the black gram is finely ground. Then the rice and the black gram batters are mixed together (2:1ratio) with addition of a little salt and allowing to ferment overnight at room temperature (about 30 °C). Finally, the fermented batter is placed in special idli pans and steamed for 5–8 min. Idli is a low calorie, starchy and nutritious food, which is consumed as breakfast or snack. Steamed idli contains about 3.4% protein, 20.3% carbohydrate and 70% moisture. The lactic acid bacteria *Leuconostoc mesenteroides*, *Streptococcus faecalis*, *Lactobacillus* are responsible for fermentation. The yeasts *Geotrichum candidum, Torulopsis holmii, Torulopsis candida* and Trichosporon *pullulans* have also been identified in idli fermentation.

KOJI: A fermented product from Japan. Polished rice is soaked in water for 17 hr at 25° C, the excess water is drained and steamed for 70 minutes and cooled to 35° C. The steamed rice is inoculated with Aspergillus and incubated at 27–28° for 50 hr. The product is dried as granules and consumed. The main enzymes that are active during fermentation are α-glycosides, glucoamylase and acid protease.

GRAM STAINING: Gram staining is a common technique used to differentiate two large groups of bacteria based on their different cell wall constituents. The name comes from the Danish bacteriologist Hans Christian Gram, who developed the technique in 1884.

Gram-positive organisms

Gram-positive bacteria have cell walls that contain thick layers of peptidoglycan, a substance that forms the cell walls of many bacteria. The peptidoglycan forms about 90% of the cell wall in gram-positive bacteria. This causes them to appear blue to purple under a Gram stain.

Gram-positive organisms include:

- *Staphylococcus* species.
- *Streptococcus* species.
- *Corynebacterium* species.
- *Clostridium* species.
- *Listeria* species.

Gram-negative organisms

Gram-negative bacteria have cell walls with thin layers of peptidoglycan (10% of the cell wall) and high lipid (fatty acid) content. This causes them to appear red to pink under a Gram stain.

Gram-negative organisms include:

- *Neisseria gonorrheae and Neisseria meningitides.*
- *Moraxella* species.
- *Escherichia coli* (E. coli).
- *Pseudomonas* species.
- *Proteus* species.
- *Klebsiella* species.

Gram staining of bacteria: One way to make bacteria stand out from their environment is a technique known as Gram staining. Bacteria are dried onto a clear glass slide then two different coloured dyes are added to stain the bacteria. The dyes are rinsed off with alcohol and water before the bacteria are observed under a microscope. If a sample of bacteria appears purple after, staining, the bacteria is a Gram-positive bacteria. If the sample it appears red after staining, it is a Gram-negative bacteria. The deeper colour of Gram-positive bacteria is due to their having thicker outer walls that are stained Some Gram-positive bacteria can form spores, also called endospores. A spore-forming bacterium encapsulates its vital structures in a tough outer coat when environmental conditions become harsh. These spores are extremely resistant to heat, chemicals, and other environmental conditions, and so help these bacteria to survive harsh environmental conditions. Bacteria don't multiply in the spore form, but if conditions become favourable again they can start to grow again. This of the vegetative form of bacteria, in which the bacteria can multiply .Examples of spore-forming bacteria of interest to the food industry are Bacillus spp. and Clostridium spp

D, Z and F Values:

Sterilizing effect or lethality: The sterilizing effect, which is also called lethality or death rate, indicates the effect of a heat treatment, expressed as the number of decimal reductions in the number of microorganisms.

When the bacterial suspension is exposed to heat, it shows logarithmic decrease in its population. It means that when microbes are exposed to heat at a particular temperature for specific time, same percentage of microbes would die every time.

Thermal Death Time (TDT) is also one of the frequently used terms, and is defined as the time required for killing specific number of microorganisms at a particular temperature. Practically, to obtain thermal death time value, the temperature is kept constant and the required time is found out to kill the specific or target number of microbial cells. In short, temperature is constant and the required time is found. TDT curve is a plot of D-value vs temperature.

Decimal reduction time (D-value):- The D-value, which denotes the decimal reduction time, is the time required at a specific temperature and under specified conditions to reduce a microbial population by one decimal. The decimal reduction time is dependent on the temperature, the type of microorganism and the composition of the medium containing the microorganism. Thus, after an organism is reduced by 1 D, only 10% of the original organisms remain. The population number has been reduced by one decimal place in the counting scheme. When referring to D values it is proper to give the temperature as a subscript to the D. For example, a hypothetical organism is reduced by 90% after exposure to temperatures of 300F for 2 minutes, Thus the D-value would be written as

$$D_{300F} = 2 \text{ minutes.}$$

$$D_{\text{reference temperature}} = \text{Time}/(\text{Log}_a - \text{Log}_b)$$

Where a = the initial population, and b = the survivors after a time interval

The Z-value: The Z-value is the increase or decrease in temperature required to reduce or increase the decimal reduction time by one decimal. It is a measure of the change in death rate with a change in temperature. The number of degrees Fahrenheit or Centigrade required for a thermal death time curve to traverse 1 log cycle. This is the temperature increase required to reduce the thermal death time by a factor of 10. The z-value gives an indication of the relative impact of different temperatures on a microorganism, with smaller values indicating greater sensitivity to increasing heat. The z-value is obtained by plotting the logarithms of at least 2 D-values against temperature or by the formula:

$$Z = (T_2 - T_1)/(\log D_1 - \log D_2)$$

Where T = temperature and D = D-value

F-value: The F value for a process is the number of minutes required to kill a known population of microorganisms in a given food under specified conditions. This F value is usually set at 12 D values to give a theoretical 12 log cycle reduction of the most heat-resistant species of mesophilic spores in a can of food. For example, if there were 10,000 spores of a species of spore in a can of food and a 12 D process was given, the initial 10,000 spores (10^4 spores) would be reduced to a theoretical 10^{-8} living spores per can, or again in theory, one living spore per 10^8 cans of product (one spore per one hundred million cans).

Toxin-producing bacteria: A toxin is a chemical poison. Bacteria are also classified by whether they produce toxins that cause foodborne illness. The infamous bacteria Clostridium botulinum produces the deadly botulinum toxin that causes botulism. One teaspoon (5 mL) of botulinum can kill up to 100 000 people. Toxins can be produced by many species of bacteria and other microbes, such as moulds and algae. Some toxins are released directly into foods, and their effects are immediate once the food is consumed. For example, S. aureus produces a toxin that causes vomiting. Other bacteria, such as V. cholera, release a toxin once they are ingested. These toxins are called enterotoxins; entero is Greek for "intestine." Enterotoxins often cause diarrhea, as they directly affect the gut function. Toxins are also problematic in the food industry, because some are very resistant to heat. For example, histamine is resistant to heat and can sometimes be found in canned foods. Some microbes can make chemical changes and toxins in foods when temperatures are high enough to allow them to grow. That is why temperature control is so important to the food industry: once a toxin is formed, there may be no way to remove it from foods.

Bacterial motility: Bacteria that can swim or move within a food can create a lot of problems. Unfortunately, most pathogenic bacteria do have this ability, and so are able to travel through high-moisture foods and other environments quite easily. This is one reason why microbiologists will look at sample bacteria on a slide under a microscope For example, Listeria is a problem in soft cheese.

Habitats of microbes Bacteria are also classified with reference to their habitat or preferred environments. Some bacteria thrive in the presence of the levels of oxygen normally in air, while others do not. Some bacteria like hot temperatures, while others survive in the freezer or in high salt conditions. Habitats can have alkaline or acidic pH. Consider, for example, the differences between a salmon and steer (cattle). These are very different looking animals that live in very different environments, so the microbes that live in and on them also prefer very different environments. Salmon live in salty, cold marine water, and they are cold-blooded. This means that a salmon adjusts its body temperature to the temperature of its environment. Wild salmon eat small marine organisms and other small fish. A steer, on the other hand, lives on land, near soil, and is warm-blooded. Steers have a vegetarian diet of grains and grasses. If we were to look at a table of microbe limits—the pH, amount of salt, and temperature range bacteria can tolerate—you might be able to guess which microbes are more commonly found in fish or cattle. Listeria is well-known for being able to grow at low temperatures, such as in a refrigerator, while Staphylococcus tolerates high acid, high salt conditions and low water activity. Moulds and fungi are well adapted to cold, moist, and fairly acidic environments, which is why you often see mould growing on the tops of food in the refrigerator.

CHAPTER 3

NUTRITION AND FOOD TYPES

3.1 BALANCED DIET

A balanced diet is defined as the diet which contains different types of foods, possessing the nutrients-carbohydrates, fats, proteins, vitamins and minerals in a proportion to meet the requirements of the body. A balanced diet invariably supplies a little more of each nutrient than the minimum requirement to withstand the short duration of leanness and keep the body in a state of good health. The basic composition of balanced diet is highly variable, as it differs from nation to nation, depending on the availability of foods. Social and cultural habits, besides the economic status, age, sex and physical activity of the individual largely influence the intake of diet.

The nutrition expert group constituted by the ICMR has recommended the composition of balanced diets for Indians. This is done by taking into account the commonly available foods in India. The composition of balanced diet (vegetarian and non-vegetarian) for an adult man and adult woman are respectively is shown in Table 1 and Table 2. The Indian balance diet is composed of cereals (rice, wheat, sorghum), pulses, roots and tubers, fruits, vegetables, milk and milk products, fats and oils, sugar and groundnut. Meat, fish and eggs are present in the non-vegetarian diets. In case of vegetarians, an additional intake of milk and pulses is recommended.

Table 1: Balanced diet for an adult man

Types of food	Sedentary work		Moderate work		Heavy work	
	Veg. (g)	Non-veg. (g)	Veg. (g)	Non-veg. (g)	Veg. (g)	Non-veg. (g)
Cereals	400	400	475	475	650	650
Pulses	70	55	80	65	80	65
Green leafy vegetables	100	100	125	125	125	125
Other vegetables	75	75	75	75	100	100
Roots and tubers	75	75	100	100	100	100
Fruits	30	30	30	30	30	30
Milk	200	100	200	100	200	100
Fats and oils	35	40	40	40	50	50
Meat and fish	-	30	-	30	-	30
Eggs	-	30	-	30	-	30
Sugar and jaggery	30	30	40	40	55	55
Groundnuts	-	-	-	-	50	50

(*Source: Report of Nutrition Expert Group, Indian Council of Medical Research, 1968*)

Table 2: Balanced diet for an adult woman

Types of food	Sedentary work		Moderate work		Heavy work		Additional allowance during	
	Veg. (g)	Non-veg. (g)	Veg. (g)	Non-veg. (g)	Veg. (g)	Non-veg. (g)	Pregnancy (g)	Lactation (g)
Cereals	300	300	350	350	475	475	50	100
Pulses	60	45	70	55	70	55	-	10
Green leafy vegetables	125	125	125	125	125	125	25	25
Other vegetables	75	75	75	75	100	100	-	-
Roots and tubers	50	50	75	75	100	100	-	-
Fruits	30	30	30	30	30	30	-	-
Milk	200	100	200	100	200	100	125	125
Fats and oils	30	30	35	40	40	45	-	15
Meat and fish	-	30	-	30	-	30	-	-
Eggs	-	30	-	30	-	30	-	-
Sugar and jaggery	30	30	30	30	40	40	10	20
Groundnuts	-	-	-	-	40	30	-	-

(Source: Report of Nutrition Expert Group, Indian Council of Medical Research, 1968)

3.2 RECOMMENDED DIETARY ALLOWANCE (RDA)

The recommended dietary allowances (RDA) represent the quantities of the nutrients to be provided in the diet for maintaining good health and physical efficiency of the body. It must be remembered that RDA is not the minimum amount to just meet the body needs, but also allowance is given for a safe margin.

RDA is useful to (*i*) assess the adequacy of national food supplies and to plan for agricultural food production both in terms of quantity and quality.

(*ii*) to provide dietary guidelines or health living individuals and groups to formulate a balanced diet.

(*iii*) for judging and deciding adequacy intake of nutrients in individuals and groups according to their weight, and other anthropometric data and to advise correct RDA for proper physical nd mental growth.

RDA had been the recognized standard globally, but from 1990s four sets of nutrient values (EAR-Estimated Average Requirement, RDA, AI-adequate intake and TUL-tolerable upper limits) are expressed as part of the dietary reference intakes. The RDAs are not recommended for use in menu planning for groups or individuals and are not used for calculation of nutrient inadequacies. Usually the EARs are approximately 80% of the RDA. And, in healthy population the distribution of nutrient requirement and dietary intake is expected to superimpose. Also, when we consider RDA as the reference the distribution shifts to the right with RDA as the mean and the entire population will shift beyond and above the requirements and a significant proportion may be at TUL. Hence, the ICMR recommended EAR for population requirement/ adequacy estimations and menu or diet planning for individuals, which is in alignment with global recommendations.

Table 3: Recommended Dietary Allowance for Indians (ICMR, 1993)

Groups	Particulars	Body wt, kg	Net energy, kcal/d	Protein, g/d	Fat, g/d	Cal-cium mg/d	Iron, mg/d	Vit. A. (µg/d) retinol	Vit. A. (µg/d) β-caro	Thia- mg/d	Ribo-mine mg/d	Nico-flavin, acid, mg/d	Pyro-Tinic Acid, mg/d	Vita, C Doxin mg/d	Folic Acid (µg/d)	Vit. B-12 (µg/d)
Men	Sedentary work		2425							1.2	1.4	16				
	Moderate work	60	2875	60	20	400	28	600	2400	1.4	1.6	18	2.0	40	100	1
	Heavy work		3800							1.6	1.9	21				
Women	Sedentary work	50	1875							0.9	1.1	12				
	Moderate work		2225	50	20	400	30	600	2400	1.1	1.3	14	2.0	40	100	1
	Heavy work		2925							1.2	1.5	16				
	Pregnant	50	+300	+15	30	1000	38	600	2400	+0.2	+0.2	+2	2.5	40	400	1
	Lactation															
	0-6 months	45	+550	+25	45	1000	30	950	3800	+0.3	+0.3	+4	2.5	80	150	1.5
	6-12 months		+400	+18						+0.2	+0.2	+3				
Infants	0-6 months	5.4	108/kg	2.05/kg		500	-	-	-	55µg/kg	65µg/kg	710µg/kg	0.1	25	25	0.2
	6-12 months	8.6	98/kg	1.65/kg			-	350	1200	50µg/kg	60µg/kg	650µg/kg	0.4			
Children	1-3 years	12.2	1240	22			12	400	1600	0.6	0.7	8	0.9	40	30	0.2-1.0
	4-6 years	19.0	1690	30	25	400	18	400		0.9	1.0	11			40	
	7-9 years	26.9	1950	41			26	600	2400	1.0	1.2	13	1.6		60	
Boys	10-12 years	35.4	2190	54	22	600	34	600	2400	1.1	1.3	15	1.6	40	70	0.2-1.0
Girls	10-12 years	31.5	1970	57			19			1.0	1.2	13				
Boys	13-15 years	47.8	2450	70	22	600	41	600	2400	1.2	1.5	16	2.0	40	100	0.2-1.0
Girls	13-15 years	46.7	2060	65			28			1.0	1.2	14				
Boys	16-18 years	57.1	2640	78	22	600	50	600	2400	1.3	1.6	17	2.0	40	100	0.2-1.0
Girls	16-18 years	49.9	2060	63			30			1.0	1.2	14				

The following factor affecting the RDA.

FACTORS Affecting RDA are : 1. Variability in nutritional requirements

2. Dietary Factors: (*i*) Bio-availability; Bioavailability of nutrients can vary widely depending upon the nutrient and the quality of diet. This factor has significance in case of certain nutrients like protein, iron, calcium, zinc Beta Catrotene and vitamin B12. Plant based diets are absorbed less due to inhiibitory factors present in plant foods like tannins, phyates and antitypsin etc.

Sex: The RDA for men is about 20% higher than that for women. Iron is an exception as the requirement is greater in menstruating women. Additional requirements (20-30% above normal) are needed for pregnant and lactating women.

Age: In general, the nutrient requirement is much higher in the growing age. For instance, the protein requirement for a growing child is about 2 g/kg body weight per day as compared to 1 g/kg body weight per day for adults.

RDI (Dietary Reference Intakes): It is average daily intake level of a particular nutrient that is likely to meet the nutrient requirement of (97-98%) healthy individuals.

3.3 CLASSIFICATION AND FUNCTIONS OF FOODS

Foods may be broadly classified in to 11 groups based on their nutritive value: (1) Cereals and millets; (2) pulses (legumes); (3) nuts and oilseeds; (4) vegetables; (5) fruits; (6) milk and milk products; (7) Eggs; (8) meat, fish and other animal foods; (fats and oils); (10) sugar and other carbohydrates foods and (11) Spices and condiments.

The body uses food to perform one or more of four main functions: to supply energy, for growth and repair, for regulation and for protection.

Energy: Food supplies the fuel or energy needed to perform the many tasks of everyday living. We need energy to think, breathe, walk, sit, speak and even sleep. We get energy from carbohydrates, proteins and fats. It is important that we eat enough food to supply all our needs. If we don't, we will feel tired and listless. Having no energy can be compared to a car that has run out of petrol. On the other hand, if we eat more energy food than our body needs, this energy will be stored in the body as fat. Too much stored energy will result in the body becoming overweight or obese.

Growth and repair: Food provides the materials needed to build, repair and maintain body tissues. Proteins, fats and minerals are the best nutrients for growth. Growing bodies need extra amounts of these nutrients. Every person whether growing or not, is going through a continual repair process of replacing injured or dead cells. It is food that supplies the nutrients necessary for this process.

Regulation: Food supplies the substances that help regulate the body's processes. Water, vitamins and minerals help regulate breathing, the nervous system, digestion, blood circulation and the elimination of waste products from the body. They help keep all the systems in the body working properly.

Protection: Vitamins, minerals and protein keep the body's tissues and organs healthy. Healthy organs are less likely to be attacked by disease.

3.3.1 Nutritional Classification of Foods

The Nutritional expert group of ICMR, India suggested a Five food group plan and nutrients supplied by each food group is given below:

S. No.	Food group	Nutrients contributed
1.	*Milk group* This includes other protein rich foods such as pulses, nuts, meat, fish, egg etc.	Rich source of protein, minerals and vitamins
2.	*Fruits and green leafy vegetables* Papaya, orange, mango, Indian goose berry, guava etc., and all green leafy vegetables	Rich sources of certain vitamins and minerals
3.	*Other vegetables* Beans, brinjal, ladies finger etc.	Fair sources of certain vitamins, minerals and roughages
4.	*Cereals, roots and tubers* Rice, wheat, maize, ragi, kaffir-corn, pearl millets etc., potato, tapioca, sweet potato etc.	-Rich source of starch -fair to good source of protein and certain B-vitamin
5.	*Fats and oils and pure carbohydrates foods* Vegetables oils, animal fats, sugar, jiggery, honey, sago, custard powder, starch etc.	• Rich source of energy. • Vegetable oils are fair to good source of essential fatty acids (EFA) and vitamin E. • Butter good source of vitamin A. Animal fats rich in cholesterol but poor source of EFA and vitamin A • Pure carbohydrates foods- rich sources of energy

3.3.1.1 Wheat Flour Terms

The Food and Drug Administration inspects and approves the use of flour treatments and additives that are used to improve the storage, appearance and baking performance of flour. The treatment additives are in no way harmful.

- **"Enriched"** flour supplemented with iron and four B-vitamins (thiamine, niacin, riboflavin and folic acid) and may be with calcium. Reconstituting the nutritional status of a processed food ingredient to match that of the original raw materials.
- **"Fortified"** implies that something is added to a product that makes its nutritional status higher than the product made from "unprocessed" raw materials. *i.e.* Cereals.
- **"Pre-sifted"** flour is sifted at the mill, making it unnecessary to sift before measuring.
- **"Bromated"** flour is largely discontinued in the United States. Ascorbic acid is now being added to strengthen the flour for bread dough's.
- **"Bleached"** refers to flour that has been bleached chemically to whiten or improve the baking qualities. No change occurs in the nutritional value of the flour and no harmful chemical residues remain. It is a process which speeds up the natural lightening and maturing of flour.
- **"Unbleached"** flour is aged and bleached naturally by oxygen in the air. It is more golden in color, generally more expensive and may not have the consistency in baking qualities that bleached flour does. Unbleached is preferred for yeast breads because bleaching affects gluten strength.

- **"Patent"** flour, bleached or unbleached, is the highest grade of flour. It is lower in ash and protein with good color. Market-wise, it is considered the highest in value and mostly used by bakers.
- **"Organic"** or chemical-free flour is not standardized, so its definition varies from state to state. It may be grown and stored without the use of synthetic herbicides or insecticides. It may also mean no toxic fumigants were used to kill pests in the grain and no preservatives were added to the flour, packaging, or food product.
- **"Gluten"** is a protein formed when water and wheat flour is mixed. Gluten gives bread dough elasticity, strength and gas-retaining properties. Wheat is the only grain with sufficient gluten content to make raised or leavened loaf of bread.

3.3.2 Recommendation on Energy Requirement

The total energy requirement or the total energy expenditure (TEE) is calculated based on a multiplication of basal metabolic rate (BMR) to physical activity level (PAL): TEE = BMR × PAL.

Physical activity level (PAL): The physical activity level (or PAL) is a way to express daily physical activity as a number and is used to estimate person's total energy expenditive (TEE). The physical activity ratio (PAR) values used by FAO/WHO/UNU were obtained from the studies conducted in Western populations. Studies carried out in India indicate that energy spent for different physical activity are lower. This could be because energy expended for a given activity (physical activity ratio-PAR) is not constant across the range of body weight and extrapolation from a heavy weight individual can overestimate energy spent for lower weight individual. Energy spent for each physical activity is lower for Indians, therefore a recalculation was performed using the PAR values reported for Indian population and this showed that the PAR was lower from 1.53 that was used in the previous recommendation (RDA2010) to 1.40 for sedentary population and was relatively lower for other physical activities as well.

BMR: The Basal Metabolic Rate (BMR) is either measured directly (using DLW or HRM methods), or predicted from body weight, gender and age specific equations that were derived from a large international dataset by the FAO/WHO/UNU. However, the comparison of BMR derived from FAO/WHO/UNU equations and BMR observed among Indians suggest that the equation can overestimate the BMR by 10-12%, because the FAO/WHO/UNU data set included young and muscular subjects. The body composition among Indians includes relatively more fat and hence would result in a lower BMR as observed in studies conducted in India. The earlier ICMR-NIN committee used 5% reduction in BMR calculation from FAO/WHO/UNU equations for deriving energy requirements for Indian adults, while the present committee reviewed the literature on BMR and based on the evidence, further reduced the BMR by another 5 % for adults.

Hence, the recommended energy requirement is lower by 3 to 8 kcal/kg/day for adults compared to the previous recommendation (RDA-2010) (Tables 2a & 4b). However, for children, since there is no recent evidence to show that the BMR of Indian children is lower than that of their Western counterparts, the present committee retained the BMR derived from the FAO/WHO/UNU 2004.

Recommendation on protein requirement

The human protein requirement should satisfy the currently established indispensable amino acid requirements as recommended by FAO/WHO/UNU Consultation of 2007.

The present Expert Group (ICMR-NIN 2020) adopted the FAO/WHO/UNU(2007) approaches to define the protein requirements for Indians of different age groups. A median obligatory nitrogen loss (WHO, 2007) has been used to compute mean (0.66 g/kg/day-EAR) and safe protein requirements (0.83 g/kg/day-RDA) for healthy Indian adults. Considering high quality protein sources as the premise for defining requirements, a newer protein quality index, digestible indispensable amino acid score (DIAAS), which is based on true ileal digestibility (instead of PDCAAS) of individual amino acids has been introduced in the current document. In addition, the cereal-legume-milk composition of the diet has been improved to 3:1:2.5 (ICMR-NIN, 2020) as compared to the earlier 11:1:3 (ICMR-NIN, 2010). Hence in the 2020 recommendation the RDA for protein is 0.83g/kg/day instead of 1g/kg/day (RDA 2010) and the EAR is 0.66 g/kg/day (Table 5a & 5b). A foot note is mentioned under the Table 5a- that for people consuming cereal-based diet with low quality protein, the protein requirements are 1 g/kg per day.

Table 4a. Summary of recommended energy requirement for Indians

Age group	Category	ICMR 2020	ICMR 2010	Difference
			Kcal/d	
Adult Men	Sedentary work	2110	2320	– 210
	Moderate work	2710	2730	– 20
	Heavy work	3470	3490	– 20
Adult Women	Sedentary work	1660	1900	– 240
	Moderate work	2130	2230	– 100
	Heavy work	2720	2850	– 130
	Pregnant	+ 350	+ 350	—
	Lactating (0-6 m)	+ 600	+ 600	—
	Lactating (7-12 m)	+ 520	+ 520	–
Infants	0-6 months	530	520	+ 10
	6-12 months	660	670	– 10
Children*	1-3 y	1070	1060	+ 10
	4-6 y	1360	1350	+ 10
	7-9 y	1700	1690	+ 10
Boys	10-12 y	2220	2190	+ 30
Girls	10-12 y	2060	2010	+ 50
Boys	13-15 y	2860	2750	+ 110
Girls	13-15 y	2400	2330	+ 70
Boys	16-18 y	3320	3020	+ 300
Girls	16-18 y	2500	2440	+ 60

*For children 1% increase over the previous recommendations.

Table 4b. Energy Requirement*

Age Group	Category	Body weights	(kcal/d)*	(kcal/kg/day)
Men	Sedentary work	65.0	2110	32
	Moderate work	65.0	2710	42
	Heavy work	65.0	3470	53
Women	Sedentary work	55.0	1660	30
	Moderate work	55.0	2130	39
	Heavy work	55.0	2720	49
	Pregnant	55.0 + GWG[b]	+ 350	
	Lactating	55.0 +	+ 600 + 520	
Infants	0-6 m	5.8	530	90
	6-12 m	8.5	660	80
Children[c]	1-3 y	12.9	1110	83
	4-6 y	18.3	1360	74
	7-9 y	25.3	1700	67
Boys	10-12 y	34.9	2220	64
Girls	10-12 y	36.4	2060	57
Boys	13-15 y	50.5	2860	57
Girls	13-15 y	49.6	2400	49
Boys	16-18 y	64.4	3320	52
Girls	16-18 y	55.7	2500	45

[a] Rounded off to the nearest 10 kcal/d [b] GWG: Energy need in pregnancy should be adjusted for actual bodyweight, observed weight gain and activity pattern for the population

[c] Energy needs of children and adolescents have been computed for reference children and adolescents; with a moderate daily physical activity level.

*The actual requirement in specific population groups should be adjusted for the actual weight and physical activity of that population

Table 5a. Summary of recommended protein requirements for Indians 2020

		Body weight (kg)	EAR (g/kg/d)	RDA (g/kg/d)	EAR (g/d)	RDA (g/d)
Adult Men	Sedentary	65	0.66	0.83	42.9	54.0
	Moderate					
	Heavy Work					
Adult Women	Sedentary	55	0.66	0.83	36.3	45.7
	Moderate					
	Heavy Work					
Pregnant Women	2nd Trimester				+ 7.6	+ 9.5
	3rd Trimester				+ 17.6	+ 22.0
Lactating Women	0-6 months				+ 13.6	+ 16.9
	6-12 months				+ 10.6	+ 13.2
Infants	0-6 months	5.8	1.16	1.40	6.7	8.1
	6-12 months	8.5	1.04	1.23	8.8	10.5
Children	1-3 y	12.9	0.79	0.97	10.2	12.5
	4-6 y	18.3	0.70	0.87	12.8	15.9
	7-9 y	25.3	0.75	0.92	19.0	23.3
Boys	10-12 y	34.9	0.75	0.91	26.2	31.8
Girls	10-12 y	36.4	0.73	0.90	26.6	32.8
Boys	13-15 y	50.5	0.72	0.89	36.4	44.9
Girls	13-15 y	49.6	0.70	0.87	34.7	43.2
Boys	16-18 y	64.4	0.70	0.86	45.1	55.4
Girls	16-18 y	55.7	0.67	0.83	37.3	46.2

For people consuming cereal-based diet with low quality protein, the protein requirements are 1 g/kg per day

Note: The cereal-legume-milk composition of the diet should be 3:1:2.5 for good protein quality.

Table 5b. Recommended protein for vegetarians

Protein recommendation: RDA 2010	Body weight kg	Protein g/kg/d	Total daily Requirement (g)
Males	60	1.0	60
Females	55	1.0	55

Note: The cereal-legume-milk composition of the diet should be 3:1:2.5 for good protein quality.

Table 6a. (Males) Nutrient values comparison ICMR-2010/2020 and IOM

Nutrients	ICMR-NIN			IOM
	RDA 2010	RDA 2020	EAR 2020	
Calcium (mg)	600	1000	800	1000
Magnesium (mg)	340	440	370	400
Iron (mg)	17	19	11	8
Zinc (mg)	12	17	14	11
Iodine (µg)	150	150	95	150
Thiamine (mg)	1.4	1.8	1.5	1.2
Riboflavin (mg)	1.6	2.5	2.1	1.3
Niacin (mg)	18	18	15	16
Vitamin B6 (mg)	2	2.4	2.1	1.3
Folate (µg) DFE	200	300	250	400
Vitamin B12 (µg)	1	2.2	2	2.4
Vitamin C (mg)	40	80	65	90
Vitamin A (µg)	600	1000	460	900
Vitamin D (IU)	400	600	400	600

Table 6b. (Females) Nutrient values comparison ICMR-2010/2020 and IOM

Nutrients	ICMR			IOM
	RDA 2010	RDA 2020	EAR 2020	
Calcium (mg)	600	1000	800	1000
Magnesium (mg)	310	370	310	310
Iron (mg)	21	29	15	18
Zinc (mg)	10	13.0	11	8
Iodine (µg)	150	150	95	150
Thiamine (mg)	1.1	1.7	1.4	1.2
Riboflavin (mg)	1.3	2.4	2.0	1.3
Niacin (mg)	14	14	12	1
Vitamin B6 (mg)	2	1.9	1.6	1.3
Folate (µg) DFE	200	220	180	400
Vitamin B12 (µg)	1	2.2	2	2.4
Vitamin C (mg)	40	65	55	75
Vitamin A (µg)	600	840	390	700
Vitamin D (IU)	400	600	400	600

Recommendation on fats and oil requirement

There are three types of fatty acids (FA) in our diets, saturated fatty acids (SFA), mono unsaturated fatty acids (MUFA) and poly unsaturated fatty acids (PUFA). Our body can synthesize SFAs, MUFAs besides obtaining them from the diet, while the PUFAs, namely, linoleic acid (also known as n-6 or omega 6 or LA) and alpha linolenic (also known as n-3 or omega 3 or ALA) cannot be synthesized. Hence, n-6 and n-3 are termed essential fatty acids (EFAs). Our body depends on dietary sources for n-3 and n-6 FA as they are not made in our body. Hence, one should take adequate amounts of nuts, oilseeds along with recommended levels of diverse foods (My Plate for the Day), to meet the required amounts of 6.6 grams of n-6 PUFA and 2.2 grams of n-3 PUFA for all the essential functions in the body. The visible fat (cooking oil) must be limited to 20-50g (4 to 10 teaspoon full) per person/ day depending on the level of energy (calorie) requirement, which is based on physical activity and physiological status. (For example, not more than 27g visible fat/ cooking oil is recommended for a 2000 kcal diet/ day).

Recommendation on vitamins and mineral requirement

For vitamins and minerals, the EAR and RDA are determined among normal individuals by using approaches such as (1) Factorial: calculate losses in feces, urine, sweat and estimate the bioavailability, then add the requirement for growth in children or milk output in lactating women (2) balance studies: minimum required to maintain homeostasis; intake – losses = 0, (3) or calculate from maintenance of optimal function, such as BP and sodium, calcium and bone density etc. The present committee has done extensive deliberations on recommendations for minerals like iron, calcium, phosphorus, zinc, selenium and iodine, and vitamins such as B vitamins and vitamin A. Data available on dietary intakes, balance studies, fecal loss- urinary loss in different geographical states, absorption studies, turnover studies were considered. For some nutrients (B1, B2, B6) enzyme activity coefficient studies were considered. As can be seen from the Tables 6 (a) (males) and 6 (b) (females) the RDA for all the vitamins and minerals are higher in the ICMR-NIN 2020 recommendation compared to the 2010. However, as the distribution of nutrient requirement and dietary intake is expected to superimpose among healthy population groups, considering RDA as the reference the distribution shifts to the right with RDA as the mean and the entire population will shift beyond and above the requirements and a significant proportion may be at TUL. Hence, the present committee recommended EAR for population requirement/ adequacy estimations, menu or diet planning for individuals, which is in alignment with global recommendation.

3.3.3 Energy Values of Foods

$$\text{Carbohydrates or fats} \xrightarrow[\text{Oxidation}]{O_2} CO_2 + \text{Water} + \text{heat}$$

$$\text{Protein} \xrightarrow[\text{Oxidation}]{} CO_2 + \text{Water} + \text{urea} + \text{heat}$$

The human body utilizes the potential energy contained in foods for maintaining life and doing work. The energy yielding factors are: (1) carbohydrates, (2) fats and (3) protein. Within the body, these nutrients are oxidized in the cells with the help of catalysts such as enzymes, co-enzymes (containing certain vitamins) and hormones. The process is one of continuous utilization of oxygen and production of CO_2, water and heat.

The energy or calorific value of foods depends on the quantity of carbohydrates, fats and proteins present in them. This can be determined by oxidizing a known weight of food in an instrument called **Bomb calorimeter** and measuring the heat produced.

The energy value of foods can be expressed in terms of kilo calories (Kcal) or mega joules (MJ). The unit *Kilo Calorie* has been in use till now. The International Union of Nutritional Sciences has suggested the use of Mega Joule (MJ) as the energy unit in place of Kcal.

Kilo Calorie: One kilogram calorie is the quantity of heat required to raise the temperature of 1 kg of water through 1°C. It is one thousand times the small calorie used in physics.

Mega Joule: One kilo calorie equals to 4.186 kilo joules. Hence, 1000 kilo calorie equals to 4.186×10^3 kilo joules or 4.186 mega joules.

1 Mega Joules = 1000 kilo joules

1 Mega joules = 239 Kcal

1Kilo calorie = 4.186 kilo joules

The average calorific values of pure carbohydrates, fats and proteins determined with bomb calorimeter are given below:

Macromolecules	Calorie
1g carbohydrate	4.10
1 g fat	9.45
1 g protein	5.65

Table 7: Physiological energy value of carbohydrates, fats and proteins from gross energy value

Nutrient	Gross energy value (Kcal/g)	Loss of food energy in digestion, %	Energy available after digestion (Kcal/g)	Loss of energy in metabolism (Kcal)	Physiological energy value of foods (Kcal/g)
Carbohydrates	4.10	2.0	4.0	Nil	4.0
Fats	9.45	5.0	9.0	Nil	9.0
Proteins	5.65	8.0	5.2	1.2	4.0

Relation between oxygen required and calorific value: It is of important to know the heat produced when 1 litre of oxygen is used for the oxidation of carbohydrates, fats or proteins. This can be calculated from the data obtained by the oxy-calorimeter and bomb calorimeter as explained below:

Table 8: Relation between oxygen required and calorific value from per g nutrient

Nutrient	Required O_2 for complete-oxidation	Yielding energy
1 g carbohydrates	0.8 litre	4.1 Kcal
1 g fat	2.2 litre	9.5 Kcal
1 g protein	1.2 litre	5.5 Kcal

Table 9: Yield of calorific value from nutrients from per litre oxygen

Amount of Oxygen	Nutrient to be Oxidizes	Produced Heat Energy
0.8 litre	1 g carbohydrate	4 Kcal
1.0 litre	1.25 g carbohydrate	5 Kcal
2.2 litre	1 g fat	9.5 Kcal
1.0 litre	0.49 g fat	4.5 Kcal
1.2 litre	1 g protein	5.5 Kcal
1.0 litre	0.83 g protein	4.6 Kcal

One litre of oxygen oxidizing carbohydrates, fats or protein produces nearly the same amount of heat *i.e.* 4.5 to 5.0 Kcal. This is an important conclusion as this is the basis for indirect determination of energy requirements from oxygen consumed.

3.3.4 Basal Energy Metabolism

The energy metabolism of a subject at complete physical and mental rest and having normal body temperature and in the post absorptive state (*i.e.* 12 hours after intake of fast meal) is known as Basal energy metabolism. Basal metabolism is usually determined using the apparatus of Benedict and Roth.

Studies carried out by various workers have shown that basal metabolism is most closely related to the body surface area and less directly related to either to the weight or height of the individual. The body surface area can be calculated according to the formula of Du Bois given below:

$$A = W^{0.425} \times H^{0.725} \times 71.84$$

Where,

A = body surface area in cm^2

H = height in cm

W = weight in kg

$$\log A = (\log W \times 0.425) + (\log H \times 0.725) + 1.8564$$

Table 10: Surface area in square meter for different height and weights (DuBois-DuBois)

Height	Weights (kg)								
(cm)	40	45	50	55	60	65	70	75	80
180	-	-	-	-	1.77	1.83	1.89	1.95	2.00
175	-	-	-	1.67	1.73	1.79	1.85	1.91	1.96
170	-	-	1.57	1.63	1.69	1.75	1.81	1.86	1.91
165	-	-	1.54	1.60	1.66	1.72	1.78	1.83	1.88
160	-	1.44	1.50	1.56	1.62	1.68	1.73	1.78	1.83
155	1.33	1.40	1.46	1.52	1.58	1.64	1.69	-	-
150	1.30	1.36	1.42	1.48	1.54	1.60	1.65	-	-
145	1.27	1.33	1.39	1.45	1.51	1.56	-	-	-
140	1.24	1.30	1.36	1.42	1.47	-	-	-	-

3.3.4.1 Biological Value: A method for determining the biological value of proteins was developed by Mitchell in 1925. It measures *the quantity of dietary proteins utilized by the animal for meeting its protein needs for maintenance and growth.*

$$\text{Biological value} = \frac{(\text{Nitrogen digested} - \text{Nitrogen lost in metabolism}) \times 100}{\text{Nitrogen digested}}$$

Nitrogen digested = N intake (In) – N in faeces (F_n) on the protein diet + N in faeces (F_e) on protein diet-free diet; *i.e.* Nitrogen digested = $I_n - (F_n - F_e)$

Nitrogen lost in metabolism = N in urine (U_n) on protein diet – N in urine (U_e) on protein free diet = $(U_n - U_e)$

$$\text{Biological value} = \frac{\text{In} - (F_n - F_e) - (U_n - U_e)}{\text{In} - (F_n - F_e)} \times 100$$

3.3.4.2 Digestibility coefficient: It is a measure of the proportion of a feed that is digestible. Dietary proteins are hydrolyzed to amino acid during digestion. The digestion begins in the stomach by the action of pepsin and later completed in intestines by trypsin, erepsin and other enzymes. Protein differs in their digestibility. In same period of say, 1 to 2 hours, certain proteins *e.g.*, proteins of milk and eggs, are easily digested and converted into amino acids, while certain other proteins *e.g.*, proteins of pulses are slowly digested to amino acids. Some amino acids are absorbed into blood stream from the intestine only unhydrolyzed portion of the protein is wasted in faeces. The term *digestibility coefficient of protein refers to the percentage of ingested protein absorbed into the blood stream after the process of digestion is complete.*

When an animal is fed on N-free diet, certain amount of nitrogen is excreted in the faeces. This is derived mainly from the digestive juices. This called endogenous faeces N. When a protein food is given, the N found in faeces consist both of endogenous N and food N lost in digestion. To find out N lost in digestion, endogenous faecal N should also be determined, For the determination of digestibility coefficient, the following data are required: (1) Food nitrogen intake (I_n); (2) Total faecal nitrogen excreted (F_n) and (3) Endogenous faecal nitrogen (F_e). The digestibility coefficient can be calculated using following formula:

$$\text{Digestibility coefficient} = \frac{N\ \text{intake} - (N\ \text{in faeces} - \text{endogenous faecal}\ N)}{\text{Nitrogen intake}} \times 100$$

$$= \frac{\text{In} - (F_n - F_e)}{\text{In}} \times 100$$

Where $(F_n - F_e)$ is the food nitrogen lost in digestion

The digestibility coefficient of protein are influenced by several factors, the most important of these being: (1) the presence of indigestible carbohydrates like cellulose and hemicelluloses, and (2) the presence of proteolytic enzyme inhibitors

3.3.4.3 Net protein Utilization (NPU): Mitchell (1922) introduced the term 'net utilization of dietary protein' which is a product of digestibility coefficient and biological value divided by 100.

$$\text{NPU} = \frac{\text{Digestibility coefficient} \times \text{biological}}{100}$$

Miller and Bender (1955) developed a direct method of estimating 'net protein utilization (NPU) of proteins. They calculated the NPU according to the following formula as experiments was done on a groups of albino rats of 28 days old.

$$\text{NPU} = \frac{\text{(Body N of the test group)} - \text{(Body N of the non-protein group)} + \text{(N consumed by Non protein group)}}{\text{N consumed by test group}} \times 100$$

The main advantage of determining NPU of a food or diet is that it helps in the calculation of the net available protein of the diet. A comparative statement of the PER, BV, NPU and chemical score of some dietary protein is given in Table 8. It will be seen that there is good correlation between the values for PER, NPU and chemical score.

3.3.4.4 Net protein ratio (NPR): this method is introduced by Bender and Doell (1957) is a modification of PER method. In this method, an allowance is made for protein requirement for maintenance. The method consists in feeding a group of meaning rats on a diet containing 10 percent of the test protein and another comparable control group on a non protein diet for a period of 10 days. The NPR is calculated by adding the loss in weight of the control group to the gain in weight of test group and dividing the total weight (g) by the quantity (g) of protein consumed by the test group according to the following formula:

$$\text{NPR} = \frac{\text{Grain in weight (g) of the test group} + \text{Loss in weight (g) of the non protein group}}{\text{Protein intake (g)}}$$

NPR values have been reported to correlate closely with NPU values. Data regarding the PER, BV and NPU of some dietary protein determined using albino rats are given in Table 8.

Chemical score: *The chemical score is the ratio between the content of the most limiting amino acid in the test protein to the content of the same amino acid in egg protein expressed as a percentage.* For example, the most limiting amino acid in milk is S-amino acids. Chemical score of milk proteins

$$= \frac{3.4}{5.5} \times 100 = 65$$

The chemical scores of gelatin and zein are zero.

Table 11: PER, BV, NPU and chemical score of some proteins

Foods	PER	BV	NPU	Chemical score	Limiting amino acids
				Animal foods	
Eggs	4.5	96	91	100	Nil
Cow's milk	3.0	84	75	65	Sulphur amino acids
Liver	2.9	77	65	66	Sulphur amino acids
Meat	2.8	80	76	70	Sulphur amino acids
Fish	3.0	85	72	60	Tryptophan
				Cereals	
Rice	2.0	64	57	60	Lysine, threonine
wheat	1.7	58	47	42	Lysine, threonine

Pulses					
Bengal gram	1.7	58	47	44	Sulphur amino acids
Pea, dried	1.6	56	45	42	Sulphur amino acids
Nuts and oil seeds					
Ground nuts	1.7	54	45	44	Lysine, Sulphur amino acids and threonine
Soybean	2.0	64	54	57	Sulphur amino acids
Cottonseed	2.1	63	53	55	Sulphur amino acids and lysine
Coconut	2.5	67	56	52	Sulphur amino acids, Lysine and threonine
Sesame	1.7	60	51	40	Lysine
Incomplete proteins					
Gelatin	0	-	-	0	Lacking in Tryptophan
Zein	0	-	-	0	Lacking in lysine and tryptophan

Protein Efficiency Ratio (PER): This method developed by Osborne, Mendel and Ferry in 1919 is based on the growth of young rats

$$\text{PER} = \frac{\text{Gain in body weight (g)}}{\text{Protein intake (g)}}$$

3.3.5 Protein Quality

The primary function of dietary proteins is to provide amino acids to meet the needs of the body. These include:

1. The replacement of endogenous loss of body proteins due to wear and tear
2. The synthesis of new tissue proteins during growth, pregnancy and lactation, and
3. The synthesis of enzymes, blood protein, hormones of protein nature, etc.

The essential amino acid content of some common foods is discussed below:

Cereals: Cereals contribute more than 70% of the protein in the diets of low income group in India. They contain 6-14% protein depending on the cereals. The limiting amino acid in different cereals proteins are lysine and threonine while in maize in addition in tryptophan also.

Legumes: common legumes are rich source of protein with 18 to 25%. Soybean is very rich containing from 35 to 40% protein. Legume protein is good source of lysine and threonone but deficit in sulphur containing amino acid and tryptophan.

Oilseed and nuts: Oilseeds and nut (except coconut) are rich source of protein (18 to 40%). Soybean proteins are rich in lysine and threonine but deficit in methionine. Sesame seed proteins are rich in methionine but are limiting in lysine. Groundnut are limiting in lysine, threonine and methionine.

Eggs: The protein of egg is rich source of all essential amino acids. Eggs contain 13.5% proteins.

Milk: Fresh milk contains only 3.5% protein due to its high water content. Milk proteins are rich in all essential amino acid except S-amino acids in which they are deficit to a small extent.

Meat and Fish: the proteins of meat and fish are rich in all essential amino acid. Meat is deficit in S-amino acid while fish is in tryptophan to a small extent.

A large number of methods have been proposed by various researchers for the evaluation of protein quality. Only a few of them measures overall nutritive value of protein *e.g.*, protein efficiency ratio (PER), net protein utilization (NPU) and biological value (BV). During recent years, only three methods, *i.e.* PER, NPR and NPU have been widely used as the most suitable methods for the evaluation of dietary proteins. All are discussed earlier.

Methods available for the evaluation of protein quality

1. *Methods based on growth and body weight changes*
   - Protein efficiency ratio
   - Net protein ratio
   - Gross protein value
   - Rat repletion method
   - Nitrogen growth index
   - Slope ratio method
2. *Methods based on carcass nitrogen analysis*
   - Nitrogen retention method
   - Net protein utilization
   - Rat repletion methods
3. *Methods based on nitrogen balance*
   - Nitrogen balance
   - Digestibility coefficient: biological vale and net utilization of dietary proteins
   - Nitrogen balance index
   - Egg repletion method
4. *Methods based on regeneration of blood and liver constituents*
   - Liver protein regeneration
   - Blood protein regeneration
   - Regeneration of liver enzyme
5. *Determination of availability of amino acid*
   - Chemical methods
   - Enzymatic methods
   - Microbiological methods
   - Animal assays
6. *Miscellaneous methods*
   - Plasma amino acids levels
   - Microbiological methods
7. *Chemical scoring methods*
   - Chemical scores
   - Essential amino acids
   - Simplified chemical scores

3.4 ASSESSMENT OF HUMAN NUTRITION STATUS

A large majority of the population in the developing countries suffer from malnutrition and under-nutrition. Data relating to the extent of prevalence and severity of malnutrition among the different age groups are not, however, available. The national nutritional policies for overcoming malnutrition in different countries should be based on knowledge of nutritional status and socio-economic factors (FAO/WHO Expert Committee on Nutrition, 1950).

Nutritional status is considered as a condition of health of a individual as influenced and outcome of utilization of the nutrients.

Anthropometry uses a measurement index to determine a person's nutritional status , which include height, length, weight, body mass index(BMI), head circumference, skin fold thickness, an arm circumference.

Methods for assessing nutritional status: Methods used in the assessment of nutritional status are:

1. Population sampling
2. Collection of data on nutritional adequacy of diets consumed
3. Anthropometric measurements
4. Clinical examination for ascertaining nutritional deficiencies
5. Radiological and biophysical deficiencies
6. Biochemical assessment

Malnutrition is a serious condition that happens when diet of a person does not contain the right amount of nutrients

Malnutrition, in all its forms, includes undernutrition (wasting, stunting, underweight), inadequate vitamins or minerals, overweight, obesity, and resulting diet-related noncommunicable diseases

Various forms of malnutrition

Under nutrition: It is the condition results from insufficient nutrients and food intake over an extended period of time. There is a decreased physical and mental development with low immunity.

There are 4 broad sub-forms of undernutrition: wasting, stunting, underweight, and deficiencies in vitamins and minerals. Undernutrition makes children in particular much more vulnerable to disease and death.

Low weight-for-height is known as *wasting*. It usually indicates recent and severe weight loss, because a person has not had enough food to eat and/or they have had an infectious disease, such as diarrhoea, which has caused them to lose weight.

Low height-for-age is known as *stunting*. It is the result of chronic or recurrent undernutrition, usually associated with poor socioeconomic conditions, poor maternal health and nutrition, frequent illness, and/or inappropriate infant and young child feeding and care in early life. Stunting holds children back from reaching their physical and cognitive potential.

Children with low weight-for-age are known as underweight. A child who is underweight may be stunted, wasted, or both.

Over nutrition: Consumption of excessive quantity of food over an extended period of time which results in overweight, obesity and other diet related health conditions such as type 2 diabetes mellitus and cardio-vasucular diseases etc.

Micrountrient deficiency in the individuals or groups due to insufficient intake of vitamins, proteins and minerals required for sustained physical growth.

Nutrigenomics: Nutrigenomics is the study of the effects of foods and food constituents on gene expression. It is about how our DNA is transcribed into mRNA and then to proteins and provides a basis for understanding the biological activity of food components. Nutrigenomics has also been described by the influence of genetic variation on nutrition by correlating gene expression or single-nucleotide polymorphisms with a nutrient's absorption, metabolism, elimination or biological effects. By doing so, nutrigenomics aims to develop rational means to optimize nutrition, with respect to the subject's genotype. By determining the mechanism of the effects of nutrients or the effects of a nutritional regime, nutrigenomics tries to define the causality relationship between these specific nutrients and specific nutrient regimes (diets) on human health. Nutrigenomics has been associated with the idea of personalized nutrition based on genotype. While there is hope that nutrigenomics will ultimately enable such personalized dietary advice, it is a science still in its infancy and its contribution to public health over the next decade is thought to be major.

Nutrigenomics is applying the sciences of genomics, transcriptomics, proteomics, and metabolomics to human nutrition in order to understand the relationship between nutrition and health. Nutrigenomics is a new science and has several different definitions. Nutrigenomics has been defined as the application of high-throughput genomic tools in nutrition research.

3.5 CAUSES AND PREVENTION OF MALNUTRITION

Malnutrition is not a condition that occurs rapidly; it is a chronic condition that develops slowly over time. It is widely accepted that malnutrition from any etiology is not a positive factor in health status, and may have a negative impact on other health conditions. Malnutrition is a condition that results from eating a diet in which nutrients are not enough or are too much such that it causes health problems. The nutrients involved can include: calories, protein, carbohydrates, vitamins orminerals. It is often used specifically to refer to undernutrition where there is not enough calories, protein or micronutrients; however, it also includes over nutrition. If undernutrition occurs during either pregnancy or before the age of two years of age it may result in permanent problems with physical and mental development. Extreme undernourishment, known as starvation, may have symptoms that include: a short height, thin body, very poor energy levels, and swollen legs and abdomen. People also often get infections and are frequently get effect of cold. The symptoms of micronutrient deficiencies depend on the micronutrient that is lacking.

3.5.1 Effects of Malnutrition

Malnutrition increases the risk of infection and infectious disease, and moderate malnutrition weakens every part of the immune system. For example, it is a major risk factor in the onset of active tuberculosis. Protein and energy malnutrition and deficiencies of specific micronutrients (including iron, zinc, and vitamins) increase susceptibility to infection. Malnutrition affects HIV transmission by increasing the risk of transmission from mother to child and also increasing replication of the virus. In communities or areas that lack access to safe drinking water, these additional health risks present a critical problem. Lower energy and impaired function of the brain also represent the downward spiral of malnutrition as victims are less able to perform the tasks they need to in order to acquire food, earn an income, or gain an education.

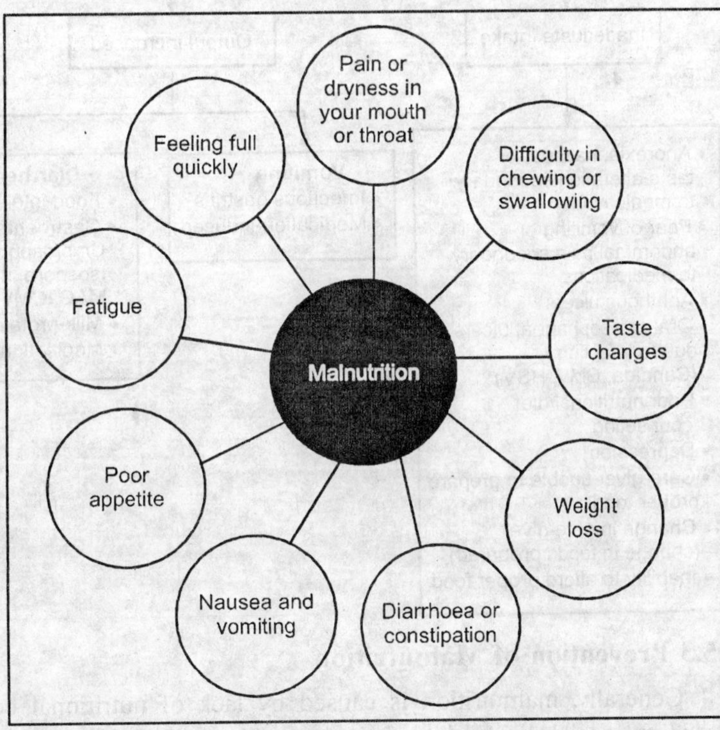

Vitamin-deficiency-related diseases (such as scurvy and rickets).

Hypoglycemia (low blood sugar) can result from a child not eating for 4 to 6 hours. Hypoglycemia should be considered if there is lethargy, limpness, convulsion, or loss of consciousness. If blood sugar can be measured immediately and quickly, perform a finger or heel stick.

3.5.2 Causes of Malnutrition

Major causes of malnutrition include poverty and food prices, dietary practices and agricultural productivity, with many individual cases being a mixture of several factors. Clinical malnutrition, such as in cachexia, is a major burden also in developed countries. Various scales of analysis also have to be considered in order to determine the sociopolitical causes of malnutrition. For example, the population of a community may be at risk if the area lacks health-related services, but on a smaller scale certain households or individuals may be at even higher risk due to differences in income levels, access to land, or levels of education

Malnutrition can be a consequence of health issues such as gastroenteritis or chronic illness, especially the HIV/AIDS pandemic. Diarrhea and other infections can cause malnutrition through decreased nutrient absorption, decreased intake of food, increased metabolic requirements, and direct nutrient loss. Parasite infections can also lead to malnutrition. People may become malnourished due to abnormal nutrient loss (due to diarrhea or chronic illness) or increased energy expenditure (secondary malnutrition).

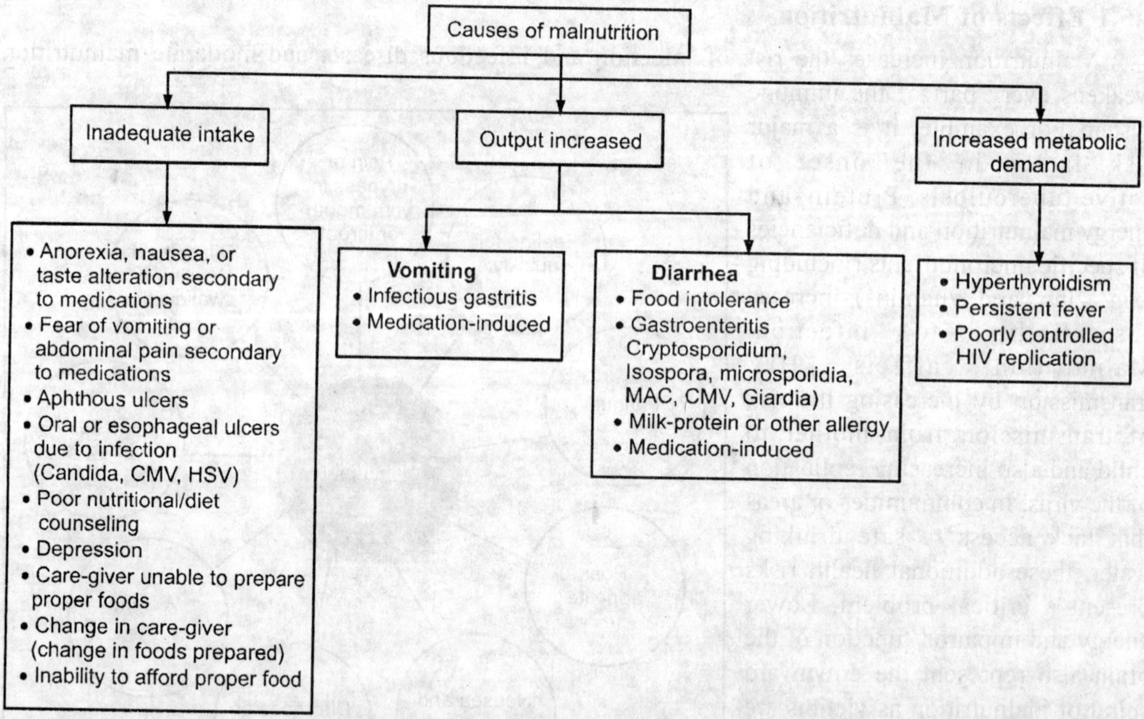

3.5.3 Prevention of Malnutrition

Generally, malnutrition is caused by lack of nutritional components it can be prevented by providing special diet such as fruit, vegetable, milk product, oils, meat and beans etc. with sufficient amount at proper time. There are primary prevention, secondary prevention and tertiary prevention for malnutrition.

Primary prevention

1. ***Health promotion***
   - Health education to mothers about good nutrition and food hygiene health workers
   - Distribution of supplements (distribution of iron, folic acid and vitamin a).
   - Promotion of breastfeeding
   - Development of low cost weaning foods
   - Measures to improve family diet
   - Nutritional education
   - Home economics
   - Family planning and birth spacing
   - Family environment
2. ***Specific protection***
   - specific protein diet, eggs, milk, fresh fruit
   - immunization
   - fortification of food

Secondary prevention; early diagnosis and adequate treatment

- Periodic nutrition surveillance
- Early diagnosis of any lag of growth.
- Early diagnosis and treatment of infection including diarrhea.
- Developing the program for early dehydration of children with diarrhea.
- Developing supplementary feeding program during epidemics.
- Regular deworming of school and preschool children.

Tertiary prevention; nutritional rehabilitation

- Nutritional rehabilitation services.
- Hospital treatment.
- Follow up of cases.

3.6 NUTRITION AND IMMUNITY

Nutrition plays an essential role in the regulation of optimal immunological response, by providing adequate nutrients in sufficient concentrations to immune cells. There are a large number of micronutrients, such as minerals, and vitamins, as well as some macronutrients such as some amino acids, cholesterol and fatty acids demonstrated to exert a very important and specific impact on appropriate immune activity. Thus, among many, some relevant case in point examples are brought and discussed: (1) The role of vitamin A/all-trans-retinoic-acids (ATRA) in acute promyelocytic leukemia, being this vitamin utilized as a very efficient therapeutic agent via effective modulation of the immune function (2) The involvement of vitamin C in the fight against tumor cells via the increase of the number of active NK cells. (3) The stimulation of apoptosis, the suppression of cancer cell proliferation, and delayed tumor development mediated by calcitriol/vitamin D by means of immunity regulation (4) The use of selenium as a cofactor to reach more effective immune response to COVID vaccination (5). The crucial role of cholesterol to regulate the immune function, which is demonstrated to be very sensitive to the variations of this macronutrient concentration. Other important examples are reviewed as well.

Vitamin D controls calcium and phosphorus levels in the blood and aids calcium absorption. Lactose improves calcium transfer through the intestinal wall and into the blood.

Table 12: Summary of recommended protein requirements for Indians 2020

		Body weight (kg)	EAR (g/kg/d)	RDA (g/kg/d)	EAR (g/d)	RDA (g/d)
Adult Men	Sedentary Moderate Heavy Work	65	0.66	0.83	42.9	54.0
Adult Women	Sedentary Moderate Heavy Work	55	0.66	0.83	36.3	45.7
Pregnant	2nd Trimester				+ 7.6	+ 9.5
Women	3rd Trimester				+ 17.6	+ 22.0
Lactating	0-6 months				+ 13.6	+ 16.9
Women	6-12 months				+ 10.6	+ 13.2
Infants	0-6 months	5.8	1.16	1.40	6.7	8.1
	6-12 months	8.5	1.04	1.23	8.8	10.5
Children	1-3 y	12.9	0.79	0.97	10.2	12.5
	4-6 y	18.3	0.70	0.87	12.8	15.9
	7-9 y	25.3	0.75	0.92	19.0	23.3
Boys	10-12 y	34.9	0.75	0.91	26.2	31.8
Girls	10-12 y	36.4	0.73	0.90	26.6	32.8
Boys	13-15 y	50.5	0.72	0.89	36.4	44.9
Girls	13-15 y	49.6	0.70	0.87	34.7	43.2
Boys	16-18 y	64.4	0.70	0.86	45.1	55.4
Girls	16-18 y	55.7	0.67	0.83	37.3	46.2

For people consuming cereal-based diet with low quality protein, the protein requirements are 1 g/kg g per day

Note: The cereal-legume-milk composition of the diet should be 3:1:2.5 for good protein quality.

- Consumption of proportions of food groups indicated in the plate helps prevent macronutrient & micronutrient malnutrition (Hidden Hunger)
- The proportion indicated in the plate ensures adequate intake of all micronutrients (vitamins & minerals), bioactive compounds, functional foods, antioxidants etc.
- No vitamin or mineral (micronutrients) supplements will provide the adequacy of all nutrients that can be met from this model plate
- Routine consumption of certain nutrients as supplements will interfere with absorption of other nutrients
- Micronutrients from food are better absorbed and more bioavailable than vitamin and mineral supplements/tablets/capsules/fortification
- A complete diet as indicated in the model plate provides many unknown substances/ nutrients that cannot be met from supplements or fortified foods

Regular consumption of foods in proportions as per the model plate

- improves immunity and resistance to infections
  maintains good microbial flora (beneficial bacteria in the intestine)
- prevents Diabetes Mellitus, Cardiovascular Diseases (CVDs) such as heart attack, stroke and many other diseases
- maintains appropriate alkalinity and thereby reduces inflammation and decreases chances of kidney stone formation
- prevents insulin resistance and maintains appropriate insulin sensitivity and glycaemic index
- ensures adequate intake of fibre and therefore prevents constipation prevents adverse effects of environmental pollution and toxins such as heavy metals and pesticides by working as a detoxifying diet.
- 'My Plate for the day' represents proportions of different food groups for meeting —2000 Kcal
- Individuals trying to reduce weight may cut-down on cereal intake
- The meal plan is not for any specific medical condition

Note: All raw vegetables and fruits should be thoroughly washed before — cutting or peeling

3.7 FOOD ADULTERATION

Food is one of the basic necessities for sustenance of life. Pure, fresh and healthy diet is most essential for the health of the people. It is no wonder to say that community health is national wealth. Good food includes nutritionally balanced food free adulteration. An adulteration free diet makes us healthy and strong while nutritionally adequate diet but adulterated makes us unhealthy.

"Food adulteration is defined as the process by which the quality or the nature of a food substance is reduced through the addition of a foreign or an inferior substance and the removal of a vital element such as addition of water to milk and removal of fat from milk."

3.6.1 Types of Food Adulteration

Food adulteration is mainly two types:

1) **Intentional adulteration**: Intentional adulteration is a willful act on the part of adulterator intended to increase the margin of profit. It includes the intentional addition or substitution or obstruction of substance which adversely affect the nature, substance and quality of foods. *Examples*: Sand, Marble chips, Stones mud, Chalk power,

2) **Incidental adulteration**: It is usually due to ignorance, negligible or lack of proper facilities. It may take place at any time during growth, harvesting, storage, processing, transport or distribution of foods. *Example*: Pesticide residue, droppings of larvae in food, rodent .

3) **Metallic contaminants:** *Example*: Arsenic from pesticide and lead from water, effluent from chemical industries.

3.7.2 Definition as per Prevention of Food Adulteration Act, 1954

In this Act unless the context otherwise requires,—

(*i*) **"adulterant"** means any material which is or could be employed for the purposes of adulteration;

(*ia*) **"adulterated"**—an article of food shall be deemed to be adulterated—

a) if the article sold by a vendor is not of the nature, substance or quality demanded by the purchaser and is to his prejudice, or is not of the nature, substance or quality which it purports or is represented to be;

b) if the article contains any other substance which affects, or if the article is so processed as to affect, injuriously the nature, substance or quality thereof;

c) if any inferior or cheaper substance has been substituted wholly or in part for the article so as to affect injuriously the nature, substance or quality thereof;

d) if any constituent of the article has been wholly or in part abstracted so as to affect injuriously the nature, substance or quality thereof;

e) if the article had been prepared, packed or kept under insanitary conditions whereby it has become contaminated or injurious to health;

f) if the article consists wholly or in part of any filthy, putrid, rotten, decomposed or diseased animal or vegetable substance or is insect-infested or is otherwise unfit for human consumption;

g) if the article is obtained from a diseased animal;

h) if the article contains any poisonous or other ingredient which renders it injurious to health;

i) if the container of the article is composed, whether wholly or in part, of any poisonous or deleterious substance which renders its contents injurious to health;

j) if any colouring matter other than that prescribed in respect thereof is present in the article, or if the amounts of the prescribed colouring matter which is present in the article are not within the prescribed limits of variability;

k) if the article contains any prohibited preservative or permitted preservative in excess of the prescribed limits;

l) if the quality or purity of the article falls below the prescribed standard or its constituents are present in quantities not within the prescribed limits of variability, but which renders it injurious to health;

m) if the quality or purity of the article falls below the prescribed standard or its constituents are present in quantities not within the prescribed limits of variability but which does not render it injurious to health:

There is a greater need that consumer should be aware of the menace of food adulteration and their effect on health. For avoiding food adulteration consumer should have knowledge about detection of contamination or adulteration in Foods and Prevention of Food Adulteration Act (1954) and Consumer Protection Act (1986). Prevention of Food Adulteration (PFA) Act (1954) is setup by Government of India to prevent food adulteration and to maintain the health stadards of consumers.

3.7.3 Categories of Food Adulteration

Replacement: Complete or partial replacement of a food ingredient or valuable authentic constituent with less expensive substitute with the intention of circumventing on *"origin"* and false declaration of the *"process"*.

Addition: Addition of small amounts of non-authenticated substances to mask inferior quality ingredient.

Removal: Removal of authentic and valuable constituent without purchaser's knowledge.

3.7.4 Reasons of Food Adulteration

- When supply is less than demand
- To cut down the product costs to meet the market competition.
- To earn more profits.
- Shortage of authentic ingredients at affordable prices.
- Shortage of qualified personnel and no updation of processing techniques.
- Inadequate knowledge on the consequences and associated food safety risks.
- Lack of awareness and updation of the information on the adulteration related food safety outbreaks.
- Adulteration in general is done to increase the value of a commercial attribute / characteristic of the products.
- Sometimes Adulteration, even though not hazardous, may lead to severe contamination issues, *e.g.* spraying of water on dry
- Chilies to cope with the excess weight loss may lead to Aflatoxins.
- Blending is not Adulteration, unless origin of the product is significant.

Table 15: Common Adulterants in foods and their detrimental effects

S. No.	Name of adulterants	Foods commonly involved	Detrimental effects
1.	Sand, muds, marble chips, stone, soapstone bits and other filth	Cereals, pulses, spices and condiments, sugar and salts.	On the teeth and soft lining of the digestive tract.
2.	Talc, chalk powder	Wheat flour, semolina, split dehusked pulses, powdered spices, sugar and salts	They are indigestible and can impair normal digestion.
3.	Starch	Khoa, milk and milk powder, butter, turmeric powder, asafetida (hing)	When starch is pure, no harmful effects on health whereas starch coloured with toxic pigments like lead chromate, it is harmful.
4.	Ergots	Bajra seeds	No data available
5.	Black gram husk, tamarind and date powder, tea dust, artificial dye	Tea dust/tea leaves and coffee	No data available
6.	Resins, other plant gums	Asafetida (hing)	No data available
7.	Dried papaya seed, thick bark of'cassia	Black pepper, cinnamon	No data available
8.	Iron fillings	Semolina (suji), tea leaves	No data available
9.	Sugar	Honey	No data available
10.	Khesari dal	Small khesari dhal in red gram dhal, larger khesari dhal in pigeon pea dhal	Disease called lathyrism, crippling paralysis, mainly in boys and men in the age group of 5-45 years
11.	Argemone seeds (dhatura)	Mustard seed and rye	Epidemic drops, swelling of limbs, pitting odema.
12.	Argemone oil	Vegetable oils	Epidemic drops, loss of eye sight, nausea, vomiting, diarrhea, swelling of limbs, pitting odema
13.	Castor oil	Ground nut oil	Impairs digestive and absorptive functioning
14.	Linseed oil	Mustard oil	Gastric disturbances.
15.	Vanaspati ghee	Desi ghee, milk, butter, curd.	
16.	Mineral oil	Edible oil and black pepper	Results in loss of fat soluble vitamins, carcinogenesis.

17.	Water	Milk, fruits beverages	Harmful only if contaminated water is used and effect will be as per contaminants.
18.	Strips of jute or corn tassles	Saffron	
19.	Washing soda	Bura sugar	
20.	Colours– lead chromate, ultramarine blue, metanil yellow	Spices, turmeric powder, chilies powder, Bengal gram flour, tea, coffee, sweets, red gram dhal etc.	Anemia, abortion, paralysis, mental retardation. Some time affects brain. All dyes are toxic and intake in excess than permitted limit of 0.2 g of dye/ kg of the final food or beverage can lead to abnormalities which are teratogenic. It effects eye, bones, skin lungs and ovaries etc.
Food Additives			
21.	Sodium bicarbonate	milk	
22.	Stabilizers and emulsifiers	Ice-cream, creams.	
23.	Sachharin	Sweets and confectionary, soft drink.	Oncogenic
24.	Tin, mineral acid	Canned food, vinegar	Colic, vomiting, photophobia.

3.8 IMPORTANT CHEMICALS IN FOOD

Probiotics: Probiotics are live bacteria and yeasts that are good for us , especially our digestive system. Probiotics are often called "good" or "helpful" bacteria because they help keep your gut healthy. You can find probiotics in supplements and some foods, like yogurt. Doctors often suggest them to help with digestive problems

Some Indian Probiotic Foods;

- Yogurt. Yogurt, or curd (dahi), is one of the best available and natural probiotic foods that you can add to your daily diet.
- Kefir — Idli — Indian Cheese (Paneer)
- Fermented Soybean — Akhuni — Miso
- Green Peas — Kimchi.

Prebiotics are classified as the non-digestible food ingredients that probiotics can feed off. They are used in the gut to increase populations of healthy bacteria, aid digestion and enhance the production of valuable vitamins. Good bacteria play a significant role in regulating our immune system, inhibiting the growth of pathogens (disease causing bacteria) and digesting food. *Galactooligosaccharides* (GOS) are the most advanced form of prebiotics which belong to a group of particular nutrient fibres that feed and encourage the growth of good bacteria in the gut.

Phytochemicals

Phytochemicals are non-nutritive plant chemicals and one of the bioactive components that have protective or disease preventive properties. There are more than thousand known phytochemicals are produced by plants. It is well-known that plant produces these chemicals to protect itself but recent research demonstrates that they can protect humans against diseases. Some of the well known phytochemicals are lycopene in tomatoes, isoflavones in soy and flavanoids in fruits. They are not essential nutrients and are not required by the human body for sustaining life. There are many phytochemicals and each works differently. These are some possible actions:

- **Antioxidant:** Most phytochemicals have antioxidant activity and protect our cells against oxidative damage and reduce the risk of developing certain types of cancer. Phytochemicals with antioxidant activity: allylsulfides (onions, leeks, garlic), carotenoids (fruits, carrots), flavonoids (fruits, vegetables), polyphenols (tea, grapes).
- **Hormonal action:** Isoflavones, found in soy, imitate human estrogens and help to reduce menopausal symptoms and osteoporosis.
- **Stimulation of enzymes:** Indoles, which are found in cabbages, stimulate enzymes that make the estrogen less effective and could reduce the risk for breast cancer. Other phytochemicals, which interfere with enzymes, are protease inhibitors (soy and beans), terpenes (citrus fruits and cherries).
- **Interference with DNA replication:** Saponins found in beans interfere with the replication of cell DNA, thereby preventing the multiplication of cancer cells. Capsaicin, found in hot peppers, protects DNA from carcinogens.
- **Anti-bacterial effect:** The phytochemical allicin from garlic has anti-bacterial properties.
- **Physical action:** Some phytochemicals bind physically to cell walls thereby preventing the adhesion of pathogens to human cell walls. Proanthocyanidins are responsible for the anti-adhesion properties of cranberry. Consumption of cranberries will reduce the risk of urinary tract infections and will improve dental health.

Phyto-nutrients in food

Alkaloids: Alkaloids are naturally occurring chemical compounds containing basic nitrogen atoms. The name derives from the word alkaline and was used to describe any nitrogen-containing base. Alkaloids are produced by a large variety of organisms, including bacteria, fungi, plants, and animals and are part of the group of natural products (also called secondary metabolites). Many alkaloids can be purified from crude extracts by acid-base extraction. Many alkaloids are toxic to other organisms. They often have pharmacological effects and are used as medications and recreational drugs. Examples are the local anesthetic and stimulant cocaine, the stimulant caffeine, nicotine, the analgesic morphine, or the anti-malarial drug quinine. Some alkaloids have a bitter taste.

Terpenoid: The terpenoids sometimes called isoprenoids, are a large and diverse class of naturally-occurring organic chemicals similar to terpenes. Most are multicyclic structures that differ from one another not only in functional groups but also in their basic carbon skeletons. Plant terpenoids are used extensively for their aromatic qualities. They play a role in traditional herbal remedies and are under investigation for antibacterial, antineoplastic, and other pharmaceutical functions. Terpenoids contribute to the scent of eucalyptus, the flavors of cinnamon, cloves, and ginger, and the color of yellow flowers. Well-known terpenoids include citral, menthol, camphor, Salvinorin A in the plant Salvia divinorum, and the cannabinoids found in Cannabis. The steroids and sterols in animals are biologically produced from terpenoid precursors. Sometimes terpenoids are added to proteins, e.g., to enhance their attachment to the cell membrane; this is known as isoprenylation.

Phenols: Phenols sometimes called phenolics, are a class of chemical compounds consisting of a hydroxyl group (-OH) bonded directly to an aromatic hydrocarbon group. The simplest of the class is phenol (C6H5OH). Although similar to alcohols, phenols have unique properties and are not classified as alcohols (since the hydroxyl group is not bonded to a saturated carbon atom). They have relatively higher acidities due to the aromatic ring's tight coupling with the oxygen and a relatively loose bond between the oxygen and hydrogen. Some phenols are germicidal and are used in formulating disinfectants. Others possess estrogenic or endocrine disrupting activity.

Flavonoid pigment: Flavonoids or bioflavonoids are structurally derived from parent substance flavones. About ten classes of flavonoids are recognized. These are anthocyanins, leucoanthocyanidins, flavonols, flavones, glycoflavones, biflavonyls, chalcones, aurones, flavones and isoflavones. Flavonoids are mainly water soluble compounds and can be extracted with 70% ethanol and remain in aqueous layer during partition with petroleum ether. They usually bound to sugar as glycosides. Flavonoids are now considered as an indispensable component in a variety of nutraceutical, pharmaceutical, medicinal and cosmetic applications. Preventing the formation of free radicals is not the only beneficial effect of flavonids. These compounds exhibit a number of other health benefits. When supplied with food for the human body, the flavonoids exhibit high biological activity, display antioxidant, anti-inflammatory and antiallergic properties.

Indoles: Indoles are a phytochemical mix extracted from cruciferous vegetables, which include cabbage, broccoli, kale, turnips and bok choy and others. Cruciferous vegetables contain a variety of Indoles such as indole-3-carbinol, ascorbigen and others. Indole-3-carbinol assists in detoxifying human tissues, promotes hormonal balance, boosts immunity against diseases like cancer and provides excellent cellular nourishment.

Chlorophyll: Chlorophyll is the molecule that catches the biggest power source in our universe, viz the sun. Chlorophyll acts as a photo receptor creating the special chemical reaction in plants known as photosynthesis. Chlorophyll is found in the chloroplasts of green plants, and is what makes green plants, green. The basic structure of a chlorophyll molecule is a porphyrin, coordinated to a central atom. Chlorophyll has been well known for its anticancer effects for over 70 years now. It is widely known that eating a diet consisting of a large amount of greens can not only prevent many types of cancer but will also assist in detoxifying the body and increase immunity and energy levels.

Carotenoids: Carotenoids are organic pigments that are naturally occurring in chromoplasts of plants and some other photosynthetic organisms like algae, some types of fungus and some bacteria. There are over 600 known carotenoids reported; they are split into two classes, xanthophylls and carotenes. They absorb blue light. Carotenoids serve two key roles in plants and algae: they absorb light energy for use in photosynthesis, and they protect chlorophyll from photo damage. In humans, carotenoids such as beta-carotene are a precursor to vitamin A, a pigment essential for good vision, and carotenoids can also act as antioxidants.

Lycopene: Lycopene is a bright red carotenoid pigment and phytochemical found in tomatoes and other red fruits. Lycopene is not an essential nutrient for humans, but is commonly found in the diet, mainly from dishes prepared with tomato sauce. When absorbed from the stomach, lycopene is transported in the blood by various lipoproteins and accumulates in the liver, adrenal glands, and testes. Because preliminary research has shown an inverse correlation between consumption of tomatoes and cancer risk, lycopene has been considered a potential agent for prevention of some types of cancers, particularly prostate cancer. However, this area of research and the relationship with prostate cancer have been deemed insufficient of evidence for health claim approval by the US Food and Drug Administration.

Phytonutrients:	Found in:	Great for:
Allicin	Garlic, onions, jicama	Eliminating toxins from the body
Capsaicin	Cayenne peppers, red peppers	Preventing toxic molecules from invading cells; reducing inflammation
Carotenoids	Carrots, tomatoes, cantaloupe,.arugula, spinach, collard greens, kale, mustard greens, Swiss chard, turnip greens, broccoli, Brussels sprouts, sweet potatoes, butternut squash, pumpkin, red peppers	Removing damaging free radicals from the cells, slowing macular degeneration, preventing cataracts, repairing DNA and blocking carcinogens from entering cells
Catechins	Green and black teas	Inhibiting the activation of carcinogens
Ellagic Acid	Grapes, strawberries, blackberries, cranberries, walnuts	Preventing cancer
Genistein	Tofu, soymilk, soybeans	Inhibiting the formation of the blood vessels that help tumors grow
Indoles and Isothiscyanates	Collard greens, kale, broccoli, cauliflower, cabbage	Blocking carcinogens and interfering with the action of a precancerous form of estrogen
Isoflavones	Kudzu, soybeans, peas, peanuts, legumes	Modulating estrogen levels; preventing breast, uterine and prostate cancers; and reducing the risk of heart disease and osteoporosis
Lignans	Seeds and grains, especially flaxseed	Inhibiting excessive estrogen action, and possibly reducing breast, colon and ovarian cancer
Limonoids	Citrus fruit peels	Clearing congestive mucus from the lungs, detoxifying enzymes in the liver, and supporting detoxification of hormones and other substances that cause cellular decay
Lycopene	Tomatoes	Fighting heart disease and prostate cancer, plus reducing the risk of stomach, lunh and prostate cancers
Phenols	Black and red berries, celery, cabbage, grapes, eggplant, peaches, nectarines	Preventing cancer, blocking specific enzymes that cause autoimmune diseases, protecting against heart attacks and strokes, preventing platelets in the blood from clumping, reversing nerve-cell aging, and destroying hepatoxins, which damage the liver
Phytosterols	Pumpkin, rice, soybeans, yams, all green and yellow vegetables	Blocking "bad" cholesterol uptake, reducing inflammation and blocking the growth of tumors
Polyphenols	Buckwheat, wheat germ	Restoring a lagging immune system
Saponins	Alfalfa, legumes	Lowering cholesterol and inhibiting the growth of cancer cells by interfering with their DNA
Zeaxanthin	Kale, daikon, collard greens, green sorrel, arugula	Enhancing immune function and preventing several types of cancer

3.9 FOOD TYPES AND THEIR EFFECT

Many people seek out foods that provide the greatest health benefits. This trend is giving rise to the idea of **functional foods**, which not only help meet basic nutritional needs but also are reported to fight illness and aging. According to the Academy of Nutrition and Dietetics (AND), formerly known as The Academy of Nutrition and Dietetics, functional foods may reduce the risk of disease or promote optimal health. The AND recognizes four types of functional foods. They are: conventional foods, modified foods, medical foods, and special dietary use foods.

The first group, **conventional foods**, represents the simplest form of functional foods. They are whole foods that have not been modified. Examples include whole fruits and vegetables (which are abundant in phytochemicals and antioxidants), yogurt and kefir (which contain natural probiotic bacteria that can help maintain digestive system health), and dark chocolate (which contains antioxidants).

Modified foods have been fortified, enriched, or enhanced with additional nutrients or bioactive compounds. Foods are modified using biotechnology to improve their nutritional value and health attributes. Examples of modified foods include calcium-fortified orange juice, breads enriched with B vitamins, iodized salt, cereals fortified with vitamins and minerals, margarine enhanced with plant sterols, and energy drinks that have been enriched with herbs (ginseng or guarana) or amino acids (taurine). It is important to consider that the health claims of some modified foods may be debatable, or entirely fraudulent. Check with a health professional regarding the effects of modified foods on your health.

Medical foods are designed for enteric administration under the guidance of a medical professional. (During enteric administration, food is treated so that it goes through the stomach undigested. Instead, the food is broken down in the intestines only.) Medical foods are created to meet very specific nutritional requirements. Examples of medical foods include liquid formulas for people with kidney disease, liver disease, diabetes, or other health issues. Medical food is also given to comatose patients through a gastronomy tube because they cannot eat by mouth.

Special dietary use foods do not have to be administered under a doctor's care and can be found in a variety of stores. Similar to medical foods, they address special dietary needs and meet the nutritional requirements of certain health conditions. For example, a bottled oral supplement administered under medical supervision is a medical food, but it becomes a special dietary use food when it is sold to retail customers. Examples of special dietary use foods include gluten-free foods, lactose-free dairy products, and formulas and shakes that promote weight loss.

The Gluten-Free Diet helps people whose bodies cannot tolerate **gluten**, a protein found in wheat, barley, and rye. One of the most important ways to treat this condition is to avoid the problematic foods, which is not easy. Although following a gluten-free diet is challenging, it is prescribed for patients with gluten intolerance and celiac disease, an autoimmune disorder with a genetic link. People who have celiac disease cannot consume gluten products without damaging their intestinal lining. Eating a gluten-free diet means finding replacements for bread, cereal, pasta, and more. It also means emphasizing fresh fruits, vegetables, and other foods without gluten. However, it is important to note that the gluten-free trend has become something of a fad even for those without gluten intolerance. Celiac disease is a relatively rare condition found in only 1 percent of the population. Therefore, a gluten-free diet should be followed only with a physician's recommendation.

Low-Carb Diets which focus on limiting carbohydrates—such as grains, fruit, and starchy vegetables—to promote weight loss. The theory behind the low-carb diet is that insulin prevents the breakdown of fat by allowing sugar in the form of blood glucose to be used for energy. Proponents of this approach believe that because limiting carbs generally lowers insulin levels, it would then cause the body to burn stored fat instead. The benefits of this kind of diet include an emphasis on whole, unprocessed foods and a de-emphasis of refined carbohydrates, such as white flour, white bread, and white sugar.

The Raw Food Diet is followed by those who avoid cooking as much as possible in order to take advantage of the full nutrient content of foods. The principle behind **raw foodism** is that plant foods in their natural state are the most wholesome for the body. The raw food diet is not a weight-loss plan, it is a lifestyle choice. People who practice raw foodism eat only uncooked and non-processed foods, emphasizing whole fruits and vegetables. Staples of the raw food diet include whole grains, beans, dried fruits, seeds and nuts, seaweed, sprouts, and unprocessed produce.

Functional Foods and Nutraceuticals

The terms "functional foods" and "functional food ingredients/nutraceuticals" are applied broadly to foods and food constituents, respectively, that provide specific health or medical benefits, including the prevention and treatment of diseases, as well as nutritional value (the term nutraceuticals is synonymously used for functional food ingredients in several countries). Functional foods and nutraceuticals include food additives, vitamin and mineral supplements, herbs, phytochemicals, and probiotics. Nutraceuticals can be derived from plant, animal, and microbial sources, including those from the aquatic environment. Phytochemicals are chemical compounds produced by plants such as alkaloids, polyphenols, uncommon amino acids, and so on. Several of these compounds are non-nutritive, but effective in preventing or combating diseases. More than 900 different phytochemicals have been identified as components of different plants. The disease-preventing and disease-combating properties of phytochemicals have been investigated intensively, but further research is needed to enable mankind to benefit from the medicinal properties of as yet unknown plants.

Major Food categories and their functional components

S. No.	Category	Functional Components
1.	Cereals	Minerals, vitamin E and γ-oryzanol (rice bran), insoluble fibre (wheat bran), beta-glucan (oats)
2.	Legumes and pulses	Isoflavones and dietary fibre
3.	Oil	Omega-3 fatty acids (flax seed oil), γ-oryzanol (rice bran oil), oleuropein (olive oil)
4.	Fruits and vegetables	Dietary fibre, carotenoids (carrot), dithiolthiones (cruciferous vegetables), beta-carotene and lutein (green leafy vegetables), lycopene (tomato), resveratrol (grapes), sulphur compounds (alliums), wide range of polyphenols
5.	Fishes	Omega-3 fatty acids (Tuna, salmon, mackerel)
6.	Dairy products	Probiotics
7.	Spices and herbs	Curcuminoids (turmeric), piperine (pepper), Eugenol (clove, bail and cinnamon), gingerol and shogol (ginger), disogenin, 4-hydroxyisoleucine and galactomannan (fenugreek), flavonoids and diallyl sulphate, alliin, ajoene, and allicin (garlic), cinnamtannin B1 (cinnamon).

Source: K BHASKARACHARY, SUDERSHAN R VEMULA, SUBBA RAO M GAVARAVARAPU and APURVA KUMAR R JOSHI. (2016). Traditional Foods, Functional Foods and nutraceuticals. Proc Indian Natn Sci Acad 82 No. 5 December 2016 pp. 1565-1577.

Nutraceuticals

The term "nutraceutical" is combination of – "nutrient" (a nourishing food component) and "pharmaceutical" (a medical drug). The name was coined in 1989 by Stephen DeFelice, founder and chairman of the Foundation for Innovation in Medicine.

Nutraceuticals, as defined by Wildman (2000), are naturally occurring substances in foods that have been found to be effective in the prevention or treatment of one or more diseases, or the improvement of physiological performance, thereby enhancing human health. The term functional food ingredients has also been synonymously used for nutraceuticals. Essential nutrients can be considered as nutraceuticals required by the human body. Examples include vitamins C and E, which function as antioxidants. The most prominent nutraceuticals in the Western world have included plant fibers, beta-carotene, omega-3 (n-3 or w-3), and polyunsaturated fatty acids, polyphenols, and so on, and the number of known nutraceuticals has been increasing progressively.

Nutraceuticals is a broad term that is used to describe any product derived from food sources with extra health benefits in addition to the basic nutritional value found in foods. They can be considered as non-specific biological therapies used to promote general well-being, control symptoms and prevent malignant processes from human body.

Health Benefits of Nutraceuticals: Nutraceuticals have attracted considerable interest due to their potential nutritional, safety and therapeutic effects. They could have a role in a plethora of biological processes, including antioxidant defenses, cell proliferation, gene expression, and safeguarding of mitochondrial integrity. Nutraceuticals may be used to improve health, prevent chronic diseases, postpone the aging process (and in turn increase life expectancy), or just support functions and integrity of the body. They are considered to be healthy sources for prevention of life threatening diseases such as diabetes, renal and gastrointestinal disorders, as well as different infections.

A wide range of nutraceuticals have been shown to impose crucial roles in immune status and susceptibility to certain disease states. They also exhibit diseases modifying indications related to oxidative stress including allergy, Alzheimer's disease, cardiovascular diseases, cancer, eye conditions, Parkinson's diseases and obesity.

Summary of mechanisms and biological effects of important nutraceuticals

S. No.	Nutraceutical	Mechansims/Biological Effects
1	Omeg3 fatty acids	Anti-inflammatory action, activation of PPARá and PPARã, interaction with G-Protein coupled receptors, and influence on membrane phospholipid content and fluidity. Neuroprotection, improvements in cardiovascular health, improvement of insulin sensitivity
2	Curcumin	Activation of AMP-activated protein kinase, inhibition of protein-tyrosine phosphatase 1B, activation of nrf2 pathway, anti-cancer, anti-oxidant, anti-diabetic, and anti-inflammatory activities and neuro-protective properties
3	Resveratrol	Activation of AMP-activated protein kinase, prevention of LDL oxidation, Anti-oxidant activity, anti- cancer attributes, cardio-protective effects, and anti-diabetic effects

4	Quercetin	Free radical scavenger, nrf2 activation, Anti-oxidant, topoisomerase inhibition, anti-cancer, cardio-protectant, anti-inflammatory and antidiabetic effects, modulation of drug metabolizing enzymes. Known to promote bone health.
5	Eugenol	Anti-mutagenic, anti-cancer, anti-fungal, anti-viral, anti-bacterial, anti-parasitic, anti-inflammatory, and anti-diabetic effects
6	Piperine	Anti-oxidant, anti-mutagenic, anti-cancer and anti-depressant effects. Best known for enhancing bio-availability of drugs and nutraceuticals via inhibiting p-glycoprotein mediated efflux.

Source: K BHASKARACHARY, SUDERSHAN R VEMULA, SUBBA RAO M GAVARAVARAPU and APURVA KUMAR R JOSHI. (2016). Traditional Foods, Functional Foods and nutraceuticals. Proc Indian Natn Sci Acad 82 No. 5 December 2016 pp. 1565-1577.

Junk Foods and its drawbacks for health

Unfortunately, today's world has been adapted to a system of consumption of foods which has several adverse effects on health. Lifestyle changes has compelled us so much that one has so little time to really think what we are eating is right! Globalization and urbanization have greatly affected one's eating habits and forced many people to consume fancy and high calorie fast foods, popularly known as 'Junk foods'. Research into the possible health hazards on consumption of such high calorie foods has given an insight to avoid them, but unfortunately measures taken are not as effective as they need to be. Diseases like coronary artery disease and diabetes mellitus have seen a profound rise in developing countries and such unhealthy junk food consumption is one of the notable factors to its contribution. This global problem of consuming junk food on a large scale and its impact on health needs emphasis and health education which can greatly contribute to its limited consumption and switching over to healthy eating habits for the better living. Knowledge highlighting about the eating habits, nutritional aspects, and quality of unhealthy foods, their health impact and preventive measures should be given to create awareness and render health education for a change towards good eating practices. Junk food and its impact on health have been reviewed from various resources and have been systematically presented, so as to emphasize its ill effects and measures to be adapted towards healthy living.

Junk food simply means an empty calorie food. An empty calorie food is a high calorie or calorie rich food which lacks in micronutrients such as vitamins, minerals, or amino acids, and fiber but has high energy (calories). These foods don't contain the nutrients that your body needs to stay healthy. Hence, these foods that has poor nutritional value is considered unhealthy and may be called as junk food. Junk food' is an informal term applied to some foods which are perceived to have little or no nutritional value, but which also have ingredients considered unhealthy when eaten regularly, or to those considered unhealthy to consume at all. *The term 'junk food" was coined as a slang in the public interest in 1972 by Michael Jacobson, Director of the Center for Science, Washington D.C.*

Health impact of junk foods Junk food allows people to eat without planning eats not only when it is pre-set meal time, but also when they have spare time. Ingredients of junk foods give great taste and make them addictive. Fat and sugar in combination are capable of producing a dopamine-driven surge of intense pleasure in people with a propensity for addictive behaviour. On the other side, it must be noted that they are hazardous to health too. High fat content, particularly cholesterol, sugar and salts have their adverse effects on health. Soaring calorie content with sugar can lead to obesity. Dense sugar content can cause dental cavities and type 2 diabetes mellitus. A short-term adverse effect as a result of eating junk foods 'lack of energy which occurs because junk foods don't provide essential nutrients, even though they can be very much sufficing, due to which one feels weakened. Unfortunately, meals consisting of junk food don't fill up for long. Because they are lacking in fibre, and are made of processed foods, they are rated high on the glycaemic index, which means they provide a quick rise in blood sugar, but this also falls quickly, and giving rise to hunger. Cholesterol and salt are known to set off blood pressure, stroke and heart diseases in a chain. Excessive salts can affect functioning of kidneys too. Excess fats and oils along with spices added in these foods act as an irritant to gastric mucosa leading to excess secretion of hydrochloric acid, landing in gastritis. Poor concentration is another result of junk food habit known to affect in immediate and medium term periods. When a sumptuous junk meal rich in oil is taken, there is a feeling of drowsiness and failure to concentrate. The junk food eating over a l period of time can drop blood circulation due to fat accumulation. Lack of vital oxygen, nutrients and proteins particularly can stale the grey (brain) cells temporarily. Most of the times these junk foods contain colours, which are often inedible, carcinogenic and harmful to the body. Flavourings and colourings can be allergic causing asthma, rashes and hyperactivity.

Junk foods Effects on children's health

Children find themselves amidst a complex society that is undergoing breaths taking changes. Wafers, chips, colas, pizzas and burgers are suddenly the most attractive food items among children. Children rapidly seem to have stepped into a world of fast foods and vending machines, totally unaware of the havoc they are creating for themselves and their impact on their health. Good nutrition is of utmost priority in children at the time of steady growth between the ages of 6 12 years. In a study done in Beijing, China and published in the year 2008 revealed eating junk food is a popular event among children and adolescents between the age of 8 and 16. Eating habits in such age group not only has an impact on their growth but also on their concentration, feeling and behaviour. With vast majority of women with school children are working class which has led to leaving behind the traditional foods at home and offering of fast foods by parents to their children. The commonest scenario noticed in most homes is a child who returns from school hangs himself in front of the television, faithfully accompanied by a bowl of wafers, a packet of chips and a can of cola. Such nutritionally weak foods become quickly addictive and can sow the seeds of infirmity and debilitating disease, which ultimately leads to many an incurable disease. Studies reveal:

- Beginning of clogging of arteries as early as at the age of 30
- Risks of prostate and breast cancer linked to their eating habits at puberty
- Setting of hypertension and osteoporosis at an early age
- Vulnerability to slow growth, tooth decay and obesity.

Priobiotic dairy foods

LAB can be used in the milk to enhance nutritive quality and can be consumed safely by all ages. Dairy and dairy products are the most common food products among the probiotic foods. Among the probiotic dairy foods are cultured butter milk, and fermented milk products and many more. Mesophilic LAB such as *Lactoccus lactis* and *Leuconstoc cremoris* strains are fermented at

30°C for 16-20 hrs. Starter cultures other than mesophilic culture such as *Lactobacilli* are also utilized in milk products to enhance nutritional quality of products. Kefir is a traditional fermented milk product containing *Lactoccus, Leuconostoc, Lactobaccilus, Acetobacter* and yeasts. These also provide a special flavor and aroma. Yogurts are prepared by fermenting *Streptococcus thermophilus* and *Lactobacillus delbruekii* sub sp *bulgaricus* growing in synergy, the temperature of fermentation is in the range of 30-43 °C and fermentation time is kept for 20 hrs.

Strain selection is specific and so is the fermentation time which imparts a specific flavor to the product. Whey is separated after milk coagulates during fermentation using different starter cultures. Depending on the live starter culture the process of production varies. Probiotic fermented milk contain live microorganisms. After fermentation if the milk is pasteurized they may be killed. At present fermented milk and yogurt are consumed in large amounts world wide.

Some Indian Probiotic Foods

Some Indian food preparations which are a part of the regular diet already contain probiotics and can be added to your diet as required. Most of these dishes are fermented, and hence, have live bacteria or yeast naturally in them. A few examples of these preparations and their probiotics benefits are mentioned below.

Dahi: Enjoy a bowl of the good old dahi or drink chaas/ lassi with your meals. Prepared by mixing starter cultures containing strains of *lactobacillus* in milk, curd contains live active cultures that are extremely beneficial for one's digestive system. But experts say it is best to stick to the homemade version and let it ferment for a full 24 hours so that majority of the lactose (milk sugar) is used up and the strength of the probiotic culture has been established. Commercial versions are often made using chemical agents and not fermented long enough.

Idlis and dosa: These South Indian staples are prepared by fermenting rice and urad daal, which makes them a rich source of live cultures of good bacteria. Plus, they are low in calories too.

Kaanji: This traditional Punjabi drink made with black carrots, mustard seeds, sea salt and water is left to ferment for up to a week leading to the growth of bacteria. But drink in moderation to avoid excess salt intake.

Achaar: Most people avoid pickle considering it a big bad lump of oil and salt. But the process of making this tasty concoction – vegetables and fruits mixed with sugar, salt, herbs and oil are allowed to ferment under the sun – favours the growth of good bacteria. Store-bought pickles often lack the natural enzymes so relish the one your grandma makes.

Dhokla: The dish is made using a batter of fermented besan (gram flour), daal or rice. Plus, the recipes use curd which adds an additional shot of probiotics.

Rajasthani Dahi or Chach Ki Rabdi

Rajasthani Dahi or Chach ki Rabdi is a regular serve in every house hold of the rural areas of Rajasthan. Rabdi is a beverage that is made by using Dahi (curd) or Chach (Buttermilk) and Bajra or Barley flour. After mixing of bajra or barley flour in butter milk it is fermented under sun in earthen pot for minimum 5-6 hrs.

Health Benefits of Rajasthani Dahi or Chach Ki Rabdi

1. It has a cooling effect on the Digestive Tract.

2. Presence of Buttermilk or Dahi provides Calcium without Fats.
3. Helps in wash down Oily Food.
4. It encourages Digestion.
5. It helps in boosting the Immune System.
6. Bajra is high in fibre, so it takes long time to move from Stomach to intestine, so it curbs hunger for long time and thus helps in weight reduction.

Some other probiotic foods

Tempeh is a fermented soybean product. It forms a firm patty whose flavor is described as nutty, earthy or similar to a mushroom.

Tempeh is originally from Indonesia but has become popular worldwide as a high-protein meat substitute.

Kimchi Kimchi is a fermented, spicy Korean side dish

Cabbage is usually the main ingredient, but it can also be made from other vegetables.Kimchi is flavored with a mix of seasonings, such as red chili pepper flakes, garlic, ginger, scallion and salt. Kimchi contains the lactic acid bacteria *Lactobacillus kimchii*, as well as other lactic acid bacteria that may benefit digestive health. Kimchi made from cabbage is high in some vitamins and minerals, including vitamin K, riboflavin (vitamin B_2) and iron

Brined Cucumbers

The process is favored by the introduction of starter cultures with the control of undesirable microbial activity. Brining treatments, environmental conditions, and initial microbial populations are the primary factors that decide the course of microbial activity. The fermentation is mainly by homofermentative LAB.

Probiotic Fermented Dairy Beverages

These are prepared mixing with the fruits such as strawberry, mango, banana and sapota. This mixed beverage on evaluation showed a reduction in the levels of pathogenic microorganisms. Fortification of products with ascorbic acid, amylase or inulin had shown significant growth and higher viability of probiotic cultures.

Now in India also awareness and demand can been seen for probiotic dairy beverages and many companies have started manufacturing them.

Yankut Danone- India has launched YAKULT

Nestle India- has launched low fat NEVITA dahi

(*L. acidophilus* and *B. Lactis* stain Bb12)

Mother dairy- has introduced a probiotic curd with dietary fiber "b-Active plus" and Nutrifit

Amul- has launched prbiotic lassi and ice cream. ("Profile" and "Amul sugar free")

Cereal Based Probiotic Fermented Beverages

Mineral value and fiber in milk can be increased with addition of cereals with high fiber content like, sorghum, millets and ragi. Fermentation with probiotic enhances not only the nutritive value but also palatability and functionality of cereals and antinutritional factors are also reduced.

Organic foods

Organic foods are made without Synthetic pesticides, Genetic modification, or fertilizers without any synthetic component. Genetic modification means that there is the "production of heritable improvements in plants or animals for specific uses, like genetic engineering". Organic foods must also not contain any type of antibiotic or growth hormone. The Organic Foods Production Act (1990) was designed to do three things:

- Create standards that would regulate the marketing of organically made foods and products;
- Give consumers a guarantee that the products labeled organic were in fact organic;
- To make possible the interstate exchanges in foods that are organic.

These foods can be both fresh and processed. The USDA does not require that organic foods be labeled as such or display the percentage of organic ingredients that they contain. According to FAO (2008), Food security exists when all the people have physical and economic access to sufficient, safe and nutritious food that meets their dietary needs and food preferences for an active and healthy life. For realizing the food security objective, all four dimensions like

- Physical Availability of food,
- Economic and Physical Access to food,
- Food Utilization.
- Stability and sustainability of the former three dimensions over time needed.

Sustainable food system built on principles that further the ecological, social, and economic values of a community and region. It is a phenomenon which emphasizes on Environmental Health, Economic Vitality, and Human Health & Social Equity.

3.10 FOOD FORTIFICATION AND MODIFICATION

Food fortification aims at bridging the gap between dietary intake and nutrient requirement without any dietary modification by fortifying commonly consumed food stuff with appropriate amount of nutrients. Food fortification is the preferred public health intervention to combat nutrient deficiencies due to low nutrient intake in large segments of the population, high prevalence of micro-nutrient deficiency and well documented adverse health consequences of such deficiency. Appropriate technologies have to be developed for fortifying the chosen food stuff with chosen micro-nutrients and the product has to be tested to assess safety, efficacy and acceptability. This has to be followed up with research studies to document the benefits of the usage of these fortified food stuffs. Once products with proven benefit are identified, production has to be scaled up and the fortified food has to be supplied through appropriate programmes. All public health food fortification programmes should be monitored using process and impact indicators.

Micro-nutrient deficiencies are major public health problems that affect all segments of the population both in developed and developing countries. A third of the global population and majority of Indians suffer from micro-nutrient deficiencies. Six decades ago India had recognized that iodine deficiency resulting in cretinism and goitre, Vitamin A deficiency leading to blindness in young children and iron and folic acid deficiency resulting in anaemia with adverse health consequences to the mother child dyad were major public health problems. The country embarked on intervention programmes to combat these deficiencies through dietary diversification, micro-nutrient supplementation and food fortification.

Types of Food Fortification: Food fortification is "the practice of deliberately increasing the content of an essential micro-nutrient (vitamins or minerals) in a food stuff so as to improve the nutritional quality of the food supply and to provide a public health benefit with minimal risk to health" (WHO 2006). The terms 'food enrichment' and 'replacement fortification' refer to the addition of micro-nutrients which are lost during processing of a food *e.g.*, vitamin A from milk during preparation of low-fat milk. There are three major categories of food fortification: (*a*) fortification as a public health intervention to bridge the gap in nutrient intake across population groups; (*b*) targeted food fortification aimed at bridging the nutrient gaps in specific "at risk" population groups with nutrient deficiencies and (*c*) market driven fortification aimed at increasing product appeal without nutritional rationale.

Fortification of Cereals with Iron, Folic Acid and Vitamin B12: Fortification of cereals (rice and atta) with iron, folic acid and vitamin B12 has been advocated for combating anaemia. The FSSAI has notified the standards for rice and "atta" fortification with iron folic acid and vitamin B12. Voluntarily fortification of rice and wheat flour ("atta") with iron, folic acid and vitamin B12 is being taken up. Large-scale studies are currently underway to explore feasibility and the impact of using rice and "atta" fortified with iron, folic acid and vitamin B12. The Department of Women and Child Development has sent a communication to the state governments requesting them to use fortified "atta" for the hot cooked meal in MDM and ICDS programmes.

Fortification of Wheat Flour with Folic Acid for Prevention of Neural Tube Defects: It has been well documented that genetic polymorphisms affecting folate metabolism in the mother is associated with an increased risk of neural tube defects (NTD). Medical Research Council, UK, carried out a study on the effectiveness of periconceptional folic acid supplementation for prevention of the recurrence of NTD in the subsequent pregnancy. This study showed that there was a 79% reduction in the recurrence of NTD in subsequent pregnancy following administration of high doses of folic acid (4 mg daily (MRC 1991). Subsequent studies have confirmed that folic acid supplementation does reduce NTD. Based on these findings, many countries initiated peri-conceptional folic acid supplementation especially in women with previous history of NTD. But compliance with peri-conceptional folic acid supplementation was low. In an effort to substantially reduce NTDs in the country, USA initiated mandatory fortification of wheat flour with folic acid. This resulted in a 19 to 32% reduction in the incidence of NTD in USA.

Fortification of Milk and Oil with Vitamins A and D: Diet surveys carried out by NNMB have shown that the intake of Vitamin A is significantly lower than the RDA in young children, adolescent girls and pregnant women in India. Over the last three decades there has been a decline in clinical vitamin A deficiency in under-five children in the country but the biochemical deficiency of vitamin A continues to be common especially in children. Vitamin D is manufactured in skin exposed to sun light. India is a sun drenched country; but plasma vitamin D assays have shown that majority of Indians across all states, and all age, sex and economic groups have blood vitamin D levels indicative of deficiency. Fortification of edible oils and milk with vitamins A and D is a simple, easy and inexpensive process. The FSSAI has notified the standards for fortifying vegetable oils with vitamins A and D. Voluntary fortification of edible oil is being taken up by some manufacturers. Feasibility, sustainability and efficacy of fortifying oil and milk with vitamins A and D is being explored. White revolution has resulted in India becoming the number 1 milk producer in the world. Average milk production is 300 ml/per capita and this is projected to increase to 350 ml/day by 2020. About 20% of milk is processed in organized sector. The standards for fortification of milk with vitamins A and D have been notified by the FSSAI. Some of the large scale milk producers have voluntarily started fortification of toned, double-toned and skimmed milk with these vitamins.

Multiple Micro-nutrient Fortification: It is well documented that the diets of poorer segments of our population might be deficient in many micronutrients and several micro-nutrient deficiencies coexist in vulnerable segments of the population. In view of this, there have been efforts to fortify a variety of food stuffs with multiple micro-nutrients. In addition, micro-nutrient powders which could be added to home food prior to consumption have also been investigated. A systematic review of these studies suggests that, though there may be some improvement in individual nutrient levels as shown by biochemical parameters after several months of consumption of fortified foods, such fortification may not reduce multiple micro-nutrient deficiencies, and there were no substantial health benefits. In segments of the population who have adequate intake of one or more nutrients from food, the consumption of multiple food stuffs fortified with multiple nutrients, may result in a higher than required intake of some nutrients. Excessive intake of nutrients or imbalance of intake between nutrients due to multiple micro-nutrient fortification of multiple food stuffs may have adverse health consequences.

Food fortification does represent a sustainable method of increasing the population's intake for selected micro-nutrients. However, fortification of multiple food stuff with multiple micro-nutrients is not advisable because of the potential adverse health consequences of excessive intake of some micronutrients and/or imbalance of intake of inter-related micro-nutrients by segments of the population who are already consuming one or more of these nutrients in sufficient amount in their daily diets.

CHAPTER 4

FOOD PROCESSING

Introduction

Food science is the discipline in which engineering, biological and physical science are used to study the nature of foods, causes of deterioration, the underlying principle and the improvements of food for the consuming publics. It helps us to understand the principles and/or mechanism involved in changes occurring during preparation of curd and the reason behind the shelf life of pickles i.e. why do not pickles spoil for years together even at room temperature?., etc.,

Food technology is the application of food science to the selection, preservation, processing, packaging, and distribution and use of safe, nutritious and wholesome food

Food processing is any conscious unit operation resulting in minor or major alterations in the natural shape, size, form, sensory and chemical characteristics of natural produce and that adds value in terms of preservation quality of the produce and convenience of its use.

Before we discuss food processing letus first get introduced to various crops/grains.

4.1 MAJOR CROPS OF INDIA

If we consider the varieties of crop grown from Kashmir to Kanyakumari and western coast of Gujarat to extreme north eastern states of Arunachal Pradesh, there would be hundreds of crops. We group all these crops into four broad types.

Table 1: Let us discuss the main crops under each type in detail

S. No.	Types of	Meaning	Major Crops
1.	Food grains	Crops that are used for human consumption	Rice, Wheat, Maize, Millets, Pulses and Oil seeds etc.
2.	Commercial Crops	Crops which are grown for sale either in raw form or in semi-processed form	Cotton, Jute, Sugarcane, Tobacco and Oilseeds
3.	Plantation Crops	Crops which are grown on Plantations covering large estates	Tea, Coffee, Coconut and Rubber
4.	Horticulture Crops	Sections of agriculture in which Fruits and Vegetables are grown	Fruits and Vegetables

4.1.1. Food Grains

(*i*) **Rice:** Rice is the most important food crop of India. It is predominantly a Kharif or summer crop. It covers about one third of total cultivated area of the country and provides food to more than half of the Indian population. Maximum population of India is of rice consumers. Rice requires hot and humid conditions. The temperature should be fairly high *i.e.* 24°C mean monthly temperature with average temperature of 22°C to 32°C. Rainfall ranging between 150-300 cm is suitable for its growth in areas of Punjab, Haryana and Western Uttar Pradesh where rainfall is less than 100 cm, rice is cultivated with the help of irrigation. Rice is grown in varied soil conditions but deep clayey and loamy soil provides the ideal conditions.

(ii) **Wheat:** Wheat is the second most important staple food crop of India next to rice. It is a Rabi or winter crop. Normally (in north India) the sowing of wheat begins in the month of October-November and harvesting is done in the month of March-April. This is the staple food of millions of people particularly in the northern and north-western regions of India. Unlike rice, wheat is grown mostly as a rabi or winter crop. The ideal temperature is between 10°C to 15°C at the time of sowing and 21°C to 26°C at the time of ripening and harvesting for wheat crop. Wheat thrives well in areas receiving annual rainfall of about 75cm. Annual rainfall of about 100cm is the upper limit for wheat cultivation. Although wheat can be grown in a variety of soils but well drained fertile loamy and clayey loamy soil is best suited for wheat cultivation. The main regions of wheat production in India are U.P., Punjab, Haryana, Rajasthan, Madhya Pradesh, Gujrat, and Maharashtra. U.P., Punjab and Haryana together produce more than 66% of the total wheat of the country.

(iii) **Millets:** Millets are short duration warm weather crops. These are coarse grain crops and are used for both food and fodder. These are kharif crop. These are sown in May-August and harvested in October-November. Today millets are mostly consumed by poor people as their staple food. In India, lots of millet is grown and these are known by various local names. Some of these are *Jawar, Bajra, Ragi, Korra, Kodon, Kutki, Hraka, Bauti, Rajgira.* In India, *Jawar, Bajra and Ragi* are grown.on large areas. But unfortunately area under these crops has drastically reduced over the years. These crops are grown where the temperature is high which ranges between 27°C to 32°C. Therefore, rainfall ranging from 50 to 100cm is ideal for their cultivation. They can be grown in inferior alluvial or loamy soil.*Jawar, Bajra,* is grown both in north and south India whereas *ragi* is generally concentrated in the southern India. *Jawar, Bajra,* is grown in Madhya Pradesh, Gujrat, Rajasthan, Maharastra, Karnataka, Tamil Nadu, Andhra Pradesh, Haryana and Punjab. *Ragi* is generally concentrated in the southern India *i.e.* Tamilnadu, Karnataka and Andhra Pradesh. Recent millets are considered very important.

(iv) **Pulses:** It includes a number of crops which are mostly leguminous and provide invaluable proteins to the vegetarian population of India. As they have fewer sources of proteins in comparison to those who consume meat and fish. They also serve as excellent forage and grain concentrates in the cattle feed. Apart from that these leguminous crops have the capacity to fix atmospheric nitrogen in the soil and are normally rotated with other crops to maintain and restore soil fertility. A large variety of pulses are found in India. These are gram, *tur or arhar* (Pigeon Pea or Red Gram), *urd* (black gram), *mung* (green gram), *masur* (lentil), *kulthi* (horse gram), *matar* (peas) etc. But among these gram and *tur or arhar* are more important pulses. Gram is the most important of all the pulses. It accounts for about 37% of the production and about 30% of the total area of pulses in India. It is a *rabi* crop which is sown between September and November and is harvested between February and April. It is either cultivated as a single crop or mixed with wheat, barley, linseed or mustard. Mild cool and comparatively dry climate with 20°C-25°C temperature and 40-45 cm rainfall is suitable for its cultivation on loamy soils. Although gram is cultivated in several parts of the country, however, 90% of the total production comes from five states. These states are Madhya Pradesh, Uttar Pradesh, Rajasthan, Haryana and Maharashtra.

4.1.2. Commercial Crops

Commercial crops are those crops which are grown for sale either in raw form or semi processed form. In this section we will learn more about selected cash crop *i.e.* sugarcane, cotton and jute; two beverages- tea and coffee; three oil seeds *i.e.* groundnut, mustard and rapeseed.

(*i*) **Sugarcane:** It is a *Kharif* crop used for sugar, gur and khandsari. It also provides raw material for the manufacturing of alcohol. Bagasse, the crushed cane residue, has also multiple uses. It is used for manufacturing of paper. It is also an efficient substitute for petroleum products and a host of other chemical products. A part of it is also used as fodder. It requires deep rich loamy soil, hot and humid climate with an average temperature of 21°C to 27°C and 75-150 cm rainfall. India has the largest area under sugarcane cultivation in the world and the second largest producer next to Brazil. As far as distribution of sugarcane cultivation in India is concerned, there are three distinct geographical regions in the country. These regions are: (*i*) The Satluj-Ganga plain from Punjab to Bihar containing 51% of the total area and 60% of the country's total production. (*ii*) The black soil belt from Maharashtra to Tamil Nadu along the eastern slopes of the western Gahats, and (*iii*) Coastal Andhra Pradesh and Krishna river valley.

(*ii*) **Cotton:** Cotton is the most important fibre crop not only of India but also of the entire world. It not only provides a raw material for cotton textile industry but also its seed is used in Vanaspati oil industry. The cotton seed is also used as part of fodder for milch cattle for better milk production. Cotton is basically a kharif crop and grown in tropical and sub-tropical areas. It requires uniformly high temperature varying between 21°C and 30°C, at least 210 frost free days as well as rainfall of 50 to 100cm and well grow in black soils. India has the largest area under cultivation and third largest producer of cotton next only to China and the USA. Within the country two third of total area and production is shared by four states. The main states for cotton production are Punjab, Maharashtra, Gujarat and Haryana.

(*iii*) **Oilseeds:** It is one of the important groups of commercial crops in India. In fact, India has the largest area and production of oilseeds in the world. Oil extracted from oilseeds not only forms an important item of our diet but also serves as raw material for the manufacturing of hydrogenated oils, paints, varnishes, soaps, lubricants etc. Oil-cake (the residue after the oil is extracted from the oilseeds) forms an important cattle feed and manure. **Groundnut** is the most important oilseed of India. Groundnut is grown both as kharif and rabi crop but 90-95% of the total area is devoted to kharif crop. It requires 20°C to 30°C temperature and 50-75 cm rainfall. Well drained light sandy loams, red, yellow and black soils are well suited for its cultivation. It is the most important oilseed of India and accounts for about half of the major oilseeds produced in the country. India is the largest producer of groundnut in the world and accounts for about one third of the world's to the production. Andhra Pradesh, Tamil Nadu and Gujarat are three main producer of groundnut in India and account for about 60% of the total production. Another 30% of the total production comes from Maharashtra, Karnataka and Odisha.

4.1.3. Plantation Crops

(*i*) **Tea**: India is famous for its tea gardens. You must have heard about tea gardens of Assam and Darjeeling in West Bengal. It is being said that tea plantation in India was started by the Britishers in 1923 when wild tea plants were discovered by them in the hilly and forest areas of Assam. Tea is made from tender sprouts of tea plants by drying them. At present, India is the leading tea producing country in the world. China and Sri Lanka are respectively second and third largest producers of tea. The ideal temperature for the growth of tea bushes and leaf varies between 20°C to 30°C and rainfall ranging between 150-300 cm. Tea bush grows well in well drained, deep, friable loamy soil. Assam is the leading producer that accounts for more than 50% of tea production of India. Tea producing areas of Assam are the hill slopes bordering the Brahmaputra and Surma valleys. West Bengal is the second largest producer of tea where tea is mostly grown in the districts of Darjeeling, Siliguri, Jalpaiguri and Cooch Bihar districts. Tamil Nadu is the third largest producer where tea growing areas are mostly restricted to Nilgiri hills.

(ii) **Coffee:** It is the indigenous crop of Ethiopia (Abysinia Plateau). From Ethiopia, it was taken to Yemen in 11th Century. From Arabia, the seeds were brought by Baba Budan in 17th Century and were raised in Baba Budan hills of Karnataka. But it was British planters who took keen interest and large coffee estates were established in the hills of Western Ghats. It requires hot and humid climate with temperature varying between 15°C and 28°C and Rainfall between 150 to 250 cm and well drained, rich friable loamy soil containing good deal of humus and minerals like iron and calcium are ideal for coffee cultivation. Karnataka, Kerala and Tamil Nadu are the main states of coffee production in India.

4.1.4. Horticultural Crops

A large variety of fruits are grown in India. Of these mango, banana, citrus, pineapple, papaya, guava, sapota, jackfruit, litchi and grape among the tropical and sub – tropical fruits; apple, pear, peach, plum, apricot, almond and walnut among the temperate fruits and anola, ber, pomegranate, annona, fig, phalsa among the arid zone fruits are important. India accounts for about 10 per cent of the production of fruits in the world. It leads the world in the production of mango, banana, sapota and acid lime and has recorded highest productivity in grape.

More than 40 kinds of vegetables belonging to different groups, namely, solanaceous, cucurbitaceous, leguminous, cruciferous (cole crops), root crops and leafy vegetables are grown in India in tropical, sub – tropical and temperate regions.

Important vegetable crops grown in the country are tomato, onion, brinjal, cabbage, cauliflower, okra and peas. India is next only to China in area and production of vegetables.

India contributes about 13 per cent to the world vegetable production and occupies first position in the production of cauliflower, second in onion and third in cabbage in the world.

Spices constitute an important group of horticulture crops. India is known as the home of spices and produces a wide variety of spices like black pepper, cardamom (small and large), ginger, garlic, turmeric, chilly and a large variety of tree and seed spices.

Among various spices grown in the country, chilly is the most widely grown spice with a share in the total production of 33.7 per cent. The demand for chilly as a spice and its oleoresins as a natural colouring material is growing in the domestic as well as international market. Turmeric has a share of 21.6 per cent in the total production of spices.

Though flower cultivation has been practiced in India since time immemorial, floriculture has blossomed into a viable business only in recent years. Considering the potential this sector has in generating income and employment opportunities, promoting greater involvement of women and enhancement of exports, it has been identified as an Extreme Focus Area for exports by the Government.

India is known for growing traditional flowers such as jasmine, marigold, chrysanthemum, tuberose, crossandra and aster. Commercial cultivation of cut flowers such as rose, orchids, gladiolus, carnation, anthurium, gerbera and lilies has also become popular.

4.1.5 Classification of Food Based on Perishability

Some food items deteriorate/spoil easily as compared to others and need to be consumed in a day or two after the purchase. While others can be kept for a longer time without being spoilt. In fact, on the basis of the quickness with which a food item gets spoilt, we can place them into three categories:

i) Perishable foods ii) Semi-perishable foods iii) Non-perishable foods.

Perishable foods: These are foods which spoil easily unless special methods are used to prevent such spoilage. All animal foods like meat, fish, poultry , eggs, milk and milk products and most vegetables and fruits come in this category. The speed with which some of these spoil varies with the temperature, moisture and/or dryness of the environment; for example while in the cold season milk can remain at room temperature for a whole day without spoiling, in the hot season it would not last more than 3 to 4 hours. Fresh eggs, meats and fish spoil very fast in the hot weather unless refrigerated. As for vegetables and fruits. They spoil faster as the day progresses. Fresh coriander, lettuce and spinach plucked from the garden wilt within a matter of minutes unless stored adequately.

Semi-perishable foods: These are foods that can survive without any perceptible signs of spoilage for a couple of weeks or for a few months. Here again, the temperature and humidity of the environment makes a big difference. Example of this category are all cereal and pulse products like wheat flour; refined wheat flour, semolina, vermicelli, broken wheat, Bengal gram flour, onions, potatoes, garlic, apples, citrus fruits, fats and oils. If properly handled and stored these will remain unspoiled for a fairly long - period. In the cold climate like in most of the western countries these food items are considered non-perishable, but during the hot and humid seasons in our country there can be no absolute classification of foods into these categories. With the exception of sugar and salt; there is nothing which would not spoil unless taken special care of. Even sugar and salt absorb moisture and become soggy during the rainy season unless we are careful.

Non-perishable foods: These foods keep for months or years without spoiling unless handled or stored carelessly. These foods are self stable at room temperature. Examples of such foods are all preserved food products (canned, dried, pickled etc.), whole cereal, pulse and millet grains, oil seeds, nuts, fats and oils, honey, sugar, jaggery, salt, some spices and essence.

4.2 FOOD PROCESSING

Food processing is the use of equipment, energy and tools to safely and efficiently transform food ingredients like grains, meats, vegetables, or fruits with minimal waste into more value-added ingredients or in combination to obtain more convenient processed food products for sale.

Some food processing techniques utilize enzymes to modify food components to improve their flavor, nutritional quality or other characteristics. Nanoparticles are used as a source to immobilize these enzymes which may aid in the dispersion throughout the food matrices and enhance their activity. Nano-silicon dioxide particles with reactive aldehyde groups which covalently bind to a porcine triacylglycerol lipase effectively hydrolyze olive oil. This helps in improving the stability, adaptability, and reusability. Nanocharcoal adsorbent is a nanoparticle product used for the decoloration of food products.

The food processing technology differ from food to food which we will read in next chapters. Here we discuss few important technique/methods only.

4.2.1 Objectives of Food Processing

Food technology is a very vast domain concerning with the production and processing of food. Food processing has certain objectives, such as:

- It boosts the shelf life of food products.
- Prevent food-contamination.
- Food storage and Transportation.
- Turns raw food materials into attractive, marketable products.
- Provide employment to a large population.

4.2.2 Food Processing Methods

There are certain criteria that have to be compiled for the appropriate processing of food, right from the possibility of a pest or bacteria to invade and multiply on foods to the biological activity of foods. The following methods are applied for the proper processing of food:

- Peeling off the outer layers of the raw materials.
- Mincing
- Fermentation
- Cooking
- Gasification such as the addition of a gas in bread or soft drinks.
- Spray drying
- Packaging
- Chopping or slicing
- Liquefaction
- Emulsification
- Mixing
- Proofing
- Pasteurization

4.2.3 Benefits of Food Processing

- Mass production of food is much cheaper overall than individual production of meals from raw ingredients. Therefore, a large profit potential exists for the manufacturers and suppliers of processed food products.
- Individuals may see a benefit in convenience.
- The food industry offers products that fulfil many different needs: From peeled potatoes that only have to be boiled at home to fully prepared ready meals that can be heated up in the microwave oven within a few minutes.
- Benefits of food processing include toxin removal, preservation, easing marketing and distribution tasks, and increasing food consistency.
- It increases seasonal availability of many foods.
- Enables transportation of delicate perishable foods across long distances.
- Makes many kinds of foods safe to eat by de-activating spoilage and pathogenic micro-organisms.
- Modern food processing also improves the quality of life for people with allergies, diabetics, and other people who cannot consume some common food elements. Food processing can also add extra nutrients such as vitamins.
- Processed foods are often less susceptible to early spoilage than fresh foods and are better suited for long distance transportation from the source to the consumer.

4.2.4 Drawbacks of Food Processing

- In general, fresh food that has not been processed other than by washing and simple kitchen preparation, may be expected to contain a higher proportion of naturally-occurring vitamins, fiber and minerals than an equivalent product processed by the food industry. Vitamin C, for example, is destroyed by heat and therefore canned fruits have a lower content of vitamin C than fresh ones.
- Food processing can lower the nutritional value of foods, and introduce hazards not encountered with naturally-occurring products.
- Processed foods often include food additives, such as flavourings and texture-enhancing agents, which may have little or no nutritive value, or be unhealthy.
- Preservatives added or created during processing to extend the 'shelf-life' of commercially-available products, such as nitrites or sulphites, may cause adverse health effects. Use of low-cost ingredients that mimic the properties of natural ingredients (*e.g.* cheap chemically-hardened vegetable oils in place of more-expensive natural saturated fats or cold-pressed oils) have been shown to cause severe health problems.
- Processed foods often have a higher ratio of calories to other essential nutrients than unprocessed foods, a phenomenon referred to as "empty calories". So-called junk food, produced to satisfy consumer demand for convenience and low cost, are most often mass-produced processed food products.
- Because processed food ingredients are often produced in high quantities and distributed widely amongst value-added food manufacturers, failures in hygiene standards in 'low-level' manufacturing facilities that produce a widely-distributed basic ingredient can have serious consequences for many final products.
- The addition of these many chemicals for preservation and flavor have been known to cause human and animal cells to grow rapidly, without going into Apoptosis.

4.2.5 Enzymes in Food Processing

The use of enzymes in the food industry is a well-established approach, in particular due to the specificity of enzyme action and their green, environmentally friendly nature. Enzymes are currently used in several different food products and processes and new areas of application are constantly being added. The introduction of enzymes as effective biocatalysts working under mild conditions results in significant saving in resources such as energy and the environment.

More and more enzymes for food technology are now derived from specially selected or genetically modified microorganisms grown in industrial scale fermenters and Table 1 enlist the range of examples and applications. About 158 enzymes are used in food industry, 64 enzymes in technical applications and 57 enzymes in feedstuff, of which 24 enzymes are used in three industrial sectors. Almost 75% of all industrial enzymes are hydrolytic enzymes. Carbohydrases, proteases and lipases dominate the enzyme market, accounting for more than 70% of all enzyme sales. Table 2 gives the representative examples of enzyme applications based on different industrial sectors, and discusses the technical benefits in various fields.

Table 1: Enzymes derived from microorganisms and used in food technology

Enzyme	Source	Action	Application
α-Amylase	*Aspergillus* spp., *Bacillus* spp.*, *Microbacterium irnperiale*	Wheat starch hydrolysis	Dough softening, increased bread volume, aid production of sugars for yeast fermentation
Lipase and Esterase	*Aspergillus* spp.*, *Candida* spp., *Rhizomucor miehei, Penicillium roqueforti, Rhizopus* spp., *Bacillus subtilis**	Hydrolyses triglycerides to fatty acids and glycerol; hydrolyses alkyl esters to fatty acids and alcohol	Flavour enhancement in cheese products; fat function modification by interesterification;synthesis of flavour esters
Pectinase (polygalacturonase)	*Aspergillus* spp., *Penicillium funiculosum*	Hydrolyses pectin	Clarification of fruit juices by depectinization
Pectinesterase	*Aspergillus* spp.*	Helps in de-esterification of pectin into pectate and methanol units in pectin	With pectinase in depectinisation technology
Hemicellulase andxylanase	*Aspergillus* spp.*, *Bacillus subtilis**, *Trichoderma reesei**	Hydrolyses hemi-celluloses (insoluble non-starch poly-saccharides in flour)	Bread improvement through improved crumb structure
Glucose oxidase	*Aspergillus niger**, *Penicillium chrysogenum*	Oxidises glucose to gluconic acid	Oxygen removal from food packaging; removal of glucose from egg white to prevent browning
Glucose isomerase	*Actinplanes missouriensis, Bacillus coagulans, Streptomyces lividans,* * *Streptomyces rubiginosus*	Converts glucose to fructose	Production of high fructose corn syrup (beverage sweetener)
β-glucanase	*Aspergillus* spp., *Bacillus suhtilis**	Hydrolyses beta-glucans in beer mashes	Filtration aids, haze prevention in beer production
β-galactosidase (lactase)	*Aspergillus* spp., *Kluyvennnvces* spp.	Hydrolyses milk lactose to glucose and galactose	Sweetening milk and whey; products for lactose-intolerant individuals; reduction of crystallisation in ice cream containing whey; improving functionality of whey protein concentration; manufacture of lactulose

Cyclodextrin glucanotransferase	*Bacillus* spp.*	Synthesise cyclodextrins from liquefied starch	Cyclodextrins are food-grade micro-encapsulants for colours, flavours and vitamins
Chymosin	*Aspergillus awamori** *Kluyvemmyces lactis**	Hydrolyses kappa-casein	Coagulation of milk for cheese making
α- Acetoluctute decarboxylase	*Bacillus subtilis**	Converts acetolactate to acetoin	Reduction of wine maturation time by circumventing need for secondary fermentation of diacetyl to acetoin
Cellulase	*Aspergillus niger, Trichoderma* spp.	Hydrolyses cellulose	Fruit liquefaction in juice production
Catalase	*Aspergillus niger** *Micrococcus luteus*	Breaks down hydrogen peroxide to water and oxygen	Oxygen removal technology, combined with glucose oxidase
Aminopeptidase	*Lactococcus lactis, Aspergillus* spp., *Rhizopus oryzae*	Releases free amino acids from N-terminus of proteins and peptides	De-bittering protein hydrolysates accelerating cheese maturation
Amyloglucosidase	*Aspergillus niger, Rhizopus* spp.	Hydrolyses starch dextrins to glucose (saccharification)	One stage of high fructose corn syrup production; production of Mite' beers
Pentosanase	*Humicola insolens, Trichoderma reesei*	Hydrolyses pentosans (solublenon-starch poly-saccharides in wheat flours)	Part of bread dough improvement technology
Pullulanase	*Bacillus* spp.*, *Klebsiella* spp.*	Hydrolyses 1-6 bonds that form'branches' in starch structure	Starch saccharification (improves efficiency)
Protease (proteinase)	*Aspergillus* spp.*, *Rhizomucor miehei, Cryphonectria parasitica, Penicillium citrinum, Rhizopus niveus, Bacillus* spp.*	Hydrolysis of kappa-casein;hydrolysis of animal and vegetable food proteins; hydrolysis of wheat glutens	Milk coagulation for cheese making;hydrolysate production for soups and savoury foods; bread dough improvement

Table 2: Enzyme application in Food processing

Application fields of Food rocessing	Enzymes	Technical Benefits
Dairy Industry	Chymosin, lipases, lysozymes	Cheese manufacturing.
	β-galactosidase, lactases	Breaking down lactose to glucose and galactose in milk processing to avoid lactose intolerance.
	lactoperoxidase	Cold sterilisation of milk: milk replacers for calves
	Acid proteinases	Milk coagulation
	Neutral proteinases and peptidases	Accelerated cheese ripening; de-bittering; enzyme modified cheese; production of hypoallergenic milk-based foods
Baking Industry	α-amylases	Degrading starch in flours and controlling the volume and crumb structure of bread.
	β-xylanases	Improving dough handling and dough stability.
	Oxidoreductase	Giving increased gluten strength.
	Lipases	Improving stability of the gas cells in dough.
	Proteases	Reducing the protein in flour
	Maltogenic á-amylases	Improves shelf-life of bread and cake
	Glucose oxidase	Oxidative reaction with gluten to make weak doughs stronger, drive and more elastic
	Asparginase	Reduces the amount of acrylamide formed during baking
	Lipoxygenase	Bleaching and strengthening dough
Juice industry	Amylases, glucoamylases	Breaking down starch into glucose.Clarifying cloudy juice, especially for apple juice.
	Pectinases	Degrading pectins which are structural polysaccharides present in cell wall. Increase the overall juice production.
	Cellulases, hemicellulose	Acting on soluble pectin hydrolysis and on cell wall components with pectinases. Lowering viscosity and maintenance of texture.
	Laccase	Increasing the susceptibility of browning during storage.
	Naringinase and limoninase	Acting on compounds that cause bitterness in citrus juices.
Starch processing	α-amylases	Cleaving α-1, 4-glycosidic bonds in the inner region of the starch.Causing a rapid decrease in substrate molecular weight and viscosity.
	Pullulanases	Attacking α-1, 6-linkage, liberating straight-chain oligosaccharides of glucose residues linked by α-1, 4-bonds.
	Neopullulanases,	Acting on both α-1, 6-and α-1, 4-linkages.
	Amylopullulanases	Cleaving α-1, 4-linkages fron non-reducing ends of amylose, amylopectin and glycogen molecules.

	β-amylases	Producing low-molecular weight carbohydrates, such as maltose and "β-limit dextrin".
	Glucoamylases	Attacking α-1, 4-linkages and α-1, 6-linkages from the non-reducing ends to release β-d-glucose.
	Isoamylases	Hydrolysing α-1, 6-linkages in glycogen and amylopectin.
	Glucose isomerases	Catalysing isomerization of glucose to fructose.Transferring a segment of a 1, 4- α-D-glucan chain to a primary hydroxyl group in a similar glucan chain to create 1, 6-linkages.
	Glycosyltransferases	Increasing the number of branched point to obtain modified starch with improved functional properties such as higher solubility, lower viscosity and reduced retrogradation.
Brewing industry	α-amylases	Hydrolysing starch to reduced viscosity; Liquefying adjunct; Increasing maltose and glucose content;
	β-glucanases	Hydrolysing glucans into oligomers and leading to lower viscosity and better filterability; Improving wort separation.
	Pullulanases	Hydrolysing α-1, 6 branch points of starch. Securing maximum fermentability of the wort.
	Amyloglucosidases	Increasing glucose content.Increasing 1% fermentable sugar in "light" beer.
	Proteases	Increasing soluble protein and free amino-nitrogen (FAN).Malt improvement.Improving yeast growth.
	Pentosanases, xylanases	Hydrolyzing pentosans of malt, barley and wheat.Improving extraction and beer filteration.
	α-acetolactate-decarboxylases (ALDC)	Converting α-acetolactate to acetoin directly. Decreasing fermentation time by avoiding formation of diacetyl. Making beer taste right
Meat processing	Acid proteases	Improve flavouring, nutritional and functional properties of proteins. Converts animal carcasses into flavourous compounds under mild condition without by-product formation.
	Tyrosinase	Cross-link meat protein, enhances functional properties of enzymes.
	Glutaminase	Enhances flavour of the meat protein due to L-glutamic acid.
	Elastase	Tenderize meat; improve the commercial value of the low value meat.
	Papain/ficin/bromelain	Meat tenderization.Hydrolyze both animal and plant proteins.Increases protein dispersability, palpability, solubility and digestibility.
	Transglutaminase	Improves the structural properties of the processed or cooked meat.
	Lipase	Hydrolyze triglycerides; Improves flavour in sausages.
	Actidin	Improve tenderness in processed meat.

4.2.8 Magnetic Resonance Imaging in Food

Magnetic Resonance Imaging (MRI) is a nondestructive and noninvasive technique that can be used to acquire two-dimensional and even three-dimensional images of biological products, even if they are opaque systems.

Most foods (initial/final) and food components are disperse multiphase systems (suspensions, foams, emulsions, porous/dry/wet bulk solids). Aspects of the material properties essential for both consumer and producer are the structure (different length-scales) and flow behavior. MRI offers the possibility to perform measurements non-invasively, non-destructively, and highly selective (*in situ*, online) in order to study the structure or trace structural changes or inner transport processes in different phases/states of aggregation (without preparations) during production, storage, transportation, and consumption (temporal, spatial, chemical resolved). Samples may be studied several times under identical or changed conditions, which is a great advantage (time saving, higher accuracy, interior surface) compared to preparative microscopy.

Quality of food processing and preparation is increasingly important factor of a healthy living. Important problems in food industry are proper preservation and conservation of food (legumes drying, food freezing,...) as well as preparation of precooked or instant food in order to preserve its quality, taste and usefulness. Nuclear magnetic resonance enables a non-destructive determination of concentration of hydrogen nuclei and therefore water concentration in a sample, mobility of water molecules (the ration between bound and free water), the proportion of fat and the ratio between fat and water in the sample. Magnetic resonance imaging (MRI) is capable to determine the distribution of nuclei under investigation inside the sample and by using the appropriate methods also their mobility in different sample parts. Whereas the method is non-invasive, it can be used for studying the dynamical processes, such as cooking, soaking, drying, freezing or food preservation, where the content or mobility of the observed nuclei are changing.

4.2.9 Ultrasonics in Food Processing

Ultrasonic is a one of the fast, versatile, emerging, and promising non-destructive green technology used in the food industry from last few years. The ultrasound is being carried out in various areas of food technology namely crystallization, freezing, bleaching, degassing, extraction, drying, filtration, emulsification, sterilization, cutting, etc. Ultrasound is being applied as an effective preservation tool in many food-processing fields viz. vegetables and fruits, cereal products, honey, gels, proteins, enzymes, microbial inactivation, cereal technology, water treatment, dairy technology, etc.

From the past many years, food industry demand for minimal processed food leads to significant alterations in the processing methods as some processing techniques applied under critical conditions lower their nutrient level and bioavailability by inducing physical and chemical changes, thereby reducing organoleptic acceptability of the food. Thus, in lieu of such techniques, newer mild processing methods in food industry have been devised in order to retain nutrient, non nutrient (bioactive) and sensory characteristics of the food products. Ultrasonic method is one among those rapidly emerging techniques that were devised to minimize processing, enhance quality, and safeguard the safety of food products.

Ultrasound are sound waves having frequency beyond the audible range of human capacity (~20 kHz). It has a variety of applications with many advantages as compared to conventional methodologies used in food industries. Ultrasound is similar to 'normal' (audible) sound based on physical properties. Ultrasound is one of the emerging technologies that were developed to minimize processing, maximize quality and ensure the safety of food products. It is one of the new technologies which increases and ensures quality and reduces the time of processing and cost of the food products. So ultrasound is used in food technology for processing, preservation and extraction steps. It makes use of physical and chemical phenomena which marks the difference with conventional techniques. It offers great advantage in various fields like productivity, yield, better quality, less time and being environmental friendly.

Ultrasound has been emerged as a revolutionary technology in the field of food industry. Its use is continuously increasing in various steps of processing of food products. Ultrasonic is a fast growing area of research, which has been found to be used increasingly in the food industry for analysis as well as modification of various food products. The use of ultrasound in food industry involves various novel ideas and methods which are interesting as compared to conventional methods or techniques. This introduces us to the food processing methods which are alternatives to conventional ones. The use of ultrasound is an active subject within the food industry for both of the research and development. When the ultrasound propagates through a material it induces compressions and decompressions (rarefactions) in the particles of the medium, due to which high amount of energy is produced. Sound is a mechanical wave that travels in a straight line and also it requires a medium through which it travels. Ultrasound is a wave with a frequently exceeding the upper limit of human hearing which is greater than 20,000 Hz (Hertz). In ultrasound, the sound ranges can be broadly divided into two different categories. The one is low energy, high frequency diagnostic ultrasound in the MHz range and another one is high energy, low frequency, power ultrasound in the kHz range. So it is possible that ultrasound can be used for processing. The basic principle behind working of ultrasound is that it utilizes interaction between high-frequency sound waves and matter to obtain information about the composition, structure and dimensions of materials through which it propagates. Ultrasound has mainly two distinct categories of frequency ranges. They are high frequency, low energy diagnostic ultrasound in MHz range and low frequency high energy power ultrasound. Low energy (low intensity, low power) ultrasound has frequencies greater than 100 KHz with intensities down 1W.cm^2. These can be used as monitoring of food products while processing and storage with high quality and safety. It is used for evaluation of the composition of meat products, poultry and fish of raw and fermented stages. It is also used for the quality check or control of fruits, vegetables, cheese, oil, bread, cereals etc. High energy (high intensity, high power) ultrasound has frequencies between 20 and 500 kHz with intensities more than 1W.cm^2 . These are disruptive in nature and have effect on mechanical, physical or biochemical properties of foods. This is used for controlling microstructures and modification, emulsification, defoaming of food products. It also has role in freezing, thawing, microbial inactivation, drying etc.

4.2.10 Nanotechnology in Food Industry

Nanotechnology is the technology of manipulation of matter at the nanometer scale. The application of nanotechnology in food has gained great importance in the recent years in view of its potential in the development of novel and healthier food. Food nanotechnology opens up new possibilities for development of innovative food products. Application of nanotechnology in food includes improvement of packaging, processing, nano-additives, cleaning and sensors for detection of contaminants.

Food nanotechnology is an area of rising attention and unties new possibilities for the food industry. Nanotechnology can be used in all the phases of the food production chain, from the agricultural production to the industrial processing and finally the packaging of foods material. Nanoparticles can also be used in food to enhance the nutritional aspects, by means of nano-supplements and nano-delivery systems for bioactive compounds.

4.2.10.1 Nano-sized supplements and nutraceuticals: These have been developed to enhance nutrition, andto improve health and well-being. Nano- sized supplement relates to processing of foodstuffs to develop nano- scale structures and stable emulsions/mixtures to improve the consistency, taste and texture attributes of the food. Nano-textured foodstuffs enable reduction of fat usage thereby contributing to healthier food. An example of product would be a ice cream, mayonnaise or spread which is nano-textured, which could low in fat but as "creamy". These products would render healthy but still tasty food products. Development of micronized starch, cellulose, wheat and rice flour, and spices for food applications are currently on going.

5.2.10.2 Nano-sized additives in food: The main benefits that could be attributed to the nano – sized additives would be better dispersibility of water insoluble additives (*e.g.* colours, flavours, preservatives, supplements) in food products without the use of additional surfactants/emulsifiers. This is believed to enhance the taste and flavour due to the larger surface areas of the nano-sized additives, enhanced absorption and bioavailability in the body. Currently available products are vitamins, antioxidants, colours, flavours, and preservatives. Nano-sized carrier systems for nutrients and supplements are also developed for use in food products. These are based on nanoencapsulation of the active in the form of liposomes, micelles, or protein based carriers. These nano-carrier systems are used to mask the undesirable taste of certain additives and supplements, or to protect some them from degradation during processing. Enhanced bioavailability, antimicrobial activity is the added claims of the nanoencapsulated nutrients and supplements. Inorganic nano-sized additives like silver, iron, calcium, magnesium, selenium and silica are also finding applications in food area. It is claimed that these additives improve the taste and flavours as a result of larger surface areas. Nano-salt enables consumer to enjoy the salt better even when used at a lower levels. A food-grade polypeptide, e-Polylysine is used to protect oil from oxidation. These Polylysine nanoparticles are much smaller than phytoglycogen octenyl succinate nanoparticles, allowing them to fill in the gaps between phytoglycogen octenyl succinate nanoparticles.

4.2.10.3 Nanoencapsulation: Nanoencapsulation is the technology of enclosing substances in miniature by using nanocomposite, nanoemulsification, and nanoestructuration techniques. This allows the controlled release of the core active molecule. The protection of compounds like vitamins, antioxidants, proteins, and lipids as well as carbohydrates may be attained by use of Octenyl succinic anhydride-e-polylysine. This acts as bifunctional molecules as either surfactants or emulsifiers in the encapsulation of nutraceuticals or drugs or as antimicrobial agents. Hydrophobically modified starch formed micelles encapsulating the active ingredient of turmeric, curcumin. The performance of antioxidants are enhanced by Lipid-based nanoencapsulation systems thereby by improving their solubility, bioavailability, stability, and preventing unwanted interactions with other food components. Nanoliposomes, nanocochleates, and archaeosomes are efficient lipid-based nanoencapsulation systems that can be used for the protection and delivery of foods and nutraceuticals.

4.2.11 Some More Processing Methods and Approaches

Retrogradation: The process of re-association of the starch granules on cooling of the gelatinized starch or the starch paste is called retrogradation. It depends on the relative proportions of amylose and amylopectin in starch as linear amylose molecules re-associate faster than the highly branched amylopectins. Reheating starchy foods also influences this process. The digestibility of starch in the small intestine is reduced by the degree of processing and retrogradation. The staling of bread is due to retrogradation of starch and the rate of staling is temperature dependent.

Food Antimicrobials: Food antimicrobials are compounds used to extend the lag phase or kill microorganisms. If antimicrobials and sanitizers are to play a major role in effective control of foodborne pathogens, food manufacturers and others within the food industry must know more about the potential for development of resistance among target microorganisms. They are different than therapeutic antibiotics (*e.g.*, penicillin, tetracyclines) used to treat human or animal disease. Food antimicrobials are sometimes called "*preservatives*." Antimicrobials may be classified as "traditional" or "naturally occurring." A number of traditional antimicrobials, *e.g.*, acetic acid and benzoic acid, are approved for use in foods by most international regulatory agencies. Naturally occurring antimicrobials include compounds that originate from microbial, plant and animal sources. A subgroup of naturally occurring antimicrobials is the bacteriocins, proteins produced by lactic acid bacteria, *e.g.*, Lactococcus, Lactobacillus, and Pedicoccus species, and a few other bacteria. Only a few naturally occurring antimicrobials, such as nisin, natamycin, lactoferrin and lysozyme, have regulatory approval for application to foods.

Fortification: Fortification usually refers to the addition of nutrients to foods from which they were either absent, or present in unimportant amounts. This is carried out because deficiencies or potential deficiencies have been shown in the population. It also includes additions to fulfil the role of another food in the diet. Thus margarine is fortified with vitamin A in many countries to replace that 'lost' when margarine is substituted for butter. Vitamin D is added at higher levels than are found in butter as a public health measure, since extra is considered necessary for the population as a whole.

Restoration: Restoration is self-evident, involving the replacement, in full or in part, of losses incurred in processing (*e.g.* loss of B vitamins and iron in milling of cereals to low extraction rates; loss of vitamin C in the preparation of instant potato). It should be noted that, up to now, restoration has been limited; for example, white bread has thiamin, niacin and iron added back, although other vitamins such as pantothenate, folate, pyridoxine and tocopherol are also partly lost in the milling process. Similarly, fruit juices might have vitamin C added back, but juices also supply folate and thiamin. In some countries, calcium and riboflavin are also added to bread: this is fortification, since wheat contains only small amounts of these two nutrients.

Enrichment: Enrichment is increasing the level of nutrients present to make the food a 'richer' source. Enrichment has frequently been interchanged with restoration and fortification as a general term. However, for labelling purposes the use of the term 'enriched' is controlled.

Standardization: Standardization is sometimes used to mean additions to compensate for natural or seasonal variations in nutrient content.

Substitution: Substitution is the nutrient addition to a substitute product to the levels found in the food which it is designed to resemble in appearance, texture, flavour and odour and which it is intended to replace partially or completely. An example is the addition of vitamins A and D to fat replacers.

Supplementation: Supplementation is the supply of nutrients (normally micronutrients) singly or in combination in a quantified dose form. Supplements can take a variety of forms such as tablets, capsules, pastilles, measured amounts of liquid or small sachets of powder.

Cleaning and disinfection: Titanium dioxide is used as a disinfecting agent as it generates reactive oxygen species in the presence of UV light that cause degradation of pathogenic microorganisms. However, this efficiency of the titanium dioxide is impaired as most of the excited electrons recombine and do not produce radicals. Deposition of silver on nanoparticles of titanium dioxide improves the antibacterial activity of titanium dioxide against E. coli whereas when combined with carbon nanotubes it exhibits enhanced activity against Bacillus cereus spores. Silver-doped titanium dioxide nanoparticles also inactivated B. cereus spores on aluminum and polyester surfaces and destroyed airborne bacteria and molds when incorporated into an air filter. Nanoparticles of silver when stabilized with SDS or PVP effectively inhibitsthe pathogenic bacteria like *E. coli* and *Staphylococcus aureus*. Surfaces of refrigerators and storage containers are coated with silver nanoparticles to prevent growth of pathogens and spoilage bacteria.

Sensors: Biosensor technology have been extensively used to detect gases in packaged foods to evaluate the integrity of the packaging material, release of compounds during spoilage of food items and the presence of pathogens or toxins in foods. Methods for identification of bacteria, viruses, toxins or other organic compounds have been developed based on nanotechnological methods and devices. Immunosensing of Staphylococcus enterotoxin B (SEB) in milk was achieved using poly(dimethylsiloxane) (PDMS) chips with reinforced, supported, fluid bilayer membranes. Antibodies to SEB were attached to the bilayer membrane in PDMS channels to form a biosensor with a detection limit of 0.5 ng/mL. A Universal G-liposomal nanovesicles based immune-magnetic bead sandwich assay was developed to simultaneously detect E. coli O157:H7, Salmonella spp., and Listeria monocytogenesin food. An electrochemical glucose biosensor, with detection and quantification limits of 0.035 and 0.107 mM, respectively, was nanofabricated by layer-by-layer self assembly of polyelectrolytes on an electrode platform. Multi-walled carbon nanotubes dispersed in the perfluorosulfonated polymer, Nafion, were deposited on a glassy carbon electrode followed by adsorption of a chitosan derivative as a polycation and glucose oxidase as a biorecognition element. Glucose in solution was detected by changes in current. Allergic protein of peanut in chocolate and other pathogenic microorganisms are detected by liposome nanovesicles.

CHAPTER 5

FRUIT AND VEGETABLE PRODUCTS TECHNOLOGY

5.1 THE INDIAN FRUITS AND VEGETABLES INDUSTRY

India is the second largest producer of the fruits and vegetables in the world after China. The country has diverse topography and climate, which ensures availability of fruits and vegetables in every season. During 2021-22, India produced 204.61 million metric tonnes of vegetables and 107.10 million metric tonnes of fruits. The area under cultivation of fruits stood at 7.09 million hectares in 2021-22, while vegetables were cultivated at 11.28 million hectares. In addition, India leads the world in the production of ginger and okra, along with banana, papaya, mango and guava.

Production and export of Indian fruits and vegetables have increased in recent years. During 2021-22, India exported fresh fruits and vegetables worth US$ 1.527.60 million, which comprised fruits worth US$ 750.7 million and vegetables worth US$ 767.01 million. India mostly exports to its neighbours, namely the UAE, Bangladesh, Pakistan, Saudi Arabia, Sri Lanka and Nepal. India's global market share is still only about 1%, but its horticulture products are becoming increasingly popular due to advancements in cold chain infrastructure, research, contemporary post-harvest technologies, supportive governmental policies and quality control procedures.

5.1.1 Production of Fruits and Vegetables in India

According to the United Nations' Food and Agriculture Organization (FAO), India was the world's second-largest producer of fruits and vegetables. India's food industry is large, and the biggest fruit-producing states are Andhra Pradesh, Maharashtra, Madhya Pradesh, Uttar Pradesh, Tamil Nadu, Karnataka and Gujarat. The major vegetable-producing states are Uttar Pradesh, Madhya Pradesh, West Bengal, Bihar, Gujarat, Odisha and Maharashtra.

Fruit production in India increased to 107.10 million tonnes in 2021-22 from 97.97 million tonnes in 2018-19, at a CAGR of 3.0%. Further, the vegetable market production expanded by 3.8% CAGR to 204.61 million tonnes during this period.

5.1.2 Fruits and Vegetable Exports from India

The large production base provides India significant export potential. It exported fresh produce worth Rs. 11,412.50 crore (US$ 1,527.60 million) over 2021-22, with fruits valued at Rs. 5,593 crore (US$ 750.7 million) and vegetables at Rs. 5,745.54 crore (US$ 767.01 million). During this period, processed fruits and vegetables (including pulses) were exported for a total of Rs. 12,858.66 crore (US$ 1,724.88 million), of which Rs. 8,308.04 crore (US$ 1,114.19 million) and Rs. 4,550.62 crore (US$ 610.69 million) were processed vegetables, including pulses.

The major fruits exported are grapes, pomegranates, mangoes, bananas and oranges, while the major vegetables exported are onions, mixed vegetables, potatoes, tomatoes and green chilies.

According to preliminary data from the Directorate General of Commercial Intelligence and Statistics, processed fruits and vegetables saw considerable growth of 51% between April and July 2022 compared to the same period last year, while fresh fruits and vegetables saw an increase of 3.79%. Fresh fruit and vegetable exports totalled US$ 498 million during this period, rising to US$ 517 million in the comparable months of the current fiscal year. In the first four months of the current fiscal year, processed fruits and vegetables exports more than doubled to US$ 665 million from US$ 441 million in the equivalent months of the previous year.

5.1.3 Government Initiatives to Promote Exports of Fruits and Vegetables

Fruits and vegetables are significant components of the agricultural and industrial economies. Due to their significance for the country's economic growth, the government has announced several changes to improve opportunities in the fruits and vegetables industry and encourage exports. Some of these reforms are listed below:

- **100% Foreign Direct Investment (FDI) permitted for the food processing sector:**
  The government had approved 100% FDI under the automatic route in the food processing sector. The intention was to make the FDI policy more investor friendly and remove the policy blockages hampering the investment inflows into the industry and the country.
- **Agriculture Export Policy (AEP):**
  The Government of India released its Agriculture Export Policy in 2018, emphasising agriculture export-oriented production, export promotion, greater farmer realisation, and synchronisation with government policies and programmes. The AEP places importance on farmer-focused mobile applications. During implementation of AEP, considerable progress has been made in giving Farmer-Produce Organizations (FPOs) and farmers a stake in the export of their produce. Due to the need to serve foreign markets, direct connectivity of FPOs/farmers with the export market has boosted farmers' incomes and led to better farming practices.
- **Direct Involvement of Farmers in Exports:**
  - ❖ **Farmer Connect Portal** – On the Agricultural and Processed Food Products Export Development Authority (APEDA) website, a Farmer Connect Portal has been created to provide FPOs/ Farmer Producer Companies (FPCs) and cooperatives a platform to communicate with exporters. There are currently 2,360 FPOs/FPCs and 2,324 exporters registered in the portal.
  - ❖ **Traceability Systems** – Traceability to the farm level is essential to guarantee the quality of exports and establish India as a trustworthy provider of high-quality goods. Many digital platforms for traceability have been created to facilitate easy business flow and ensure system transparency.
    - **HortiNet-Mango:** More than 38,000 farmers and over 66,000 farms have been registered.
    - **HortiNet-Vegetables:** The system covers 43 vegetables. To date, over 10,000 farmers and 10,000 farms have been registered.
    - **HortiNet-Citrus Fruit:** This system was implemented in July 2018. So far, a large number of farmers and farms have been registered.

- **Addressing Transport and Logistics Issues:**
  - ❖ In order to help farmers and producers transport their agricultural products from rural areas to major towns and cities, the Indian Railways has introduced the Kisan Rail service, under which trains are run with multiple commodities (perishables, agriproducts and seeds), consignors and consignees. The Indian Railways has run 157 Kisan Rail services on 18 routes so far to transport perishable goods such as fruits, vegetables and other foods.
  - ❖ The Ministry of Food Processing Industries (MoFPI)'s Operation Greens (TOP to TOTAL) programme provides 50% subsidy on the Kisan Rail delivery of fruits and vegetables.
  - ❖ The Ministry of Food Processing Industries (MoFPI)'s Operation Greens (TOP to TOTAL) programme provides 50% subsidy on the Kisan Rail delivery of fruits and vegetables.

5.1.4 Value Added Products from Fruits and Vegetables

Low cost technologies are available for producing value added products from fruits and vegetables such as juices, squashes, purees, jams, jellies, pickles and chutneys, resins and prunes. New techniques for extending shelf life of fruits have been developed and commercialized like waxing, packaging in perforated LDPE bags, cold and controlled atmosphere (CA) storage.

A wide variety of value added products can be made from fruits and vegetables as shown in Table 1. The choice of the products to be manufactured will depend on the readily availability of the raw materials in the area where the processing unit is proposed to be set up and the consumer preferences in the neighbouring markets.

Table 1: Suggestive products prepared from fruits and vegetables

S. No.	Commodity	Value added products
Fruits		
1.	Aonla	Preserve, Jam, Candy, Syrup, Juice, Pickle, Chutney, Triphala Powder, Fried Shreds.
2.	Apple	Preserve, Jam, Juice, Cider, Dried Apple, Chutney.
3.	Bael	Preserve, Nectar, Squash, Canned Bael, Cider
4.	Ber	Candy, Preserve, Canned Ber, Jam
5.	Citrus Fruits	Juice, Pickle, Marmalade, Squash, Cordial, Barley Water, Candy
6.	Grape	Wine, Juice, Raisin, Munakka
7.	Guava	Jelly, Cheese, Toffee, Nectar, RTS, Squash, Vinegar, Canned Guava
8.	Litchi	Juice, Syrup, Canned Litchi
9.	Mango	Natural And Sweetened Juice, Ready To Serve (RTS), Squash Nectar, Jam, Preserve, Pickle, Chutney, Toffee, Amchur, Mango Pulp, Mango Concentrate, Leather, Papad, Canned Mango
10.	Papaya	Jam, Candy, Nectar, Pickle, Sauce, Canned Papaya, Papain, Leather
11.	Peach	Jam, Chutney, Canned And Dried Peach
12.	Pear	Jam, Chutney, Pickle, Preserve, Canned Pear
13.	Pineapple	Canned Pineapple, Juice, Squash, Syrup, Jam, Dried Pine Apple.
14.	Plum	Jam, Chutney, Sauce, Dried Plum
15.	Pomegranate	Juice, Squash, Syrup, Anardana (Dried Products)

Vegetables

S. No.	Commodity	Value added products
16.	Brinjal,	Pickles
	Green Chilli,	—do—
	Radish, Turnip,	—do—
	Cucumber,	—do—
	Bitter Guard,	—do—, Power, Juice
	Beet Root	Power, Juice, Candies
17.	Cabbage	Sauerkraut, canned cabbage
18.	Carrot	Jam, Preserve, Pickle, Canned, Canned Carrot, Halwa
19.	Cauliflower	Pickle, Dried and Canned Cauliflower
20.	Ginger	Pickle, Preserve, Candy, Dried Ginger, RTS, Syrup, Flakes
21.	Mushroom	Pickle, Sauce, Chutney, Canned and Dried Mushroom, Mushroom Powder
22.	Onion and Garlic	Pickles, Paste and Dried Powder, Flakes
24.	Peas	Canned Pea, Frozen Pea, Dried Pea, Pickles
25.	Potato	Chips, French-Fry, Papad, Starch, Canned Potato, Dried Potato, Potato Flour, Flakes
26.	Tomato	Sauce, Chutney, Pickle, Puree, Paste, Juice, Soup, Jam, Canned Tomato, Powder

5.2 FRUITS AND VEGETABLES AS LIVING COMMODITY

Fruits and vegetables, fresh or processed, form an important component of our diet and there is an ever increasing demand for these. Fruits are harvested at slightly immature or mature greens stages and yet their physiological activities continue. Harvesting of fruits and vegetables at appropriate maturity level is important and one of the basis of close observations, maturity indices is fixed for various commodities.. Commonly following criteria have been utilized for fixing maturity standards:

Computation of days from bloom to harvest

- Measurement of heat units
- *Visual means*- skin colour, persistence or drying of parts of plant, fullness of fruit
- *Physical methods*- ease of separation, pressure test, density, grading etc
- *Chemical methods*- total solids, sugars, acid, sugar-to-acid ratio, starch content etc.
- *Physiological methods*- respiration methods etc.

Chemical composition:

Most fresh vegetables and fruit are high in water content, low in protein, and low in fat. In these cases water contents will generally be greater than 70% and frequently greater than 85%. Commonly protein content will not be greater than 3.5% or fat content greater than 0.5 %. Exceptions exist in the case of dates and raisins which are substantially lower in moisture but cannot be considered fresh in the same sense as other fruits. Legumes such as peas and certain beans are higher in protein; a few vegetables such as sweet corn which are slightly higher in fat and avocados which are substantially higher in fat

5.2.1 Pre and Post Harvest Changes and Maturity Standards for Storage

Post-harvest physiologists distinguish three stages in the life span of fruits and vegetables: **maturation, ripening**, and **senescence**.

Maturation is indicative of the fruit being ready for harvest. At this point, the edible part of the fruit or vegetable is fully developed in size, although it may not be ready for immediate consumption.

Ripening follows or overlaps maturation, rendering the produce edible, as indicated by taste.

Senescence is the last stage, characterized by natural degradation of the fruit or vegetable, as in loss of texture, flavour, etc. (senescence ends at the death of the tissue of the fruit). Some typical maturity indexes are

Skin colour: This factor is commonly applied to fruits, since skin colour changes as fruit ripens or matures. Some fruits exhibit no perceptible colour change during maturation, depending on the type of fruit or vegetable colour charts are available for cultivars, such as apples, tomatoes, peaches, chilli peppers, etc.

Optical methods: Light transmission properties can be used to measure the degree of maturity of fruits. These methods are based on the chlorophyll content of the fruit, which is reduced during maturation. The fruit is exposed to a bright light, which is then switched off so that the fruit is in total darkness. Next, a sensor measures the amount of light emitted from the fruit, which is proportional to its chlorophyll content and thus its maturity.

Shape: The shape of fruit can change during maturation and can be used as a characteristic to determine harvest maturity. For instance, a banana becomes more rounded in cross-sections and less angular as it develops on the plant. Mangoes also change shape during maturation.

Size: Changes in the size of a crop while growing are frequently used to determine the time of harvest. For example, partially mature cobs of *Zea mays saccharata* are marketed as sweet corn, while even less mature and thus smaller cobs are marketed as baby corn. For bananas, the width of individual fingers can be used to determine harvest maturity.

Aroma: Most fruits synthesize volatile chemicals as they ripen. Such chemicals give fruit its characteristic odour and can be used to determine whether it is ripe or not.

Fruit opening: Some fruits may develop toxic compounds during ripening, such as ackee tree fruit, which contains toxic levels of hypoglycine. The fruit splits when it is fully mature, revealing black seeds on yellow arils.

Leaf changes: Leaf quality often determines when fruits and vegetables should be harvested. In root crops, the condition of the leaves can likewise indicate the condition of the crop below ground. For example, if potatoes are to be stored, then the optimum harvest time is soon after the leaves and stems have died. If harvested earlier, the skins will be less resistant to harvesting and handling damage and more prone to storage diseases.

Abscission: As part of the natural development of a fruit an abscission layer is formed in the pedicel.

Firmness: A fruit may change in texture during maturation, especially during ripening when it may become rapidly softer. Excessive loss of moisture may also affect the texture of crops.

5.2.2 Physical and Chemical Treatment to Increase the Shelf life Conditions for Transportation and Storage:

The preliminary processing operations of fruits and vegetables are sorting, grading, washing, peeling, sizing, blanching, etc.

1. **Sorting and grading-** Sorting is a separation based on a individual physical properties of raw materials such as weight, size, shape, density, photo metric property, etc. while grading is classification on the basis of quality incorporating commercial value, end use and official standards.. After this preliminary sorting, the fruits and vegetables are graded. This is necessary to obtain a pack of uniform quality as regards size, colour, etc. It is done manually or with the help of grading machines.
2. **Washing-** The graded fruits and vegetables are washed with water in different ways, such as soaking and subsequent washing in running water or sprayed with water or dry air to remove surface adhering material. A thorough wash is very essential for improved microbiological quality of final product..
3. **Size reduction** -Fruits and vegetables are processed either as whole or into small pieces by size reduction. Size reduction involves peeling, coring and sizing. Peeling is done to remove unwanted or inedible material and to improve the appearance of the final product using a peeler while coring is done to remove central inedible portion using a corer. There are five main methods of peeling. They are flash peeling (*e.g.* for root crops), knife peeling (*e.g.* for citrus fruits), abrasion peeling (*e.g.* for potato), caustic peeling (*e.g.* for guava, orange segments) and flame peeling (*e.g.* onion and garlic).
4. **Blanching-** Blanching refers to the mild heat treatment given to fresh produce such as vegetables to inactivate enzymes. Blanching also improves colour, flavour and nutritional quality. Usually it is done with boiling water or steam for short periods, followed by cooling. In small scale industries, the fruit or vegetable to be blanched is placed in a wire of perforated basket, which is first dipped in hot water (88-99 °C) for about 2-5 minutes.
5. **Ripening** -Ripening before processing may be required for certain fruits such as avocado, banana, kiwifruit, mango, nectarine, papaya, peach, pear, plum, melons, etc. that are picked immature. Ethylene treatment can be used to obtain faster and more uniform ripening. The optimum temperature range for ripening is 15-25 °C and within this range, the higher the temperature the faster the ripening. Relative humidity should be maintained between 90 and 95% during ripening.

Canning

The process of sealing fruits and vegetables or any other foodstuffs hermetically (air tight) in containers and sterilizing them by heat for long storage is known as canning. In 1904, Nicholas Appert of France invented this process and he is called as "*Father of Canning*". The process of canning is also known as Appertization. Fruits and vegetables are canned in the season when the raw material is available in plenty. The canned products are sold in off-season and give better returns to the growers. The preliminary operations of canning are selection of the raw material, washing, sorting and grading and blanching.

Can filling

Can filling is the process of aseptically filling whole or sized fruit or vegetables into the containers. The cans are washed with water or subjected to steam jet to remove any adhering dust or foreign matter. Tin cans made of thin steel plate of low carbon content, lightly coated on either side with tin metal to a thickness of about 0.25 mm are usually used in canning. The thickness of coating varies from 0.31 mm to 1.54 mm.

Lacquering

it is necessary to coat the inside of the can with some material like lacquer, which would prevent discolouration, but would not impart its own flavour or injure the wholesomeness of the contents. The process of coating of inner side of the can to prevent discolouration of the product is called as lacquering. Lacquers include oleo-resinous material, synthetic resins, phenolic resins, epoxy resins and vinyl resins. There are two types of lacquers: (*a*) acid resistant and (*b*) sulphur resistant. The acid-resistant lacquer is ordinary gold coloured enamel and the cans treated with it are called as *A.R-enamel cans*. The sulphur-resistant lacquer is also of golden colour and the cans coated with it are called *C-enamel cans* or *S.R. cans*. Acid-resistant cans are used for packing of fruits of the acid group with soluble colouring matter such as raspberry, strawberry, red plum, coloured grapes, etc. Sulphur resistant cans are used for non-acid products like peas, corn, beans, etc.

Syruping and brining

In canning, syrups are added to fruits whereas brine (salt solution) is added to the vegetables. Purpose of adding syrups or brine is to improve the flavour, fill the space between the pieces of canned product and aid in the heat transfer during sterilization. Cane sugar, glucose syrup, invert sugar and high fructose corn syrups are used for canning. Brine containing 1 to 2 percent of common salt is generally used for vegetables.

Exhausting

Exhausting usually means heating the can and can contents before sealing. Sometimes it may also refer to the treatment of the container under a mechanically produced vacuum. But in either case it is done to remove air from the can interior and prevent corrosion. It also prevents undue strains upon the can during sterilization and prevents overfilling of can contents. Removing of air also helps in better retention of vitamins especially of vitamin C. The other advantages of the exhaust process are prevention of bulging of the can when stored at high altitudes or in hot climates.

5.3 QUALITY LOSSES IN FRUITS AND VEGETABLES

Fruits and vegetables are important supplement to the human balanced diet as they provide the essential minerals, vitamins and dietary fibre (roughage) for maintaining the tear and wear of the body. Fresh fruit and vegetables have a short shelf life under ambient conditions of temperature and humidity due to their highly perishable nature. They soon lose their freshness and become subjected to mould and bacterial attack, and consequently decay and become useless as articles of human diet. Fresh fruits and vegetables are valued for their quick sources of available energy. Fresh fruits have high water content (70-96%), varying amount of carbohydrate (3-27%) and fibre (0.2-3.1%) and a low content of protein, fat and minerals. Fruits are important source of Pro-vitamin A and vitamin C. In addition, vegetables also supply fair amount of carbohydrates, protein and energy and add colour, flavour and aroma to human diet.

Losses of nutrients in fruit and vegetables after harvest are a major source of human food loss. Carbohydrates are lost especially when the fruit and vegetables are subjected conditions which increase their respiration rate. The survival of fruit and vegetables organs depends considerably upon their nature, structure, natural biological function, metabolism and susceptibility to external attack.

Most of the problem encountered in the handling and preservation of fruit and vegetable and their products come from the fact that they are living organs.

The external surface are contaminated with various microorganisms (fungi, bacteria) that can grow at the expense of the product in the presence of spoilage, wounds or other portals of entry to cellular and tissue fluid.

The quality of fresh fruit and vegetables depends upon the selection, careful handling of food products, physiological, biochemical; and microbiological changes and storage conditions after harvest. The important measures to be taken are: (1) harvesting at optimum maturity, (2) minimum injury during handling, (3) reduced microbial infection, (4) maintenance of proper humidity and temperature. Horticultural commodities are different from other processed food products, as they are living organism. The high respiration rate and other metabolic processes associated with maturation and ripening of these products continue throughout the marketing cycle. This creates a special problem in the handling, storage and packaging of fresh produces. Harvesting at proper stage of maturity, regulation of the physiological and biochemical changes and control of microbial infection are of paramount importance in the post harvest handling of fruit and vegetables.

Horticultural maturity: It can be defined as "that stage at which a commodity has reached a sufficient stage of development that after harvesting and post harvest handling (including ripening), its quality will be at least at the minimum acceptability. The distinction between maturation and senescence has never been clearly established. It is defined as the collection of processes that follow the growth and development stage up to the first stages of senescence and produces the desired aesthetic and food quality characteristics (*e.g.* colour, texture or flavour). Maturation usually commences before growth ceases and includes different activities in different commodities. Growth and maturation are often collectively referred to as the development phase. Senescence is defined as the process that follows maturity that ultimately leads to death. It is also defined as "the period, when anabolic (synthesis) biochemical processes give way to catabolic (degradative) processes, leading to aging and finally death of the tissues".

Development and maturation of fruit are completed only when it is attached to the plant, but ripening and senescence may proceed on or off the plant. Fruit are generally harvested either when mature or when ripe. There are two type of fruit due to respiratory crisis or climacteric crisis (1) Climacteric fruits (2) Non climacteric fruits. The climacteric fruits (*e.g.* apples, pear, banana etc.) have the property of being able to ripen after they have picked up. When they are harvested too soon (*i.e.* before the minimum climacteric), their maturation is often difficult and incomplete. If they are picked too late (*i.e.* after the minimum climacteric), then their maturation is already ongoing and their survival time is reduced. The development status at the time of harvest is very important for refrigerated storage. Non-climacteric fruit (*e.g.* cherries, grapes, citrus, etc.) mature without having a respiratory crisis, and, without special treatment, they do not mature after being picked. Maturation, the most remarkable phenomenon in the life of fruit is characteristics by colour changes (*i.e.* chlorophyll depletion), acquisition of agreeable flavours, development of characteristics odours, and modification of texture accompanied by a loss of firmness. These are the result of biochemical; transformation that most often take place simultaneously.

Most vegetable are harvested at immature stages of maturity. Vegetables toughen as they mature and while yield is increasing the vegetable product is losing tenderness. The speed of change or development of maturity varies enormously with the crop and product. The exact point of harvest for the vegetables is critical in order to obtain desired good quality. For slower maturing products such as root crops and leafy vegetables, where the vegetables parts of the plants are harvested, the rate of developments is much slower and need to measure maturity is less critical, harvest can be judge by eye. The rate and time at which vegetables mature is largely dependent on genetic factors. A given commodity may be horticultural matured at any stage of development. In most vegetables optimum horticultural maturity coincides with optimum eating quality. Yet, for many vegetables, the optimum eating quality is reached before full maturity (*i.e.* full development) *e.g.*, leafy vegetables, immature fruit (cucumbers, sweet corn, green beans, peas) etc. In this problem of frequently delayed harvest which results in over-maturity and consequently lower quality is possible. Fruits and vegetables are consumed ripe and attain their best quality when ripened on the plant.

Respiration: In the post harvest life of the fruit and vegetables, respiration plays a very significant role. Respiration is the overall process by which stored plant reserves (carbohydrates, fats and proteins) are broken down to simple end products with release of energy in the form of heat. Respiration, in which oxygen is consumed and carbon dioxide is released, is commonly used as an indicator of metabolic activity. The uptake of oxygen and the release of carbon dioxide can be easily measured. The energy produced by the breakdown of glucose-6-phosphate during respiration is employed for the synthesis of adenosine tri-phosphate (ATP), which is essential for the respiratory oxidation chain. However, part of this energy is lost in the form of heat, which increase the temperature of the organism and is even generated during refrigerated storage. Glucose-6-phosphate, which is derived from the breakdown of starch and sucrose, enters into a series of the reactions that take place either in the cytoplasm (glycolysis) or in the mitochondria (Kreb's cycle and a chain of respiratory oxidations), producing carbon dioxide, water and energy as the ultimate end products. Respiratory carbon dioxide is produced in successive steps by the Kreb's cycle. The oxygen is necessary at the chain of respiratory oxidations and the production of water. Some fruits and vegetables have high respiration rates and require considerably more refrigeration than more slowly respiring. *Respiring rate is a good index of the post harvest life of fruits and vegetables.* To extent the post harvest life of fruit and vegetables, its respiration rate should be reduced as far as possible.

Ripening: The ripening of fruit undergoes many physiological changes after harvest. Among the important substitutes of the fruits are enzymes. These bring about changes, such as softening of the edible tissues, change in colour, flavour, odour, pectic substances, protein, carbohydrate, organic acids, ethylene production and also in respiration rate during the ripening of fruits. With ripening, changes occur in colour, flavour and texture which render the fruit acceptable to the consumer. Pectic substances are cementing substances in cell fruit cell which decompose to pectin and pectic acid. This decomposing partially responsible for the softening of fruit tissues during ripening. Compositional changes in fruits during ripening are ideal if the fruits are harvested at proper maturity. Immature fruit will have unsatisfactory quality. Colour changes in fruit and vegetable is due to degradation or break down of chlorophyll and consequent unmasking of carotenoid pigments in case of orange. During ripening, there is decrease in starch and increase in fructose, glucose and sucrose resulting in sweetness of the fruit. Ripening also decrease the organic acids and phenolics to reduce the acidity and astringency of produce and makes it more acceptable.

Ethylene Biosynthesis: Ethylene plays an important role in fruits and vegetables by regulating a number of processes during their entire life from germination to senescence. Ethylene plays a hormonal role in vegetables. During the early stages of the development of the tomato while the fruit is still green, ethylene is not produced. A sudden increase in the rate of its synthesis is observed at the onset of maturation. Increased ethylene production also occurs when plant is submitted to stress (*e.g.* wounds). All living vegetables organs are capable of producing ethylene to various degrees, sometimes in very low quantities but significantly to have spectacular physiological effects. After harvest, this gas always has some adverse consequences, such as decreasing product survival by accelerating senescence, initially and stimulating fruit maturation, disrupting growth and provoking specific alternations (reddish colouration of lettuce, bitterness in carrots). Certain organism, while they synthesis none or very little ethylene, can be very responsive if it only produced when they have been stressed (*e.g.* wounds or dehydration). Sometimes ethylene is beneficial, improving the quality prior to retail distribution. Ethylene is physiologically active in trace amounts (less than 0.1 ppm). Generally, ethylene production rates increase with maturity at harvest, physical injuries and stress. Ethylene exempted from the requirement of a residue tolerance when used as a plant regulator either before or after the harvest.

Oxidation of Phenolic Compounds: Vegetable cells often contain abundance off phenol compounds that are easily oxidized in the presence of oxygen by the action of enzymes of which the principals are the poly phenol oxidases (PPO). Vegetables organs become brown only when their tissues are wounded or if their function is severely disrupted. When the cells are wounded, such as with cut, bruised, subjected to parasitic attack, or even when they are killed in some fashion or other. The vacuolar membrane is disrupted and the poly phenol oxidases contact the phenols. Oxygen must be available for the reaction to take place (which in the case of when the organs are exposed to air) and the browning occurs. In addition, any cellular disinfections (except mechanical wounding) that leads to a modification of the membrane permeability risks causing the same results and is observed to occur in certain physiological diseases.

Microbiological aspects: Several sources of contamination are linked to the growth environment: soil and atmosphere microflora, microbiological quality of the water used for irrigation, dispersion by the rain propagated by the washing or projection of soil, horticultural processes, insect movement (*e.g.*, plant lice, mites, worms etc). Microbial pollution can be intensive during the various horticultural processes, such as fertilization or the spreading of manure. The microflora present at the time of harvest is a major factor determining the microbiological quality of raw material and this varies considerably. The major factors affecting fruit and vegetables deterioration including following:

(*i*) Growth and activities of microorganisms, principally bacteria, yeast and molds,

(*ii*) Activities of food enzymes and other chemical reactions within fruit and vegetables itself;

(*iii*) Infestation by insects, parasites and rodents.

Wastage of fruit and vegetables by consumption can be rapid and severe, particularly in tropical areas where high temperatures and high humidity favour rapid microbial growth. Many bacteria and fungi can cause the post harvest decay of fruit and vegetables. However, it is well established that the major post harvest losses of fruit and vegetables are caused by species of the fungi *Alternaria, Botrytis, Diplodia, Monilinia, Penicillum, Phomopsis, Rhizopus* and *Sclerotinia* and of the bacteria *Erwinia* and *Pseudomonas.* The growth of spoilage bacteria is favoured by higher water contents of vegetables whereas when much of this water is in available forms suggests relatively low carbohydrate and fat content. The pH range of most vegetables is within the growth range of large number of bacteria, and it is not surprising, therefore, that bacteria are common agents of vegetables spoilage.

The causative organisms break down pectin giving rise to a soft, mushy consistency, sometimes a bad odour, and a water soaked appearance. The quantities of nitrogenous compounds present, the vitamins (especially the B-complex group), and minerals are adequate to sustain the growth of the invading organism until the vegetables have been essentially consumed or destroyed. The bad odours that are produced probably the direct result of volatile compounds (*i.e.*, Ammonia, volatile acids and the like) produced by the microflora. Many *Erwinia spp.* such as *E. carotovora* are capable of fermenting many of the sugars and alcohols that exist in certain vegetables such as rhamnose, cellobiose, arabinose, mannitol and so far that the compounds which are not utilized by many of the more common bacteria. While most *Erwinia* spp. grows well at about 37°C, most are also capable of good growth at refrigeration temperature with some strains reported to grow at 1°C. Most of organism are weak pathogens in that they can only invade damaged produce; a few such as *Colletotrichum,* are able to penetrate the skin of healthy produce. Often the relationship between the host (fruit or vegetables) and the pathogen is reasonably specific, for example, *Penicillum digitatum* rots only in citrus and *P. expansum* rots in apple and pear, but not in citrus.

Phytopathogens attack fruits and vegetables reducing, their organoleptic and nutritional quality, and causing the appearance of mechanical quality defects. For example, the tomato can be attacked by eight types of parasites that belong to the species *Pseudomonas, Xanthomonas and Clavibactor* and green beans by *Corynebacterium*, *Pseudomonas* and *Xanothomonas*. The lesions caused by these bacteria continue to expand after the harvest, but adjacent healthy products are not affected as long as there is no entertainment by way of water or infections inoculum. *Erwinia carotovora* and *Pseudomonas fluorescens*, which are favoured by free water or elevated relative humidity (RH) , are those most often found and are frequently the cause of soft rot in market vegetables. The molds are by far most important group of organisms in vegetables spoilage whereas the genera *Erwinia* and *Pseudomonas* are the most important bacteria that cause vegetable spoilage.

The average water content in fruit is about 85 % and the average carbohydrate is about 13%. The fruit differ from vegetables in having less water content but more carbohydrates. On the basis of nutrition, these products would appear to be capable of supporting the growth of bacteria, yeast and molds. Bacteria growth is generally favoured when pH of fruits is suited by the wider pH growth range of molds and yeast. Much yeast is capable of attacking the sugar found in fruits and bringing about fermentation with the production of alcohol and carbon dioxide. Many molds are capable of utilizing alcohol as sources of energy and when these and other simple compounds have been depleted, these organisms proceed to destroy the remaining parts of fruits such as structural polysaccharides and rinds.

5.3.1 Quality Deterioration Factors

The following factors affect the quality of fruits and vegetables.

Effect of Temperature: Temperature is the single most important environmental factors that influence the deterioration rate of harvested fruit and vegetables. Respiration in produces involves many enzymatic reactions. The rate of these reactions, within the physiological temperature range, increases exponentially with increase in temperature. Temperature influences respiration, ethylene production, metabolism, moisture loss, compositional changes, development of physiological disorders, growth rate of pathogens and undesirable growth in fruit and vegetables. Reduction in temperature will give some reduction in the rate of change of any given parameter whether it the respiration, change in texture or loss of vitamin C. Lowering the temperature of non-climacteric produce merely lowers the rate of deterioration, whereas in climacteric fruits low temperature can also be used to delay the onset of ripening. *For maximum storage life, the optimum safe temperature for the horticultural produce should be maintained.*

Effect of Water loss and Relative humidity: Fresh fruit and vegetables can be regarded as essentially ,water infancy and expensive package. This water is costly to put into those packages. Water loss of saleable weight and thus is a direct loss in marketing. Measures that minimize water loss after harvest can be profitable. The high water content of fruit and vegetables is held within produce by osmotic forces within the cells, mostly as free water, although a small proportion is chemically bound and therefore, is more tightly held and more stable. Water in plant tissue contains varying amounts of solutes which slightly depress the vapour pressure of the water. The small reduction in equilibrium relative humidity due to the presence of solutes can also be related to the terms *water activity* and *water potential*.

At low storage temperatures, where a high humidity is required small fluctuations in temperature can result in excessive condensation on cooling surfaces and accentuated water loss from produce. There is a great loss by evaporation from produce with a high surface area to unit volume ratio. Many types of produce have a waxy coating of the surface (cuticle) that is resistant to the passage of water or water vapour. The loss of water or vapour, and respiratory gas exchange take place only by diffusion through cuticle. The rate of transpiration thus depends on the number and size of the pore openings and the nature of the wax coating. Mechanical damage can greatly accelerate the rate of water loss from produce. Bruising damage the surface organization of the tissues and allows a much greater flow of gaseous material through the damage area. An effective way for reducing water loss from fruit and vegetables is to increase the relative humidity of the air. This reduces the vapour pressure difference between the produce and the air, hence the amount of water required to be evaporated from the produce before the air is saturated with water vapour. The addition of water vapour to a cold storage chamber can be controlled automatically with humidistat.

Air movement over the produce is a significant factor influencing the rate of moisture loss, air movement required to remove heat from produce, but it effect on moisture loss must also considered. Air movement tends to sweep away this moist air from around the produce. Increasing the rate of air movement reduces the thickness of the boundary layers, increases the vapour pressure difference near the surface, and so increases the rate of moisture loss. The faster that air moves across the surface of the fruit and vegetables the greater is the rate of water loss from the produce. Water loss can be reduced by placing a physical barrier around the produce to reduce air movement across its surface.

Harvesting and Field Handling: When vegetables are maturing in the field, they are changing from day to day. There is time when the vegetable will be at peak quality from the stand point of colour, texture and flavour. Much of thee harvesting of most fruit crops are still done by hand. This labour may represent about half of the cost of growing the fruit. Mechanical damage can be subtle. Harvested fruit and vegetables are washed to remove soil, microorganism and pesticides reduces and sorted according to size and quality. Only the unique combination of eyes, intelligence and hands can permit rapid harvest of delicate and perishable materials with minimum loss and bruising.

Mechanical harvest can be used comfortably with commodities that can harvest at one time and are not sensitive to mechanical injury and with vegetable designed for immediate processing. Although, mechanical harvesting has the potential for rapid harvest, and reduce the problem associated with hiring and managing of hand labour. In order to maintain fruit and vegetable quality and avoid heating, the fruit and vegetable should be harvested and removed from the field as rapidly as possible. The produce once harvested should be protected from the adverse weather conditions. Fast transport of fruit and vegetables with minimum handling damage during shipment is very important in marketing of perishables. The present system of handling of fruit and vegetables in road trucks and railway wagons is highly defected and needs through improvement.

Water transport is much more energy efficient than other methods of transportation. By far the largest portion of vegetables transported by sea now travels in sea going inter-modal 'marine' container. These containers are well insulated may or may not have their own refrigeration capacity.

In general, railway wagons are heavily insulated and fairly airtight, so that a major problem can be providing enough air exchanges to prevent injurious atmospheric modifications in pathway.

5.3.2 Selection Criteria for Some Fruits

- *Citrus fruits:* firm, thin skinned, heavy, blemish-free, fresh aroma and smell.
- *Bananas:* clean, blemish-free, crack-free, complete, attached to stalk, a brown stalk not black, soft but not soggy.
- *Apples:* crisp, bright coloured, heavy, clean, bruise-free, shiny and well shaped.
- *Grapes:* plum, shiny, bright coloured, attached to stem, no discolouration, blemish-free, bruise-free, clean, firm and sweet.
- *Cherries:* bright red, firm, blemish-free, clean, attached with stem, without holes and having fresh aroma.
- *Papayas:* orange to reddish orange in colour, firm, not soggy to touch, blemish-free, clean, heavy and not over ripe.

Table 2: Criterion for selection of vegetables

Vegetables	Characteristics
Potatoes	Firm, clean, smooth surface, neither soggy nor have eyes.
Tomatoes	Firm, bright red, uniform and smooth surface without any holes, cracks, black colourations or soggy and soft to touch.
Carrots	Orange to yellow, firm, smooth, fresh, without any holes, cracks, dirt or soggy surface
Beans, peas	Bright green, firm, tender, fresh, break easily with a snap, clean, smooth to touch.
Cabbage	Green, fresh, compact, leaves as a whole mass, without any holes, yellow or withered leaves.
Brinjal	Bright purple, oval or round in shape, without any scars or decay or holes. Surface smooth and firm to touch not soft or soggy.
Green leafy	Fresh, without any yellow or withered leaves, vegetables no insect infestation, free of dirt or mud.

5.3.4 Mushroom

In India, mainly three species viz., white button, oyster or dhingari and paddy straw mushrooms are commercially cultivated at large scale. The edible mushrooms are rich source of vitamins, minerals, amino acids and high quality of proteins and are also low in fat, calories and carbohydrates, hence suggested as a balanced food for human consumption. Mushroom and their products are engaged as delicacy and its consumption is rapidly increased as they have remarkably taste, flavour and nutritive value. The White button mushrooms (*Agaricus bisporus*), Shiitake mushroom (*Lentinus edodes*), Pleurotus species (*Pleurotus osteatus, P. flabellatus, P. sajor caju etc.*), Paddy straw mushrooms (*Volvariella volvacea*), Winter mushrooms (*Flammulina velutipis*), Jew's ear mushrooms (*Auricularia polytricha*) are commercially cultivated species of mushroom. Mushrooms have achieved significant importance due to their nutritive and medicinal values and as an income generating industry in the world. Its products can serve to improve the nutritional status and helping in alleviating protein deficiency in children. In forthcoming period, development and introduction of new products with wider acceptability and comparatively at low price will further increase the demand

and consumption of value added mushroom products due to their therapeutics values. Mushrooms are edible fungi assume considerable importance in human diet, as they are good source of non-starchy carbohydrate, dietary fibre, minerals and vitamins-B and essential amino acids. The fresh mushroom contain about moisture (85-95%), protein (3.0%), carbohydrate (4.0%), fat (0.3-0.4%) and mineral/vitamins (1.0%). Mushrooms are popular due to their delicacy and flavour rather than food value. Fleshy nature of mushroom is responsible for its main attraction to human being as a source of food. Like other fruit and vegetables, mushrooms are soft textured and highly perishable in nature. Mushroom proteins are comparable to muscle protein in nutritive value. However, it is now a well-established fact that they are excellent source of vitamins and minerals also.

The vitamins in mushroom are well retained during cooking, canning, and dehydration. Mushrooms are highly perishable commodities and they start deteriorating immediately after their harvest. They develop brown discolouration on the surface of mushroom caps due to enzymatic action of polyphenol oxidase and they quickly become soft at high temperature. Mushroom have poor shelf-life and dehydration appears to be a promising cost effective method of preservation in Indian conditions as dehydrated mushroom are easy to transport as compared to canned, pickled and frozen product. Development of appropriate storage and post harvest technology in order to extent their marketability and availability to consumers in fresh as well as processed form is of great significance. Even in this century of vegetarian consciousness and healthy eating, the mushroom is, in fact, providing to be an excellent meat substitute to consumers.

Shiitake mushrooms have antimicrobial effects along with lipid lowering effects. It has been shown to improve liver function in individuals with hepatitis. It is felt to lower serum cholesterol by binding it in the gut and increasing its excretion in the stool. It can decrease the blood pressure of high blood pressure patient. In recently research, the red mushroom can cure and prevent the diabetes, paralysis, asthma, jaundice, cancer, heart disease, thyroid, sinus, migraine, blood pressure, piles, arthritis, tumor, kidney disorders, skin problems, anemia, tiredness, constipation, sleeplessness, gas formation, children diseases, loss of hairs and also other relative diseases. Anticancerous extract of shiitake causes recession of some kinds of cancer and inhibits the growth of some viruses like influenza. It has been found that various edible mushrooms (cultivated or wild) show anti-bacterial, anti-fungal, anti-protozoal and anti-viral effects. They have been reported to posses significant anti-cancer and blood cholesterol reducing properties.

Mushrooms are a simple form of plant like which lack chlorophyll and hence cannot produce their own food. They depend upon other living or dead plants and organic matter. Mushrooms are a rich source of proteins, vitamins and minerals. Their low content of carbohydrate and fat makes them an ideal food for diabetics and persons who wish to shed excess fat. They are also a good sources of energy, about 454 g of fresh mushrooms provides 120 kcal.

Most of the edible varieties of mushroom belong to the family Agricaceae of the class Basidiomycetes. However, gucchi (Morchellaesculentii) belongs to the class Ascomycetes. It grows wild and has not been cultivated under artificial conditions. Commonly cultivated species of mushroom are:

(*i*) Button mushrooms (*Agaricusbisporus*, *A. compestris*),

(*ii*) Oyster mushroom or dhingree (*Pleurotussajorcoju*, *P. columbinus*, and

(*iii*) Paddy straw mushroom (*Volvriellavolvacea*)

Of these, button mushroom is the most important for the preservation industry because products prepared from it are much superior in texture and cooking quality than those from other species. Besides, this species is easily digestible and rich in proteins and vitamins.

Because of highly perishable nature of fresh mushrooms and poor transportation facilities for marketing, growers do not get a proper return. It is, therefore, essential to consume mushrooms immediately or preserve them in various forms.

Processing : Pickling and sun-drying are economically viable methods of preserving mushrooms. However, freezing and freeze-drying give them an excellent quality. They can be used commercially for export market. Mushrooms can be processed in a number of ways. Different technologies which have a potential for processing mushrooms are described.

5.4 PROCESSED FRUIT AND VEGETABLE PRODUCTS

Some of the well known processed products of fruits and vegetables are discussed here:

5.4.1 Fruit Beverages

In India, the pure fruit juice industry is still in its infancy. Preparation of these juices is limited to small scale productions only, because the equipment required for production of the best quality fruit juices is rather sophisticated and costly. Quite recently, however, a few units have come into existence to package fairly large quantities of pure fruits juices from citrus fruits, pineapples, grape, apples etc. Fruits such as apple, grape, pomegranate, mulberry, jamun, phalsa, mango, litchi, pineapple etc are generally utilized for the preparation of juices.

Fruits juices are preserved in different forms such as pure juices, squashes, cordials, fermented juices etc. The fruit beverages are broadly classified as follows:

Unfermented juice or pure fruit juice: This is the natural juice pressed out of the fruit, and remains practically unaltered in its composition during preparation and preservation.

Fruit juice beverage: this is a fruit juice which is considerably altered in composition before consumption. It may be diluted before it is served as a drink.

Fermented fruit beverage: This is a fruit juice which has undergone alcoholic fermentation by yeast. The product contains varying amount of alcohol. Grape wine, apple ciders, berry wines are typical examples of this kind of beverage.

Fruit juice squash: This consists essentially of strained juice containing moderate quantities of fruit pulp to which cane sugar is added for sweetening, e.g. orange squash, lemon squash, pine apple squash and mango squash.

Fruit juice cordial: This is a sparkling, clear sweetened fruit juice from which all the pulp and other suspended materials have been completely removed. Example: lime juice cordial.

Sherbet or syrup: This is clear sugar syrup which has been artificially flavoured, *e.g.* sherbets of sandal, sangtra, almond rose, khuskhus, sarsaparilla, kewra etc.

Fruit juice concentrate: This is a fruit juice which has been concentrated by the removal of water either by heat or by freezing. Carbonated beverages and other products are made from its.

Fruit juice powder: This is fruit juice which has been converted into free flowing, highly hygroscopic powder to which natural fruit flavor in powder form is incorporated to compensate for any loss of flavor in concentration, dehydration etc. freeze dried fruit juice powders form the last word among sophisticated fruit juice products. They are reconstituted readily to yield full-strength, full-fruit, fruit juice drink.

Production of fruit beverage on a commercial scale was practically unknown till about 1930, but since then it has gradually become an important industry. Fruits beverage provide delicious cold drinks during summer season. Due to their nutritive value they are becoming more popular than synthetic drinks which at present have a very large market in our country.

Fruit beverages are easily digestible, highly refreshing, thirst quenching, appertizing and nutritionally far superior to many synthetic and aerated drinks. They can classify into fermented and unfermented fruit beverage.

1. Fruit Juice: Juices are two types-

(*a*) **Natural juice:** It is the juice, as extracted from ripe fruits and contains only natural sweetness, colour and aroma.

Pure fruits juices such as apple juice and orange juice are commercially produced in several countries. Apple juice is generally bottled while other juices are canned.

(*b*) **Sweetened juice:** It is a liquid fruit product which contains at least 85 % fruit juice and 10% total soluble solids (TSS).

(*c*) **Blended juice:** Sometimes two or more fruits juices are mixed to yield a well balanced, rightly flavoured, highly palatable and refreshing drinks. Juices as blended so as to utilize a too sweet fruit (grape), a bitter fruit (grape fruits), too acidic or tart fruit (sour lime, sour plum, galgal, sour cherry etc); bland and insipid fruits like pear or apple and strongly flavor fruit (guava and banana). Some of the common commercial blends of juices are

- Grape (97%) + lime (3%)
- Grape (50%) + orange (50%)
- Orange (50-75%) + grape fruit (20-50%)
- Apple (97%) + lime (3%)
- Apple (74%) + grape fruit (25%) + sugar (1%)
- Apple (50-75%) + pine apple (25-50%) + sugar (1%)
- Apple (37%) + plum (62%) + sugar (1%)

The quality of the juice will be depending on the manner in which these several processes are carried out. The most important steps in processing of fruits juices are

i. ***Selection and preparation of fruits:*** the variety, maturity and locality of cultivation influenced the taste, flavor and storability of the juice. Only fully ripe fruits should be selected. Over ripe and unripe (raw or green) fruit, diseased, damaged, decayed or trimmed if used, adversely affect the final quality of the fruit juice, so avoided. Dirt and spray residues of arsenic, lead etc are removed by washing with water or dil. HCl acid (1 part acid and 20 part water).

ii. ***Extraction of juice:*** Generally fruit juice is extracted from fresh fruit by crushing and pressing them. Screw types extractor, basket press or fruit pulper are mostly used.

iii. ***Deaeration***: fruit juice contains some air, most of which is present on the surface of the juice and some is dissolved in it. Most of the air as well as other gases are removed by subjecting the fresh dearation and the equipment used for the purpose is called a deaerator.

iv. ***Straining, filtration and clarification***: Fruits juice always contain varying amount of suspended matter consisting of broken fruit tissues, seed, skin, gums, pectic substances and colloidal protein. Seeds, pieces of pulp and skins are removed by straining through a thick cloth or sieve.

Fine suspended particles in the juices are removed with special equipment known as 'filter-press'. The filtering media may be finely woven cloth, canvas, fibre, asbestos pads, cotton or wood pulp discs, porous porcelain wares. The colloidal suspension tends to clog the filters in the press. In order to minimize this, filter aids such as diatomaceous or infusorial earth, also known as supercel, kieselguhr, Spanish clay and bentonite, which are added to the extent of 0.1 to 0.2%. Recently china clay has been demonstrated to be a good filter aid.

Completely removal of all suspended materials from juices, as in lime juice cordial is known as clarification which closely related to the quality, appearance and flavor of the juices. The following methods of clarification of juice are employed are Settling, filtration, freezing (– 18°C in carboy), cold storage (– 2 to – 3°C for month), high temperature (82°C for a minute), chemicals (gelatin, albumen, casein, mixture of tannin and gelatin), enzymes like pectinase and amylases. Pectinase lowers the viscosity and causes the cloud particles to aggregate and sediment and can be easily centrifuged off. Amylased are used to remove the unwanted haze in the juice and also responsible for the gel formation in the juice during storage.

v. ***Preservation***: fruits juices and other fruit beverages are preserved by pasteurization but sometimes chemical preservatives (sodium benzoate, potassium petbisulphite or KMS) are used. Fruits juices are pasteurized at about 85°C for 25 to 30 minutes according to the nature of fruits and the size of container.

After pasteurization juice is filled in pre-sterilized bottles with leaving 1.2-2.5 cm head space. They are then sealed either by crown corking machine or with caps.

2. **Ready to Serve (RTS):** This is type of fruit beverage which contains at least 10 percent fruit juice and 10 percent TSS beside about 0.3 % acid. It is not diluted before serving; hence it is known as ready to serve (RTS). Commercial RTS contains 13% TSS and 0.3 % acid and pasteurized at about 90 °C for 25 minutes. RTS can be prepared from bael, lemon/lime, guava, aonla, mango, ginger etc.
3. **Nectar:** This contains at least 20% fruit or pulp and 15% TSS with 0.3% acid. It is not diluted before serving. This is prepared from mango, papaya, guava, bael, jamun blend aonla etc.
4. **Cordial:** it is sparkling, clear, sweetened fruit juice from which pulp and other insoluble substances have been completely removed. It contains at least 25 % juice and 30 % TSS. It also contains about 1.5% acid and 350 ppm sulphur dioxide as a preservative. This is very suitable for blending with wine. Lime and lemon are suitable for making cordial. In homes, cordial can be prepared using following recipe: lemon/lime juice (1.0 litre), sugar (1.25 kg), water (1.0 litre) and KMS (Potassium metabisulphite) (2.0 g).
5. **Squash:** This contains at least 25% fruit or pulp and 40 to 50% TSS, commercially. It also contains about 1.0% acid and 350 ppm sulphur dioxide or 600 ppm sodium benzoate as a preservative. It is not diluted before serving. This is commercially prepared from mango, orange, guava, bael, pineapple etc.
6. **Crush:** This type of fruit beverage contains at least 25percent fruit juice or pulp and 55 percent TSS. It is more or less similar to squash, contains about 1.0 % acid and is diluted before serving.
7. **Syrup:** This type of fruit beverage contains at least 25 percent fruit juice or pulp and 65 percent TSS. It also contains about 1.3 -1.5 % acid and is diluted before serving. Fruits like phalsa, aonla, jamun, pomegranate, grape, lemon, orange and sometimes ginger can be used for preparation of syrup. Syrup (with 68% TSS and 1.3% acid) can be prepared commercially. Rose syrup, sandal syrup and almond syrup made from extracts are very popular.
8. **Synthetic syrup**: Heavy sugar syrup of 70 to 75% strength is used as the base of all synthetic syrups and they are flavored and colored with artificial essence/flavours and colours. They

never contain fruit juice or pulp. A large proportion of these syrup can however be replaced by real fruit juice, squash and syrups which are more nutritious. These can be prepared by using 1.5 kg sugar, 500 ml water and 1.5 g citric acid. Different colour and flavours are added as required.

9. **Fruit juice powder:** Fruit juice can be converted into a free flowing, hygroscopic powder by puff-drying, freeze drying, vacuum drying, spray drying or drum drying. The powder has the advantage of long shelf life and soluble in cold water. But during the drying process much of the characteristics of fresh flavor are lost which are compensated by adding to natural fruit flavor in powder form. Reconstitution of the fruit powder mixture yield full strength fruit juice drink. CFTRI Mysore has developed fruit juice powder technology for mango, orange, lemon, guava, passion fruit, banana, avocado, tomato etc.

10. **Barley water:** Fruit juice which contains at least 25% fruit juice, 30 % TSS and 0.25% barley starch is known as barley water. It also contains about 1.0 % acid. Barley water is prepared from citrus fruits such as lime, lemon, grape fruits and orange while lime and lemon are mostly used. It is prepared by using about 1 litre of fruit juice, 2.0 kg sugar, 15 g of barley flour and 1.3 litre of water. Essence and potassium meta-bisulphate may also be added if desired.

Still beverages

Juice and juice drinks, sport and energy drinks and ready-to-drink teas and coffees are still beverages that have not been carbonated. The range produced covers an increasing variety in many tastes and flavours.

Tea beverages: Ready-to-drink teas are an increasingly popular beverage group in range of still beverages, and in recent years their appeal has broadened as an increasingly preferred option. Nestea is available across most of our markets in a variety of flavours including Green Tea, Lemon, Peach, Blackcurrant and Fruits of the Forest. Consumer demand for more choice and variety within the tea category has led to the introduction of Nestea Vitao. Nestea Vitao is a range of green, red and white teas with all the natural goodness of tea combined with delicious fruit flavours to help improve the overall wellbeing. In 12 countries, Nestea products were launched with stevia, an innovative new natural sweetener derived from the leaves of the stevia plant.

Juice beverages: Fruit juices and fruit drinks provide consumers with vitamins and nutrition as well as the liquid needed to maintain good levels of hydration, necessary to sustain a healthy, well-balanced life. The range of fruit drinks can be categorized as:

- fruit juice, a juice obtained by simple pressing of the fruit, with vitamin content restored if lost during processing;
- fruit juice from concentrate, obtained by evaporating most of the water contained in the initial juice and then replacing it during the bottling process;
- fruit nectar, a juice or a juice pulp to which water and varying amounts of sugar (depending on the fruit involved) are added; and
- fruit drinks, which are soft drinks that contain variable quantities of fruit juice, as well as water and sugar or sweeteners. On average, these have a fruit juice content of between 5 per cent and 12 per cent.

Energy drinks: Energy drinks remain a highly dynamic segment, offering fun and functionality and usually contain. Energy-enhancing products, mainly carbonated and containing taurine, guarana, glucose, caffeine and other exotic herbs and substances, as well as added minerals and vitamins. The category includes still or carbonated, ready to drink (rtd) products, non-ready to drink (non-rtd) powders and concentrates. All powders and concentrates are expressed in ready. Sugar, a source of energy. Caffeine, a mild stimulant in combination with sugar, it is known as being particularly energising and invigorating Vitamin B Taurine, glucuronolactone and inositol (depending on the local adaptation).

Sports drinks: Performance-enhancing products, described as 'isotonic', 'hypertonic' or 'hypotonic', meaning 'in balance with', 'lighter than' and 'heavier than' body fluids, respectively. Products must contain sodium citrate (acidity regulator), sweetening agents and either glucose or dextrose, and minerals such as calcium dicitrate, potassium chloride, magnesium phosphate or zinc sulphate. The category includes still or carbonated, ready to drink (RTD) products, non-ready to drink (non-rtd) powders and concentrates. It also contains fruit and non-fruit flavoured products. All powders and concentrates are expressed in ready to drink (RTD) volumes. Sports drinks have been designed to provide:

- *Water:* for proper re-hydration. The body loses water during physical exercise in order to regulate body temperature and prevent it from rising
- *Carbohydrates:* during physical activity carbohydrates (or sugars) are the main fuel used by our body. Sports drinks contain an appropriate amount of carbohydrates to provide energy for muscular activity.
- *Mineral salts:* (particularly sodium) to enhance the absorption of water and carbohydrates and to compensate for the loss of sodium caused by perspiration.

It's important that sports drinks are pleasant tasting in order to encourage their consumption and ultimately hydration.

Sports drinks have been specially designed to ensure proper hydration and provide carbohydrates and mineral salts needed to help people achieve their best performance.

Carbonated beverages

Carbonated soft drinks are known for their thirst quenching and refreshing properties. However, they lack nutritional content. On the other hand, fruit juices, packed in cans, bottles or pouches are also very popular in the country which contain the nourishing properties and goodness of the fruit. Carbonated fruit based beverage is a new concept which provides nutritional elements of the fruit along with natural pigments and flavour in addition to carbonation effects.

Carbonation is the process of dissolving sufficient carbon dioxide in water or beverage so that the product when served gives off the gas as fine bubbles and has a characteristic taste. Carbonation adds to the life of a beverage and contributes in some measure to its tang. Fruit juice beverages are generally bottled with carbon dioxide content varying from 1 to 8 g per litre. Carbonation has many advantages such as it creates anaerobic condition of microbial activity, reduces oxidation of ascorbic acid and also prevents browning. The keeping quality of carbonated beverages is enhanced by adding about 0.005 percent sodium benzoate.

Carbonated soft drinks constitute the major category in "Aerated Soft Drinks", the other two categories being juice based soft drinks and squash, sharbat and syrup. Various types of soft drinks including orange, lime and lemon based drinks as well as soda water fall in the category of aerated soft drinks. These water drinks consist of water, carbon dioxide, colour, additives and preservative. In a tropical country like India, which has oppressive summers, there is substantial market for aerated soft drinks. The main process steps are:

i) Making concentrate of sugar, glucose, citric acid, essence and preservatives.

ii) Feeding the concentrate into dosing machine.

iii) Releasing the concentrate in each bottle in a required proportion.

iv) Filling the bottle with treated water.

5.4.2 Fruit Jam

Jam is a product made by boiling fruit pulp with sufficient sugar to reasonably thick consistency, firm enough to hold the fruit tissues in position. Jam contains 0.5-0.6 percent acid and sugar should not less than 68.5 percent total soluble solids as determined by Refractometer. Apple, apricot, mango, pineapple, plum, strawberry, carrot and tomato are used for preparation of fruit jam. It can be prepared from one kind of fruits or from two or more kinds. Apple jam can be prepared by using 1.0 kg apple pulp with 0.75 kg sugar, 2.0 g citric acid and 100 ml water (if needed). The following procedure is adopted for the development of fruit jam.

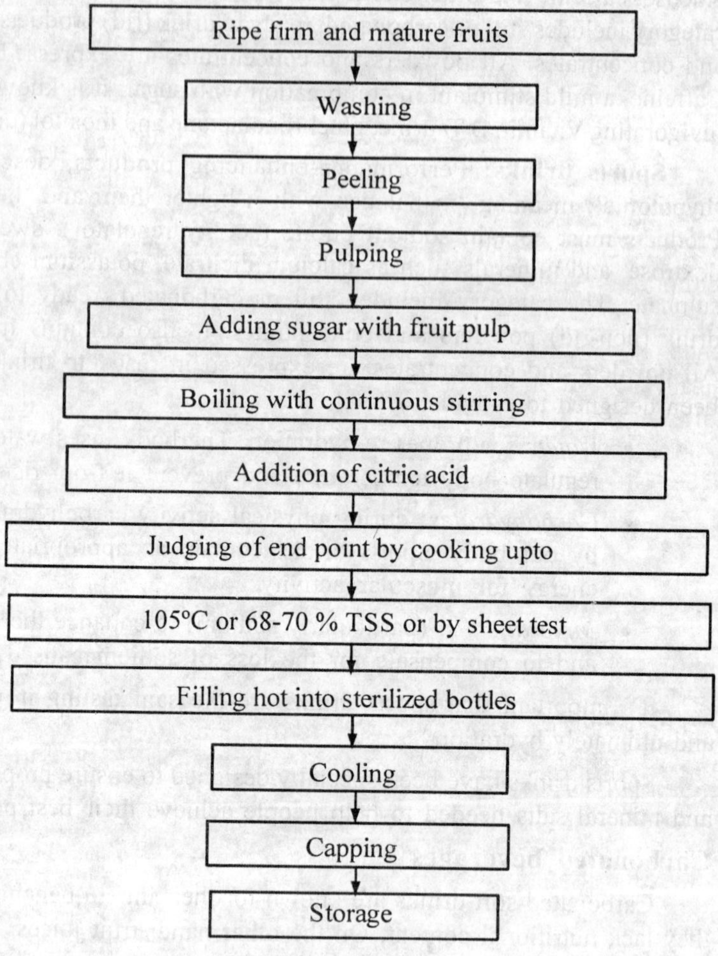

Fig. 1: Process chart of Fruit Jam

Problems in jam during processing and storage:

a) **Crystallization:** The final product should contain 30 to 50 percent invert sugar. If the percentage is less than 30, cane sugar may crystallize out on storage and if it is more than 50, the jam will be honey like due to the formation of small crystals of glucose. Corn syrup or glucose may be added along with cane sugar to avoid crystallization.

b) **Sticky or gummy jam:** Because of high percentage of total soluble solids, jam tends to become gummy or sticky. This problem can be solved by addition of pectin or citric acid or both.

c) **Premature setting:** This is due to low TSS and high pectin content in the jam and can be prevented by adding more sugar. If this cannot be done a small quantity of $NaHCO_3$ is added to reduce the acidity and thus prevent pre-coagulation.

d) **Surface graining and shrinkage:** this is caused by evaporation of moisture during storage of jam. Storing in a cool place can reduce it.

e) **Microbial spoilage:** sometimes mold may spoil the jam during storage, but they are destroyed if exposed to less than 90 percent humidity. Hence, jam should be stored at 80 percent humidity. Mold growth can be prevented by hot sealing the filled jar and covering the surface of jam with a disc of wax paper. It is also advised to add 40 ppm SO_2 in the form of KMS.

5.4.3 Jelly

A jelly is a semi solid product made by boiling a clear, strained solution of pectin containing fruit extract, free from pulp, after addition of sugar and acid. A perfect jelly should be transparent, well set but not too stiff and should have the original flavor of fruit. It should be of attractive colour and keep its shape when removed from the mould. It should be firm enough to retain a sharp edge but tender enough to quicker when pressed. It should not be gummy, sticky or syrupy or have crystallized sugar. The jelly should be free from dullness, with little or no syneresis (weeping), and neither tough, not rubbery. Guava, sour apple, plum, loquat, pineapple, strawberry, are used for preparation of jelly which is rich in pectin content. A good jelly should have 65% TSS, 1.0% pectin and 0.5-0.6 % acid. A good quality jelly is prepared from ripe guava due to higher content of pectin.

The end point of the jam and jelly can be judged in the following procedures:

Sheet or flake test: A small portion of jam or jelly is taken out during boiling, in a spoon or wooden ladle and cooled slightly. It is allowed to drop. If the product falls off in the form of sheet or flake instead of flowing in continuous steam or syrup, it means that the end point ha been reached and the product is ready, otherwise, boiling is continued till the sheet test is positive.

Drop test: A drop of the concentrated mass is poured into a glass containing water. Setting down of the drop without breaking or dilution or disintegration denotes the end point.

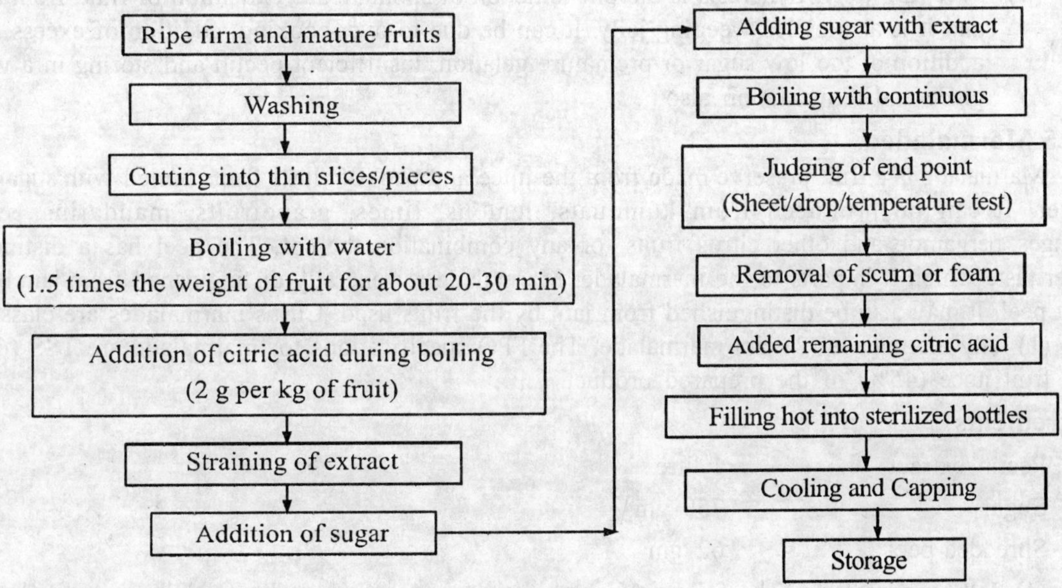

Fig. 2

Temperature test: A solution containing 65 percent total soluble solids (TSS) boils at 105°C. Heating of the jelly to this temperature would automatically bring the concentration of solids to 65 percent or degree Brix. This is the easiest way to ascertain the end point.

Problems in jelly making

The most important difficulties in that are experienced are as follows:

(*a*) **Failure of jelly to set:** It is the main problem encountered with jelly making. Often, it is due to impcrtant balance between various constituents of jelly *e.g.* lack of acid or pectin, addition of too much sugar, inaccurate measurement, insufficient cooking, overcooking and slow prevents the pectin from building a proper network of gel.

(*b*) **Cloudy or foggy jelly:** Unclarified juice or pectin extract, under ripe fruit, non-removal of scum, premature gelation, over-cooking or pouring so slowly into containers can results in a cloudy jelly.

(*c*) **Colour changes:** Darkening at the top of the jars can be caused by storing them in too warm a place or by an imperfect jar seal.

(*d*) **Crystal formation:** It is due to addition of excess sugar and also to over concentration of jelly.

(*e*) **Gummy jelly:** Gummy jelly is the results of prolonged or overcooking in which more than desired inversion of sugar occurs.

(*f*) **Presence of mold:** The appearance of mold can be the results of imperfectly sealed jars and air borne contamination if insufficient sugar is used. The availability of water makes a favorable environment for contamination from the jars if they are not properly sterilized or left under processed. Mold is visible before the taste is affected.

(*g*) **Stiff jelly:** Over-cooking or using too much pectin makes too tough jelly which fails to spread when applied on bread.

(*h*) **Weeping jelly:** Syneresis is the phenomenon of spontaneous exudation of fluid from a gel and it is also called weeping jelly. It can be due to over-cooking, addition of excess acid, addition of too low sugar or premature gelation, insufficient pectin and storing in a warm place and fermentation also.

5.4.5 Marmalade

Marmalade is a fruit preserve made from the juice and peel of citrus fruits boiled with sugar and water. It can be produced from kumquats, lemons, limes, grapefruits, mandarins, sweet oranges, bergamots and other citrus fruits, or any combination thereof. The peel has a distinctive bitter taste which it imparts to the marmalade. Marmalade is generally distinguished from jam by its fruit peel. It may also be distinguished from jam by the fruits used. Citrus marmalades are classified into (1) jelly marmalade (2) jam marmalade. The FPO specifications for marmalade are TSS (65%) and fruit juice (45%) of the prepared product.

Ingredients

Pectin extract	-	1 litre
Sugar	-	750 gm
Shredded peel	-	62 gm

(1) Jelly marmalade: The following combinations give good quality of jelly marmalade:

i. Sweet orange (Malta) and khatta or sour orange (Citrus aurantium) in the ratio of 2: 1 by weight. Shreds of Malta orange peel are used.

ii. Mandarin orange and khatta in the ratio of 2: 1 by weight. Shreds of Malta orange peel are used.

iii. Sweet orange (Malta) and galgal (Citrus iimonia) in the ratio of 2: 1 by weight. Shreds of Malta orange peel are used.

(2) Jam marmalade: The method of preparation is practically the same as that for jelly marmalade. In this case the pectin extract of fruit is not clarified and the whole pulp is used. Sugar is added according to the weight of fruit, generally in the proportion of 1: 1. The pulp-sugar mixture is cooked till the TSS content reaches 65 per cent.

Problems in marmalade making: Browning during storage is very common which can be prevented by addition of 0.09 g of KMS per kg of marmalade and not using tin containers. KMS dissolved in a small quantity of water is added to the marmalade while it is cooling. KMS also eliminates the possibility of spoilage due to moulds.

5.4.6 Preserve

A mature fruit/vegetable or its pieces impregnated with heavy sugar syrup till it becomes tender and transparent is known as a preserve. Apple, pear, mango, cherry, karonda, strawberry, pineapple, papaya, etc., can be used for making preserves.

In the home they can be prepared using 1 kg of fruit, 1 liter of water and 1 kg of sugar. A little quantity of acid (citric or tartaric) is added during the preparation to prevent crystallization of the syrup.

General considerations: Cooking of fruit in syrup is difficult because the syrup has to be maintained at a proper consistency so that it can permeate the whole fruit without causing it to shrink or toughen. Cooking directly in syrup causes shrinking of fruit and reduces absorption of sugar. Therefore, the fruit should be blanched first to make it soft enough to absorb water, before steeping in syrup. However, highly juicy fruits may be cooked directly.

Fruits may be cooked in syrup by three processes as given below:

a) **Rapid process:** Fruits are cooked in low-sugar syrup. Boiling is continued with gentle heating until the syrup becomes sufficiently thick. Soft fruits such as strawberries and raspberries, 'which require very little boiling for softening, unlike hard fruits like apples, pears, and peaches, which require prolonged heating, can be safely cooked in heavy syrup. Rapid boiling should, however, be avoided as it makes the fruit tough, especially when heating is done in a large shallow pan with only a small quantity of syrup. The final concentration of sugar should not be less than 68 per cent which corresponds to a boiling point of 106°C. This is a simple and cheap process but the flavour and colour of the product are lost considerably during boiling.

b) **Slow process**: The fruit is blanched until it becomes tender. Sugar, equal to the weight of fruit, is then added to the fruit in alternate layers and the mixture allowed standing for 24 hours. During this period, the fruit gives out Water and the sugar goes into solution, result in a syrup containing 37-38 per cent total soluble solids. Next day the syrup is boiled after removal of fruits to raise its strength to about 60 per cent total soluble solids. A small quantity of citric or tartaric acid (1 to 1.5 g per kg sugar) is also added to invert a portion of the cane sugar and thus prevent crystallization. The whole mass is then boiled for 4-5 minutes and kept for 24 hours. On the third day, the strength of syrup is raised to about 65 per cent, total soluble solids by boiling. The fruit is then left in the syrup for a day. Finally, the strength of the syrup is raised to 70 per cent total soluble solids and the fruits are left in it for a week. The preserve is now ready and is packed in containers. In practice, the number of steps may be varied.

c) **Vacuum process**: The fruit is first softened by boiling and then placed in the syrup which should have 30-35 per cent total soluble solids. The fruit- syrup blend is then transferred to a vacuum pan and concentrated under reduced pressure to 70 per cent total soluble solids. Preserves made by this process retain the flavour and colour of the fruit better than by the other two methods. In all these processes, the fruit is kept covered with syrup during cooking as well as afterwards otherwise it will dry up and the quality of the product would be affected. The product should be cooled quickly after the final boiling to prevent discolouration during storage. The fruits are drained free of syrup and filled in dry containers or glass jars. Freshly prepared boiling syrup containing 68 per cent total soluble solids is then poured into the jars/ containers which are then sealed airtight. In commercial scale production, however, it is better to sterilize the cans to eliminate any possibility of spoilage of product during storage.

5.4.7 Pickles

The process of preservation of food in common salt or vinegar is called as pickling. Spices and edible oils also may be added to the product. Salt, vinegar, lactic acid and oil are the important ingredients used in pickle production. These substances when used in sufficient quantities, act as preservatives either singly or in combination. The preservative action of these substances are given below:

Salt

Vegetables do not ferment when they are covered with strong brine or packed with a fairly large quantity of salt. Spoilage is prevented by adding sufficient common salt, bringing its final concentration in the material from 15 to 20 percent. At this high salt concentration, mould and even lactic acid-forming bacteria do not grow. This method of preservation is only applicable to vegetables which contain very little sugar because sufficient lactic acid cannot be formed by fermentation to act as preservative.

Vinegar

In vinegar pickles, vinegar acts as a preservative. In order to ensure satisfactory results, the final concentration of acid as acetic acid, in the finished product should not be less than 2 percent. To avoid dilution of the vinegar by the water liberated from the tissues, the vegetables are generally placed in strong vinegar of about 10 percent acidity for several days before final packing..

Lactic acid

Bacteria prefer for their growth media with little or no acid. The lactic acid bacteria, however, can grow in acid media and can also produce acid through their action on the substrate. They can grow in the presence of 8 – 10 percent salt. The growth of undesirable organisms is inhibited by adding salt while allowing the lactic fermentation to proceed. In fermented pickles, microorganisms ferment sugars to lactic acid. When vegetables are placed in brine, the soluble material present in them diffuses into the salt water owing to osmosis and the liquid penetrates into the tissues.

Oil

In oil-based pickles, fruits or vegetables are completely immersed in the edible oil. It acts as a barrier for air and creates an anaerobic condition which is utilized by the native bacteria for the production of lactic acid. Oil prevents growth of spoilage yeasts and moulds. Generally mustard

Oil is used.

In India, the Food Safety and Standards (FSS) Rules (2006) defines pickles as "preparation made from fruits and vegetables or other edible plant material including mushrooms free from insect damaged or fungal infection, singly or in combination preserved in salt, acid, sugar or any combination of the three. The pickle may contain onion, garlic, ginger, sugar, jaggery, edible vegetable oil, green or red chillies, spices, spice extracts/oil, lime juice, vinegar/acetic acid, citric acid, dry fruits and nuts. It shall be free from copper, mineral acid, alum, synthetic colours and shall show no sign of fermentation". Pickles may be of following combinations confirming to the requirements as given below:

Pickles in citrus juice or brines

a) Drained weight: Not less than 60 percent
b) Sodium Chloride content when packed in brine: Not less than 12 percent
c) Acidity as Citric acid when packed in Citrus Juice: Not less than 1.2 percent

Pickles in oil

a) Drained weight: Not less than 60 percent
b) Fruit and vegetable pieces shall practically remain submerged in oil

Pickles in vinegar

a) Drained weight: Not less than 60 percent
b) Acidity of vinegar as acetic acid: Not less than 2.0 percent

Some of the famous pickles with processing flow chart

(i) Lime pickle : Lime1kg, salt 200 g, red chili powder 15 g, cinnamon, cumin, cardamom (large) and black pepper (powdered) each 10 g, clove (headless) 5 numbers

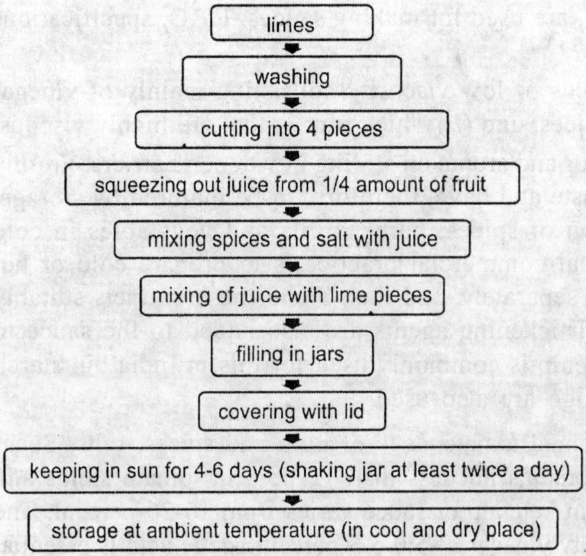

Fig. 3: Processing Flow-sheet For Lime Pickle

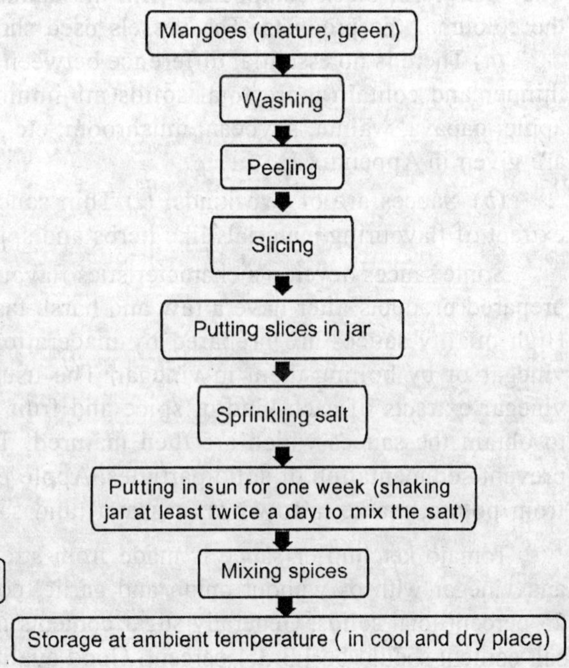

Fig. 4: Processing Flow-sheet For Mango Pickle

(*ii*) Lime and green chillies pickle : Lime 750 g, green chillies 250 g, salt 200 g, cinnamon, cumin, cardamom (large) and black pepper (powdered) each 10 g,clove (headless) 8 numbers.

(*iii*) **Mango pickle :** Mango peeled and sliced 1 kg, salt 200 g, red chilli powder 10 g, asafoetida 5 g, fenugrrek, black pepper, cardmom (large), cumin and cinnamon (powdered) each 10 g, clove (headless) 6 numbers.

(*iv*) **Sweet mango pickle :** Mango slices 1 kg, salt 120 g, red chillies, cumin, cardamom (large), aniseed, cinnamon, black pepper, coriander (powdered) each 10 g, clove (headless) 6 numbers, jaggery or sugar.

5.4.8 Sauce/Ketchup

Chutney and sauce/ketchup are important products prepared both in home and commercially in India. They improve the digestion and are good appetizers. Fruits such as mango, apple, plum, apricot and peach and vegetables like tomato, cauliflower, turnip and carrot are the raw materials used. Ginger, garlic, onion, herbs, spices etc are added for flavor and aroma in the final products. Sometimes powdered cloves are added. Since the flower head of clove contains tannin which causes browning, black neck ring formation takes place in products if whole cloves are used. Hence clove should be used only after removing the flower head. Vinegar, tamarind pulp and pomegranate seed impart acidity. Sweetness is given by adding sugar or jaggery and salty taste by only common salt. Chutney or sauces do not get spoilt due to presence of vinegar, salt, sugar and some spices. Chemical preservatives are sometimes added to prevent spoilage. Iron and copper equipments should not be used in the preparation of sauces and chutneys as these metals are acted upon by vinegar. Further, traces of these metals dissolved in oil, catalyze the development of rancidity in the final products. They also form black compounds with the tannin of fruits and spices and thereby adversely affect the colour of the products. The vessels used should be glass-lined or made of nickel or stainless.

(*a*) There is no essential difference between sauce and ketchup. However, sauces are generally thinner and contain more total solids(minimum 30%) than ketchups (minimum 28%). Tomato, apple, papaya, walnut, soybean, mushroom, etc., are used for making sauces, F.P.O. specifications are given in Appendix IX.

(*b*) Sauces are of two kinds: (*i*) Thin sauces of low viscosity consisting mainly of vinegar extract of flavouring materials like herbs and spices, and (*ii*) Thick sauces that are highly viscous.

Some sauces develop a characteristics flavour and aroma on storing in wooden barriers. Freshly prepared products after have a raw and harsh taste and have, therefore, to be matured by storage. High quality sauces are prepared by maceration of spices, herbs, fruits and vegetables in cold vinegar or by boiling them in vinegar. The usual commercial practice is to prepare cold or hot vinegar extracts of each kind of spice and fruit separately, and then blend these extracts suitably to obtain the sauces which are then matured. Thickening agents are also added to the sauce to prevent sedimentation of solid particles. Apple pulp is commonly used for this in India but starch from potato, maize, arrowroot (cassava) and sago are also used.

Tomato ketchup or sauce is made from strained tomato juice or pulp and spices, salts. Sugar and vinegar with or without onion and garlic, contains not less than 12 percent tomato solids and 25 percent total solids. Generally sugar contents in ketchup or sauce varies from 10-26 percent. The salt content should be 1.3-3.4 percent. Good quality vinegar of 5.0-5.5 percent acetic acid is essential for the preparation of high quality sauce/ketchup.

Some of the other sources are:

(*i*) ***Apple sauce*** : Apple pulp 1 kg, sugar 250 g, salt 10 g, onion (chopped) 200 g, ginger (chopped) 100 g, garlic (chopped) 50 g, red chilli powder 10 g, clove (headless) 5 numbers, cinnamon, cardamom (large), aniseed(powdered) 15 g each, vinegar/acetic acid 50 ml and sodium benzoate 0.7 g per kg finished product.

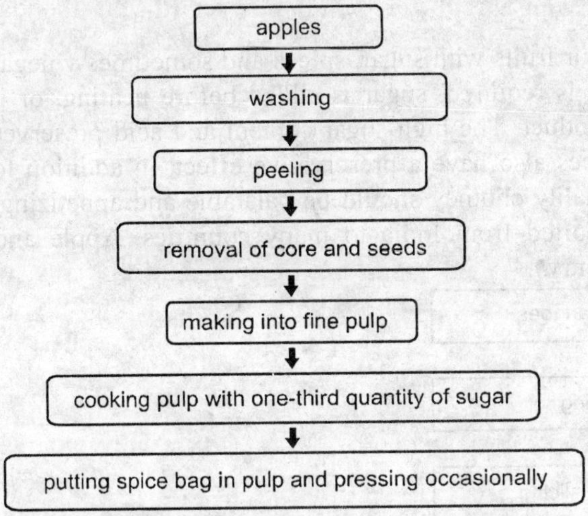

Fig. 5: Processing Flow-sheet for Apple Sauce

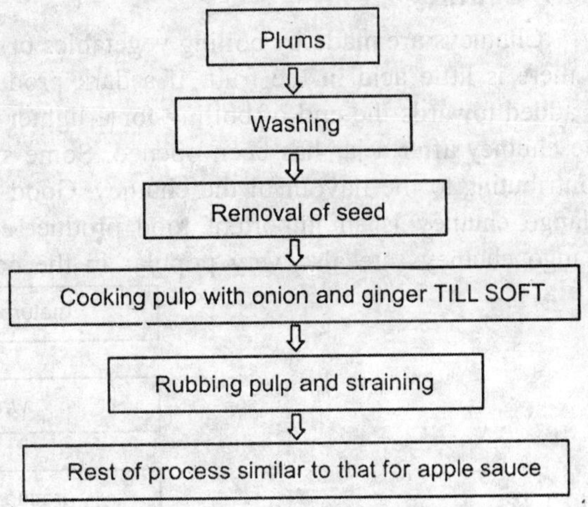

Fig. 6: Processing Flowchart for Plum Sauce

(*ii*) ***Plum sauce*** : Plum pulp 1 kg, sugar 100 g, salt 20 g, onion (chopped) 15 g, ginger (chopped) 25 g, garlic (chopped) 10 g, red chilli powder 10 g, clove (headless) 5 numbers, black pepper, cardamom (large), cinnamon (chopped) 10 g, aniseed (powdered) 15 g each, vinegar/ acetic acid 40 ml and sodium benzoate 0.7 g per kg finished product.

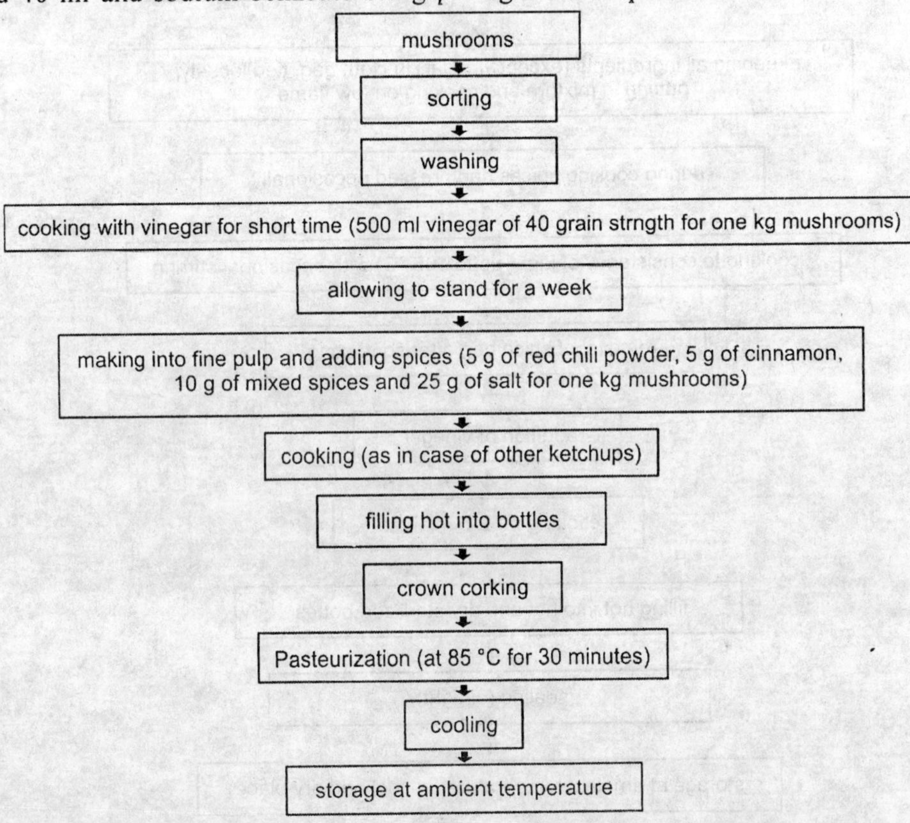

Fig. 7: Flow-sheet for Processing of Mushroom Ketchup

5.4.9 Chutney

Chutneys are made by boiling vegetables or sour fruits with sugar, spices and sometimes vinegar if there is little acid in the fruit. If a dark product is required, sugar is added before heating, or it is added towards the end of boiling for a lighter product. The high sugar content and acid preserves the chutney after a jar has been opened. Some spices also have a preservative effect, in addition to contributing to the flavour of the chutney. Good quality chutney should be palatable and appetizing. Mango chutney is an important food product exported from India to many countries. Apple and mango chutneys are also very popular in the country.

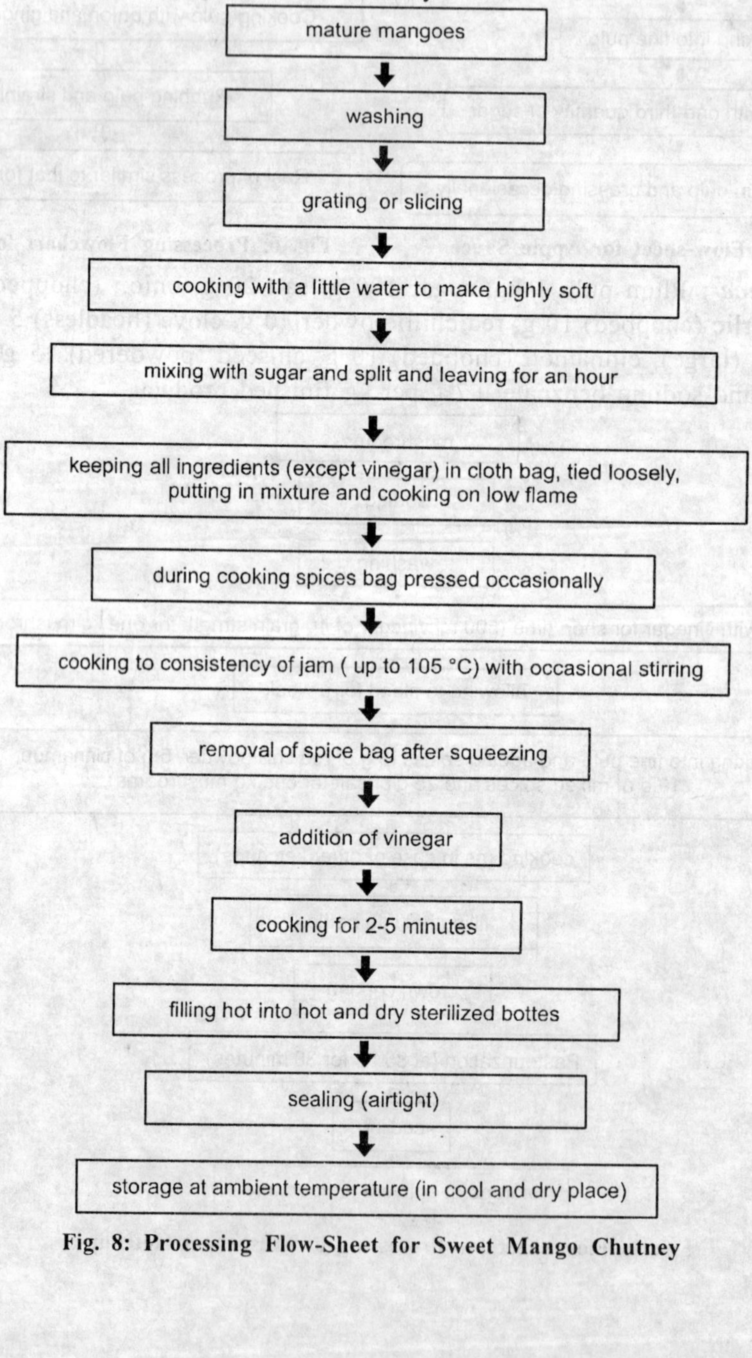

Fig. 8: Processing Flow-Sheet for Sweet Mango Chutney

Recipes for chutneys : Some common recipes for preparation of chutney are given below. However, it is always possible to go beyond a recipe, ignoring conventional tasters and creating something new. In mango and apricot sweet chutneys, where vinegar is used in large quantity, the amount of sugar added may be reduced, because vinegar itself acts as a preservative. These chutneys are cooked to the consistency of jam to avoid fermentation.

Sweet mango chutney : Mango slices or shred 1 kg, sugar or gur 1 kg, salt 4 g, onions (chopped) 50 g, garlic (chopped) 15 g, red chili powder 10 g, black pepper, carddamom (large), cinnamon, cumin, aniseed (powdered) 10 g each, clove (headless) 5 numbers and vinegar 170 ml.

5.4.10 Tomato Products

The manufacture of processed fruits and vegetables is controlled by the Fruit Products Order (FPO), 1955 of the Govt. of India. The Fruit Products Order, 1955 is mandatory for tomato products. The tomato products should conform to specifications laid down in FPO. The FPO specifications are as follows:

i) Tomato Juice : 5% total solids.

ii) Tomato Puree : 9% total solids. Sodium Benzoate 250 ppm

iii) Tomato Ketchup : 25% total solids. Acidity: 1.0% Sodium Benzoate: 750 ppm

The Bureau of Indian Standards has laid down the following specifications for tomato products:

i) Tomato Juice : IS:3881:1966.

ii) Tomato Ketchup : IS:3882:1966.

iii) Tomato Puree : IS:3883:1966.

Now in this era, the entrepreneurs may adopt HACCP and ISO 9000 certification also.

(*i*) Soup

A liquid food prepared from meat, fish, or vegetable combined with various other ingredients and often containing solid pieces. Some soups are served with large chunks of meat or vegetables left in the liquid, while a broth is a flavored liquid usually derived from boiling a type of meat with bone, or a vegetable for a period of time in a stock. A common type of broth is consommé, which are crystal clear broths or stock that have a full flavor, aroma, and body. Tomato soup is becoming very popular in homes. Stored soup is warmed at the time of serving. **Recipe:** Tomato pulp 1 kg, salt 20 g, sugar 20 g, butter or cream 20 g, flour/starch 10 g, onion (chopped) 20 g, garlic (chopped) 5 g, clove (headless) 5 numbers, cumin, cardamm (large), black pepper, cinnamon (powdered) 1 g each and water 350 ml.

The main steps in tomato soup preparation are as

→ Tomato pulp/juice (strained) → Boling to concentrate → Putting spice bag in cooking pan (as in sauce) → Preparing paste of butter and flour/starch → Addition to concentrate cooking to desired consistence with continuous stirring (to prevent coagulation of starch) → Addition of sugar and salt then cooking fro 2 min. → Removal of spice bag (after squeezing) → Filling into cans (plain cans) → Sterilization (at 115°C for 40-45 min) → Cooling → Storage at ambient temperature (in cool and dry place)

(ii) Tomato Puree

Fully ripe well developed colour tomatoes or other are washed, trimmed, steamed; crushed in a crusher or cut into pieces with knives. The crushed pieces are heated in the steam jacketed kettle till they become quite soften. The heated tomatoes are passed through the pulping machine using a fine mesh sieve to separate juice from seeds and the skin. The juice obtained as above is concentrated under vacuum to about 9% to 12% total solids so as to get tomato puree. The product is filled in bottles, crown corked and processed in boiling water for 30 min. and cooled.

(iii) Tomato Paste

Tomato paste is a thick paste that is made by cooking tomatoes for several hours to reduce moisture, straining them to remove the seeds and skin, and cooking them again to reduce them to a thick, rich concentrate. In contrast, tomato purée is a liquid with a consistency between crushed tomatoes and tomato paste, and consists of tomatoes that have been boiled briefly and strained. It contains not less than 25 percent tomato solids. On further concentration to 33 percent or more solids, it is called **concentrated tomato paste**. The difference between tomato paste, tomato purée, and tomato sauce is consistency, and the thicker the consistency, the deeper the flavor. Depending on its manufacturing conditions, tomato paste can be the basis for making ketchup or reconstituted tomato juice.

- Hot break: heated to about 100 °C; pectin is preserved > thicker-> ketchup
- Warm break: heated to about 79 °C; colour is not preserved, but flavour is
- Cold break: heated to about 66 °C; colour and flavour is preserved -> juice

Problems in tomato products during storage:

Black neck: Formation of a black ring in the neck of bottles is known as black neck. It is caused by the iron which gets into the product from the metal of the equipment and the cap/crown cork through the action of acetic acid. This iron coming into contact with tannins in spice forms ferrous tannate which is oxidized to black ferric tannate. Black neck can be prevented by:

a) Filling hot sauce at a temperature not less than 85°C;

b) Leaving very little head space in bottles (the more the air the greater is the blackening);

c) Reducing contamination by iron, sources of iron being salt and metal equipment;

d) Partial replacement of sugar by corn syrup or glucose syrup which contain sulphur and prevent blackening;

e) Addition of 100 ppm sulphur dioxide or 100 mg ascorbic acid;

f) Storing bottles in horizontal or inverted position to diffuse the entrapped air (02) throughout the bottle thus reducing its concentration in the neck sufficiently to prevent blackening;

g) Using cloves only after removing the flower/head.

5.4.11 Candied Fruits/Vegetables

A fruit/vegetable impregnated with cane sugar or glucose syrup, and subsequently drained free of syrup and dried, is known as candied fruit/vegetable. The most suitable fruits for candying are aonla, karonda, pineapple, cherry, papaya, apple, peach" and peels of orange, lemon, grapefruit and citron, ginger, etc. Pineapple cores, which are a waste product in the canning of pineapples, can be candied directly without any preliminary treatment. There is scope for developing this useful byproduct. F.P.O. specifications. The process for making candied fruit is 'practically similar to that for preserves. The only difference is that the fruit is impregnated with syrup having a higher percentage of sugar or glucose. A certain amount {25-30 per cent} of invert sugar or glucose, viz. confectioners glucose (corn syrup, crystal syrup or commercial glucose), dextrose or invert sugar is substituted for cane sugar. The total sugar content of the impregnated fruit is kept at about 75 per cent to prevent fermentation. The syrup left over from the candying process can be used for candying another batch of the same kind of fruit after suitable dilution, for sweetening chutneys, sauces and pickles, and in vinegar making.

5.4.12 Glazed Fruits and Vegetables

Covering of candied fruits/vegetables with a thin transparent coating of sugar, which imparts them a glossy appearance, is known as glazing. The preparation of glazed fruits has been described by Cruess as under: Cane sugar and water (2 : 1 by weight) are boiled in a steam pan at 113-114°C and the scum is removed as it comes up. Thereafter the syrup is cooled to 93°C and rubbed with a wooden ladle on the side of the pan when granulated sugar is obtained. Dried candied fruits are passed through this granulated portion of the sugar solution, one by one, by means of a fork, and then placed on trays in a warm dry room. They may also be dried in a drier at 49°C for 2-3 hours. When they become crisp, they are packed in airtight containers for storage.

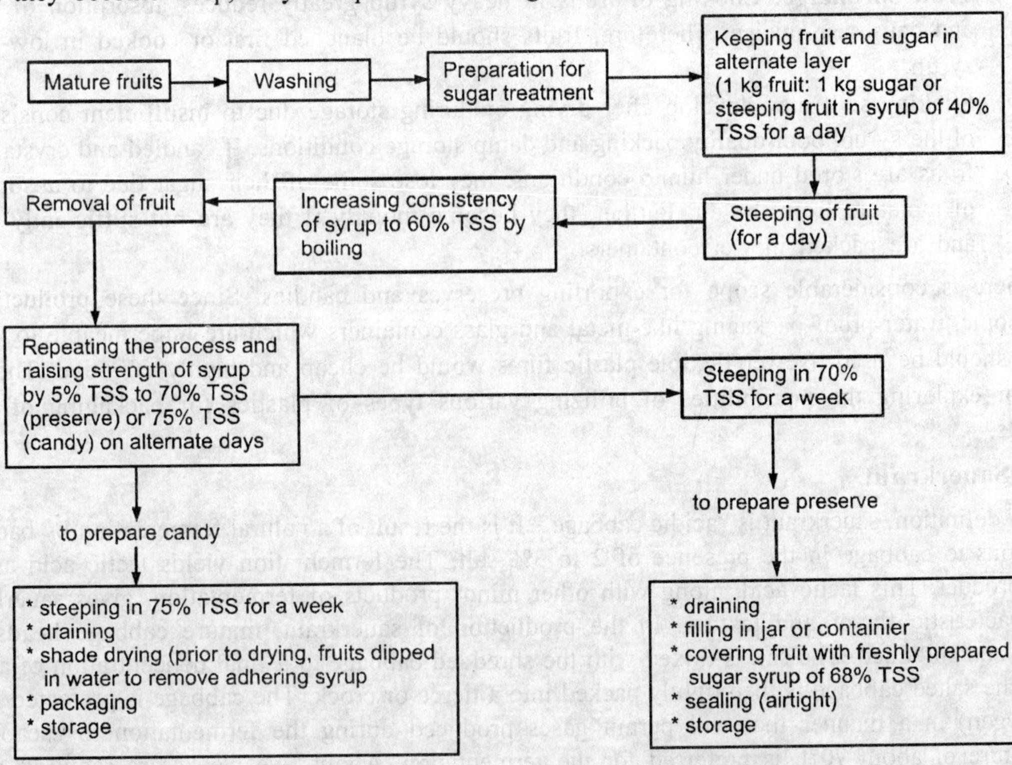

Fig. 9: Processing sheet of preserve and candy

5.4.13 Crystallized Fruits/Vegetables

Candied fruits/vegetables when covered or coated with crystals of sugar, either by rolling in finely powdered sugar or by allowing sugar crystals to deposit on them from a dense syrup are called crystallized fruits. The candied fruits are placed on a wire mesh tray which is placed in a deep vessel. Cooled syrup (70 per cent total soluble solids) is gently poured over the fruit so as to cover it entirely. The whole mass is left undisturbed for 12 to 18 hours during which a thin coating of crystallized sugar is formed. The tray is then taken out carefully from the vessel and the surplus syrup drained off. The fruits are then placed in a single layer on wire mesh trays and dried at room temperature or at about 49°C in driers.

Problems in preparation of preserves and candied fruits

(*i*) **Fermentation:** It is due to low concentration of sugar used in the initial stages of preparation of preserves. Sometimes fermentation also occurs during storage due to low concentration of sugar and insufficient cooking. This can be prevented by boiling the product at suitable intervals, by adding the required quantity of sugar and by storage in a cool and dry place.

(*ii*) **Floating of fruits in jar**: It is mainly due to filling the preserve without cooling and can be avoided by cooling the preserve prior to filling.

(*iii*) **Toughening of fruit skin or peel:** It may be due to inadequate blanching or cooking of fruits hence blanching till tender is necessary. Toughness may develop when cooking is done in a large shallow pan with only a small quantity of syrup.

(*iv*) **Fruit shrinkage:** Cooking of fruits in heavy syrup greatly reduces absorption of sugar and causes shrinkage. Therefore, fruits should be blanched first or cooked in low-sugar syrup.

(*v*) **Stickiness:** It may develop after drying or during storage due to insufficient consistency of the syrup, poor quality packing and damp storage conditions. If candied and crystallized fruits are stored under humid conditions, they lose some of their sugar due to absorption of moisture from the air. Further, they become mouldy if they are not sufficiently dried and are packed in wet containers.

There is considerable scope for exporting preserves and candies. Since these products are hygroscopic, water-proof packaging like metal and glass containers which are impermeable to water vapour should be used. Newer flexible plastic films would be cheap and highly effective. There is need for exploring the possibilities of utilizing various types of plastics for packaging of such products.

5.4.14 Sauerkraut

By definition, sauerkraut is "acidic cabbage." It is the result of a natural fermentation by bacteria indigenous to cabbage in the presence of 2 to 3% salt. The fermentation yields lactic acid as the major product. This lactic acid, along with other minor products of fermentation, gives sauerkraut its characteristic flavor and texture. In the production of sauerkraut, mature cabbage heads are washed and shredded. The salt is mixed with the shredded cabbage to a final concentration of about 2.5%. The salted cabbage is then tightly packed into a tierce or crock. The cabbage is protected from air (oxygen) in a manner that will permit gases produced during the fermentation to escape. A temperature of about 70°F is preferred for the fermentation. About five weeks are required for a complete fermentation. The salting of the cabbage serves two major purposes. First, it causes an osmotic imbalance which results in the release of water and nutrients from the cabbage leaves. The fluid expelled is an excellent growth medium for the microorganisms involved in the fermentation. It is rich in sugar and growth factors. Second, the salt concentration used inhibits the growth of many spoilage organisms and pathogens. It does not, obviously, inhibit the desired floral succession. As cabbage is approximately 90% water and the salt is dissolved entirely in the water, the actual salt concentration (brine strength) experienced by the microorganisms in their aquatic milieu is around 2.8%. Thorough and even distribution of the salt is critical. Pockets of low or high salt concentration would result in spoilage and/or lack of the desired fermentation. Throughout the fermentation, it is critical that oxygen be excluded. The presence of oxygen would permit the growth of some spoilage organisms, particularly the acid-loving molds and yeasts. As no starter cultures are added to the system, this is referred to as a wild fermentation. The normal flora of the cabbage leaves is relied upon to include the organisms responsible for a desirable fermentation, one that will enhance preservation and organoleptic acceptability. The floral succession is governed mainly by the pH of the growth medium. Initially, a coliform starts the fermentation. Coliforms which have contributed to our lab-made sauerkraut in recent years have included *Klebsiella pneumoniae*, *K. oxytoca* and *Enterobacter cloacae*. As acid is produced, an environment more favorable for *Leuconostoc* is quickly formed. The coliform population declines as the population of a strain of ***Leuconostoc*** builds. As *Leuconostoc* is a hetero-fermentative lactic acid bacterium, much gas (carbon dioxide) accompanies the acid production during this stage. The pH continues to drop, and a strain of ***Lactobacillus*** succeeds the *Leuconostoc*. (On occasion a strain of *Pediococcus* arises instead of *Lactobacillus*.) The complete fermentation, then, involves a succession of three major groups or genera of bacteria, a succession governed by the decreasing pH.

cabbage (immature, white and sound headed)
↓
removal of core
↓
trimming (removal of outer leaves and defective portion)
↓
washing
↓
slicing (fine threads)
↓
putting threads in jars or vats
↓
addition of 25% salt
↓
covering mouth of jar with plastic cover
↓
allowing to ferment for a week at 16-22 °C
↓
removal of scum
↓
draining out juice
↓
pasteurizing herds (sauerkraut) at 75-80 °C for 10 minutes)
↓
filling hot into sterilized jars or wide mouthed bottles
↓
pasteurizing previously drained out juice at 90 °C
↓
pouring hot juice on to sauerkraut
↓
sealing
↓
storage

Fig. 10: Flow Chart for Making Sauerkraut

5.4.15 Fruit Toffee

Pulpy fruits like mango, guava, papaya, etc. can be used for making toffee. It is prepared by using 1 kg fruit pulp, 700 g sugar, 100 g glucose, 150 g skimmed milk powder and appropriate amounts of butter or ghee, essence and colour.

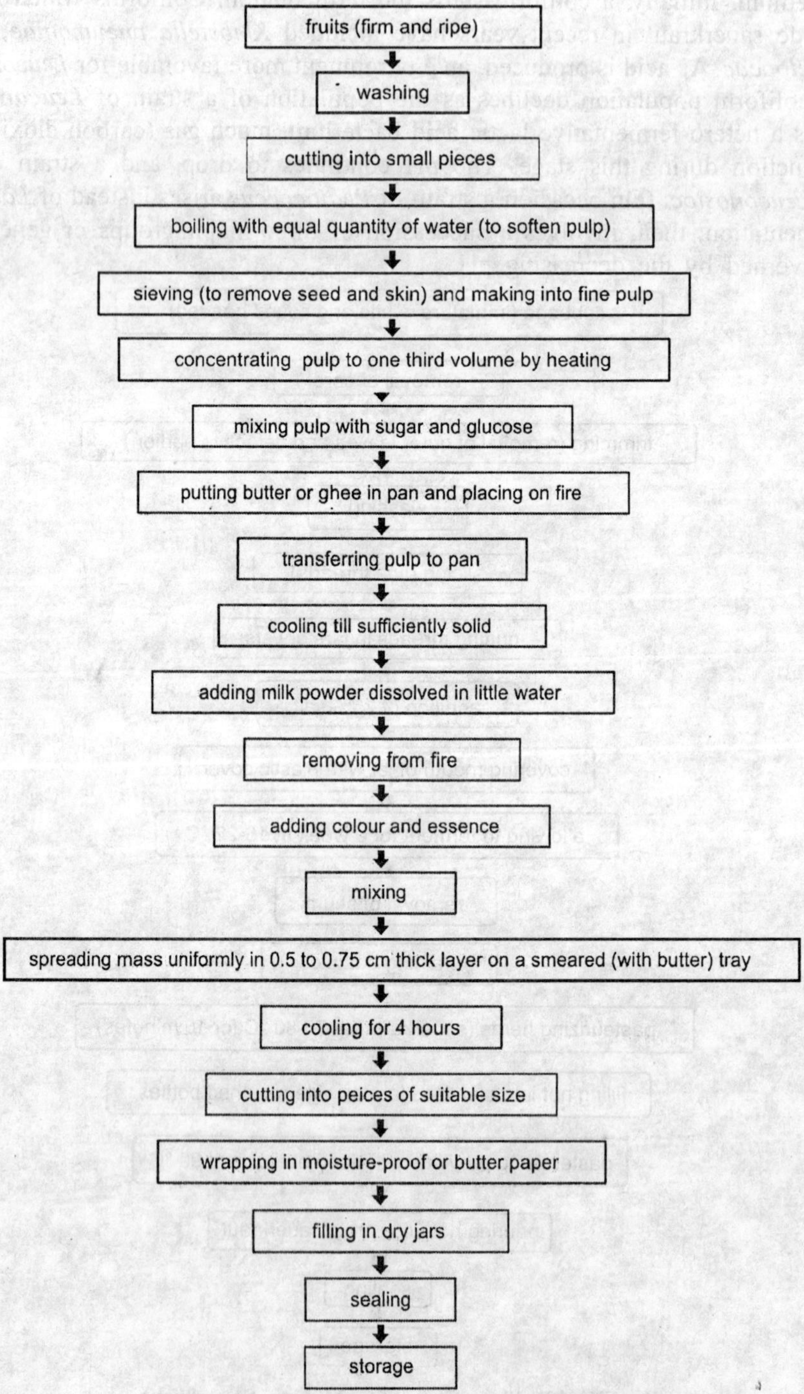

Fig. 11: Flow Sheet for Processing of Fruit Toffee

5.4.16 Fruit Butter

Fruit butters are prepared from apples, peaches, pears, apricots, plums, grapes, etc., or a combination of these fruits. They have a soft butter-like consistency and can be spread easily on breads. They are made by cooking 750 g of sugar with 1 kg of pulp and adding 1 pieces like nutmeg, cinnamon, clove, etc. On account of mild spicy taste and flour fruit butters, specially apple butter are very popular. The preparation of fruit butter is similar to that of jam except that fine pulp is used to which small quantities of spices are added.

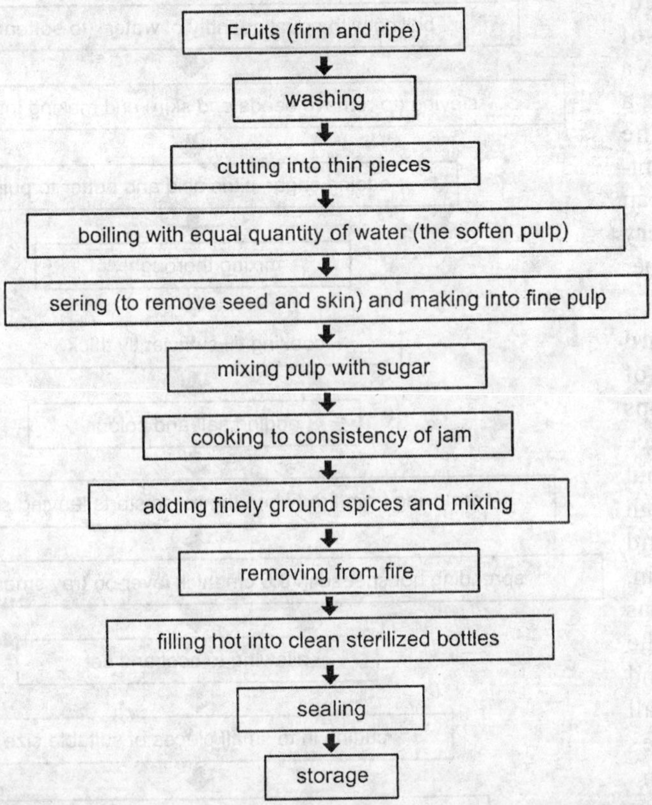

Fig. 12: Flow-sheet for Processing of Fruit Butter

5.4.17 Fruit Cheese

Fruit cheese has recently become very popular. It is a confection of the type of karachi Halwa and is prepared from fruits like guava, apple, pear and plum. Fruit cheeses have a long shelf-life and are at their best after 3 to 6 months storage. They can be prepared by using fruit pulp 1 kg sugar 1.25 gk, butter 70 g, citric acid 3 g, salt 2 g and appropriate amount of colour.

5.4.18 Other Vegetables Derived Products

Fresh Frozen Vegetables: There are thousands of frozen foods available. Before freezing, it is necessary to blend the product to destroy enzymes, which would result on off flavours and consequent quality deterioration. As frozen food preserves the vegetables, they don't get spoiled even after months once they are kept in cold storage, some 250000 retail stores have frozen food departments and 75% of the industry output is sold through super markets

Potato Powder, Granules & Flakes: Potato is one of the important tuber vegetables, which is consumed throughout the year. Indian vegetable basket is incomplete without mentioning the king of vegetables-potato-a sustaining force and a culinary delight. The tantalizing taste of nutrient-rich potatoes makes it an essential part of every breakfast, lunch and dinner worldwide.

Garlic Oil and Powder: Garlic is one of the important bulb crops grown and used as spice and condiment throughout India. It possesses a high nutritive value and medicinal property. Allicin, the principle of garlic has antibiotic properties. The plant is a small herb and produces a group of small bulbs called cloves covered with a thin skin

Bitter Gourd (Karela) Powder: Karela is a vegetable which is grown in every part of India. Karela is especially grown in India in from April to August. In the session it is abundantly available. It is generally used as vegetable throughout India. It has also good medicinal value. It is generally bitter in taste. Karela powder is now special product which can be produced by spray drying process.

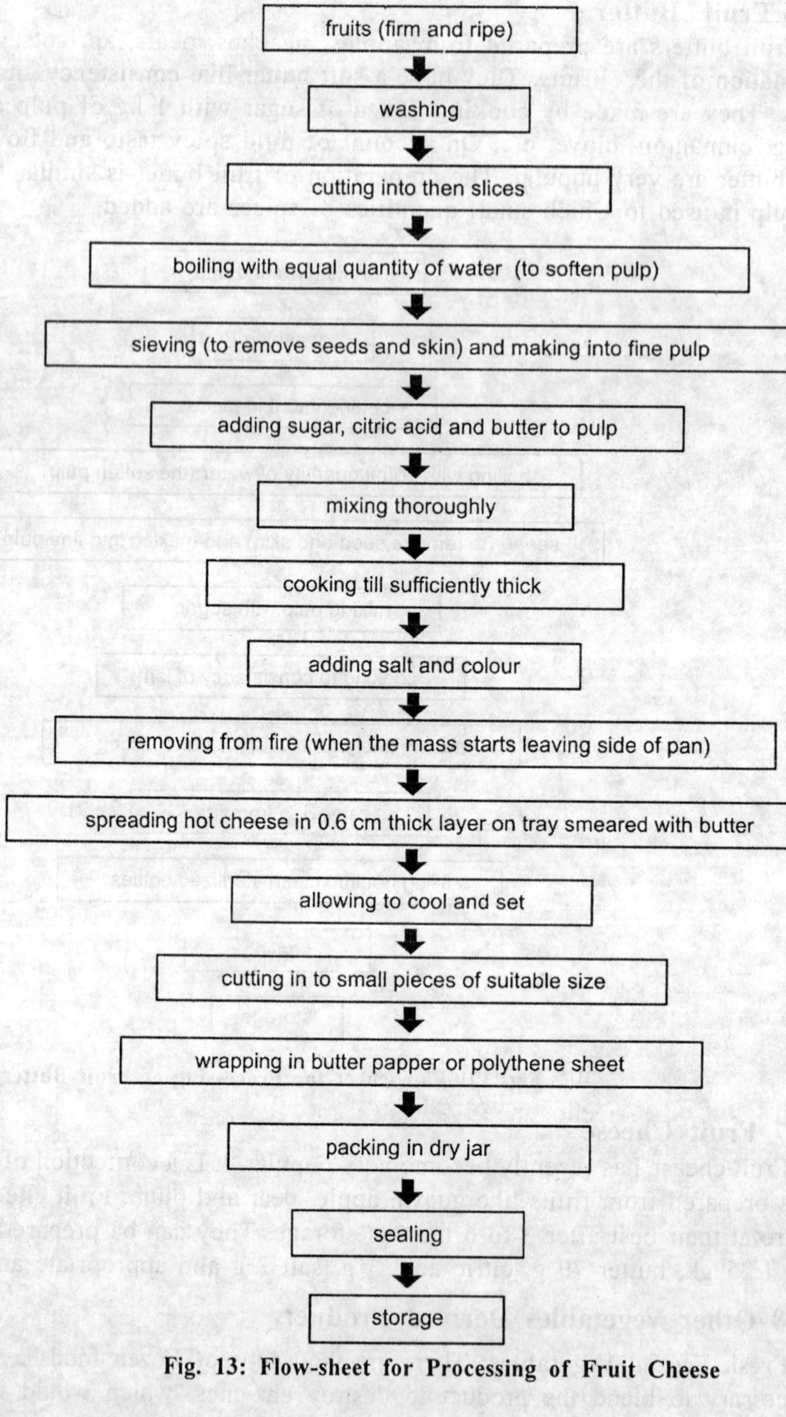

Fig. 13: Flow-sheet for Processing of Fruit Cheese

CHAPTER 6

VEGETABLE OIL PROCESSING

INTRODUCTION

The oils and fats are composed of different mixtures of glycerides of various fatty acids. It may be noted that the main constituents of the vegetables oils are 16 and 18 carbon acids. Easters containing more unsaturated esters constitute fats. All fats and oil are broadly classified into edible and non-edible. Ground nut, cotton seed, linseed, soybean, mustard are some of the sources of the edible oil. The edible oils are mainly used for cooking table's uses and salad dressing, besides this non-edible oils are used for soap industry, drying oil industry etc.

India's oilseeds production in marketing year (MY) 2023/2024 (October-September) is forecast to remain flat at 41.5 million metric tons (MMT), mostly unchanged from MY 2022/2023. Unseasonably heavy spring precipitation and a predicted El Niño weather pattern in the wake of severe April-June heatwaves will expose summer oilseed crops to greater incidences of plant stresses and thus impact yields. Oil meal production will remain steady at 20 MMT while exports will fall to 1.9 MMT, following an exceptional increase in exports in the current MY as southeast Asian demand has favoured competitively priced Indian oil meals against other origins. India will remain among the largest consumers of edible oils and is forecast to import 14.5 MMT of various oil commodities in the out year. Global decline in oilseed prices and relatively low import duties have stabilized domestic edible oil prices, leading to record ending stocks in the current year.

India's MY 2023/2024 oilseed production, which includes soybean, rapeseed-mustard, peanut, sun flower seed, cottonseed, and coconut (copra) is forecast to remain flat at 41.5 MMT, averaging approximately 1.03 MT/ha with near normal yields (Table 1). This estimate assumes a normal monsoon, favourable weather conditions and sufficient fertilizer availability throughout the growing season. Post expects continued high acreages of soybean, peanut, and rapeseed mustard, as farmers shift from cotton to other oilseed and pulse crops. Copra acreages are predicted flat in the out year, while farmers will continue to slowly reduce sunflower cultivation toward more remunerative crops.

Table 1: Oil content and average yield of some oil seed

S. No.	Oil seed	Oil content (%) wt	Average oil (kg)	Yield (kg/ha)
1.	Cotton seed	18 - 20	140	863
2.	Shelled ground nut	45 - 50	790	2494
3.	Rape seed	40 - 45	409	1166
4.	Soy bean	18 - 20	319	1788
5.	Oil palm kernel	40 - 45	3895	4455
6.	Safflower	30 - 35	762	2119
7.	Seasame	50	260	—
8.	Flax seed	35 - 42	230	650
9.	Sun flower	35 - 45	589	1469

6.1 OIL AND FATS

Oil and fats are important sources of energy requirements. Weight for weight, they furnish 2.25 times more energy than protein and carbohydrates. Thus, they help reduce the bulk of food, we take. Fat soluble vitamins A, D, E and K play a part in the biosynthesis of several long chain alcohols.

6.1.1 Linoleic Acid

Oils provide the essential fatty acid, linoleic acid, which is needed for human health. Excessive intake of saturated fatty acids increases the level of serum lipids and the incidence of arteriosclerosis and heart disease. A high level of consumption of unsaturated acids is thus necessary for normal health.

Linoleic acid (9,12-Octadecadienoic acid) has structural formula

$$CH_3\ (CH_2)_4\ CH = CH\ CH_2CH = CH(CH_2)_7\ COOH$$

Linoleic acid is a polyunsaturated omega-6 fatty acid. It is a colorless liquid that is virtually insoluble in water but soluble in many organic solvents. It typically occurs in nature as a triglyceride (ester of glycerin) rather than as a free fatty acid. It is one of two essential fatty acids for humans, who must obtain it through their diet, and the most essential, because the body uses it as a base to make the others.

Linoleic acid (LA: $C_{18}H_{32}O_2$; 18:2, ω-6) is a precursor to arachidonic acid (AA: $C_{20}H_{32}O_2$; 20:4, ω-6) with elongation and unsaturation. AA is the precursor to some prostaglandins, leukotrienes (LTA, LTB, LTC), thromboxane (TXA) and the N-acylethanolamine (NAE) arachidonoylethanolamine (AEA: $C_{22}H_{37}NO_2$; 20:4, ω-6), and other endocannabinoids and eicosanoids.

The metabolism of LA to AA begins with the conversion of LA into gamma-linolenic acid (GLA), effected by Δ6-desaturase. GLA is converted to dihomo-γ-linolenic acid (DGLA), the immediate precursor to AA.

LA is also converted by various lipoxygenases, cyclooxygenases, cytochrome P450 enzymes (the CYP monooxygenases), and non-enzymatic autoxidation mechanisms to mono-hydroxyl products viz., 13-Hydroxyoctadecadienoic acid, and 9-Hydroxyoctadecadienoic acid; these two hydroxy metabolites are enzymatically oxidized to their keto metabolites, 13-oxo-octadecadienoic acid and

9-oxo-octadecdienoic acid. Certain cytochrome P450 enzymes, the CYP epoxygenases, catalyze oxidation of LA to epoxide products viz., its 12,13-epoxide, vernolic acid, and its 9,10-epoxide, coronaric acid. These linoleic acid products are implicated in human physiology and pathology.

Hydroperoxides derived from the metabolism of anandamide (AEA: $C_{22}H_{37}NO_2$; 20:4,n-6), or its linoleoyl analogues, are by a lipoxygenase action found to be competitive inhibitors of brain and immune cell (Fatty Acid Amide Hydrolase) FAAH, the enzyme that breaks down AEA and other endocannabinoids, and the compound linoleoyl-ethanol-amide ($C_{20}H_{37}NO_2$; 18:2,n-6), an N-acylethanolamine,[*clarification needed*] - the ethanolamide of linoleic acid (LA: $C_{18}H_{32}O_2$; 18:2, n-6) and its metabolized incorporated ethanolamine (MEA: C_2H_7NO), is the first natural inhibitor of FAAH, discovered.

Uses and reactions

Linoleic acid is a component of quick-drying oils, which are useful in oil paints and varnishes. These applications exploit the lability of the doubly allylic C"H groups ("CH=CH"CH_2"CH=CH") toward oxygen in air (autoxidation). Addition of oxygen leads to crosslinking and formation of a stable film.

Reduction of the carboxylic acid group of linoleic acid yields linoleyl alcohol.

Linoleic acid is a surfactant with a critical micelle concentration of 1.5×10^{-4} M @ pH 7.5.

Linoleic acid has become increasingly popular in the beauty products industry because of its beneficial properties on the skin. Research points to linoleic acid's anti-inflammatory, acne reductive, skin-lightening and moisture retentive properties when applied topically on the skin.

Linoleic acid is also used in some bar of soap products.

6.1.2 Method of Oil Processing

Three well known oil processing methods are described here.

(1) Bullock driven chaki (Ghani), (2) Mechanical expression, (3) Solvent oil extraction

1. Bullock Driven Ghani

In India, the most popular method of extraction is by ghani, which is basically a large pestle and mortar. The mortar is an inverted cone, the pestle is heavy bank of timber seated at the bottom of the cone and inclined at an angle so that meal is crushed against the mortar during rotation. The timber bank is pulled against the sideway mortar by weight and is rotated by a pole inserted through it at right angle. One or two bullocks yoked to the pole provide power walking blind folded in a circle round the mortar, but ghani are now being modernized by adopting the pestle to mortar drive. Mortars are often hollowed out tree trunks but more recently of wood lined concrete or cast iron. Many small farmers have their seed pressed on contract paying either cash or a percentage of oil. Press cake as right is considered by some millers others allow farmers to remove it extraction. One bullock ghani can operate six charges of sunflower per day or 80 kg of meal (approximately 160 kg of seed). The produce of 45 kg of seed with a seed oil content of 30% would be 23 kg hulls, 13 kg of oil, 9 kg meal and the pressed cake containing some of 10 % oil.

2. Mechanical Expression

There are two steps involves in expulsion of oil through expeller, (1) disintegration and (2) pressing. Under the disintegration process, oil globules are separated. The tough membrane surrounding the oil droplet is exposed and burst under pressure enabling the oil to ooze out.

Expression is the process of mechanically pressing liquid out of liquid containing solids. Screw presses, roll presses and mill, collapsible plate and frame filler presses, disk mill are some of the example of a wide range of equipment used for expression liquids. The advantage of mechanical expression system over chemical extraction is that it gives the liquid free of dissolved chemical and thus a safer process.

Hydraulic Press: The hydraulic press is considered of a series of horizontal corrugated iron plates. These plates are separated by 4 to 14 pre-moulded oil seed cakes. Pressing is completed in two stages. In first stage the oil samples are pressed at approximately 5 MPa for 15-20 minutes. After wards a pressure of 28 MPa is applied for 5-10 min to complete the expression process. The out put of the press varies depending on the size and seed being used. In recent time at commercial level processing the hydraulic pressure has been replaced by screw type presses.

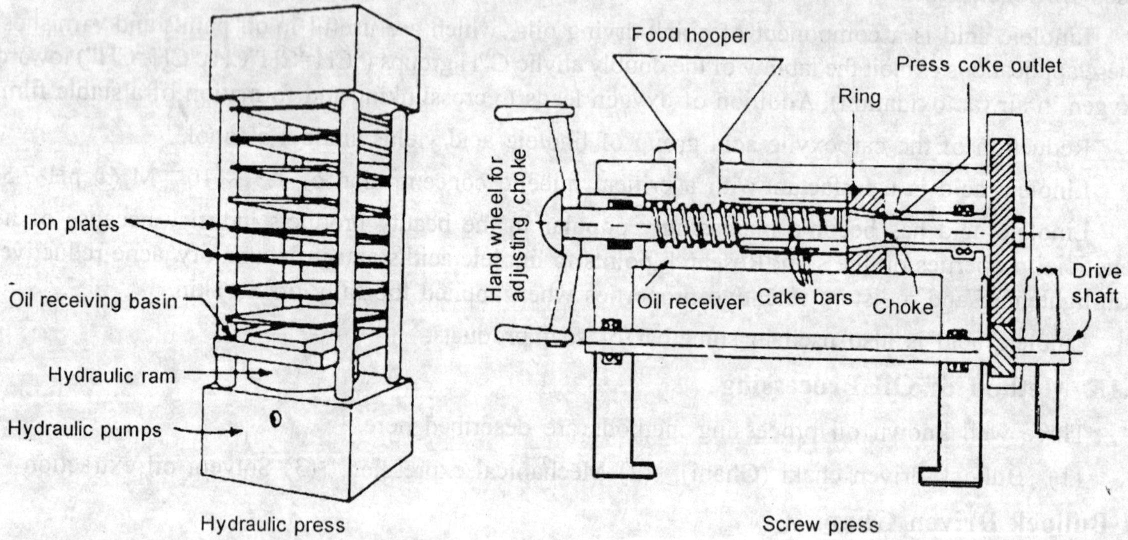

Fig. 1

Screw Press: The press has a horizontal main shaft. The screw assembly is formed integrally with this shaft. This screw rotates within a cage or barrel. The barrel is made of case hardened rings. Spacers are used between the lining bars or rings to allow drainage of the oil as the pressure on the feed material is increased. At the discharged end, a movable choke or cone controls the operating pressure. It is achieved by changing the width of annular space through which the oil cakes pass. The choke is adjusted by a hand wheel on the opposite end of the screw. Most screw presses have "feed gear" a means of running meal into the press, the choke gear, a means for adjusting the choke thickness.

3. Solvent Oil Extraction

Extraction is the process of separating a liquid from a liquid solid system with the use of a solvent. Extraction may also be said as a process to extract oil from oil bearing materials through the process of diffusion with the help of low boiling point solvent. This process gives a higher recovery of oil and a drier cake than expression. Extraction processing or solvent extraction is capable of removing nearly all of the available oil from oil seed meal or flakes. Apart from giving higher yields of oil, the extraction process may provide meal of better preservation qualities and with higher protein quantities.

In solvent extraction process, the solvent is added to well prepared materials. It is then followed by the diffusion of oil solvent mixture to the surface of solid for recovery of oil. The most commonly used solvent in Indian plants is the ***n–hexane***. The boiling point of ***n-hexane*** is about 65.5°C. A screw stirrer is provided in the extractor unit to prevent accumulation of material at one place during the process. The extracted meal which comes out of the extractor bottom is removed by metering screw conveyor. The deoiled cake coming out of the extraction unit has 25% to 40% solvent by weight. This has to be removed and recovered. This is normally done by evaporation either through the direct or indirect heating by steam or a combination of both.

6.1.3 Pretreatments of Oilseeds

Pretreatment in oilseed is done to improve the appearance of the oilseeds for the convenience of making oil.

1) **Drying:** The oilseeds should be dried before pressing. Proper water content will result in high oil yield, high output and high quality oil.
2) **Cleaning:** Inevitably, there will be impurities in the oilseeds that enter into the oil plant. If the soil, stem and leaves are not removed before pressing, the quality of oil and seed cake will be affected, some oil will be absorbed by these impurities so that oil yield will decline. Sand not only affects the normal work of **oil press**, but also largely shortens the service life of pressing screw, pressing bar and cake outlet. Stone, metal and other hard materials in the oilseeds will damage the pressing screw at once. There are many ways to remove the impurities. For light materials such as grass, stem and leaves, air classification can be adopted. If the impurities are small, we could remove them by screening separation. For those materials whose size and relative density are similar with oilseeds, clod can be smashed in sand machine first and then screened. Irony impurities can be separated by electromagnet or permanent magnet.
3) **Hulling:** For oilseeds with husk, we should remove the shell before pressing, so the throughput and oil yield can be improved. Dehulling can also be called sheling or decorticating
4) **Flaking:** Flaking ruptures seed cellular structure and increases surface area for incrased contact between solvent and seed during the solvent extraction process. Typical flake thickness is in the ranges 0.25-0.37 mm. Oil from the flaked seeds should be extracted as quickly as possible (within 24 hours) to minimize meal and oil quality.
5) **Puffing:** Sometimes this process will be adopted to optimize the leaching property of oilseeds.
6) **Crushing:** The aim of crushing is to reduce the size of the seeds, ensuring the uniformity of cooking. Too big or too small sizes are all to the disadvantage of oil outlet. Too big oilseed will obstruct the oil path. Too small oilseed will be brought way when pressing, increasing the resistance of oil flowing, and even blocking the oil path. Meanwhile, small oilseeds will make the plasticity of pressing material larger, which goes against the pressure's increasing, causing unnecessary reclaim. Large plasticity will also make the oil come out in advance in the form of solid cake or oil of bad quality. Some oilseeds can be pressed in its whole form, but after crushing and flaking, oil yield is obviously improved.
7) **Cooking:** This process is not only important for the oil yield, but also closely linked with the service life of oil press. Pressing material should contains proper amount of water and have good fluidity. It should have necessary temperature, lowering the viscosity and surface tension of oil in it, ensuring the good fluidity of oil when pressing. The method

that often adopted is wetting the oilseeds first, and then drying them by roasting machine, adjusting the water content to an ideal state. One of the matched equipment is **oilseeds roasting** machine. It is indispensible as well as crucial in the oil press production line. Different oilseeds has different characteristics, they shall be cooked to a certain extent accordingly. (It is said 70% yield lies in roasting and 30% lies in pressing. Therefore roasting or cooking is a key factor.)

6.1.4 Vegetable oil Refining

Crude vegetable oil contains various minor components, such as oxidation products of triacylglycerols and terpenes, polar lipids, trace metal derivatives, which deteriorate its sensory and functional properties. Therefore, it is processed by refining.

The first refining step is the *degumming.* Oil is treated with hot water, usually containing phosphoric or citric acid. Most phospholipids present in crude oil are hydrated and become insoluble in oil. Some phospholipids are not precipitated unless special procedures are used, such as super degumming. The precipitate, containing co-precipitated components other than phospholipids and some oil, is removed, dried, and used as commercial lecithin. The membrane filtration is another approach to degumming. The degummed product may be treated in two ways. If the free fatty acid content is high, it is alkali refined by a solution of sodium hydroxide or, less often, by sodium carbonate.

Degumming efficiency (g/100 g) = $\frac{P_0 - P_d}{P_0} \times 100$ where P_0 is phospholipids of crude oil (ppm) and P_d is phospholipids of degumming (ppm)

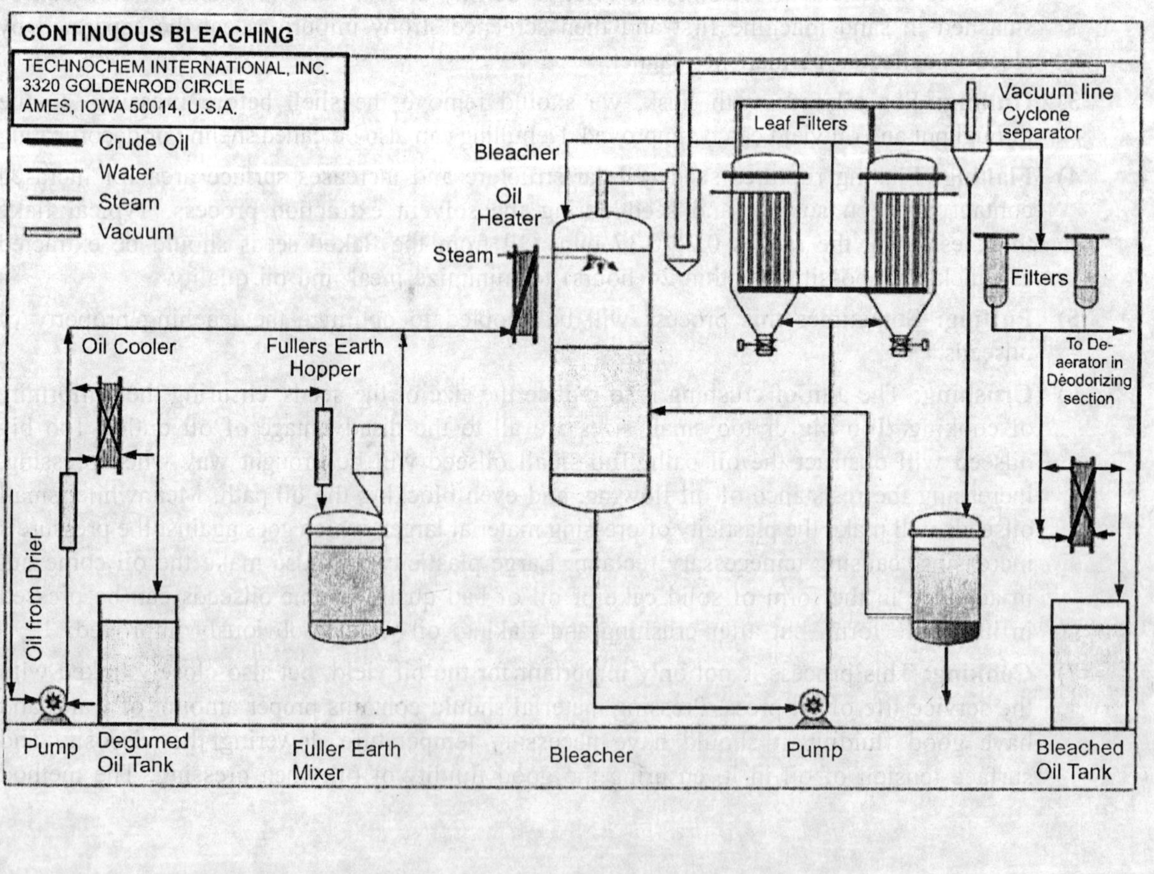

Free fatty acids are converted into water soluble sodium salts, which are washed out of oil with hot water. Natural pigments and other impurities are partially removed, too. After the alkali refining, oil is dried by heating at reduced pressure, and treated with bleaching earth or a mixture of bleaching each and with active carbon. In the process of *bleaching*, natural pigments (mainly carotenoids, pheophytins and chlorophylls) and the last traces of sodium salts are removed. Dimers of polyunsaturated fatty acids or sterols and trans-isomers may be formed in the course of *bleaching*.

Bleached oil is deodorized by treatment with overheated steam under reduced pressure in nitrogen at temperatures of 220–250°C. Volatile substances, formed by oxidation of unsaturated fatty acids during seed storage or seed processing, are removed during the process, and both the sensory value and the resistance against oxidative sensory deterioration (called rancidity) are thus substantially improved. Other relatively volatile substances are also removed at least partially, such as sterols or tocopherols. The deodorized oil has a bland neutral flavor.

Crude oils containing less than about 1% free fatty acids may be refined in a simpler way, *i.e.*, by physical refining. After degumming, crude oil is deodorized in a similar way as in the case of alkali refined oils to remove all relatively volatile components, including free fatty acids. The resulting oil is bleached. The alkali refining step is thus eliminated, which is advantageous from the environmental standpoint. The resulting refined oil is of about the same quality as alkali-refined oil, *e.g.*, as in the case of rapeseed oil.

During the process of *deodorization cis,cis*-diunsaturated fatty acid bound in triacylglycerols is partially isomerized into *cis,trans* and *trans,cis*-dienoic isomers in the case of linoleic acid. Several other trienoic isomers are formed in oils containing linolenic acid, such as soybean or rapeseed oil. As the nutritional value of these isomers is doubtful, the deodorization temperature should be lower than 240°C to minimize the isomerization. The best results are obtained using thin-film deodorization. In this process the temperature may be lower and the heating time is shorter.

Vapors removed during deodorization are collected as deodorization sludge. They contain free fatty acids, sterols, and tocopherols so that they can be used for the production of tocopherol concentrates suitable as antioxidants. Sterols may be isolated, too, and used either directly or after hydrogenation in stanols in margarines as an additive lowering blood pressure and decreasing the cholesterol content in blood plasma. Refined oils are either used directly as salad oils or frying oils, or after emulsification as mayonnaise and salad dressings, or are added to margarines. If fresh fish oils are properly refined, they are acceptable for margarines even without hydrogenation, even when their oxidation stability may still be a problem.

6.1.4.1 Hydrogenation: Hydrogenation is probably the most commonly used optional processing step. The purpose of hydrogenation is the saturation of fats, which is the addition of hydrogen to the double bonds in the fats. Hydrogenation can be either partial or full. Full hydrogenation converts the vegetable oils into fully saturated fats, vegetable oils partially saturated so the melting point increases to the point where solid fat is present at room temperature. Fats are hydrogenated for various reasons, including changing the plastic properties of the fat. However, most importantly, hydrogenation lowers the degree of unsaturation, which makes the fat more resistant to oxidation. A classical example is the partial hydrogenation of soybean oil. Soybean oil contains small amounts of linolenic acid (C18:3), which are responsible for flavor reversion (off flavor development). Partial hydrogenation of the oil eliminates the linolenic acid, resulting in a much more stable fat. Because of the differences in reaction rates, highly unsaturated fatty acids are hydrogenated quicker than fatty acids with fewer double bonds. In hydrogenation, the fat is mixed with hydrogen gas and a catalyst. The most commonly used catalyst is nickel. Hydrogenation is usually done in a closed vessel at high temperatures and pressures. A problem with hydrogenation that has recently gained considerable attention is the development of *trans* fatty acids. In nature, fatty acids contain almost exclusively *cis* double bonds. However, during hydrogenation the double bond is cleaved due to the addition of the catalyst at the double-bond site. Especially in partial hydrolysis situations, the catalyst may split off the fatty acid without hydrogenation taking place. In this case, the double bond may be reestablished in the *trans* configuration because, for the short time span that the catalyst is bound to the fatty acid, the original double bond becomes a freely rotatable single bond, allowing for *trans* fatty acid formation. Over the last decade, the hydrogenation process has undergone numerous modifications to reduce the formation of *trans* fatty acids because of their health implications.

6.1.4.2 Winterizing/Fractionation

The term fractionation is almost self-explanatory: the fat is divided into fractions. Fractionation is based on the differences in melting point among the various triacylglycerides. Because the fractionation of the fat is based on temperatures well below room temperature, the process has also been termed winterizing. In winterizing, the temperature of the fat is lowered, which causes triacylglycerides with a high melting point to crystallize, that is, solidify. Triacylglycerides with high melting points contain a relatively larger share of either saturated fatty acids or *trans* fatty acids. Thus, winterization can be used to reduce the amount of *trans* fatty acids that were formed during hydrogenation, although there is no selectivity for *trans* fatty acids. Fats with a wide melting range, such as cottonseed oil and palm oil, require winterizing, but winterizing is also practiced with animal fats such as lard and tallow. The effect of winterizing can be easily modeled in a home setting by placing olive oil in a refrigerator. The commercial process often involves "seeding" the liquid fat (oil) with a solid fat, allowing for faster crystallization. The fat is then chilled via cooling coils at a specific rate that depends on the type of fat. The chill rate and agitation rate are crucial for proper crystallization. The solid, crystallized fat is then separated from the liquid fraction by means of filtration.

6.1.4.3 Interesterification: Although interesterification can dramatically change the functionality of a fat, it is not commonly practiced because of a lack of control over the resulting fat. Unlike hydrogenation or winterizing, interesterification does not change the overall fatty acid profile of the fat; it rearranges the fatty acids within and among triacylglycerides by hydrolyzing and re-esterifying ester bonds between the fatty acids and the glycerol molecules. The result is a fat with a narrower melting range due to more random distribution of fatty acids among the triacylglycerides. Because of the formation of *trans* fatty acids in hydrogenation *interesterification*, in combination with blending, has recently received considerable attention as a possible replacement for hydrogenation.

6.1.4.4 Industry description and practices: The vegetable oil processing industry involves the extraction and processing of oils and fats from vegetable sources. Vegetable oils and fats are principally used for human consumption but are also used in animal feed, for medicinal purposes, and for certain technical applications. The oils and fats are extracted from a variety of fruits, seeds, and nuts. The preparation of raw materials includes husking, cleaning, crushing, and conditioning. The extraction processes are generally mechanical (boiling for fruits, pressing for seeds and nuts) or involve the use of solvent such as hexane. After boiling, the liquid oil is skimmed; after pressing, the oil is filtered; and after solvent extraction, the crude oil is separated and the solvent is evaporated and recovered. Residues are conditioned (for example, dried) and are reprocessed to yield by-products such as animal feed. Crude oil refining includes degumming, neutralization, bleaching, deodorization, and further refining.

6.1.4.5 Waste characteristics: Dust is generated in materials handling and in the processing of raw materials, including in the cleaning, screening, and crushing operations during processing. For palm fruit, about 2–3 cubic meters of wastewater is generated per metric ton of crude oil (m^3/t). The wastewater is high in organic content, resulting in a biochemical oxygen demand (BOD) of 20,000–35,000 milligrams per liter (mg/l) and a chemical oxygen demand (COD) of 30,000–60,000 mg/l. In addition, the wastewaters are high in dissolved solids (10,000 mg/l), oil and fat residues (5,000–10,000 mg/l), organic nitrogen (500–800 mg/l), and ash residues (4,000 to 5,000 mg/l). Seed dressing and edible fat and oil processing generate approximately 10–25 m^3 of wastewater per metric ton (t) of product. Most of the solid wastes (0.7–0.8 t/t of raw material), which are mainly of vegetable origin, can be processed into by-products or used as fuel. Molds may be found on peanut kernels, and aflatoxins may be present.

6.1.4.6 Pollution prevention and control: Good pollution prevention practices in the industry focus on the following main areas:

- Prevent the formation of molds on edible materials by controlling and monitoring air humidity.
- Use citric acid instead of phosphoric acid, where feasible, in degumming operations.
- Where appropriate, give preference to physical refining rather than chemical refining of crude oil, as active clay has a lower environmental impact than the chemicals generally used.
- Reduce product losses through better production control.
- Maintain volatile organic compounds (VOCs) well below explosive limits. Hexane should be below 150 mg/m^3 of air (its explosive limit is 42,000 mg/m^3).
- Provide dust extractors to maintain a clean workplace, recover product, and control air emissions.
- Recover solvent vapors to minimize losses.
- Optimize the use of water and cleaning chemicals.
- Recirculate cooling waters.
- Collect waste product for use in by-products such as animal feed, where feasible without exceeding cattle-feed quality limits.

Continuous sampling and measuring of key production parameters allow production losses to be identified and reduced, thus reducing the waste load.

Odor problems can usually be prevented through good hygiene and storage practices. Chlorinated fluorocarbons should not be used in the refrigeration system.

6.1.4.6 Pollution reduction targets: Since the pollutants generated by the industry are very largely losses in production, improvements in production efficiency, as described above, are recommended to reduce pollutant loads. Wastewater loads are typically 3–5 m^3/t of feedstock; plant operators should aim to achieve lower rates at the intake of the effluent treatment system. Hexane, if used, should be below 50 mg/l in wastewater. The BOD level should be less than 2.5 kg/t of product, with a target of 1–1.5 kg/t.

6.1.5 De-Oiled Cake Processing

Mustard oil cake: There is a great potential for preparation of high quality oilseeds protein concentrate from mustard, though there are number of problems too. The oil from mustard is known for its pungent flavor which is developed during milling through the control of moisture. While this flavour is highly appreciated by the consumers, it is very much undesirable in the protein concentrate. The presence of iso-thyocyanates and their toxicity is not desirable in the protein meal. Mustard oil cake powder can be used to irrigate the plants and also provide nutrition

Sunflower cake: The deoiled meal/cake of sunflower is used as animal feed. It has high nutritional value and rich its vitamin E. Laboratory defatted sunflower flours have been reported as possessing high protein contents, bland flavours, white colour at acid pH levels and containing no anti—nutritive factors. Functional test data show that sunflower flours and concentrates have high salt solubility, oil absorption and oil emulsification. High weight gains in rat fat feeding trials were obtained for sunflower blends with legume and animal proteins, suggesting their applications in milk and meat extenders and in soybean based infant formulas. Heat treatments, mechanical agitation and emulsification are reported to be effective in stabilizing 80% of sunflower proteins. Sunflower flour slurries show excellent whippability and foam stability, comparable to that of soybean protein isolate but lack the ability to form a firm gel. Spun sunflower protein casein (1 : 1) blends are superior to other vegetable proteins in shear strength. swellability and firmness. Sunflower proteins in particular have unique organoleptic and functional properties which could expand the range of food uses for concentrated seed protein, and blends with cereals, legume, animal products and lysine. Bakery products can also be prepared from sunflower and wheat flour.

Soybean cake: Soybean contains about 40% protein and 20% oil. Soy protein is the most economical protein produced in the world. The high quality of soy-protein is illustrated by its content of all the essential amino-acids with the exception of sulphur containing amino-acids. This imbalance is adequately offset in a traditional cereal based mixed diet in India. Supplementation of the cereal based diet with soy-protein gives an amino-acid complementation which results in increased protein quality and quantity approaching to that of animal protein.

Soy-protein concentrates and isolates: Soy-protein concentrates are produced from defatted flakes or flour by immobilizing the major protein component during separation of the low molecular weight carbohydrates, mineral matters and other major constituents. The soy protein concentrates contain not less than 70% protein. Soy protein isolate is prepared from defatted soyflour or flakes by extracting the proteins with an aqueous medium which may vary in pH from near neutrality to an alkaline pH. The aqueous extract is separated from the fibrous residue by centrifugation. The pH of the clarified extract is then adjusted to about 4.5 with food grade acid to precipitate the proteins. The protein curd is concentrated and washed with water. The concentrated protein can be dried as such or neutralized with food grade alkali and dried.

Textured protein: Textured or texturized vegetable protein (TVP), also known as textured soy protein (TSP), soy meat, or soya chunks is a defatted soy flour product, a by-product of extracting soybean oil. It is often used as a meat analogue or meat extender. It is quick to cook, with a protein content equal to that of meat.

TVP is usually made from high (50%) soy protein soy flour or concentrate, but can also be made from cotton seeds, wheat, and oats. It is extruded into various shapes (chunks, flakes, nuggets, grains, and strips) and sizes, exiting the nozzle while still hot and expanding as it does so. The defatted thermoplastic proteins are heated to 150–200°C, which denatures them into a fibrous, insoluble, porous network that can soak up as much as three times its weight in liquids. As the pressurized molten protein mixture exits the extruder, the sudden drop in pressure causes rapid expansion into a puffy solid that is then dried. As much as 50% protein when dry, TVP can be rehydrated at a 2:1 ratio, which drops the percentage of protein to an approximation of ground meat at 16%. TVP is primarily used as a meat substitute due to it's very low cost at less than a third the price of ground beef, and when cooked together will help retain more weight from the meat by absorbing juices normally lost.

Many TVP producers use hexane to separate soy fat from soy protein, and trace amounts of the solvent are left after manufacturing. But the few rodent studies that have been done suggest it would be almost impossible to get enough hexane from TVP to cause harm. Measured levels of residual hexane in TVP are around 20 parts per million; and rodent studies suggest that a dosage of 5g/kg is the minimum level where adverse effects were observed. As such one would have to consume around 2.5 metric tons of TVP per kilogram of body weight to reach a toxic dose.

Margarine and spreads

Margarine was invented and patented by the French chemist, Hippolyte Mege Mouries, in 1868 as a substitute to butter. The margarine was traditionally based on animal fats and the process was a relatively simple mixing process that included simultaneous cooling. Margarine and related products contain a water phase and a fat phase. Depending on the nature of the product the recipe will typically consist of a fat blend, emulsifier(s), flavour(s), colour(s), water, salt, sugar, and preservatives. Stabilizers are often added to fat spreads. Margarine, like butter, can be characterized as a water-in-oil (w/o) emulsion in which the water phase is finely dispersed as droplets in the continuous fat phase. The fat crystals form a three-dimensional network resulting in products with properties of plastic semisolid nature. The major ingredients in the fat phase, the fat blend, consist normally of a blend of different fats and oils. In order to achieve margarine with the desired characteristics and functionalities, the ratio of fats and oils in the fat blend is very important.

The ingredients used in the formulation of the fat blend can be derived from any animal, vegetable, or marine oil source. The choice of fats will depend on legislation, price, quality, functionality, and market demands. However, the availability of fats can be limited due to legislation, religious prohibitions, or trade barriers. Apart from the fat blend, the fat phase typically consists of minor ingredients such as emulsifier, lecithin, flavour, color, and antioxidants. Emulsifiers are surface-active compounds used to reduce the interfacial tension between the water and the fat phase. The emulsifier stabilizes the liquid emulsion before crystallization to secure a homogeneous product and provide fine and stable water distribution in margarine and spreads. The microbiological keeping properties in the final product are thereby improved. The most commonly used emulsifiers in margarine are *distilled monoglycerides* or *mixtures of mono- and diglycerides*. The best water binding effect in margarine is achieved by using saturated monoglycerides. Soya lecithin can be used with the emulsifier to improve the effects of the emulsifier. To achieve the maximum effect of the emulsifier–lecithin system, the emulsifier is heated with the lecithin and liquid oil before the mixture is dissolved in the melted fat blend.

Additionally, lecithin reduces spattering in frying margarine, and it prevents burning of sediment compounds (lactose and casein), because lecithin incorporates these compounds. Lecithin is also a good antioxidant. Fat-soluble butter flavour and color (*i.e.*, β-carotene) are added to achieve a product that tastes and looks like butter. In addition, β-carotene has pro-vitamin A activity. Antioxidants can be added in order to improve the shelf-life of the product, because these substances can delay the onset or slow the rate of oxidation. In margarine production the following antioxidants can be added to the water or fat phase according to solubility: natural tocopherols, BHA (butylated hydroxyanisole), BHT (butylated hydroxytoluene), TBHQ (tertiary butyl-hydroquinone), ascorbic acid, and ascorbic palmitate . The use of food additives, such as emulsifiers, flavors, colors, and antioxidants, is controlled by health authorities and governmental agencies. The use and the maximum dosages permitted in food vary. Thus, local legislation should always be consulted before using food additives in food products.

6.2 QUALITY PARAMETERS OF FATS AND EDIBLE OILS

Peroxide value: The peroxide value is defined as the amount of peroxide oxygen per 1 kilogram of fat or oil. Detection of Peroxide gives the initial evidence of rancidity in unsaturated fats and oils. The double bonds found in fats and oils play a role in autoxidation. Oils with a high degree of unsaturation are most susceptible to autoxidation. The best test for autoxidation (oxidative rancidity) is determination of the peroxide value. Peroxides are intermediates in the autoxidation reaction. Autoxidation is a free radical reaction involving oxygen that leads to deterioration of fats and oils which form off-flavours and off-odours. Peroxide value, concentration of peroxide in an oil or fat, is useful for assessing the extent to which spoilage has advanced.

Iodine Number: It is defined as the grams (number) of iodine absorbed by 100 gram of fat or oil. Iodine number is useful to know the relative unsaturation of fats and is directly proportional to the content of unsaturated fatty acids. Thus lower is the iodine number, less is the degree of unsaturation. The determination of iodine number will help to know the degree of adulteration of given oil. **Higher the iodine number the more C = C bonds are present in the fat.**

If the iodine number is 0-70, it will be a fat and if the value exceeds 70 it is an oil. Starch is used an indicator for this reaction so that the liberated iodine will react with starch to give purple coloured product and thus the endpoint.

Saponification: The hydrolysis of triacylglycerols by alkali to produce glycerol and soaps is known as Saponification.

$$\text{Triacylglycerols} + 3\text{NaOH} \longrightarrow \text{Glycerol} + 3\ \text{R-COONa (soaps)}$$

Saponification value: It is defined as the mg of KOH required to hydrolyze (saponify) one gram of fat or oil. Saponification value is a measure of the average molecular size of the fatty acid present. The value is higher for fats containing short chain fatty acids. The Saponification numbers of a few fats and oils are as Human fat (195-200), Butter (230-240) and Coconut oil (250-260).

The magnitudee of saponification value gives an idea about the average molecular weight of the fast or oil. **Higher the molecular weight of the fat smaller is the saponification value.**

Reichert-Meissel (RM) Number: It is defined as the number of 0.1 N KOH required to completely neutralize the soluble volatile fatty acids distilled from 5 gram fat. RM number is useful in testing the purity of butter since it contains a good concentration of volatile fatty acids (butyric acids, caproic acid and caprylic acid). This is in contrast to other fats and oils which have a negligible amount of volatile fatty acids. Butter has a RM number is the range of 25-30, while it is less than one (1) for most other edible oils. Thus any adulteration of butter can be easily detected by this sensitive RM number.

Acid number: It is defined as the number of mg of KOH required to completely neutralize free fatty acids present in one gram of fats or òils. In normal circumstances, refined oils should be free from any free fatty acids. Oils, on decomposition -due to chemical or bacterial contamination-yield free fatty acids. Therefore, oils with increased acid number are unsafe for human consumption. It is an indicator of indequate processing and storage conditions (*i.e.* high temperature and relative humidity, tissue damage etc.)

Polenske number: Also known as the *Polenske value*. It is an indicator of how much volatile fatty acid can be extracted from fat through saponification. It is number of milliliters of 0.1 N NaOH required to neutralize the insoluble fatty acids (*i.e.* those which are not volatile with steam distillation) obtained from 5 gram of fat.

Kirschner value: The Kirschner value is an indicator of how much volatile fatty acid can be extracted from fat through saponification. It consists of the number of milliliters of 0.1 normal sodium hydroxide necessary for the neutralization of water-soluble silver salts made from the water-soluble volatile fatty acids distilled from 5 grams of a given fat.

Acetal number: It is the number of milligrams of KOH required to neutralize the acetic acid obtained by Saponification of 1 gram of fat after it has been acetylated (The treatment of fat or fatty acid mixture with acetic anhydride results in acetylation of all alcohols OH groups). The acetyl number is, thus, a measure of the number of OH groups in the fat. For example, the castor oil has a high acetyl number (146) because of high content of a hydroxyl acid, ricinoleic acid, in it.

Table 2: Analytical values for some fats and oils

Fats/ oils	Sapon. value (mg KOH/g)	Iodine value (g I_2/100 g)	RM Number	Acetal Number	Acid value (mg KOH/g)
Animal fat					
Halibut liver oil	170 -180	120 - 135	-	-	1.0
Cod liver oil	180 - 190	140 - 180	-	-	0.5 - 5.0
Human fat	194 - 198	65 - 69	0.4	-	-
Lard	195 - 203	47 - 66	0.5 - 0.8	2.6	-
Beef fat	196 - 200	35 - 42	-	2.7 - 8.6	-
Butter	210 - 230	25 - 40	17 - 35	1.9 - 8.6	0.5 - 3.0
Cow's milk	216 - 235	26 - 45	-	-	-
Vegetable fat					
Castor oil	175 - 187	80 - 90	1.4	146 - 150	0.2 - 4.0
Corn oil	187 - 195	104 - 128	-	-	1.0 - 2.0
Linseed oil	188 - 195	170 - 195	1.0	4.0	1.04 - 4.0
Olive oil	190 - 195	80 - 90	0.6 - 1.5	10 - 11	0.2 - 3.0
Coconut oil	254 - 262	7 - 10	0.6 - 7.5	2.0	2.5 - 6.0
Palm oil	188 - 195	114 - 138			

Table 3: Fatty acid composition of some common fats and oil (g/100 g)

Fats/oils	Saturated	Mono saturated	Polysatuarted		*Predominant Fatty acids
			Linoleic	α-Linoleic	
Coconut[a]	90	7	2	< 0.5	SFAs
Palm kernel	82	15	2	< 0.5	SFAs
Ghee [a, b]	65	32	2	< 1.0	SFAs
Vanaspati [b]	24	19	3	<0.5	SFAs
Red palm oil	50	40	9	< 0.5	SFAs + MUFAs
Palm oil	45	44	10	< 0.5	SFAs + MUFAs
Olive	13	76	10	<0.5	MUFAs
Ground nut	24	50	25	< 0.5	MUFAs
Rape/mustard	8	70	12	10.0	MUFAs
Sesame	15	42	42	1.0	MUFAs + PUFAs
Rice bran	22	41	35	1.5	MUFAs + PUFAs
Cotton seed	22	25	52	1.0	PUFAs
Corn	12	32	55	1.0	PUFAs
Sunflower	13	27	60	< 0.5	PUFAs
Safflower	13	17	70	< 0.5	PUFAs
Soybean	15	27	53	5.0	PUFAs

Note: SFAs = saturated fatty acids, MUFAs = mono unsaturated fatty acids, PUFAs = Polyunsaturated fatty acids, a = Mainly short medium –chain fatty acid (ground nut 77 %, ghee 25%), b = trans fatty acid (ghee 2 %, vanaspati 53%), c = long chain monounsaturated fatty acid (50 % Erucic acid; 5% Eicosenoic acid) Rape/ mustard and soybean are good source of 2-linoleic acid

Table 4: Physico-chemical characteristics of ghee

S. No.	Parameters	Cow ghee	Buffalo ghee
1.	RM Value	26.7	32.3
2.	Polenske value	1.76	1.41
3.	Iodine Number	33.7	29.4
4.	Butryorefractometer reading	42.3	42.0
5.	Saponification Number	227.3	230.0
6.	Kirschner value	22.1	28.4
7.	Melting Point, °C	28 - 41	32 - 43
8.	Refractive Index at 60 °C	1.4465	–
9.	Specific Gravity at 60 °C	0.887	0.887
10.	Unsaponifiable matter, %	0.4	–
11.	Smoking Point, °C	20.8	–

6.3 RANCIDITY

Rancidity is the term used to represent the deterioration of fats and oils resulting in an unpleasant taste. Fats containing unsaturated fatty acids are more susceptible to rancidity. Rancidity occurs when fats and oils are exposed to air, moisture, light, bacteria etc.

Hydrolytic rancidity occurs due to partial hydrolysis of triacylglycerols by bacterial enzymes (lipase). In hydrolytic rancidity, moisture and enzymes cause splitting of the triglyceride molecules into glycerol and free fatty acids. The rate of lipolysis of the fat is strongly influenced by temperature. Optimum temperatures for such reactions are usually near 38°C. Hydrolytic rancidity can be controlled by bringing the product to low moisture content, storing the product at a low temperature, and inactivating the enzymes by heat treatment. The high processing temperatures to which most snacks are subjected are usually sufficient to destroy the enzymes which would otherwise lead to hydrolysis of fats

Oxidative rancidity in fats and oil is due to oxidation of unsaturated fatty acids. This results in the formation of unpleasant products such as dicarboxylic acids, aldehydes, ketones etc. Oxygen is required through the formation of intermediate namely, peroxides. Rancid fats and oils are unsuitable for human consumption. Oxidative rancidity is unquestionably the more important of these two mechanisms so far as effects on food acceptability are concerned. The susceptibility of a fat to oxidation depends to a considerable extent on the number of unsaturated bonds in fatty acids moiety. Polyunsaturated fats are very prone to oxidation, whereas fully saturated fats and oils are much more stable. Other minor difficulties are found in light struck oils and ketonic degradation. Of the deterioration of fats and oils, oxidative rancidity is most always present. Oxidative rancidity is influenced by air, light, heat, heavy metals ions, moisture and the presence of natural antioxidants.

The more common test for detection of rancidity in fat/oils are (*i*) peroxide value, (*ii*) determination of carbonyl, (*iii*) active oxygen determination, (*iv*) thiobarbituric acid test (TBA), and (*v*) Schaal oven test ,whch is used primarily in the baking industry.

6.4 LIPID (EDIBLE FAT/OIL) OXIDATION or AUTOOXIDATION

Edible fats containing unsaturated molecules are susceptible to attack by molecular oxygen. This process is referred to as lipid oxidation and can give rise to undesirable volatile flavour compounds, potentially toxic oxidation products and a general deterioration in the quality of the fat containing foods. Fat oxidation is influenced by a range of parameters, including light exposure, temperature, and presence of per oxidant metals, presence of antioxidant compounds, and the degree of unsaturation of the fat. The volatile flavour products of lipid oxidation include aldehydes, ketones, alcohols, esters, lactones and hydrocarbons, of which the unsaturated aldehydes and ketones are primarily responsible for undesirable oxidized (rancid) flavour.

Lipid oxidation is a chain reaction involving initiation, propagation and termination stages. Oxidation of unsaturated fatty acids results in the formation of odourless, tasteless intermediate products known as fatty acid hydroperoxides. These compounds are unstable and can degrade via a variety of pathway, ultimately yielding volatile flavour products. Inhibiting the progress of lipid oxidation in foods, including milk and milk products, is a key factor in maintaining quality and extending shelf life. Milk is a complex biological matrix which contains many factors that can exert antioxidant and/

or prooxidant effect. Subsequent processing and storage of milk may also exert a profound influence on the progress of lipid oxidation.

Oxidation of unsaturated edible fats (RH) is a free radical process that involves initiation, propagation and termination steps. The initiation reaction generally involves removal of a hydrogen atom from the methylene (CH_2) group adjacent to a double bond in an unsaturated fat molecule. This generates the fatty acid radical (alkyl free radical, R*). The formation of R* from the RH is influenced by light exposure, metal catalysts, heat, active oxygen species and other factors. The alkyl radical (R*) is extremely reactive and can combine with molecular oxygen to produce a peroxy-radical (ROO*) which can combine with another unsaturated fatty acid molecule (RH) and generate the corresponding hydroperoxides (ROOH) and a new alkyl radical. Hydroperoxides are unstable and degrade to produce volatile, non-radical end products, many of which result in off flavours. Alternatively, the hydroperoxide can be degraded to produce an alkoxy radical (RO*) and a hydroxyl radical (*OH), both of which are extremely reactive and can propagate the chain reaction by reacting with further RH molecules. The decomposition of hydroperoxides is commonly catalyzed by prooxidant metals, such as copper and iron.

Initiation

$RH \longrightarrow R^\bullet + H^\bullet$

(fatty acid, free or esterified) (alkyl radical)

Propagation

$R^\bullet + O_2 \longrightarrow ROO^\bullet$ (peroxy radical)

$ROO^\bullet + RH \longrightarrow ROOH + R^\bullet$ (hycroperoxide)

$ROOH \longrightarrow RO^\bullet + {}^\bullet OH$ (alkoxy radical) (hydroxy radical)

$RO^\bullet + RH \longrightarrow ROH + R^\bullet$

${}^\bullet OH + RH \longrightarrow H_2O + R^\bullet$

$RO^\bullet + ROOH \longrightarrow ROH + ROO^\bullet$

$ROOH \longrightarrow$ **Nonradical end products, e.g. aldehydes**

Termination

$R^\bullet + R^\bullet \longrightarrow RR$

$RO^\bullet + RO^\bullet \longrightarrow ROOR$

$RO^\bullet + R^\bullet \longrightarrow ROR$

$ROO^\bullet + R^\bullet \longrightarrow ROOR$

The reaction ultimately terminates if the supply of RH molecules is exhausted, if Oxygen becomes limiting, if radicals react with each other to generate nonradical end products. Food lipids typically exhibit a lag phase (induction) during which the rate of lipid oxidation is low. However, as the autocatalytic chain reaction accelerates, hydroperoxides accumulate rapidly and reach a maximum, following which hydroperoxide decomposition reactions and generation of volatile off-flavoured (rancid) compounds become more important. The longer the induction period, the more stable is the food to oxidation. The addition of an antioxidant minimizes the extent of lipid oxidation by inhibiting the initiation of propagation steps, thereby prolonging the shelf life of the food products.

6.5 ANTIOXIDANT

Antioxidant are defined by the United States Food and Drug Administration Act(FDA) as "The substances used to preserve food by retarding deterioration, rancidity or discolouration caused due to oxidation" (Code of Federal Regulation, CFR). The prominent effects of oxidation include the development of rancid off-flavour by fat, oils and lipid containing foods, possibility of toxic oxidation products, discolouration of pigments, loss of product flavour or odour, changes in texture and the loss of nutritional value from the destruction of vitamin (A, D and E) and essential fatty acids (*e.g.* linoleic acid). Aldehydes and ketones which are generated from the chain reactions are responsible for the off flavour and odour. Addition of antioxidant compounds is widely used in food products to inhibit the progress of lipid oxidation. Antioxidant is a substance which when added to fat and fat containing foods prevents their oxidation and thus prolong their shelf-life, wholesomeness and palatability. Without them, fatty foods (*e.g.* potato chips, salted nuts, fat containing dehydrated foods) cannot be stored for any length of time without becoming rancid. The function of antioxidants by interrupting the free radical reaction involved in lipid oxidation. An antioxidant should not have any harmful physiological effect and should not impart an objectionable flavour, odour or colour to the food in which it is present. It should be effective in low concentration (0.01 to 0.02%) and be fat soluble. Some antioxidants used in foods are butylated hydroxyanisole (BHA), butylated hydroxytoluene (BHT), tertiary-butylated hydroquinone (TBHQ) and propyl gallate (PG), thiodipropionic acid, dilauryl thiodipropionate, stannous chloride, tocopherols, more expensive naturally occurring vitamin E, sulphur dioxide and ascorbic acid. Ascorbic acid prevents browning caused by enzymatic oxidation of phenolic compounds. Acids such as citric and phosphoric increase the effectiveness of ascorbic acid.

There is now a growing interest in the development of natural antioxidant for foods because of consumer preference and some queries regarding the toxicity of chemical antioxidant such as butylated hydroxtoluene (BHT). The presence of highly unsaturated fatty acids in microbial cells and their relative stability have prompted many researchers to turn to microorganisms as a possible source of natural antioxidant.

In terms of packaging material a study shows that opaque nylon LLDPE was the most stable followed by transparent PET bottles and lastly HDPE jerry can
However, this deterioration may have occurred due to auto-oxidation by oxygen in the headspace of packaging materials which is highest in HDPE jerrycan followed by PET clear bottles and lastly opaque nylon LLDPE.

Table 5: List of permissible chemical antioxidant used in dairy and food industry

Name of Antioxidants	
Ascorbic acid	Butylated hydroxyanisole (BHA)
Na/Ca Ascorbate	Butylated hydroxytoluene (BHT)
Citric Acid	Lecithins
Na/Ca/K Citrate	Na/Ca/K lactate
Tartaric acid	Na/Ca/K malate
Na/Ca/K Tartarate	Ammonium citrate
Succinic acid	Ammonium perric citrate
Phosphoric acid	Calcium disodium EDTA
Na/Ca/K salt of Phosphoric acid	Stannous chloride
Nicotinic acid	Phospholipids
Propyl-octyl/dodecyl gallate	Dilauryl-thiodipropionate
	α, γ, δ-tocopherols

6.6 ADULTERATION IN OILS / FATS AND THEIR DETECTION

Adulteration of food commodity defined as the addition or subtraction of any substance to or from the food, so that the natural composition and quality of food substances is affected. Adulterated food is dangerous because it may me toxic and can affect health and it could deprive nutrient essential for proper growth and development. Some adulteration is used in oil fats (as per FASSAI manual).

Table 6:

Food Articles	Adulterant	Method of Detection	Remark
Ghee	Vanaspati or margarine	Take about one tea spoon full of melted sample of ghee with equal amount of Con. HCl in stoppered test tube and add to it a pinch of sugar. Shake for one minute and led it for 5 minutes. Appearance of crimson colour in lower (acid) of vanaspati or margarine.	The test is specific for sesame oil which is compulsory added to vanaspati and margarine. Some coal tar colour also gives a positive test. If test is + ve *i.e.* red colour develops only by adding strong HCl (without adding crystals of sugar) then the sample is adulterated with coal tar dye. If the crimson or red colour develops after adding and shaking with sugar, then alone vanaspati or margarine is present.
	Mashed potatoes, sweet potatoes and other starches	The presence of mashed potatoes and sweet potatoes in ghee can be easily be detected by adding a few drops of iodine, which is brownish in colour turns to blue if mashed potatoes/sweet potatoes/other starches are present.	—
Butter	Vanaspati or margarine	Take about one tea spoon full of melted sample of ghee with equal amount of Con. HCl in stoppered test tube and add to it a pinch of sugar. Shake for one minute and led it for 5 minutes. Appearance of crimson colour in lower (acid) of vanaspati or margarine.	The test is specific for sesame oil which is compulsory added to vanaspati and margarine. Some coal tar colour also gives a positive test. If test is +ve *i.e.* red colour develops only by adding strong HCl (without adding crystals of sugar) then the sample is adulterated with coal tar dye. If the crimson or red colour develops after adding and shaking with sugar, then alone vanaspati or margarine is present.
	Mashed potatoes, sweet potatoes and other starches	The presence of mashed potatoes and sweet potatoes in ghee can be easily be detected by adding a few drops of iodine (which is brownish in colour) turns to blue if mashed potatoes/sweet potatoes/other starches are present.	
Edible oil	Prohibited colour	Take 5 ml sample in a test tube and add 5 ml of Conc. HCl. Shake gently, let it stand for 5 minutes. Colour will separate separate in the upper layer of the solution.	
Coconut oil	Any other oil	Place a small bottle of oil in refrigerator. Coconut oil solidifies leaving the adulterant as a separate layer.	

CHAPTER 7

MILK AND MILK PRODUCTS PROCESSING

7.1 DEFINING MILK

- Codex Alimentarius defined milk as 'the normal mammary secretion of milking animals obtained from one or more milkings without either addition to it or extraction from it, intended for consumption as liquid milk or for further processing'.
- Milk can be defined as a complex consisting of fat, proteins lactose, minerals in continuous phase of water, as major constituents, and vitamins, enzymes pigments, gases and several other organic and inorganic substances." The milk fat exists in the form of emulsion which is stabilized by the presence of phospholipid membrane on the surface of the fat globules. Protein, particularly casein is found in the form of colloidal dispersion, lactose and certain minerals are present in true solution.
- Milk could be defined as "fresh clean lacterace sucretion obtained by complete milking of one or more healthy milk animals, properly fed and kept excluding that obtained within 15 days before and 5 days after calving".

India is now the largest producer of milk in the world with a production of 221.06 million tonnes in 2021-22 with a percent share of 24% in the world production. Per capita availability of milk in India in the year was 444 gm/person/Day.

Dairy is a place on farm where milk is processed and milk products (viz. butter, cheeses etc.) are:

7.2 NUTRITIONAL COMPOSITION

Milk contains several substances which could be classified under two major heads viz. liquid and solid. Milk is a colloid containing liquid water as *dispersion medium* and *various solids* are dispersed phase. Milk solids such as fat, protein, lactose and minerals, all taken together are termed as total solids (TS) in milk. The solids can be regrouped as fat and solid-non-fat. The fat consists of true fat and substances associated with fat viz. lecithin, carotene, cholesteral, glycerides and vitamins like A,D,E and K. The SNF can be grouped as lactose (alpha and beta); protein like casein (alpha, beta gamma and Kappa), lactalbumim and actoglobulin; minerals like phosphates, citrates and chlorides of Na, Ca and Mg with traces of Fe, Cu and I_2, and minor constituents of importance like vitamins, B_1, b_2, and B_6 and dissolved gases, enzymes and microorgan.

It is a well known fact that the composition of milk varies from species to species. The composition of milk of each species is given below:-

Table 1: Composition of milk

Species	Moisture/Water %	Fat %	Protein %	Lactose %	Ash %
Human	87.4	3.5	2.0	6.8	0.25
Cow	87.2	4.9	3.2	4.6	0.75
Buffalo	84.1	7.2	3.8	4.8	0.76
Goat	87.0	4.8	4.2	4.1	0.89
Sheep	83.2	6.0	5.2	4.7	0.90
Ass	89.0	2.5	2.0	6.1	0.41
Camel	87.6	5.4	3.0	3.3	0.70

Milk contain approx. 3.4% total fat. Which contains approx. 65% saturated, 30% monosaturated and 5% polyunsaturated fatty acids.

Milk fat melts over a wide range of temperature from approx. – 40°C to 40°C. Milk fat can be degraded by enzyme action, exposure to light and oxidation.

Enzymes that degrade fat are called lipases and the process is called *lipolysis*. Milk lipases can come from various sources like, native milk, airborne, bacterial contaminants, bacteria that are added for fermentation or somatic cells present in the milk. Stomatic cell count (SCC) *i.e.* total number of cells per litre of milk is the main indicator of milk quality.

7.3 ROLE OF CONSTITUENTS OF MILK

1. **Water:** The water in the milk is the same as any other water. Its function is to hold the solids of the milk partly in solution and partly in suspension.
2. **Milk Fat:** Fat is a mixture of the glycerides of certain fatty, acids. Milk fat contains 15 to 20 fatty acids. Milk fat is the lightest portion of milk. It is because of this fact that the cream, which contains most of the milk fat in milk, rises to the top to form the cream layer. It is very rich sources of energy and also a good source of vitamin A and D. The size of fat globules in milk varies from 1 μm to 10 μm.
3. **Protein:** The Principal classes of proteins of milk are casein, lactoglobulin and lactalbumin. The casein account for 80% of total protein content, lactalbumin and lactoglobulin (whey proteins).
   - **Casein:** casein is a phospho-protein which is found only in milk. It exists in milk in combination with calsium, hence is often spoken as calcium caseinate phosphate complex. The casein is precipitate by acids at its iso-elctric point of pH 4.6. It is precipitated out of milk, when the milk sources or when acid or rennet is added to it. Because casein is a protein, it supplies the body with muscle-building material. Casein, when converted into sodium caserinate, is used as source of protein in many of the imitation milk products.
   - **Whey protein:** The proteins, lactalbumin and lacto globulin are present in small amounts, dispersed in the water of milk. The so called whey protein that remain in solution or suspension after the precipitation of the casein by acid or rennet may be salted out by various combination of inorganic salts.

4. **Lactose:** Lactose is a disaccharide carbohydrate found only in milk in the form of glucose and galactose, which are liberated when lactose is hydrolyzed either by the enzyme lactose of the digestive tract or by lactose of bacterial origin. Lactose serves the body as a source of energy, but is not as rich as butterfat. Lactose is easily changed by bacterial action to lactic acid. A change causes milk to taste sour.
5. **Minerals constituents:** The mineral constituents or salt of milk constitute 0.6 to 0.8% of the total weight. The potassium and chlorides of milk are in solution whereas the calcium, phosphorus and magnesium are partly in solution and partly in colliadal suspension. Minerals of milk are very essential as a food for young, as they help to build bone and promote the proper development of the teeth. Although the average minerals content in milk is 0.7%.
6. **Minor constituents:** The water, milk fat, protein, lactose and minerals are termed the major constituents of milk because they are present in comparatively large quantity and makeup the bulk of the product, while other substances present in milk are called minor constituents.
   - **Pigments:** Milk contains two fat soluble pigments "carotene" and "xanthophylls" and one water soluble "lactoflavin" (Lactochrome). Carotene is mainly responsible for yellow colour of cow milk.
   - **Cholesterol:** The amount of cholesterol in milk varies directly with the the butter fat content of the milk. It is a yellow white fatty chemical compound found in such food as eggs, meats and dairy products.
   - **Phospholipids:** The principal phospholipids found in milk is called "lecithin". Lecithin is a fat like substance containing nitrogen and phosphorus. The lecithin is closely associated with milk fat.
   - **Enzyme:** Enzyme are complex organic compound which initiate the chemical reaction. Lipase acts only upon fat, and proteins acts only upon protein decomposition products. High temperature, unfavorable pH, light and certain chemicals tends to inactivate them.

(*a*) **Catalase**: This enzyme, which splits hydrogen peroxide into water and molecular oxygen, is detected by the liberation of oxygen in a fermentation tube. A temperature of 65°C to 67°C for 30 min. destroys this enzyme.

(*b*) **Amylase**: Amylase, a starch splitting enzyme is considered to be the least variable in quantity of all the enzymes in normal milk.

(*c*) **Phosphotase**: It is always present in milk. Its concentration is fairly constant. It has the ability to free phenol from alcoholic esters of phosphoric acid.

(*d*) **Lipase:** Lipase is an enzyme in milk fat that breaks down fats and then causing a strong or "rancid" flavor. Lipase perform essential roles in digestion, transport and processing of dietary lipids into all, living organisms.

(*e*) **Galactase:** It slowly reduces milk protein to simple compounds, hence it plays a part in the "ripening" of some cheeses.

(*f*) **Lactase:** Lactase hydrolyzen lactose into simpler sugar like glucose and gelactose.

(*g*) **Olienase:** It plays a part in the development of oxideized or cappy flavour of milk.

7.4 PROPERTIES OF MILK

(A) Chemical Properties:

1. **Chemical reaction:** Freshly drawn milk normally shows an amphoteric reaction, that is, it turns red litmus blue, and blue litmus red. This property in milk is due to the presence of different amino-acids in milk protein. Amino-acids consist of NH^{2+} as well as COOH group which show alkaline as well as acidic reactions.
2. **Acidity:** The acidic nature of milk is due to the presence of phosphates, protein, citrates and dissolved dioxide. This acidity is called in milk is called natural acidity and range from 0.13% to 0.21%. This is always expressed as percent lactic acid. When milk is kept under atmospheric conditions for sometime, an increase in acidity in milk is noticed. This increase in acidity known as developed acidity is due to production of lactic acid as well as a result of microbial activity.
3. **pH of milk:** Normal fresh milk has a hydrogen in concentration of approx. pH 6.5-6.7, which indicates that the milk is slightly acidic.
4. **Buffering action of milk:** Fresh milk acts as a complex buffer because it contains several substances which contribute to this property of milk. CO_2, protein, phosphate citrates and a number of minor constituents are responsible for buffering capacity of milk.
5. **Oxidation-reduction potential**: In practice, the potential difference created by platinum electrode in a solution of an oxidant or reductant is measured by completing a circuit through calomel half cell and a potentiometer. In this measured potential is called oxidation-reduction potential or Redox-potential. It is noted by Eh of milk about +0.2 to +0.3 volt.

(B) Physical Properties

6. **Taste and odour:** Normal milk tastes slightly sweet and has a milk aromatic flavour and aroma. The sweet taste comes from the flavour and aroma principally from milk sugar and buffer fat.
7. **Colour:** Cow milk is always yellow in colour due to the carotene. Buffalo milk is white due to absence of carotene and white opaque colour seen in reflected light is caused by the interference with passage of light caused by fat and colloidal dispersed substances. Buffalo have a tendency to convert all carotene into vitamin A.
8. **Specific gravity:** It means the weight of given volume of milk compared with the weight of the same volume of water at the same temperature. Sp. gravity of milk is determined at 15°C. Lactometer is used to determine the sp. gr. of milk. Milk contains many constituents whose sp. gr. is less than one.

   Increase in the fat content of milk results in lowering of sp. gr., and decrease in fat content of milk, causing increase in sp. gr. of milk. Milk normally varies in sp. gr. between 1.028 to 1.034. Generally cow milk has 1.028-1.032 and Buffalo milk 1.030 to 1.034 of sp. gr.

   $$\text{Sp. gravity} = 1 + \frac{CLR}{1000}$$

   CLR = Corrected Lactometer reading at 15.5°C
9. **Boiling point:** Water boils at 100°C under normal ambient temperature and pressure. The presence of dissolved substances increases the boiling point of a solution. Since milk contains several dissolved substances it has higher boiling temperature than that of water.

The boiling point of both cow and buffalo milk ranges from 100.2°C to 101°C with an average of 100.5°C.

10. **Freezing point:** The (FP) of milk of cow or buffalo ranges from – 0.535°C to – 0.550°C with an average of – 0.545°C. The addition of 1% water to milk will raise the FP by 0.006°C. Milk freezes at temperature slightly lower than that of water due to soluble constituents such as lactose, soluble salt etc. which lower or depress the freezing point.
11. **Refractive index:** The refractive index of milk is sometimes used to indicate adulteration, especially watering. It is the refractive index of solvent plus the indices of the solutes. The RI of the milk ranges from 1.3440 to 1.3485. The freezing point determination is more reliable than RI for detecting added water. It can be used to estimate total solids.
12. **Electrical conductivity:** In a pure solution, the conductivity is a function of ionic concentration. It increases with increase in temperature. The average values at 300°C are in milli-mhos per centimeter, 3.67 for buffalo milk and 4.67 for cow milk.
13. **Specific heat:** The specific heat of milk usually ranges between 0.920 and 0.930. It changes with change in temperature. Milk has highest specific heat, 0.938 at 15°C.
14. **Coefficient of thermal expansion:** Milk expands when heated and contracts when cooled, the ratio of increase in volume per degree of increase in temperature is known "coefficient of expansion".
15. **Viscosity:** The viscosity of a substance refers to its resistance to flow. The viscosity of a heterogeneous substance such as milk at given temperature depends upon its composition and the physical state of its colloidally dispersed substances, including milk fat. The viscosity decrease with increase in temperature, that is, it has a negative temperature coefficient. At normal temperature, viscosity of milk varies from 1.5 to 2 centipoises (m pas). The viscosity of milk is always higher than the viscosity of water. This is due to the pressure of dissolved solids in the milk. Homogenization increases the viscosity of milk. Viscosity of milk is important in determining: 1. the rate of creaming, 2. rates of mass and heat transfer, 3. the flow conditions in dairy processes.
16. **Thermal conductivity:** Increasing temperature increase the milk thermal conductivity. It decreases as concentration level increases and for a given temperature and concentration, the higher the fat content the lower the thermal conductivity. At 30°C the thermal conductivity of milk is 13.5×10^4 cal $cm^{-1}s^{-1}c^{-1}$ or For milk with a lowr moisture percentage, the experimental conductivity ranged from 0.568 to 0.637 $Wm^{-1}k^{-1}$ and for these samples with a higher moisture percentage, conductivity ranged from 0.584 to 0.562 $Wm^{-1}k^{-1}$.
17. **Surface tension:** The surface tension of milk at 20°C is 54.5 dynes/cm. It decreases as the temperature is raised, at 60°C it is about 40 to 50 (dynes/cm). The presence of fat lowers the surface tension, whole milk has a slightly lower surface tension than skim milk and that of cream is still lower. Milk and cream on again undergo a slight decrease a surface tension. Surface tension of milk varies with temperature and total solids. Development of acidity and churning lower the surface tension of milk.

(C) Germicidal Property of Milk:

Fresh milk exhibits quality to retard the growth of microorganisms of milk. This property milk last on heating the milk. The germicidal effect is conducted by lactenin work against organism. This property varies with the milk of different animals and also with the milk of same animal at different times.

7.5 MILK PROCESSING

7.5.1 Milk Collection and Reception

Milk may be supplied to the dairy in milk cans (churns) or by a tanker after it has been cold-stored at the farm (tank milk). During transport, *milk in cans* usually has a temperature of >10°C, but may vary between 0 and 40°C according to the climate. Consequently, bacterial growth often occurs between milking and the milk's arrival at the dairy, as this may take as long as a day. Spoilage of the milk is mainly by mesophilic bacteria and usually involves lactic acid fermentation; however, heavy contamination with polluted water (mainly pseudomonads) may cause a non-souring spoilage. On reception at the dairy plant, milk is cooled to < 6°C, which helps to more or less stabilize its bacteriological quality for at most 2 days.

On reception, the quantity of milk is recorded first. At the dairy, milk in cans is weighed by a platform balance. The quantity of tank milk is determined by metering the intake line of the milk tanker. Milk volume is then converted to weight. It is advisable that the reception of milk in cans at the dairy occur as soon as possible after milking. This implies twice-a-day milk collection. Often this is not practical, and the evening milking is cooled by mains or well water. Once a-day collection may, however, seriously impair the milk quality in cans. Tank milk should be refrigerated to < 4°C. After 4 or 5 d storage, substantial growth of psychrotrophs may occur. Consequently, tank milk can normally be kept on the farm for 3 days, *i.e.*, six milkings, and stored for another day at the dairy before processing. Depending on the age of the milk supplied to the dairy, it can be stored for another 1 or 2 d without further treatment. All milk supplies should, however, be cooled to – 4°C because the temperature may increase during transport from the farm to the dairy and the generation time of bacteria is markedly shorter at high temperatures.

7.5.2 Cooling of Milk

A food is generally cooled or frozen to retard spoilage. Fresh milk is routinely cooled to about 5°C in many regions of the world. For liquid milk products cooling may extend the shelf life by days or weeks. Cooling of milk is also applied for specific purposes, such as inducing fat crystallization or enhancing the creaming tendency. Freezing is mostly done to make a specific product, such as ice cream, and occasionally as a concentration process. Freezing is sometimes used to substantially retard deterioration of fresh milk or liquid milk products. Cooling of milk causes several changes, the most important ones are:

a) The growth of most microorganisms is much slower, if not stopped, and so are the changes induced in milk by their metabolism.

b) Nearly all chemical and enzymic reactions are retarded.

c) Autoxidation of lipids, whether induced by light or Cu^{2+}, is enhanced, presumably because the activity of the enzyme superoxide dismutase is decreased.

d) Changes in solubility and association of salts occur. The amount of micellar calcium phosphate decreases and the pH increases.

e) The casein micelles attain a higher voluminosity and part of the casein, especially α-casein, goes into solution. This results in an increased viscosity and an enhanced susceptibility to attack by plasmin.

f) The fat globule membrane loses some components, and its structure is altered. These changes are irreversible.

g) Cold agglutination (clumbing of particles) of fat globules occurs, *e.g.*, enhancing creaming rate.

h) The triglycerides in the fat globules will partly crystallize.

Cooling of packaged products can also take a long time, especially if it involves viscous products. For the most part, air cooling is used. It is better to package the product after cooling, if possible.

7.5.3 Pasteurization of Milk

"Pasteurization of milk is a heat treatment process in which to partially kill the micro organisms or harmful pathogens present in milk at predetermined time and temperature".

The pasteurization is the heating of every particle of milk or milk product to at least 63°C and holding at such temperature continuously at least 30 min or heating it to at least 71.5°C and holding at such temperature continuously for at least 15 sec or an approved temperature time combination that will serve to give a negative phosphatase test. The time and temperature treatment used in pasteurization depends upon.

- The heat resistance of the particular vegetative or pathogenic micro organisms.
- The sensitive of product quality to heat.

Main objectives of pasteurization:

- To make milk safe for human consumption
- To increase the keeping quality of milk

Normally, milk develops acidity which causes spoilage of milk within 4-5 h of milking. In order to improve the shelf life of this milk, it is necessary that the milk is properly pasteurized. Heating process destroys most of the organisms and the growth of those micro organisms which survive heat treatment is retarded due to proper cooling. When the milk is properly pasteurized and the bacterial load is controlled for nearly 48-50 hr.

Disadvantages:

1. The nutritive value of milk is to some extent adversely affected.
2. It affects the creamline.
3. Adversely affects clotting of milk with rennet.
4. Increase the cost of milk due to processing changes
5. This process does not destroy bacterial toxins in milk
6. The process masks inferior quality milk

Time-temperature combination: The temperature-time for pasteurization process is principally based on the thermal death point of the pathogenic organisms particularly.

Mycobacterium tuberculosis: This organism is one of the most heat resistant pathogenic organisms which might be present will be destroyed. The phosphatase enzyme requires slightly higher temperature time treatment for its inactivation than the **Mycobacterium tuberculosis** does for its destruction. The temperature time combination should therefore be slightly higher than required for inactivation of phosphatase enzyme. The various temperature time combinations for pasteurization process as effective against **Mycobacterium tuberculosis** and phosphatase enzymes are as given below:

Operation Name	Temperature	Time
Low temperature longtime (LTLT)	62.8°C or 63°C	30 min
Higher temperature short time (HTST)	71.7°C or 72°C	15 sec.
Ultra high temperature (UHT)	89°C	1 sec.
	90°C	0.5 sec.
	94°C	0.1 sec.
	95°C - 100°C	0.05 sec.
Ultra pasteurization or Super pasteurization	135 - 150°C	0.001 sec.

Methods of Pasteurization:

1. In Bottle pasteurization: Raw milk is filled in glass milk bottles which are tightly sealed with special caps. These bottles are subjected to heat treatment ranging from 63-66°C for a period of 30 min. Later on, they are passed through a spray of cold water which cools the milk to 5-7°C.

Demerits:

(*a*) More chances of bottles breakage

(*b*) Heat transfer during heating as well as cooling is very low.

(*c*) Special caps/machines are required

(*d*) Oversized bottles, are required to allow expansion of milk during heating

2. Batch pasteurization: This method is also called vat pasteurization, holding method or low temperature longtime (LTLT) pasteurization method. In this, milk is heated to 63°C for 30 min. immediately after heating milk is cooled to 4-5°C. The process of heating as well as cooling may be done in the same vat. During heat transfer milk is agitated mechanically. The vat pasteurizer consist agitator and thermometer with the provision of hot water and chilled water inlets and outlets.

Advantages:

- Suitable for small operation
- Does not involve sophisticated equipment
- Process is simple
- Technically trained person are not required
- No milk is lost during pasteurization process

Disadvantages:

- Time taken for pasteurization is too long.
- There are no automatic controls to check the operation
- The growth of thermophilic organisms is encouraged
- Involves cleaning of vat after pasteurization of each lot
- In-place-cleaning is not convenient
- Operating cost per litre of milk handled is more
- Can not handle large quantity of milk

3. High temperature short time (HTST) pasteurization: Process involves heating of milk to 71.5°C. This process of pasteurization of milk is most commonly practiced in modern dairies particularly where large volume of milk is handled. This process is also called continuous process or plate pasteurization process. In this process, milk is pumped either from the dump tank or from the storage tank to float control tank from where it is pumped to the pasteurizer. Pasteurizer has four different sections through which milk passes during pasteurization. First of all, milk enters into the regeneration section where its Temperature is raised to about 45°C by out going heated milk on the other side of the plates and then it goes either to filters or clarifier as the case may be for removal of extraneous materials if present. Then milk comes to the heating section where the temperature of milk is raised to at least 71.5°C by hot water or intermittent steam and this hot milk enters in the holding section of the pasteurizer. At the end of the holding section, a flow diversion valve (FDV) is fixed to control proper heating and holding and milk passes through the valve. FDV automatically checks the flow of milk; if it has not been properly heated to the required temperature then FDV diverts the milk to the flow control tank and milk comes to the regeneration and follows the same path again. In case milk has been properly pasteurized then through the FDV milks enters the regeneration section where it heats the incoming raw milk and its temperature is reduced (partial cooling) and finally this process to the cooling section where it is cooled about 4°C-5°C. Thus, the milk is pasteurized and it is now ready for packing, storage or conversion into other products.

Advantages:

1. Large volume of milk can be pasteurized without interruption
2. Milk is readily available for packing or further processing, once the operation has started, milk can be filled in bottles or sachets within 15 min.
3. Less flour space is required because this equipment is compact with increasing or decreasing the plates
4. Heating, holding and cooling are done in the same unit
5. Provides economy of operation because of regeneration

Disadvantages:

1. Initial cost is higher
2. Requires an experienced and technical operator
3. Some milk is lost in the pipe lines which gets dilated due to flushings
4. Gaskets used in pasteurizer (HTST) are damaged and require replacement more frequently.
5. Due to higher heating temperature more chilled water is required for cooling of milk which in turn increases the cost of refrigeration

Vacuum Pasteurization

This process of pasteurization is also called vacreation. The advantages of pasteurizing milk by this process is to remove off flavour from milk as well as from cream. *Machine used for New Zealand by M/s Murray Deodorizers Ltd.*

The principal of vacuum pasteurization is mixing milk with pressure steam and immediately followed by sudden and spontaneous expansion into a finely divided state with a chamber maintained at reduced pressure. This effects separation of off-flavours along with water vapour (which acts as a carrier) state to the expansion state. transition from a compression state to the expansion state. At the same time instantaneous cooling effect upon the product is an important factor in preserving the desirable characteristics of the product, even when high temperature is adopted. Vaporization removes the off-flavours effectively.

Vacreator is an equipment generally used for vacuum treatment of milk or cream. Due to time lapse between the production stage in the farm and processing in dairy plant, the cream quality deteriorates and pasteurization in vat or HTST unit is not found satisfactory. This led to the adoption of processing the aged, sour cream under vacuum condition.

Flash Pasteurization

This process is similar to HTST but in this method temperature of milk is raised to 80°C for practically no holding period. This process destroys all the pathogens organisms that might be present in milk and makes it safe for human consumption. The major advantages of this process are-

(*i*) The reduction in nutritive value of milk due to heat treatment is less in this process than other methods.

(*ii*) Time taken for pasteurization is less as compared to other methods of pasteurization

Ultra High Temperature Pasteurization (UHT Process)

In the UHT process, milk is heated either by direct steam injection, swept surface, heat exchanger or turbulent heat exchanger. Milk is heated to about 135-150°C for practically no holding time (fraction of a second). Heating of milk is usually done in two stages. The second stage is being UHT process under pressure etc. Milk is aseptically packed while it is still hot. Milk pasteurized by UHT process has additional advantages such as maintaining the nutritive value, colour and flavour similar to that raw milk.

Effect of Pasteurization on Nutritive Value of Milk

Heating process destroys certain vitamins, reduces cream line and causes partial precipitation of certain minerals. It has been found that in the holding method of pasteurization, destruction of vitamin C between 5 to 10%. Cream line is reduced by 5-10%. Cream line refers to the amount of fat which has risen to the top of a bottle of milk. Cream line is usually regarded as important criteria for judging the compositional quality of milk. However, the advantages of pasteurization of milk are more important than the slight reduction in the nutritive value of milk.

7.5.4 Sterilization of Milk

Sterilization is heat treatment in which to destroy the microorganism and harmful pathogens completely from food material at specified time and temperature combination. 121.1°C for 2-5 min.

Concept: The term sterilization, when used in association with milk means heating milk continuously to a temperature of 115°C for 15 min or 145°C for 3 sec. or equivalent approved temperature time combination to ensure preservation at room temperature for a period of not less than 15 days from the date of manufacture. Sterilized milk shall show absence of albumin by a negative turbidity test. Sterilized milk shall be sold only in the containers in which the milk was sterilized.

Strictly speaking the term sterilization means making it sterile. Any substance could be considered sterile when it is completely free from living organism. If milk becomes sterile and there is no subsequent contamination it should be understood that such milk can be kept for a long period without having any change due to microbial activities. This concept of making the milk sterile may be practically possible because such milk may not be suitable for human consumption. Therefore, commercial sterilized milk will always have limited shelf life. The basic requirement for sterilized milk should therefore be free from spoilage type of microorganisms and fairly acceptable flavour and colour. In order to achieve both the above objectives prevention of Food Adulteration Act has prescribed a minimum of 15 days keeping quality at room temperature.

Methods of producing sterilized milk: There are different methods of producing sterilized; (*i*) In bottle sterilization (*ii*) Ultra high temperature short time (UHT ST) process (*iii*) Sterilization by the two stage methods.

(*i*) **In bottle Sterilization**: The flow diagram of manufacture include receiving milk, cooking to 115°C and bulk storage preheating (38-40°C) filtration /clarification, cooling to 50°C standardization and storage (5°C), preheating (60°C), Homogenization, clarification, filling and capping (In cleaned and sanitized bottles) sterilizing (108-111°C 125-30 min) cooling milk is heated (room temperature) storage (room temperature). In this process the milk is heated in a bottle by system at a temperature between 110-120°C the temperature of milk rises slowly due to slow heat transfer especially when the bottles are not agitated in the sterilizers. The glass milk bottles used for preparation of sterilized milk do not with stand sudden and extreme temperature change. It is advisable to sterilize milk by a time temperature combination in which the temperature is low and time is long. This process causes changes in flavour as well as colour of milk. Milk normally develops strong cooked or burnt flavour and brownish colour which is not linked by the consumers.

(*ii*) **Sterilization by UHTST Method**: In this method milk in heated to 135-150°C for a few seconds. The holding period may range from 1-20 seconds. The process of sterilization is generally carried out in a plate or a tubular heat exchanger. This process of sterilization has been found to be most effective in destroying the heat resistant spores such as *bacillus subtilis spores*. Due to higher temperature treatment the colour of milk is not impaired whereas it acquires cooked or burnt flavours. After heat treatment milk should be filled in containers aseptically. The keeping quality of the product is fairly long provided proper precautions are taken during filling or packing.

(*iii*) **Sterilization by two stage process**: In this process the milk is sterilized in two stages. Milk is first treated by UHTST process and then filled in bottles which are further subjected to in bottle Sterilization process. The process has been found to be most effective and the keeping quality of the product has been found to fairly long. The best result can be obtained only if the in bottle treatment is as mild as possible to avoid impairing the taste and colour of milk.

The taste and colour of the product prepared by this process is better than those of milk sterilized according to complete in bottle sterilization. The capacity of the equipment for in bottle treatment is greater when used for two stage method than the complete in bottle method. This method has greater reliability as compared with complete in bottle treatment.

Types of Sterilizers: Generally two types of sterilizers are in use. They are the batch type and the continuous type:

(*i*) **Batch Type**: batch type sterilizer is either an autoclave or steam cabinet. In the simplest type of sterilizers the bottles are not agitated, as a rule treatment is carried out by steam and temperature of milk increase slowly. The process involves heating of milk at relatively low temperature which greatly impairs the colour and taste of the product.

The batch sterilizers may be rotary or stationary, rectangular, horizontal, bailer shaped with provision of steam inlet and condensate outlet fitted with clampdown covers into which steam is adjusted for the required temperature and time for sterilization. The capacity of batch sterilizer is generally small and the process is considered suitable for a small scale operation.

Advantages of Batch sterilizers:

(1) The operation of batch sterilizers is simple, (2) Initial capital investment is less.

(3) Recurring expenditure is less, and (4) Floor space required is less.

Disadvantages of Batch Sterilizers:

(1) The quality of sterilized milk is generally inferior. The colour of milk is decidely brownish and has pronounced cooked flavour

(2) The process is time consuming, and (3) Suited only for small scale operation.

Continuous sterilizers: Continuous sterilizers are most for suited for large scale operation. There is variation in the capacity of different plants ranging from 500 bottles of one l per h to about 6000 bottle per h. The continuous sterilizers may operate with steam or hot air.

After filling (providing enough head space for expansion) and crown corking the hot milk bottle are transferred to the conveyor system of the sterilizer. Then vertical sterilizer is an insulate lower with 3 or 4 internal chambers for pre-heating sterilizing and stepwise cooling. The conveyor in the vertical loop passes through the chambers having loaded milk bottles which are in horizontal position. In the upward movement, milk bottles which are in horizontal position. In the upward movement, milk gets heated by vapour as it reaches the top of the chambers. When it travels in the down wards direction, milk gets heated to around 80°C at the top and 90°C at the bottom thorough water heated by steam pressure from the second chamber. The bottles then moves up in the first cooling chamber containing water and by time they come down the temperature may be around 55°C. The bottles are then cooled by a spray of water to around 35°C. The bottles are then come back through the conveyor to the unloading platform.

7.5.5 Homogenization of Milk

Homogenization refers to the process of forcing the milk through a homogenizer with the object of subdividing the fat globules. The primary *function* of ***homogenization*** is to *prevent creaming*, or the rising of fat to the top of the container of milk (whole or some low-fat milk). The *result* is that milk maintains a more uniform composition with improved body and texture, a whiter appearance, richer flavor, and more digestible curd. Homogenization *mechanically* increases the number and *reduces* the size of the fat globules. The size is reduced from 18m to less than 2 m, or 1/10 of their original size. The process of homogenization permanently *emulsifies* the fine fat globules by a method that pumps milk under high pressure [2000–2500 psi] through small mesh orifices of a homogenizer. Homogenizer reeduces the fact globule to a average of < 1μm diameter.

Homogenization offers a *permanent* emulsification because as the surfaces of many new fat globules are formed, each fat globule becomes coated with a part of the lipoprotein membrane and additional proteins from casein and whey. Thus, these proteins adsorb onto the freshly created oil surface, *preventing* globules from reuniting or coalescing, and the fat remains homogeneously distributed throughout milk. Milk may be homogenized *prior* to or *subsequent* to pasteurization. The homogenization process is completed at a *fast* rate to ensure the control of bacteria and loss of quality. Some characteristics of homogenized milk include the following:

- *No creaming* or separation of cream to the top of the container.
- *Whiter* milk due to a finer dispersions of fat. There is an increase in the absorption and reflection of light due to the smaller fat particles.
- *More viscous* and creamy milk due to a greater number of fat particles.
- *More blend* due to smaller fat particles.
- *Decreased fat stability* as fat globule membranes are broken.
- *Less stable to light* and may exhibit light-induced favor deterioration by sunlight or fluorescent light. Thus, paperboard cartons and clouded plastic bottles are used for milk.

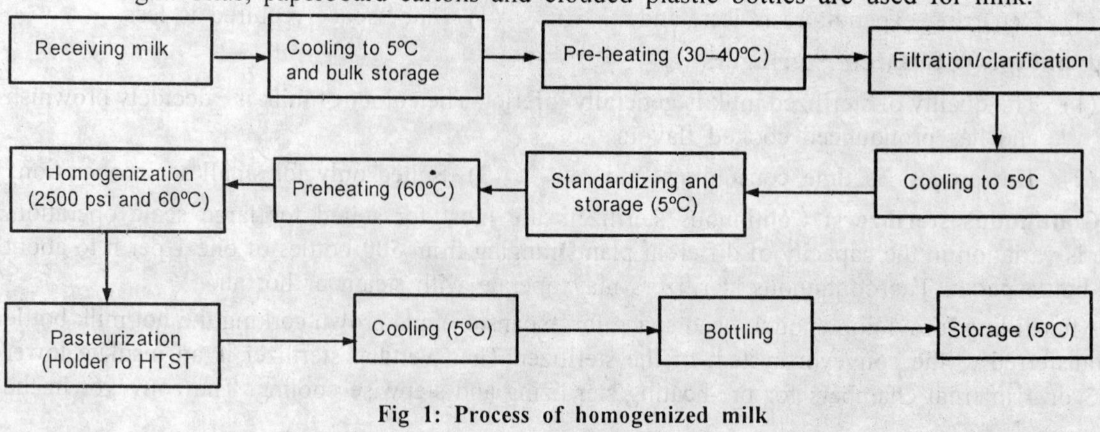

Fig 1: Process of homogenized milk

Sequence of various processes involved in production of homogenized milk. The possible sequences are:

1. Clarification, pre-heating, homogenization, pasteurization, cooling.
2. Clarification, pre-heating, pasteurization, homogenization, cooling.
3. Pre-heating, homogenization, clarification, pasteurization, cooling. *(for Indian condition)*
4. Pre-heating, clarification, homogenization, pasteurization, cooling.
5. Pre-heating, clarification, homogenization, pasteurization, cooling.

7.6 TYPES OF MILK

Depending on level of different constitute there are milk with various names as follows:

7.6.1 Standardized Milk

This is milk whose fat and /or solid non fat content have been adjusted to a certain predetermined level. The standardization can be done by partially skimming the fat in the milk with a cream separator, or by admixture with fresh or reconstituted skim milk in the proper proportions. As per FSSAI, the standardized milk or liquid consumption should contain a minimum of 4.5 % fat and 8.5 % solid non fat throughout the country. The initial reaction of the consumer may be that the standardized milk is 'thinner' than whole milk.

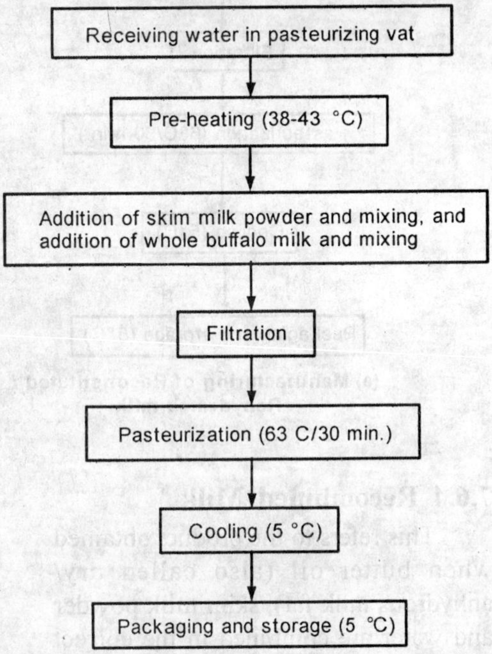

Fig 2: Manufacturing of Toned milk

7.6.2 Toned Milk

Toned milk (also called single toned milk) refers to milk obtained by addition of water and skim milk powder to whole milk and increase the quantity of availability milk and tone up the nonfat solids level to the original amount. As per FSSAI it should contain minimum milk fat 3% and minimum milk SNF of 8.5%. In practice, whole buffalo milk is admixed with reconstituted spray dried skim milk for it preparation. Toned milk is the brainchild of D.N. Khurody (India) in 1946 in the Central dairy of Aarey milk colony and marketed in Mumbai city. Under PFA Rules.

7.6.3 Double Toned Milk

Same as toned milk except that FSSAI rules, double toned milk should contain a minimum of 1.5 % fat and 9.0 % solid non fat throughout India. Manufactured same as toned milk.

This refers to milk by dispersing whole milk powder (also called dried whole milk) in water approximately in the proportion of 1 part powder to 7-8 part water. (Usually spray dried powder is used, since it is more soluble and produces less sediments.

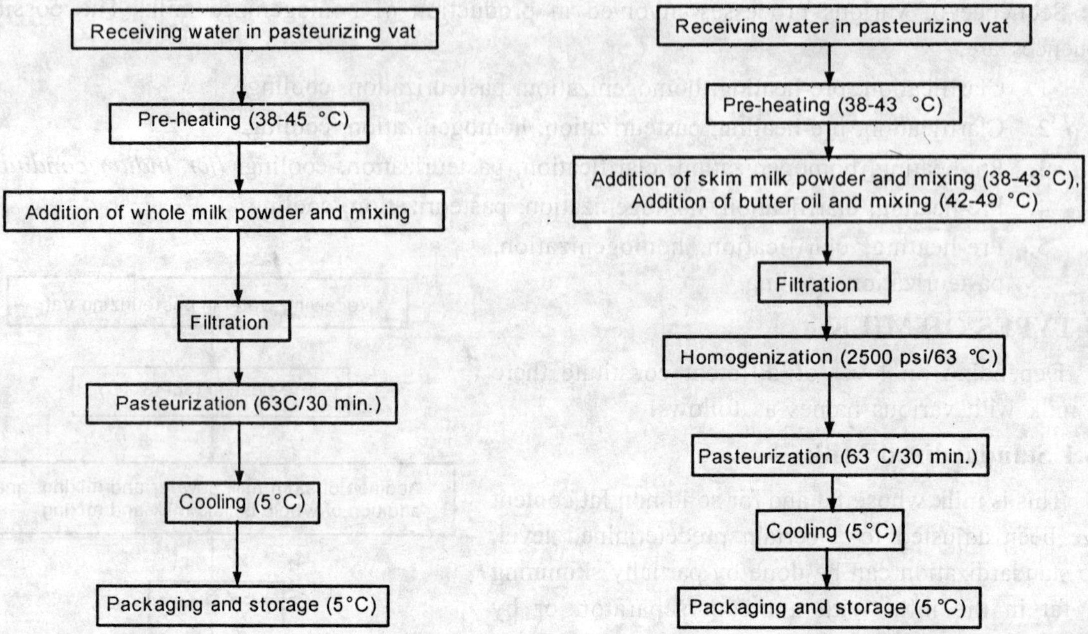

(a) Manufacturing of Reconstituted / Rehydrated milk **(b) Process of Recombined Milk**

Fig. 3.

7.6.4 Recombined Milk

This refers to the product obtained when butter oil (also called dry/ anhydrous milk fat), skim milk powder and water are combined in the correct proportions to yield fluid milk. The milk fat may also be obtained from other sources, such as unsalted butter or plastic cream. Under FSSAI rules, recombined milk should contain a minimum of 3.0 percent fat and 8.5 percent solid non fat. It shows negative to phosphotase test.

7.6.5 Flavoured Milk

Flavoured milks are milks to which some flavours have been added. When the 'milk' is used, the product should contain a milk fat percentage at least equal to the minimum legal requirement for market milk. But when the fat level is lower (1-2 percent), the term 'drink' is used. In this case, milk is to make

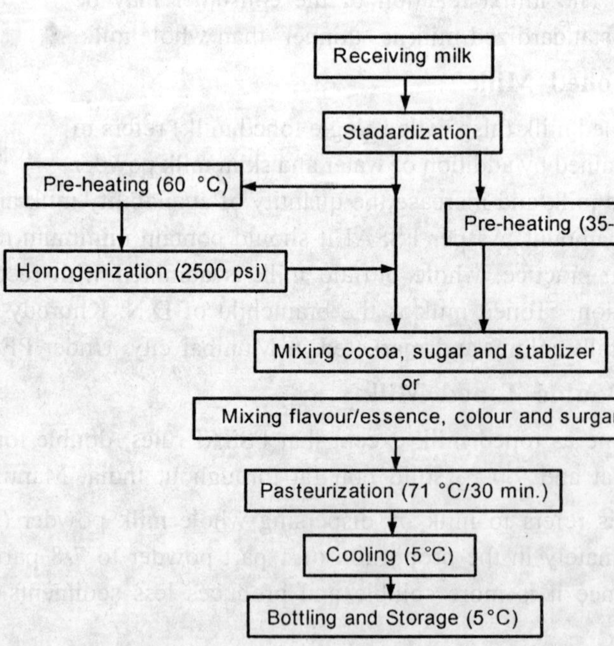

Fig. 4: Manufacturing of flavoured milk

more palatable to those who do not relish it as such; to stimulate the sale of milk, and to put skim milk to profitable use. The main types of flavoured milk are (*i*) chocolate milk/drinks, (*ii*) fruit flavoured milk/drinks, and (*iii*) sterilized flavoured milk/drinks. Flavoured milk is subjected to heat treatment as prescribed in sub-regulation 2.1.1. (General standards for milk and milk products of FSSAI).

7.6.6 Acidophilus Milk

Acidophilus milk is produced by fermentation of milk by *Lactobacillus acidophilus.* This product possesses therapeutic value. Its therapeutic properties are attributed to the ability of the organisms to become transplanted in the intestinal tracts. *Lactobacillus acidophilus* is a slow fermenting organism and to get a reasonably fast growth rate it is customary to ultra heat milk (98ºC for 30 min or 145ºC for 2-3 sec) before incubation. Continued incubation may result in 1% or more acidity. Acidophilus milk should be cooled to 5ºC immediately. Fresh acidophilus milk contains in excess of 500 million cells/ml, although the viable count decreases rapidly with storage.

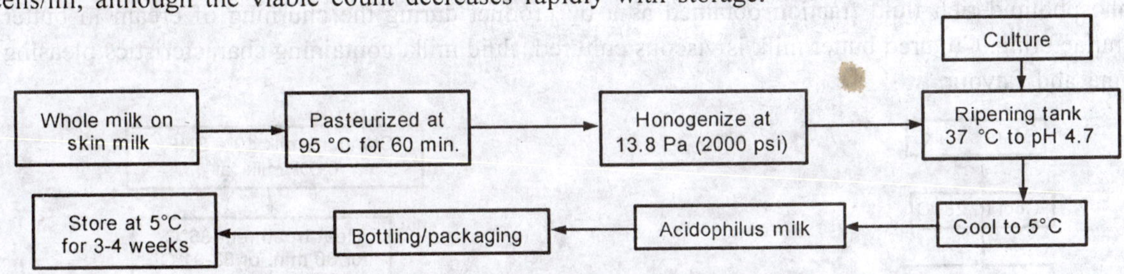

Fig. 5: Processing of acidophilus milk

7.6.7 Kefir

Kefir belongs to the class of acid and alcohol fermentation milk. It is produced by fermentation with kefir grains. The grains are white to yellow in colour and insoluble in water and common solvents. However, when added to milk, their size expands by imbibing water and their colour changes to white. The grains contain 24 % slimy polysaccarides secreted by the culture. The symbiotic micro-flora contains yeasts (*saccharomyces kefir and Torula kefir*), lactobacilli (*Lactobacillus caucasicus*), leuconostocs and lactic streptococci. The product is foamy and fizzy due to its carbon dioxide content. Kefir is rich in probiotics.

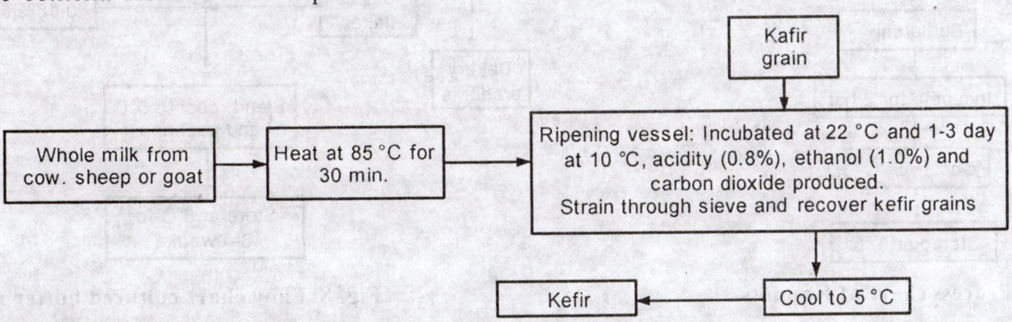

Fig. 6: Production of Kefir

7.6.7.1 Koumiss: Koumiss is similar to kefir except that mare's milk is used in its manufacture. Russians use koumiss for the treatment of pulmonary tuberculosis in doses of 1.4 litre per day for 2 months. The product is alcoholic and produces slight intoxication. The alcoholic content of koumiss may vary from 1 to 2.5 %, depending upon whether the product is of the weak or strong type. Corresponding to the alcoholic content, the titrable acidity varies from 0.7 to 1.8 % lactic acid. Mare's milk is low in casein content and does not curdle like cow's milk. Accordingly, koumiss is a grayish white wholesome drink. Bacteria in koumiss play a major role in pH decreasing and reducing spoilage.

The starter for koumiss consist of *Lactobacillus bulgaricus and lactose fermenting yeast, Torulopsis holmii.* Lactic acid, ethanol and carbon dioxide are the major products giving koumiss a sour alcoholic flavour and fizzy appearance. In view of the production of CO_2 in the product, appreciably pressure is developed in the capped bottles.

7.6.8 Cultured Butter Milk

Cultured butter milk is produced from pasteurized skim milk or part skim milk cultured with lactic and aroma producing organism. *Streptoccus lactis* and/or *Streptoccus cremoris*, *S. lactis subsp. diacelylactis* and *Leuconostoc cremoris* are frequent cultures. The term butter milk is also used for a phospholipid rich fluid fraction obtained as a by product during the churning of cream in butter manufacturing. Cultured butter milk is viscous cultured, fluid milk, containing characteristics pleasing aroma and flavour.

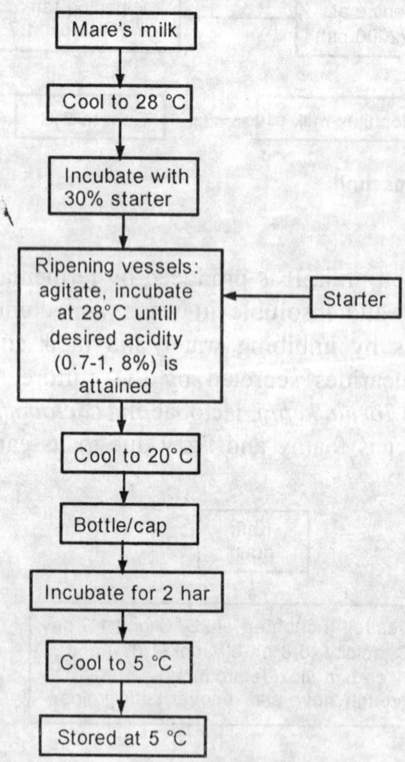

Fig. 7: Process chart of Koumiss

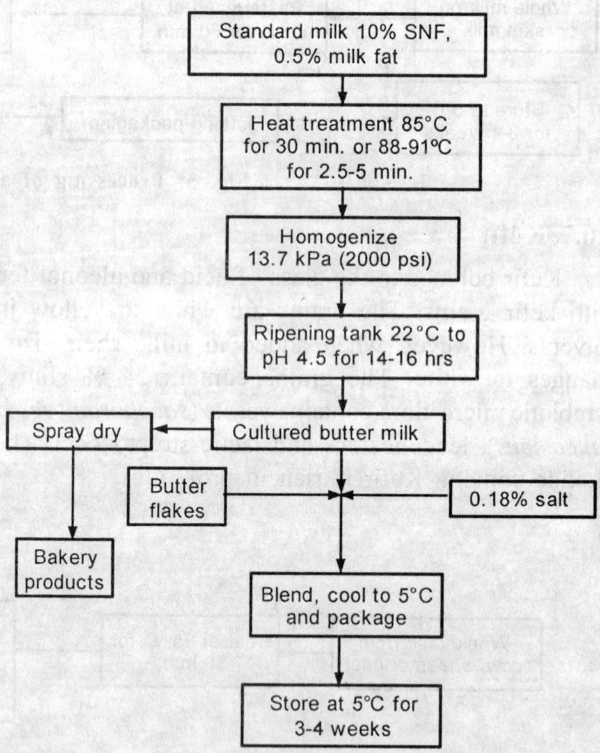

Fig. 8: Flow chart cultured butter milk

The processes used in the manufacture of cultured butter milk include pasteurization, homogenization and culturing system. The ingredients are skim milk, low fat milk, cream, condensed skim milk, non-fat dry milk, cultured and salt. The addition of 0.20-0.25% sodium citrate to milk provides a precursor to enhance flavour production by culture. Milk fat level ranges from 0.5 to 1.8%. The standard also requires a minimum titrable acidity of 0.5% calculated as lactic acid.

Cultured milk shall be obtained from milk containing not less than 2.0% milk fat. For standardizing the milk solid non fat level to 8.25%, butter granules or flakes may be added to butter milk either by churning 18-20% fat cream or by spraying melted butter oil on chilled butter milk. Under refrigeration, the keeping quality of cultured butter milk is extended to 3-4 weeks.

7.6.9 Evaporated Milk

Evaporated milk is sterilized, concentrated, homogenized milk. The product can be kept without refrigeration and has a long shelf life; it is completely safe for the user. After dilution, flavor and nutritive value of the product are not greatly different from that of fresh milk. A major problem with sterilization is the heat stability; the higher the concentration of the milk, the lower its stability. That is why concentrating cannot be by more than about 2.6 times, which corresponds to a level of about 22% solids-not-fat in the evaporated milk. Currently, bottled evaporated milk is often used in coffee in certain countries. It can be added while cold because a fairly small amount is involved as compared to non-evaporated milk. After the bottle has been opened, the milk can be kept in a refrigerator for up to 10 days because it initially contains no bacteria at all and because contaminating bacteria grow somewhat more slowly owing to the reduced water activity, which is about 0.98. Several variations are possible. Some process steps are discussed in more detail in the following text..

Preheating serves to enhance the heat stability of the evaporated milk, inactivate enzymes, and kill microorganisms, including a significant proportion of the bacterial spores present. Currently, UHT treatment is generally preferred. It reduces the number of spores in the milk considerably, and therefore a less intensive sterilization suffices.

Concentrating of the milk is usually done by evaporation. Standardization to a desired dry-matter content is of much concern. A higher concentration causes a lower yield and a poorer heat stability. After concentrating, the manufacturing processes for in-bottle-sterilized and UHT-sterilized evaporated milk differ.

Homogenization serves to prevent creaming and coalescence. It should not be too intensive because the heat stability becomes too low. *Stabilization*. To ensure that the evaporated, homogenized milk does not coagulate during sterilization and at the same time does acquire a desirable viscosity, a series of sterilization tests is often done on small quantities of the evaporated milk to which varying amounts of a stabilizing salt (for the most part, Na_2HPO_4) are added. The stabilizing salt is added as an aqueous solution, which dilutes the evaporated milk slightly. Therefore, the milk is often concentrated somewhat too far and is restandardized to the correct dry-matter content during stabilization.

Packaging in cans is common. The tin plate of the cans is coated (provided with a protective layer of a suitable polymer) to prevent iron and tin from dissolving in the product. After filling, the cans may be closed by soldering, but mechanical sealing is currently preferred. Evaporated milk intended for use in coffee is usually packaged in bottles that are closed with a crown cork or a screw cap.

Sterilization. In-bottle or in-can sterilization can be applied batch-wise (in an autoclave) or continuously. Machines that have rotary air locks (to maintain the pressure) may be applied for cans and hydrostatic sterilizers for bottles. The sterilization is primarily aimed at killing all bacterial spores — reduction to, say, 10^{-8} spores/ml — and inactivating plasmin. If the sterilizing effect is adequate for *B. stearothermophilus*, then *B. subtilis*, *Clostridium botulinum*, and *C. perfringens* are also absent. *UHT sterilization* kills bacterial spores more effectively than in-bottle sterilization.

7.6.10 Sweetened Condensed Milk

Sweetened condensed milk is milk that is concentrated by evaporation, to which sucrose is added to form an almost saturated sugar solution, after which it is canned. The high sugar concentration is primarily responsible for the keeping quality of the product and for its fairly long shelf life, even after the can has been opened, although it then will eventually become moldy. The product is somewhat glassy in appearance because the fat globules show little light scattering as the refractive index of the continuous phase is almost equal to that of fat. The turbidity of the product is largely due to lactose crystals. Most of the lactose crystallizes because of its supersaturation. The process steps are briefly discussed in the following text:

Heating: Pathogens and potential spoilage organisms must be killed. Among the enzymes, milk lipase should primarily be inactivated; bacterial lipases are not inactivated and, if present, can cause severe rancidity. UHT heating at about 130 to 140°C is commonly applied.

Homogenization: Creaming is often not a major problem, and therefore homogenization is not always done. Currently, however, sweetened condensed milk is made less viscous (and exhibits less thickening) than previously.

Addition of Sugar: This can simply be added to the original milk. The amount added can be adjusted readily, and the sugar is pasteurized along with the milk. The sugar should be refined and be devoid of invert sugar to prevent excessive Maillard reactions.

Concentration: This is usually done by evaporation. A falling-film evaporator is generally used to remove the bulk of the water and a circulation evaporator to remove the remainder. Relatively high temperatures (up to 80°C) are often applied, which implies a lower viscosity in the evaporator but a higher initial viscosity of the final cooled product. The low water content of the sweetened condensed milk implies a high viscosity and boiling point.

Cooling and seeding: In these steps, formation of large lactose crystals must be avoided. Consequently, seed lactose is added. Before that, the condensed milk must be cooled to a temperature at which lactose is supersaturated so that the seed lactose does not dissolve.

Packaging: Packaging in cans is common. The cans are then covered with a lid and the seams are sealed. Cans and lids are first sterilized, *e.g.*, by flaming. The packaging room is supplied with air purified through bacterial filters.

Sweetened condensed milk is not sterile. It contains living microbes and spores. The low water activity (about 0.83) or, rather, the high sugar content prohibits growth of most but not all microorganisms. Deterioration usually occurs by osmophilic yeasts, most of which belong to the genus *Torulopsis*. The yeasts often cause gas formation (bulging cans), a fruity flavor, and coagulation of protein. Some molds, especially strains of *Aspergillus repens* and *A. glaucus*, can grow as long as oxygen is present. If so, fairly firm colored lumps are formed and an off-flavor develops. One spore in one air bubble can cause such a lump.

The main change in sweetened condensed milk during storage is presumably *age thickening* and, finally, gelation. Sweetened condensed milk is far more concentrated than evaporated milk. Nevertheless, it does not thicken markedly faster with age. It is usually assumed that added sucrose inhibits age thickening; other sugars or hexitols have a similar effect. A difference with evaporated milk is that an initial decrease in viscosity before age thickening is not observed. The viscosity increases almost linearly with time.

7.6.10.1 Frozen concentrated milk: Frozen concentrated milk refers to the milk which has been partially concentrated and then solidified by freezing. Advantages of this milk are long keeping quality and easy transportation. But destabilization of fat and casein results in oiling-off and sediment formation.

7.6.10.2 Fermented milk: Fermented milk refers to the milk which has been made by employing selected microorganisms to develop the characteristic flavours, body and texture. Fermentation is defined as the metabolic process in which chemical processes are brought about on an organic substratum, whether protein, carbohydrates or fat through the enzymes liberated by specific living micro-organisms. A number of different kinds of starters or cultures are available in dairy industry. The starter species most commonly used in industry are: *Str. diacetilactis, Str. lactis,Str. cremoris, Leuc. Citrovorum* and *Leuc. dextrancium.* A starter may contain a single lactic strain or a mixture of lactic streptococci with or without Leuconostoc species.

An active starter performs three important functions in manufacturing: (1) acid production, (2) desired characteristic and flavour production, (3) Prevention of growth of undesirable microorganisms. Some fermented milk are natural butter milk, cultured butter milk, acidophilus milk, Bulgarian butter milk, Kumiss, kefir, yoghurt and dahi

The merits are: (1) much more palatable than milk, (2) nutritive value increased, (3) more easily assimilated by human system than milk, (4) may contain some beneficial antibiotics and regular intake increases human longevity and (5) may possess therapeutic properties.

7.7 GRADING OF MILK

Judging of milk refers to the act of evaluating its eating quality on basis of various attributes. The eating quality is determined by organoleptic/ sensory tests which include all the five senses of sight, smell, taste, touch and sound. Of these taste and smell are the most important in judging and grading.

The consumer acceptability of dairy product is determined primarily by its eating quality. It is well known that dairy products cannot be of a higher quality than the raw materials from which they are made. Hence, milk producers should have a definite knowledge as to what constitutes desirable and undesirable flavours in milk, as well as the factors causing them. The procedure for examination or scoring is given below.

(*a*) ***Sampling*** : secure a representative sample aseptically by the standard procedure for bacterial count determination.

(*b*) ***Sequence of observations*** : it includes the following steps:

(I) *Sediment* – the sediment discs should be compared with a standard charts for scoring.

(II) *Closure* – after having scored for sediment, the closure should be carefully observed and scored.

(III) *Container* – the glass container is examined

(IV) *Flavour* – the well mixed milk at 16-21°C has been taken; sip a sufficient amount of it (5-10 ml). To yield a normal taste reaction. By placing the nose directly over the milk when it has been shaken, any off- smell may be detected.

Different grades of milk

The different grades of milk are:

(*a*) **Grade 1 :** Milk with clear pleasant flavour, MBR (Methyl Blue Reduction) time over 5 hours and 30 minutes and practically no sediment on sediment disc. Mainly used for production of Market milk, Sterilized milk, Evaporated milk, Sweetened condensed milk, Milk powder, Infant foods, Cheese etc.

(*b*) **Grade 2 :** milk having off- flavours such as; definitely feed, flat or salty: slightly barny, bitter, foreign, malty, metallic, musty, oxidized or rancid; or very slightly weedy; MBR time between 2½ and 5½ hours; or milk which shows a medium amount of sediment. Mainly used for production of Butter, Ice cream, Flavoured milks, Fermented milk, Khoa, Chana/ Paneer, Butter oil, Ghee etc.

(*c*) **Grade 3:** milk having off- flavours such as; definitely barny, bitter, foreign, malty, metallic, musty, oxidized or rancid; or slightly high- acid; MBR time between 20 minutes and 2½hours; or definitely high in sediment. Mainly used for production of Ghee, Casein etc..

(*d*) **Reject or no grade** - milk with high – acid, rancid, weedy, or foreign flavours; MBR time less than 20 minutes and containing an extremely high amount of sediment or any noxious foreign matter.

7.8 OTHER MILK PRODUCTS

7.8.1 Cream

Cream is known as the fatty layer that rises to the top of milk. Cream is sold in many varieties. The fat content may range from 10% (half-and half) to 48% (double cream). Although used for several purposes, it is primarily something of a luxury and, therefore, an excellent flavor is of paramount importance. Because of the high fat content, any off-flavor of the fat becomes concentrated. For instance, milk with a fat acidity of 1 mmol per 100 g fat will not be perceived to have a soapy, rancid flavor by most people, but a whipping cream made from it will definitely taste rancid. Therefore, the milk should be impeccable with regard to lipolysis and fat oxidation. Sometimes anhydrous milk fat is used in cream products and recombination is applied. Such a fat may have an oxidation flavor, and even if impeccable in this respect, the taste of the product may be somewhat less rich because of the absence of components from the milk-fat-globule membrane.

7.8.1.1 Cream production: The basic principle of cream separation is based on the fact that milk fat is lighter than the skim milk portion. Cream is obtained by either gravity or centrifugal methods:

Gravity method : The milk is allowed to stand for some time; there is a tendency for fat to rise. The velocity or rate at which fat rise is given by Stocke's law;

$$V = \frac{2G\,(ds - df)\,r^2}{9n}$$

where V = velocity or rate at which a single fat globule rises.

G = Acceleration due to gravity ds = density of skim milk

df = density of fat r = radius of fat globule

n = viscosity of skim milk

The important factors affecting the rate of rise are size of fat globules. Temperature, clumping and addition of adhesives.

Centrifugal method: When milk enters rapidly revolving bowl of cream separator, it is subjected to centrifugal force, which is 3000 to 6000 times greater than gravitational force. While both fat and skim milk are subjected to centrifugal force, the difference in density affect the heavier portion more intensely than the lighter portion, there by the skim milk is forced to the periphery while fat portion moves towards centre. The cream and skim milk both form vertical walls within the bowl and are separated by being led through separate outlets. The various type of cream separators are warm milk separator, cold milk separator, power driven milk separator, hand driven milk separator, open bowl or gravity fed separator, semi enclosed separator etc.

7.8.1.2 Different factors affecting fat percentage of cream

(*a*) Position of cream screw–by altering position of the cream screw, the ratio of skim milk to cream changes. When cream screw is moved in towards the axis of rotation, a higher fat percentage in cream is obtained and vice versa.

(*b*) Fat percentage–the higher the fat percentage in milk, the higher the fat percentage in cream and vice versa.

(*c*) *Speed of bowl*–the higher the speed of bowl, the higher the fat percentage in cream, and vice versa.

(*d*) *Rate of milk inflow*–the higher the rate of milk inflow, the lower the fat percentage in cream, and vice versa, the lower the rate of milk, the higher the fat percentage in cream, and vice versa

(*e*) *Temperature of milk*–The optimal milk separation temperature is 35-40°C. It is also recommended to not warm milk above 45°C.

(*f*) *Amount of water or skim milk added to flush the bowl*–the greater the amount of water or skim milk added to flush the bowl, the lower the fat percentage in cream, and vice versa

7.8.1.3 Fat Determination in Milk and Milk Products

The **Gerber method** is primary and historic chemical test for determination of fat in milk and milk products depends on the liberation of the fat by the action of sulphuric acid on milk or milk products in specially shaped, calibrated glass containers, called butyrometers which are then centrifuged to aid the separation of fat, the volume of which is finally read off against the percentage scale etched on the butyrometer. This method is widely used in India for the rapid determination of fat in milk and other milk products when a large number of samples is to be analysed at a time. (IS 1224 Part1, 1977).

Rose Gottlieb Method: Weigh accurately about 10 gram well mixed sample of milk and 5-10 grams of milk product into the Rose Gottlieb or Mojonnier tube. Add 1.25 ml of concentrated ammonia and mix well by gentle rotating. Add 10 ml ethyl alcohol and mix thoroughly again. Add 25 ml diethyl ether and close the tube with pre wetted bark cork and shake well for 1 minute then add 25 ml of light petroleum ether. Shake the contents thoroughly for 30 seconds. Then allow the tube to stand for at least 30 minutes. When there is a separation of ether layer siphon or decant the ether layer into a clean, dry and weigh conical flask. Repeat the extraction process using 15 ml each of diethyl ether and petroleum ether 2 times more. The cork of the tube is washed with solvent mixture often before each removal. Evaporate the solvent of the conical flask by keeping it on water bath being heated. Residual fat is dried at 102 ± 2°C in a hot air oven till its weight is constant. In case of milk products the following amount of the sample is taken and mix with boiling or hot distilled water and rest of the method is same as in case of milk.

1. Cream: 1- 2 grams of sample is taken. **2. Butter:** 1- 1.5 grams of sample is taken.

3. Paneer and Khoa: For both the products generally 2- 2.5 grams of sample is taken.

Hot Extraction

E-500: Hot Extraction after hydrolysis with the HydrolEx H-506 A simple and fast procedure for fat determination is introduced. The sample is hydrolyzed with the HydrolEx H506, followed by an extraction with the FatExtractor E-500 Hot Extraction. The total fat content is determined gravimetrically, after the extract has been dried to a constant weight. This application follows official methods (ISO 1444:1996, ISO 11085:2016, AOAC 2003.05, AOAC 991.36).

7.8.2 Butter

Butter, a water-in-oil emulsion, comprises of >80% milk fat, but also contains water in the form of tiny droplets, perhaps some nonmilk fat, with or without salt (sweet butter); texture is a result of working/kneading during processing at appropriate temperatures, to establish a fat crystalline network that results in desired smoothness (compare butter with melted and recrystallized butter). It is used as a spread, a cooking fat, or a baking ingredient. Salt, flavorings, or preservatives are sometimes added to butter. When refrigerated, butter remains a solid, but softens to a spreadable consistency at room temperature, and melts to a thin liquid consistency at 32°C–35°C. Butter generally has a pale yellow color, but varies from deep yellow to nearly white. As a water-in-oil emulsion it contains 80%–82% milk fat and 18%–20% of an aqueous phase. Butterfat is very complicated in its fatty acid and triacylglycerol composition. In addition to the usual C16 and C18 acids, it contains short-chain and medium-chain acids (C4–C14), a range of trans monoene acids, mainly 18:1, and oxygenated and branched-chain acids. The trans acids represent 4%–8% of the total acids.65 Butter contains some cholesterol (0.2%–0.4%). Spreads with lower levels of fat are also available. Butter that spreads directly from the refrigerator is made by removing some of its higher melting glycerol esters or by blending with a vegetable oil.

The pH of sweet cream butter (unfermented) is about 6.4–6.5. Many countries allow sodium chloride and lactic cultures as the only nonmilk additives in butter (Milner, 1995). Some countries allow neutralization of cream and addition of natural coloring agents to adjust for seasonal variation in colorant in the cream (*e.g.*, annato, carotene, and turmeric). There are two kinds of butter: sweet cream, which may or may not be salted, and ripened-cream butter. In ripened cream butter, citrate in cream is fermented by certain lactic acid bacteria to produce acetoin and diacetyl; the latter imparts a characteristic flavor to the product. Ripened-cream butters are more popular in Europe, whereas unripened or sweet-cream butter is preferred in the United States, Ireland, England, Australia, and New Zealand.

When whey produced during cheese making is passed through a separator, the result is whey cream. Whey cream is processed into butter, usually as a blend with sweet cream. Butter from a _20% whey cream and sweet cream blend may be indistinguishable from that made from 100% sweet cream. Butter is also manufactured from neutralized or non-neutralized whey cream, usually as a blend with sweet cream.

Thus, butter manufacture involves partial or complete separation of cream from raw milk, pasteurization, possible fermentation by added lactic acid bacteria (when ripened-cream butter is manufactured), churning, working, salting, packaging, storage, and perhaps later repackaging.

The *skimming* is mainly done for economical reasons: (1) reduction of fat loss (*e.g.*, the fat content of buttermilk is 0.4% and that of skim milk is 0.05%; this means that removal of 1 kg of skim milk from the liquid to be churned will result in an additional yield of about 4 g of butter), (2) reduction of the size of the machinery (especially the churn), and (3) reduction of the volume of buttermilk. Hence, a high fat content of the cream (*e.g.*, 40%) has advantage, also because it counteracts development of off-flavors. If a continuous butter-making machine is used, the fat content of the cream is often taken even higher, for example, up to 50%.

Pasteurization serves to kill microorganisms, inactivate enzymes, make the cream a better substrate for the starter bacteria, and render the butter more resistant to oxidative deterioration. Over intense heating causes a cooked or gassy flavor. Sometimes the cream is pasteurized in a vacreator, which involves the hot cream being put under vacuum to cool, due to which some compounds causing off-flavors are removed.

The *starter* should produce lactic acid and 'aroma' (*i.e.*, primarily diacetyl). Moreover, the starter should not be strongly reducing, because this causes loss of diacetyl (by reduction to acetoin and 2,3–butanediol). Use is made of a mesophilic mixed-strain starter culture, containing the acid producers *Lactococcus lactis* sspp. *lactis* and *cremoris*; and the aroma producers *Leuconostoc mesenteroides* ssp. *cremoris* and *Lactococcus lactis* ssp. *lactis* biovar. *diacetylactis*. Moreover, a careful selection of strains is needed, with respect to the reducing capacity of the starter, and the formation of acetaldehyde by the *diacetylactis* strains, because too much of it causes a yogurt-like flavor. The starter is usually cultured from a frozen concentrate. The inoculum percentage is high because the bacteria have to grow at a sub-optimal temperature.

The purpose of *ripening* is to sour the cream and to crystallize fat. Without solid fat, churning is impossible, and too little solid fat goes along with excessive fat loss in the buttermilk. The method of cooling (temperature sequence) affects the butter consistency.

The *churning* is in most cases achieved by beating in of air. It can be done in a churn, mostly consisting of a large vessel (tub, cylinder, cube, or double-ended cone) with so-called dashboards, which is partly (at most half) filled with cream, and which is rotated at several revolutions per minute (rpm.). The churning then takes, say, 20 min. There are also churns with a rotary agitator (for example, 20 rpm).

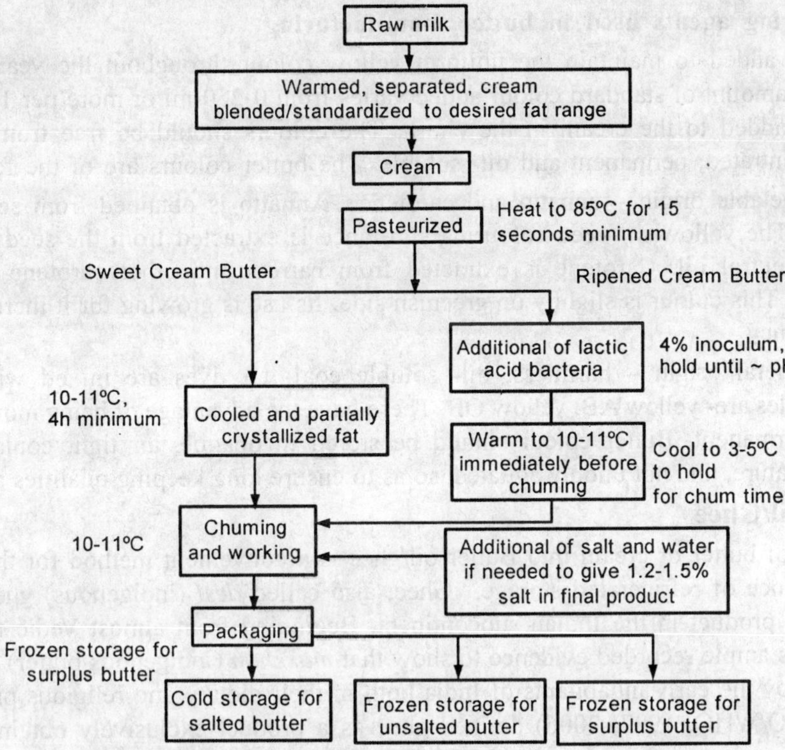

Fig. 9: Flow chart showing manufacturing of butter

The churning should proceed rapidly and completely (low fat content in the buttermilk), and the formed butter grains should have the correct firmness to allow for efficient working. The size of the butter grains can be varied by continuing the churning for various lengths of time after grains have formed. Very fine butter grains (on the order of 1 mm) are hard to separate from the buttermilk, especially in continuous machines.

If the butter grains are not too large, their firmness can to some extent be affected by *washing*, that is, via the wash-water temperature. The washing consists of mixing the butter grains with cold water, after which the water again is drained off. This reduces the dry-matter content of the butter moisture. Formerly, washing was done to improve the keeping quality of the butter, but nowadays it is only done to control the temperature, if needed.

The *working* (kneading) is done (1) to transform the butter grains into a continuous mass; (2) to finely disperse the moisture in the butter; (3) to regulate the water content; and (4), if desired, to incorporate salt. Working consists of deforming the butter. This can, for instance, be achieved by squeezing the butter through rollers, by allowing it to fall from a height, or by squeezing the butter through perforated plates (in the continuous machines).

Classification of Butter

There are different types of butter. A brief description of several kinds of butter is as follows:

(*a*) *Pasteurized cream butter* - made from Pasteurized sweet cream. Usually has a milder flavour than that made from similar unpasteurized cream.

(*b*) *Ripened cream butter* - made from cream in which a pleasant delicate aroma has been developed before churning by ripening.

(*c*) *Unripened cream butter* - made from unripened cream. Usually have mild flavour.

Different colouring agents used in butter manufacturing

Colours are added to maintain the uniform yellow colour throughout the year for consumer satisfaction. The amount of standard colour added varies from 0-250 ml or more per 100 kg of butter fat. Colours are added to the cream in the churn. The colours should be free from off- flavours, non- toxic, concentrated, permanent and oil- soluble. The butter colours are of the following types:

(1) Of vegetable origin – annatto and carotene. Annatto is obtained from seeds of annatto plant. The yellowish – red colouring substance is extracted from the seeds by dissolving it in neutral oil. Carotene is extracted from carrots and other carotene rich vegetable matter. This colour is slightly on greenish side. Its use is growing for it increase in vitamin A potency

(2) Of mineral origin – harmless, oil- soluble coal- tar dyes are mixed with neutral oil. Examples are- yellow AB, yellow OB. These have the advantage of being more concentrated and permanent. Butter colour should be stored in opaque, air tight containers at room temperature, and not unduly agitated, so as to ensure long keeping qualities and usefulness.

7.8.3 Butter Oil/Ghee

Conversion of butter or cream into Butter oil/ghee is a convenient method for the preservation of fat in the absence of refrigerated storage. Ghee, also called *desi* (indigenous) ghee, is the most widely used milk product in the Indian subcontinent. Beginning from almost Vedic times (3000 to 2000 BC), there is ample recorded evidence to show that *makkhan* (indigenous butter) and ghee were extensively used by the early inhabitants of India both in their dietary and religious practices Codex Alimentarius (FAO/WHO, 1997, 2006) defined ghee as a product exclusively obtained from milk, cream or butter by means of processes, which result in almost total removal of water and non-fat solids, with an especially developed flavour and physical structure. Since ghee is primarily distinguished from butteroil by its flavour characteristics, the definition proposed by Codex Alimentarius (FAO/WHO, 1997, 2006) describes the product more closely. However, considering ghee as a product in its own right, it can more appropriately be defined as a pure clarified fat exclusively obtained from milk, cream or butter, by means of processes involving application of heat at atmospheric pressure, which result in the almost total removal of moisture and SNF and which gives the product a characteristic flavour and physical structure and texture.

Ghee is a solid fat-based product made in India from cow- or buffalo-ripened milk. It is less perishable than butter and, therefore, more suitable for a tropical climate. Milk is curdled. The curd is then manually churned until it precipitates butter and leaves behind some whey. The butter is then heated on a low flame until a layer of white froth covers the surface. This state indicates the end of the process, and the liquid obtained on filtering the suspension is pure ghee. Ghee is made by simmering unsalted butter in a large pot until all water has boiled off and protein has settled to the bottom. The cooked and clarified butter is then spooned off to avoid disturbing the milk solids on the bottom of the pan. Unlike butter, ghee can be stored for extended periods without refrigeration, provided it is kept in an airtight container to prevent oxidation and remains moisture-free.

A major portion of ghee is utilized for culinary purposes, for example, as a dressing for various foods and for cooking and frying of different foods. It is considered as the supreme cooking or frying medium. In the Indian context, ghee is a product of the sacred cow, 'born of fire', and hence pure and confers purity to other foods when used in making them. Almost the entire range of Indian sweets, prepared with admixtures of milk, cereals, fruits, vegetables and nuts, are preferably cooked using ghee as the medium. Ghee is one of the four basic elements in the Indian cooking. Sweets and meals cooked in ghee enjoy special status and are recognized for their distinguished flavour attributes derived from ghee. Meals for special occasions are cooked in ghee. Butter oil/ghee contains butter fat (99.5 to 99.8%), moisture (0.1 to 0.3%), acidity (0.2 to 0.5 % as oleic acid) and peroxide value (0.0 to 0.1%).

Methods of manufacturing: Butteroil refers to the fat concentrate obtained mainly from butter or cream by the removal of practically all the water and solid- not- fat content. The terms of milk fat, anhydrous milk fat, dry butter fat and dehydrated butter fat are used synonymously with the butteroil but the raw material for preparation is usually cream.

The different methods are:

(*a*) Direct evaporation:

(1) At atmospheric pressure (2) Under vacuum

(*b*) Decantation

(*c*) Centrifugation followed by vacuum drying

(*d*) Direct from cream by de-emulsification and centrifugation.

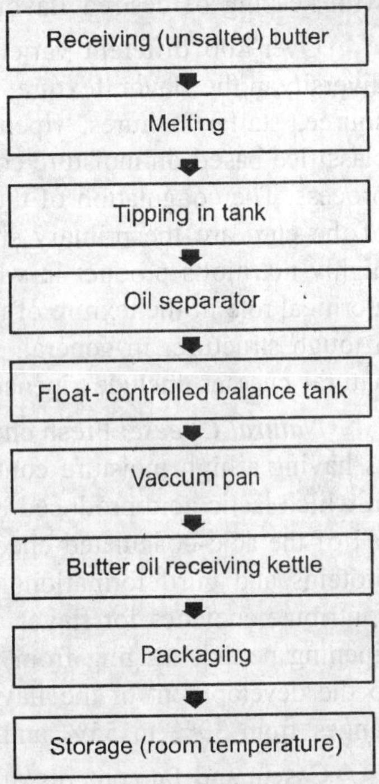

Fig. 10: Butter oil manufacturing

Direct evaporation : This is a batch process and may be carried out at atmospheric pressure or under vacuum. Butter is placed in a steam jacketed large open vat/ pan. At first heat is applied slowly till butter melts. The temperature is then gradually raised, and butter is stirred, usually to 108 – 110 °C. When all moisture evaporated, the residual butter fat is drained from curd and filtered. The product has somewhat darker colour compared to other methods; it has a cooked flavour. Direct evaporation under vacuum does not yield much but it gives good quality final product.

Decantation : This is also a batch process. Butter is melted and allowed to stand undisturbed for sufficient time, until it stratifies to three different layers, viz., top- scum, middle fat and bottom serum. The fat layer is drawn off from the top and cooled. A clean separation cannot be obtained by this method and also have low fat recovery. This is an uneconomical when employed in large scale.

Centrifugation followed by vacuum drying : This is a more or less continuous method and yields high quality product. A typical method has given below. Butter is dumped in the butter melter, which is a vertical jacketed stainless steel cylindrical tank fitted with agitator. If butter is very cold and hard, it should be cut into small pieces before heating. Then steam inlet to the jacket is opened and the agitator runs at low speed.

The tipping tank, which is jacketed at the bottom, filled with clean water and heated to 77-79 °C. The centrifugal oil separator is then started and when it attains full speed, the hot water from tipping tank is run to it. When the water is completely run out, the discharge valve of butter melter is gradually opened to allow the melt to enter the separator. The melt is separated into oil and serum.

The oil flows into Float- controlled balance tank and thence into vacuum pan due to suction. Here it is dehydrated at 56-63°C under a vacuum of 57-62 cm of mercury. At the end of the operation, the vacuum is broken and butteroil allowed to flow by the gravity into the receiving kettle for subsequent cooling, packaging and storage temperatures.

Direct from cream by de- emulsification and centrifugal separation.

This process utilizes the principle of de-emulsification of cream used in various continuous butter making processes. De-emulsified fat may then have melted and clarified by centrifuging and vacuum heating.

7.8.4 Cheese

Cheese refers to a group of dairy products in which casein, fats and other milk nutritional compounds remains in clot. Cheese origin estimates over 7000 years ago (B.C.).

The main goal of cheese production is keeping of nutrient compounds in non-spoiling conditions with keeping of desired flavour.

Over 400 different varieties of cheese have been recognized throughout the world. The wide diversity in the flavor, texture, and appearance of these cheeses is attributed to differences in the milk source, starter cultures, ripening conditions, and chemical composition. Cheeses are frequently classified based on moisture content, method of precipitation of the cheese proteins, and the ripening process. The coagulation of the casein proteins, separation of the curds from the whey, and ripening of the curd are the primary steps involved in the processing of cheese. The resulting product is a highly nutritious product in which the casein and fat from the milk are concentrated. The fat plays a critical role in the texture of the cheese by preventing the casein molecules from associating to form a tough structure. In general, most cheeses can be classified as natural or processed cheeses. The natural cheeses include ripened or unripened cheeses.

Natural Cheese: Fresh cheeses are consumed immediately after processing and are characterized as having a high moisture content and mild flavor. Most fresh cheeses are acid-coagulated cheeses, in which lactic acid produced by the starter cultures causes the precipitation of the caseins. The final pH of the acid-coagulated cheeses is 4.6. Rennet is primarily used for the coagulation of the casein proteins and curd formation in ripened cheeses. Starter cultures are added to produce acid and contribute enzymes for flavor and texture development during ripening. Ripened cheeses undergo a ripening period, ranging from 3 weeks to more than 2 years, following processing that contributes to the development of the flavor and texture of the cheese. The moisture content of these cheeses ranges from 30% to 55% and the pH ranges from 5.0 to 5.3.

Casein and fat contents of the milk are standardized to minimize variations in the quality of the cheese due to seasonal effects and variation in the milk supply. The casein-to-fat ratio can be adjusted by the addition of skim milk, cream, milk powder, or evaporated milk or the removal of fat. Calcium chloride (0.1%) may also be added to improve coagulation of the milk by rennet and further processing of the cheese.

In most natural, aged cheeses, coagulation of the casein proteins by the addition of rennet is most common. This process is temperature dependent, with no coagulation occurring below 10°C, and an increase in coagulation rate accompanying an increase in temperature until the optimal temperature for coagulation at 40–45°C. The production of acid by lactic acid bacteria or the direct addition of hydrochloric or lactic acid can also result in the aggregation of the casein micelles and formation of clots. As the pH of the milk is reduced, the casein micelles become insoluble and begin to aggregate. Lactic acid bacteria cultures are added to the milk in conjunction with the rennet in ripened cheeses.

Frequently, mixed-strain cultures, which contain unknown numbers of strains of the same species, are used. Mesophilic L cultures contain *Leuconostoc* species, including *Ln. mesenteroides* ssp. *cremoris* and *Ln. lactis,* while the main species in mesophilic D cultures *Lactococcus lactis* ssp. *cremoris* with lesser amounts of *Lc. lactis* ssp. *lactis.*

The pressure and time of pressing range from a few g/cm^2 for a few minutes for moist cheeses, to 200 to 500 g/cm^2 for up to 16–48 hours for cooked and hard cheeses. The temperature (20–27°C) and humidity (95% relative humidity) of the pressing room is controlled to optimize the growth of the lactic acid bacteria and facilitate the deformation and shaping of the curd.

The salting step reduces the moisture content of the curd, inhibits the growth of starter bacteria, and affects the flavor, preservation, texture, and rate of ripening of the cheese. Final salt contents of cheeses range from 0.7% to 4% (2–10% salt in moisture contents).

Fresh, green cheese has a bland flavor and a smooth, rubbery texture. During the ripening process, the characteristic texture and flavor of the cheese develop through a complex series of biochemical reactions. Ripening starter cultures are selected to develop the texture and flavor characteristics of the specific cheese type. Protease and lipase activity during the ripening is probably most important to the development of the flavor and texture of the cheese. Lipases break down triacylglycerols into free fatty acids, and mono- and diacylglycerols. The short-chain free fatty acids contribute to the sharp, pungent flavor characteristics of the cheese.

Processed Cheese: Processed cheeses are produced by blending and heating several natural cheeses with emulsifiers, water, butterfat, whey powder and/or caseinates to form a homogeneous mixture. The proportion of cheese used in the formulation ranges from 51% for cheese spreads and cheese foods to 98% in processed cheeses. Different types of natural cheeses will produce processed cheeses with different flavor and textural characteristics. The formulation of these ingredients affects the consistency, texture, flavor, and melting characteristics of the processed cheese. The heating process inactivates the microorganisms and denatures enzymes to produce a stable product. The flavor of the processed cheese is generally milder than the natural cheeses, due to the effects of the heat. However, the melting properties of the processed cheese are much improved due to the addition of the emulsifiers. Processed cheeses range in consistency from block cheese to sliced cheese to cheese for spreading.

7.8.4.1 Cheese cultures: Cheese cultures are a group of specific bacteria strains that are combined in order to make a particular type of cheese. They are also used to help good bacteria in the milk flourish and lead to a more rich and developed flavor. All cultures accomplish the same basic task—their primary function is to raise the acidity of milk by absorbing the lactose (a natural sugar found in milk) and transforming it into lactic acid. This part is especially beneficial in the cheesemaking process for three reasons:

1. The acid helps the milk split into particles called curds—an essential ingredient to produce cheese.
2. Lactic acid causes milk to become more acidic by consuming the sugar inside the milk.
3. After this process, the cheese begins to formulate its unique flavor, texture, and smell.

While most cheese cultures have a very similar makeup, they can be differentiated by the temperature at which they work, the type of bacteria strains they contain, and the ratio of each strain present. Depending on the type of cheese you want to make, the type of bacteria strain and ratio of each strain will vary.

Temperature: Cheese cultures can be classified by the temperature at which they work. The two **most** common type of cheese cultures are:

Mesophilic culture: This type of cheese culture is best suited to work in moderate or medium temperatures up to 90°F. It is ideal for making a variety of hard cheeses such as Monterey, Cheddar, Jack, Edam, Gouda, etc. Mesophilic is also the most common of the two cultures as it is used to produce the majority of cheeses that cannot be heated up to a high degree.

Thermophilic culture: This type of cheese culture works well with warmer temperatures between 68-125° F range as it is a heat-loving bacteria. It's used to make a variety of cheeses like Mozzarella, Parmesan, Provolone, Swiss, Romano, and more that can withstand higher temperatures.

For each individual culture, the growth and flavor production range will vary depending on not only the temperature but how many strains of bacteria is used and the ratio of each strain used.

Starter Culture vs. Non Starter Culture: Although it is possible to make cheese without a cheese culture like certain types of fresh, unaged cheeses (cream cheese, cottage cheese, rennet, etc.), most require a starter culture of some sort. Starter culture is specially grown bacteria (LAB or lactic acid bacteria) that is used to start the transformation of milk into cheese. These are great for beginners or if you're just simply looking for a straightforward way to get started on making your own cheese! Most starter cultures come with a specific blend of bacteria that can be used to make a particular type of cheese. However, some starter cultures have a more broad use such as Mesophilic culture that can be used for a variety of cheese recipes ranging from semi-soft to hard. Many cheese recipes also typically list out the type of cheese culture that is needed in order to create your own, taking the guesswork out of your hands.

By contrast, non-starter culture (NSLAB or non-starter lactic acid bacteria) is made out of the microbial groups that are lower in curds and have different conditions than that of their counterparts. According to the National Center for Biotechnology Information, this type of culture dominates the cheese microbiota during the ripening process by being able to tolerate a hostile environment which strongly influences curd maturations and contributes to the development of the cheese's final characteristics.

7.8.4.2 Curing of cheese: The curing/ripening/souring/maturing of cheese refers to the storage of cheese for at least 2 to 3 months at a given low temperature (0-16 °C), during which its physical, chemical and bacteriological properties are profoundly changed, resulting in the development of characteristic flavour, body and texture. The term green cheese is applied to hard – pressed cheese in early stages of ripening before the characteristic flavour and texture of ripened cheese have developed. The ripening agents influence the rate, extent, and nature of ripening. The common agents are bacteria, molds and enzymes.

7.8.4.3 Enzyme modified cheese: These are concentrated cheese flavours produced enzymatically from cheeses of various ages EMC is obtained by incubation of milk proteins and lipids with selected enzymes and micro-organisms in a slurry system under controlled condition. The main ingredients for EMC as cheese curd medium aged cheeses, selected micro-organisms and a blend of enzymes, proteinases, peiptidases, lipases and esterases. Specific combination of micro-organisms and enzymes can be exploited to yield flavours typical of chedder, Parmesan, Swiss, Gouda, blue and Mozzarella cheese. Enzyme preparation used in the production of EMC are mainly acidic and neutral proteineses of microbial origin Baccilus spp and Aspergillus pp, with lipase and esterase activities naturally associated or intentionally added.

7.8.5 Yoghurt

Generally, the definition of yogurt requires that it is a milk product that is fermented by the action of both *Lactobacillus bulgaricus* and *Streptococcus thermophilus*. In addition other lactobacilli and bifidobacteria are sometimes added during or after culturing yogurt. The milk fat content of yogurt is regulated by the CFR (Code of Federal Regulations) with definitions for yogurt, low fat yogurt, and nonfat yogurt (21 CFR 131.200–206. 2003). The basic steps required for manufacture of yogurt include:

1. Raw ingredient receiving and quality inspection
2. Milk standardization
3. Culture handling
4. Yogurt mix blending
5. Mix homogenization and pasteurization
6. Inoculation, fermentation, and cooling
7. Fruit, flavor, and/or color addition
8. Packaging and storage

The general goal of yogurt production is to create a semisolid, long shelf-life food from perishable, fluid milk. Development and retention of the appropriate texture is critical to good yogurt quality. Yogurt mix preparation (particularly heat treatment and fortification), fermentation conditions (particularly culture type), and post-fermentation handling all have a great impact on product texture.

The milk is initially standardized to the desired fat (0.5–3.5% fat) and milk solids-not-fat (12.5%) contents. The increase in the protein content is most commonly achieved through the addition of nonfat milk powder and improves the body and decreases syneresis of the final product.

The denaturation of the whey proteins and subsequent interactions between the whey proteins and casein and/or fat globules improves the stability of the gel and increases water-binding capacity of the caseins to decrease syneresis. Following heat treatment, the milk is cooled to 43–45°C for inoculation of the starter cultures. The fast acid-producing thermophilic lactic acid bacteria, *Streptococcus salivarius* ssp. *Thermophilus* and *Lactobacillus delbrueckii* ssp. *bulgaricus* are the primary microorganisms used in the production of yogurt. These bacteria have a synergistic effect on each others' growth and should be present in approximately equal numbers for optimal flavor development. *Lb. delbrueckii* ssp. *bulgaricus* has important protease activity and hydrolyzes the milk proteins to small peptides and amino acids.

The acid produced by the yogurt cultures decreases the pH of the milk to cause the aggregation of the casein micelles. As the pH decreases to less than 6.0, the colloidal calcium phosphate that stabilizes the casein micelle structure is solubilized and micelle undergoes partial rearrangement. Solubilization of the colloidal calcium phosphate is essentially completed when the milk reaches a pH of 5.0. With further acid production, the pH of the milk reaches the isoelectric point of casein (pH 4.6) and electrostatic repulsion of the charged groups on the casein proteins decreases as these groups become protonated. Complete solubilization of colloidal calcium phosphate prior to the initiation of gel formation results in the formation of yogurt with stronger gels and reduced tendency for syneresis. Higher inoculation rates for the starter cultures (2%) and a lower incubation temperature (40°C) contribute to stronger interactions between casein molecules and a more stable gel structure and reduced syneresis.

Two types of yogurt, set-style and stirred-style are produced. Set-style yogurt is fermented following packaging, with color and flavors added to the container prior to the addition of the inoculated milk, resulting in a gel that forms a firm, unbroken coagulum. Stirred-style yogurt is fermented in a vat prior to packaging, with the gel structure broken following fermentation during the addition of flavors and colors, cooling and packaging stage. For both types of yogurt, either a short incubation period at 40–45°C for 21/2–3 hours or a long incubation period at 30°C for 16–18 hours may be used to attain a pH of 4.5 or titratable acidity of 0.9% lactic acid prior to cooling.

The metabolism of the yogurt cultures contributes to the characteristic flavor of yogurt. Both bacteria are heterofermentative and produce lactic acid from glucose, yet are unable to metabolize galactose. Acetaldehyde, a key flavor component of yogurt described as having a fruity aroma, is produced by the degradation of threonine to acetaldehyde and glycine by the enzyme threonine aldolase. Although *S. thermophilus* forms a majority of the acetaldehyde produced, the proteolytic activity of *Lb.delbrueckii* ssp. *bulgaricus* generates the precursors for the formation of acetaldehyde.

7.10.6 Khoa

Khoa refers to the partially dehydrated whole milk product obtained by continuous heating of milk in a karahi over direct fire while also constantly stirring- cum- scraping by using a khunti till it reach a semi solid consistency. There after pan contents are removed from the fire and worked up into a solid mass known as Khoa- pat.

According to PFA rules, Khoa is the product obtained from cow or buffalo milk, or a combination of thereof, by rapid drying. The milk fat content should not be less than 20% of a finished product. Mainly three types are there;

Type	Gross composition		Specific sweets
	Fat %	Moisture %	
Pindi	21-26	31-33	Burfi,peda
Dhar	20-23	37-44	Gulabjamun,pantooa
Danedar	20-25	35-40	Kalakh and, Gourd Burfi

7.8.7 Curd (Dahi)

It is the major product obtained from milk in India. Milk is fermented by Lactobacillus and streptococcus bacteria which convert the lactose in milk to lactic acid responsible for sour taste of curd. The difference in the flavor of the curds is believed to be due to microorganisms involved in fermentation. The preparation of curd is a way of preserving milk. The growth of acid forming bacteria prevents the growth of other microorganisms which cause milk to spoil. During curd formation, the lactose of milk is converted into lactic acid. There is some breakdown of protein increasing the non protein nitrogen. The fat globules coagulate and distribute themselves on the top physically during curd formation. Milk proteins are jellied and thin exudates of clear serum on the curd is seen.

7.8.8 Ice Cream

The Code of Federal Regulations (21 CFR135.110) specifies both compositional and manufacturing requirements for a product to be called ice cream. The compositional requirements state that the product cannot contain less than 20% total milk solids including 10% milk fat. No more than 25% of the nonfat milk solids can be derived from whey, and caseinates may be used only after reaching the 20% milk solids minimum. Some allowances are made for bulky flavors such as chocolate and certain fruit flavors, and the requirements for milk solids level is reduced by 20%. The manufacturing requirements defined in law are that the freezing should occur under agitation; the mix should be pasteurized, may contain safe and suitable non-milk derived ingredients, may be sweetened with safe and suitable sweeteners, and may be flavored.

The term "ice cream" in its generic sense includes all whipped dairy products that are manufactured by freezing and are consumed in the frozen state, including ice cream that contains either dairy or non-dairy fats, premium (higher-fat) versions, "light" (lower-fat) versions, ice milk, sherbet and frozen yogurt. Ice cream mix formulations specify the content of fat, milk solids-not-fat, sweeteners, stabilizers, emulsifiers and water that are desired. Dairy and other ingredients used to supply these components are chosen on the basis of availability, cost, legislation, and desired quality. Common ingredients include: cream, butter or vegetable fats, as the main sources of fat; condensed skim or whole milk, skim milk powder, and/or whey powder or whey protein products, as the sources of concentrated milk solids-not-fat; sucrose and corn starch hydrolysates, as the sweeteners; polysaccharides, such locust bean gum, guar gum, carboxymethyl cellulose, and/or carrageenan, as the stabilizers; monoglycerides and diglycerides and polysorbate 80, as the emulsifiers; and milk or water, as the main sources of water in the formulation to balance the components.

The manufacturing process for most of these products is similar and involves the following steps: preparation of a liquid mix by blending of ingredients, pasteurization (65°C for 30 min or 80°C for 25 s), homogenization, cooling to 4°C and ageing of the cold, liquid mix for 4–24 h; concomitantly whipping and freezing this mix dynamically under high shear to a soft, semi-frozen slurry with an air phase volume of 45–52% (overrun of 80–110%) at a temperature of about – 5°C; incorporation of flavoring ingredients to this partially frozen mix; packaging the product; and further quiescent freezing (hardening) of the product in blast air to – 30°C. Homogenization is responsible for the formation of the fat emulsion by forcing the hot mix through a small orifice under a pressure of 14–18 MPa, perhaps with a second stage of 3–4 MPa. Ageing allows for hydration of milk proteins and stabilizers (increase viscosity and decrease melting rate), crystallization of the fat globules, and membrane rearrangement due to competitive displacement of adsorbed proteins by low molecular mass surfactants. The concomitant aeration and freezing process involves numerous physical changes, including the action of proteins and surfactants in forming and stabilizing the foam phase, partial coalescence of the fat emulsion, causing both adsorption of fat at the air interface and the formation of fat globule clusters that stabilize the lamellae between air bubbles, and freeze concentration of the premix by the removal of water from solution in the form of ice.

7.8.8.1 Cheddaring: This refers to the combined operations of packaging, turning, piling, and repiling the curd cubes in cheddar cheese manufacturing.

(*a*) *Packing* – after the bulk drainage of whey, the curd cubes are kept closely together into two heaps with a channel in between. This takes 5 to 15 minutes. It results in the formation of two long slabs of curd. These slabs are cut with a cheese knife into blocks or strips 15 to 20 cm wide.

(*b*) *Turning* – as soon as blocks of curd can be handled without breaking, they are rolled bottom- side up in the vat. This is called turning and it is carried out every 15 minutes till the curd is ready for milling and salting.

(*c*) *Pilling and repiling* – within 30 to 45 minutes of packing, blocks of curd are turned and laid over another in twos or threes. This is called pilling. Then the position of curd is altered this is called repiling.

The cheddar operation lasts for two hours or more and is very important not only for moisture control but also for improving body and texture. After cheddaring cheese become dried, more mellow and silky and changes from a sorbo rubber like material to one resembling chicken breast meat. In the later stages, it tends to tear apart in fibrous shreds and develops a characteristic nutty and buttery aroma. The end of cheddaring operation is indicated by:

(I) *Titratable acidity* : 0.30-0.35% more than at cutting.

(II) *Hot iron test* : long threads, 12 mm or slightly more.

(III) *pH* : about 5.4

7.8.9 Milk Powder

The main purpose of the manufacture of milk powder is to convert the liquid perishable raw material to a product that can be stored without substantial loss of quality, preferably for some years. Decrease in quality mainly concerns formation of gluey and tallowy flavors (due to Maillard reactions and autoxidation, respectively) and decreasing nutritive value (especially decrease in available lysine). If the water content becomes very high and the storage temperature is high, caking (due to lactose crystallization) and enzymic and even microbial deterioration can occur; however, such problems are avoidable.

After adding water the powder should be reconstituted completely and readily to a homogeneous mixture, similar in composition to the original product. Complete reconstitution means that no undissolved pieces or flakes are left and that neither butter grains nor oil droplets appear on top of the solution. 'Readily reconstituted' means that during mixing of powder and water no lumps are formed, because these are hard to dissolve. In the ideal situation the powder will disperse rapidly when scattered on cold water; this is called *instant powder*. Special processing steps are needed to achieve this property. The importance of instant properties closely depends on the kind of application.

Many steps involved will be self-evident. Intense pasteurization is needed to obtain resistance to autoxidation. The concentrate is not always homogenized, especially if atomization is done by means of a nozzle, because the fat globules are effectively disrupted in the nozzle. Homogenization of highly concentrated milk considerably increases its viscosity (because the transfer of large casein micelles to the fat globules gives the latter such an irregular shape as to increase the effective volume fraction of fat globules plus casein micelles). This increase leads to coarser droplets during atomization, with all drawbacks involved.

For the manufacture of *skim milk powder* the pasteurization can be less intense (at least phosphatase negative), according to the intended application. Homogenization is omitted, and the milk can be concentrated to a somewhat higher solids content. Nor are lecithinizing and gas flushing carried out. Sometimes vitamin preparations are added, especially vitamin A. This can be achieved by dry mixing afterward, or by emulsifying a concentrated solution of vitamin A in oil into a part of the skim milk.

The manufacture of *whey powder* is largely similar to that of skim milk powder. At first, curd fines should be removed from the whey by filtration or by means of a hydrocyclone, and the whey should be separated. A problem is the processing of sour whey, which causes rapid fouling of the machinery. Sour whey (or skim milk) can be neutralized with alkali.

Whey can be evaporated to at least 60% dry matter, but then crystallization of lactose readily occurs. An alternative operation is to allow the lactose in the evaporated whey to crystallize as completely as possible, *e.g.*, by keeping it for 3 h at 25°C while stirring. If the dry-matter content is over 60%, seeding with lactose crystals is not necessary. Atomization should be with a disk, as a spray nozzle would become blocked. The precrystallized whey powder then obtained has some attractive properties, especially in regard to caking. An additional advantage for the manufacturer is the higher yield: The conventional methods for determining the water content of powders do not remove the bulk of the water of crystallization of á-lactose monohydrate; crystallization of 80% of the lactose yields up to a maximum of 3% more whey powder. In this way precrystallized skim milk powder also can be made, but then a longer crystallization time and seeding with lactose crystals are needed.

Malted milk powder: According to PFA rules malted milk food is product obtained by mixing whole milk or partially skimmed milk or milk powder with malt extract and cereal grain flour in such a manner as to secure complete hydrolysis of starchy material. It should not contain added sugars, foreign fat, added colours and preservatives. It may contain cocoa powder. Malted milk food should be in the form of power.

7.8.10 Manufacturing of Lactose

Lactose is the principal carbohydrate in the milks of all mammals; non-mammalian sources are very rare. Milk contains only trace amounts of other sugars, including glucose (50 mg/l), fructose, glucosamine, galactosamine, neuraminic acid and neutral and acidic oligosaccharides. The lactose content of cows' milk varies with the breed of cow, individuality factors, udder infection and especially stage of lactation. The concentration of lactose decreases progressively and significantly during lactation. Lactose, along with sodium, potassium and chloride ions, plays a major role in maintaining the osmotic pressure in the mammary system. Thus, any increase or decrease in lactose content (a secreted constituent, *i.e.* formed within the mammary gland) is compensated for by an increase or decrease in the soluble salt (excreted) constituents. This osmotic relationship partly explains why certain milks with high lactose content have low ash content and vice versa. Lactose plays an important role in milk and milk products:

- it is an essential constituent in the production of fermented dairy products;
- it contributes to the nutritive value of milk and its products; however, many non-Europeans have limited or zero ability to digest lactose in adulthood, leading to a syndrome known as ***lactose intolerance***;
- it affects the texture of certain concentrated and frozen products;
- it is involved in heat-induced changes in the colour and flavour of highly heated milk products.

Lactose is a disaccharide consisting of galactose and glucose, linked by a β-l-4 glycosidic bond. Its systematic name is β-*O*-D-galactopyranosyl-(1- 4)-α-D-glucopyranose(α -lactose) or β-*O*-D-galactopyranosyl-(1-4)-β-D-glucopyranose(β -lactose). The hemiacetal group of the glucose moiety is potentially free (*i.e.* lactose is a reducing sugar) and may exist as an α or β-anomer. In the structural formula of the α-form, the hydroxyl group on the C_1 of glucose is ***cis*** to the hydroxyl group at C_2 (oriented downward).

Production of lactose essentially involves concentrating whey or ultrafiltration permeate by vacuum concentration, crystallization of lactose from the concentrate, recovery of the crystals by centrifugation and drying of the crystals. The first-crop crystals are usually contaminated with riboflavin and are therefore yellowish; a higher grade, and hence more valuable, lactose is produced by redissolving and recrystallizing the crude lactose. Lactose may also be recovered by precipitation with $Ca(OH)_2$ especially in the presence of ethanol, methanol or acetone. Lactose has several applications in food products, the most important of which is probably in the manufacture of humanized infant formulae. It is used also as a diluent for the tableting of drugs in the pharmaceutical industry (which requires high-quality, expensive lactose) and as the base for plastics. Among sugars, lactose has a low level of sweetness, which is generally a disadvantage but is advantageous in certain applications. When properly crystallized, lactose has low hygroscopicity, which makes it an attractive sugar for use in icings for confectionary products.

Food applications of lactose are as follows:

- Humanized baby foods
- Confectionery products
- Agglomeration due to lactose crystallization
- Anticaking agent at high relative humidity
- Maillard browning, if desired
- Flavour adsorbant
- Flavour enhancement
- Instantizingifree-flowing agent in foods
- Determineralized whey powder or lactose
- Improves functionality of shortenings
- Certain types of icing
- Accentuates other flavours (chocolate)
- Flavour volatiles
- Sauces, pickles, salad dressings, pie fillings

7.8.11 Manufacturing of Casein

Casein is the major protein in cows' milk, and comprises about 80 % of the total protein content of which the rest, some 20 %, are the whey or serum proteins.

Casein is the basic component of ordinary cheese. In the cheese-making process, casein is precipitated by the action of rennet enzymes, and a coagulum is formed consisting of casein, whey proteins, fat, lactose and the minerals of the milk.

It exists in four subtypes: αs1-casein, αs2-casein, β-casein, and κ-casein. α-Casein (mix of αs1- and αs2-casein) is the main fraction of milk protein. Casein solubility depends on casein type and is strongly influenced by medium pH

All caseins are relatively small molecules, ranging in molecular weight from about 20 to 25 kDa

Casein is usually divided into the following types: (*i*) Rennet casein, obtained by enzymatic precipitation (*ii*) Acid casein, obtained by acidifying skim milk to the isoelectric point (pH 4.6 – 4.7)

In addition to these two main types, there are other commercially available casein products of importance, such as:

- Co-precipitate, made by heating skim milk to a high temperature and then precipitating the casein/whey protein complex, usually with calcium chloride.

The co-precipitate also contains whey proteins and calcium

Commercial casein is made from skim milk by one of two general methods – precipitation by acid or coagulation by rennet. As much of the fat, whey proteins, lactose and minerals as possible must be removed by multistage washing in water, as they reduce the quality of the casein as well as its keeping quality. Dried, properly produced casein has a relatively good keeping quality and is used mainly in the food and chemical industries.

Micellar casein is the purest form of casein there is. In milk, casein is contained within micelles, essentially solid particles floating in liquid.

Casein micelles consist of water, casein, salts (primarily calcium phosphate magnesium, and citrate), and enzymes. On a dry basis, casein micelles have about 6.6% inorganic material, (Colloidal calcium phosphate) 35.6% α_{sl}-casein, 9.9% α_{s2}-casein, 33.6% β-casein, 11.9% κ-casein, and 2.3% casein fragments.

7.9 DEFECTS IN DAIRY PRODUCTS

Quality can be defined as 'fitness for purpose', the interpretation of which depends on the buyer,.the user of the product and the agency that regulates the product. In relation to dairy products this generally involves availability, safety (chemical and microbiological), convenience, freshness, integrity and nutritional value. The quality of all dairy products at the end-point of the handling chain depends on all stages along the chain from milking to processing and finally to the consumer. The end-point of the handling chain is where the consumer makes the final assessment of quality, judging the product, largely on its sensory properties of smell, sight, touch and taste. Off-flavours in milk are a major problem for dairy producers and processors. Potentially, these off-flavours can result in the final manufactured dairy product being rejected at great expense to the processor. An understanding of potential off-flavours in milk provides an insight into how they impact on the quality of manufactured dairy products.

- ***Transmitted flavours:*** Off-flavours in milk caused by the transfer of substances from the cow's feed or environment into the milk while it is in the udder are known as transmitted flavours. They include flavours commonly described as 'feed', 'weed', 'cowy' and 'barny'. The compounds causing the off-flavours may enter the milk through the respiratory tract and/or digestive system and bloodstream.
- ***Feed flavours:*** Undesirable feed flavours can enter milk and cause taints through the cow's consumption of certain types of feed or through the inhalation of the aroma of such feeds. The problem can be controlled by withholding such feeds for 4 to 5 hours before milking. Thus, a feeding regime which restricts the intake of noxious and odorous weeds (*e.g.* wild garlic, onion weed, carrot weed) and roughage is essential for the production of milk free of undesirable feed taints.
- ***Cowy, barny and unclean flavours***: The term 'cowy' is often used to describe an 'unclean' flavour usually associated with barn odours and poor ventilation. The 'barny' or 'unclean' odours are transferred to the milk through the cow's respiratory system in the same manner as feed flavours. The physical condition of the cow may also contribute to off-flavours in milk. Cows suffering from ketosis or acetonemia produce milk with a 'cowy' odour.
- ***Chemical flavours:*** Chemical flavours in milk may result from the contamination of milk through various environmental sources during milking and processing. These include sanitisers in improperly

rinsed equipment, usually chlorine, iodine-based and quaternary ammonium salt compounds. Some dairy producers and processors have had difficulties when using phenols and chlorine compounds in combination. These can react to form chlorophenols, which produce a flavour taint with much lower flavour thresholds than either phenols or chlorine alone.

- ***Flavours associated with oxidation:*** The sensory quality of fat-containing dairy products is largely dependent on the chemical stability of milk lipids during storage. The major milk lipids, namely the glycerides, phosphoglycerides, glycolipids and cholesterol esters, contain fatty acids as common building moieties. The unsaturated fatty acids are susceptible to oxidation which gives rise to off-flavours and limits the shelf-life of many fat-containing dairy products.
- ***Flavours associated with heat treatment:*** The primary purpose of heat treatment of raw milk is to destroy pathogenic microorganisms including *Salmonella* spp., *Escherichia coli*, *Campylobacter* spp., *Yersinia enterocolitica*, *Listeria monocytogenes*, *Cryptosporidium parvum*, *Streptococcus* spp., *Staphylococcus aureus*, *Brucella abortus* and *Mycobacterium tuberculosis*, to make it safe for human consumption. At the same time, heat treatment prolongs shelf-life by destroying spoilage micro-organisms and enzymes. However, off-flavours may be produced by heat processing, the time and temperature of which govern the nature and intensity of the flavours. Heat-induced flavours have been described as 'cooked' or sulphurous', 'heated', 'scorched' and 'caramelised'. The slight 'cooked' or 'sulphurous' flavour of pasteurised milk results from the formation of such volatile substances as ammonia, hydrogen sulphide, mercaptans, and volatile phosphorus compounds that occur with protein breakdown reported that β-lactoglobulin degradation accounts for practically all of the free SH groups in heated milk and is the source of the 'cooked' flavour. The sweet caramel flavour of heat-treated milk has been attributed to non-enzymic browning while a scorched flavour is due to localised overheating in a heat exchanger creating excessive 'burn on'.
- ***Bacterial flavours:*** The fresh milk from a healthy cow drawn aseptically contains only a few bacteria (10^2–10^3cfu mL^{-1}). Off-flavours in the milk from bacterial metabolism can occur at any stage of production or processing. They are not detectable until large numbers of bacteria are present, usually millions per millilitre. Off-flavours of bacterial origin in raw milk are an indication of inadequate hygiene and sanitation, or of the milk having been stored for too long or at too high a temperature. The flavour defects from bacterial growth in both raw and pasteurised milk are described as 'acidic', 'sour', 'malty', 'fruity', 'unclean', 'bitter' and 'putrid'. The production of lactic acid or a combination of other acids by the principal acid-producing bacterial species in milk, such as *Streptococcus, Pedicoccus, Leuconostoc, Lactobacillus*, and members of the Enterobacteriaceae family, cause an acidic flavour in raw and pasteurised milk. A 'malty' flavour in milk, sometimes described as 'cooked', 'caramelised' and 'burnt' can be associated with the metabolism of *Lactococcus lactis* biovar *maltigenes* while a fruity flavour in pasteurised and processed dairy products is associated with post-pasteurisation contamination by *Pseudomonas fragi* producing ethyl esters. Spoilage by psychrotrophic organisms often produces 'unclean', 'bitter', 'putrid' and 'rancid' flavours.
- ***Lipolysed flavor:*** Hydrolysis of milk fat, or lipolysis, catalysed by lipases, is a major dairy industry problem because of the production of flavour defects in milk, cream and manufactured dairy products. The flavours produced are often described as 'soapy', 'rancid', 'butyric', 'bitter', 'unclean' and 'astringent'. Lipolysis produces free fatty acids (FFA) and mono- and diacylglycerols. Short-chain free fatty acids, particularly butyric acid (C_4) and caprylic acid (C_6), are mostly responsible for the unpleasant rancid. The lipases responsible for lipolysis in milk and milk fat products are of two types, the *endogenous milk lipase* and *exogenous bacterial lipases*.
- ***Proteolysis:*** Proteinases act on milk proteins, particularly the caseins, to form peptides and amino acids. Certain small peptides impart a bitter or astringent taste to milk and milk products. The action of proteinases may also change rheological properties by destabilising the casein micelles resulting in defects such as gelation.

7.10 MILK QUALITY COUNTS

Measures of Raw Milk Quality: Somatic Cell Count (SCC): The number of somatic cells in milk, referred to as the somatic cell count or SCC, is used throughout the world as an indicator of milk quality. The current regulatory limit for somatic cells in milk in the United States defined in the Grade "A" Pasteurized Milk Ordinance is 750,000 cells per milliliter (mL). Somatic cells originate only from inside the animal's udder.

Poor quality milk has a high number of somatic cells and is an inferior product with reduced processing properties resulting in dairy products with a reduced shelf-life. On the other hand, high quality milk has a very low number of somatic cells, a longer shelf-life, tastes better and is more nutritious. One characteristic feature of cows with mastitis is a significant elevation in the number of somatic cells in milk. Milk from uninfected mammary glands contains less than 100,000 somatic cells per mL. A milk SCC of more than 200,000 per mL suggests that an inflammatory response has been elicited, a mammary quarter is infected or is recovering from an infection, and that milk has reduced manufacturing properties. It is not uncommon for milk from cows with subclinical and/or clinical mastitis to contain several hundred thousand and even millions of somatic cells per milliliter of milk. Thus, an increase in the SCC of milk is a good indicator of mastitis or inflammation in the udder. Infection of the udder by mastitis pathogens alters milk composition and reduces milk yield.

Standard Plate Count (SPC): The SPC is an estimate of the total number of viable aerobic bacteria present in raw milk. This test is done by plating milk on a solid agar, incubating plates for 48 hours at 32 °C (90 °F), followed by counting bacteria that grow on plates. The SPC is used to monitor progress since consistent application of proper milking system cleaning practices, proper milking practices, udder hygiene and good mastitis prevention and control practices should allow dairy producers to produce milk with a low SPC, which is less than 5,000 colony forming units (cfu)of bacteria per milliliter.

Pasteurized Milk Ordinance mandate that the milk SPC should not exceed 100,000 cfu/mL. However, most segments of the dairy industry feel that more stringent standards (SPC ≤ 10,000 cfu/mL) will result in higher quality milk. Though it is impossible to eliminate all sources of bacterial contamination of milk, milk from clean, healthy cows that has been properly collected generally has a SPC less than 1,000 cfu/mL.

The preliminary incubation (PI) count is a test that can detect bacteria, called psychrotrophic bacteria, that grow in cold environments. Technicians can detect this type of bacteria by holding milk at 55°F (12.8°C) for 18 hours after that SPC or Plate Loop Count (PLC) is formed.

It is suggested that a maximum allowable PI count should be 200,000 CFU/ml. Some milk handlers use counts of 50,000-100,000/ml or even lower as their limits. Another approach sometimes used is to consider a milk suspect if the PI count is higher than the SPC by a designated amount (*e.g.* 3-4 times higher)

Laboratory Pasteurization Count (LPC): This is not a regulatory test required by govt. agencies. The LPC, also known as the thermoduric count, is an estimate of the number of bacteria that can survive laboratory pasteurization at 62.8°C (143°F) for 30 minutes. This process destroys most of the mastitis causing pathogens, selecting for those bacteria that can survive pasteurization temperatures (thermoduric bacteria).

Coliform Count (CC): The CC is a test that estimates the number of bacteria that originate from manure or a contaminated environment. Milk samples are plated on Violet Red Bile agar or MacConkey's agar and incubated for 48 hours at 32°C (90°F), after which typical coliform colonies are counted. Coliform counts reflect hygiene and sanitation practices followed on the farm.

Table 1. Interpretive Criteria for Bulk Tank Milk Monitoring

Parameter	Low	Medium	High
Bulk tank SCC	<200,000	200,000-400,000	>400,000
Standard Plate Count (SPC)	<5,000	5,000-10,000	>10,000
Preliminary Incubation Count (PIC)	<10,000	10,000-20,000	>20,000
Lab Paseurized Count (LPC)	<100	100-200	>200
Coliform Count	<50	50-100	>100

Fig. Troubleshooting Sources of Bulk Tank Milk Contamination

CHAPTER 8

MEAT PROCESSING

8.1 LIVESTOCK IN INDIA

Livestock play an important role in Indian economy and provide livelihood to two-thirds of rural community. Livestock and poultry including cattle, water buffalo, sheep, goat, pig and chicken are primarily produced by the masses for milk, meat, egg, draught power and biomass. Few other species viz, yak, mithun, camel, rabbit, duck, emu, Japanese quail, etc. are also produced in some parts of India as livelihood activities. India has around 42 sheep breeds, 26 goat breeds, 13 buffalo breeds, 40 cattle breeds, 6 pig breeds and 17 chicken breeds registered with Indian Council of Agricultural Research-National Bureau of Animal Genetic Resources (ICAR-NBAGR). India has a huge livestock wealth and ranks 1st, 2nd, 2nd and 4th in the world for water buffalo, cattle, goat and sheep population, respectively during the year 2019 (FAOSTAT). In the year 2018-19, India has produced 8.1 million tonnes of meat and has the distinction of producing largest amount of buffalo meat in the world (42.15%). It is also the 2nd largest producer of goat meat in the world. Per capita consumption of meat in India still remains relatively low at less than 6.5 kg/person/annum. Meat sector activities includes live animal transport, marketing, slaughtering of animals, processing, value addition, by-products utilization, disposal of solid and liquid waste, distribution and retailing of meat and offals. India has around 4000 registered slaughterhouses/places maintained by local bodies, where animals are slaughtered for domestic consumption. Slaughtering is performed in designated abattoirs or slaughterhouses and most of the meat is consumed on the same day or kept in a refrigerator in the households.

Egg production in the country is growing at a rate compound annual growth rate (CAGR) of 7.4 per cent per annum. The per capita availability of eggs is at 95 eggs per annum in 2021-22. Meat production in the country has increased from 6.69 million tonnes in 2014-15 to 9.29 million tonnes in 2021-22.

There are about 303.76 million bovines (cattle, buffalo, mithun and yak), 74.26 million sheep, 148.88 million goats, 9.06 million pigs and about 851.81 million poultry as per the 20th Livestock Census in the country.

There are about 27 modern meat processing plants (approved after due inspection) for the export of meat. All export oriented units (EOU) are registered with the Agricultural and Processed Food Products Export Development Authority (APEDA) of India.

Meat, fat and other carcass parts used as raw materials for the manufacture of processed meat products are mainly derived from the domesticated animal species cattle, pigs and poultry and to a lesser extend from buffaloes, sheep and goats. In some regions other animal species such as camels, yaks, horses and game animals are used as meat animals but play only a minor role in meat processing.

8.2 MEAT

Meat can be defined as "the muscle tissue of slaughter animals". The other important tissue used for further processing is fat. Other edible parts of the slaughtered animal and often used in further processing are the internal organs1 (tongue, heart, liver, kidneys, lungs, diaphragm, oesophagus, intestines) and other slaughter byproducts (blood, soft tissues from feet, head). A special group of internal organs are the intestines. Apart from being used as food in many regions in particular in the developing world, they can be processed in a specific way to make them suitable as sausage casings. Some of them are eaten with the sausage; others are only used as container for the sausage mix and peeled off before consumption. The skin of some animal species is also used for processed meat products. This is the case with pork skin and poultry skin, in some cases also with calf skin (from calf heads and legs).

Red meat refers to the meat from mammalian skeletal muscle tissue with distinctive red color including beef, pork, and lamb. Although muscle and meat are used interchangeably on many occasions, there are differences between the two terms. Muscle refers to a tissue responsible for contraction and movement in live animals, while meat is a broad term referring to edible tissues from animals consisting of muscle, adipose, and other connective tissues. The major components of meat include water, proteins, lipids, carbohydrates, minerals, soluble non-protein substances, vitamins, and some incidental compounds such as feed additives or contaminants. The composition of meat is dependent on the species, breed, sex, age, activity, the anatomical location of the cut, the relative proportions of tissues in the retail cut, and other factors. However, the composition of lean meat is fairly consistent even across different species. Lean meats contain less adipose tissue than well-marbled cuts of meat. The location of the cut of meat on the animal, muscle contraction, and postmortem changes all influence the degree of meat tenderness. Individual cuts vary in inherent tenderness, requiring different cooking methods All meat is subject to mandatory *inspection* by the USDA and voluntary *grading*. After inspection, alteration may occur by processing methods including curing, smoking, restructuring, and tenderizing. Kosher and Halal inspections mean much more than having a religious official blessing.

Incomplete plant proteins of animal feed are resynthesized in meat and it is important to know that only animal protein is a *complete* protein. Thus, if meat consumption is minimized or omitted from the diet, for any number of reasons, an individual must obtain similar nutrients from a nonmeat source, such as combination of various plants. Yet, some individuals may have environmental, religious, vegetarian, health, or other concerns related to the consumption of meat; thus, they might choose to avoid meat products or consume meat minimally. Meat must satisfy the requirements of appearance, texture, and flavor, as well as nutrition, safety, and convenience. Therefore, if eating meat, it becomes important to know the effects of cooking meat on its various components.

8.2.1 Types of Tissues in Meat

Meat is composed of three tissues: muscle tissue, connective tissue, and adipose or fatty tissue.

Muscle Tissue. Muscle is the predominant component of most meat and meat products. Muscle tissue is referred to as the *lean* tissue of meat. It includes *cardiac, skeletal, and smooth muscle. Cardiac* muscle is located in the heart. *Skeletal* muscle, the primary component of the carcass, provides support for the weight of the body and movement, or locomotion. When a muscle is used, it serves to strengthen the bone to which it is attached (true in humans, too). *Smooth* muscle is the visceral muscle located, for example, in the digestive tract, reproduction system, and throughout the blood vessels of the circulatory system. Inside the muscle cell membrane, there are ***myofibrils*** containing alternating thin and thick protein filaments, namely, the *actin* and *myosin*, which contract and relax in the living animal. They are varied in length, perhaps 1 or 2 inches long, and are very small in diameter. Each fiber is cylindrical with tapered ends and is covered by a thin connective tissue sheath called ***endomysium***. Small bundles of 20–40 fibers make up one primary bundle that represents the "***grain***" of meat. This primary bundle is surrounded by ***perimysium*** connective tissue.

Connective Tissue. This meat component is made up of protein and mucopolysaccharides. It is located throughout the muscle and determines the degree of meat tenderness. Less is more tender. As mentioned, muscle bundles are surrounded with various types of connective tissue—endomysium, perimysium, and epimysium—structures that bind muscle fibers in bundles to form muscle. The connective tissue extends beyond the muscle fibers to form *tendons*, which attach the muscle to bones and hold and connect various parts of the body. Connective tissue also forms *ligaments*, attaching one bone to another. Additionally, the tough skin or hide of an animal is connected to underlying animal tissue by connective tissue.

Collagen

Collagen is a substantial part of connective tissue and is found in ligaments, tendons, skin and many other types of tissue serving mechanical and structural functions. Collagen accounts for almost one third of the total protein and is made from several different proteins. One of the major components is the amino acid hydroxyproline and this particular amino acid is present within collagen in a concentration of 12.5%. The amino acids proline and glycine are present at around 45–50% within collagen. The building blocks for collagen are units of tropocollagen, which is a right-handed triple helix made out of three intertwined proteins, and numerous molecules of tropocollagen align themselves next to each other to form collagen.

Collagen is the most abundant protein found in mammals—in bone, cartilage, tendons, and ligament, enveloping muscle groups, and separating muscle layers. It also is in horns, hooves, and skin. Collagen is a triple-coil protein structure that is white in color and contracts to a thick mass when heated. Yet, it becomes tenderized when cooked with *moist* heat. This tenderization may be referred to in several manners. For example, collagen may be "*converted to*," "*solubilized to*," or "*gelatinized to*" water-soluble ***gelatin***. (This is the same gelatin that may in turn be used for edible gels in the diet.) In older animals, the collagen is increased and may form many crosslinkage, thus *preventing* solubilization of collagen to the tenderer gelatin. The meat from older animals therefore is tough.

8.2.2 Composition of Meat

In general, meat is composed of water, fat, protein, minerals and a small proportion of carbohydrate. The most valuable component from the nutritional and processing point of view is protein. Protein contents and values define the quality of the raw meat material and its suitability for further processing. Protein content is also the criterion for the quality and value of the finished processed meat products. Table 1 shows the chemical composition of fresh raw and processed meats.

Table 1: Content of water, protein, fat, ash (in percent) and calories (approximate values for selected raw and processed food products)

	Product	Water	Protein	Fat	Ash	Calories / 100g
FRESH	Beef (lean)	75.0	22.3	1.8	1.2	116
	Beef carcasss	54.7	16.5	28.0	0.8	323
	Pork (lean)	75.1	22.8	1.2	1.0	112
	Pork carcass	41.1	11.2	47.0	0.6	472
	Veal (lean)	76.4	21.3	0.8	1.2	98
	Chicken	75.0	22.8	0.9	1.2	105
	Venison (deer)	75.7	21.4	1.3	1.2	103
	Beef fat (subcutaneous)	4.0	1.5	94.0	0.1	854
	Pork fat (back fat)	7.7	2.9	88.7	0.7	812
PROCESSED	Beef, lean, fried	58.4	30.4	9.2		213
	Pork, lean, fried	59.0	27.0	13.0		233
	Lamb, lean, fried	60.9	28.5	9.5		207
	Veal, lean, fried	61.7	31.4	5.6		186
	Raw-cooked sausage with coarse lean particles (ham sausage)	68.5	16.4	11.1		170
	Raw-cooked sausage finely comminuted, no extender	57.4	13.3	22.8	3.7	277
	Raw-cooked sausage (frankfurter type)	63.0	14.0	19.8	0.3	240
	Precooked-cooked sausage (liver sausage)	45.8	12.1	38.1	395	
	Liver pate	53.9	16.2	25.6	1.8	307
	Gelatinous meat mix (lean)	72.9	18.0	3.7	110	
	Raw-fermented sausage (Salami)	33.9	24.8	37.5		444
	Milk (pasteurized)	87.6	3.2	3.5		63
	Egg (boiled)	74.6	12.1	11.2		158
	Bread (rye)	38.5	6.4	1.0		239
	Potatoes (cooked)	78.0	1.9	0.1		72

8.2.3 Meat Colouring

The red pigment that provides the characteristic colour of meat is called myoglobin. Similar to the blood pigment haemoglobin it transports oxygen in the tissues of the live animal. Specifically, the myoglobin is the oxygen reserve for the muscle cells or muscle fibres. Oxygen is needed for the biochemical process that causes muscle contraction in the live animal. The greater the myoglobin concentration, the more intense the colour of the muscle. This difference in myoglobin concentration is the reason why there is often one muscle group lighter or darker than another in the same carcass. Myoglobin concentration in muscles also differs among animal species. Beef has considerably more myoglobin than pork, veal or lamb, thus giving beef a more intense colour The maturity of the animal also influences pigment intensity, with older animals having darker pigmentation. The different myoglobin levels determine the curing capability of meat. As the red curing colour of meat results from a chemical reaction of myoglobin with the curing substance nitrite, the curing colour will be more intense where more muscle myoglobin is available

8.2.4 The Nutritional Value of Meat and Meat Products

(*a*) **Proteins:** The nutritional value of meat is essentially related to the content of high quality protein. High quality proteins are characterized by the content of essential aminoacids which cannot be synthesized by our body but must be supplied through our food. In this respect the food prepared from meat has an advantage over those of plant origin. There are vegetable proteins having a fairly high biological value (for instance soy protein, the biological value of which is about 65% of that of meat).). The contractile proteins or myofibrillar proteins are quantitatively the most important (some 65%) and are also qualitatively important as they have the highest biological value.

(*b*) **Fats Animal fats are principally triglycerides.** The major contribution of fat to the diet is energy or calories. The fat content in the animal carcass varies from 8 to about 20% (the latter only in pork, see table 1). The fatty acid composition of the fatty tissues is very different in different locations. External fat ("body fat") is much softer than the internal fat surrounding organs due to a higher content of unsaturated fat in the external parts. The unsaturated fatty acids (linoleic, linolenic and arachidonic acid) are physiologically and nutritionally important as they are necessary constituents of cell walls, mitochondria and other intensively active metabolic sites of the living organism. The human body cannot readily produce any of the above fatty acids, hence they have to be made available in the diet. Meat and meat products are relatively good sources, but in some plant sources such as cereals and seeds, linoleic acid is usually present at about 20 times the concentration found in meat.

Vitamins: Meat and meat products are excellent sources of the B-complex vitamins (see table. Lean pork is the best food source of Thiamine (vitamin B1) with more than 1 mg/100 g as compared to lean beef, which contains only about 1/10 of this amount. The daily requirement for humans of this rarely occurring vitamin is 1-1.5 mg. Plant food has no vitamin B12, hence meat is a good source of this vitamin for children, as in their organisms deposits of B12 have to be established. On the other hand, meat is poor in the fat soluble vitamins A, D, E, K and vitamin C. However, internal organs, especially liver and kidney generally contain an appreciable percentage of vitamin A, C, D, E and K. Most of the vitamins in meat are relatively stable during cooking or processing, although substantial amounts may be leached out in the drippings or broth.

Table 2: Average content of vitamins in meat (micrograms per 100g)

Food	B1	B2	B6	B12	A	C
Beef, lean, fried	100	260	380	2.7	20	1
Pork, lean, fried	700	360	420	0.8	10	1
Lamb, lean, fried	105	280	150	2.6	45	1
Veal, lean, fried	70	350	305	1.8	10	1
Pork liver, fried	260	2200	570	18.7	18000	24

(*c*) **Minerals:** The mineral contents of meat (shown as "ash" in table 1) include calcium, phosphorus, sodium, potassium, chlorine, magnesium with the level of each of these minerals above 0.1%, and trace elements such as iron, copper, zinc and many others. Blood, liver, kidney, other red organs and to a lesser extent lean meat, in particular beef are good sources of iron. Iron intake is important to combat anaemia, which particularly in developing countries is still widespread amongst children and pregnant women. Iron in meat has a higher bio-availability, better resorption and metabolism than iron in plant products.

8.3 MEAT PROCESSING

Meat processing technology comprises the steps and procedures in the manufacture of processed meat products. Processed meat products, which include various different types and local/regional variations, are food of animal origin, which contribute valuable animal proteins to human diets. Animal tissues, in the first place muscle meat and fat, are the main ingredients, besides occasionally used other tissues such as internal organs, skins and blood or ingredients of plant origin.

All processed meat products have been in one way or another physically and/or chemically treated.

1. **Grinding or mincing :** Lean meat and fat are minced separately in a meat mincer. The choice of mincer plate or sieve depends on the type of meat.
2. **Mixing :** Meat and fat to be used for the preparation of coarse ground sausage are mixed uniformly in a mixer. Extender, condiments and spices should also be run in the mixer for even distribution.
3. **Chopping and emulsifying :** For emulsion preparation, lean meat is first chopped for few minutes in a bowl chopper with salt to extract Myofibrilar proteins. This is followed by addition of fat and running for a few minutes again to get desired emulsion consistency. Now all other ingredients are added and chopper is run for some time for uniform distribution. The entire operation is conducted at a low temperature by addition of ice flakes in place of chilled water.
4. **Stuffing :** Sausage emulsion or batter is taken to suffer for extrusion into casings. The casings are first collected on the stuffing horn or nozzle and released to coincide with the extrusion.
5. **Linking and tying :** In small sausages, the encased mass is twisted to produce links either manually or mechanically whereas in large sausages, the encased mass is tied with thread at regular intervals.
6. **Smoking and cooking :** Sausage links are hung on the smokehouse trolley and transferred to smoke house. The temperature of smokehouse is usually maintained at 68-70°C which is enough for coagulation of sausage emulsion, cooking and requisite drying of sausages.
7. **Chilling :** The cooked product is showered with chilled water to an internal temperature of about 4°C.
8. **Peeling and packaging :** While artificial or synthetic casings are peeled off before the product is packed, small sized natural casings need not be removed. The product is generally unit packed for retail outlets.

8.3.1 Primary Factors in Meat Processing

When we process meat to make products, the following factors are to be considered:

Cohesiod : The product should retain its physical integrity after processing.

Fat : Like water, maximum amount of natural and added fat should be retained during processing till consumption.

Moisture : Maximum amount of natural moisture (water) of meat and added water should be retained during processing. This is very important for yield and quality of pH : The pH of meat governs the functional properties of meat, which is very important for product preparation.

Protein : The quality of protein is important particularly in emulsion type meat products. WHC: Water holding capacity of meat plays important role to get good quality meat products.

8.3.2 Equipment used in Meat Processing

In modern meat processing, most of the processing steps can be mechanized.

Meat grinder (Mincer)

A meat grinder is a machine used to force meat or meat trimmings by means of a feeding worm (auger) under pressure through a horizontally mounted cylinder (barrel)

Bowl cutter (bowl chopper)

The bowl cutter is the commonly used meat chopping equipment designed to produce small or very small ("finely comminuted") lean meat and fat particles. Bowl cutters consist of a horizontally revolving bowl and a set of curved knives rotating vertically on a horizontal axle at high speeds of up to 5,000 rpm.

Filling machine ("sausage stuffer") These machines are used for filling all types of meat batter in containers such as casings, glass jars, cans etc. The most common type of filling machine in small and medium size operations is the piston type.

Clipping machine

Clipping machines place small aluminium sealing clips on the sausage ends and replace the manual tying of sausages. They can be used for artificial or natural casings. Clipping machines can also be connected to filling machines. Such machines work with so called casing brakes, which are devices for slow release of the shirred casings from the filling horns ensuring tight filling.

Smokehouses

Simple smokehouses are used for smoking only (In traditional and small-scale operations the most common methods of smoke generation include burning damp hardwood sawdust, heating dry sawdust or heating pieces of log. But technological progress has changed the smoke generation and application techniques. Methods used in modern meat processing include the following:

- Burning/smouldering of saw dust
- Smoke generation through friction
- Smoke generation through steam

Combined equipment : Modern facilities can combine smoking, cooking and cooling operations for meat products in one continuous process. By means of automatic stirring systems processing parameters such as smoke generation, temperature (up to 100 °C) and relative humidity (up to 100%) required to dry, smoke, or steam-cook any type of product, can be pre-set. With additional refrigerated units installed in the smokehouse, it is also possible to use it as a fermenting/ripening room for the first crucial steps in production of fermented sausages or raw ham products, where air temperature and air humidity have to be accurately controlled

Brine injector: This equipment serves for the injection of brine into meat. Brine is water containing dissolved salt and curing substances (nitrite) as well as additives such as phosphates, spices, sugar, carrageenan and/or soy proteins The injection is done by introducing pointed needles into the muscle tissue. Brine injection is mainly used for the various types of ham, bacon and other whole muscle products.

Tumbler or Massager: Tumblers are used for the processing of meat products such as whole-muscle or reconstituted hams. Such machines resemble in principle a drum concrete mixer. Vacuum packaging machine For vacuum packaging the meat product has to be placed into a vacuum bag (multi-layer synthetic bag. Air is removed from the bag by means of the vacuum packaging machine and the bag then sealed

Mixer / blender: Mixers are used to blend meat and spices, or coarse and finely chopped meat. The machine generally consists of a rectangular or round bottom vessel through which two parallel shafts operate. Various paddles are mounted on those shafts to mix the meat.

Emulsifying machine (colloid mill): The emulsifier serves for the preparation of very fine meat emulsions. Its functional parts are a perforated plate, attached to which two edged blades are rotating (rotor blade). Next to the blades there is a centrifugal pump that forces the pre-ground meat through the perforated plate

Ice flake: In these machines ice flakes are continuously produced from potable water. Ice is needed in meat processing for some types of meat products. Water, added in the form of ice, is an important ingredient in order to enhance protein solution.

Frozen meat cutter: The purpose of cutting frozen meat blocks into smaller pieces is to make frozen meat suitable for immediate comminuting in grinders, bowl cutters etc. without previous thawing.

8.4 SLAUGHTERING OF MEAT

One common humane method of rendering an animal insensible is by striking it on the head with air or gunpowder driven blunt or penetrating device. This has largely replaced stunning with a sledge hammer. Another method employs electric shock, and a third uses a tunnel filled with carbon dioxide through which the animal passes. Each of these various methods can differently affect blood hormone levels, muscle chemistry, and meat properties.

After stunning, hoisting and blooding, a modern slaughter house is an efficient continuous disassembly line. Virtually every component of the animal body is utilized including the hide, viscera, blood and carcass. The skinned, washed and eviscerated carcass is then moved by monorail into chill room, where the deepest part of the meat is chilled to 2°C in about 36 h. This prevents rapid bacterial spoilage.

The practice of resting animals before slaughter can help delay bacterial spoilage of meat. Animals store glycogen in their muscles as a source of reserve energy. After an animal killed, this glycogen in converted under the anaerobic condition in the muscles into lactic acid which lowers the pH and acts as mild preservatives. But, if animals are excited or excersed before slaughter, the glycogen is largely consumed and there is very little left to be converted to lactic acid in the post mortem tissues.

The tenderness of meat

The tenderness of meat ranks as the second most important criterion to ensure repeat customer purchase of meat, the first being attractive colour and appearance. A lack of tenderness in meat is caused by a combination of toughness in the fibre structure of meat and toughness in the connective tissue. The degree of toughness of meat can predominantly be linked to the age of the animal and to a small degree to the species of animal. Muscle tissue of older animals shows signs of an increased number of cross-links between actin and myosin as well as increased numbers of cross-links within collagen. To obtain tender meat, a certain temperature–pH relationship should be adhered to post-slaughter; the pH value must be at or below 5.7 once a temperature of 7°C is present within meat. If the meat or carcass cools too quickly and the temperature is below 7°C, once a pH value of 5.7 is reached, there is a risk of cold shortening. To avoid cold shortening, another temperature– pH relationship to be observed is that thc internal temperature of meat must not be below 14°C if the pH is still at 6.2 or above. Of course, a carcass must also not be cooled too slowly for microbiological reasons; microbial growth must be kept under control.

Tenderizing meats may be desirable prior to cooking. *Young* animals are *naturally* tender and do not need *artificial* tenderizing. Recall that the connective tissue of *older* animals contains more covalent cross-links, is less soluble, and less readily converted to gelatin. Therefore, meat from older animals may require tenderization. In addition to the age, the origin of the cut on the animal also is a factor influencing tenderness.

The less tender cuts of meat may be *artificially* tenderized to break down the proteins of muscle or connective tissue. This may be achieved by mechanical, electrical, or enzymatic treatment as discussed below.

The *mechanical* tenderization includes chopping, cubing, and grinding. Meat may cubed, ground, or pounded prior to stuffing or rolling or used in a recipe. These techniques break the surface muscle fibers and connective tissue. A special instrument that pierces the meat with multiple thin, tenderizing needles is involved in the "needling" or "blade tenderizing" of meat.

Electrical stimulation such as ultrasonic vibration indirectly tenderizes meat by the physical vibrations that stimulate muscles to breakdown ATP to lactic acid. It also decreases the pH. The electrical stimulation of a carcass tenderizes without degrading the muscle fibers and texture of meats to a mushy state.

Natural *enzyme* tenderizers derived from tropical plants are available as powders or seasoning compounds that may be applied by dipping or spraying meat. They are more effective in tenderizing than marinades, which only penetrate approximately one-fourth inch into the interior of the meat. Enzymes include papain from the papaya plant, bromelain from pineapple, and ficin from figs.

Some of these enzymes treat the muscle tissue and others treat the connective tissue. For example, the enzymes chymopapain, or papain, and ficin exert a greater effect on tenderizing *muscle fibers* than *connective tissue*, while bromelain degrades *connective tissue* more than the myofibrils. Any overapplication of natural enzyme tenderizers to meat surfaces or allowing the treated meat to remain at temperatures conducive to enzymatic activity could produce an *overly* soft meat consistency.

The natural enzyme tenderizer papain also may be injected into the jugular vein (bloodstream) of an animal a few minutes before slaughter. It is distributed throughout the animal tissue. The enzyme is heat activated [by cooking at 140–160°F (60–71°C) and eventually denatured in cooking.

Meat products Numerous processed meat products in the form of convenience foods', ready-to-cook or ready-to-eat items are available in retail stores. Meat products can be divided into several groups based on their product characteristics and processing procedures, viz., canned meats, frozen meats, dry preserved meats, cured meats, sausages, frozen dinner meats, fermented meats and luncheon meats:

i) **Canned meats:** Canning is a thermal process employing steam to sterilize the food material in a sealed container. Pasteurized canned products have to be kept refrigerated while sterilized products can be kept at room temperature. Processing procedure involves commercial sterilization in retorts at 121°C. Product may be fully cooked, cured or noncured. Cured products are usually pasteurized at 65-75°C. Metal cans are coatedwith sulphur resistant resins and nylon cans are used for packing. Examples of canned meats are canned ham, corned beef, beef stew, beef in chili sauce, etc.

ii) **Frozen meats:** Frozen meat products may be prepared from cooked or raw meat. Products are quick frozen at –20 to – 40°C by blast freezing and vacuum packaged to prevent development of rancidity. Some of the products include *e.g.*, home meal replacement items and breakfast items like meat loaf, breaded boneless pork/beef cutlet, pork sausage, meat ball, etc.

iii) **Dry preserved meat:** Drying of meat is an old process to keep meat at ambient temperature for longer time. Sun drying and hot air drying is prevalent commercially. Ethnic dried meat is available in some states especially buffalo meat, ostrich, etc. Dried beef item, biltong, is a popular product from South Africa. It is dried after marination with salt, seasoning and spices or after cooking. The reduced water activity increases shelf life. The dried meat is smoked to impart flavour and to increase shelf life. But texture will be hard.

iv) **Cured meats:** Meat cured with salt, sodium nitrite/nitrate, other adjuncts like ascorbate, erythorbate, alpha tocopherol, sugar/corn syrup and polyphosphates by injection or dry rub or as immersion pickle for preservation and getting desirable colour and flavour. They include pork products such as ham and bacon and beef product such as corned beef. Corned beef is being exported in bulk from India. The domestic consumption of the traditional products ham and bacon is comparatively higher although innumerable cured sliced restructured ready-to-eat products are in the retail stores and restaurants.

8.5 HAM

Ham is from pork thighs while conventional **bacon** is from pork bellies. Bone-in hams and boneless hams or bacon are cured by injection followed by immersion in pickle in stainless steel vats at 4°C. Hardwood or liquid smoke is used for smoking and cooking of cured products. Ham slices and bacon rashers must be cooked to ensure destruction of possible microorganisms. **Corned beef** is prepared using thin strips of precooked beef cured and cooked in cans and is the major value added meat product that is exported.

Fermented meat products: Fermented meat products, very popular with European consumers, are prepared by microbial fermentation and dehydration to develop specific flavour and texture. Selected bacterial starter cultures like Lactobacillus, Pediococcus, Lactococcus and Micrococcus are added to the minced meat in the preparation of such products. Meats which are most commonly used for fermented products are pork and beef. The minced meat-bacterial mixture is kept at specific temperature and humidity for specified period. This allows the maximum growth of the added bacteria. During the fermentation, the bacteria utilizes the sugar and produce lactic acid, which causes decrease in pH. After completion of fermentation, the product is dried to specific moisture level. After drying, products are cooked and/or smoked as per requirement. Lower moisture content, lower water activity and low pH do not allow spoilage bacteria to grow. Based on the pH level, the fermented meat items can be divided into two groups: low acid and high acid products. Fermented dry sausages do not require refrigeration for storage. However, semi-dry sausages require refrigeration temperature to prevent microbial spoilage during storage. Fermented sausages are very popular in Goa.

8.6 SAUSAGES

Traditionally, this term means a product consisting of a mince of ground meat and fat, which is stuffed into a casing. It also involves the use of a curing salt (sodium chloride þ nitrate/nitrite) that contributes to its characteristic color and flavor. Basically, sausages can be arranged into several groups based on the main preservation practices of fermentation, drying, or cooking.

Classification system of sausages.

Sausages are such a large number of varying kinds of products that it is not possible to cover them in any classification system. Some overlapping is always there. Some of popular classification systems are:

1. Based on degree of chopping:
   (*a*) Coarse ground sausage (*b*) Emulsion type sausage
2. Based on moisture content:
   (*a*) Fresh sausage (*b*) Smoked uncooked sausage
   (*c*) Cooked sausage
3. Based on fermentation:
   (*a*) Fermented sausage (*b*) Non-fermented sausage

Fresh Sausages: Fresh sausage may also be known as moist sausage, because its moisture content is high, at between 50 and 60%. These sausages are stored for a few days under refrigeration and are cooked before eating. Fresh sausages can differ in texture, seasoning, type of casings, and meat content .Some of the most well known are mettwurst and bockwurst, which were originally fresh, but more recently are cooked. Others, like country-style sausages, may be smoked.

Raw Fermented Sausages: These sausages are fermented at high temperatures so that lactic acid bacteria may grow and drop the pH towards acid values. Merguez-type sausages are produced in North African countries and Southern European countries and can be briefly dried after fermentation. Raw fermented sausages can be smoked (*e.g.*, Lebanon Bologna) or cooked. They are preserved under refrigeration and are cooked before eating.

Semidry Sausages: There are many varieties of semidry sausages. As their denomination indicates, their moisture content is intermediate, between 35 and 50%, as a result of a mild drying and short ripening step. The water activity is above 0.86 and pH near 5.0. These sausages are fermented rapidly for a few hours in the United States or more slowly in Europe. They are smoked and can be cooked for pasteurization. The summer sausage is quite popular in the United States. Longaniza is typical in Spain and France. Semidry sausages are preserved under refrigeration unless the combination of low pH (below 5.0), and a moisture to protein ratio of less than 3.1:1 are achieved to guarantee the shelf-life.

Dry Sausages: There are many dry types of sausage. In general, they have a moisture content below 35%. The denominations may vary according to the geographical area where they are produced. In other cases, the names may be applied depending on the physical or chemical characteristics of the sausages like form, diameter, size of fat particles, application of smoking, addition of specific spices, presence of molds on the external surface, and so on.

Cooked Sausages: There are also many types of cooked sausages, including garlic sausages, frankfurters, mortadella, and so on. Italian mortadella, or Bologna sausage, is fermented at 30–38°C for 2–7 days. Then, it is cooked until it reaches an internal temperature of 65–70°C, cooled, and dried for maturation. German Bruhwurst is smoked and scalded. Kochwurst is also scalded and may contain large chunks of meat; it is eaten either sliced or spread. Frankfurters, wieners, and hot dogs are coarsely minced or finely chopped. Cotto salami is cooked, contains peppercorns, and may be smoked. This type of cooked salami is refrigerated before eating. Colour enhancer in cooked sausages is ascorbic acid.

Ingredients and processing of sausages:

Pork meat, either alone or in combination with beef, is the main ingredient of sausages. In other products like poultry sausages, the main ingredient is poultry. It is important to control the characteristics of all these raw meats, in particular hygienic quality. Beef meat contributes to a better red color of the product. The other main ingredient is fat which must be fresh or stored under frozen storage.

Salt is an essential ingredient of sausages, usually added at 2–3%. It contributes to the technological and sensory quality through

- Selection of the microbial flora by inhibition of the growth of undesirable microorganisms;
- A characteristic salty taste of the sausage;
- An increase of myofibrillar protein (actin and myosin) solubility; and
- Control of enzyme activity

Nitrite constitutes an essential additive for sausage preservation. Sodium nitrite is formulated in a curing salt. In some cases, potassium nitrate can also be added in the formulation when sausages are ripened for a long time. Nitrite is very reactive and interacts rapidly with proteins, such as myoglobin, and inhibits the growth of undesirable microorganisms, in particular Clostridium botulinum. Ascorbic and erythorbic acids or their sodium salts are used to accelerate the reduction of nitrite to nitric oxide, assuring the absence of residual nitrite in the products and thus avoiding the risk of nitrosamine formation.

Carbohydrates are added as the substrate for microbial fermentation. Lactic acid is the main compound resulting from fermentation by lactic acid bacteria. If an excessive amount of carbohydrates is added, pH can drop to values below 4.7 and most of the enzymes responsible for the generation of flavor compounds can be inhibited and the sensory quality seriously affected.

There is a wide variety of spices and flavorings that can be used for seasoning the sausages. Spices can also contribute to a specific flavor or color. This includes mustard, oregano, rosemary, garlic, onion, pepper, or paprika. Spices can be used either in a natural form (whole or ground) or as flavoring extracts (essential oils and oleoresins). Flavoring agents and flavor enhancers may be used to accentuate a specific flavor. Smoke flavoring may be applied on the surface as an oil or water solution to give a smoke flavor.

8.7 POULTRY MEAT PROCESSING

Poultry, especially chicken broilers and turkey, is one of the most widely consumed muscle foods in the world. It is an important source of dietary energy and nutrients, such as high quality proteins, essential fatty acids, vitamins and highly bio-available minerals.

Poultry refers to any domesticated avian species, and poultry products can range from whole carcasses to cut-up carcasses, portions, boneless meat, or any further processed meat. Poultry production and consumption all over the world has increased considerably during recent years. Several variables influence buying decisions and eating patterns in the short or long term, including ethnic or religious traditions, diet and health concerns, and price and availability. Recently, consumer attitudes about eating meat have been greatly influenced in relation to the saturated fat and cholesterol intake and their contribution to arteriosclerosis and heart attacks. Additionally, recent outbreaks of bovine spongiform encephalopathy (BSE) and foot-and-mouth disease have modified consumer's attitudes against red meats.

Poultry meat has a high protein content varying from 18-25 percent, and is comparable in quality and nutritive value to other meats. It contains all essential amino acids required for body building. Chicken fat is more unsaturated than the fat of red meat and this has nutritional advantage. Poultry flesh is a good source of vitamin B and minerals. The dark meat of chicken is richer in riboflavin than the light, but the light colour meat is richer in niacin. Processed meats, including canning products, now contain less fat (under 25% or lower), where poultry, especially chicken and turkey, are popular as an alternative for manufacturing healthy low fat meat products.

Raw chicken has little or no flavor, it develops during cooking. The cooking method is selected on the basis of the tenderness of poultry and its fat content. Moist heat methods are applied to older and tougher birds in order to them tender and palatable. Dry heat methods are applied to young tender birds. Young tender poultry is cooked by broiling, frying, baking or roasting.

Chicken Processing

Dressing : Dressing of chicken includes all the steps involved in obtaining ready to cook (RTC) meat from live birds. The procedure being scientific ensures hygienic meat to the consumers.

Starvation : The fed birds till slaughter will have feed in the intestines, which will increase the chances of microbial contamination of the carcass.

Therefore, birds are starved for 4 to 12 hour but cool drinking water is provided during starvation, which helps in obtaining clean and better meat.

Killing : The different slaughter methods (Jhatka, halal, Kosher's) are being adopted for killing the birds. Jhatka method is the most humane method since the bird is decapitated, the struggling is less and bleeding is also less. In halal method, the blood vessels are severed through an incision just behind the earlobe and a part of spinal cord and severed. This is the inhumane method and the bird feels pain, struggle violently thereby effecting a perfect bleeding. There is also possibility of contamination by secretions of respiratory and digestive system in halal method. In stunning method the head of the bird will be made to come in contact with water or saline bath where they are subjected to 100 to 200 volts electric shock for 1-2 second. Stunning accelerates rate of pH fall and increase tenderness.

Poultry meat products: Further processing of dressed poultry includes portioning (making cut up parts), seasoned cut, batter-breaded patties and nuggets, sliced meat for delis in fast food outlets and restaurants, luncheon meats for sandwiches, varieties of cooked, cured items like turkey ham and turkey bacon, frankfurters, bologna, etc. Processed whole chicken will be either halved or quartered. The various cut- up- parts of poultry are wings, breast, leg (thigh and drumstick), back and neck. Normally only the breast and thighs are hand deboned from chilled carcass. Chicken and turkey are deboned mechanically, as well.

Marinated poultry products: New poultry products have been evolved on marination, curing and cooking. Marination is by soaking/rubbing salt, vinegar/lemon juice/wine, oil in combination with spices to improve flavour and yield and to increase tenderness and other eating quality. All types of poultry - whole birds, cut up parts, boneless meat, chopped and formed items can be marinated. Some pieces of the product may pickup more ingredients and produce detectable variations in flavour and juiciness and may exceed the permissible levels. Good manufacturing practices have to be adopted to maintain consistency in the product. Vacuum tumbling enables commercial marination.

Thawing of meat

Thawing is the reverse process of freezing. The major difficulty when thawing is that the difference between the temperatures of the source of heat and the frozen meat cannot be too great for a prolonged period of time as this causes bacteria to grow at a fast rate, creating a microbiological risk. Thawing takes place at a slower rate than freezing as water displays less thermal conductivity than ice. During freezing, the layer of ice formed on the outside of the material to be frozen removes energy quickly from the water still present within the inner layers of the material and, as a result, the water turns fairly quickly into ice. During thawing, however, water is present first on the surface on the outer layers of the material to be defrosted. As water is a poor conductor of heat, the heat penetrates very slowly through the layer of surface water first before finally reaching the ice in the inner layers and core. This is why thawing takes place at a slower rate than freezing and also why a long period of time is required to thaw large pieces of meat fully; a large amount of water is already present in most areas of a large piece of meat, but water in the core remains as ice for a long time as the surrounding water acts as a barrier against heat.

8.8 FISH PROCESSING

Seafood species come in a bewildering variety of shapes and forms which are the product of a long period of evolution. They can be grouped in various ways. The first and most obvious division is between fish and shellfish, where the main biological difference is the position of the skeleton. True fish possess a recognized internal skeleton and swimming is the usual method of locomotion, whereas shellfish species are without a backbone and have a hard external shell or exoskeleton to compensate. Most shellfish, with the exception of the crustacea and cephalopods, remain stationary throughout their adult life. Fish can be differentiated according to whether they live in salt water (marine) or fresh water, whether they live on the bottom or near the surface of the sea and whether or not the flesh is fatty. These oily fish are normally not eaten fresh in western Europe and the USA, but are sold preserved in some way such as smoked, cured, marinated or canned.

Chilling of fish: One of the most perishable of all foods, fish begin to deteriorate immediately they are caught. The prime method of retarding this process is to reduce the temperature by chilling, or freezing, as soon as possible after capture. The simplest way is to surround the fish with ice, but mechanical refrigeration is now widely used and there is some usage of refrigerated sea water, particularly for pelagic species such as mackerel. The bacteria responsible for fish spoilage are psychrophilic, *i.e.* cold loving, and even if fish are kept chilled at 0°C (32°F) under the best conditions of handling, the activities of these bacteria result in severe loss of palatability. Species such as cod and haddock approach inedibility after about 14-16 days. At 5-6°C (42°F), a temperature at which many domestic refrigerators operate, spoilage will be about twice as fast, whereas at U°C (52°F) it will be 4-5 times faster. Chilled temperatures much below 0°C are to be avoided because of the detrimental effect of slow freezing on the texture of the flesh. The most satisfactory storage temperature is -20C which results in an extension of the shelf life of white fish by several days.

Frozen fish: Freezing as a general preservation process is dealt with elsewhere. It is now well known that rapid freezing is essential for good quality. This is defined as taking no more than 2 h to pass from 0 to –5°C (32 to 23°F) in the thickest part of the fish, and freezing at this rate or faster is now normal good commercial practice. Most fish begin to freeze at about – 1°C (30°F), but multiplication of the putrefactive bacteria is only completely arrested at about – 9°C (15°F). Although bacterial spoilage is then suspended and there is some reduction in bacterial numbers, not all the bacteria are destroyed by freezing. The quality of the frozen product is closely related to the freshness of the raw fish: the fresher the fish before freezing the better it keeps in frozen storage. Whole fish of age equivalent to 3-4 days in ice will show some signs of deterioration on thawing and the staler the fish the more noticeable are the deteriorative changes that occur on storage.

Fish products: An extremely diverse range of products can be manufactured from fish and shellfish, depending on the species and the method of preservation of the raw material.

Salting: Apart from the use of salt as a flavouring agent for smoked fish, its two principal uses as a preservative are brine pickle salting, chiefly of fatty fish such as herring, and dry salting, as applied to cod and similar species. Cod and other white fish can also be pickle salted, but fatty fish cannot be satisfactorily dry salted because the fat easily becomes rancid on exposure to air, whereas if immersed in a saturated brine pickle they are protected by a liquid barrier from the inroads of oxygen. In the case of products such as red herring, where fairly heavy salting is combined with drying in warm smoke, the antioxidants absorbed protect the fat. In brine pickling, the fish is first 'gripped', *i.e.* partly eviscerated in a special manner, the purpose of which is to remove the intestine but leave the pyloric caeca intact. These organs contain powerful enzyme systems which are responsible for the characteristic flavour of herring.

Cod for salting (to produce 'klippfisk' as it is called in Norway) are usually headed, split and cleaned so as to leave a piece of the backbone at the tail end for strength. They are then packed in layers with solid salt to form stacks. The saturated brine formed is allowed to run away. The fish eventually become impregnated with a saturated salt solution (containing 26% salt) which amounts to a salt content of about 18% in the product. At a suitable stage in the curing process, the fish are removed from the stack, washed and allowed to drain, and are then hung up to dry for a few days at a time, with several intermediate periods of pressure in the stack to bring further moisture from the centre to the surface for the subsequent drying stage.

Curing: A term widely used in the fish industry to denote the process of preservation by drying, salting, smoking, fermenting, acid curing or any combination of these.

Marinating: The marinating of fish and shellfish involves its treatment with acid and salt. Not only does this process preserve the product by retarding the action of spoilage bacteria and enzymes, it also gives it a characteristic texture and flavour. The precise nature of the process is complex. The concentration of salt in a marinade will normally be lower than that required if salt alone were used as the preserving agent and the action of the acid, usually acetic or lactic, is essential in effecting preservation. At a pH of 4.5 or below, all food poisoning and most spoilage bacterial are prevented from growing and at such levels of acidity marinated products will keep for several months at 40C. In practice, the shelf life will vary from a few weeks to several months depending on the nature of the product, the way in which it has been processed and packed and the storage temperature. Methods of marinating vary, but the process usually consists of a two-stage process, the second of which may include the addition of sugar, spices and herbs depending on the final product.

Fish pickles: These include traditional craft products such as herring marinades, rollmops, pickled cockle and mussels, etc. In general, they are made by marinading in an acetified brine prior to packing in vinegar with appropriate spicing. Their microbial stability is related to the salt and acid contents (acetic with possibly some lactic acid); the general principles covering vegetable pickles apply. Acid hydrolysis of the protein during storage and the cooking effects of pasteurization may tend to shorten shelf life, but there is still a high demand for these products.

Smoking: The smoking of fish, as with meat, was originally a preservation process, almost certainly discovered by accident. Today, the reasons for smoke preservation are less important and the main reason for smoking is to produce a pleasant tasting alternative form of fish. The modern smoked products nevertheless do have somewhat longer shelf life than the unsmoked equivalents. Most of the common white and oily fish can be smoked, including eels, and a number of shellfish such as mussels and oysters. Cold smoking, in which the smoke temperature does not exceed 33°C, to avoid coagulating of proteins cold smoking require cooling except for smoked salmon fish gives a yellow colour to the fish but does not supply sufficient heat to cook the flesh. In hot smoking the smoke temperature is 70°C or higher, thus the fish is cooked in the process. Fish are prepared for smoking by washing, usually removing the guts, beheading ('nobbing'), splitting, filleting and sometimes skinning, depending on the product. Salt is added by dry salting or immersing in a prepared brine.

Drying: Natural drying in the sun and wind, and artificial drying over wood fires were the principal means of preserving fish in former times. Large fish are usually split along the backbone into two portions, connected at the tail end. Drying takes several weeks, depending on the size of fish and the weather, and the final water content is about 15%. Above this water content moulds can grow and spoil the fish. The water content is reduced from about 55% in the wet stacked state, to between 35 and 45% depending on the product and the market intended. In all the producing countries, mechanical dryers are now replacing natural drying for salt fish.

Canned fish: More than a million tonnes of fish a year are canned throughout the world. Tuna and salmon head the list, but other pelagic species such as mackerel, herring, pilchard and sardine are also popular to some degree. Demersal white fish are not usually preserved by canning as the sterilization process usually produces a browning of the fish flesh. Shellfish species which may be canned include crab, shrimp, lobster, octopus, oyster and mussel meats.

Fish for canning are normally prepared by nobbing (*i.e.* removing the heads), removing the tails, gutting, then either washing to remove loose scales or skinning completely. The fish may then be salted by soaking in 50-100% brine (13-26% salt by weight) and in some cases may be smoked. Brining has the effect of washing out the insides of the fish and getting rid of blood residues and most of any broken gut; it also reduces the moisture content of the flesh thus reducing the amount of cook out during sterilization and the dilution of any sauce. The prepared fish may be packed into the cans and then The cans are topped up with brine, oil or prepared sauce, as required, then closed and sterilized in the usual way. It may be necessary to wash the seamed cans before sterilizing, using hot detergent followed by a water rinse.

Potted fish: Potted fish use a recipe for short-time preservation of fish by cooking in vinegar, salt, spices, etc., often with a protective layer of butter. It is applied to herring, sardines, shrimp and salmon.

Fish pastes: The usual starting material is cooked fish, normally canned. It is mixed with cereal (breadcrumbs), spices and usually with artificial colour, filled into jars or cans and sterilized by cooking in retorts under pressure. A 'botulinum cook' is necessary.

Fish sausage: In Japan, fish hams and fish sausages are popular products. The sausage typically contains minced fish flesh with 10% pork fat, 10% starch and 2.5% salt, seasoning and preservatives. Chemical preservatives, such as furyl furamide and nitrofurazone, have been used to give a storage life at ambient temperature of a month or more. Fish sausages were originally made from fish species such as tuna, but there was a switch to lower priced Alaska pollack surimi when tuna became expensive due to a combination of lower catches and an upgrading in quality which led to its use as sashimi. As well as the slicing sausage, the product could be canned after the fashion of frankfurters.

Fish flour: Ethanol or isopropanol may be used to extract water, fat and some of the fishy flavoured substances from fishmeal, to produce fish flour with a protein content of 80-85%. The process is operated at ambient temperature, therefore there is minimum protein degradation and the product can be of suitable quality for human food use. It is more commonly used, however, for animal feed. For the manufacture to be economic it is essential to recover and re-use the solvent employed.

8.9 EGG PROCESSING

Most freshly laid eggs are sterile, at least inside, but the shells soon become contaminated by fecal matter from the hen, by the cage or nest, by wash water if the eggs are washed, by handling, and perhaps by the material in which the eggs are packed. The total number of microorganisms per shell of a hen's egg has been reported to range from 10^2 to 10^7 with a mean of about 10^5. The types of microorganisms recovered from the shell are diverse. *Salmonella* sps may be on the shell or in the egg as laid, build up during processing, and appear in significant numbers in frozen or dried eggs. On average, a hen lays more than 260 eggs per year.

Eggs contain about two parts white to one part yolk by weight. The whole mixed egg contains about 65% water, 12% protein and 11% fat. The yolk is rich in fat soluble vitamin A, D, E and K and in phospholipids including the emulsifier lecithin. Nutritionally, eggs are a good source of fat, protein, vitamins and minerals, especially iron. Eggs also contain about 240 mg of cholesterol which is all contained in the yolk. The most common method of egg grading is by candling, in which the egg is held up to a light source. Candling well reveal many defects- a cracked shell, a fertilized egg yolk, a blood spot, an enlarged air cell, firmness of white which become thinner on ageing, and a position of yolk which tends to drift off centre when the eggs becomes stale. Storage of egg is best at a temperature slightly above the freezing point of the egg. A temperature of –1°C in warehouse is ideal; to minimize moisture loss from eggs, the relative humidity may be as high as 80%. In proper cold storage, Grade A quality can be maintained for as long as 6 months.

8.9.1 Quality of Eggs by Candling

Handling the egg against a light source is called candling. This helps in determination of internal and external quality characteristics of egg. In candling the egg quality is assessed based on

(A) Shell quality, (B) air cell characteristics, and (C) yolk and albumin quality.

Shell quality : Cleanliness, porosity and quality of the shell can be observed. Cracks in the shell which are not visible to the naked eye can be identified while candling.

Aircell : Size, shape and condition of the air cell are useful in assessing the interior quality of eggs. In stored/aged eggs, there will be increased loss of moisture. The increased size is inversely related to egg shell quality and humidity and directly related to temp. and air movement during storage.

Yolk : Yoik colour, visibility and movement of the yolk during candling indicate yolk quality. The centred yolk cause of thick albumen indicates good quality. Egg yolk contain phosvitin protein. Phosvitin consists of 4% of egg yolk dry matter and 11% of egg yolk proteins.

Defects identifiable by candling : The main defects are: thin shelled egg, mottled shell, body checked egg, corrugated egg, tremulous air cell, bubbly air cell, addled, rots, mottled yolk, blood spots, meat spots, double yolk, egg in egg etc.

The specifications for standard egg are—(*a*) weight 55-58 gm (*b*) volume 62-65 ml (*c*) Specific gravity 1.072-1.09 (*d*) long circumference 14-16 cm (*e*) short circumference 12-14 cm (*f*) shape index 74-77 (*g*) surface area 65-70 cm^2.

Before freezing egg yolk, it is should be treated with enyme protecolytic to prevent gel formation.

8.9.2 Different Egg Products

Boiled egg: Eggs are kept for 12 min (full boiling)/6 min(half boiling) at water above 80°C. Egg are cooled in cold portable water for easy removal of shell over cooking results in greenish colour

Pickled eggs: Small pullets/quail eggs are preferred. The hard cooked peeled eggs are placed in pickle solution (vinegar or 5% acetic acid). Pickling solution can penetrate albumen in 1 day and yolk in 6 days. Red beet juice is used for red colour

Scotch eggs: They are hard cooked peeled eggs (HCPE) wrapped in layer of sausage which are deep fat fried. HCPE are kept moist, then rolled in wheat flour and wrapped in ready sausage. Then they are again rolled in breading flour and subjected to deep fat frying at 177°C/7min.

Shelf life - 30 days at 4°C.

Fried Eggs: Eggs with higher thick albumen are soft pride in oil with slide cooking of yolk. The cooking is done on a grindle inside a 10 diameter ring so as to have a uniform size product.

Scrambled eggs: Contains mix of eggs and milk in the ratio of 7:3. Eggs are beaten gently and pepper. Before butter begun to sizzle, the eggs are poured onto the pan while flame is kept low.

8.10 INDIAN MEAT SECTOR

8.10.1 Important Issues in Indian Meat Sector

- Lack of specific breeds for meat production/absence of selection process/poor genetic potential
- Non-availability of quality feed and reducing of grazing land
- Non-availability of basic minimum facilities for live animal marketing and absence of animal grading system
- Limited number of environmentally controlled poultry farms, absence of HACCP measures and inadequate biosecurity implementation
- Movement of animals between states, absence of disease free zones and lack of traceability system
- Poor recording of antibiotic and hormonal use and enforcing withdrawal mechanism
- Limited transportation vehicles for live animal, carcasses and meat
- Inadequate cold-chain logistics and additional tax on frozen meat products
- Limited market intelligence (both domestic and export) and shortage of skilled manpower

8.10.2 Some Suggested Solutions of Issues/ Problems

1. Slaughterhouse construction/modernization, byproducts utilization and effluent treatment must be an important component and must be incorporated in Smart City plans.
2. Banning/restricting of scattered poultry processing in wet market within city limits and popularization and promotion of chilled and packaged poultry meat through central processing facilities.
3. Municipalities to create better facilities at service abattoirs: Roads, potable water supply, composting, rendering and waste disposal facilities. Each municipal abattoir/ slaughterhouse must have Rendering/Composting and Effluent treatment plant for solid and liquid waste management
4. Skill development programmes and hands-on trainings to various stake-holders in meat value chain viz, butchers, meat processors, retailers, veterinarians, quality control inspectors and other meat processors in the area of clean and safe meat production, waste utilization, value added meat products etc.
5. Creation of agencies/NGO's to link all the small and medium-scale entrepreneurs and stake-holders to market in a value chain: Farmers, Producers, Primary Processors, Secondary Processors, Transportation, Storage, Wholesalers, Retailers,Quick Service Restaurants, Super-Markets and Service Providers etc.
6. Market infrastructure.
   (*a*) Establishment of livestock trading mandis in each district/clusters.
   (*b*) Regulate movement of live animals between states and encourage establishment of disease-free zones, quarantine stations and mobile sanitizing vehicles.
   (*c*) Policies to restrict the movement of live animals and birds and encouragement for transportation and sale of chilled, packed and frozen meat.
   (*d*) Promotion of e-commerce and online meat marketing entrepreneurs to create better processing, storage, transportation and other logistics in meat value chain.
7. Cold chain and storage infrastructure along the meat value chain

CHAPTER 9

CEREAL PROCESSING

9.1 PADDY (RICE) PROCESSING

Paddy – Rice System

Rice is consumed either as raw or parboiled. An estimate of the quantity of parboiled as well as raw rice consumed in India can be made taking into account that-the states of Assam, West Bengal, Odisha, A.P., Tamil Nadu and the states of Bihar, Chhattishgarh, Madhya Pradesh and Uttar Pradesh produce both parboiled rice and raw rice in equal proportions and the rest of the states being predominantly raw rice consuming areas. At present there are about 10852 rice mills in India. In this chapter technology of parboiling and milling of rice and cereals and pulses has been discussed briefly.

Some of the important terms used in rice milling industry are as follows :

(*i*) *Paddy–Rice* in the hull (Husk) after threshing is known as paddy or rough rice.

(*ii*) *Husked Rice*-Kernels without husk are known as brown rice or husked rice.

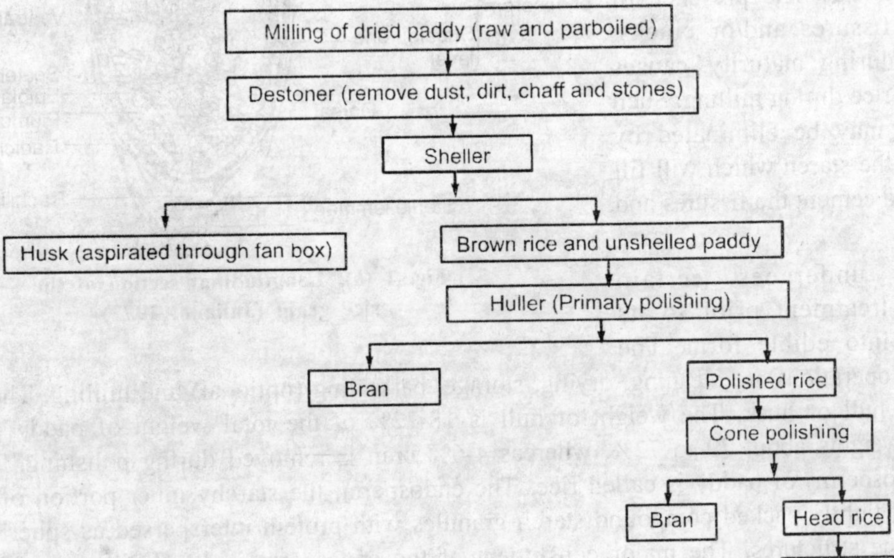

Fig. 1 (*a*)

(*iii*) *Milled Rice*–Brown rice after having been subjected to milling operation is left with white rice. The bran may be present partly in case of under polished rice.

(*iv*) *Degree of Milling*–It is a measure of the extent to which the bran layers and germ have been removed. Generally 4-6 per cent milling is acceptable by industry.

(*v*) *Milling yield*–The total quantity of head rice plus broken of all kinds received after milling are known as milling yield. The milling yields vary between 64 and 75 per cent depending upon the variety, quality of grain, pre-treatments and the type of mill.

Milling process of paddy can be shown in Fig. 1 (*a*).

Paddy production is widely scattered through the world. Paddy is harvested as a covered grain in which the kernel (caryopsis) is enclosed in a protecting layer is called hull or husk. The hull is a two piece structure (lemma and palea), which tightly attached with kernel, providing security against many microorganism, insects and a barrier to rapid change in moisture content of kernel as changes in humidity occurs. One hundred kg of paddy would yield about 22 kg of husk, 4 kg bran and about 74 kg of white rice if nothing is lost in the process of conversion of paddy into white rice. Total production 90 million tones are milled in home and in traditional and modern mills.

The structure of paddy grain Fig. 1. (*b*) shows that the endosperm which covers the major volume of rice grain, is mainly composed of polygonal starch granules. The voids or intergranular spaces are filled with air and moisture. The presence of voids and fissures and/or cracks, developed during maturity, causes breakage of rice during milling. Such a breakage may be eliminated by gelatinizing the starch which will fill the voids and cement the fissures and cracks.

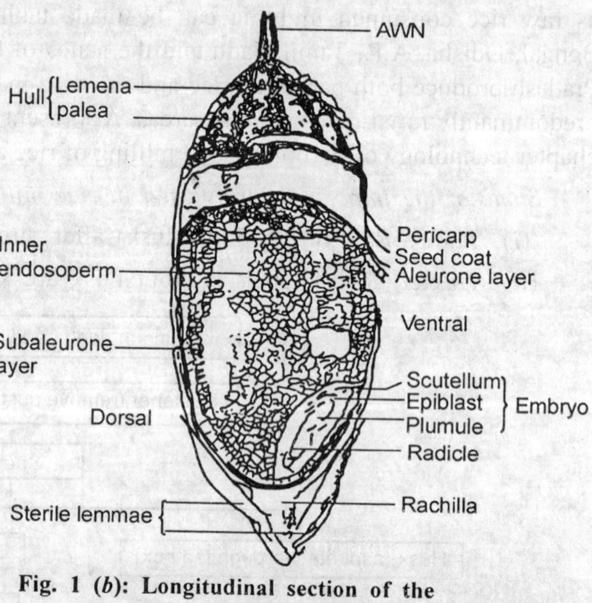

Fig. 1 (*b*): Longitudinal section of the rice grain (Juliano, 1972)

Paddy undergoes certain processing treatment prior to its conversion into edible form. The various unit operations are cleaning, drying, storage, parboiling (optional) and milling. The kernel is enclosed by hull or husk. The weight of hull is 18-22% of the total weight of paddy grain. The endosperm weights about 70 to 72%, whereas 4-6% bran is removed during polishing. The edible portion (endosperm) of paddy is called rice. The endosperm, the starchy inner portion of kernel, is composed of tightly packed compound starch granules with protein interspersed as spherical bodies and crystalline structures. The major constituent of the endosperm is starch (approx. 90 percent). The outermost most layer of the endosperm is the aleurone. This structure is botanically part of the endosperm; however, rice millers consider it as a part of the bran because it is mostly removed in milling operation. The area between endosperm and husk is composed three distinct layers *i.e.* pericarp, tegmen (seed coat), and nucleus. These three layers plus the aleurone layer account for approximately 3% of the brown rice weights and together are known as the bran. The remaining 4 % of the brown rice kernel is comprised of the germ (embryo). The content of selected nutrients of Brown rice and milled rice at 12 % moisture content is given in Table 1.

Table 1: Content of selected nutrients of Brown rice and milled rice at 12 % moisture

S. No.	Nutrients	Milled Rice	Brown rice
1.	Crude ash (%)	0.5	1.0
2.	Crude fat (%)	0.3	1.9
3.	Crude fibre (%)	0.3	0.7
4.	Crude protein (N × 5.95) (%)	5.8	7.2
5.	Neutral detergent fibre (%)	0.8	2.7
6.	Starch (%)	67.0	57.0
7.	Iron (mg/g)	0.2	0.3
8.	Calcium (mg/g)	13.0	24.0
9.	Total phosphorus (mg/g)	1.2	2.5
10.	Phytin phosphorus (mg/g)	0.5	2.0
11.	Potassium (mg/g)	1.0	1.7
12.	Sodium (mg/g)	45.0	315.0
13.	Niacin (mg/g)	18.0	43.0
14.	Riboflavin (mg/g)	0.4	0.9
15.	Thiamine (mg/g)	0.7	4.4
16.	Tocopherol (mg/g)	trace	17.0

The primary objective in rice milling is to remove the hull or husk and bran with minimum breakage of the endosperm to produce acceptable white rice. Processing steps influences the milling quality of rice. After harvest, paddy grain is to be dried upto 12-13 percent moisture content (wet basis). The dried product is dehulled and milled. Rice quality involves the head rice yield (HRY) and milled rice yield (MRY). HRY is the percentage of rough rice that is left after complete milling operation. Head rice is defined as 'unbroken kernels of rice and broken kernel of rice that are at least three fourths of an unbroken kernel'. Head rice is generally worth twice as much as broken kernels. MRY is the percentage of rough rice remaining as milled rice that contains both head and broken kernels.

The degree of milling (DOM) is the extent to which the bran layers are removed by milling. Milling influences the MRY, HRY and DOM. Clean and good quality paddy can give a yield of 74% rice. But due to several reasons, it has not been possible to achieve 74% yield of rice by traditional methods and machines. Use of modern machines like rubber roll sheller along with improved method of drying, paddy bran removal and grader can give higher out turn. The terminology related to rice milling is given as

Bold Rice: Rice with whole milled kernels having length breadth ratio between 2.0 and 3.0.

Bran: the outer covering of the brown rice. It consists of the pericarp seed coat and part or whole of aleurone layer depending upon the polish given. It is removed during milling process; sometime, small pieces of endosperm and germ are present.

Bran Oil: The oil that is extracted form rice bran.

Brokens: Pieces of kernel that is less than ¾th of the size of full kernels.

Brown Rice: When paddy or rough rice is separated in to husk and kernel, the kernel is called brown rice or shelled rice, or dehusked rice or cargo rice.

Head Rice: It refers to the kernels of milled rice, which is more than ¾th of the full kernel.

Head Yield: It is the amount of head rice obtained by milling a unit amount of clean paddy, expressed in %ages.

Milled Rice: Rice obtained from paddy after milling operation i.e. removal of husk and also removal of bran layers.

Milling Yield: It is the outturn of rice after milling expressed in percentage with respect to clean paddy.

Polished Rice: The rice is obtained after removing the bran layer from brown rice. It is also called white rice or milled rice or polished rice.

Red Rice: Rice kernel whole or brokens which have 25% or more their surface having red pericarp.

Rice/Quick-cooking Rice.

Quick-cooking rice is those that require significantly less cooking time than raw milled rice (15-25 min). Because of the demand from the modern customer, many processes have been developed for quick-cooking rice. The most common processes, all starting with milled rice are:

(*i*) Rice is cooked as above but is dried at a low temperature, the rice is then heated rapidly to expand or puff off the grains

(*ii*) Pre-soaked rice freeze dried. The product reconstitutes very well in hot water

(*iii*) Precooked rice is frozen, thawed, drained and then dried. Much of the water is removed at thawing and this cuts down the cost of drying

Flaked Rice

Flaked rice is made from parboiled rice. Paddy is soaked in water for 2-3 days (or hot water at 70-80°C for 20 min) to soften the kernel, followed by boiling in water for a few minutes. After cooking, the water is drained off and paddy is heated (250-275°C) in a shallow earthen vessel till the husks break open, after which it is pounded by a wooden pestle, heavy iron rollers which flatten the rice kernel and remove the husk

Milling is an ancient technique that has been used to make the cereals more palatable. Milling generally involves removal of husk, bran, seed coat and aluerone layer. The germ is also removed usually because of its high content of fat, which tends to make the product liable to become rancid and less palatable. Thus milling helps to increase the storage life of the product.

The various milling operations and equipments used in a modern rice mill are given in Table 2 and discussed below:

Table 2: List of milling operations and equipments used in Paddy Processing

Unit operations	Equipments	Function of machines
Cleaning	Cleaner	Removing foreign matter from paddy
Shelling	Rubber roll sheller	Separating husk from the paddy grain
Husk separation	Husk aspirator	Separation of husk from the product obtained from sheller
Paddy separation	Paddy separator	Removal of paddy from brown rice
Bran removal	Polisher/whitener	Removal of bran layer from brown rice
Bran aspiration	Bran aspirator	Removal of bran adhering to the rice kernel
Grading	Grades	Separation of broken rice from head rice
Handling and transportation	HandlingEquipments	Conveying of paddy rice to various processing units

1. Paddy Cleaning: Cleaning of paddy is the first step in paddy rice milling. Cleaning adds to the quality of paddy and it is desirable for further processing operations. Cleaning refers to removal of all types of foreign matters and other impurities. These matter can cause damage to rice processing machines and their presence lower the quality of milled rice. The foreign matters can be grouped into following categories

- big impurities like stems, paddy ear heads, stones, iron pieces etc.
- small impurities *e.g.* weed seeds, dust, mud particles etc. and
- impurities of equal size as to paddy like immature grains stones and other matters.

For cleaning of paddy, generally the difference in physical properties of impurities and paddy are used e.g. size, weight or length of grains. Lighter foreign matters are removed or separated by air aspiration, while the bigger and smaller impurities from paddy are separated with the help of suitable screens. Impurities similar to the shape and size of paddy are broken during milling operation and then could easily be separated from the rice. Impurities equal in both weight and size as paddy are difficult to separate by other mechanical means. The machines used for cleaning operation of paddy are described below:

Cleaner: The paddy is fed into this machine through a cleaner opening in the top. The suction fan draws air through the film of grain and separates all dust and light impurities, which drop to the cone – shaped bottom of the aspiration housing for automatic discharge. The paddy falls to a vibrating sieve with large perforations which removes large impurities such as straws, big stones, and the paddy and remaining small impurities. The over flow from this sieve is again subjected to strong aspiration to remove the last traces of light impurities.

Destoner: The destoner consists of a perforated deck mounted at an angle and operated by a reciprocating motion. A large amount of air is blown from below through the sieve. When a mixture of paddy and stones is fed at the top of the sieve, the air coming through the sieve stratifies the materials according to their density (or heaviness). The heavier stones remain on the deck and are carried backward to the top end by the reciprocating motion of the deck and discharged. The lighter paddy remains floating and slides can be controlled by adjusting the rate of feed, air flow and sieve tilt.

2. Parboiling: It is a permitting (optional) treatment given to paddy prior to its milling to achieve maximum recovery of head rice and to minimize breakage. In this process paddy is soaked and the wet paddy is heated and then dried. The paddy grain is mainly composed of polygonal starch granules. The voids or inter-granular spaces are filled with air and moisture. Due to these voids cracks develop and it cause breakage during milling. This breakage may be reduced by gelatinizing the starch. During gelatinization process starch swell and fill the voids. During soaking of paddy water penetrates into starch granules and results in swelling of grains. In heating the energy weakens the granule structure and more surfaces become available far water absorption and results in irreversible granule swelling. This phenomenon is called *gelatinization of starch.* The temperature at which gelatinization takes place is known as the *gelatinization temperature* and it is specific for particular variety in the near hood of 70°C. *Parboiling is a hydrothermal treatment.*

The main objective of parboiling are: (*i*) to increase the total and head rice yield of paddy, (*ii*) to prevent the loss of nutrients during milling (*iii*) to salvage wet or damaged paddy and (*iv*) to mill the rice according to refinement of consumers.

Advantages of Parboiling

Parboiling process developed by tradition in India and then improved by various researchers into its present form, provides a unique tool for improving not only the milling quality of paddy but also the other qualities. In general, parboiling process has the following advantages :

(*i*) Due to the splitting of the husk in the process of parboiling, the shelling of parboiled paddy becomes easier.

(*ii*) The extra strength acquired by the rice kernel during parboiling helps in reducing the brokers to a considerable extent.

(*iii*) It has been claimed that parboiled rice retains more proteins, vitamins and minerals than raw milled rice of the same variety.

(*iv*) Due to its acquired hardness, parboiled rice is more resistant to insect infestation during storage as compared to raw rice.

(*v*) During cooking, the loss of solids in gruel is less in parboiled rice when compared to raw rice.

(*vi*) Parboiled rice can withstand overcooking without becoming pasty.

(*vii*) Rice bran from parboiled rice is of superior quality. It contains about 25-30 per cent oil whereas raw rice bran contains about 15-20 per cent oil. Further, due to heat treatment of paddy during parboiling, the enzyme lipase which is mostly responsible for the hydrolysis of oil (development of free fatty acids) is destroyed to a certain extent and the oil is, therefore, of a superior quality having low free fatty acids (FFA).

Disadvantages of Parboiling

(*i*) The heat treatment during parboiling, causes a destruction of some natural antioxidants, the parboiled rice, therefore, develops more rancidity than raw rice during storage.

(*ii*) Parboiled rice takes more time to cook to the same degree of softness than raw rice and may have a characteristics flavour and colour which is not liked by many raw rice eaters. Besides, it is usually not preferred by them due to the changes in taste and texture.

(*iii*) The presence of high moisture, in parboiled paddy for a long duration, may cause the development of micotoxins in rice which are hazardous to the human health.

(*iv*) Parboiled paddy has to be dried again from 45 – 50 per cent moisture to 14-16 per cent for proper milling and storing, thus adding an extra drying cost to the total processing.

(*v*) The shelled parboiled rice is harder, therefore, more difficult to polish, resulting in lower mill throughput capacity and increases milling power. This increases the milling cost. Moreover, it also chokes the polisher due to the higher oil content of the bran.

(*vi*) The parboiling process needs an extra investment of capitals.

Inspite of the different disadvantages mentioned above and of extra expenditure involved in the process, the higher out-turn of the total (about 1-2 %) as well as head rice brings an additional profit to the miller and at the same time ensures a rice at an economical price to consumer.

There are certain varieties of paddy which inherently have poor milling quality. For them parboiling is must in order to obtain a good amount of head rice. It also provides a special flavored rice for people who are accustomed to and like parboiled rice. Generally scented and fine varieties of paddy which have good milling quality are not parboiled.

3. Milling: The rice kernel is composed of four primary components viz., hull or husk, seed coat or bran, embryo or germ and endosperm. The primary objective of milling rice is to remove the indigestible hull and additional portions of bran to field whole unbroken endosperm. Rice milling operations are relatively uncomplicated abrasive and separatory procedures which produce a variety of products dependant on the degree of bran removal or the extent of endosperm breakage.

Milling is a series of mechanical operations which remove the hull, embryo and outer layers of the rice kernel. The husk, pericarp and outer layers of aleurone are removed. This is called polishing of rice. Dehuskers, hullers and pearling machines are used in milling.

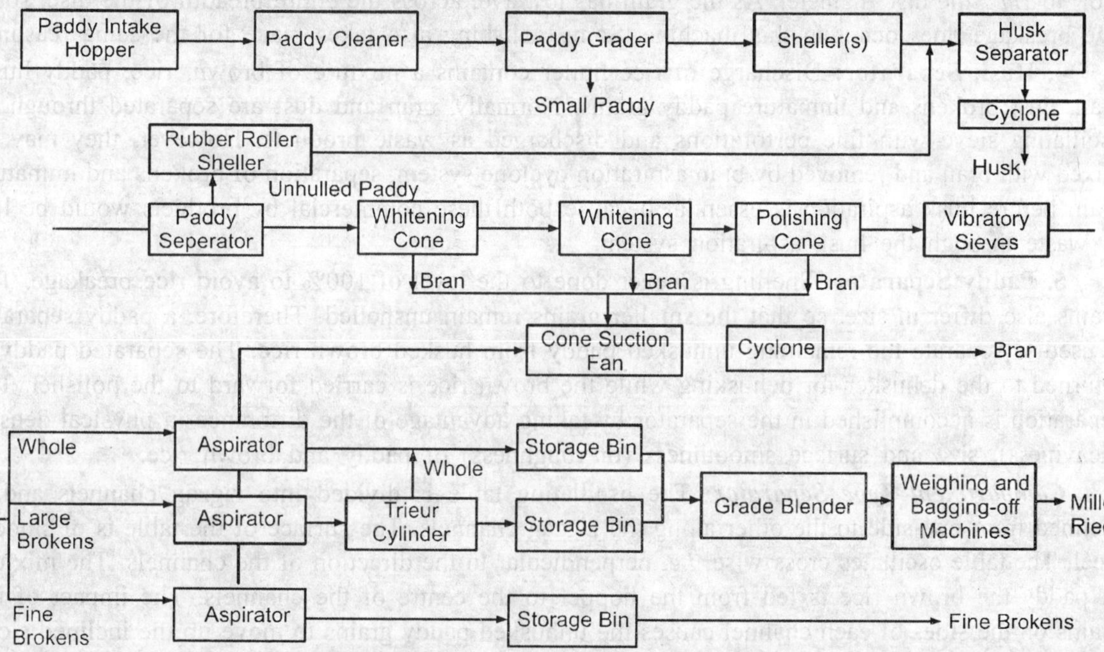

Fig. 2: Flow chart of the rice milling process

Huller Equipment: The purpose of hulling machine is to remove the husk from paddy grain with minimum damage to the bran layer and as far as possible not to break the brown rice.

Hullers may be of three types: (*i*) Stone disk, (*ii*) Rubber roll and (*iii*) Impeller

Impeller huller: The impeller huller is designed based on centrifugal and coriolis forces, whereby paddy is thrown against the liner part of the impeller housing.

***Rubber roll sheller**:* This consists of two rubber rolls rotating in opposite direction at different speeds. A feeder feeds paddy uniformly to the m/c. Paddy is fed in this layer between the rotating roll by the feeder. One of the roll is fixed while the other is adjustable to obtain desired clearance between them. The rolls are driven mechanically and the adjustable roll normally runs about 25% slower than the fixed one. The clearance between the roll is kept smaller than the thickness of paddy grain. The clearance should be about half the thickness of paddy and may be adjusted subsequently by judging the shelling efficiency. If the gap between rolls is properly adjusted. This equipment can shell up to 95% of paddy fed to it. During shelling, the faster roll should have a peripheral surface speed of 10 to 13 m/s, while the slower roll 8-10 m/s. Rubber roll machine performance depends upon the size and shape of rough rice.

Disc Sheller: It consists of two horizontal iron discs coated with emery. The top disc is fixed to the frame housing, and the bottom disc rotates. The rotating disc can be moved vertically up or down to adjust the clearance between the two discs. The clearance is thus adjusted to the size of the paddy grain. Paddy is fed into the centre of the machine. As it reaches the rotating disc, it moves outward by centrifugal force. During its travel outward, whenever it is up-ended, it is caught between the top (stationary) and bottom (rotating) discs and is dehusked by shear. The clearance between the two discs is critical to avoid excessive breakage. Quite often, the effective width of the emery coating is made too large causing unnecessary breakage of the grain. The width should be $1/6^{th}$ to $1/7^{th}$ the disc diameter. As the grain has to travel across the entire breadth of the disc, some rice breakage does occur in this machine. Some polishing also takes place for the same reason.

4. Husk Separator: Discharge of rice huller contains a mixture of brown, rice, paddy husk, bran, dust brokens and immature paddy grains. Normally, bran and dust are separated through an oscillating sieve with fine perforations and discharged as waste products. However, they may be mixed with bran and removed by bran aspiration cyclone system, separation of brokens and immature grain before husk aspiration is essential because both these commercial by products would be lost as waste through the husk aspiration system.

5. Paddy Separator: Shelling is never done to the level of 100% to avoid rice breakage. The grains also differ in size, so that the smaller grains remain unshelled. Therefore, a paddy separator is used to separate the remaining unhusked paddy from husked brown rice. The separated paddy is returned to the dehusker for dehusking while the brown rice is carried forward to the polisher. The separation is accomplished in the separator by taking advantage of the difference in physical density (heaviness), size and surface smoothness (or roughness) of paddy and brown rice.

Compartment–Type Separator: The oscillating table is divided into zigzag channels and is inclined from one side to the other along the zigzag channels. The surface of the table is of smooth steel. The table oscillates cross wise, *i.e.* perpendicular to the direction of the channels. The mixture of paddy the brown rice is fed from the hopper to the centre of the channels. The impact of the grains on the sides of each channel causes the unhusked paddy grains to move up the inclined slope toward high side of the table. The dehusked brown rice slides down the slope to the low side of the table. The slope and stroke of the table are adjusted to meet the needs of paddy of different size or condition and to ensure complete separation. Usually there are several decks one above the other.

Tray Separator: It consists of several indented trays (*i.e.* trays having a large number of depressions) mounted one above the other, all attached to an oscillating frame. The tray section moves up and forward, making a slight jumping movement. The mixture falls on each tray at the top corner from the inlet hopper. The smooth, smaller and heavier brown rice tends to go below and paddy to float up due to the motion of the tray. Further, the brown rice, being smaller, is caught in the indentations (depressions) and moves upward along with each jump of the tray. Thus it is carried to the upper side of the tray and discharged there. The free-flowing paddy slides downwards and is discharged there. Unseparated paddy and brown rice remaining at the middle portion are discharged in between and are returned to the hopper for re circulation. The table inclination is adjustable to meet different grain sizes and conditions. For efficient paddy separation, feed rate, speed, stroke and table inclination should be carefully set. Improper setting would result in brown rice going with return paddy or return paddy going with brown rice, or both, affecting capacity of the plant and the yield and quality of milled rice.

6. Whitening: Whitening is the removal of silver skin and bran layer followed by polishing. Three kinds of whitening machines, viz. vertical abrasive whitening cone, horizontal abrasive whitening cone, horizontal jet pearler are used.

7. Polishing: The brown rice is next polished to remove bran layers. Some amount of polishing is essential for easy cooking and storage, although excessive polishing reduces the nutritive value of rice. There are two types of polishers, one of emery and other of metal. The emery polishers (called whiteners) polish the grains by abrasion with emery while the metal polishers (called pearler) polish by friction between the rice grains. The emery polishers are again of two types – vertical (cone polishers) & horizontal.

Cone Polisher: It consists of a vertical truncated cone, covered with energy, which rotates inside a wire screen. The clearance between the cone and screen can be adjusted by raisin or lowering the cone. At regular intervals around the cone, the wire screen is divided into segments by vertical adjustable rubber brakes. The brown rice enters at the top centre and moves outward by centrifugal force to the edge of the cone. As the brown rice moves down between the cone and the screen around the cone, the abrasive action of the emery peels the bran off the grains. The bran goes out through the screen and is collected separately. The polished rice is discharged at the bottom.

Horizontal Abrasive Polisher: The machine consists of an abrasive cylindrical emery stone attached to a steel shaft rotating in a cylindrical, perforated metallic screen mounted horizontally. Broom rice enters at one end, and moves round and round the abrasive roll to the opposite discharge end. The pressure on the grain is controlled by hanging different weights on the discharge gate. As the grain passes through the space between the roll and the perforated screen, the bran layers are peeled off from the grain. The bran passes out through the perforated screen and polished rice is discharged through the outlet. The abrasive roll is made of carborandum.

Pneumatic Bran Separator: This equipment separates rice germs and brokens from bran also conveys the bran pneumatically (*i.e.* by air). It consists of a powerful centrifugal fan which aspirates the bran from the polisher and delivers it to a cyclone. A blower and an auxiliary cyclone aspirate the bran from the outlet of the main cyclone. Thus fine bran is separated from coarse materials (germs and brokens).

8. Glazing: It is a coating with talcum powder and glucose after polishing to give a transparent look to rice. Dry talc powder about 1-1.2% by weight is required. Glucose is added to the rice as 1:1 solution with water. About 1.0 kg glucose solution is required for 1000 kg of rice.

9. Grading: Grading in rice milling usually refers to the separation of broken from the head rice and the further classification of brokens. After polishing operation, the milled rice contains, in addition to whole grains, broken grains of different sizes as well as some bran and dust. Separation of these materials, termed 'Grading', must now be done. Bran and dust particles are removed by aspiration. Brokens may be separated either by a 'Plan sifter' or by a 'Trieur'.

Plan sifter: It is a single or double-decked sieve which is given a swinging motion produced by an eccentric drive. It consists of two sheets of different perforations (first small and then large) to separate two grades of brokens from the polished rice. The grain moves across the swinging sieve in a continuous, spiral path. A plan sifter, being of sieve type, cannot separate all broken grains from head rice. Big brokens remain along with head rice, while small brokens (less than half size) are removed. Sieves of the grader should be kept free from clogging for maximum removal of brokens.

Trieur: This is slightly inclined rotating cylinder containing indentations, like small pockets, all along its inner body. The mixed (head and broken) rice is unload into the raised end of the cylinder. As the rice passes along the slowly rotating cylinder, the broken grains sit nicely in pockets and are therefore picked up by the rotating cylinder. But as the cylinder rotates upward, the sitting broken grains finally fall out at a high point and are caught by a collector through fixed inside the cylinder and discharged separately. The unbroken grains, being too long, cannot sit in the pockets which are too small. Hence they move along undisturbed down the cylinder as it rotates. Whole and broken grains are thus separated into two streams. By adjusting the size of the indentations and the position of the through, broken rice of different size can be separated. Broken grains of half or more is permitted in market rice in India, Indian mills generally use only plan sifters and not trieures.

Circular purifier: It is used for removing pieces of husk, bran and dust particles that remain adhering to milled rice after grading. Rice grains are kept suspended in a strong stream of air, when adhering particles are sucked away. Often purifiers are installed also to cool the rice between polishing passes.

Table 3: Nutritional comparision

	Parboiled rice	White rice	Brown rice
Calories	194	205	194
Total fat	0.5 grams	0.5 grams	1.5 grams
Total carbs	41 grams	45 grams	40 grams
Fiber	1 gram	0.5 grams	2.5 grams
Protein	5 grams	4 grams	4 grams
Thiamine (vitamin B1)	10% of the RDI	3% of the RDI	23% of the RDI
Niacin (vitamin B3)	23% of the RDI	4% of the RDI	25% of the RDI
Vitamin B6	14% of the RDI	9% of the RDI	11% of the RDI
Folate (vitamin B9)	1% of the RDI	1% of the RDI	3.5% of the RDI
Vitamin E	0% of the RDI	0% of the RDI	1.8% of the RDI
Iron	2% of the RDI	2% of the RDI	5% of the RDI
Magnesium	3% of the RDI	5% of the RDI	14% of the RDI
Zinc	5% of the RDI	7% of the RDI	10% of the RDI

* RDI: Recommended Dietary Intakes

10.2 WHEAT PROCESSING

1. Structure and Classification

The grain of wheat (Fig. 3) consists of an outer covering. The pericarp and testa which is hard and indigestible; an aleurone layer, which contains a higher proportion of protein than flour; an embryo attached to a small structure; the sculentum, at the lower end of the grain; and finally, the endosperm comprising 85% of the whole grain from which the flour is derived.

2. Wheat Selection and Blending

The chemical composition and quality of individual lots of wheat vary widely, depending upon the variety and environment conditions under which they are grown. Since the miller must produce of flour of definite characteristics for the particular market. He is serving and endeavor to maintain uniform quality from day to day, month to month and year to year, the of wheat he purchases and the binding of them according to quality are essential phases of modern milling.

3. Storage:

Grain should have moisture content less than 20% before it is harvested. If it is stored in a moist conditions bacteria and moulds will grow and will cause the temperature of the bulk grain to rise. The quality of wheat will consequently be damaged. In order to store it successively, it is, therefore, necessary to reduce the moisture content to, say, and 13 % by a process of drying. This can be done in simple of the grain is not allowed to exceed 50^0C. The use of excessive temperature damages the wheat enzymes which are essential in flour during the baking process.

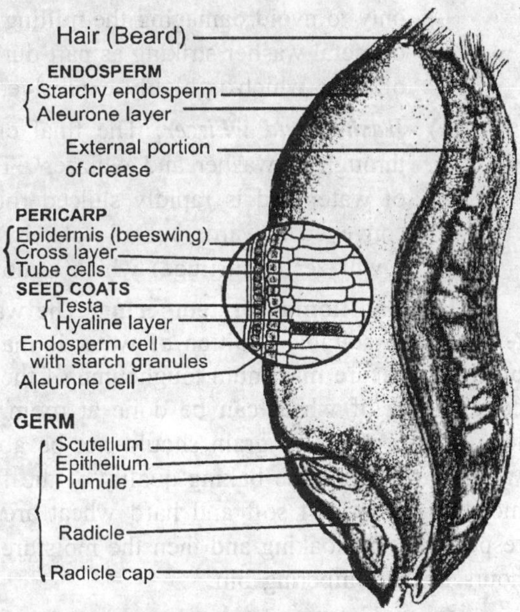

Fig. 3: Diagrammatic longitudinal section of wheat grain through crease and germ

4. Flour Milling

The milling process as a whole can be divided into two parts, the preliminary cleaning of the grain and the adjustment of its moisture content to an optimum level and separation of the husk and outer layers of the grain from the flour. The main am of the modern milling is to obtain maximum recovery of white flour from endosperm without any part of bran or germ. The yield of white flour and by products from flour milling are approximately 70 percent and 30 percent respectively. The byproduct (mill feed) is composed of bran (12%), germ (3%) and shorts (15%).

Wheat contains bran (12%), germ (3%) and endosperm (85%). Flour milling is the continuous process that is used to transform the wheat into a form which is of use to the baking and other industries and the domestic consumer. A small portion of production is geared towards the production of whole-wheat flours, employing a simplified process flow sheet, but most demand and effort is directed towards the production of white flour.

(A) Cleaning: Commercially wheat as received at the mill contains various impurities, such as stinking smut, weed seeds, other cereals grains, soils etc. The cleaning operation is carried in the following machines in that sequence:

(*i*) ***Rubber separator***: The grain is passed over a set of sieves in a 'rubber separator' in order to free it from gross contamination. This machine is fitted with fans to blow off dust. The first separator may be followed by a second to remove impurities still remaining.

(*ii*) ***Disc separator***: The grain is then allowed to pass to disc separator. The machine is fitted with discs containing lots or indents, designed to pick up and hold the grain while allowing oats, barley and other grains to pass through; other discs with smaller indents separate seeds and broken wheat grains.

(*iii*) ***Scourer***: In dry scouring, the wheat is forced against a perforated iron casing by beaters fixed to a rapidly revolving drum. This severe treatment removes foreign materials lodged in the creases of the kernels as well as the brush hairs.

(*iv*) ***Magnetic separators***: The wheat, cleaned so far, is then passed over magnetic separators to remove any nails or pieces of metal. The complete removal of iron is important, not only to avoid damaging the milling machinery but also to prevent any possibility of a nail or metal washer striking as part during later stages of the process and igniting a dust cloud of flour which is highly explosive.

(*v*) ***Washer and whizzer***: The final cleaning operation is carried out by passing the grain through a 'washer and whizzer'. The wheat is carried out into the machine in a stream of water and is rapidly sluiced round at high speed. The wheat separated from dirt, is conveyed upwards out of water by means of inclined vanes. This is then passed through a whizzer (centrifuge) which removes the build of the liquid water.

(B) Conditioning or tempering: The washed wheat is immediately sent into a conditioner. In tempering, a suitable addition of water is made and wheat allowed standing for a sufficient length of time to secure maximum toughening of the bran with optimum mellowing of the endosperm. The conditioning of wheat can be done at room temperature, elevated or higher temperature. But the temperature of wheat grain should not be above 47°C because the gluten quality will be affected which deteriorates the baking quality of the flour for bakery products manufacturing. Generally the moisture content of soft and hard wheat are increased to 15 to 17 percent and 16 to 19 percent respectively by soaking and then the moisture of the grain is equilibrated by tempering for 18 to 72 hours in the tempering bin.

(C) Separation of flour: In the manufacture of white flour, the aim is separation of the endosperm of the grain from the bran and germ followed by pulverizing it to very small particles.

(D) Grinding: The grinding or milling of wheat is performed by roller flour mill. The roller milling system is classified into breaking system and reduction roll system. In addition most of the flour mills consist of a stand – by system of scratch roll system. The scratch roll system is only extension of breaking roll system. The basic difference between break roll and reduction roll system is due to variation in their surface conditions. The surface of reduction roll is smooth while break roll has corrugated surface.

(*i*) Breaking system

a) **Break rolls**: The first part of the grinding process proper is carried out in corrugated rollers known as 'break rolls'. These are horizontal rollers of usually 60 to 75 cm length and 20 to 25 cm diameter and not in actual contact with each other. They are operated in opposite directions at a differential in speed of about 2.5:1. Upper roll revolves at a higher speed. Each stands has two pairs of rollers. In the first break rolls, the corrugations are usually 4.5 per cm, this number increasing in progressing through the break system, to as high as 10-11 corrugations to the on the fifth break roll. As the roll turn rapidly the edges of the corrugations of fast roll out across those of the slow roll, so that there is a shearing as well as crushing action on the wheat which falls is a rapid steam between them. The coming from the rolls is sifted through a sifter. Only a small amount of flour is produced by the first break rolls. The broken grain from the plan-sifter associated with the first break rolls will passes to a second break rolls which are set a little closer together than the first break rolls, so that the materials is crushed a little finer and fragments of endosperm are released. The crushed stock is sifted and the coarser material passed through the third break rolls, and the stock again sifted and the process may go ahead. These rolls are set progressively closer together and are each more finely fluted than the pair before.

b) **Sieving**: After each grinding on the break rolls, the crushed materials, called stock or chop or semolina is conveyed to sifter or bolter. It is a large box fitted with a series of slopping sieves. The break sifters have a relatively coarse wire sieve at the top and progressively finer silk sieves arranged below. The sifter is given a gyratory motion. Three general classes of material are separated: coarse fragments, fine particles or flour, and granular particles of intermediate size which are called middling.

c) **Purification**: The middlings consists largely of fragments of endosperm, mixed with small pieces of bran and the released embryos. All three graded streams are put through a purifier which is an arrangement or sieves coupled to suction fans to draw off branny particles.

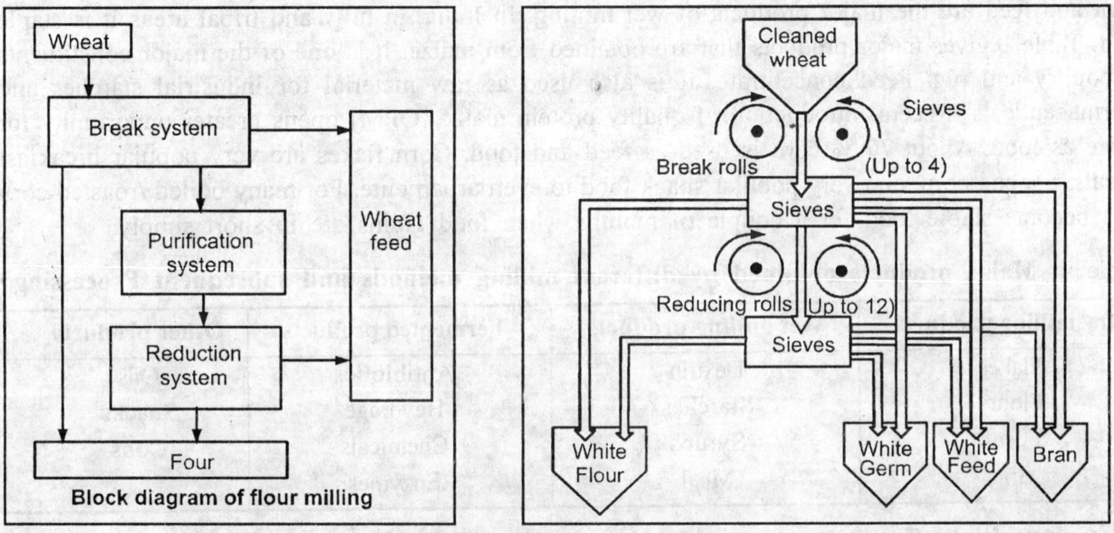

Fig. 4: The basic layouts of the wheat roller mill

d) **Reduction rolls**: The purified and classified middlings are gradually ground to flour between smooth rolls, called reductions, which revolves at a differential of about 2.5:1. This produces a crushing and rubbing action which powders and granular of semolina into flour. It also flattens out the embryo of the grain and any branny particles which are then more readily removed by the sieves.

End Product of Wheat Milling and Their Application

(*i*) Semolina is a milling product consisting of coarse particles of mainly endosperm with a diameter of 300-750 μm.

(*ii*) Middlings are a product consisting of intermediate-sized endosperm particles with a diameter of 125-300 μm. Both semolina and middlings are used as ingredients in porridges and for the production of pasta

(*iii*) Flour consists of fine endosperm particles of less than 125 μm diameter. It is used for making white bread, confectionery products and certain pasta products.

Milling of Soft and Hard Wheat

In the milling of soft wheats, the meanly endosperm is fragmented indiscriminately. Therefore, the flour particles consist mainly of fragments of single cells or fragments of clusters of two or three neighbouring cells. The flour easily sticks together and sifts with difficulty, tending to close the apertures of sieves.

In the milling of hard wheats, fracturing of the grain follows the middle lamellas of the mealy endosperm cells. Hard wheat yield a coarse, gritty flour which is freely flowing and easily sifted

9.3 MAIZE (CORN) MILLING

Corn (maize) can be processed into various food feed ingredient, industrial product and alcoholic beverages. At present, there are two types' modern methods of milling of corn, *i.e.* dry milling and wetting milling. Besides germ for corn oil extraction and husk and deoiled germ etc for feed, grits (mainly used for break fast cereals) are the main product of corn dry milling where as pure starch, germ and feed are the major products of wet milling. In India, in hilly and tribal areas it is staple food. Table 1 gives major products that are obtained from maize. It is one of the major constituents of poultry and pig. Feed concentrate. It is also used as raw material for industrial starches and pharmaceuticals. Recent introduction of quality protein maize (QPM) opens greater opportunity for maize as food. About 70 % corn is used as feed and food. Corn flakes are very popular breakfast cereals, popped corn, and very popular snack food to even urban elite. For many boiled /roasted corn cabs become staple food for a couple of months when food grains are in short supply.

Table 4: Maize products obtained by different milling methods and subsequent Processing

Dry milling products	Wet milling products	Fermented products	Other products
Flakes Flours Feeds Grits	Dextrin Starches Syrups Meal	Antibiotics Beverage Chemicals Enzymes	Oils Snacks Cobs

Composition: The mature corn kernel is composed of four major parts; (*a*) endosperm, 82 %; (*b*) germ, 12 % (*c*) pericarp, 5% and (*d*) tip cap, 1%.

Fraction	Kernel, %	Starch, %	Protein, %	Lipid, %	Ash, %	Sugar, %
Whole grain	-	71.5	10.3	4.8	2.0	1.4
Endosperm	82.3	86.4	9.4	0.8	0.6	0.3
Germ	11.5	8.2	18.8	34.5	10.8	10.1
Bran	5.3	7.3	3.7	1.0	0.3	0.8

Method of Corn Milling

(*i*) Wet milling

(*ii*) Drying milling:

a. Non degerming process *b.* Degerming process

(1) Corn Dry Milling

i) **Non degerming:** The whole corn is ground into meal of high fibre as well as high protein content without of germ by stone grinder.

ii) **Degerming process:** The corn is moistened with a little amount of water and tempered for moisture equilibrium. The purpose of all dry degerming corn milling methods is to remove hull, germ and tip cap from the corn kernel as far as practicable and primarily produce corn grits with some meals and flours. The yield of endosperm product and honey feed are about 70 % and 30 % respectively.

Tempering-Degerming (TD) process or Dry milling: They have several objectives:

a. To remove essentially all germ and hull so that endosperm contains as low fat and fibre as possible.

b. To recover a maximum amount of the endosperm as large clean grits without any dark speck, and

c. To recover a maximum amount of pure particles of germ.

Unit operations in Degerming dry milling

(*i*) **Cleaning:** Thorough cleaning of corn is essential for the subsequently milling operation. The pieces of iron etc. are removed by magnetic separators. Dry cleaner consists of sieves and aspirators and some times a wet cleaner consisting of washing destining unit and a mechanical type dewatering unit, known as whizzer are used for cleaning of corn.

(*ii*) **Tempering/conditioning:** Predetermined amount of moisture is added to the corn in the form of cold or hot water or steam in one, two or three stages with appropriate tempering times after each stage. The tempering times (rest periods) vary according to the hydration methods, so called tempering temperature vary from room temperature to about 50^0C accordingly.

The optimum moisture content for degerming in the Baell degermer is 21-25%. Either cold or hot water is used for the addition of moisture. A little heat in the form of open steam is added as and when necessary.

(*iii*) **Degerming:** It is a process in which endosperm is separated (detached) from other components of corn kernels is namely, germ, hull and tip cap. There are several devices used for degerming the corn with varying degree of efficiency. In modern tempering process Beall degermer device is used which consists of a truncated cone type rotor and cylinder.

(*iv*) **Drying and Cooling:** The degermer products are to be dried to 15% to 18% moisture content for proper grinding and sifting. Generally, rotary steam tube dryers are used for drying the products. Rotary louver type dryer can be also employed. The stock is heated to about 50°C. Counter flow or cross flow rotary vertical gravity or fluidized belt type or cooler can be used for cooling the dried products.

Sifting is a process to pass corn, sugar or any other product through a sieve in order to remove any lumps or unwanted materials.

(*v*) **Separation:** The germ, husk and endosperm fragments are then separated by means of sifters, aspirators, specific gravity table separator or purifiers.

(*vi*) **Rolling and Grading:** The releasing of germ and husk from the endosperm products occurs during their gradual size reductions roller mills. Grading or classification is the separation of a single stock (usually endosperm particles) into two or more group according to particle size.

Cleaning ⟶ Tempering ⟶ Degerming ⟶ Drying & Cooling
↓
Product ⟵ Rolling & Grading ⟵ Separation ⟵

2. Corn Wet Milling: The pure starch, pure germ and feed are the basic products of corn wet milling. The raw corn for wet milling should contain 15-16% moisture and it should be physically sound. The heat damaged corn affects the quality of oil extracted form its germ. Corns are treated at temperatures of 75°C during drying.

Sufficient amount of moisture is added to the corn during steeping in the wet milling process in order to prepare the corn for subsequent degerming, grinding and separation. The wet milling process consists of following steps (*i*) cleaning (*ii*) soaking (*iii*) germ separation and recovery (*iv*) grinding and hull recovery (*v*) separation of starch and gluten.

1. **Cleaning:** All impurities such as dust, chalf, cobs, stones, insects-infests grain and broken and other foreign materials are removed from corn by screening and aspirating. The clean grains are conveyed to the storage bins.
2. **Steeping:** The major objectives of steeping are
   a. To soften the kernel for grinding
   b. To facilitate separations of germ
   c. To facilitate separation of gluten from to starch granules
   d. To remove soluble, mainly from starch

Water impregnated with sulphur dioxide (*i.e.* acidulated water with H_2SO_3) is used for steeping. It helps in arresting certain fermentation during long steeping process. The steeping is carried out at about 50°C for a period varying from 28 to 48 hr in different plants. After steeping corn attains a moisture content of about 45%.

3. **Germ recovery:** the wet and soften corn kernels containing about 45% moisture are conveyed to the degerminating unit. This machine consisting of a metallic stationary plate and a rotating plate with projecting teeth is employed only for tearing the soft kernels apart and freezing the germs without grinding.

   The pulpy mixture containing germs, husk, starch and gluten is passed through hydro-clones, where the germ being lighter is separated from other heavier ingredients by centrifugal force.
4. **Milling and Fibre recovery:** After separation of germ and screening of the coarse particles, the mixture contains starch gluten and hulls.

   Mainly horny endosperm and hull are then generally ground by either traditional ***Burstone mill or modern entolelor impact mills*** to release the rest of the starch. Materials to be ground enter the machine through spinning rotor and are thrown out with great force against the impactors at periphery of the rotor and also against a stationery impactor resulting in considerable reduction in size. Here only the starch is readily released with a very little size reduction of hulls.

   The milled slurry containing the ground starch, gluten and hulls is passed through a series of hexagonal reels where the coarse hulls and fibres are removed.
5. **Starch-Gluten separation:** In the modern process, the slurry containing starch and gluten is concentrated and then the lighter gluten particles are separated from the relatively heavier starch particles by the centrifugal force in high speed centrifuges. The centrifuging of starch is carried out in two stages. In many modern mills, the second stage of centrifugation is performed by a number of hydroclone types of equipment.

   The starch obtained from the second stage of separation is filtered and then dried to produce dry starches.

9.4 SAURGHUM (JOWAR) PROCESSING

Decortication to attrition milling : In areas where sorghum and other millets are consumed as food mainly in India and Africa, they are often milled by decortications process because of two reasons. First, the grains are nearly round and do not have a crease. Second, the decortication process is similar to hand pounding which is traditional processing of grains. PRL dehuller successfully removes the hulls from millet, sorghum and maize. The dehuller consists of a metal shaft on which a number of grinding stones or abrasive disks are evenly spaced about 2 cm apart. This rotor is enclosed by a semi-circular sheet material barrel that is filled with grain. The abrasive disks spinning at 1500-2000 rpm rub against the freely moving mass of grain and abrade away the outer layers. The product is separated by mechanical winnowing into the hulls and endosperm

Grinding and pulverizing : Dehulled sorghum is milled to meal or flour using a hammer mill or burr mill. Whole sorghum is also milled in this way as in sorghum malt

Dry milling : The clean and moistened grain is milled by the conventional roller mills to separate the endosperm, germ and bran from each other. The products of dry milling are:

1. Grit – 76.7%
2. Bran – 1.2%
3. Germ – 11%
4. Fibre – 10%

Wet milling : Sorghum can be wet milled by the same method as used for maize wet milling. However wet milling of sorghum is more difficult than that of maize because:

- Sorghum is small sized spherical grain
- It has a small germ
- Grain has dark layered outer layers as pericarp contains polyphenolic pigments. These pigments leach out and give the starch an off colour during wet grinding
- Bran of sorghum breaks into small pieces that interfere with the separation of protein and starch

9.5 PROCESSING OF OATS

The oat grain is harvested with its hull on. After the removal of hull, oat is known as groat.

Milling : During milling, the main objective is to remove the hull from the groat and to obtain high yield of clean groats. The steps involved in oat milling are:

1. **Cleaning :** The oat grain samples are cleaned of the extraneous matter *i.e.* loose hulls, weed seeds, straw, dust, thin and light grains and extraneous metals etc. This is achieved in a multistage cleaning process that uses magnetic separators, sieves, aspirators and indented cylinders
2. **Grading :** The heat treated oats are graded for size before impact dehulling. It is carried out using automated sieves with rectangular slots of increasing size
3. **Impact dehulling :** Separation of the hulls and groats is achieved by impact and abrasion. The graded grain is fed into the huller onto the rotor, which rotates at 1500-2000 rpm. Through impact and abrasion, hull is detached. The rubber liner reduces the breakage and assists in separation of the hull from the groat
4. **Stabilization :** Groats contain 5-9% oil content which is evenly distributed throughout the groat and remains unchanged under normal storage conditions. The lipase enzyme is present in the outer bran layers of the groat which causes hydrolytic rancidity. Hence, inactivation of lipase is known as stabilization which is achieved by the use of heat. *Advantages of this process are:*

- Lipase is completely inactivated
- It destroys bacteria and fungi on the surface
- Typical nutty oat aroma and flavour develop

9.6 PULSE MILLING

In India, people are mostly vegetarian depending largely on cereals and pulses, as their staple food, which provide the main source of dietary protein and calories. The protein from pulses are known to be of inferior quality, due to the deficiency of sulphur containing amino acids as well as due to other factors like digestibility, availability of amino acids, anti nutritional factors etc. However, pulses are rich in protein and are mainly consumed in the form of dehusked split pulses. Pulses are the major source of proteins to vegetarian masses in the country. There are about 10,000 pulses mills (Dhal mills) in India. Pulses consumed as Dhal have about 17-25% protein with Dhal yield potential of 83-85 %. However, existing commercial Dal mills have a Dhal recovery of 65-70% where as modern Dhal mills yield about 70-75%. Milling of pulses means removal of the outer husk and splitting the grain in to two equal halves. Generally, the husk is much more tightly held by the kernel of some pulses than most cereals. Therefore, a large amount of abrasive force is applied for the complete dehusking of the grain which results in high losses in the form of brokens and powder. The yield of split pulses in traditional mills is only 65% to 70% while potential yield may be 80 to 85% and broken loss varies 15 to 20%.

Chemical composition: In general, pulses contain 20-30 percent protein, about 60 percent carbohydrates, 1.0-2.5 percent fat, and are fairly good source of thiamine, nicotinic acids, calcium and iron (Table 5). Pulse carbohydrates (mainly starch) are well absorbed and utilized, providing equivalent energy value in terms of calories on unit weight basis as that of cereals.

Table 5: Chemical composition of selected pulses

Pulses	Energy Cal./100g	Crude protein, %	Fat, %	Carbo-Hydrates, %	Minerals (mg/100g)			Vitamins (mg/100g)		
					Ca	Fe	P	B_1	B_2	Niacin
Chickpea	361	20.6	2.2	61.2	190	9.8	280	0.30	0.51	2.6
Pigeon pea	343	24.1	1.7	62.9	129	5.8	288	0.52	0.14	2.3
Lentil	346	25.1	1.8	60.8	130	6.1	250	0.50	0.21	1.8
Peas	315	26.1	1.5	56.6	150	5.2	300	0.45	0.50	1.3
Blackgram	350	26.2	1.2	56.6	185	8.7	345	0.42	0.37	2.0
Green gram	334	24.0	1.3	56.6	140	8.4	280	0.47	0.39	2.0
Cow pea	342	32.4	1.8	60.3	76	5.7	430	0.92	0.18	1.9
Kidney beans	341	22.1	1.7	61.4	137	6.7	410	0.54	0.18	2.1
Horse beans	322	22.0	0.5	57.3	280	7.6	390	0.42	0.20	1.5

(*Source:* Aykroyd and Doutly, 1964; Gupta 1982a)

Composition of pulse (Arhar)

Moisture	=	10.35%
Protein	=	24.19%
Ether extract	=	1.89%
Ash	=	3.55%
Crude Fibre	=	1.01%
Carbohydrate	=	59.21%

Average percentage of husk and endosperm in 'Arhar' is 15% and 85% respectively.

Table 6: Husk content and maximum possible dhal yield from some of the selected pulses

Pulse	Husk content, %	Gota yield, %	Dhal yield, %	Germ yield, %
Bengal gram	12	88	84	4
Pigeon pea	13	87	83	4
Green gram	11	89	84	5
Black gram	13	87	83	4
Cowpea	12	88	83	5
Kidney beans	11	89	84	5
Horse gram	12	88	83	5
Soybean	11	89	84	5
Average	**12**	**88**	**84**	**4**

Method of pulse milling:

(1) Wet milling, (2) Dry milling

1. Dry milling: There is no common processing method for all types of pulses. However, some general operations of dry milling method are such as:

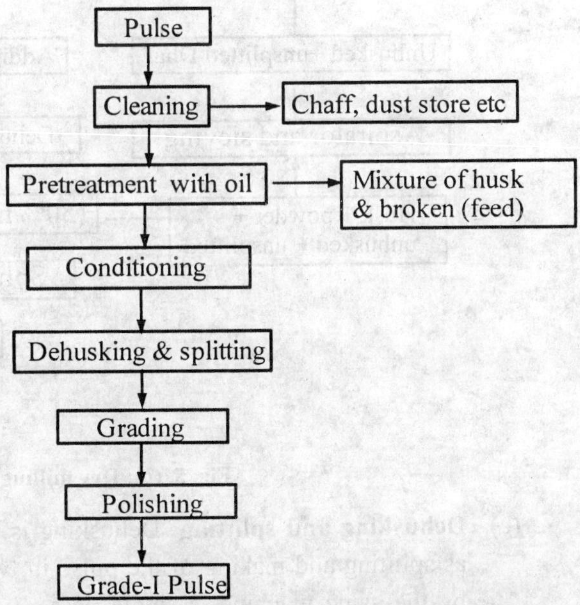

Fig. 5. (*a*): Flow diagram of dry milling of Pulse

(*a*) **Cleaning and grading**: Cleaning and grading operation may be accomplished using the sets of sieves of suitable mesh size, and aspiration system to remove dust, chaff, stone, iron pieces and other foreign materials.

(*b*) **Pitting and scarification**: This is to facilitate the oil penetration process for the loosening of husk. Emery rolls with outer cage used for making scratch over the husk of pulse.

(*c*) **Penetration of oil:** The scratched or pitted pulses are passed through a screw conveyor and mixed with some edible oil like linseed oil (1.5 to 2.5 kg/tonnes of pulse). After the oil treatment, the pulses are kept for about 12 hours to allow proper penetration to take place in the pulse kernel (*i.e.* called tempering).

(*d*) **Conditioning:** It is done by alternate wetting and drying. Under the sun drying for 2 to 4 days about 3.5 to 5 % moisture content is added to the pretreated pulses and heaped overnight and spread over a paved or cemented yard under the sun. Process is repeated till 2 to 4 days depending upon the type of pulse. The final drying of the pulse is done to bring its moisture content is about 10 to 20%, and then pulse is ready for dehusking

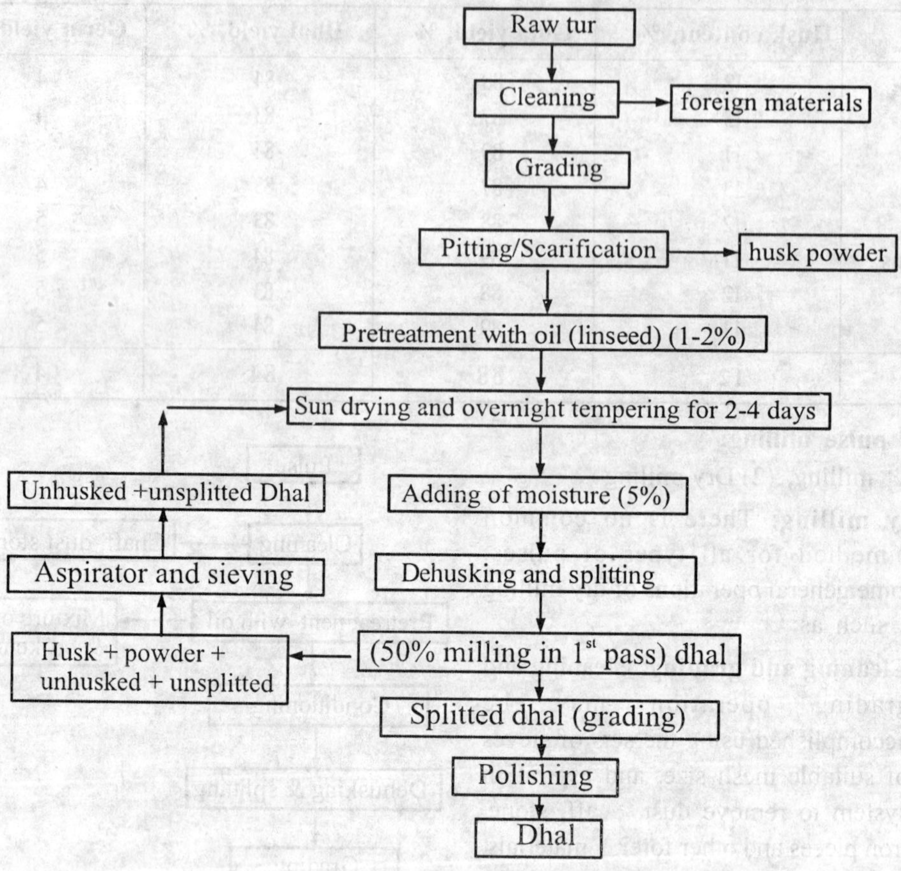

Fig. 5. (*b*): Dry milling of Arhar (Tur) dhal

(*e*) **Dehusking and splitting**: Dehusking is the operation in which to remove the outer husk as splitting and making of the pulse in two equal halves. Both the operation is carried out by the same machine is single pass.

An emery roller and concave type machine commonly is known as Gota machine. However, give better yields. About 50% of pulses are dehusked and dehusked and splitted single pass by Gota machine. Splitted dhal are separated from the mixture of husk, powder, unhusked dhal and unsplitted dhal by using the aspirator and sieves. Unhusked and unsplitted dhal may be pretreated and conditioned. If so required, whole process is repeated 2-3 times until the remaining pulse are dehusked and splitted.

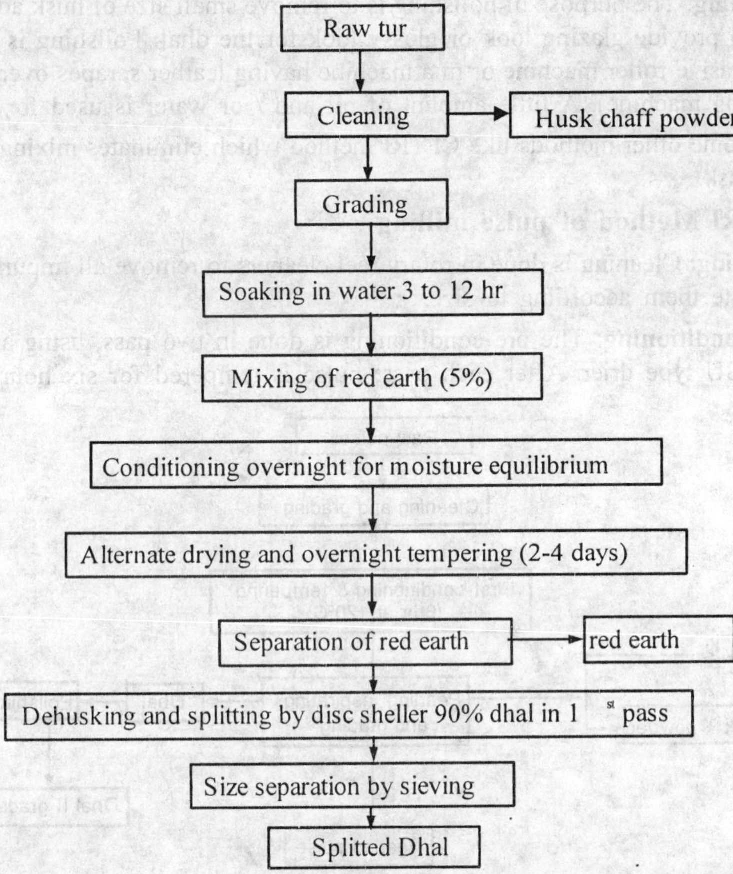

Fig. 5. (c): Wet milling of Tur (Arhar)

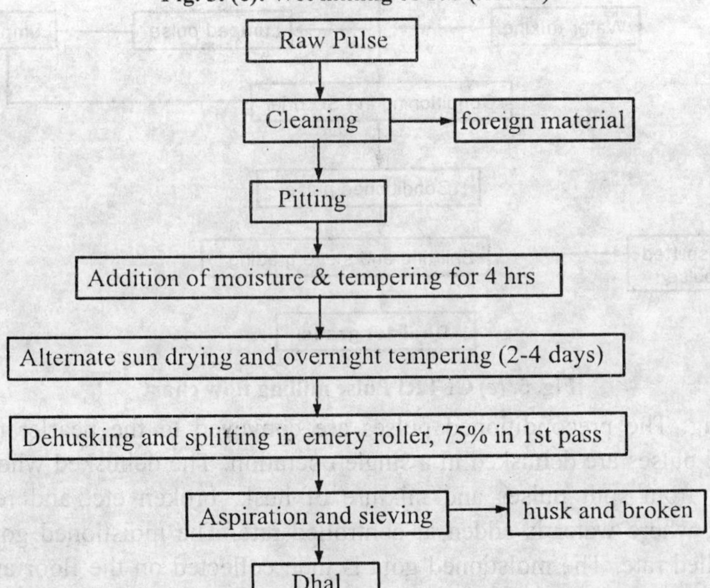

Fig. 5. (*d*): Flow chart of dry milling of Bengal gram, Lintel, Peas

(*f*) **Polishing**: The purpose of polishing is to remove small size of husk adhering to cotyledons and to provide glazing look or glossy look for the dhal. Polishing is carried out either in an abrasive roller machine or in a machine having leather scrapes over the cylindrical rotor (buffing machine). A little amount of oil and / or water is used for proper polishing.

There are some other methods like CFTRI method which eliminates mixing of oil and water for loosening the husk.

Modern CFTRI Method of pulse milling

1. **Cleaning**: Cleaning is done in rotary reel cleaners to remove all impurities from pulses and separate them according to size.
2. **Pre conditioning**: The pre conditioning is done in two pass, using a hot air of 120°C in the LSU type drier. After each pass, pulse is tempered for six hours.

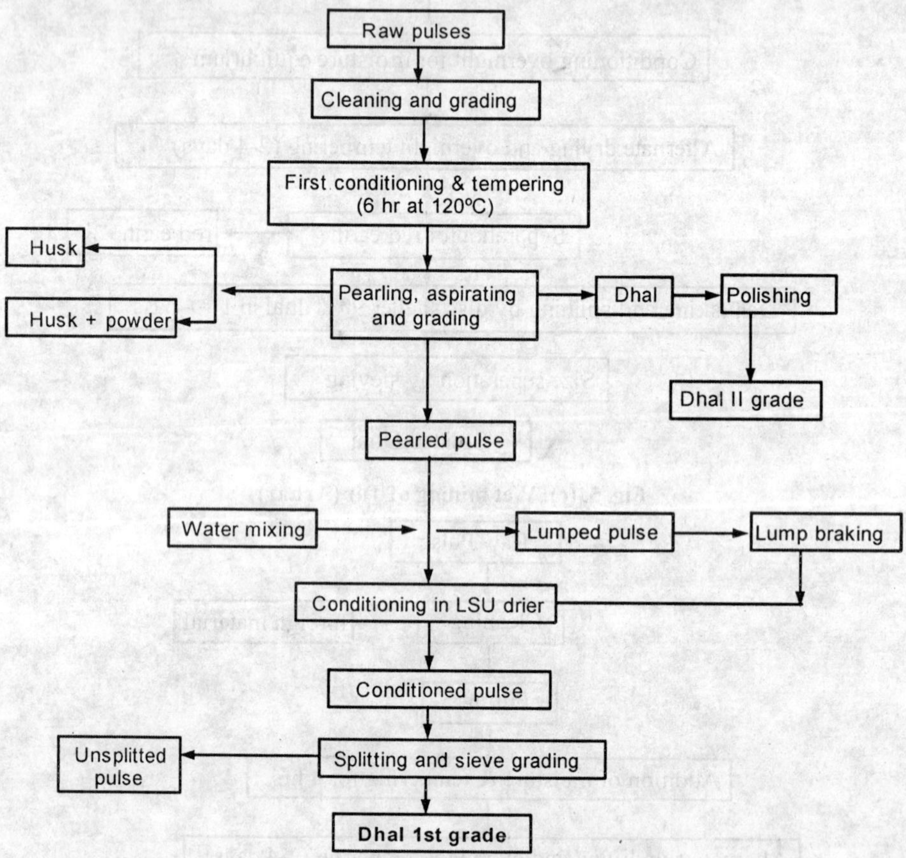

Fig. 5. (*e*) CFTRI Pulse milling flow chart

3. **Dehusking**: The preconditioned pulses are conveyed to the pearler or dehusker, where almost all pulses are dehusked in a single operation. The dehusked whole pulses (gota) are separated from split pulses and mixture of husk, broken etc, and received in a screw conveyor, where water is added at controlled rate. The moistioned gota is then collected at controlled rate. The moistioned gota is then collected on the floor and allow remaining as such for about an hour.

4. **Lump breaking**: Due to moistioning gota, the sticky coating over the cotyledons leads to formation of lumps. Before splitting, it is necessary to break the lump breaker.
5. **Conditioning and splitting**: After lump breaking, the gota is conveyed to LSU drier, where it is exposed to hot air for a few hours. The gota is thus dried to the proper moisture level for splitting. The hot conditioned and dried gota is splitted in emery roller mills in one pass. The splitted dhal is due to grade in first pulse and dehusked whole pulses and small broken by using a proper sieving. The unsplitted dehusked pulse again fed to conditioner for splitting.

9.7 BARLEY PROCESSING

The mature barley grain is an elongated oval structure, although more spherical and globular kernels. The hull comprises about 13% of the kernel, the pericarp plus testa about 3%, the aleurone about 5%, the starchy endosperm about 76%, and the embryo plus the scutellum about 3.0%. Kernels may weigh anywhere from 5 to 80 mg; however, most hulled barley kernels will weigh between 35 and 45 mg, whereas typical hulless kernels will weigh between 25 and 35 mg. Most soluble carbohydrates are deposited and stored within cells in the starchy endosperm tissue during the maturation of the kernel. The largest component of the carbohydrate group is starch, considered a soluble polysaccharide and the major source of energy in barley for food and growth of the new plant after germination. Starch is also the most variable constituent of all nutrients in barley, varying from a low of 45% or less to as much as 65% of the kernel. Barley starch is composed of two structural types, amylopectin and amylose. Amylopectin is a branched-chain polysaccharide in which α-(1,4)-d-glucose units are branched through α-(1,6)-d-glucose linkages, and amylose is primarily a straight chain of α-(1,4)-d-glucose units. In most barley, amylopectin is the major starch type, making up 72 to 78% of the total, with amylose making up the remaining 22 to 28%.

As with other cereal grains, barley requires one or more processing procedures in order to reduce or change the kernels into a usable, edible form. Modern processing methods do one or more of the following: alter physical form or particle size, isolate and concentrate specific parts of the grain, improve mouthfeel and palatability, alter nutrient digestibility, and improve product stability or shelf life. Some form of milling, either dry or wet, is the processing most commonly applied to cereal grains. With the exception of malting and extrusion, we deal primarily with dry milling processes in this chapter. Dry milling encompasses a variety of abrasion, grinding, flaking, and separation procedures utilizing numerous types of specialized mills.

A multitude of food products can be produced from barley using one or more of several processing or milling procedures that are available in commerce. Barley may be milled by blocking (dehulling), pearling, flaking, cutting, grinding, roller milling, and further processed by air classifying, sieving, extruding, and infrared heating. Malting is a separate process used to prepare barley as a specialty food additive and in alcoholic beverage production.

The first step in processing barley is cleaning to remove foreign grains, weed seed, and impurities such as dirt, sand, dust, straw, chaff, and string, and to remove broken kernels. This is accomplished by use of specialized equipment, including screens, magnets, de-stoners, gravity tables, separators, and scourers, and aspiration with air currents. A process of sieving with selective screens is effective in separating small, less hazardous impurities once larger contaminants are removed. Specific-gravity separations utilizing air currents may also be accomplished once the partially decontaminated grain leaves the sieving process. This will separate lighter material, such as dust, chaff, straw, and string, from the grain.

In most processing centers, cereal grains are no longer cleaned by washing with water, although there is a pretreatment process called *damping*, which means the controlled addition of moisture. This process is often referred to as *conditioning* or *tempering* of the grain, which alters some of the physical properties. Conditioning is not a single process for all grains, being specific for the individual grain and the milling process. The volume and temperature of the water added will have major effects on processing. Considerably less is known about conditioning barley for milling compared to wheat and oats. Recent research has focused on understanding conditioning of barley, especially in the production of flour through roller milling; however, recommendations are limited for barley milling other than for pearling.

Blocking and pearling are processes whereby the outer barley grain tissues are gradually removed by an abrasive scouring action to produce an edible product for food. *Blocking*, sometimes referred to as *hulling* (*dehulling*), is usually the next processing step after cleaning. Blocking is designed to remove the tough, fibrous, and largely indigestible hull that adheres strongly to the kernel. The hull represents 10 to 13% of the dry weight of the kernel, but under some conditions, blocking in a commercial dehulling or pearling machine may remove as much as 20% of the kernel weight.

Dehulling machines are comprised of circular abrasive stones rotating on a vertical or horizontal axis in a cylindrical chamber surrounded by screens. The cylinder is strongly aspirated, and the degree of abrasion is governed by the counter pressure applied at the outlet, the abrasiveness of the stones, and the distance between the rotor and the surrounding screens. The *pearling* process that follows blocking is commonly done in three or more stages. The latter stage or stages are sometimes referred to as *polishing*. The degree of pearling, typically stated as a percentage, refers to the amount of the kernel removed during processing.

The primary food product of the pearling process is pearl barley. Commercially pearled barley usually represents approximately 60 to 70% of the original barley kernel and is the typical product used for soups and pilafs (a nutritional dish). It is also the material for further processing, including grinding, flaking, cutting, and roller milling. Blocked and pearled barley may be used for soups, stews, pilafs, and other dishes and also as a rice extender, as noted without further processing. Pearled barley may be lightly cooked or roasted through various processes to produce "quick-cooking" barley products. Pearling fractions can be produced utilizing various extraction rates that vary widely in their physical, chemical, and functional characteristics. Thus, the various layers removed as by-products in the pearling process can be utilized in formulating numerous end products, especially for the production of functional foods with defined health benefits.

10.8 PASTA/MACRONI PROCESSING

The basic forms of pasta products such as spaghetti, lasagna, macaroni, and other types of short goods, have not altered much over the centuries. Similarly, pasta continues to be made using the same ingredients: durum wheat semolina or flour, common wheat farina or flour, or various combinations of these, water and optional ingredients such as egg, spinach, tomato, herbs, etc. Modern processing technology, however, has changed dramatically. The large automated, computer controlled plants that we are familiar with today are very different from the small factories seen in the infancy of the modern pasta processing industry. Large amounts of pasta can now be processed in a day in modern plants that are run by only a few personnel. There are many reasons for the popularity of pasta but the most important ones are as follows:

- Pasta has an excellent nutritional profile. It is a good source of complex carbohydrates and a moderate source of protein and some vitamins. For example, a two-ounce portion of dry pasta contains about 210 calories and is about 75 percent carbohydrate, 13 percent protein, and 1.5 percent fat. In

- Pasta represents good consumer value and, as such, it sells well in both good and bad economic times.
- Dry packaged pasta is virtually non-perishable if stored appropriately.
- Pasta is easy to cook, has a wholesome taste, and an extensive variety of dishes can be prepared using the many different pasta shapes and sizes available.

Pasta manufacturers today produce many varieties of dried products with hundreds of shapes and sizes available. These products may be broadly classified as either short or long goods. Internationally, the most well-known long goods are spaghetti (of various diameters), fettuccini, and linguini. Elbowshaped- macaroni is probably the most familiar short good, along with penne and the many types of shells. Stamping the forms such as bow ties from an extruded thin sheet of dough produces another familiar group of short goods, Bolognatype pasta.

All types of pasta are prepared using a few common elements. In each instance, a semolina or flour is mixed with water to form a stiff dough. The dough is then shaped, usually by extrusion through various shaped dies. For dried pasta the formed product is dried to between 12 percent to 13 percent moisture content.

The main ingredient of premium quality pasta is 100 percent durum wheat semolina. Semolina, which originates from the endosperm of durum wheat, is essentially coarse flour. Good quality pasta can also be made with durum wheat flour or a blend of semolina and durum wheat flour (granular). Pasta can be produced using common (soft or bread) wheat farina or flour, but is generally inferior in appearance (color) and cooking quality to pasta made from durum wheat.

In the first stage of the process, semolina and water are initially combined in a premixer (normal range 25–30 kg of water per 100 kg semolina15). The amount of semolina, water and other optional ingredients (such as eggs, enrichment, spinach, herbs, etc.) are measured and dispensed using various types of dosers depending on equipment manufacturer. The product of a conventional pasta mixer is not a cohesive dough, but rather a mixture of agglomerated lumps of semolina. This mixture, through the action of mixing paddles or kneading blades, passes from the mixing chamber to the extrusion chamber and extrusion worm where the dough is formed and developed under pressures in the range of 80–120 kg/cm^2.

Dough temperature during the extrusion process should not increase above about 50°C to prevent damage to the gluten network, and consequently to final product cooking quality. Heat, generated by the pressure and friction created during the extrusion process, must be dissipated through cooling to prevent inordinately high dough temperatures. Mixing and extrusion chambers operate under vacuum to minimize oxidation of the carotenoid or xanthophyll pigments. Oxidation of these pigments is known to decrease the yellow color of finished pasta.

In addition, the vacuum prevents air bubble formation, which can give rise to defects and an unsightly appearance in the dried product. The product must now be dried down to a moisture of around 12.5 percent to ensure that it is strong and will have a long storage life. The drying process itself must be managed carefully to attain a uniform rate of water removal. Cooled short goods are conveyed into bins in preparation for packaging. In the case of long goods, following cooling the product passes through the stick stacker where the product is removed from the sticks, and onto the stripper-saw that then cuts the pasta with high-speed saws. Packaging is a most important process since it protects the product from breakage or contamination before delivery and sale.

9.9 BAKED PRODUCTS

Baked products are foods manufactured from recipes largely based on or containing significant quantities of wheat or other cereal flours which are blended with other ingredients, are formed into distinctive shapes and undergo a heat-processing step which involves the removal of moisture in an oven located in a bakery.

Classification of Bakery Ingredients based upon their Functions

1. **Structure Builders :** They provide the structure and texture to the cake *e.g.* flour, eggs, milk
2. **Tenderizers :** They provide softness and shortness in the product *e.g.* fat, sugar, baking powder
3. **Moisteners :** They provide moisture and keeping quality *e.g.* milk, water, eggs, syrup
4. **Driers :** They absorb and retain moisture and provide the body of the product *e.g.* milk solids and starches
5. **Flavours :** They provide natural flavour *e.g.* cocoa, chocolate, butter, eggs and other natural flavour bearing ingredients.

Various Ingredients used in Baking

The different ingredients used in baking are:

1. Flour : Wheat flour is the basic structural component of most batter and dough products. It performs the textural function because of gluten content, which allows expansion of air cells and provide rigidity after baking. pH of satisfactory flour is usually between 5.5-6.5. Commercially flour is obtained from two types of wheat:

(*a*) ***Hard Wheat*** : It is mostly desirable in bread production. They mill well and yield good quantities of flour that is high in good quality protein from which strong elastic dough can be made. Hard wheat dough has high water absorption capacity, excellent gas holding properties and will yield bread with good volume, grain and texture

(*b*) ***Soft Wheat*** : It is low in protein and yields flour having low water absorption capacity and poor tolerance to mixing and fermentation. They are undesirable for bread production but are highly desirable in production of cakes, pastries and cookies

2. Sugar : It imparts sweet taste. It has tenderizing action on flour proteins and it makes the cake tender. Sugar helps to retain moisture in cakes, which improve its shelf life. Other uses of sugar are:

- Serves as a form of food for yeast in fermentation
- Assists in the creaming and whipping process of mixing
- Provides good grain texture in the product
- Promotes a good crust colour
- Adds nutritional value to food
- Increases gas production
- Used in preparation of icings

3. Shortenings : Fat lubricates the structure of a baked product. These are essential ingredients of most types of bakery products which shorten pastry, cake, *i.e.* any fat fit for such use *e.g.* lard, butter and some vegetable oils like coconut oil, corn oil, peanut oil and soyabean oil. Uses of shortenings are:

- Impart shortness, richness and tenderness to the product
- Provide aeration
- Promote a desirable grain and structure
- Act as emulsifiers for holding liquids
- Improve the eating qualities
- Contribute to flavour
- Develop flakiness in product

4. Leavening Agents : Leavening agents contribute significantly to the textural properties of baked goods by expanding the batter or dough, sometimes during mixing and always during baking. Various leavening agents used are:

(*a*) ***Yeast* :** Function of yeast in bread making is to lighten the dough and impart it a characteristic aroma and flavour. Generally four kinds of yeasts are available to the bakers- living yeast for leavening, dead dried yeast for nutritional and flavour enhancement, baker's yeast for white bread and food yeast for rye bread. Baker's yeast is an oval shaped, one-celled and colourless microscopic plant called *Saccharomyces cerevisae.*

(*b*) ***Baking Soda* :** It is chemically known as 'sodium bicarbonate'. It liberate CO_2 gas, a leavening gas when heated. If soda alone is used as a leavening agent, a residue of washing soda will remain in the cake. This residue when present in excess gives the dark colour and taste

(*c*) ***Baking Powder* :** Baking powder is the combination of sodium bicarbonate and an acid salt when moistened and heating will evolve gas which leavens the product giving it volume and making light and easy to digest. Baking powder is of 3 type:

- *Fast Acting* : It releases most of its CO_2 gas during bench operation and all the gas is released during baking *i.e.* mixing operation
- *Slow Acting* : They do not release much of gas during bench operation and all the gas is released when it comes in contact with heat
- *Double Acting* : This is most widely used by bakers. This baking powder releases part of gas during bench operation, increasing fluidity of cake batter. The remaining of CO_2 gas is released in the oven, which gives volume to the end product.

5. Eggs : Most important function of eggs is to provide structure to the cake. Other functions of eggs are:

- Binding action
- Emulsifying action
- Colour
- Leavening action
- Flavour
- Nutritive value

6. Salt : Common salt is used for bringing out the flavour of other ingredients, which are used in cakes and to impart taste to the bread and other products. Functions of salt are:

- Increases gluten stability
- Develops flavour
- Contributes to the crust and crumb formation
- Controls fermentation
- Retains water

Common English dictionary definitions for groups of baked products include:

- Bread – *n.* food made of flour or meal (and) baked
- Cake – *n.* baked, sweetened bread
- Biscuit – *n.* dry, small, thin variety of cake
- Pastry – *n.* article of food made chiefly of flour, fat, sugar and water

Table 8. Types of wheat flour and their characteristics

Sr. No.	Type of Wheat Flour	Specific Characteristics
1.	Bread flour	• Flour with high level of good quality protein • Protein content: 10.8 - 11.3% (Mechanical process) 11.8- 12.3% (Fermentation process)
2.	Biscuit flour	• Milled from weak wheat of low protein content • Protein content: 8 - 9.5%
3.	Household flour	• Weak wheat of low protein content with admixture of up to 20% of strong wheat
4.	Self-raising flour	• Flour with added raising agents • Moisture should not exceed 1330. to avoid premature reaction of aerating chemical
5.	Flour forconfectionery	*Cakes* • Undamaged starch granules, free from adhered protein and unattached by amylases • Protein content: 8.5-9.5% • Panicle size 90 μ *Buns* • Bread nuking flour *Pastry* • Strong baker's flour
6.	Flour for soups	• Steamed flour in which enzymes have been inactivated
7.	Flour for sausagerusk	• Low protein flour milled from weak wheat
8.	Batter flour	• Low protein flour milled from grist comprising 90% weak wheat and 10% strong wheat

9.8.1 Bread Making

Ingredients and their Functions in Bread Making

Essential ingredients

1. **Flour:** Flour is essential to the structure of dough and subsequently the bread. Gluten (Gladin and Glutenin) is the principle functional protein of wheat flour. Gluten forms fibrillar frame work when hydrated and mechanically worked. Thus the wheat live is converted into cohesive, elastic, extensible dough. This viscoelastic three-dimensional gluten network retains gas formed by sugar fermentation and contributes to structure of dough and bread.

   Starch plays important role in dough during baking. When heat is applied, gas cells expand gluten networks stretches, starch granules take up water and get partially gelatinized. This viscous paste sets to gel after baking. Satisfactory protein content for bread flour is 11 - 13% and moisture content not mote than 14%.

2. **Water:** Water hydrates gluten proteins during mixing, gelatinizes starch during baking and serves as a dispersion medium for other ingredients such as yeast. Quality of water such as pH and hardness of water play important role in dough formation. Excessively alkaline water can retard the activity of yeast enzymes. Hard water containing calcium and magnesium ions, may have a "tightening" effect and soft water a "loosening" effect on dough.

3. **Veen:** Yeast produces carbon dioxide and ethanol by fermentation of fermentable sugars. During fermentation it also helps in formation of flavour precursors. Rate of fermentation of dough by yeast is controlled by temperature, nutrient supply, water, pH, sugar concentration, salt and level and type of yeast. Generally two type of yeasts are used in baking: Compressed yeast and dried yeast. Both the types consist of living cells of *Sorcharomyces cerevisiae*
4. **Salt:** Salt eats a flavour enhancer and helps control the fermentation by yeast. It also toughens the gluten and gives less sticky dough.

There are two procedures of bread making:

1. **Straight Dough Method :** It is the simplest method for bread making. In this method, all the formula ingredients are mixed into developed dough that is then allowed to ferment. During fermentation, the dough is usually punched one or more times. After fermentation, it is divided into loaf-sized pieces, round moulded into loaf shape and placed into the baking pan
2. **Sponge and Dough Process :** In this, part of the flour, part of the water and the yeast are mixed just enough to form a loose dough (sponge) which is allowed to ferment upto 5 hrs. Then it is combined with the rest of the formula ingredients and mixed into a developed dough.

Basic operations in bread making are:

1. Sieving
2. Weighing
3. Preparation of Different Solutions
4. **Mixing :** The main purpose of mixing a dough is to make and develop gluten. The different stages of mixing are:
   (*a*) Pick-up stage (*b*) Clean-up stage
   (*c*) Development stage (*d*) Final stage
   (*e*) Let-down stage (*f*) Break-down stage
5. **Fermentation :** Bread fermentation is an anaerobic process. Thus, little growth of yeast occurs during dough fermentation. The process of fermentation starts just after mixing and it increases during interproofing and final proofing
6. **Knock Back :** It has the objective of equalizing the dough temperature throughout the mass, reducing the retarding effect of excessive accumulation of CO_2 within the dough mass and introduces O_2 for the stimulation of yeast activity
7. Scaling or Dividing
8. Rounding
9. **Intermediate Proof :** The loss of gas during scaling and rounding is compensated by submitting the dough pieces to an extra fermentation period of 5-30 min at 80-85°F and 75% RH.
10. **Moulding:** It is also called panning. The pan should be greased with 0.1-0.2% pan oil. The pan temperature is 90°F. The optimum panning should be carried out so that seam of the dough is placed on the bottom of the pan. Moulding is done for the removal of extra gas formed by fermentation at the time of intermediate proofing

11. **Final Proof :** Final proofing is done at a temperature of 95°F at 85% RH for 55-65 min. The objectives of final proofing are:
   - To relax the dough from the stress received during fermentation operation
   - To facilitate production of gas in order to give volume to the bread
   - To change tough bulky gluten to a good mellow extensible character
12. **Baking :** Normally, bread is baked at a temperature of 240-250 °C for 30 min. During baking, the dough volume will continue to increase. The purpose of baking is to transform unpalatable dough into a light porous and readily digestible flavoured product.
13. **Cooling and Slicing :** After baking, the loaves have to cool down to room temperature so that they do not dry excessively. Other purposes of cooling before slicing and wrapping are to:
   - Facilitate slicing
   - Prevent condensation of moisture in the wrapper
   - Desirable temperature of bread during slicing is 95-105 °F
14. **Packaging :** For bread wrapping, mostly wax paper or polypropylene is extensively used

The process of bread manufacturing is shown by flow diagram in Fig,. 6.

Major Bread Faults and Causes

1. **Volume :** A small volume of bread may be due to:
   - Tight dough
   - Little yeast and fermentation time
   - Low temperature
   - Under proofing
   - Lack of diastatic activity

   Excess volume can be due to:
   - Over fermentation
   - Lack of salt in formula
   - Excessive yeast and proofing time
   - Loose moulding
   - Lack of temperature in oven
2. **Crust Colour :** Pale crust is caused due to:
   - Yeast is added in excess
   - Insufficient humidity during proofing
   - Underbaking
   - Poor diastatic activity
   - Old dough

   Crust colour shall be too dark due to:
   - Addition of more sugar
   - Addition of more milk
   - Over baking
   - High oven temperature
   - Old dough

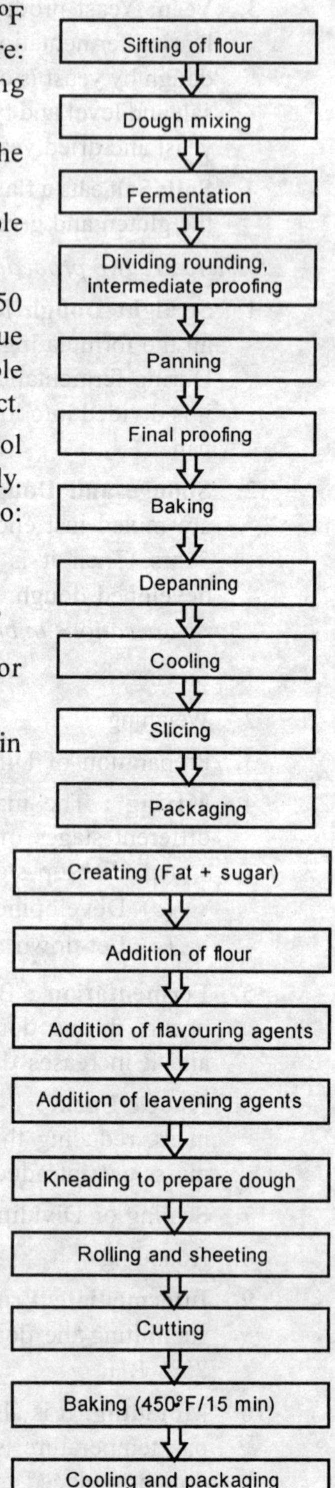

Fig. 6: Flow diagram for bread manufacture

3. **Leathery Crust :** The crust of bread should be crisp and should easily break but if the crust becomes tough and is not easily pulled, it is leathery. It is due to insufficient conditioning of gluten or if crust absorbs a lot of moisture

4. **Blisters under crust :** This can be due to:
   - Over proofing
   - Excessive steam or humidity in proof box
   - Improper handling during baking
   - Tight moulding

5. **Very Thick Crust :** It is caused due to:
   - Use of less shortening in the formula
   - Less sugar in the formula
   - Less moisture during proofing
   - Low oven temperature
   - Overbaking

6. **Flinty Crust or Shell Tops :** Sometimes crust of bread is hard and breaks like an egg shell called as flinty crust. This is generally with strong wheat's flour where the flour is insufficiently fermented.

7. **Wild Break :** If the gluten is not adequately conditioned during fermentation, the top crust instead of rising gradually will burst open under pressure of expanding gas. Insufficient proofing and excessive heat are likely to give wild break

8. **Sticky Crumb :** It may be due to sprout damaged wheat flour if it is proved or baked in excessive humid conditions and under baked

9. **Crumbiness of the crumb :** It may be due to:
   - Too slack or tight dough
   - Excessive use of fat
   - Low salt oontent
   - Excessive use of mineral improvers

10. **Holes and tunnels in bread:** It may be due to:
    - Use of weak flour
    - High yeast content in formula
    - Improper dispersion of ingredients
    - Too hot oven base
    - Under mixing or over mixing

11. **Irregularity :** Loose moulding or moulding with uneven pressure results in large air pockets in the folds

12. **Deficiency of Bloom :** It is due to poor diastatic activity of flour

13. **Colour Spots :** It is due to carelessness on the part of baker, unclean moulds, handling bread with unclean hands, etc.

14. ***Poor Flavour and Taste*** **:** It is due to:
    - Improper storage of raw ingredients
    - Poor quality ingredients
    - Unfermented or over proofed dough
    - Dirty moulds or pans
    - Cooling of bread under unsanitary conditions

15. **Ropy Bread :** It is caused by *Bacillus mesentricus*

16. **Staling of Bread :** If the bread is stored for a number of days, certain changes occur which causes staling of bread. These are:

    (*i*) ***Crust Staling*** **:** During crust staling, moisture from the crumb is transferred to the crust and due to hygroscopic properties, the crust absorbs moisture and becomes soft and leathery (*ii*) ***Crumb Staling*** : It is associated with the gradual and spontaneous aggregation of the amylopectin giving rise to crystalline structure. Due to loss of moisture, the crumb becomes hard and more crumbly

9.8.2 Baked Product Made from Soft Wheat (Biscuits, Cake)

Types of Cookies

Cookies : Cookies are one of the best known quick snack products. They are characterized by a formula high in sugar and shortening and low in water.

Crackers : Cracker is a term used for biscuits of low sugar and fat content; frequently bland or savoury. They are usually made from strong flour and developed dough. Crackers and crisp breads are used as bread substitutes usually topped with savoury foods like cheese, meat preparations, etc.

Biscuits : This is one processed wheat product which has found acceptability in rural areas in our country. The raw materials for biscuits are flour, sugar and shortening. The steps involved in biscuit making are:

(*i*) Mixing and Kneading (*ii*) Sheeting and Shaping

(*iii*) Baking and Cooling (*iv*) Packaging

Cakes: Cakes are characterized by high levels of sugar in the formula in which starch gelatinizes during baking. There are 2 types of cakes:

(*i*) **Unshortened :** These cakes do not contain fat as a basic ingredient. They are leavened by air or steam *e.g.* sponge cake

(*ii*) **Shortened :** These cakes contains shortening or butter as an essential ingredient. They are leavened with baking powder. *e.g.* chocolate cake, pound cake, etc.

Suggestions for Cookies Making

- Cookie dough should be mixed just enough to blend the ingredients homogenously. When the dough is slightly overmixed, gluten tends to develop which will retard the spread of cookies. Improper mixing of ingredients will produce cookies that are spotted
- Proper mixing of sugar and shortening is very important for optimum cookie spread.
- Cookies should be placed enough apart on the pans to avoid sticking during baking
- If the cookie is cut thick, the finished cookie will lose the appearance and flavour also
- When the pans are greased, the cookie will spread more. To retard spreading, dust the pans with flour after they are greased
- In order to obtain best results, cookies should be removed from the oven while they are still soft as they will continue to bake in hot pans

9.8.3 Cake Making Methods

Sugar batter method

In this method fat is creamed and then sugar is added gradually. When adequate aeration is achieved, flour is added in the mixture along with raising agents. There should be minimum mixing action to avoid gluten formation. When all flour is mixed, remaining liquid is added to the batter to necessary consistency.

Flour batter method

In this method fat and quantity of flour not exceeding the weight of fat is creamed together. Eggs and an equal quantity of sugar are whipped to a stiff froth. Then remaining sugar is dissolved in water or milk and added to the mixture. Lastly remaining flour along with baking powder is added and mixed gently.

Blending method

This is used for formulations containing more sugar than quantity of flour. All ingredients except sugar and milk are mixed together. Sugar, milk, colour and flavours are mixed and added to previous mixture followed by eggs and mixed to form a smooth batter.

Boiled method

Flour (more than two third portions) is added to melted butter or margarine and mixed well. Eggs are whisked with sugar followed by addition of colour and flavor. This is added to flour- fat mixture in equal parts, mixing thoroughly at each stage. Remaining flour is also added at this stage.

Sugar water

Method Initially sugar is dissolved in water followed by addition of all other ingredients except eggs. Finally eggs are added and whisked well.

All in process

In this method, all the ingredients are put into the mixing bowl together. Aeration of the mixture is achieved by controlling the speed of mixer as well as mixing time. The batter is then put in greased pan. Only 2/3rd height of mould should be filled. Load the batter containing pan into oven as soon as possible. Bake the cake at 375° - 400°F for 25-30 min.

Different Types of Cakes Made

1. **Sponge Cake :** They do not contain any added fat or shortening. Whole egg is used in sponge cake. Sponge cakes depend mainly upon the whipping of eggs for their lightness on aeration. There are 2 types of sponge cakes:
   (*a*) *Straight Sponge* : These contain eggs, sugar, flour, salt and flavour
   (*b*) *Short Sponge* : These contain the ingredients of a straight sponge and milk, shortening, water, leavening, etc.
2. **Angel Cake :** It is a foam-type cake which depends mainly on egg white protein for the bulk of the structure of the finished volume. It is a cake without shortening. The basic ingredients for angel cake are flour, sugar and egg. They should be free from fat and yolk in order to give a good volume. Granulated sugar gives good results
3. **Pound Cake :** It is a shortened cake with fat as an essential ingredient. Air is used for leavening purpose. The original formula for a pound cake was one pound each of flour, butter, eggs and sugar. This made a very heavy, rich and expensive cake. A good shortened cake has fine grain cells of uniform size, thin cell walls and a crumb that is more elastic than crumbly.

9.8.4 Kulcha Bread

1. Mix 2.5 cups all-purpose flour (maida), ¾ teaspoon salt, 2 to 2.5 teaspoons sugar, ½ teaspoon baking powder and ¼ teaspoon baking soda in a bowl. Make a well in the center.
2. Add 4 tablespoons yogurt (curd), 2.5 tablespoons oil and approximately ¾ cup water.
3. Begin to mix the flour with the liquids first and then start to knead.
4. Make a smooth, supple and soft dough.
5. In the same bowl or pan, cover the dough with a wet kitchen napkin. You can also lightly brush some water on the dough and cover the pan with a lid.
6. Let the dough leaven for 2 hours.
7. Lightly knead the leavened dough again.
8. Make small balls of the dough and lightly flatten them. Sprinkle some nigella seeds or sesame seeds on the dough ball.
9. Heat a skillet or tawa on medium-high to high heat. The tawa or skillet has to be very hot. Place the kulcha on the tawa.
10. Flip and cook the other side till it is ½ cooked. Apply oil or ghee on both sides of kulcha while cooking.
11. Flip a few times as needed and roast till the kulcha gets golden spots and is evenly cooked. Prepare more kulchas in a similar way.

9.8.5 Idli Making

Firstly there are two basic ways you can make idli with the traditional method of soaking the ingredients, grinding them to a batter and fermenting.

With Idli Rice: Traditionally idli rice and urad dal are used to make the idli batter. Idli rice is parboiled rice and used specifically for making idli and dosa. This recipe post shares the method of making idli with idli rice and regular white rice.

With Idli Rava: A second easier way is to use idli rava with urad dal. Idli rava is coarsely ground idli rice and is easily available in shops and online.

Soaking rice and lentils: For making simple traditional idli, both the rice and the urad dal are rinsed a couple of times with fresh water and soaked separately for 4 to 5 hours.

Quality of rice and urad dal: Make sure to use both rice and urad dal within their shelf-period. Always use urad dal which is fresh and within its shelf-life. Aged urad dal does not ferment well and makes the idli dense.

Grinding: Then the lentils (urad dal) are ground to a soft, fluffy batter and the rice to a semi-fine consistency. Both the batters are mixed and allowed to ferment.

The amount of water to be added in a stone-grinder is more than what is added in a mixer-grinder. For ½ cup soaked urad dal, you can add about 1 cup water. Add water in parts while grinding urad dal. For 2 cups of soaked rice, add about 1.5 to 2 cups of water.

Fermentation: Both the ground lentil batter and rice batter are mixed thoroughly. Then the batter is kept to ferment overnight or for 8 to 9 hours or more till the batter doubles or triples in volume having a pleasant sour aroma. The fermentation largely depends upon the temperature and climate. A warm temperature is conducive for a good fermentation in the batter.

Steaming: Special pans are used to steam the idli. You can buy these pans online. This idli pan is brushed or greased with some oil. The batter is poured in the pan and then steamed.

Steaming time: The steaming time varies from 12 to 15 minutes. Idli should never be oversteamed as then they become dry and dense.

CHAPTER 10

SPICES PROCESSING

10.1 INTRODUCTION

A spice is a seed, fruit, root, bark, berry, bud or other vegetable substance primarily used for flavouring , colouring or preserving food. Spices are distinguished from herbs, which are parts of leafy green plants used for flavouring or as a garnish. Many spices have antimicrobial properties. Spices produce a vast and diverse assortment of organic compounds, the great majority of which do not appear to participate directly in growth and development. Condiments are added to a dish to add or complement its flavour. They are often prepared mixes (like mustard or soy sauce), although the broad definition can include spices (*e.g.* pepper).

Spices and condiments are defined as "Vegetable products or mixtures, free from extraneous matter, used for flavouring, seasoning or imparting aroma in foods." Herbs are a subset of spices, generally derived from fresh or dried leaves, but in this guide no distinction is made between spices and herbs, in keeping with the International Standards Organization (ISO) definition. Essential oils or extracts are also derived from these plant sources either as a primary processing or a secondary opportunity.

Spices are used for flavour, colour, aroma and preservation of food or beverages. Spices may be derived from many parts of the plant: bark, buds, flowers, fruits, leaves, rhizomes, roots, seeds, stigmas and styles or the entire plant tops. The term 'herb' is used as a subset of spice and refers to plants with aromatic leaves. Spices are often dried and used in a processed but in complete state. Another option is to prepare extracts such as essential oils by distilling the raw spice material (wet or dry), or to use solvents to extract oleoresins and other standardized products.

A spice may be available in several forms: fresh, whole dried, or pre-ground dried. Generally, spices are dried.

There are a large number of various spices, used along with food such as pepper, chill, cardamom, cinnamon, mustard, cloves, ginger, turmeric, coriander etc. These spices give taste to the prepared food and at the same time give attractive colours and smell to the food. So the usage of some or all of these spices during cooking is now became an unavoidable one.

Essential oils are liquid products of steam or water distillation of plant parts (leaves, stems, bark, seeds, fruits, roots and plant exudates). Expression is used exclusively for the extraction of citrus oil from the fruit peel, because the chemical components of the oil are easily damaged by heat. Citrus oil production is now a major by-product process of the juice industry. An essential oil may contain up to several hundred chemical compounds and this complex mixture of compounds gives the oil its characteristic fragrance and flavour. An essential oil may also be fractioned and sold as individual natural components. Other processing options can also produce further products that can be sold alongside essential oils. The plant parts can be extracted with organic solvents to produce oleoresins, concretes and absolutes or extracted with a near or supercritical solvent such as carbon dioxide to produce very high quality extracts. These oleoresins and extracts contain not only the volatile essential oil but also the concentrated non-volatile flavour components and these have wide application in the food and pharmaceutical industries. The solvent extraction processes are more difficult and complex than steam distillation and will normally be beyond the financial resources of most small scale processors.

Spices can be added to foods in several forms: as whole spices, as ground spices, as essential oils, as oleoresins or as prepared and filtered vinegar infusions. A more recent alternative is spice extracts. These consist of the flavour components of a spice, dispersed on one of several types of base, the most suitable bases for pickle and sauce use, for example, being salt or dextrose. Natural materials used in flavour creations are still most often isolated from essential oils. Extraction of oils and oleoresins is accomplished using a range of methods, including:

Grinding an herb or spice to a specified particle size using standardized sieve apertures is a normal processing activity. Grinding gives easier mixing in the final food product and aids the dispersion of flavour throughout the food. A food manufacturer will have specific particle size requirements and the processor will have to mill the herb or spice through sieves that will obtain the fineness required. There are specific examples. White pepper is produced by removing the pericarp (fruit wall) from ripe pepper fruits, and then grinding. White pepper is traditionally prepared by steeping ripe fruits in water for a few days, rubbing to remove the pericarp, washing and drying. The berries that are beginning to ripen are put into bags and soaked in water to soften the pericarp, which is then washed off and the seeds dried in the sun. Soaking tanks and clean water produces pepper of higher quality.

For black pepper, berries are harvested when mature green, de-spiked and dried in the sun. For both black and white pepper, the quality of the product is dependent on the weather, as almost all the pepper is sun-dried. Efforts to improve quality by cleaning out foreign matter, stalks, and light berries by simple sieves and blowers reduce the amounts transported and increase the value. Ground pepper is obtained by grinding pepper with equipment like a hammer-mill. The pepper is first fluidized for the removal of extraneous matter and then passed through screens.

Extraction of essential oils: The extraction of essential oils from plant material can be achieved by a number of different methods . There are five main methods of extraction:

- steam distillation
- hydrocarbon extraction
- chlorinated solvent extraction
- enzymatic treatment and fermentation
- Super critical carbon dioxide extraction.

Functional foods have been defined as "foods that provide benefit beyond basic nutrition." The definition applies to foods rather than drugs and implies a benefit beyond that supplied from calories or basic nutrition alone, including the provision of minimum required levels of vitamins and minerals. The Dietary Guidelines have recognized the concept of foods being eaten not only for the prevention of deficiencies, but to provide optimal health and to reduce the risks of common age-related chronic diseases. These benefits are likely to result from healthy dietary patterns, and the interaction of multiple compounds found in foods such as fruits, vegetables, nuts, grains, and spices. This is a relatively new area of nutrition science investigation but one that holds great promise.

Table 1: Important flavour compounds in spices

Sr. N.	*Common Name*	*Botanical Name*	*Family*	*Origin*	*Plant Part Used*	*Important Chemical content*	*Essential oil%*	*2n. no.*
1.	Black pepper	*Piper nigrum*	Piperaceae	Indo-burma	Fruit, seed	Piperine	1-3	128
2.	Cardamom (small)	*Elettaria cardamomum*	Zingibraceae	India	Fruit seed	Cineol		48
3.	Ginger	*Zingiber officinale*	Zingibera-ceae	South east Asia	Rhizome	Zingiberene	1.9-2.2	22
4.	Turmeric	*Curcuma longa*	Zingibera-ceae	South east Asia	Rhizome	Curcumine	0.24	62
5.	Cinnamon	*Cinnamomum verum*	Lauraceae	Srilanka	Bark	Cinamaldehyde	.5-2	24
6.	Nutmeg	*Myristica fragrans*	Myrsticaceae	Indonesia	Seed, Aril	Terbein	–	–
7.	Clove	*Syzygium aromaticum*	Myrtaceae flower	Indonesia	Unopened flower bud	Eugenol	–	44
8.	All spice	*Pimenta dioca*	Myrtaceae	West Indies	Fruit seed	Phenol	–	–
9.	Curry leaf	*Murraya koenigi*	Rutaceae	India	Leaves	Koenigine	–	18
10.	Asafoetida	*Ferulla foetida*	Apiaceae	Iran	Oleoresin Gum	Ferumine	10-17	–
11.	Saffron	*Crocus sativus*	Iridaceae	India	Stigma	Cicrocrocin	0.5-1.0	–
12.	Dill	*Anethum graveolens*	Apiaceae	Eurasia	Fruit	Carvone	1.5-4.0	–
13.	Coriander	*Coriandrum sativum*	Apiaceae	Mediteranean region	Leaves, seed	Linalool	0.1-1.0	22
14.	Cumin	*Cuminum cyminum*	Apiaceae	Mediteranean region	Fruit	Cuminol	2.5-3.5	14
15.	Fennel	*Foeniculum vulgare*	Apiaceae	Mediteranean region	Fruit	Limone	0.7-1.2	–
16.	Aniseed	*Pimpinella anisum*	Apiaceae	Mediteranean region	Fruit	Anithol	–	–
17.	Bishop's weed		Apiaceae	Mediteranean region	Fruit	Thynol	–	–
18.	Vanilla	*Vanilla planifolia*	Orchidaceae	America	Fruit	Vanillin	–	–
19.	Fenugreek	*Trigonella foenum-graceum*	Fabaceae	Europe	Seed	Diosgenin	–	–
20.	Large cardamom	*Amomum subulatum*	Zingiberaceae	India	Fruit seed	Cineal		

10.2 PROCESSING OF IMPORTANT SPICES

10.2.1 Processing of Coriander Powder

- Coriander is an aromatic spice, popularly referred to as Dhania.
- Coriander, *Coriandrum sativum*, is an erect annual herb in the family Apiaceae.
- Coriander is an annual plant, surviving only one growing season and reaches up to 50 cm
- Within 90 to 135 days, the coriander crop matures.
- To prevent shedding losses, the correct harvesting time is in the morning hours.
- Coriander is commonly found both as whole dried seeds and in ground form.
- Ground coriander seed loses flavor quickly in storage and is the best ground fresh.
- The fruit is globular, 3 to 4 mm in diameter, and splits into two locules of one seed each when pressed.
- To sweet and savory food recipes, it gives a slight flavor and fragrance.

Traditional methods:

- Cleaning of seed is done through a wind-based separator.
- Seeds are further dried in the shade to bring the moisture levels down to 9%.
- The second drying stage should be in the shade to prevent over-heating of the seeds.
- Traditionally, grading has been done through sieves by laborers.
- Traditional Chakki has lower yield efficiency which leads to a loss in form of ground powder.
- The packaging of coriander is done in polybags.

Modern method:

- This method involves Pre-Cleaner, Gravity Separator.
- There are modern machines like color sorters available for grading the coriander seeds not only on the basis of shape and size but also shape.
- The latest type of pulverizer includes classified material is conveyed into the cyclone for collection and bagging.
- The packaging is involved in pouch is developed using quality materials.
- Sun drying is necessary to remove the moisture from plants and seeds under the sun. Threshing of seed spices:
  - After proper drying, the coriander plant is taken to the threshing process.
- The typical aroma and flavor of coriander seed are not fully developed until it is completely dry.

Grinding: The process is the final stage where the dried seeds of coriander are grounded. It is turn into a fine powder which is further processed by Pulverizing

Pulverizing: It's a type of grinding process which grinds the given product to a very fine-sized powder. A dust collector is provided in the system for ensuring dust-less operation and for no loss of ground powder.

Packaging: The finished product is then packaged and stored for supply.

10.2.2 Chilli Processing

Traditionally, matured gathered chillies are dried in the open yards for 15 to 20 days. The cycle includes dunking the red chillies in an uncommonly arranged "Dipsol" arrangement followed by sun drying. Dipsol is a water-based emulsion containing potassium carbonate,

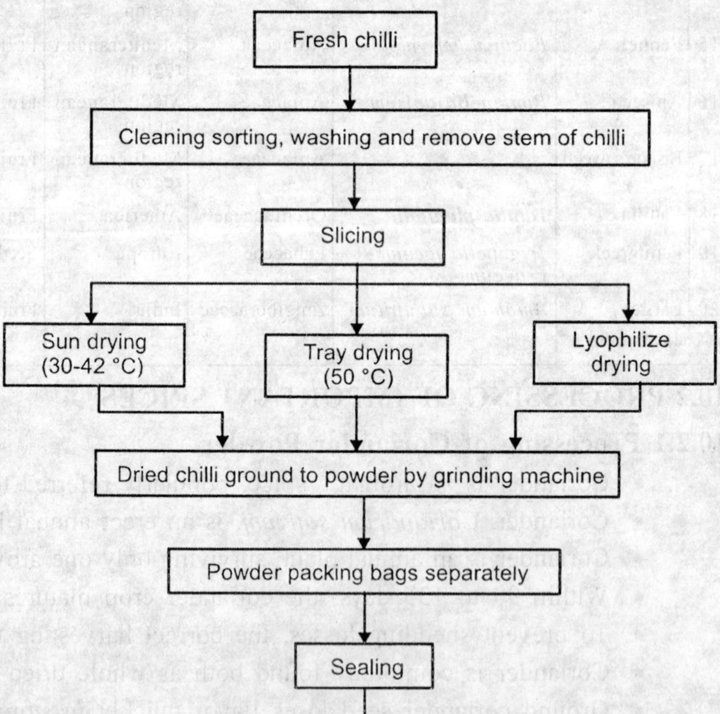

Fig. 1: Diagrammatic Reepresentation for Processing of Chilli Powder

refined groundnut oil, gum acacia and butylated hydroxyanisole. This cycle holds the sharpness and normal tone bringing about better yields. The method guarantees a steady finished result. Depending upon the type and size of chilli, drying time varies. Wash chillies thoroughly under running tap water. Wipe off the water droplets and arrange chillies lengthwise on the baking tray. Turn on the oven then put it on a low temperature around 100°C. Keep turning the pods every hour for uniform drying. Ideal temperature for drying is 80 °C for 8 hours for most of chilli varieties. After drying store them in an airtight container in cool and dark place.

Processing of Chilli Powder: It is shown diagrametically in Fig. 1.

10.2.3. Cardamom Processing

Types of cardamom There are two main types of cardamom:

(*i*) Small green cardamom (*Eletteria cardamomum*)

(*ii*) Large red/black cardamom (*Amomum subulatum Roxb*).

The most common type is the small green cardamom while large cardamom is mainly grown in India, with some in Nepal and Bhutan. They both come from the Zingiberaceae family of plants.

Harvesting: Harvesting at the correct stage of maturity is essential to produce high quality cardamom capsules. The fruits should only be harvested once they are fully ripe and mature.

Cleaning: The crop should be cleaned before processing. The first stage is to remove dust and dirt using a winnowing basket. This can be made locally from bamboo, palm or other leaves.

Washing: The capsules are washed throughly in water to remove any soil that has adhered to them.

Pre-treatment: After washing, the stalks are removed from the cardamom capsules by hand. The capsules can be soaked in a solution of sodium bicarbonate (2-5%) for ten minutes to help retain the green colour. This is an optional step. A 2% solution of sodium bicarbonate is prepared by dissolving 20g (about 4 tea spoons) of sodium bicarbonate in 1 litre of water

Drying: This is the most important part of the process as it affects the quality of the final product. It is important to dry the cardamom capsules as soon after harvest as possible to prevent the loss of flavour. It is also important that the drying process is as short as possible so that mould does not grow on the capsules and the bright green colour is retained. The drying temperature should not be above 50°C as this affects the colour and delicate flavour of the final product. In most places, cardamom capsules with a good green colour can be sold for a premium price. The moisture content of a fresh cardamom capsule is about 85%. This needs to be reduced to 10% in the dried product so the cardamom capsules can be stored. If the drying period is too long mould can start to grow on the cardamom. There are several options available to the smallscale processor, depending upon the size of the business and the local weather conditions at the time of processing.

Each method has different advantages and disadvantages.

- Sun drying.
- Solar drying (Solar cardamom dryer)
- Wood-fired dryer.
- Electric or gas dryer.
- Humidity-controlled drying.

Grading: Cardamom is graded by colour and size. The deeper the green colour and the larger the capsule size, the higher the grade. All grading is done by hand. The Indian grading system for cardamom capsules separates them into different types:

- Alleppey Green Cardamom
- Coorg Green Cardamom
- Bleached or Half-bleached Cardamom
- Bleached White Cardamom

- Mixed Cardamom

Grinding : Cardamom capsules are usually sold whole. Grinding can be a method of adding value to a product. However, it is not advisable to grind spices. After grinding, spices are more vulnerable to spoilage.

Packaging: Cardamom capsules can be packaged in polythene bags of various sizes according to the market demand. The bags should be sealed to prevent moisture entering. Sealing machines can be used to seal the bags. Attractive labels should be applied to the products.

Storage: Dried cardamom capsules must be stored in moisture-proof containers away from direct sunlight. For long term bulk storage, polythene-lined gunny bags (strong sacks made from jute fibres) inside wooden boxes are used.

11.2.4 Clove Processing

Harvesting Clove trees are first harvested when the tree is 6-8 years old. The timing of harvest of the clove buds is critical. The buds should be harvested before the purple or crimson flowers start to develop. The correct time of harvest is when the outer green leaves (the calyx) of the flower bud change from olive green to yellow pink and before the petals fall to expose the stamens. Clusters of flower buds are hand-picked from the branches. It is important that the branches are not removed or damaged as this will reduce the yield of future crops.

Pre-treatment: After harvest the buds are detached from the stalks by holding a cluster in one hand, pressing it against the palm of the other hand and slowly twisting so that the buds fall off. The hands of the processor and the room in which the buds are separated must be very clean to prevent contamination of the cloves. The stems and buds are separated and dried separately. The stems can be used for oil distillation.

Drying: The buds have to be dried quickly or they will start to ferment. They are usually dried in the sun, spread on clean mats. The cloves should be raked and turned frequently to ensure they develop an even brown colour. The colour of buds changes from pale russet to a darker brown as the clove dries. The drying process takes about four to five days. It cannot be speeded up or the cloves will become dry, brittle and withered rather than plump. The final moisture content of the dried cloves should be 8-10%. Experienced clove driers will know when the cloves are fully dry as the buds will snap easily. During the rainy season, cloves should be dried using a mechanical drier such as a tray drier. Badly dried cloves are pale brown and classified as khuker.

Winnowing: The dried buds are winnowed using a traditional winnowing basket to remove dust and other foreign matter. Small cleaning machines are available that use a blower to remove the dirt and dust.

Grinding: Grinding can be a method of adding value to a product. However, it is not advisable to grind spices. After grinding, spices are more vulnerable to spoilage. The flavour and aroma compounds are not stable and will quickly disappear from ground products. The storage life of ground spices is much less than for the whole spices.

Packaging: Cloves can be packaged in polythene bags of various sizes according to the market demand. The bags should be sealed to prevent moisture entering. Sealing machines can be used to seal the bags.

Storage: Dried cloves must be stored in moisture-proof containers away from direct sunlight. It is essential that the cloves are fully dry before they are stored. Any moisture within the bags will cause the cloves to rot. The stored cloves should be inspected regularly for signs of spoilage or moisture. If they have absorbed moisture, they should be re-dried to a moisture content of 10%.

Uses: To flavor foods and drinks to produce essential oil for dentistry and cleaning agent in microscopy.

10.2.5 Cinnamon Processing

The cinnamon tree is a bushy evergreen tree that is cultivated as low bushes (about 2-3m tall) to make harvesting easier. The bushes grow well in shaded places with an average rainfall and without extremes of temperature. The optimum temperature for production is between 27 and 30°C. The soil should not be waterlogged as this produces a bitter-tasting bark. Eight or ten side branches grow on the bush and these are harvested after about three years to obtain the cinnamon bark.

Harvesting: Cinnamon bark is harvested twice a year immediately after each of the rainy seasons when the humidity makes the bark peel more easily. The trees are first harvested when they are three years old, one year after pruning. The side stems that are about three years old are removed and the bark is stripped off. Cinnamon bark is only obtained from stems that are between 1.2 and 5 cm in diameter.

Processing: Processing accounts for about 60% of the cost of production of cinnamon. This is because the peeling of bark from the stems is labour intensive and is usually done by hand, by skilled peelers. The quality of cinnamon depends on how well the bark is removed from the stems. The larger pieces or quills can be sold for more than the smaller broken pieces.

Drying is also an important stage of the processing of cinnamon. It contributes to the quality of the final product.

Remove the tender stems (with diameters less than 1.2 cm) and use these for mulching.

- Stems with diameters of more than 5 cm are not used to prepare cinnamon bark. Remove these and use for oil distillation.
- Remove the soft outer bark using a fine rounded rasp knife.
- Rub the stripped stem with a brass rod to loosen the inner bark. It is important to use a brass rod so that the bark does not become discoloured.
- Make cuts around the stem at 30 cm intervals using a small pointed knife. The knife blade should be stainless steel or brass to prevent staining the bark.
- Make long cuts along the length of the stem, so that the bark can be carefully eased off the stem. Use the pointed knife and the rubbing rod to help ease off the bark.
- The pieces of removed bark are known as quills. Place these curled quills inside one another to make long compound quills (up to 1m long). Use the best whole quills on the outside and fill in the centre with broken pieces of bark.

Drying : The compound quills are placed on coir rope racks and dried in the shade to prevent warping. After four or five days of drying, the quills are rolled on a board to tighten the filling and then placed in subdued sunlight for further drying. In humid climates or during the rainy season it will be necessary to use a mechanical dryer to complete the drying process.

Grinding: Grinding can be a method of adding value to a product. However, it is not advisable to grind spices. After grinding, spices are more vulnerable to spoilage. The flavour and aroma compounds are not stable and will quickly disappear from ground products.

Quality of cinnamon is judged by the thickness of bark (broken or entire quills) and the aroma and flavour.

Packaging: Cinnamon quills are cut into pieces up to 10cm in length and packed into moisture-proof polypropylene bags for sale. The bags should be sealed to prevent moisture entering.

10.2.6 Processing of Turmeric

Turmeric is one of the most important spices, well known for its medicinal values since ancient times. It has antiseptic, anti- inflammatory and antioxidant properties. It also used wide for cosmetic purposes.

Processing: Processing of turmeric refers to conversion of turmeric rhizomes to powder. Following are the processing steps:

Washing:

- At first rhizomes are separated after digging out from the soil
- For this rhizomes are kept soaked in water throughout the night.
- Later on rhizomes are taken out and water is sprayed.
- First part from middle is called mother rhizomes.
- The second part of it which is long and thin is called Doctor Rhizome.
- Mother rhizome is kept for seed while Doctor rhizomes are further processed and sold. Boiling/Blanching/Cooking
- Traditionally boiling is done in metal or mud pots along with 3/4 water.
- Top of the pots are covered with a lid or dry leaves. Boiling process is continued till foams and white foams start coming out.
- Rhizomes are tested by pressing with fingers. If rhizomes are soft and inner colour has become yellow instead of red then this process is said to be complete.
- In the developed method of boiling or blanching both colour and quality improved.
- Rhizomes are treated with 0.1 percent Soda (sodium carbonate, sodium bicarbonate or ammonium carbonate) and water solution.
- In this process time spent is 30 minutes to 6 hours. This depends on the use of the method and equipments. Boiler is used in the developed method. After 30 or 40 minutes bulbs/tubers are taken up and tested along with the frame.

Drying:

- Cooked rhizomes are cooled first and spread slowly in the yard for drying.
- It takes at least 10 to 15 days for drying in the sun.
- Tubers are brought up and down in the middle of drying so that all are dried well.
- Mother rhizome takes comparatively more time while Doctor rhizome dries up quickly. Therefore these are dried separately also.
- Completely dried turmeric holds 6 percent moisture content.

Polishing:

- Dried rhizomes are rubbed against ground or below the feet to take out the hard layer over them and small roots are also remove
- By this process the colour of turmeric becomes bright.
- Machines are also used in polishing consisting of a horizontally mounted drum in which rhizomes are filled.
- Rotation of drum causes mutual rubbing of rhizomes. During the period some water is also sprinkled for improving colour.

Colouring:

- Export quality turmeric is given special colour by mixing yellow colour. Colouring is done by two methods.
- One is dry colouring in which dry colour is spread over the rhizomes after boiling is done and thoroughly mixed.

- In the wet colouring, colour solution is prepare, sprayed on rhizomes and mechanically mixed. After colouring is complete, these are dried for a week. Grinding/Powdering
- Dried and polished turmeric are crushed into large pieces in pestle mortar followed by grinding in stone, attrition mill or hammer mill.
- The particle size of turmeric powder should not exceed 300 micron.

10.2.7 Processing of Garlic

Garlic (Allium Sativum) is an important spice or condiment cultivated throughout India. It is chiefly used for flavouring and seasoning vegetable and meat dishes.

- In its medicinal use garlic preparations are given in cough and other lung diseases, stomach complaints (as ulcers of the intestines) and disorders resulting from child birth and as a specific remedy for eyes and earache.
- Dried powder is the main processed product of garlic.

Garlic Powder:

Initially garlic was consumed as such, no efforts was being made to produce dehydrated garlic or garlic powder with a result that nearly 20 percent of the crops was wasted due to respiration, transpiration and micro biological spoilage during ordinary storage of garlic bulb.

The conventional technique of making garlic powder consists of : removing outer papery layer by hand üseparation and peeling of clove manually dehydrating and powdering them before packaging.

CFTRI has developed an improved process of dehydrated garlic powder production free from husk. Garlic bulbs are broken and cloves are separated and outer papery husk of bulb is aspirated off. The cloves are peeled mechanically (Preconditioning) and the dried. Dried material is further broken in to large pieces and husk adhering to broken cloves is aspirated off. Dried meat after inspection is powdered to obtained product.

10.3 TEA PROCESSING

Tea is an evergreen shrub or tree, which grows wild fro India to China. There are about 45 species of *Camellia* of which *sinensis* considered native to India, is important one from which tea of commerce is made. The important constituents of tea contributing to flavour of tea beverage are caffeine, poly-phenols and essential oils. Analysis of fresh tea leaves shows poly-phenols 22.2, protein 17.2, caffeine 4.3, crude fibre 27.0, starch 0.5 and ash 5.6 %, little amount of carotene, B-vitamin and ascorbic acid. During manufacturing of black tea, ascorbic acid is lost. The important poly-phenols present in tea leaves are catechins and glallocatechins. The summary of the processing is given below:

1. **Withering:** The withering is carried out by spreading tea leaves thinly on racks or shelves, to dry the leaves partially. Generally withering is allowed till the water content in the leaf is lowered by about 40%.
2. **Rolling:** The withered leaves are then are rolled to break open the cells and release the juices and enzymes. Various rolling techniques are employed and the flavour characteristics inherent in various types of tea partially depend on techniques used.
4. **Fermentation:** After rolling, the leaves are sifted and spread out on suitable platform allowed to ferment for 2-6 hr at temperatures 21-27°C. During this process, the enzyme causes the oxidation of various poly-phenols present in juices, resulting in the change of colour from green to reddish copper. Two of the important poly-phenols that undergo oxidative changes are catechin and glallocatechin.
5. **Firing:** When the fermentation has proceeded to the desired degree, further change is arrested by drying or firing. This comprises passing of fermented leaves through a chamber

in which hot air is circulating. At the entrance of the chamber, the temperature is 93° which drop to about 49°C near the exit. The time required for this process is about 30-40 min and the dried production contains 3-4 % moisture. Besides halting the fermentation process, firing causes some caramelization to occur resulting in the characteristics colour of black tea leaves. The aroma of tea is believed to develop during the fermentation and firing process. Although a large number of volatile compound have been identified from tea leaves, none has been found to make any significant contribution to the tea aroma.

6. **Grading and Sorting:** The dried product is cleaned and sorted into various grades of tea of commerce. The quality of black tea is related to the poly-phenols and enzyme content of the leaves used in processing. They are of maximum in buds and the first and the second leaves (28 and 27%, respectively) and types of tea obtained from these are the most desirable. On this basis tea is categorized as leaf and broken grade. The broken grade usually gives a stronger tea than leaf grade. Besides the above the grade, there are the waste products fanning and dusting.
7. **Packing**: Tea is generally blended before it reaches the consumer. In India, the blended tea in packed in plywood boxes lined with alumunium foil and parchment paper. During packing, tea absorbs moisture. If the moisture content increases to 6%, tea is to be subjected to second firing before packing. India is also exporting tea in consumer tea packs instead of bulk tea chests

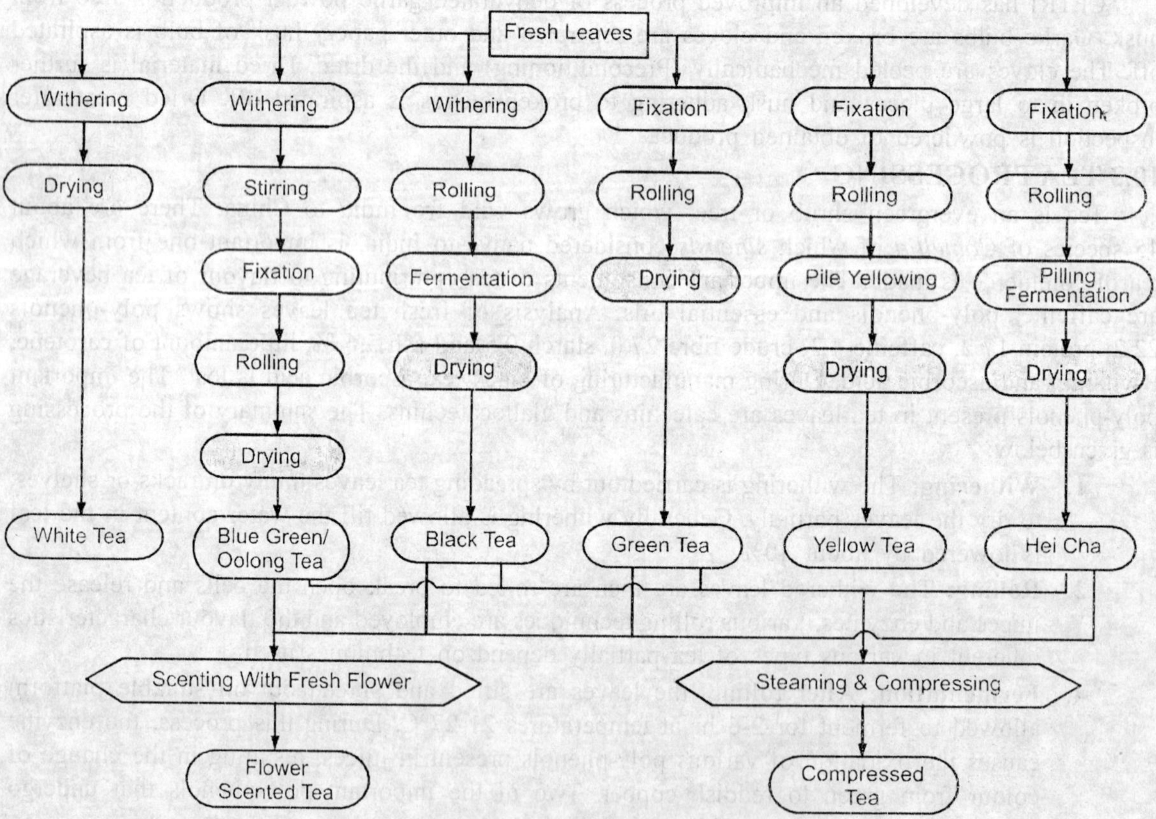

Fig. 2: Process Flow Chart of Tea Processing

At stages of manufacture the maintenance of hygienic conditions is of paramount importance not only in relation to accepted standards imposed by food regulation but in order to turn out good quality tea.

11.4 COFFEE PROCESSING

Coffee is a tropical crop and native of Africa continents but historical incidents indicates that it was first identified as beverages in Arabian continents and spread all over the world from there only. In India, It was brought from Mecca by a pilgrim. Coffee is grown in the regions of tropical and subtropical climate and it is important export commodity of these regions. Out of 90 known species of coffee, only three species have become significant in world trade namely, *Coffee arabica* and *Coffee canephora* and *Coffee luberica.*

Coffee made from the seeds of the beans of perennial shrubs of Genus *Coffea* of family *Rubiaceae.* Coffee contains virtually no food value in itself and it is consumed entirely for else representing and stimulating properties. It contains caffeine which provides its physiologically stimulating effect.

The world production of coffee is estimated to 96.6 million bags during 1997-98 in which the share of Indian coffee production was 4%. One coffee bag contains about 60-75 kg of coffee or in rare cases 50 kg. Globally production of coffee was in Brazil (29.6%), Colombia (11.8%), Indonesia (7.7%), Vietnam (5.2%), Mexico (4.4%), India (3.9%), Guatemala (3.2%) and others (34.2%). The structure of coffee cherry is shown in Fig. 3.

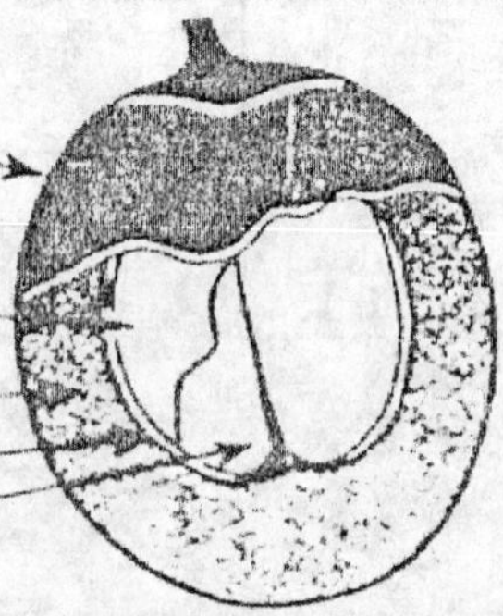

Fig. 3: Structure of Coffee Cherry

Primary processing of coffee:

Primary processing of cherry is done to obtain greenish grey colour beans embedded into the cherry. The structure of coffee cherry consists of two coffee beans covered by thin parchment like 'Hull which is further surrounded by mucilaginous pulp. The entire structure is covered by as outer skin deep red in colour when ripe. Some time a single bean kills the berry instead of two when the seed is called peppery since it is like pea". Both pulp and hull are removed to obtain this semi-finished product is known as green beans. Coffee processing consists of removing the skin pulp parchment silver skin. The quality of the final product depends upon the manners of processing there are two methods of primary processing of coffee cherry to obtain green beans, namely, (i) wet processing, and (ii) dry processing. The Fig. 3 represents the flow chart of coffee processing.

1. Harvesting: Coffee is harvested either as ripe cherry or as cherry which has ripened and then dried out. Harvesting of ripe cherry is practiced in most coffee countries which are then usually followed by wet processing. Harvesting is usually a manual process employing seasonal labour since coffee producing. Coffee is allow to dry on the trees itself and its harvested either from tree or the ground when they fall.

2. Classification and Separation: The harvested cherries are usually cleaned by sieving to remove dirt, stone twigs, leaves etc. special care is taken to separate ripe fruit which may be sorted out by hand picking, however, this involves high labour cost. A widely practiced method of separation is floatation method.

3. Processing: After classification/ separation, the processing is done by two methods *i.e.* **(A) Wet processing** and **(B) Natural/dry processing**

A. **Wet Processing:** This process is more sophisticated than the dry process and by general consent leads to better quality coffee and commands a higher price. This process requires cherries which are fully ripe or very close thereto. The cherries must be processed as soon as possible after harvesting because wet fruit start to degrade as soon as they are removed from trees.

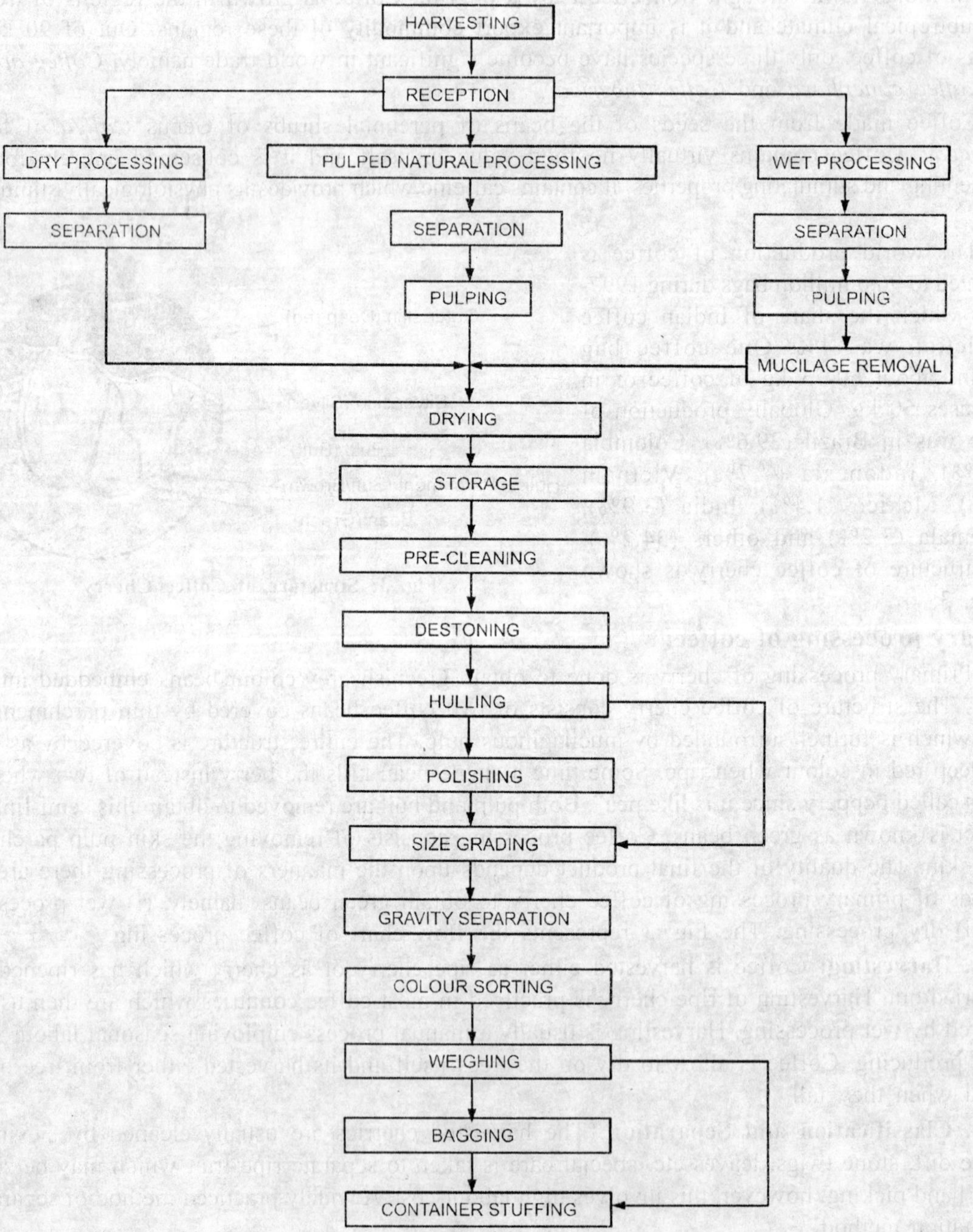

Fig. 4: Flow Chart for Processing of Coffee

A.1 Pulping: After cleaning and sorting cherries to wet processed are pulped by the pulping machines are two main types: drum pulper and disc pulper.

The pulped cherries are discharged from the pulper on to a sieve which may be in the form of an oscillating flat tray or hollow rotating cylinder. This is wet sieving operating assisted by water sprays through out. The skins and pulped cherries are sent to a further small pulper, known as a repasser.

A.2 Fermentation: The objective of the fermentation stage in the wet processing of coffee is to remove the layer of mucilage surrounding the beans before the final drying stage. If it is not removed, drying is impeded and the surface of the bean becomes sticky, causing handling problems. This mucilage layer is only around 0.8 mm thick, and is slippery, translucent and colourless when freshly pulped, but turns brown on exposure to air. It is an amorphous gel quite insoluble in water, and clings tightly to the parchment like skin surrounding itself.

Traditionally, this is achieved by transporting the beans by water into concrete tank, draining off the water and holding for 2-3 days. Each day the tank is partly refilled with water and the beans turned over thoroughly to ensure an even process. Fermentation tanks should be protected from direct sunlight. Depending on the scale of crop, tanks may be from about 0.5-30 m^3 and may have bottoms to assist washing after fermentation is complete.

B. Natural Processing/Dry processing: Some classification may follow *i.e.* removal of unripe cherries by washing in running water and screening this process will also remove adventitious non coffee rubbish, the washed cherries may still induce some unripe and overripe cherries. They are spread out to dry usually on a concrete floor, known as a barbecue.

Machines are used in some place to complete drying. The dried cherries have then to be husked which is much the same as the hulling carried out on dry parchment coffee from the wet process.

Polishing: This process is particularly important for dry process. Polishing is the removal of silver-skin, except that retained in the centre-cut of beans which is only really subsequently released as chaff on roasting and grinding is desirable to give the green beans an attractive appearance.

4. Drying

4.1 Sun drying: In Latin America, washed coffee beans are spread in layers 5-10 cm deep on large concrete terraces with frequent stirring regularly during drying. Drying of washed coffee from about 53% moisture to the required 10-12% takes approximately one week on a concrete terrace, given continuous good weather.

In Africa, freshly washed beans are first spread on portable wire mesh trays at only 2-3 mm depth and stirred regularly. The beans are frequently stirred and sorted by hand, defected beans and undesirable debris being removed. The moisture content of coffee beans is removed from 45 % to 10 %.

4.2 Hot Air Driers: Many different mechanical driers have been designed and used in the coffee industry, mostly in Latin America. The main criterion is avoided raising the temperature of the beans themselves too high. Actual bean temperatures should not be higher than about 50°C. However, because of evaporative cooling effects it is permissible for the air surrounding the beans to be as warm as 90°C during the early stages while the bean is still relatively moist. There are various driers are developed and used to dry the coffee bean viz. Wilkén drier, Guardiola drier, Torres drier, and Moreira drier etc..

5. Hulling: The purpose of hulling is to remove the parchment from washed coffee after drying, or the dry skin, pulp and parchment from natural dry processed coffee. Huller for the two operations differs somewhat in detailed design but have major features in common.

6. Grading and Sorting: The grading and sorting of coffee beans by several methods like.

i) Grading by size *ii)* Grading by density *iii)* Air lifting sorting
iv) Manual sorting *v)* Electronic sorting.

7. Packaging: Bags usually made of jute or natural fibres used for packaging the raw/cured coffee. Coffee is very sensitive to foreign odour. Therefore, Care has to be taken to use only jute bags which are free from odour: Odour free jute bags (clean used DWFB-Twill, bags size 44 × 26½) should be used for packaging raw coffee.

8. Storage and Transportation: Green coffee is sold in sacks or bags (usually of jute), generally at 60 kg net weight, or 60-75 kg and may need to be stored either in ware houses or ship transit to other countries for roasting. Green coffee is susceptible to changes affecting appearance and flavour, but especially at elevated temperature (say above 25°C and in conditions of high relative humidity where the moisture content can be rise above 12-13 %. Under the latter conditions, mould growing on beans is a particular hazard, creating a new defect of 'mouldy' beans; additional black beans may rise. Insect damage resulting in holes in the bean may also occur during unsanitary storage. Wet process Arabica coffee is less susceptible to change under unfavourable storage conditions.

9. Roasting: Raw green coffee has no flavour or aroma and has an unpleasant taste. Roasting of coffee improves the flavour and aroma. Roasting of coffee beans involves rapid heating, firstly to drive off the retained moisture, then to raise the bean temperature to about 180°C. Pyrolysis then takes place and exothermic chemical reactions occur which raise the bean temperature a further 20-30°C. Including moisture loss, the weight loss during roasting is 15-22%. The degree of roast also affects the flavour and is a matter of customer preference. There are several roaster used in different countries like. Probat–Werke Roasters, Gothot roaster, Radial turbo roaster, and Smithern roaster

10. Grinding: Before extraction with hot water, it is necessary to grind the roasted beans in order to obtain a satisfactory yield and rate of extraction. The particle size of the ground coffee influences not only yield and rate of extraction but also the actual substances extracted with hot water. Very fine grinds allow large quantities of colloidal substances, mostly carbohydrates and oils in nature; to enter the brew. Thus taste also influences by the fineness of the grind. Grinding realizes quite large amounts of carbon dioxide also some of the volatile aromatic substances. After grinding the flavour becomes rather unstable. Grinding is done mostly by the pump grinder works on the principle of tearing or crushing action.

CHAPTER 11

FOOD SPOILAGE AND PRESERVATION

11.1 INTRODUCTION

Foods are materials, raw, processed, or formulated, that are consumed orally by humans or animals for growth, health, satisfaction, pleasure, and satisfying social needs. Generally, there is no limitation on the amount of food that may be consumed (as there is for a drug in the form of dosage). Excessive amounts could be harmful, for example, salt, fat, and sugar. Chemically, foods are mainly composed of water, lipids, fat, and carbohydrate with small proportions of minerals and organic compounds. Minerals include salts and organic substances include vitamins, emulsifiers, acids, antioxidants, pigments, polyphenols, and flavor-producing compounds. The different classes of foods are perishable, non-perishable, harvested, fresh, minimally processed, preserved, manufactured, formulated, primary, secondary derivatives, synthetic, functional, and medical foods.

Foods are made from natural materials, and, like any living matter, will deteriorate in time. The deterioration of food, or food spoilage, is the natural way of recycling, restoring carbon, phosphorus, and nitrogenous matters to the good Earth. However, spoilage (deterioration, putrefaction) will usually modify the quality of foods from good to bad, in the form of poor appearance (discoloration), offensive smell, and inferior taste. Food spoilage could be caused by a number of factors, chiefly biological, but also by chemical and physical factors. Consumption of spoiled foods can cause sickness, and even death. Thus, food safety is the major concern in spoiled foods.

The preservation method is mainly based on the types of food that need to be prepared or formulated.

Preservation methods start with the complete analysis and understanding of the whole food chain, including growing, harvesting, processing, packaging, and distribution; thus an integrated approach needs to be applied. It lies at the heart of food science and technology, and it is the main purpose of food processing. First, it is important to identify the properties or characteristics that need to be preserved. One property may be important for one product, but harm to others. For example, collapse and pore formation occur during the drying of foods.

11.2 FOOD SPOILAGE

Food spoilage is the undesirable deterioration of food quality that may result in changes in odour, taste, and appearance of food. Another definition of food spoilage is **"to destroy the value or quality of a food."** Spoilage refers to the process of decay itself. Spoilage can occur through both microbial and non-microbial routes. Spoilage does not necessarily mean that the food is dangerous to eat. It just means that the food has been transformed in ways that make it less appealing for human consumption.

Major Factors Affecting Spoilage

1. Temperature, 2. Moisture content in food, 3. Humidity of storage environment, 4. Amount of light and time, 5. Presence of oxygen in the storage environment, 6. Spoilage bacteria, 7. Improper food processing.

Spoilage due to Physical Factors

1. Temperature, moisture and pressure can also cause food spoilage.
2. Physico-chemical reactions are caused by freezing, burning, drying and bruising of fruits and vegetables during storage, handling and transportation.
3. Food processing or storage causes deterioration in colour of fruits and vegetables due to degradation of chlorophyll resulting dull olive-brown colour.
4. Anthocyanins, pigment in fresh and processed foods, form complexes with metals resulting in colour change. *e.g.*, red sour cherries react with tin and form undesirable purple complex.

Manufactured (processed) and natural foods are composed mainly of carbohydrates, proteins, and lipids (fats and oils). The major constituents in vegetables and fruits are carbohydrates, including sugars (sucrose, glucose, and so on), polymers of sugars (starch), and other complex carbohydrates such as fibers. **Lipids** are the major components of oilseeds, milk and most cheeses, and proteins are the chief constituents of muscle foods. Under natural storage conditions, foods start to deteriorate once the living cells in the foods (of plant and animal origins) are dead or damaged. The exposure of foods and damaged cells to the environment would attract microorganisms (*e.g.*, bacteria, molds, and viruses), and insects, which in turn would further accelerate the decomposition of the food. Foods with contaminated microorganisms lead to food borne illnesses. For most food poisoning, the spoilage has not reached the stage where the sensory attributes (appearance, smell, taste, texture, and so on.) of the foods are abnormal. Illness from food can be mainly classified as:

- **Food borne infection** caused by pathogenic bacteria (disease-causing microorganisms, such as Salmonella bacteria, multiplying in a victim's digestive tract, causing diarrhea, vomiting, and fever, and so on), and
- **Food borne intoxication** (food poisoning resulting from a toxin produced by pathogenic microorganisms, for example, *Clostridium botulinum* and *Staphylococcus aureus*, in the food itself).

Undesirable Changes in Food due to Spoilage

- Change in colour (long storage of banana)
- Change in consistency (splitting of milk)
- Change due to mechanical damage (eggs with broken shell)
- Change in texture (rotting of carrot)
- Change in smell (rancid smell of spoiled oils

The three most important routes of spoilage are:

1. Autolysis or enzymatic spoilage, 2. Microbial spoilage, 3. Chemical spoilage (fat oxidation)

1. Autolysis or enzymatic spoilage

Autolysis (Self destruction) or enzymatic spoilage refers to natural stages of decomposition that occur in living organisms shortly after death. This can also be called self-digestion, and refers to the actions of the organisms' own enzymes that result in cellular destruction. Microbial spoilage refers to the external actions of bacteria and fungi on foods. This is the same process as microbial fermentation, except that the actions of the bacteria and fungi result in undesirable traits in the food during spoilage. Like fermentation, spoilage is a consequence of metabolic processes. Whenever microbes feed on a substrate (*i.e.*, food), they change it. Microbes also use enzymes to break down carbohydrates, fats, proteins, and other nutrients in the substrate to form molecules they can transport inside them to use as energy and building blocks.

Enzymatic spoilage

Every living organism uses specialised proteins called **enzymes** to drive the chemical reactions in its cells. After death, enzymes play a role in the decomposition of once-living tissue, in a process called **autolysis** (self-destruction) or **enzymic spoilage**. For example, some enzymes in a tomato help it to ripen, but other enzymes cause it to decay. Once enzymic spoilage is under way, it produces damage to the tomato skin, so moulds can begin to can attack it as well, speeding the process of decay.

Enzymic browning

When the cells of fruits and vegetables such as apples, potatoes, bananas and avocado are cut and exposed to the air, enzymes present in the cells bring about a chemical reaction in which colourless compounds are converted into brown-coloured compounds. This is called **enzymic browning**. If the food is cooked very soon after cutting, the enzymes are destroyed by heat and the browning does not occur. For example, apples are prone to discolouration if cut open when raw, but when cooked they do not go brown.

Lysosomes are a type of cell structure containing autolytic enzyme groups that affect lipids (fats), sugars and proteins. Following death the lysosomes structures break open releasing their enzymatic contents. When the organism is alive, its enzymes are regulated by processes in the living cells. When the organism dies, its enzymes are still active, but are no longer regulated or functioning. These enzymes begin the process of self-digestion or decomposition, and result in tissue softening and other activities. In fresh fish, for example, enzymatic spoilage begins as soon as the fish dies. Removing the guts of the fish and refrigerating it rapidly will help to lessen the effects of enzymatic spoilage. The enzymes involved in spoilage include trypsins, collagenases, and glycolytic enzymes.

Enzymatic spoilage also causes weakening of muscles and pokes holes into other tissues, such as intestinal tissues. Any breaches in the intestine will result in the release of live microbes from the gut that will perform the next stage of decomposition.

2. Microbial spoilage

Microbial spoilage can be caused by bacteria and fungi (yeast and moulds). Through fermentation or spoilage, bacteria, yeast, and moulds may change the colour, smell, and/or taste of our food. In some cases, bacteria will produce odours to ward off competitors, including humans.

Most food spoilage is a result of *microbial activity*. Visible microbial growth may be apparent in the form of surface slime, degradation of structural components of the food can cause a loss of texture, but the most common manifestation will be chemical products of microbial metabolism, gas, off odours and flavours.

Table 1: Most Common Bacteria Genera Found in Certain Food Types

Microorganisms	Foods
Corynebacterium, Leuconostoc	Dairy products
Achromobacter,	Meat, poultry, sea foods
Bacteriodes, Proteus,	Eggs and meats
Pseudomonas	Meats, poultry, eggs

We have already discussed about factor affecting microbial growth in chapter 2 (Art 2.2.1).

Microbial spoilage and foodborne illness:

Most microbial spoilage is detectable by smell, taste, or visual appearance. Some microbes can be beneficial, can cause spoilage, or cause illness, depending on the circumstances. Of importance, microbial spoilage can change foods in a way that is not detectable and creates a new hazard. Mycotoxins are chemicals produced by moulds that can cause foodborne illness if the contaminated foods are consumed. Moulds that produce mycotoxins are very common and cause significant losses of agricultural crops worldwide These moulds are usually associated with cereals, legumes, and flours. In some countries, as much as 50 % of grains are contaminated by mycotoxins. For example, aflatoxins, produced by the fungus *Aspergillus flavus*, are one of the most potent liver carcinogens known. Aflatoxins cause significant health problems in developing countries, where it commonly contaminates grains and animal feeds. Aspergillus is often associated with drought-stress in plants just prior to harvesting. Poor drying techniques and storage conditions that do not control moisture create conditions for fungal growth and mycotoxin formation in grains. Another example of a mycotoxin is ergot. Ergot is a potent alkaloid mycotoxin associated with breads and grains, which is produced by a mould called *Claviceps*. This mycotoxin was behind infamous mass poisonings during the Middle Ages, wherein it caused convulsions and gangrene. *Scombroid* or *histamine poisoning* is a foodborne illness caused by eating tuna that has undergone microbial spoilage

This type of food poisoning is entirely preventable by controlling refrigeration. Histamine is a chemical that produces facial flushing and swelling, often associated with allergic responses. Histamine is not a naturally occurring chemical in tuna. However, the muscle flesh of tuna can contain high amounts of an amino acid called histidine, which can be converted into histamine by bacteria that are present on the surface of tuna (*e.g.*, Morgonella). These bacteria will grow during temperature abuse and bacterial decomposition of the tuna, and the conversion to histamine will only take place in the presence of large numbers of these bacteria, over one to ten million bacteria per gram of tuna.

Roots of Disease Transmission

1. Air and dust, 2. Soil water and plants, 3. Gastrointenstial tract, 4. Animals,
5. Animal feeds, 6. Food utentsils, 7. Food handlars, 8. Cross containimation,
9. Unsafe temperature, 10. Poor personal hygiene

Detection of Spoilage

Spoilage is manifested by a variety of sensory cues such as off-colors, off-odors, softening of vegetables and fruits, and slime.

Early detection of spoilage would be advantageous in reducing food loss because there may be interventions that could halt or delay deterioration, and on the other hand food that had reached the end of its designated shelf life but was not spoiled could still be used.

Traditional methods of estimating bacterial populations do not provide results quickly enough to allow for interventions. Microbial population levels can be measured by real time PCR in liquids, such as Gluconobacter in an electrolyte replacement drink and yeasts in wine and fruit juices. Other methods for detecting bacteria include ATP bioluminescence and electrical impedance assays but some food matrices may contain interfering substances.

Detection of volatile compounds produced by spoilage bacteria can be a less invasive and more rapid means for monitoring spoilage. Biogenicamines (putrecine, cadaverine, histamine, and tyramine) are commonly produced during spoilage of high protein foods and can attain levels that cause illness, particularly in spoiled fish. HPLC methods have been used to quantitate different amines in fish, chicken, and cheese. Combined concentrations of these amines are expressed as a biogenic amine index that is related to the extent of food spoilage and to the concentrations of spoilage organisms.

Electronic noses were first developed about twenty years ago and have undergone many refinements since. They consist of a set of sensors that react with different volatile chemicals and produce an electrical signal. An odor profile can be analyzed by using pattern recognition files. Such systems have been used to detect spoilage in beef, bakery products, fish, and milk. Other techniques being developed to detect microbes or chemicals associated with spoilage include: (*a*) FT-IR (Fourier Transform-Infrared Spectroscopy) used with beef and apple juice; (*b*) visible and shortwavelength near-infrared spectroscopy to detect microbial load of food samples rapidly, accurately and noninvasively.

Control of Spoilage Microorganisms

Spoilage organisms are not originally an integral part of foods but are widely present in water, soil, air, and other animals. Healthy living plants and animals can ward off bacteria and fungi, but as soon as they are slaughtered or harvested their defenses deteriorate and their tissues become susceptible to spoilage microbes. Good manufacturing practices with strict attention to sanitation and hygiene can prevent colonization by many, but not all, microbes and are the most important first step in delaying the spoilage process.

Microbes require certain conditions for growth, and therefore management of the environment of foods can change these factors and delay spoilage:

- Many, but not all, microbes grow slowly or not at all at low temperatures, and refrigeration can prolong the lag phase and decrease growth rate of microbes.
- Many microbes require a high water activity and therefore keeping foods such as grains and cereal products dry will help to preserve them.
- Some microbes require oxygen, others are killed by oxygen, and still others are facultative. Managing the atmosphere during storage in packaging can retard or prevent the growth of some microbes. Several types of modified atmosphere packaging (MAP) have been developed to retard growth of pathogenic and spoilage organisms;

However, microbes are endlessly innovative and eventually seem to circumvent the barriers we set up against them. Therefore further strategies and multiple hurdles are utilized to extend shelf life. These procedures must be assessed for compatibility with different foods so that there are no significant organoleptic changes in the foods caused by the treatment or preservative. These methods for food preservation will not be covered in depth here.

Processing technologies, in addition to thermal processing, are being developed to kill spoilage microbes, including:

- high pressure processing of fruits, juices, meat and fish
- ozone
- irradiation of fruit and meat
- pulsed electric fields of juices

Formulation of processed foods may include compounds that alter the water activity or pH of foods, thereby limiting growth of many organisms.

Antimicrobial compounds may be added to foods or packaging to inhibit growth of many spoilage organisms:

- Organic acids can help control bacteria, molds and yeasts in bakery products, meat, juices, and other foods ;
- Bacteriocins, including nisin, can help control spoilage bacteria in dairy products, fish, juice,and vegetables;

- Chitosan incorporated into foods or used as a coating for fruits and vegetables inhibits growth of some spoilage bacteria and yeasts.
- Many herbs, essential oils, and spices have demonstrated some inhibitory activity against spoilage microbes in a variety of foods. Thyme, oregano, vanillin, and cinnamon are the most commonly mentioned substances in recent years.

3. Chemical spoilage

Chemical spoilage can be the last stage of spoilage for some kinds of foods stored for long periods, such as frozen foods. If they are not properly packaged or stored for too long, chemical changes can occur to make the foods unpalatable. Chemical reactions in food are responsible for changes in the colour and flavour of foods during processing and storage. Foods are of best quality when they are fresh, but after fruits and vegetables are harvested, or animals are slaughtered, chemical changes begin automatically within the foods and lead to deterioration in quality. Fats break down and become rancid (smell bad), and naturally-occurring enzymes promote major chemical changes in foods as they age.

Appearance of spoiled food

Spoiled food is generally more a problem of appearance than a problem of disease causing. In food spoilage, the changes in appearance or texture of the food, such as rottenness, softness and change in colour, taste or odour are usually obvious, whereas in contaminated food such characteristics may not be noticed. A large majority of the microorganisms responsible for food spoilage are not pathogenic to humans. However, you should advise people in your community that they should not eat`food that is spoiled because it is not nutritious and may make them sick (cause vomiting).

Rancidity (or the process of rancidification) is a form of chemical spoilage that occurs from oxidation of fats and lipids. The reaction of the food with oxygen in the air causes decomposition of fats and oils. The great tasting fats in foods are transformed into foods containing undesirable tastes, from chemicals such as aldehydes and ketones. This problem arises in foods when either the packaging is poor or the food has been in prolonged storage. Peanut butter and frozen seafoods (for example, salmon) are susceptible to this kind of spoilage. Nuts and nut butters, such as peanut butter are foods have a fairly high content of oil and fat. Prolonged storage of peanut butter at room temperature can result in rancidity. Although nuts and nut butters can be stored at room temperature, their shelf life is approximately one year, after which the oils and fats they contain will oxidize and go rancid. While this is a food quality issue and will not cause of Foodborne illness In general, for both foodborne intoxications and foodborne infections, two conditions must be met for foodborne illness to occur:

1. The pathogen or toxin must be present in the food in sufficient quantity to cause illness.
2. The food must be eaten.

For bacterial foodborne infections, conditions must also be suitable for microbial survival and/or growth. These conditions include:

- A food substrate that provides nutrients to the pathogen;
- A pH above 4.6;
- A water activity (a_w) above 0.85;
- An aerobic or anaerobic environment, depending on the pathogen; and
- A high redox potential. Depending on how a bacterial pathogen causes infection, the following two conditions are needed before or after the contaminated food is consumed:
- The temperature of the food or the host must allow for microbial growth, and

- There must be enough time for microbes to grow to disease-causing numbers and/or to produce secondary toxins. illness, the taste of rancid peanut butter is not acceptable to most consumers.

11.3 FOOD PRESERVATION

Food preservation is the process of treating and handling food in such a way as to stop or greatly slow down spoilage and prevent foodborne illness while maintaining nutritional value, texture and flavour.

11.3.1 Why Food Preservation is Essential

(*a*) Prevention of post harvest losses occurring in grains, field crops, fruits, vegetables and spice crops by introducing improved, cost effective technologies so that the incomes of the rural farming sector will be increased as results of the increase in their marketable surplus. At national level, such measures would increase the quantity of essential foods items available for consumption.

(*b*) Prevent the deterioration quality occurring in grains, other field crops, fruits, vegetables and spice crops due to adoption of improper post harvest handling, storage and processing techniques so that the quality of these essential food commodities reaching the market is significantly improved. Improvement of product quality will enable the farmers to sell their 'value added' produce at an attractive price in the competitive market and thereby increase their income agriculture.

(*c*) Prevent the nutritional losses due to use of improper food processing techniques occurring in food crops and spice crops and thereby increase the nutritional status of the country.

(*d*) Improper farm level storage and preservation facilities to enable the farmers and processors to sell their commodities during off seasons at attractive prices and thereby increase their incomes.

(*e*) Introduce improved techniques that utilize minimum labour in order to reduce production costs of food commodities.

(*f*) Develop and transfer viable agro-based industries at rural level in order to increase income and employment opportunities of the rural farming sector and thereby improve their living standard and food habits.

(*g*) Popularize the use of foods prepared from cereals grains, fruits, vegetables and spices crops among the consumers order to create a higher market demand fro the local grain production.

(*h*) Provide food with attractive packaging and nutrients required for enhancing good health, strengthening bodies and empowering minds.

(*i*) Help build communities and generate income fro farmers and manufactures.

There are many techniques used to preserve food, such as legal food additives, varying levels of food ingredients or components, traditional and new technologies. Legal food additives, among other functions, can prevent oxidation and inhibit or destroy harmful microorganisms (molds and bacteria). Vitamin E or vitamin C can serve as antioxidants in many food products and benzoate in beverages can act as an antimicrobial agent. We can preserve food by manipulating the levels of food ingredients or components to inhibit the growth of microorganisms or destroy them, for example, by keeping the food low in moisture content (low water activity), high in sugar or salt content, or at a low pH (less than pH 5). Other traditional technologies such as canning (thermal processing), fermentation, refrigeration, and freezing are well-established preservation methods. Recently, new or alternative technologies have become available to preserve food. Because they are new, their applications are carefully monitored.

11.3.2 Principles of Preservation

There are three main principles:

A. Prevention/delay the microbial decomposition of the food
B. Prevention/delay the shelf decomposition of the food
C. Prevention of damage by insects, animals, mechanical causes, etc.

(A) Prevention/delay the microbial decomposition of the food:

1. By keeping out the microorganisms – Asepsis
2. By removal of microorganisms – Filtration
3. By hindering the growth and activity of microorganisms – Anaerobic condition
4. By killing the microorganisms – Exposing to high temperature

1. *Asepsis* : It means preventing the entry of microorganisms by maintaining general cleanliness, while picking, grading, packing and transporting of fruits and vegetables, increasing their keeping quality and the product prepared from them will be of superior quality.
2. *Filtration* : Fruit juices, beer, soft drinks, wines, etc... enter through bacteria proof filters which are made of asbestos pad or unglazed porcelain type of materials. These filters contain the microorganisms and allow the water or juice to percolate through with or without pressure.
3. *Anaerobic conditions* : It can be maintained by—
   (*a*) Replacing the O_2 by CO_2 – carbonation
   (*b*) Evacuating the sealed container (fruit juice)
   (*c*) Use of oils from top of the food(pickles)
4. ***Exposing at high temperature***:
   (*a*) **Canning :** Food is exposed to a high temperature(>100ºC) which prevents spoilage and inactivate the enzymes present in the food
   (*b*) **Irradiation :** In this, the food is exposed to the radiations to kill the microorganisms present in it by ionizing and non-ionizing radiations like alpha, beta and gamma rays. Here, food is exposed to electromagnetic or ionizing radiations of various frequencies ranging from low frequency to high frequency *i.e.* gamma rays which destroy the microorganisms present in the food.

(B) Prevention/delay the shelf decomposition:

(*a*) By inactivating the enzymes – Blanching
(*b*) Prevention/delay the non-enzymatic chemical reactions – Antioxidant

(*a*) ***Blanching***:

1. It is a primary treatment which soften the tissues to facilitate packaging
2. To preserve the original colour and flavour
3. To destroy the undesirable enzymes
4. Elimination of the air
5. Mostly used for vegetables
6. Remove microorganisms
7. Remove astringent taste and toxins

(*b*) **Antioxidants :** These are the substances which are used to protect the food against deterioration caused by exposure to the air

1. BHA – Butylated Hydroxy Anisole
2. BHT – Butylated Hydroxy Toluene
3. Gellates – Animal fat, Vegetable Oil
4. Tocopherols – Animal Fat
5. Ascorbic Acid- Fruit juices, citrus oils, wine, beers, etc...
6. Lactic Acid- Processed fruits and vegetables, canned fruits
7. Phosphoric Acid- vegetable oils, animal fat and cola drinks

11.3.3 Preservation Methods

Preservation processes include:

- Heating to kill or denature micro-organisms (*e.g.* boiling)
- Oxidation (*e.g.* use of sulphur dioxide)
- Toxic inhibition (*e.g.* smoking, use of carbon dioxide, vinegar, alcohol etc.)
- Dehydration (drying)
- Osmotic inhibition (*e.g.* use of syrups)
- Low temperature inactivation (*e.g.* freezing)
- Ultra high water pressure (*e.g.* fresherized, a kind of cold) pasteurization, the pressure kills naturally occurring pathogens, which cause food deterioration and affect food safety.)
- Many combinations of these methods (Hurdle technology)
- Chelation

11.3.4 Methods of Preservation in Practice

1. COOKING

Cooking is a heating process, the primary object of which is to produce a more palatable food. The word "cooking" is broad term embodying at least six form of heating including; baking, broiling, roasting, boiling, frying and stewing. The method of applying heat energy and the duration differ somewhat for each of these processes. Baking, broiling and roasting usually required dry heat at relatively high temperature greater than 100°C), boiling and stewing are done by placing the product in boiling water and frying involves cooking oil and temperatures much greater than 100°C. Two preservative changes occur in food as a result of cooking:

(I) destruction or reduction of microorganisms and
(II) Inactivation of undesirable enzymes
(III) Destruction of potentially hazardous toxin present naturally or through micro organisms
(IV) Alteration of colour, flavour and texture and
(V) Improve digestibility of food.

Undesirable changes also may occur such as degradation of nutritive component and sensory attributes. Principles which can be applied to describe the effect of cooking on reduction of microorganisms and enzymes also can be applied to other changes occurring during cooking.

2. BLANCHING

Blanching of fruits and vegetables is done by immersing them in hot/boiled water or steam by exposing them to live steam or hot air for a proper period (2-5 min) of time followed by cooling. The extent of blanching varies with food. Fruits are generally not blanched leaving the oxidizing enzyme system active. Blanching is a thermal treatment to be done prior to freezing, drying and canning for the following purposes

(*i*) It activates most of the plant enzymes which cause harness, discoloration (polyphenal oxidase), off flavour (peroxidase), softening and loss of nutritive value.

(*ii*) The reduction of area of leafy vegetables and facilitate their easy handling.

(*iii*) Removes tissue gases which reduce sulphides.

(*iv*) To destroy the micro organisms to about 99%.

(*v*) Enhance green colour of vegetables like peas, broccoli and spinach.

(*vi*) To remove undesirable acids and astringent taste of the peel and spinach.

(*vii*) Removes the skin of vegetables such as beetroot and tomatoes which helps in their peeling.

Two of the most heat resistant and widely distributed enzymes in plant tissues are peroxidase and catalase. Activity of these enzymes, therefore, can be used to evaluate the effectiveness of a blanching treatment. The heating time necessary to destroy catalase or peroxidase depends on the type of fruits and vegetables, the method of heating medium, the size of the fruit and vegetables and the temperature of heating medium. Heating media other than water (*e.g.* steam, hot air, and microwave) and at temperatures other than 100°C can be used blanching time should not be more than 5 minutes.

3. PASTEURIZATION

The pasteurization is thermal process in which the harmful pathogen/ microorganism are partially destroyed at predetermined time and temperatures. The high temperature and short time (HTST) method involves a comparatively high temperature for a short time (71.6°C for 15 second for milk), whereas the low temperature and long time procedure involves, relatively low temperature for longer time (*e.g.* 62.7°C for 30 minute for milk)/ Optimization process depends on the relative destruction rate of organisms as compared to quality factors, but generally the HTST process results in maximum product quality. The time temperature treatment used in pasteurization depends on:

i. The heat resistance of the particular vegetative or pathogenic microorganism. The process is designed to destroy, and

ii. The sensitivity of product quality to heat.

4. STERILIZATION

Sterilization refers to complete destruction of microorganisms. Because of the resistance of certain bacterial spores to heat, this frequently requires a treatment of at least 121°C of wet heat for 15 min or its equivalent. It also means that every particle of the food must receive this heat treatment. If a can of food is to be sterilized, then immersing it at 121°C into pressure cooker or retort for 15 min will not be sufficient because of the relatively slow rate of heat transfer through the food into the can. Depending on the size of the can, effective time to achieve true sterility may be several hours. During this time there can be many changes in the food which reduce its quality. Fortunately, many foods need not be completely sterile to be safe and have keeping quality.

5. CANNING AND BOTTLING

Canning process was first developed by Nicholas Appert in France in the year 1809 and he is called as *Father of Canning*. The process of canning is also known as Appertization. Fruits and vegetables are canned in the season when the raw material is available in plenty. The canned products are sold in off-season and give better returns to the grower. Canning involves cooking fruits or vegetables, sealing them in sterile cans or jars, and boiling the containers to kill or weaken any remaining bacteria as a form of pasteurization. Various foods have varying degrees of natural protection against spoilage and may require that the final step occur in a pressure cooker. High-acid fruits like strawberries require no preservatives to can and only a short boiling cycle, whereas marginal fruits such as tomatoes require longer boiling and addition of other acidic elements. Many vegetables require pressure canning. Food preserved by canning or bottling is at immediate risk of spoilage once the can or bottle has been opened. Lack of quality control in the canning process may allow ingress of water or micro-organisms. Most such failures are rapidly detected as decomposition within the can causes gas production and the can will swell or burst. However, there have been examples of poor manufacture and poor hygiene allowing contamination of canned food by the obligate, *Clostridium botulinum* which produces an acute toxin within the food leading to severe illness or death. This organism produces no gas or obvious taste and remains undetected by taste or smell. Food contaminated in this way has included Corned beef and Tuna.

Neosartorya fischeri, *Talaromyces flavus*, and *Eupenicillium brefeldianum*. These organisms are saprophytic rather than parasitic and usually contaminate fruits on or near the ground.

Byssochlamys fulva, *Byssochlamys nivea*, and *Byssochlamys spectabilis* are associated with spoilage of pasteurized and canned fruits and fruit products due to the production of heat-resistant ascospores and pectolytic enzymes and the ability to grow under low oxygen tensions.

Besides spoilage, the heat-resistant molds produce a number of toxic secondary metabolites.

Can filling

Can filling is the process of aseptically filling whole or sized fruit or vegetables into the containers. The cans are washed with water or subjected to steam jet to remove any adhering dust or foreign matter. Tin cans made of thin steel plate of low carbon content, lightly coated on either side with tin metal to a thickness of about 0.25 mm are usually used in canning. The thickness of coating varies from 0.31 mm to 1.54 mm. The following are the different types of base plates used for can manufacture:

A) **Type L:** It is a high purity steel with low metalloid and residual content. This kind of base plate is used for highly acidic foods.

B) **Type MR:** It is a low metalloid steel with no severe restriction on residual content. It is used for moderate acid foods.

C) **Type MC:** It is similar to MR type but has high phosphorus content to give mechanical strength or stiffness. It is usually used for low acid foods.

Lacquering

It is difficult to coat steel plate uniformly with tin during the process of can manufacture. Small microscopic spaces are always left uncoated, although the coating may appear perfect to the naked eye. The content of the can may react with the exposed parts of container and cause discolouration of the product or corrosion of the tin plate. When the corrosion is severe, the steel is attacked and black stains of iron sulphide are produced. Hence, it is necessary to coat the inside of the can with some material like lacquer, which would prevent discolouration, but would not impart its own flavor or injure the wholesomeness of the contents. The process of coating of inner side of the can to prevent discolouration of the product is called as *lacquering*. Lacquers include oleo-resinous material, synthetic resins, phenolic resins, epoxy resins and vinyl resins. There are two types of lacquers: (*a*) acid resistant and (*b*) sulphur resistant. The acid-resistant lacquer is ordinary gold coloured enamel and the cans treated with it are called as *A.R-enamel cans*. The sulphur-resistant lacquer is also of golden colour and the cans coated with it are called *C-enamel cans* or *S.R. cans*. Acid-resistant cans are used for packing of fruits of the acid group with soluble colouring matter such as raspberry, strawberry, red plum, coloured grapes, etc. Sulphur-resistant cans are used for non-acid products like peas, corn, beans, etc.

Syruping and brining

In canning, syrups are added to fruits whereas brine (salt solution) is added to the vegetables. Purpose of adding syrups or brine is to improve the flavor, fill the space between the pieces of canned product and aid in the heat transfer during sterilization. Cane sugar, glucose syrup, invert sugar and high fructose corn syrups are used for canning. Brine containing 1 to 2 percent of common salt is generally used for vegetables. Strength of syrup is measured by using hydrometer or a refractometer while strength of brine is measured by salometer or salinometer. The syrup or brine should be added to the can at a temperature of about 90?C, leaving suitable headspace in the can.

Exhausting

Exhausting usually means heating the can and can contents before sealing. Sometimes it is may also refer to the treatment of the container under a mechanically produced vacuum. But in either case it is done to remove air from the can interior and prevent corrosion. It also prevents undue strains upon the can during sterilization and prevents overfilling of can contents. Removing of air also helps in better retention of vitamins especially of vitamin C. The other advantages of the exhaust process are prevention of bulging of the can when stored at high altitudes or in hot climates. In heat exhaust method, the cans are generally passed through a tank of hot water at about 92-97 °C or on a moving belt through a covered steam box. The time of exhaust varies between 5 to 25 minutes. After exhausting cans are immediately sealed with the help of double rolling operation of seamer.

Coatings: properties and alternatives

Many different can coatings are commercially available, but most of them are based on a limited number of chemicals functionalities. Coatings contain different additives, *e.g.* agents to increase surface slipping as well as abrasion and scratch resistance of can coatings, lubricants, anti-foaming agents, adhesives, scavengers for hydrochloric acids, and pigments.

Epoxy-based coatings have the highest market share of more than 90%. However, can manufacturers and food companies have started to replace BPA-based epoxy coatings by alternatives as a consequence of toxicological evidence, public discussions, and recent regulatory decisions. Acrylic and polyester coatings are currently used as first generation alternatives to epoxy coatings and, more recently, polyolefin and non-BPA epoxy coatings were developed. Further inventions include BPA capturing systems and top coatings. Most of these alternative coatings are more expensive than epoxy coatings and may not display the same array of characteristics with respect to their stability and universal applicability yet.

Epoxy coatings: In the 1950s, epoxy resins were introduced as coatings for aluminum and steel cans. Their stability, protective function, and technical properties made them the most commonly used coating material. Most epoxy coatings are synthesized from bisphenol A (BPA, CAS 80-05-7) and epichlorohydrin forming bisphenol A-diglycidyl ether epoxy resins. Many different blends of epoxy coatings were developed with epoxy-phenolic coatings being the most important subgroup. Other blended resins are *e.g.* epoxy amines, acrylates, and anhydrides.

Oleoresins: First can coatings were made of oleoresins, which are mixtures of oil and resin extracted from plants. Oleoresins are rather flexible and easily applied, but do not adhere well to metal surfaces, have a limited corrosion resistance, and need long curing times. Furthermore, they may change the organoleptic properties of food.

Vinyl: Vinyl coatings are synthesized from vinyl chloride and vinyl acetate. They are highly flexible and stable under acidic and alkaline conditions, but they do not adhere well on metal and do not withstand at high temperatures. Vinyl coatings need plasticizers and stabilizers and are often blended with other resins. Vinyl organosols are prepared from suspensions of resin in organic solvent. Organosols offer comparably higher chemical resistance, thermal stability, and adhesion properties than vinyl coatings.

Phenolic: Phenolic resins are composed of phenols and aldehydes. They are highly corrosion resistant and protect cans from sulfide staining. Phenolics have low flexibility, do not adhere well to metal, and may change the odor and flavor of foods. They are applied as coatings for drums and pails, but unblended phenolic resins are not used in food and beverage cans. However, phenolics are common crosslinkers (*e.g.* in epoxide resins) and increase their resistance.

Acrylic: Acrylic resins are most commonly synthesized from ethylacrylate. They have a clean appearance and display corrosion and sulfide stain resistance, but they are brittle and may change the taste and odor of foods.

Polyester: Isophthalic acid (IPA) and terephthalic acid (TPA) are the main carboxylic acids used in polyester coatings. Polyester resins are easy to handle during the production process and adhere well to the metal surface, but they are usually not stable under acidic conditions and have a poor corrosion resistance. Alternatively, polyethylene terephthalate (PET) coatings are used to laminate beverage cans, but adhesives are needed to bind the PET onto the metal.

Polyolefins: Coatings that are based on dispersions of polyolefins have recently entered the market. According to the manufacturer, the final polyolefin coating exhibits corrosion protection, adhesion, and flexibility without impacting the flavor of the food.

Types of Can

- Three types of cans are mainly in vogue currently and they are the three piece food can, two piece drawn and wall ironed can and drawn and redrawn can.

Three Piece Food Can

- Tinplated steel, coated with lacquer, so as to prevent contact between the tinplate and the food to be canned, and dried in ovens for 15- 20 minutees is cut into strips of specific lengths and widths as per the size of the cans desired.
- Such individual strips are then rolled into cylinders and the two edges of the cylinder drawn with an overlap, which is electrically welded.
- At this stage the cylinders are further given a coating of lacquer on the seams and dried in ovens
- A lip is next formed on each end of the of the cylinder.
- Seperate ends (lids and bases) are made in a different area and the rims of these ends are curled and a sealing compund is injected into the curl.
- The base is next joined to the cylinder body, the sealing compound forming an airtight seal.
- The cans, with the seperate lids are ready for use.

Two Piece Drawn and Wall Ironed Can

- These cans consists of two pieces of tinplate, the body and base being formed from one piece of metal and the lid from another.
- The body and base are shaped from a thick piece of tinplate which is drawn up, ironed and ridged for strength and then given a coat of lacquer.

Drawn and Redrawn Can

- Drawn and redrawn cans are manufactured from two pieces of tinplate , the body being made from a disc shaped piece lacquered on both sides and drawn up to form a shallow cup and then drawn and redrawn to form a deep cup.

6. DRYING

Drying is thermo-physical and physico-chemical operation by which the excess moisture from a product is removed. It is defined as a process of moisture removal due to simultaneous heat and mass transfer. Drying is the process of removal of moisture from the agricultural product to a safe level for preservation of quality, quantity, nutritional value and viability. It refers to removal of moisture from grains and other products to a predetermined level, whereas dehydration means removal of moisture to very low levels usually to bone dry condition. Drying makes the food grains and other product suitable for safe storage and protects them against attack of insects, molds and other microorganisms during storage. Drying makes the food grains and other products suitable for safe storage and protects them against attack of insects, molds and other micro-organisms during storage. During drying, the moisture from solid gets vaporized and diffused in dilute environment. Removal of moisture takes place by high pressure or high temperature conditions.

Drying Methods: The agricultural product drying methods can be broadly grouped into two, (1) sun/solar drying, (2) artificial drying with mechanical means.

(A) Sun drying: Sun drying is the most popular traditional method of drying. A major quantity of grain is still dried by the sun in most of the developed countries. This drying has several advantages and disadvantages:

Advantages:

- No fuel or mechanical energy is required
- Operation is very simple
- Viability, germination, baking qualities is fully preserved.
- Microbial activity and insect/pest infestation are reduced.
- Labour oriented
- No pollution

Disadvantages:

- Completely dependent on weather.
- Not possible round the clock and round the year.
- Excessive losses occur due to shattering, birds, rodents etc.
- Requires specially constructed large floor area, restricting the capacity of mill to a certain limit.
- The entire process is unhygienic.
- Unsuitable for handling of large quantity of grain within a short period of harvest.

(B) Mechanical drying: It is the process of utilizing mechanical means for drying of grains by ventilating natural or heated air through the grain mass to accomplish removal of moisture from it. Mechanical drying system has the following features.

- Rate of drying of grains can be controlled by controlling the temperature of hot air ventilating through grain mass.
- Grains can be dried in all seasons and also during night.
- The process is automatic and requires a small number of unskilled labourers, however, a trained person is required to operate the dryer.
- Losses due to insects, birds and rodents are avoided.
- The process requires fuel or electrical or mechanical power to drive the air and their accessories. Cost of drying per unit mass is comparatively higher than sun drying.
- The process requires little space for operation and is suitable for big mills.
- Mechanical drying in conjunction with early harvest improves the milling quality of grains.

The amount of moisture removed from the grain is dependent upon following factors *i.e.*

- the moisture level and the temperature of the food material
- the temperature and relatively humidity of the ventilating air, and
- the quantity of air flowing around the food material

(*i*) **Contact drying:** In this method of drying, heat is supplied to wet material by conduction. For heat transfer, a heated surface like plate, cylinder, dryer wall is used. The rate of heat transfer is dependent upon the thermal conductivity of the heated surface and also depends on the heat transfer coefficient from the heating medium to the surface. The common heating medium in conduction drying for any food materials used are steam, organic liquids, metals and other materials with high values of heat transfer coefficient. Since all the heat, which passes through the material is utilized for moisture evaporation; thermal efficiency of contact drying is higher.

(*ii*) **Convective drying:** In this method, the sensible heat of heated air is transferred to the wet product by convection. Heated gaseous medium (usually air) is ventilated through a mass of wet materials and carries with it the water vapour evaporated from the material. To save energy, some times the exit air from dryer is re-circulated. Sometimes, the partially dried material is re-circulated for further drying. In such situation the system is known as recirculatory dryer.

(*iii*) **Freeze drying:** This method of drying is based on the sublimation of frozen moisture from the wet product placed in a drying chamber. The pressure in the drying chamber is low. Heat is supplied by radiation from heated trays and the temperature of product is not raised above 0°C. The sublimated moisture is condensed on refrigerated plates in the drying chamber but these plates do not come in contact with products.

(*iv*) **Radiation Drying:** Heat energy can be supplied to wet products by elector-magnetic waves. The wave length of the electromagnetic radiation lies between 0.76 to 400 ìm. The radiation within this wavelength is also called infra-red radiation. The infra-red penetrates the surface of wet material and causes vibrations of molecules, which creates thermal effect. Since the penetration depth of infrared waves is relatively small, this method of drying is commonly used for drying of thin material. The moisture migration inside the material and diffusion of vapour follows the same laws as in convective or contact drying.

(*v*) **Super heated Steam drying:** In this method of drying, first of all the drier is filled with hot air and normal convection drying takes place. The water vapour evaporated during drying operations starts to circulate with hot air. Over pressure is released by a pressure control valve and the air is gradually replaced by water vapour. At the end of drying, water vapour with a small amount of air is circulated.

(*vi*) **Osmotic drying:** This method can be successfully applied to dewatering of cellular products such as fruits, vegetables, meat etc. For the moisture removal, osmo-active substances like 60% aqueous solution of saccharose or 25% aqueous solution of NaCl is used. The difference in osmotic pressure on both sides of the cell wall having properties of a semi-permeable membrane causes moisture removal from the products. The semi-permeable property of cell wall permits migration of water and low molecular molecules to the osmo-active liquid having higher osmotic pressure. Thus, thinner cell sap causes increase in water activity of the medium.

(*vii*) **Fluidized bed drying**: The products are being dried under fluidized condition in a dryer. The products are fluidized by drying air with sufficiently high velocity to cause suspension. In this drying process, higher rate of moisture migration takes place. Every surface of product is contact with drying air, so that uniform drying of products take place. This method is normally used for the materials which have high initial moisture content and are lighter and at the same time requires to be dried quickly such as vegetable seeds.

(*viii*) **Desiccated air drying:** In this method of drying, the ambient air is passed through a desiccated medium or source *e.g.* silica gel. The desiccator absorbs moisture from air, as a result, the relative humidity of air is reduced and at the same time there is an increase in its temperature. When such air comes in contact with wet grains, transfer of moisture from wet grains to drying air takes place. The drying action occurs due to convective heat transfer.

(*ix*) **Infrared drying:** The application of infrared radiation primarily intends the surface treatment of foods. Infrared heating offers many advantages over conventional drying under similar conditions. Comparative studies for infrared drying versus other techniques have proven these benefits. Infrared radiation energy is transferred from the heating element to the product, heating the material more rapidly and uniformly without heating the surrounding air, and hence the energy is used in a more efficient way. The irradiated surface evaporates much more water and drying time is shortened by up to half. Infrared radiation has been applied in conjunction with several drying processes because of these advantages. Combined with hot air pre-drying, infrared heating can save 20% of drying time compared with the infrared drying alone.

(*x*) **Radiofrequency drying:** The use of radiofrequency energy for dielectric heating of food materials is an important application area, which has been studied as a possible method for drying agricultural products. The radiofrequency heating addresses directly the product, so that its interior is heated faster than its surface. The water is released without overheating or dehydration of the surface. Therefore, it can be used as a complement to other drying processes, and allows to reach very low humidity levels, of the order of 1 to 2%, with minimal impact on quality. This novel drying method provides shorter time, higher energy efficiency and better product quality as compared to conventional hot air heating.

(*xi*) **Microwave drying:** This method provides a high heating rate and does not originate alterations on the surface of the food and hence no crust is formed. The industrial microwave treatment is limited due to its high cost and to the need to synchronize the generator for different foods. Thus, it is used industrially for low moisture foods, or as a final stage of the dehydration process. Microwave drying is an efficient method for postharvest processing of agricultural products due to time efficiency, low energy consumption and high product quality, which are major factors to be considered by the industry. Compared to convective drying, microwave drying can be advantageous due to its volumetric heating and reduced processing time. On the other hand, it may cause overheating of particles and undesired degradation of bioactive compounds, but the use of microwaves under vacuum may significantly prevent from quality degradation of heat-sensitive materials.

7. FREEZING

Freezing is also one of the most commonly used processes commercially and domestically for preserving a very wide range of food including prepared food stuffs which would not have required freezing in their unprepared state. Cold stores provide large volume, long-term storage for strategic food stocks held in case of national emergency in many countries. Examples: Potato waffles are stored in the freezer, but potatoes themselves require only a cool dark place to ensure many months' storage. Microbial growth is prevented completely for most action of enzymes of fruit and vegetables greatly retarded. The lower the storage temperature, the slower will be the rate of biochemical and enzymatic reaction, but most of them will still continue at any temperature. Therefore, it is a common practice to inactivate the enzymes in vegetables by scalding or blanching the latter before freezing, practicable. The rate of freezing on food depends upon a number of factors such as the method employed, the temperature, circulation of air or refrigerant, size and shape of package, kind of foods etc. Freezing is cheaper than canning and frozen products are better in quality than the canned products, but for storage of frozen products, uninterrupted supply of electricity is essential, which is a problem in many areas. There are various methods of freezing:

1) **Slow or sharp freezing:** in this method, time required is to achieve frozen condition of produce is large. The techniques involved in freezing by circulation of cold air either natural air or with the aid of fans. The temperature of air may vary from –15°C to –30°C, and freezing may take place from 3 to 72 hr. Due to larger time freezing, the ice crystals formed bigger in size that is cause of rupture of cell of food materials. At thawing of fruits frozen by this method can not regain their original moisture and texture and due to this reason, nowadays, freezer rooms are maintained at – 23 to – 29°C or even lower.

2) **Quick Freezing (Rapid Freezing):** In this process the food is exposed to blast of air at a very low temperatures of maximum ice crystal formation (0 to – 4°C) in 30 min or less and then cooled at –18°C. Such a speed results in formation of very small ice crystal and hence minimum disturbance of cell structure. The yield of a good quality product after thawing, to achieve quick freezing. The temperature to which product is exposed is much lower. This may be achieved by one method of following methods
   - By direct immersion
   - By indirect contact with refrigerant
   - By air blast

(*i*) **By direct immersion:** Since liquids have good heat conductivity, food can be frozen rapidly by direct immersion in a liquid such as a brine or sugar solution at low temperature. Solution works as a refrigeration medium. The condition required is that the product could be frozen at this temperature. The immersion freezing is done at the temperature of – 18°C or below varying from seconds to one minute. This method has several merits and demerits;

Merits

a) There is perfect contact between the refrigerating medium and product; hence the rate of heat transfer is very high.

b) Fruits and vegetables are frozen with a coating of syrup or brine which preserves the colour and flavour during storage.

c) The frozen product is not a block because each piece is separated when immersed.

Demerits

a) Refrigerant may enter the food products causing adverse changes in its quality

b) The refrigeration temperature must be carefully controlled, as at high temperature the medium will enter the product by osmosis and at low temperature the medium may freeze solid.

c) It is very difficult to keep the medium at a definite concentration and also keep it free from dirt and contamination for longer period.

d) It is difficult to make syrup that will not become viscous at low temperature.

(*ii*) **By Indirect contact with refrigerant:** Indirect freezing may be defined as freezing by contact of the product with metal surface which itself cooled by freezing brine or refrigerant media. This is an old method of freezing in which the food in block or in packages is kept in contact with the passage through which the refrigerant at – 18 to – 47°C flows. This method is popular more in form in plate freezer consisting of two parallel plates, one of which in movable and both are cooled to very low temperature. Plate freezers are often used to the freezing packed food.

(*ii*) **By Air Blast:** In this method, refrigerated air between the temperature (– 18 to – 34°C or even less is blown through the material to be frozen. If the air velocity is so high, it may cause fluidization of the product (more than the terminal velocity of the product). The freezing of each piece of product takes place separately. This method of freezing is better known as **IQF (Individual Quick Freezing)**. The requirement of this method is that velocity of air blast should be very high and the product should not be large in size. The freezing of pieces as diced carrot, diced onion, diced potato, by this method is becoming increasable popular.

(3) Cryogenic freezing: The cryogenic is a method in which the temperature of freezing medium is very low and could as well as – 76°C. Although most foods retain their quality by quick frozen, a few, such as mushroom, sliced tomatoes, whole strawberries and raspberries require ultra freezing which can be achieved by cryogenic freezing. The freezers are used for cryogenic freezing at very low boiling point. The liquid nitrogen, liquid air, liquid and solid carbon dioxide are the refrigerant used for this freezing. Freezing is done by immersing the product in liquid or by spraying refrigerant over the product or by circulating air at ultra low temperature around product.

(4) Dehydro-freezing: It is an adjunct to freezing in which a food is first dehydrated to a desirable moisture content and then frozen. It is particularly suited to fruits and vegetables, since fresh fruits and vegetables contain more water than other types of foods, like meat and cereals and their cellular structure is less elastic, they are prone to more damage during freezing than meat etc. Removing some of the water prior to freezing theoretically allows the ice crystals to form and expand without damaging the cellular structure of the produce. Reducing the water content prior to freezing also has the potential to reduce the freezing time, the initial freezing point, and amount of the ice formed within the product. The concept of dehydration was developed in 1940s. This process is commercially successful as applied to potatoes, carrots and others. This process is hard to perform at home.

(5) Freeze drying: In this method, food is first frozen at –18°C on trays in the lower chamber of a freeze drier and then frozen material dried (initially at 30°C for 24 hr and then at 20°C) under high vacuum (0.1 mm Hg) in the upper chamber. Direct sublimation of ice takes place without passing through intermediate liquid stage. The product is highly hygroscopic, excellent in taste and flavour and can be reconstitute readily, mango pulp, orange juice concentrate, passion fruit and guava pulp are dehydrated by this method. This method is also known as *lyophilization*.

8. CHILLING

Chilling is the unit operation in which the temperature of a food is reduced to between –1°C and 8°C. It is used to reduce the rate of bio-chemical and microbiological changes, and hence to extend the shelf life of fresh and processed foods. It causes minimal changes to sensory characteristics and nutritional properties of foods and, as a result, consumers as being convenient, easy to prepare, high quality and "healthy", perceive chilled foods, natural and fresh.

Chilling is often used in combination with other unit operations *i.e.* fermentation or pasteurization to extent the shelf life of mildly processed foods.

Chilling equipments are refrigerators and cryogenic systems.

Chilling foods are grouped into three categories according to their storage temperature range as follows

1. –1°C to +1°C (fresh fish, meats, sausages and ground meats, smoked meats and breaded fish.)
2. 0°C to + 5°C (pasteurized canned meat, milk, cream, yogurt, prepared salad, sandwiches, baked foods, fresh soups and sauces, pizza, pastries and unbaked dough).
3. 0° to + 8°C (fully cooked meats and fish pies, cooked or uncooked cured meat, butter margarine, hard cheese, cooked rice, fruit juice and soft fruits).

Cryogenic Chilling

A cryogen is a refrigerant that changes phase by absorbing latent heat to cool the food. Cryogenic chillers use solid carbon dioxide (CO_2) or liquefied N_2. Solid CO_2 removes latent heat of vaporization (352 KJ/kg at –78°C), and liquid cryogens remove latent heat of vaporization (358 KJ/Kg at 196°C) for liquid N_2; liquid CO_2 has a similar latent heat to the solids.

The gas absorbs sensible heat as it warms from –78°C (CO_2) or from –196°C (liquid N_2) to give a total refrigerant effect of 565 KJ/Kg and 690 KJ/Kg, respectively. The advantages of CO_2 includes:

(*i*) A higher boiling and sublimation point than N_2, and therefore a less severe effect on the food.

(*ii*) Most of heat capacity arises from the conversion of solid or liquid to gas.

9. SMOKING

Smoking is the process of flavoring, cooking, or preserving food by exposing it to the smoke from burning or smoldering plant materials, most often wood. Meats and fish are the most common smoked foods, though cheeses, vegetables, and ingredients used to make beverages such as whisky. Rauchbier, and lapsang souchong tea are also smoked. Smoke is an antimicrobial and antioxidant, but smoke alone is insufficient for preserving food in practice.

i. **Hot smoking** exposes the foods to smoke and heat in a controlled environment. Although foods that have been hot smoked are often reheated or cooked, they are typically safe to eat without further cooking.

ii. **Smoke-roasting** or **"Smoke-baking"** refers to any process that has the attributes of smoking with either roasting or baking.

iii. **Cold smoking** can be used as a flavor enhancer for items such as pork chops, beef steaks, chicken breasts, salmon and scallops.

Eating a diet high in smoked, cured, or salted meats has been shown to be a risk factor in stomach cancer. In addition to sugar and salt exposure, smoking can directly create compounds known to have long-term health consequences, namely polycyclic aromatic hydrocarbons, or PAHs, many of which are known or suspected carcinogens.

10. PRESERVATION BY SALT AND VINEGAR /PICKLING

Preservation with salting:

Salting or curing draws moisture from the meat through a process of osmosis. **Pickling**, also known as **brining** or **corning**, is the process of preserving food by anaerobic fermentation in brine (a solution of salt in water) to produce lactic acid, or marinating and storing it in an acid solution, usually vinegar (acetic acid). The resulting food is called a *pickle.* This procedure gives the food a salty or sour taste. In South Asia edible oils are used as the pickling medium instead of vinegar. Table salt, which consists primarily of sodium chloride, is the most important ingredient for curing food and is used in relatively large quantities. Salt kills and inhibits the growth of microorganisms by drawing water out of the cells of both microbe and food alike through osmosis. Concentrations of salt up to 20% are required to kill most species of unwanted bacteria.

A number of fruits and vegetables are preserved in vinegar whose final concentration, in terms of acetic acid, in the finished pickle should not be less than 2 percent. To prevent dilution of vinegar below this strength by the water liberated from the tissues, the vegetables or fruits are generally placed in strong vinegar of about 10 percent strength for several days before pickling. This treatment helps to expel the gases present in the intercellular spaces of vegetable tissue.

Vinegar pickles are the most important pickles consumed in other countries. Mango, garlic, chilies, etc. are preserved as such in vinegar.

Pickling can be broadly categorized as chemical pickling (for example, brining) and fermentation pickling (for example, making sauerkraut).

i. **Chemical pickling**, the food is placed in an edible liquid that inhibits or kills bacteria and other micro-organisms. Typical pickling agents include brine (high in salt), vinegar, alcohol, and vegetable oil, especially olive oil but also many other oils. Many chemical pickling processes also involve heating or boiling so that the food being preserved becomes saturated with the pickling agent. Common chemically pickled foods include cucumbers, peppers, corned beef, herring, and eggs, as well mixed vegetables such as piccalilli, chow-chow, giardiniera, and achar.

ii. **Fermentation pickling**, the food itself produces the preservation agent, typically by a process that produces lactic acid. Fermented pickles include sauerkraut, nukazuke, kimchi, surströmming, and curtido. Some chemically pickled cucumbers are also fermented.

iii. **Commercial pickles**, a preservative like sodium benzoate or EDTA may also be added to enhance shelf life. **Example:** Meat is cured with salt or sugar, or a combination of the two. Nitrates and nitrites are also often used to cure meat and contribute the characteristic pink color, as well as inhibition of Clostridium botulinum. Sauerkraut and Korean kimchi are produced by salting the vegetables to draw out excess water.

11. BY SUGAR

Sugar is used to preserve fruits, either in syrup with fruit such as apples, pears, peaches, apricots, plums or in crystallized form where the preserved material is cooked in sugar to the point of crystallization and the resultant product is then stored dry. Creates osmotic effect and absorbs water in the food reducing water activity (a_w). This method mostly usd for preparing jams and jellies This method is used for the skins of citrus fruit (candied peel), angelica and ginger. A modification of this process produces glazed fruit such as glazed cherries where the fruit is preserved in sugar but is then extracted from the syrup and sold, the preservation being maintained by the sugar content of the fruit and the superficial coating of syrup. The use of sugar is often combined with alcohol for preservation of luxury products such as fruit in brandy or other spirits. These should not be confused with fruit flavored spirits such as cherry brandy or Sloe gin. The concentration of sugar in sugar preserved products must be 68% or more

12. BY LYE

Sodium hydroxide (lye) makes food too alkaline for bacterial growth. Lye will saponify fats in the food, which will change its flavor and texture. Lutefisk (Norweigan dish) for preserving fish uses lye in its preparation, as do some olive recipes. Modern recipes for century eggs also call for lye. Masa harina and hominy use lye in their preparation, but not for preservation. Lye is also works as de-emulsifier.

13. EXTRUSION COOKING

Extrusion is a thermo-mechanical processing operation in which the raw material is fed into a hopper and forced through the passage between a rotating screw and a stationery barrel. The processed material comes out through a die of specific shape. The extrusion cooking technology is one process where starch foods can be processed at higher temperatures within short time so as to reduce the anti-nutritional factors without affecting quality of other constituents. Single and twin-screw extruders are widely used in the food industry for production of shaped and cooked products. The higher shear and temperature environment inside the screw channel results in mixing in the material and leads to chemical reactions that constitute the cooking process. Extrusion cooking is an emerging technology having advantages of low production cost, capable of producing end products in various shapes and sizes, from a variety of food materials with easy digestibility, maintaining hygiene and high product quality and leaving no effluents or hazardous materials. Extrusion cooking is a specialized form of processing, which is unique in food and feed processing because of the conditions that are used to transform the raw materials.

Advantages of extrusion: Extrusion technology provides several advantages over traditional methods of food and feed processing, including the following:

i. **Versatility:** Options for processing a variety of food products by changing a minor ingredient and/or processing conditions on the machine

ii. **Product shape:** Different shapes, textures, colors, and appearances obtained by minor changes in hardware and processing conditions

iii. **Low cost:** Energy efficient processing, and often lower in cost compared to other options

iv. **Production of new food:** Availability of automation with most new extruders, which can increase productivity

v. **High product quality:** Improved product quality over other processes because cooking is done in a very short time and less destruction of heat sensitive ingredients occurs.

vi. **Easy scale up:** Easy scale-up of extrusion processes from pilot plant to commercial production.

Extruded Products:

- ❖ Snack foods ❖ Ready to eat breakfast cereals ❖ Texturized vegetable proteins
- ❖ Pasta ❖ Dal analogue
- ❖ Biodegradable packaging made from starch ❖ Aqua feed
- ❖ Animal feed ❖ Poultry feed

Examples;

- ❖ Soy nuggets/granules ❖ Cheese balls ❖ Kurkure ❖ Soy fortified break fast cereals

14. MINIMAL PROCESSING

Minimal processing is used for the preservation of short shelf life of fruits and vegetables, and meat products, with minimum damage to the freshness of the products. Minimal processed foods retain their freshness and they are more acceptable to consumer than conventionally processed products. Minimal processing can be achieved by using of a combination of mild processing methods, which control the growth of spoilage and pathogenic microorganisms (hurdle technology), without serious damage to the product quality. Hurdles (obstacles) used in food preservation include temperature, water activity, pH, preservatives and competing microorganisms (*e.g.* lactic acid bacteria). Recent non thermal preservation methods such as irradiation, high pressure and pulse electric field may also be used. Minimal processed fruits can be produced using the following hurdles: steam blanching for 1-3 min, reduction of water activity (a_w) to 0.98-0.93 by sugar addition, lowering the pH to 4.1-3.0 by addition of citric acid or phosphoric acid, and addition of antimicrobials *e.g.* 1000 ppm of sorbate and sulfite. The treated fruits can be packaged and stored at ambient (room) temperature (upto 35°C) for about 4 months. Minimal processed raw vegetables can be preserved by modified atmosphere packaging (MAP) and storage at 1-8°C for 5-7 days. Vegetables and potato dishes (salads), vacuum packaged (sous vide) and heated mostly at 65-95°C, can be stored under refrigeration (1-8°C) for about 42 days. The growth of anaerobic microorganisms such as toxin producing Clostridium botulinum should be prevented by some additional hurdles. Development of minimally processed foods by hurdle technology should be combined with GMPs (good manufacturing practices) and HACCP (hazard analysis) for better process control.

15. HURDLE TECHNOLOGY

Hurdle technology is the technology, by which every preservation parameter is used at an optimum level in order to get maximum microbial inactivation by a combination of two or more such parameter so that damage to sensory properties of food is kept to be minimum.

The process used for preservation provides shelf stability to a product by laying hurdles which are difficult to overcome by microorganism causing food spoilage.

The parameters like water activity (a_w), high temp (F), low temp (t), acidification (pH) and competitive flora (K-F) are called hurdles. The use of the inhibiting factors (hurdles) in combination can be advantageous principally by allowing the less extreme use of the any single treatment. The hurdle concepts illustrate that complex interaction of temp, water activity, pH and so on, are significant to microbial stability of foods.

Various Hurdles Commonly Found in Food Preservation.

The brief classification of different hurdles is given below:

(*a*) pH = – log [H] =

- Low acid foods have pH 5.0 and more.
- Medium acid foods have pH 5.0 and 4.5
- Acid foods have pH 4.5 and 3.7
- High acid foods have pH 3.7 and less.

The acidity or alkalinity of an environment has a profound effect on the stability and activity of macromolecules such as enzymes. In general, bacteria grows fastest in the pH range 6.0 to 8.0 (i.e. near the neutral pH), Yeast grows fastest in the pH range 4.5 to 6.0. Filamentous fungi grows fastest in the pH range 3.5 to 4.0. Lactobacilli and acetic acid bacteria grow with optimum usually between pH 5 to 6.0.Most foods are at least slightly acidic (since material with an alkaline pH generally have a rather unpleasant taste).

Exception : Egg white, where the pH increases to 9.2 (as CO_2 is lost from the egg after lying) is a common exception to this.

The ability of low pH to restrict microbial growth has been deliberately employed since the earliest times in the preservation of foods with lactic acid. Therefore, for food preservation the pH should be lowered.

(*b*) **Water activity (a_w)** $= \dfrac{p}{p_{water}} = \dfrac{1}{100} ERH$

Most of the microorganisms associated with foods grow best at relatively high water activity. Therefore, a reduction in water activity would limit the growth of majority of the microorganisms. ***A limiting value of water activity for growth of any microorganism is about 0.6 and below this value the spoilage of foods is not microbiological*** (but may be due to insect damage or chemical reaction such as oxidation). Thus, stability and safety of many foods depend on or at least enhanced by reduced water activity.

The common methods for decreasing water activity of food are drying, addition of salt, humectants (like sugar or polyols) and freezing. The water activity of foods influences the multiplication, metabolic activity, resistance and survival of organisms present.

The stability and safety of many foods is not based solely on water activity, but on the combined effects of several factors. These factors could have an additive or synergistic effect.

(*c*) **Redox potential or Oxygen Reduction potential (Eh) :** The tendency of medium to accept or donate electrons, to oxidize or reduce, is termed as redox potential. The growth of microorganism in biological medium is dependent on Eh of medium. **The Lower Eh value contributes to microbiological stability of food products.**Not only aerobic but also many facultative anaerobic bacteria do not grow well at low Eh. This hurdle can be regulated by type of package and packaging material.

(*d*) **Heating (F-Hurdle) :** This is an energy **intensive** hurdle. This results into wastage of valuable resources (*i.e.* energy) and increases the production cost. The purpose of heat treatment in food preservation is to kill the microorganisms and inactivates the enzyme that become active in the subsequent storage of packaged food.

To produce "energy saving foods" the energy consuming hurdle F can be replaced partly by less energy consuming hurdles such as a_w, pH and Eh. It is found that an adjustment of foods to a_w below 0.95 would make temperatures above +100°C unnecessary in canning (because the surviving spores of bacteria cannot cause spoilage or food poisoning below this a_w).

Microbial growth can occur over a temperature range from about – 8°C up to 100 °C at atmospheric pressure.

Most bacteria, yeast and molds grow best in the temperature range of about 16°C–38°C. Some grow even at 0 °C and others at a temperature as high as 100°C.

The optimum temperature for most of the bacteria growth is 35°C,

The optimum temperature for most of the mold growth is ~ 25-30 °C,

The optimum temperature for most of the yeast growth is 35-47°C.

Some kinds of yeast can grow at even at 0 °C

Most of bacteria are killed in range of 82-93°C, but many bacterial spores are not destroyed even by 100 °C for 30 minutes heating.

When foods are high in acids (such as tomatoes, orange juice), one need not heat as severely because acid increases the killing power of heat. A temperature of 93°C for 15 minutes may be enough to gain stability if sufficient acid is present.

(*e*) **Chilling(t Hurdle) :** This is also an energy **intensive** hurdle. The energy saving can be done here also as in F hurdle. This hurdle operates by reducing the a_w, apart from the low temperature affect.

However, there is no perfect agreement between the minimum a_w and temperature for minimum growth bacteria, yeast and moulds. *e.g.*

- **For yeast** minimum a_w is 0.88 and minimum temperature should be –12 °C (but at this minimum temperature a_w is 0.89).
- **For bacteria** minimum a_w is 0.90 and minimum temperature should be –10 °C (but at this minimum temperature a_w is 0.91).
- **For moulds** minimum a_w is 0.70 and minimum temperature should be –18 °C (but at this minimum temperature a_w is 0.84).

This revealed that during freezing, some of yeast, moulds, and bacteria were inhibited by lowering of a_w instead of temperature.

However, the retardation of microbial and biochemical activities at low temperatures is the basis of preservation by cold. Cold temperature treatment only reduces the microbial activities and population but does not kill all the bacteria.

Most spoilage organisms grow above 10°C. Some food poisoning organisms grow slowly up to 3.3°C.

Cryophilic (psychrophilic) grow slowly from – 4.4 °C to – 9.4°C provided the food is not frozen. These organisms however do not produce toxins but cause deterioration.

There is no growth of organisms below –9.4°C though there may not be a total destruction at that temperature.

***(f)* Preservatives (Preservative Hurdle) :** A preservative is defined as any substance which is capable of inhibiting, retarding or arresting the growth of microorganisms. Chemical preservatives interfere with cell membrane of microorganisms, their enzymes or their genetic mechanisms. The compounds used as preservatives may be natural or synthetic. Chemical preservatives are added after the foods are processed.

Several preservatives are frequently being used in food industry within the permissible limits of legal standards *e.g.* NaCl, Sorbic acid, acetic acid, propylene, glycol, glycerol, nitrite, potassium sorbate, primaricin, parabens, butanediol, BHA, BHT, sodium metabisulphates, antibiotics etc.

Apart from above chemicals some spices and herbs are also used as preservatives.

The antimycotic agents (like potassium sorbate, sodium benzoate, propylene glycerol) are added to intermediate moisture meat (IMM) products and they prevent the mould growth.

16. NON-THERMAL PROCESSING

Non-thermal processes for the preservation of foods are under intense research to evaluate their potential as alternative or complementary processes to traditional methods of food preservation. Traditionally most preserved foods are thermally processed by subjecting the food to high temperatures of 60-100°C for a few seconds to minutes to transfer energy to foods. This energy may trigger unwanted reactions in the foods leading to certain undesirable changes as milk so processed may have a cooked flavour accompanied by a loss of certain vital nutrients and flavours. It is no the shelf-life of food but it's the quality that give with the non-thermal method which avoid quality degradation of foods that results from thermal processing. In these the losses in quality degradation expected from high temperature is minimum and utilize less energy as compared to high temperature processing.

Various non-thermal processing methods gaining importance are as discussed below:

(i) High Pressure Processing

High Pressure Processing (HPP) is a method of food processing where food is subjected to elevated pressures (9,000 atmospheres), with or without the addition of heat, to achieve microbial inactivation or to alter the food attributes in order to achieve consumer-desired qualities. Pressure inactivates most vegetative bacteria at pressures above HPP retains food quality, maintains natural freshness, and extends microbiological shelf life. High (hydrostatic) pressure in the range of 1-8 kbar (100-800 MPa) can inactivate vegetative cells of pathogenic and spoilage microorganisms without heat damage to the quality of sensitive foods. High pressure processing (HPP) can be applied to pasteurization and minimal processing. Destruction of microbial spores any require combined heat and HPP treatment.

The process is also known as high hydrostatic pressure processing (HHP) and ultra high-pressure processing (UHP). Most processed foods today are heat treated to kill bacteria, which often diminishes product quality. High pressure processing provides an alternative means of killing bacteria that can cause spoilage or food-borne disease without a loss of sensory quality or nutrients. In a typical HPP process, the product is packaged in a flexible container (usually a pouch or plastic bottle) and is loaded into a high pressure chamber filled with a pressure-transmitting (hydraulic) fluid. The hydraulic fluid (normally water) in the chamber is pressurized with a pump, and this pressure is transmitted through the package into the food itself. Pressure is applied for a specific time, usually 3 to 5 min. number of changes occur to the morphology and genetic mechanism of the microorganisms. The intracellular gas vacuoles of the microbe can collapse at 0.6 MPa. When the pressure exceeds 200MPa, the cell wall and sub cellular structure gets altered in case of yeasts. Some biochemical changes are also found to occur. As a result of denaturation of proteins present in the cell membranes, membrane malfunctions occur which ultimately leads to inhibition of amino acid uptake. Numerous studies have shown a loss of intracellular constituents from microorganisms after pressure treatment, due to which, the cellular membrane gets damaged completely leading to death and injury. The mechanism of action is better explained by the following four principles.

The processed product is then removed and stored/distributed in the conventional manner. Because the pressure is transmitted uniformly (in all directions simultaneously), food retains its shape, even at extreme pressures. And because no heat is needed, the sensory characteristics of the food are retained without compromising microbial safety. High pressure processing causes minimal changes in the 'fresh' characteristics of foods by eliminating thermal degradation. Comparison between thermal processing and HPP, HPP results in foods with fresher taste, and better appearance, texture and nutrition.

High pressure processing can be conducted at ambient or refrigerated temperatures, thereby eliminating thermally induced cooked off-flavors. The technology is especially beneficial for heat-sensitive products. Like any other processing method, HPP cannot be universally applied to all types of foods. HPP can be used to process both liquid and solid foods. Foods with a high acid content are particularly good candidates for HPP technology.

The method of pulse and oscillatory pressurization is more effective in spore inactivation than continuous pressurization. Spore inactivation can be greatly improved by increasing the oscillation cycle. Therefore Pulse pressurization is useful in decreasing spore inactivation time.

The mechanism of spore inactivation due to oscillatory pressurization is not clearly known. It is possible that the change in properties of water (*i.e.* decrease in viscosity and surface tension at 70°C) may have an effect on destruction of spores by oscillatory pressurization. The surface of spore is completely ruptured after pressurization. The physical changes in the spore wall caused by an increase in temp from 20 to 70°C may destroy spores. Also, a weakening of physical strength of spores may occur.

(ii) Oscillating Magnetic Field Processing

Strong static or oscillating fields (5-50 Tesla) have the potential to inactivate vegetative microorganisms. The impulse duration is in between 10 μs and several milliseconds and the frequencies are maximally 500 MHz because above this items begin to warm up noticeably. The preservation of foods with oscillating magnetic field (OMF) involves sealing of foods in a plastic bag and subjecting it to 1-100 pulses in can OMF at temperatures of 0°C to 50°C for a total exposure time ranging form 25 to 100 minutes. Therefore, no special preparation is required. Magnetic field treatments are carried out atmosphere pressure and at a temperature that stabilizes the food material. It does not have any influence on the organoleptic properties as the temperature raises only 2-5°C.

(iii) Pulsed Electric Fields Processing

Pulsed electric field (PEF) processing is a non-thermal method of food preservation that uses short bursts of electricity for microbial inactivation and causes minimal or no detrimental effect on food quality attributes. PEF can be used for processing liquid and semi-liquid food products. PEF processing offers high quality fresh-like liquid foods with excellent flavor, nutritional value, and shelf-life. Since it preserves foods without using heat, foods treated this way retain their fresh aroma, taste, and appearance. PEF processing involves treating foods placed between electrodes by high voltage pulses in the order of 20–80 kV (usually for a couple of microseconds). The applied high voltage results in an electric field that causes microbial inactivation. The electric field may be applied in the form of exponentially decaying, square wave, bipolar, or oscillatory pulses and at ambient, sub-ambient, or slightly above-ambient temperature. After the treatment, the food is packaged aseptically and stored under refrigeration. Application of PEF technology has been successfully demonstrated for the pasteurization of foods such as juices, milk, yogurt, soups, and liquid eggs. Application of PEF processing is restricted to food products with no air bubbles and with low electrical conductivity. The maximum particle size in the liquid must be smaller than the gap of the treatment region in the chamber in order to ensure proper treatment. PEF is a continuous processing method, which is not suitable for solid food products that are not pumpable. PEF is also applied to enhance extraction of sugars and other cellular content from plant cells, such as sugar beets. PEF also found application in reducing the solid volume (sludge) of wastewater. PEF treatment has lethal effects on various vegetative bacteria, mold, and yeast. Efficacy of spore inactivation by PEF in combination with heat or other hurdles is a subject of current research.

A series of short, high-voltage pulses breaks the cell membranes of vegetative microorganisms in liquid media by expanding existing pores (electroporation) or creating new ones. Pore formation is reversible or irreversible depending on factors such as the electric field intensity, the pulse duration, and number of pulses. The membranes of PEF-treated cells become permeable to small molecules; permeation causes swelling and eventual rupture of the cell membrane. In general, the shelf-life of PEF-treated and thermally pasteurized foods is comparable. PEF pasteurization kills microorganisms and inactivates some enzymes and, unless the product is acidic, it requires refrigerated storage. For heat-sensitive liquid foods where thermal pasteurization is not an option (due to flavor, texture, or color changes), PEF treatment would be advantageous. PEF pasteurized products currently are stored refrigerated. In some cases (for example, milk), this is necessary for safety (to prevent the growth of spores in low-acid foods). For acid foods, refrigeration is not necessary for microbial stability, but is used to preserve flavor quality for extended periods of time. Three types of factors that affect the microbial inactivation with PEF have been identified: factors depending on (1) the process (electric field intensity, pulse width, treatment time and temperature, and pulse wave shapes), (2) microbial entity (type, concentration, and growth stage of microorganism), and (3) treatment media (pH, antimicrobials, and ionic compounds, conductivity, and medium ionic strength).

(iv) Ohmic Heating Processing

Ohmic heating is an advanced thermal processing method wherein the food material, which serves as an electrical resistor, is heated by passing electricity through it. Electrical energy is dissipated into heat, which results in rapid and uniform heating. Ohmic heating is also called electrical resistance heating, Joule heating, or electro-heating, and may be used for a variety of applications in the food industry. During conventional thermal processing, either in cans or aseptic processing systems for particulate foods, significant product quality damage may occur due to slow conduction and convection heat transfer. Ohmic heating is a food processing method in which an alternating electrical current is passed through a food sample. This results in internal energy generation in foods. This produces an inside-out heating pattern, which is much faster than conventional outside-in heating. Ohmic heating is somewhat similar to microwave heating but with very different frequencies. The advantage of ohmic heating is that it uniformly heats foods with different densities, such as chicken noodle soup.

For example, liquid egg can be ohmically heated in a fraction of a second without coagulating it. Juices can be treated to inactivate enzymes without affecting the flavor. Other potential applications of ohmic heating include blanching, thawing, on-line detection of starch gelatinization, fermentation, peeling, dehydration, and extraction. The shelf life of ohmically processed foods is comparable to that of canned and sterile, aseptically processed products. Ohmic heating saves significant time and energy in hot air and freeze drying of foods and enhances extraction yields in some processing operations. The parameters used during ohmic heating, such as frequency of alternating current, applied voltage and the temperature to which the sample is heated, have a significant effect on its success. The electrical conductivity of the food or food mixture is a significant factor, too. Ohmic heating is a useful tool for value-added processing, and it has great potential for use in a wide variety of food processing operations involving heat and mass transfer.

(v) Membrane Processing

This is a technique that permits concentration and separation without the use of heat. Particles are separated on the basis of their molecular size and shape with the use of pressure and specially designed semi-permeable membranes. Membrane separation processes are based on the ability of semi permeable membranes of appropriate physical and chemical nature to discriminate between molecules primarily on the basis of size, and to lesser extent, on shape and chemical composition. Depending on the chemical/physical properties of the membrane (primarily pore size distribution) concentration or dewatering (reverse osmosis, RO), fractionation of components in solution (ultrafiltration, UF) and clarification of slurries or removal of suspended matter (microfiltration, MF) are accompanied. Membrane filtration is a pressure driven technology with pore sizes ranging from 100 molecular weight to 5 microns.

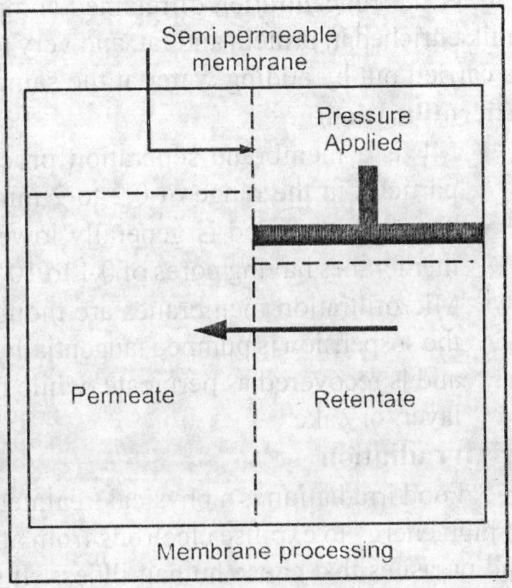

Fig. 1

Important applications:

1. Proteins can be seperated in—(*i*) Whey production (*ii*) Whey protein concentrate.
2. Milk can be concentrated prior to conservation.

1. Reverse Osmosis/Hyperfiltration: Reverse Osmosis (RO) process consists of generating an aqueous solution with a low salt content from another aqueous solution that has a high salt content, via a water-permeable membrane. It is the technology used to produce desalinated water from seawater. The separation process is due to the different solubility and diffusivity in the membrane of the aqueous solution components. Reverse osmosis (RO) designates a membrane separation process, driven by a pressure gradient, in which the membrane separates the solvent (generally water) from other components of a solution. The membrane configuration is usually cross-flow. With reverse osmosis, the membrane pore size is very small allowing only small amounts of very low molecular weight solutes to pass through the membranes.

The application of reverse osmosis in the food industry is a clear example where it is widely used; from concentrates of egg whites, fruit juices and gelatins, to removal of bacteria and brine in meat or alcohol removal from spirits. Dairy, starch and sugar industries are also users of the ro plant working process.

2. Ultrafiltration: Ultrafiltration is a fractionation process separating molecular species on the basis of size using a membrane, which retains the larger molecules and allows water and smaller molecules to pass. Ultrafiltration, UF has membranes with larger pores and will retain protein, lipids and colloidal salts, while allowing smaller molecules to pass through to the permeate phase. It designates a membrane separation process, driven by a pressure gradient, in which the membrane fractionates components of a liquid as a function of their solvated size and structure. The membrane configuration is usually cross-flow. In UF, the membrane pore size is larger allowing some components to pass through the pores with the water. It is a **separation/ fractionation process** using a 10,000 MW cutoff, 40 psi, and temperatures of 50-60°C with polysulfone membranes. In UF milk, lactose and minerals pass in a 50% separation ratio; for example, in the retentate would be 100% of fat, 100% of protein, 50% of lactose, and 50% of free minerals.

3. Diafiltration: It is a specialized type of ultrafiltration process in which the retentate is diluted with water and re-ultrafiltered, to reduce the concentration of soluble permeate components and increase further the concentration of retained components. It is more or less a purification process in producing milk enriched in protein and fat, and very low in lactose and salt content. This most efficient diafiltration, is carried out by adding water at the same rate as the permeate is removed.

Microfiltration:

- MF is a membrane separation process similar to UF but even larger membrane size allowing particles in the range of 0.2 to 2 mm to pass through.
- The pressure used is generally lower than that of UF process. MF utilizes inorganic or organic membranes having pores of 0.1 to 10 mm, although the narrow range of 0.2 to 2 mm is more typical.
- Microfiltration membranes are thought to act like a physical sieve. In cross flow microfiltration, the suspension is pumped tangentially over the medium. Clear liquid permeates the filtration medium and is recovered as permeate, while the solids accumulate at the filtration barrier to form a fouling layer, or cake.

(vi) Irradiation

Food irradiation is a physical treatment in which food is exposed to ionizing radiation, *i.e.* radiation of high energy to expulse electrons from atoms and to ionize molecules. It is used to destroy the bacteria and parasites that cause human illness. It can also make food last longer by destroying or inactivating insects, molds and yeasts that spoil food, delaying the ripening of fruits and vegetables, and limiting unwanted spouting of potatoes and other similar vegetables. Food irradiation is safe and keeps the food in fresh condition. The process is quite simple and technical. The irradiation process involves passing of food through a radiation field allowing the food to absorb desired radiation energy. The food itself never comes in contact with the radioactive materials.

Gamma rays are electro-magnetic radiations of very short wave length in the same family as x-rays, ultra violet, visible, infra red, microwaves and radio waves. The electro-magnetic energy used in food irradiation is similar to x-rays but has shorter wave length, producing grater energy and penetration. So, food processed by irradiation is not in any way made radioactive, regardless of dose absorbed or length of time the food is exposed to. Three types of ionizing radiation can be used for the treatment of food; (1) gamma rays from Cobalt-60 (Co^{60}) or cesium-137 (Ce^{137}) with respective energies of 1.33 and 0.67 million electrons volts, (2) Electronic generated from machine sources operated at maximum energy of 10 MeV, and (3) x-rays generated from machine sources operated at a maximum energy of 5 MeV. In 1981, a Joint FAO/IAEA/WHO expert Committee on Food Irradiation (JECFI) states that the irradiation of foods upto an overall average absorbed dose of 10 kilo Gray (kGy) = 1000Gy (gray), which is in SI unit of energy absorbed (1joule/kg) from ionizing radiation. 1Gy = 100 rad (1 rad = 100 erg/g), and 1kGy = 100 krad present no toxicological hazards and introduce on special nutritional or microbiological problems. Ionizing radiation may have applications in food processing and other related activities. Among the potential application are as:

i. Sterilization of foods in hermetically sealed containers. The process is called "radappertizing" and is directed to production of foods stable at room temperatures conditions for a long period of time. It may be preferable to canning for the foods which are adversely affected by heating but can tolerate sterilizing doses of radiation.

ii. Extension of shelf life of various foods to be distributed and stored at refrigerated temperature. These include fresh fruits and vegetables, milk, egg, fish, meat and also their products. This shelf life can be extended by reducing the microbial load and / or preventing potentially harmful pathogenic microorganisms. Irradiation with higher doses could allow a much longer shelf life at refrigerator temperatures for fish and other sea foods and could improve the safety of poultry by eliminating potential dangerous organisms. In case of fresh fruits and vegetables, irradiation can destroy surface molds and yeast and thus make the commodities more safe and stable.

iii. Treatment of water, sewage and food processing industries wastes. A number of application are possible in which the food itself is not treated by radiation but some materials involved in the food processing plants or in the waste disposed system are so treated.

iv. Disinfestations of grain or dried fruits and of other commodities subjected to insect attack. Doses of 25krad kill the adults and larvae of major insects infesting grain and cereals. To prevent recontamination disinfestation can be an extremely useful step in preserving grain supplies and in preventing insect infestation of the other products.

Disinfestation; it is a physical or chemical process to destroy or remove small undesirable animal forms particularly anthropods, or rodents present in food product.

v. Sprouting in onion, garlic, potatoes and carrot are major problems during storage at ambient temperature for long period of time. This can be prevented by chemical treatments, but an alternative method is provided by ionizing radiation. Only about 15 krad is required and the chemical effects of these low does are negligible.

vi. Irradiation at low doses levels can delay ripening and over ripening of tropic fruits like banana, mangoes and papaya which treated mature but unripe. The shelf life of irradiated fruits can be further extended by combining with other post harvest methods such as waxing, packaging in perforated or closed poly bags, refrigeration and modified atmosphere. Low doses of irradiation when combined with hot water dip treatment (50-55°C for 5-10 min) are found to improve the shelf life as well as reduce fungal decay in fruits.

Table 2: The application of ionizing radiations in food preservation

S.No.	Levels	Doses (kGy)	Utilization
1.	Low dose	0.03-0.15	Sprout inhibition in bulbs and tubers
		0.25-0.75	Delay in fruit ripening
		0.25-1.00	Insect disinfection and elimination of food borne parasites
2.	Medium dose	1.5-3.0	Reduction of spoilage microbes to improve shelf-life of meat, poultry and sea foods under refrigeration
		3.0-7.0	Elimination of pathogenic microbes in fresh and frozen meat, poultry and sea foods
		10.0	Reduction of microbes in spices to improve hygiene
3.	High dose	25-70	Sterilization of packaged meat, poultry and their products which are shelf stable without refrigeration
		25-70	Sterilization of hospital deals

Table 3: Approved irradiation dose and the purpose for food by Govt. of India

S. No.	Food items	Dose (kGy)	Purpose
1.	Onions	0.03-0.09	Sprout inhibition
2.	Potatoes	0.05-0.15	Sprout inhibition
3.	Ginger	0.03-0.15	Sprout inhibition
4.	Garlic	0.03-0.15	Sprout inhibition
5.	Small onion	0.03-0.15	Sprout inhibition
6.	Rice	0.25-1.00	Insect disinfestation
7.	Semolina	0.25-1.00	Insect disinfestation
8.	Wheat Atta	0.25-1.00	Insect disinfestation
9.	Maida	0.25-1.00	Insect disinfestation
10.	Raisins	0.25-0.75	Insect disinfestation
11.	Dried figs	0.25-0.75	Insect disinfestation
12.	Dried dated	0.25-0.75	Insect disinfestation
13.	Mango	0.25-0.75	Shelf life extension & quarantine treatment
14.	Spices	6.0-14.0	Microbial decontamination and insect disinfestation
15.	Meat	2.5-4.0	Shelf life extension under refrigeration and pathogen control
16.	Chicken	2.5-4.0	Shelf life extension under refrigeration and pathogen control

vii. Fruit spoilage results principally from infection by the filamentous fungi and yeast where as bacteria infection is of minor importance in fruits spoilage. Redurization of fresh fruit is aimed at control of these spoilage microorganisms.

viii. Irradiation is most effective method to sanitize spices. The processing of spices to reduce the microbial contamination, which often are of the 108 cfu/g in common spices. This facility has though out of 12000 tonnes per year at an average dose of 10 kGy.

(vii) Ultrasound Method

Ultra sound is probably the most simple and most versatile method for the destruction of cells and for the production of extracts. It is efficient safe and reliable. Ultrasound technology have the advantage of relatively low cost and robust process and associated electronics, a reasonably well –established theory of the interaction between acoustic fields and materials properties, difference to hostile environments *e.g.* corrosive or hot materials, and accessibility to materials opaque to light. In 1959, Mayer and Tiedemann was made first attempt at ultrasonic non-destructive testing of complex food system- whole egg. Other application included cell disruption, degassing of liquid, homogenization of emulsions, and dispersion of aggregated materials, cleaning, animal back fat thickness estimation, low energy ultrasonification for accelerating aging of wine and distilled liqueurs and agitation of thixotropic fluids.

(viii) Supercritical Fluid Extraction

Supercritical Fluid Extraction (SFE) is the process of separating one component (the extractant) from another (the matrix) using supercritical fluids as the extracting solvent. Extraction is usually from a solid matrix, but can also be from liquids. SFE can be used as a sample preparation step for analytical purposes, or on a larger scale to either strip unwanted material from a product (*e.g.* decaffeination) or collect a desired product (*e.g.* essential oils). Carbon dioxide (CO_2) is the most used supercritical fluid, sometimes modified by co-solvents such as ethanol or methanol. Extraction conditions for supercritical CO_2 are above the critical temperature of 31°C and critical pressure of 74 bar. Addition of modifiers may slightly alter this.

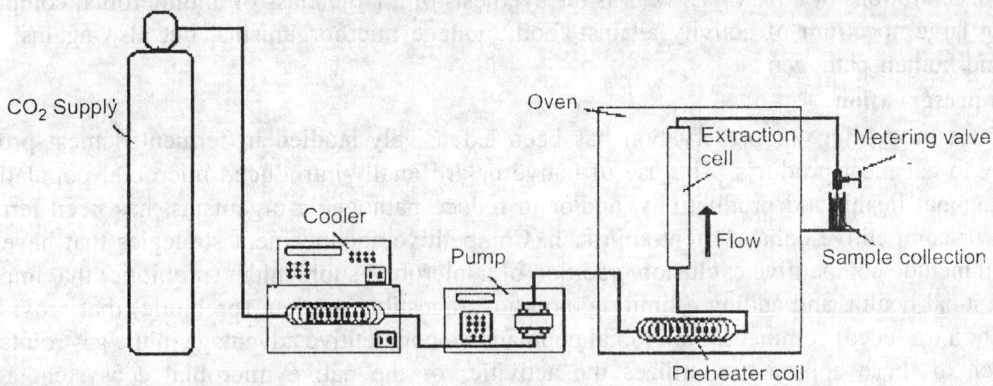

Fig. 2

11.4 BIOPRESERVATION

Biopreservation, can be defined as the extension of shelf life and food safety by the use of natural or controlled microbiota and/or their antimicrobial compounds. One of the most common forms of food biopreservation is fermentation, a process based on the growth of microorganisms in foods, whether natural or added. Traditionally, a great number of foods have been protected against spoiling by natural processes of fermentation. Currently, fermented foods are increasing in popularity (60% of the diet in industrialized countries) and, to assure the homogeneity, quality, and safety of products, they are produced by the intentional application in raw foods of different microbial systems (starter/protective cultures).

Biopreservation is the use of natural or controlled microbiota or antimicrobials as a way of preserving food and extending its shelf life. The biopreservation of food, especially utilizing lactic acid bacteria (LAB) that are inhibitory to food spoilage microbes, has been practiced since early ages, at first unconsciously but eventually with an increasingly robust scientific foundation. Beneficial bacteria or the fermentation products produced by these bacteria are used in biopreservation to control spoilage and render pathogens inactive in food. There are a various modes of action through which microorganisms can interfere with the growth of others such as organic acid production, resulting in a reduction of pH and the antimicrobial activity of the un-dissociated acid molecules, a wide variety of small inhibitory molecules including hydrogen peroxide, etc. It is a benign ecological approach which is gaining increasing attention.

Biopreservative agents

Of special interest are *lactic acid bacteria* (LAB). Lactic acid bacteria have antagonistic properties which make them particularly useful as biopreservatives. When LABs compete for nutrients, their metabolites often include active antimicrobials such as lactic and acetic acid, hydrogen peroxide, and peptide bacteriocins. Some LABs produce the antimicrobial nisin which is a particularly effective preservative. These days LAB bacteriocins are used as an integral part of hurdle technology. Using them in combination with other preservative techniques can effectively control spoilage bacteria and other pathogens, and can inhibit the activities of a wide spectrum of organisms, including inherently resistant Gram-negative bacteria." Lactic acid bacteria and propionibacteria have been extensively studied for their efficacy against spoilage causing yeasts and molds in food spoilage.

Yeast

In addition to lactic acid bacteria, yeasts also have been found to have a biopreservation effect due to their antagonistic activities relying on the competition for nutrients, production and tolerance of high concentrations of ethanol, as well as the synthesis of a large class of antimicrobial compounds exhibiting large spectrum of activity against food spoilage microorganisms, but also against plant, animal and human pathogen..

Meat biopreservation

In meat processing, biopreservation has been extensively studied in fermented meat products and ready to eat meat products. The use of native or artificially-introduced microbial population to improve animal health and productivity, and/or to reduce pathogenic organisms, has been termed a probiotic or competitive enhancement approach. Competitive enhancement strategies that have been developed include competitive exclusion, addition of a microbial supplement (probiotic) that improves gastrointestinal health, and adding a limiting, non-host digestible nutrient (prebiotic) that provides an existing (or introduced) commensal microbial population a competitive advantage in the gastrointestinal tract. Each of these approaches utilizes the activities of the native microbial ecosystem against pathogens by capitalizing on the natural microbial competition. Generally speaking, competitive enhancement strategies offer a natural 'green' method to reduce pathogens in the gut of food animals.

Seafood biopreservation

In fish processing, biopreservation is achieved by adding antimicrobials or by increasing the acidity of the fish muscle. Most bacteria stop multiplying when the pH is less than 4.5. Traditionally, acidity has been increased by fermentation, marination or by directly adding acetic, citric or lactic acid to food products. Other preservatives include nitrites, sulphites, sorbates, benzoates and essential oils.

Bacteriophages

Bacteriophages (Greek for 'bacteria eater'), or simply phages, are viruses which infect bacteria. The majority of all bacteriophages known exhibit a double-stranded DNA genome inside the virion capsid and belong to the order of tailed phages, Caudovirales. The tailed phages can be further separated into three families: Podoviridae, which are characterized by very short tails; Myoviridae, which exhibit longer, straight and contractile tails; and Siphoviridae, which can be identified due to their long and flexible tails. Another well studied group of phages with many applications, although minor in terms of species diversity, is represented by filamentous phages which exhibit a single stranded DNA genome decorated by a helical protein layer surrounding the DNA molecule. Bacteriophages are ubiquitously distributed in nature and can also be isolated from human or animal associated microflora. They outnumber their bacterial host species by a factor of ten representing the most abundant self-replicating entities on earth with an estimated 1031 phages in total. Several laboratories have been testing suitability of bacteriophage isolates to control certain bacterial pathogens. Significant advancements in this research have been made at the Bacteriophage Institute in Tbilisi, Georgia, where phage therapy is routinely applied in medicine research field. Today treatment of antibiotic resistant bacteria is a challenging task. Recently, research on bacteriophages has gained additional momentum in light of the identification of antibiotic-resistant pathogens of infectious diseases, wherein the application of antibiotics is not effectively working, therefore research on the application of bacteriophages is being reviewed intensely.

11.5 FOOD ADDITIVES

Food additives are substances added to food to preserve flavor or enhance its taste, appearance, or other qualities. Some additives have been used for centuries; for example, preserving food by pickling (with vinegar), salting, as with bacon, preserving sweets or using sulfur dioxide as with wines. With the advent of processed foods in the second half of the twentieth century, many more additives have been introduced, of both natural and artificial origin. Food additives also include substances that may be introduced to food indirectly (called "indirect additives") in the manufacturing process, through packaging, or during storage or transport.

To regulate these additives and inform consumers, each additive is assigned a unique number called an "E number", which is used in Europe for all approved additives. This numbering scheme has now been adopted and extended by the Codex Alimentarius Commission to internationally identify all additives, regardless of whether they are approved for use

Categories of Additives

Food additives can be divided into several groups, although there is some overlap because some additives exert more than one effect. For example, salt is both a preservative as well as a flavor.

Acidulents: Acidulents confer sour or acid taste. Common acidulents include vinegar, citric acid, tartaric acid, malic acid, fumaric acid, and lactic acid.

Acidity regulators: Acidity regulators are used for controlling the pH of foods for stability or to affect activity of enzymes.

Anticaking agents: Anticaking agents keep powders such as milk powder from caking or sticking.

Antifoaming and foaming agents: Antifoaming agents reduce or prevent foaming in foods. Foaming agents do the reverse.

Antioxidants: Antioxidants such as vitamin C are preservatives by inhibiting the degradation of food by oxygen. (Also refer Page No. 350)

Bulking agents: Bulking agents such as starch are additives that increase the bulk of a food without affecting its taste.

Food coloring: Colorings are added to food to replace colors lost during preparation or to make food look more attractive.

Fortifying agents: Vitamins, minerals, and dietary supplements to increase the nutritional value

Color retention agents: In contrast to colorings, color retention agents are used to preserve a food's existing color. Natural and synthetic colours are added to foods to enhance visual appeal.

Emulsifiers: Emulsifiers allow water and oils to remain mixed together in an emulsion, as in mayonnaise, ice cream, and homogenized milk.

Flavors: Flavors are additives that give food a particular taste or smell, and may be derived from natural ingredients or created artificially.

Flavor enhancers: Flavor enhancers enhance a food's existing flavors. A popular example is monosodium glutamate. Some flavor enhancers have their own flavors that are independent of the food.

Flour treatment agents: Flour treatment agents are added to flour to improve its color or its use in baking.

Glazing agents: Glazing agents provide a shiny appearance or protective coating to foods.

Sequestrants: These are chelating agents. They react with trace elements such as Iron, Copper present in foods and remove them from solutions. The trace elements are active catalysts concerned in oxidation and decolourisations of food products. Sequestrants such as EDTA, polyphosphate, and citric acid react with the trace elements and inactivate them.

Tracer gas: Tracer gas allow for package integrity testing to prevent foods from being exposed to atmosphere, thus guaranteeing shelf life.

Preservatives: Preservatives prevent or inhibit spoilage of food due to fungi, bacteria and other microorganisms.

Stabilizers: Stabilizers, thickeners and gelling agents, like agar or pectin (used in jam for example) give foods a firmer texture. While they are not true emulsifiers, they help to stabilize emulsions.

Sweeteners: Sweeteners are added to foods for flavoring. Sweeteners other than sugar are added to keep the food energy (calories) low, or because they have beneficial effects regarding diabetes mellitus, tooth decay, or diarrhea.

Thickeners: Thickening agents are substances which, when added to the mixture, increase its viscosity without substantially modifying its other properties.

Packaging: PACKAGING Bisphenols, phthalates, and perfluoroalkyl chemicals (PFCs) are indirect additives used in manufacturing or packaging. In July 2018 the American Academy of Pediatrics called for more careful study of these three substances, along with nitrates and food coloring, as they might harm children during development.

WHO response

WHO encourages national authorities to monitor and ensure that food additives in food and drinks produced in their countries comply with permitted uses, conditions and legislation. National authorities should oversee the food business, which carries the primary responsibility for ensuring that the use of a food additive is safe and complies with legislation.

Evaluating the health risk of food additives

WHO, in cooperation with the Food and Agriculture Organization of the United Nations (FAO), is responsible for assessing the risks to human health from food additives. Risk assessment of food additives are conducted by an independent, international expert scientific group – the Joint FAO/WHO Expert Committee on Food Additives (JECFA).

International standards for the safe use of food additives

The safety assessments completed by JECFA are used by the joint intergovernmental food standard-setting body of FAO and WHO, the Codex Alimentarius Commission, to establish levels for maximum use of additives in food and drinks. Codex standards are the reference for national standards for consumer protection, and for the international trade in food, so that consumers everywhere can be confident that the food they eat meets the agreed standards for safety and quality, no matter where it was produced.

Once a food additive has been found to be safe for use by JECFA and maximum use levels have been established in the Codex General Standard for Food Additives, national food regulations need to be implemented permitting the actual use of a food additive.

Additive on labels

The Codex Alimentarius Commission also establishes standards and guidelines on food labelling. These standards are implemented in most countries, and food manufacturers are obliged to indicate which additives are used in their products. In the European Union, for example, there is legislation governing labelling of food additives according to a set of pre-defined "E-numbers". People who have allergies or sensitivities to certain food additives should check labels carefully.

11.6 CHILLING AND FREEZING INJURY

Physiological disorder refers to breakdown of tissues and develops in response to adverse environment, especially temperature, or to a nutritional deficiency during growth and development. Some reactions are sensitive to low temperature and cease completely below a critical temperature. Metabolic disturbances occurring at reduced temperature are generally divided in into two main groups: ***chilling injury*** and ***physiological disorder***. Chilling injury results from the exposure of susceptible tissues to temperature below 15°C although the critical temperature at which chilling injury symptoms are produced varies among the different horticultural commodities. The injury is caused due to change in physical state of membrane lipids and dissociation of enzymes and other proteins. Chilling injury may occur in the field, in transit or distribution, in retail or home refrigerators. The effect of short periods of chilling may cumulative in some commodities.

The primary cause of chilling injury is thought to damage plant cell membranes. The membrane damage sets off a cascade of secondary reactions, which may include ethylene production, increased respiration, reduced photosynthesis, interference with energy production, accumulation of toxic compound such as ethanol and acetaldehyde and altered cellular structure. Chilling injury is a time by temperature problem. If the produce is stored below the critical temperature for short periods, the plant can repair the damage. If exposure is prolonged, irreversible damage occurs and visible symptoms often result. Injury occurs sooner and is more severe, if the lower temperature is below the threshold temperature. Detection and diagnosis of chilling injury is often difficult, as product often look sound when removed from the chilling temperature, but symptoms may occur when the produce is placed at higher temperatures. Symptoms which appear at higher temperatures may appear almost immediately, or may take several days to develop. Symptoms also may not be visible externally.

Table 5: Symptoms of chilling injury in fruits and vegetables

Fruits and Vegetables	Recommended storage temperature, (°C)	Symptoms of chilling injury
Apple	0-7	Core or flesh browning, fermented flavour, spongy texture, susceptibility and symptoms vary with cultivar
Water melon	10-15	Pitting, loss of flavour, fading of red colour
Banana	> 13	Green fruit: brown under peel discolouration; Ripe fruit: brown to black peel discolouration, off-flavour, abnormal ripening
Grapefruit	10-15	Brown pitting of rind, watery breakdown of internal and external tissues, fermented odour
Honeydew	7-13	Water-soaked of the rind, softening, grying or browning, surface becomes soft and sticky resulting in increased decaymelon
Mango	>13	Grayish skin discolouration, pitting, uneven ripening, poor flavour, increased susceptibility to Alternaria rot
Orange	2-5	As for grape fruit
Papaya	7-13	Pitting, olive or brown discolouration, abnormal ripening
Peach/Nectarine	– 0.5-1	(Critical temperature 2-8) – internal breakdown, mealiness, abnormal ripening, flesh browning or reddening
Pineapple	7-13	Flesh watery, followed by browning or blackening
Guava	4.5	Pulp injury, decay
Litchi	3	Skin browning
Pomegranate	4.5	Pitting, external and internal browning
Bael	3	Brown spot on skin

Olive, fresh	7	Internal browning
Ginger	7	Softening, tissue breakdown, decay
Okra	7-10	pitting
Sweet potato	> 13	Flesh discolouration, internal breakdown, increased decay, off-flavour, hard core when cooked
Pepper	7-13	Water-soaked appearance, sheet pitting, darkening, predisposition to Alternaria and Botrytis
Potato	3-10	Mahogany browning, sweetening
Pumpkin	10-15	Rot, primarily Alternaria
Tomato (ripe)	7-13 > 13	Rubbery texture, water flesh, irregular ripening, seed browning
Avocado	7-13	Darkening of vascular tissues, discolouration of flesh and skin, off-flavour and odour, abnormal ripening
Bean (snap)	7-10	Russeting, pitting
Asparagus	2-4	Occurs primarily at the tips-darkened and water-soaked followed by bacterial soft rot
Cucumber	7-10	Pitting of surface, lenticel area affected first, followed by *Fusarium* and other rots
Egg plant	7-13	Scald-like browning, pitting, flesh browning, decay and loosening of cap stems, Alternaria rot
Summer squash	5-10	Surface pitting, rapid decay
Lemon	10-14	As for grape fruit, plus red blotch
Lime	9-12	As for grape fruit

Freezing Injury

The recommended storage temperatures for commodities that is not susceptible to chilling injury as low as possible but slightly above the freezing point. Freezing injury occurs when ice crystals form in the tissues. Cultivar, locations and growing conditions may affect the freezing point. To be on the safe side, the highest temperature at which freezing of a specific commodity may occur should be used as a guide for recommending the optimum storage temperature. The most common symptom of freezing injury is a water soaked appearance. Tissues injured by freezing generally loose rigidity and become mushy upon thawing.

The susceptibility of different fresh fruits and vegetables to freezing to freezing injury varies widely. Some commodities may be frozen and thawed a number of times with little or no injury, whereas others are permanently injured by even at a small freezing. All fruits and vegetables can be categorized into three group based on their sensitivity to freezing: ***most susceptible***, those that are likely to be injured by even one light freezing; ***moderately susceptible***, those that will recover from one or two light freezing; and ***least susceptible***, those that can be lightly frozen several times without serious damage. Table 6 shows the relative susceptibility of a number of fruits and vegetables to freezing injury.

Table 6: Susceptibility of fruits and vegetables to freezing injury

Most Susceptible	Moderately Susceptible	Least Susceptible
Apricot, Peaches, Asparagus, Avocado, Banana, Beans, Berries, Plum, Cucumbers, Eggplant, Lemons, Lettuce, Limes, Okra, Potato, Sweet Potato, Tomato, Squash (Summer).	Apples, Broccoli, Carrots, Cauliflower, Celery, Grape, Onion, Orange, Parsley, Pear, Pea, Radish, Spinach, Squash (Winter), Grapefruits.	Beets, Brussels Sprout, Kale, Cabbage Dates, Turnip.

CHAPTER 12

FOOD PACKAGING AND STORAGE

12.1 INTRODUCTION

Packaging is the scientific method of containing food products against physical damage, chemical changes, and further microbial contamination and to display the product in the most attractive manner for consumer preferences.

Food packaging is defined as a coordinated system of preparing food for transport, distribution, storage, retailing, and end-use to satisfy the ultimate consumer with optimal cost. Food packaging is an essential part of modern society; commercially processed food could not be handled and distributed safely and efficiently without packaging. The World Packaging Organization (WPO) estimates that more than 25% of food is wasted because of poor packaging (WPO, 2009). Thus, it is clear that optimal packaging can reduce a large amount of food waste. According to Robertson (1992), packaging as the enclosure of the products, items or packages in a wrapped pouch, bag, box, cup, tray, can, tube, bottle or other containers to perform the various functions, *i.e.* containment, protection, information, promotion, etc.

Packaging provides quality and quantity assurance besides creating hygienic environment for food product. It offers security through tamper proof designs and contributes to the product image through structural and graphical design. Food safety is permanent importance as package products against biological, chemical and distribution damages. The primary objective or packaging is to protect the contents during storage, transportation and distribution against deterioration. It may be physical, chemical or biological.

Packaging of food serves many purposes such as providing effective protection to package foods against external contamination from environment; preserving the quality of food. It is one of the most important parameters that sale the product and also a communication device to provide detailed information about the product like, contents, ingredients, notional values, cooking instruction, packaging and expiry dates, etc. generally packaging material s are lighter in weight, easier to open, reseal and store, ensure safe transport and distribution, protect the product from adverse effects such as heat, cold, moisture, etc.

Storing food in the right way can be a great help in ensuring a household's food security. Food storage broadly refers to the different means through which food can be kept for longer periods without the food spoiling. The *shelf life* of a food is the length of time a food remains safe and fit for human consumption. It is essential to store food properly to ensure the following:

- Food remains in good condition for as long as possible
- Food is protected from flies, dust and other organisms that can spoil and/or contaminate food
- Food is protected from organisms like insects and rats that eat and spoil food. For instance, proper storage of grains protects it from rats and aphids which eat and spoil maize
- Reduction in post-harvest food losses Foods should be stored differently on the basis of how fast they will spoil or develop off flavours.

12.2 FOOD PACKAGING

12.2.1 Purpose of Packaging

In addition to the direct approach to food preservation, such as drying and freezing, other measures such as packaging and quality management tools need to be implemented in the process to avoid contamination or recontamination. Although these measures are not preservation techniques, they can play an important role in producing high-quality safe food. Packaging performs five main functions *i.e.* Product containment, preservation and quality, presentation and convenience, protection, and provide storage history.

1. Product Containment: The first function of packaging is its capability of containment. The primary purposes of packaging are containment and protection. It is self-explanatory; liquids, semi-liquids, and powders, as well as bulk solids, cannot be marketed without suitable containers. According to the size of the package, different amounts of the product can be delivered to consumers suiting their choice and convenience. In certain circumstances, quantification is mandatory, as in the case of medical pills or capsules that are marketed individually in a blister-type package. Containment refers to holding goods in a form suitable for transport, whereas protection refers to safekeeping goods in a way that prevents significant quality deterioration.

2. Preservation by Maintaining Quality: The second function of packaging is to control the local environmental conditions to enhance storage life and safety. The main purpose of food packaging is to protect the product from surroundings and maintain the quality of the food throughout the product's shelf life. One means of spreading the product availability over time is by the proper use of packaging. Product shelf life is controlled by three factors: product characteristics, properties, and storage and distribution conditions of individual package. Reactions causing deterioration in foods include enzymatic, chemical, physical, and microbiological changes. Additional problems include insects, pests, and rodents.

3. Presentation and Convenience: The third function is the presentation and convenience. In many cases, these are most important factors to the consumers.

Presentation: Food labels are intended by law to provide the information that consumers need to be able to make the necessary decisions about those purchases of food. It is important to display the product in an attractive manner to the potential buyer. A cleverly designed and beautifully produced packaging can help sell a product, which is an essential ingredient of an effective marketing campaign. The packaging helps in distinguishing products on the shelf, which is a trait especially important when marketing low-fat or nutritional products. Furthermore, packaging must address communication, legal, and commercial demands. For a package to be effective, it must present the product well and should do its own publicity. The protective packaging may have flaps that can be opened to give a ready-made display for the product, whereas some stores may remove the protective packaging to display the product directly on the shelves, leading to a preference for rectangular containers. The clarity (haze) and gloss optical characteristics are important in packaging presentation.

Convenience: In many cases, packaging provides convenience to the consumers, for example, paper carton for milk or juice with an ease-open and easy-pour cap, thus can also increase consumption. Eating styles, such as ready-to-eat meals, snacks, and microwaveable ready meals, have been changed over the years, which need innovation in packaging. For children, the packaging might represent innovation or fun. Today's consumer wants to buy food that is ready to eat, or needs a minimum of preparation, and is good value for money. With microwave food preparation increasing, there is a need for the packaging industry to confront the particular problems in designing packages that deliver microwave products to the dinner table. Other conveniences could be ease of opening, smaller portions, reclosable, and tamper-proof methods. Consumers want tamper-evident closures to avoid packaging being opened unnoticed.

4. Protection during Distribution and Processing: The fourth function is to protect the product during transit to the consumer. Packaging is part of the distribution process necessary to deliver goods to the consumer and facilitate handling and transportation. It also has affected international trade by making shipping of food products possible, allowing seasonal products to be more accessible out of season. Packaging can handle better when there are challenges in food distribution chain, such as heat, humidity, or dew. It is important to be aware of the distribution challenges and designing of package to suit it. In case of prepacked product, it should have the ability to stand the severity or type of process conditions, such as flexible packaging during canning, microwaveable foods, ovenable, and retortable foods. Irradiated foods are usually prepacked prior to treatment by ionizing radiation, which prevents recontamination. Packaging materials are also exposed to radiation during treatment, though in this instance it can lead to radiation-induced degradation of the packaging material, followed by interaction between the material and food product.

Protective packaging is a term applied to packaging primarily designed to protect the goods, rather than for appearance or presentation, so it is generally used to apply to the outer containers used for transporting goods from the manufacturer to the point of sale, and filling materials inside the outer containers, *e.g.*, nylon barrier-sealed bubble packaging (computer parts), urethane expanding foam, PE foam package "cushions," and PS loose-fill packaging. The most widely used protective package is the outer carton.

Thus most important functions of food packaging are as under:

12.2.2 Functions of Food Packaging

1. It contains the food product for ease and safety during transport.
2. Protects against spillage, evaporation or pilferage losses.
3. Protection from contamination.
4. Prevention of degradation from exposure to environmental factors.
5. Convenient means of dispensing.
6. Attraction of consumer.
7. Identification of manufacturer's brand, quantity, quality and type of product.
8. Educate the consumer.

12.2.3 Characteristics of Food Package

1. **Colour:**

Blue	:	Cleanliness and coolness
Green	:	Tranquillity
Orange	:	Warmth

Yellow : Strength and cheerfulness
White : Mourning
Cherry blossom : Japanese favour it.
White and black : Controversial

2. **Shape:** ➢ Rectangle ➢ Triangular ➢ Cylindrical ➢ Oval

Strength Properties :

1. Tensile strength – Stretch the film to see the strength 2. Bursting strength
3. Tearing strength 4. Water vapour permeability 5. Grease permeability
6. Oil permeability 7. Heat

Requirements of containers:

1. Nontoxic 2. Compatible 3. Sanitary protection
4. Moisture and fat protection
5. Gas and odour protection - Bad odour – out - Aroma – in

12.3 PACKAGING MATERIALS

In choosing the appropriate packaging for their product, packers must consider many variables. For example, *canners* must make packaging choices based on cost, product compatibility, shelf life, flexibility of size, handling systems, production line filling and closing speeds, processing reaction, impermeability, dent and tamper resistance, and consumer convenience and preference. Processors who use *films* for their product must select film material based on its "barrier" properties that prevent oxygen, water vapor, or light from negatively affecting the food.

12.3.1 Properties of Ideal Packaging Materials

An ideal packaging material should have following qualities:

- It should contain the content within it
- It should not affect the flavour of the product packed.
- Stable performance over large range of temperature.
- Adequate compulsive strength and sufficient impact and puncture strength.
- Sufficient thickness of cushioning materials with sufficient ventilation, space for rapid cooling of product.
- Protect the product from O_2, moisture and light.
- Protection of the content form adulterations.
- Closure characteristics such as opening, sealing, resealing and pouring.
- Low cost and availability.
- It should non-toxic in nature.
- Proper labeling, storing, marketing appeal to sale, etc.

12.3.2 Requirements of Packaging Materials

Packaging provides a barrier between the food and environment. It controls light transmission, transfer of heat, moisture and gases and movement of micro-organisms or insects. Major requirement of food packaging materials are briefly described below.

1. Moisture and gases : Rate of moisture and oxygen transfer are the main factors that control the shelf life of dehydrated foods and those that contains appreciable quantities of lipids or other oxygen sensitive components. Transfer of oxygen, moisture and carbon dioxide through packaging materials is critically important in determining the shelf life and quality of chilled fresh foods and foods packaged in modified atmosphere. This mainly depends on permeability property. Thickness, chemical composition, structure and orientation of molecules in a packaging material influence the barrier properties. Permeability is also related to both temperature and relative humidity of the atmosphere in which permeability measurements are made.

2. Microorganisms : In fact, packaging materials are barrier to microorganisms, and seals the area of potential source of contamination. Main causes of microbial contamination of adequately processed food are air or water drawn through pinholes in hermetically sealed containers, contamination of heat seals by products, poorly aligned lids or caps and damage to packaging materials (tears, creases).

3. Mechanical strength : Ability of packages to protect the foods from mechanical damage is measured by tensile strength, impact strength and other mechanical strength properties. Each of these factors is influenced by temperature of material and length of time that the force is applied. Orientation of molecules in one direction (bi-axial) improves mechanical properties of some films (for example polyethylene, polypropylene, polyethylene terephthalate and polystyrene).

4. Light : Light transmission is required in packages that are intended to display contents but is restricted when foods are susceptible to deterioration by light (for example, by oxidation of lipids, destruction of riboflavin and loss of colour). Pigments are incorporated into glass containers or polymer films, or they are printed to reduce light transmission to sensitive products.

5. Heat : Insulating effect of a package is determined by its thermal conductivity and its reflectivity. Materials which have low thermal conductivity (*e.g.* paper board, polyurethane) reduce conductive heat transfer, and reflective materials (*e.g.* aluminium foil) reflect radiant heat.

12.4 COMMONLY USED FOOD PACKAGING MATERIAL

The most common food packaging materials include metals, glass, paper, and plastic.

Metal: Metals such as steel and aluminum are used in cans and trays. A metal can forms a hermetic seal, which is a complete seal against gases and vapor entry or escape and it offers protection to the contents. The trays may be reusable or disposable recyclable trays and either steam table or No. 10 can size. Metal also is used for bottle closures and wraps. New microwavable steel cans are available for packaging. Steel cans that are capable on running on a manufacturer's steel can filling lines are now also capable of microwave heating by the consumer. In some case, *retort packaging* may provide more consistent flavor and texture than food in cans. The requirement on film used in retort packaging is that it must hold up to varied thermal processing, and the subsequent processes of distribution and storage. **Aluminum** is formed easily into cans with hermetic seals. It also is used in trays and for wraps such as aluminum foil, which provide an oxygen and light barrier. It is lighter in weight than steel and resists corrosion.

Glass: Glass is derived from metal oxides such as silicon dioxide (sand). It is used in forming bottles or jars (which subsequently receive hermetic seals), and thus protects against water vapor or oxygen loss. The thickness of glass must be sufficient to prevent breakage from internal pressure, external impact, or thermal stress. Glass that is *too* thick increases weight, and thus freight costs, and is subject to an increased likelihood of thermal stress or external impact breakage.

Paper: Paper is derived from the pulp of wood and may contain additives such as aluminum particle laminates, plastic coating, resins, or waxes. These additives provide burst strength (strength against bursting), wet strength (leak protection), and grease and tear resistance, as well as barrier properties that assure freshness, protect the packaged food against vapor loss and environmental contaminants, and increase shelf life. Varying thicknesses of paper may be used to achieve thicker and more rigid packaging.

- *Paper* is thin (one layer) and flexible, typically used in bags and wrappers. Kraft (or "strong" in German) paper is the strongest paper. It may be bleached and used as butcher wrap or may remain unbleached and used in grocery bags.
- *Paperboard* is thicker (although still one layer) and more rigid. Ovenable paperboard is made for use in either conventional or microwave ovens by coating paperboard with PET polyester.
- Multilayers of paper form *fiberboard*, which is recognized as "*cardboard*."

Paper board grades used in food packaging

- **Linerboard :** Board having at least two plies, the top layer being of relatively better quality; usually made on a Fourdrinier machine with 100% virgin pulp furnish.
- **Food board :** Board used for food packaging having a single- or multi-ply construction, usually made from 100% bleached virgin pulp furnish.
- **Folding Boxboard (Cartonboard) :** Multi-ply board used to make folding boxes; top ply (liner) is made from virgin pulp, and the other plies are made from secondary fibre.
- **Chipboard :** Multi-ply board made from 100% low-grade secondary fibre.
- **Base Board :** Board that will ultimately be coated or covered.
- **Folding Cartons :** Folding cartons are containers made from sheets of paperboard (typically with thicknesses between 300 and 1100 mm), which have been cut and scored for bending into desired shapes.

Note: It is common practice at dhabhas or street thelas, that food items viz roties, parathas are packed in news paper which is risky because ink used in news papers contain various bioactive materials with known negative health effects which can contaminate food and lead to health issues when injested.

FSSAI packaging rules 2018 prohibits use of newspapers or similar materials for storing and wrapping food items.

Plastic: Plastic has shrink, nonshrink, flexible, semirigid, and rigid applications, and varies in its degree of thickness. Important *properties* of the many types of plastics that make them good choices for packaging material include the following:

- Flexible and stretchable
- Lightweight
- Low-temperature formability
- Resistant to breakage, with high burst strength
- Strong heat sealability
- Versatile in its barrier properties to O_2, moisture, and light

Plastic has multiple *functions* as a packaging material, including use in bottles and jars, closures, coatings, films, pouches, tubs, and trays. It also may be used *in combination* with other packaging materials such as metal (for lining cans), paper (for moisture resistance), and glass (reduces bottle breakage). Some of the more commonly used plastics for food products are discussed in the following:

Polyethylene (PE): Polyethylene is the most common and the least expensive plastic comprising 63% of total plastic packaging. It is a water-vapor (moisture) barrier and prevents dehydration and freezer burn. Use of this PE may be recommended for less plasticizer migration into food.

Polypropylene (PP): Polypropylene has a higher melting point and greater tensile strength than polyethylene. It often is used as the inside layer of food packages that are subject to higher temperatures of sterilization (*e.g.*, retort pouches or tubs).

Polystyrene (PS): Polystyrene is a versatile, inexpensive packaging material and represents 8% of total plastic packaging. When foamed, its generic name is expandable polystyrene (EPS). This styrofoam has applications in disposable packaging and drinking cups. It offers thermal insulation and protective packaging. EPS is used in "clam shell" fast-food packaging, egg cartons, bowls, cups, and meat trays and is the "peanuts" in packages. Approximately 30% less energy is required to form polystyrene cups than paperboard cups.

Polyvinyl chloride (PVC or vinyl): Polyvinyl chloride comprises 6% of total plastic packaging. It blocks out air and moisture, preventing freezer burn, and offers low permeability to gases, liquid, flavors, and odors. PVC prevents the transfer of odor and keeps food fresh by controlling dehydration and is capable of withstanding high temperatures without melting. PVC has good puncture resistance and "cling" properties. It is used to prevent splattering in microwave food preparation.

Polyvinylidene chloride (*PVDC*, Saran_): ***Polyvinylidene chloride*** is a thermoplastic resin used for household wraps and has excellent barrier properties. *Cryovac* is a Saran film used in vaccum-sealing (*Kryos* = cold *Vacus* = empty in Latin).

Many manufacturers specify proprietary molded and shaped bottles to hold the food contents. The appropriate plastic may be chosen to satisfy this highly specialized demand.

There also are *food-based* materials used to produce thermal plastic resins. They are made from natural sugars found in corn and other plants. For example, wheat starch and corn sugar are being developed for packaging purposes.

Plastic permeability

When the gas or vapour compounds pass through the plastic, they must solubilize at first, diffuse through the material, and finally desorb on the other side. Such vapour or gas mass transfer (or permeability) has a significant impact on the shelf life, quality, and safety of foods. For example, the expected loss of moisture from juice or of CO_2 from carbonated beverages, depending on storage conditions, can be estimated through quantitative evaluation of the package permeability. Similarly, the time required to reach certain atmospheric conditions in the package that favour the growth of aerobic or anaerobic pathogens can also be estimated through calculation of the permeability

Other Packaging Materials

Cotton or **burlap** (jute) may be used for grains, flour, legumes, and some vegetables, primarily in transport.

Edible films are subject to FDA approval because they become part of the food. Natural edible films extend shelf life, although for shorter time than synthetic non-edible packaging materials. Edible films are a unique type of packaging material. As stated in a publication of the Institute of Food Technologist's Expert Panel on Food Safety and Nutrition: These films are defined as a thin layer of edible material formed on a food as a coating or placed (preformed) on or between food components. Its purpose is to inhibit migration of moisture, oxygen, carbon dioxide, aromas, and lipids, etc; carry food ingredients (*e.g.*, antioxidants, antimicrobials, flavor); and/or improve mechanical integrity or handling characteristics of the food".

Antimicrobials may be included in films or containers. Antimicrobial activity may be due to the addition of specific substances, radiation, or gas-flushing. Irradiation sterilization of packaging materials may be forthcoming with approval from FSSAI.

Examples of edible films include those used as the sugar shell on individual chocolate covered candies (M&Ms_); casings, such as in sausage; and *edible waxes*, such as those applied to fruits and vegetables. Serving in the role of edible films, the casings "contain" and the waxes function to improve or maintain appearance, prevent mold, and contain moisture while still allowing respiration.

As well, food may be coated with a thin layer of polysaccharides such as cellulose, pectin, starch and vegetable gums, or proteins, such as casein and gelatin. Cut, dried fruit pieces are often sprayed with an edible film prior to their inclusion into items such as breakfast cereal.

Foil is a packaging material that may be used in snack bags (chips, etc) or as a laminate in aseptic packaging (see Aseptic Packaging). It is used as a wrapping for dry, refrigerator, or freezer storage. It provides a moisture-proof and vapor-proof barrier.

Laminates are multilayers of foil, paper, or plastics that may be utilized selectively according to the specific food packaging need. In combination, the various laminates may provide more strength and barrier protection than the individual laminate material. Laminates provide barriers useful in controlling O_2, water vapor, and light transmission and they provide good burst strength. The laminates may resist pinholes and flex cracking. Retort pouches are examples of laminates used in packaging and contain polyester film, aluminum foil, and polypropylene.

Resins are used for sealing food packages. They must withstand the stress of processing and offer seal integrity that prevents product contamination.

Wood may be used in the manufacture of crates that contain fresh fruits and vegetables.

Bag-in-a-box: A bag-in-box or BiB is a container for the storage and transportation of liquids. It consists of a strong bladder (or plastic bag), usually made of several layers of metallised film or other plastics, seated inside a corrugated fiber-board. It is now offered in five-gallon bags with snap-on caps over a 1" polyethylene spout. There is a high barrier film, with heat-resistance up to 88°C. Regardless of the materials that are selected for use, *source reduction, reuse*, and *recycling* should be important considerations of packaging manufacturers. The food industry challenge is to provide the appropriate materials to accomplish packaging functions at reasonable cost.

12.4 PACKAGING SYSTEMS

We can categorize packaging systems into four groups: primary packaging, secondary packaging, distribution or tertiary packaging, and unit load.

1. Primary packaging the first-level package that directly contacts the product is referred to as the "primary package." For example, a beverage can or a jar, a paper envelope for a tea bag, an inner bag in a cereal box, and an individual candy wrap in a pouch are primary packages, and their main function is to contain and preserve the product Primary packages must be non-toxic and compatible with the food and should not cause any changes in food attributes such as colour changes, undesired chemical reactions, flavour, etc.

2. Secondary packaging the secondary package contains two or more primary packages and protects the primary packages from damage during shipment and storage. Secondary packages are also used to prevent dirt and contaminants from soiling the primary packages; they also unitize groups of primary packages. A shrink wrap and a plastic ring connector that bundles two or more cans together to enhance ease of handling are examples of secondary packages.

3. Tertiary package the tertiary package is the shipping container, which typically contains a number of the primary or secondary 250 Food Processing: Principles and Applications packages. It is also referred to as the "distribution package." A corrugated box is by far the most common form of tertiary package. Its main function is to protect the product during distribution and to provide for efficient handling.

4. Unit load: A unit load means a group of tertiary packages assembled into a single unit. If the corrugated boxes are placed on a pallet and stretch wrapped for mechanical handling, shipping and storage, the single unit is referred to as a "unit load." The objective is to aid in the automated handling of larger amounts of product. A fork-lift truck or similar equipment is used to transport the unit load.

Consumer/Industrial Packaging System

Consumer packaging means a package that will be delivered to the ultimate consumer in the retail store. Usually, primary and secondary packages fit in this category.

Industrial packaging means a package for warehousing and distribution to the retail store. Tertiary packages and unit loads fit in this category.

12.5 DIFFERENT PACKAGING TECHNIQUES / METHODS

12.5.1 Controlling Atmosphere Packaging

Reduced *temperature* remains as the primary means of food protection. However, controlling the known elements in the package environment, such as O_2, CO_2, water vapor, and ethylene concentration, also may reduce spoilage and contamination (*e.g.*, enzymatic, biological), thus extending shelf life (the time required for a food to become unacceptable from a sensory, nutritional, or safety perspective). The creation of a packaging environment with little or no oxygen has beneficial applications for the food industry. However, microbiological concerns arise simultaneously. Proper controls need to be in place for reduced oxygen packages.

The function of CO_2 addition in packaging is to inhibit growth of many bacteria and molds. The O_2 maintains respiration and color and inhibits growth of anaerobic microorganisms. Nitrogen (N_2) is used to flush the package and rid it of air (O_2 specifically). Nitrogen also prevents a collapse of the loose-fitting packaging material.

Providing control in packaging is needed by fruits and vegetables. They continue to breathe and require oxygen after harvesting and processing, thus the package must contain oxygen. Yet it needs to be controlled, as *too high* a level causes oxidation and spoilage and *too low* a level leads to anaerobic spoilage. In extending shelf life of fruit, oxygen levels should approximate 5% and carbon dioxide at 1–3% (with refrigeration maintained at temperature-specific levels). Packaging environments must match the respiration rate as closely as possible.

12.5.2 Modified Atmosphere Packaging

Modified atmosphere packaging (MAP) modifies the internal package atmosphere of food and helps preserve packaged food. It replaces the air in the package with nitrogen or carbon dioxide and the shelf life of the product can increase by as much as 200%. Gas flushing and sealing reduces oxygen coming through respiration of vegetables. MAP is a *one-time modification* of gases so that it is different from air, which normally contains 78.08% nitrogen, 20.96% oxygen, and 0.03% carbon dioxide.

MAP *primarily* is applied to fresh or minimally processed foods that are still undergoing respiration, and it is used for the packaging of a variety of foods. Such foods include baked goods, coffees and teas, dairy products, dry and dehydrated foods, lunch kits, and processed meats (to keep the meat pigment looking desirable). It also is used for nuts, snack food applications, and pasta packaging. This type of packaging with high CO_2 levels inhibits many aerobic bacteria, molds, and yeasts.

MAP is one of the most widely used packaging technologies, as it functions to enhance appearance, minimize destructive waste, extend shelf life, and reduce the need for artificial preservatives. MAP's pure gas or gas mixture environment varies with the type of food and its packaging, temperature, and microbial load. In particular, nitrogen is used in bread products while carbon dioxide is best suited to high-fat products.

The addition of *nitrogen* gas, which is odorless, tasteless, colorless, nontoxic, and nonflammable, is introduced into the food package *after* all atmosphere has been removed from the pouch and vacuum chamber and just *prior* to hermetic sealing of the package. It increases the package's internal pressure. This modification, by a predetermined dose of liquid nitrogen (LN), offers protection from spoilage, oxidation, dehydration, weight loss, and freezer burn and extends shelf life, as nitrogen consumes oxygen.

The three main gases used for MAP are nitrogen (N_2), carbon dioxide (CO_2), and oxygen (O_2). They are used either alone or, in most cases, in combination. Mixtures of carbon dioxide (CO_2) and argon (Ar) are also utilized commercially. Examples of gas mixtures that are used for fresh and processed foods Nitrogen (N_2) Nitrogen is the most commonly used gas in MAP. It is an inert gas with no odour or taste. Nitrogen also has low solubility in water (0.009 g/kg at 20 °C). Nitrogen does not directly provide any microbial retardation but it delays aerobic microbial growth and oxidation by replacing oxygen.

Carbon dioxide (CO_2): Carbon dioxide is colourless with a slightly pungent odour. The most important function of this gas is related to its bacteriostatic and fungistatic properties. Usually, a higher concentration is more effective against microorganisms. However, colour changes and acid tastes have been reported by several researchers due to exposure to high CO_2. Carbon dioxide has high solubility in water (1.69 g/kg at 20 °C). Thus, packages containing moist foods with CO_2 in their headspace may collapse.

Oxygen (O_2): Oxygen is a colourless, odourless, and highly reactive gas. It promotes food deteriorative reactions such as fat oxidation, browning reactions, and aerobic microbial growth. For this reason, the desired oxygen content in the headspace of most foods is often extremely low. However, oxygen is still needed for the retention of colour in red meat and for fruit/vegetable respiration.

Carbon monoxide (CO) Carbon monoxide is a colourless, tasteless, and odourless gas. When carbon monoxide combines with myoglobin, a bright red pigment (carboxymyoglobin) is formed, which is more stable than normal red meat pigment (oxymyoglobin). The use of carbon monoxide is not for quality issues but for its visual effect. Since carbon monoxide is a toxic and highly flammable gas, its commercial use is limited. In the US, carbon monoxide is currently used for red meat but the maximum concentration is 4% in MAP.

Argon (Ar): Argon is a chemically inert, colourless, tasteless, and odourless gas which is denser and heavier than air. Compared to nitrogen, argon is a more effective gas for use in flushing out air. However, due to the high cost of argon, nitrogen is mostly used for flushing.

Examples of MAP for Same foods:

12.5.2.1 Modified atmosphere packaging for meat: For red meat, oxygen is necessary to maintain the red colour of oxymyoglobin in unprocessed meats. On the other hand, a low oxygen level is desired to prevent the growth of microorganisms and oxidative rancidity of fat. Typically, the shelf life of fresh red meat is extended by packaging it in an atmosphere of 20% CO_2, 60–80% O_2, and up to 20% N_2. However, off-odours and rancidity have been reported in meats stored at high O_2 concentrations Thus, maintaining a low temperature (0–2 °C) is desired when high-O_2 MAP is used. Poultry has low myoglobin content so it does not need oxygen to maintain its colour. A higher CO_2 concentration (20–100%) is possible to extend the shelf life. However, a few studies report colour change with high CO_2 concentration in poultry products (Dawson, 2004).

12.5.2.2 Modified atmosphere packaging for seafood: Seafood such as fish and shellfish is highly perishable owing to its high water activity (*aw*), pH, and the presence of autolytic enzymes, which cause rapid development of undesirable odours. A low oxygen atmosphere can delay the occurrence of undesirable odour and growth of aerobic microorganisms. For example, packaging tilapia fillets in 75% CO_2:25% N_2 extended their shelf life up to 80 days at 4 °C)

However, fresh fish may be contaminated with the anaerobic *C. botulinum* either as a result of being present in the microbiota of the fish ecosystem or due to post catch contamination during processing. A low oxygen atmosphere poses a potential threat for a packaged fish to become toxic prior to spoilage. To assure the safety of MAP fish products, the product must be maintained at or below 3 °C at all times. Since chilled storage control is a critical factor to determine the shelf life, some companies use time temperature indicators (TTI) to monitor for temperature abuse.

12.5.2.3 Modified atmosphere packaging for fresh fruits and vegetables Fresh fruits and vegetables keep consuming O_2 and emitting CO_2 even after harvest. The purpose of MAP for fresh fruits and vegetables is to minimize the respiration and senescence without causing suffocation and damage to metabolic activity that rapidly reduces their shelf life. However, a low oxygen and high CO_2 atmosphere that develops inside the package due to respiration of the product may result in the accumulation of ethanol and acetaldehyde, and fermentation could start. Thus, the package material needs to be somewhat permeable to oxygen and CO_2 to allow the transfer of the gases from outside and inside. The change in gas composition during storage depends on the permeability of the container to water vapour and gas, storage temperature, and the mass of the food.

Advantages:

1. Shelf life will be increased by 50 to 400%.
2. Reduced economic losses due to longer shelf life.
3. Provides a high quality product.
4. Centralized packaging and product control.
5. Improved presentation – clear view of product and all –around visibility.
6. Little or no need for chemical preservatives.
7. Sealed packages are barriers against product recontamination and drip from package.
8. Odorless and convenient packages.
9. Longer freshness cycles.

Disadvantages:

1. Added costs for gases, packaging materials and machinery.
2. Temperature control is necessary.
3. Different gas formulations for each product type.
4. Special equipment and training is required.
5. Increased pack volume adversely affects transport costs and retail display space.
6. Loss benefits once the pack is opened or leaks.
7. CO_2 dissolving into the food could lead to pack collapse and increased drip.

12.5.3 Active Packaging

Active packaging began as *"smart" packaging* in 1980s, and was referred to as *"interactive"* packaging almost from the start. All three terms describe the same thing, which is packaging that could "sense" changes in the internal environment and respond by adapting as necessary. Sachets may be added to a package in order to control elements such as ethanol, oxygen, or microbes. By its inherent design, packaging typically serves in a *passive* role by protecting food products from the external environment. It provides a physical barrier to external spoilage, contamination, and physical abuse in storage and distribution.

Today, packaging more *actively* contributes to the product's development, controls maturation and ripening, helps in achieving the proper color development in meats, and extends shelf life. Thus it is considered to play an *active* (not passive) role in protecting foods . Yet, despite the many attributes and benefits of smart/interactive/active packaging, it generally does not actually "sense" the environment conditions and change accordingly. Examples of ***active packaging*** technologies are listed in the following text. Active packaging for *fresh and minimally processed* foods provide the following:

- Edible moisture or oxygen barrier (to control loss of moisture and enzymatic oxidative browning in fresh cut fruits and vegetables and to provide controlled permeability rates matched to the respiration rate of the fruit).
- Edible antimicrobial (biocidal) polymer films and coatings (which may release controlled amounts of chlorine dioxide into the food, depending on temperature and humidity; or destroy *E. coli* 0157:H7 in meats, and prevent mold growth in fruits).
- Films that are scavengers of off-odors.
- Oxygen scavengers for low-oxygen packaging.

Active packaging for *processed* foods provides the following:

- Edible moisture barrier.
- O_2, CO_2, and odor scavenger.

Oxygen Scavengers

Oxygen scavengers are a type of active packaging technique which absorb the dissolved oxygen or oxygen in the héadspace leading to extended shelf life and retainment of the original food quality. Oxygen scavenging films extend the shelf life of foods while maintaining their nutritional quality and preventing discoloration, microbial spoilage, rancidity, and organoleptic deterioration, thereby ensuring food safety.

Oxygen scavengers are becoming increasingly attractive to food manufacturers Overall, oxygen absorbing technology is based on oxidation or combination of one of the following components: iron powder, ascorbic acid, photosensitive polymers, enzymes, etc. These compounds are able to reduce the levels of oxygen to below 0.01%, which is lower than the levels typically found (0.3-3%) in the conventional systems of modified atmosphere, vacuum or substitution of internal atmosphere for inert gas. An appropriate oxygen scavenger is chosen depending on the O_2-level in the headspace, how much oxygen is trapped in the food initially and the amount of oxygen that will be transported from the surrounding air into the package during storage.

The most well known oxygen scavengers take the form of small sachets containing various *iron based powders* containing an assortment of catalysts. However, non-metallic oxygen scavengers have also been developed to alleviate the potential for metallic taints being imparted to food products and the detection of metal by in-line detectors. Non-metallic ıvengers include those that use organic reducing agents such as ascorbic acid, ascorbate salts or catechol. They also include enzymatic oxygen scavenger systems using either glucose oxidase or ethanol oxidase.

Ethylene Scavenging Systems: The use of active packaging with ethylene scavenging characteristics aids in mitigating ethylene's detrimental effects. Based on minimizing ethylene-induced deterioration, ethylene scavenging methods help to extend the shelf life of fresh foods.

The use of **carbon dioxide scavengers** is particularly used in packing fresh roasted or ground coffees that produce significant volumes of carbon dioxide. A mixture of **calcium oxide** and **activated charcoal** has been used in polyethylene coffee pouches to scavenge carbon dioxide.

12.5.4 Passive Packaging

Fruits and vegetables continue to respire after harvest, consuming oxygen and producing carbon dioxide and water vapour. If the respiration characteristics of commodity can be accurately matched to permeability of film used for packaging, then a favourable modified atmosphere concentration of oxygen and carbon dioxide is established. By achieving optimal or equilibrium modified atmosphere composition passively, operating and maintenance cost can be reduced drastically.

12.5.5 Aseptic Packaging

In order to destroy any *C. botulinum* spores and extend the shelf life of low-acid foods, ***aseptic packaging*** may be utilized. Independent sterilization of both the *foods* and *packaging material,* with assembly under *sterile environmental* conditions, is the rule for aseptic packaging which now shows more main stream technology.

In an aseptic system of packaging, the packaging material consists of *layers* of polyethylene, paperboard, and foil. It is sterilized by heat (superheated steam or dry hot air) or a combination of heat and hydrogen peroxide and then roll-fed through the packer to create the typical brick/block shape. The container is filled with a sterile (no pathogens or spores) or commercially sterile (no pathogens, but *some* spores) liquid food product and sealed in a closed, sterile chamber. Once packed, the product requires no refrigeration. Liquids such as creamers, milk, or juices may be packed in this manner. Triple or multiple packs of flavored milk and juice, with attached straws, are available on grocery shelves. The market leaders of aseptic packages have introduced easy-open, easy pour features into their cartons. The plastic devices are injection molded and adhere to the package tops.

The sterility of packaging material has formerly relied on *chemical* technologies of sterilization (principally heat with hydrogen peroxide). *Nonchemical* techniques have been explored in order to avoid chemical sterilant residues. Ionizing and nonionizing radiation have been tested for use in aseptic packaging.

Aseptic packaging can be broadly characterized into 5 basic types:

Fill and Seal: Performed sterile containers are filled and sealed in an aseptic environment. Thermo formed or blow mould systems, which utilize preformed containers and aseptic canning operations are representative of this group

Form, Fill and Seal : In this system, a roll of incoming material is sterilized and formed, filled and sealed in an aseptic environment. A typical system is the tetra pack operation

Erect, Fill and Seal : A knocked down blank of incoming material is erected, sterilized. filled and sealed. *e.g.* combination-block operation

Thermoform, Fill and Seal : Rollstock is sterilized which is heated, thermoformed, filled and sealed in an aseptic environment. It appears that this will be tremendous development area in the foreseeable future.

Blow Mould, Fill and Seal : In this, an extrudable material is blow moulded. The product is filled into the package and sealed bore the moulds are open or the sterile bottle is closed in the mould and delivered to a separate operation where the sterile container is opened, filled and sealed in an aseptic environment. This can be applied to either formed bottles or flexible containers.

12.5.6 Flexible Packaging

Flexible packaging is available for packaging use in the foodservice industry and is finding more applications at the *retail* level, including packaging for bagged cereals and sliced deli meat. Nonrigid packaging containers such as stand-up pouches or tubes and zippered bags are examples of flexible packaging used for peanuts, peanut butter, or produce such as fresh-cut lettuce and peeled baby carrots. The same packaging also might need to be *resealable* to meet consumer demands and may require zipper handles or spouts with *easy open* screw-off tops.

"Flexible packaging uses less material, is more cost effective, and packaging speeds are getting higher. Large flexible packages have replaced cans and rigid packaging." Whether it is attributable to flexible packaging alone, or marketing, and so forth, one manufacturer of snack mix has said "Sales of the product more than doubled just by changing the package".

Flexible packaging is adequate for the plethora of low-fat/no-fat food products such as salty snack foods that are available in the marketplace. It keeps these products fresh by providing flavor and aroma barriers, which keep outside odors out and flavors in. It is used for fresh fruits and vegetables and matches respiration rate as closely as possible.

Test to assess functional properties of flexible packaging materials

The *functional properties include*:

Thickness : Thickness or caliper is the perpendicular distance between the two principal surfaces of the paper. Caliper of craft liner for a grammage should be uniform across the sheet. Micrometer Screw Gauge apparatus is used to test the thickness of the paper. The values obtained from apparatus are measured in mm or mils or points. (1 mil = 1 point = 1/1000 inch = 0.025 mm).

Grammage (GSM) or Basis Weight : The weight per unit area of paper is defined as basis weight in g/m^2, or grammage. For determine the grammage of paper or paper board, substance indicator apparatus is used. *Procedure*: A specimen is cut into a size of 10x10 cm after conditioning the sample and kept in the substance indicator. Weight of the paper is expressed as gram per square meter.

Bursting Strength : Bursting strength is the hydraulic pressure in kg/cm^2 or lb/in^2, required to produce rupture of material when the pressure is increased at a controlled constant rate through a rubber diaphragm of 1.2 inch in diameter. Bursting strength is widely used as measure of resistance to rupture in many kinds of paper. It gives an indication of stretch of paper. The apparatus used for testing bursting strength is bursting strength tester.

Procedure: Clamp the sample of approximate size of 12 × 12 cm after conditioning in position, apply hydrostatic pressure with the instrument until the specimen ruptures and record the maximum registered reading in the pressure gauge. Make at least 10 acceptable tests to each side of the samples. The obtained values are a measure of pressure and are expressed in kg/cm^2 or ib/in^2.

Determination of Burst Factor : It can be obtained from the formula,

Burst factor (BF = Bursting Strength (kg/cm^2) × 1000/Grammage (GSM) of paper.

Puncture resistance : The resistance of paper board to puncture is extreme important in manufacturing of shipping containers, because of the hazards involved in transportation, handling and storing, Containers frequently are punctured by corners of the other containers, lumbers, fork trucks etc. The each puncture test gives an indication of the ability of container components or combined board to resist the damage caused by these various objects. The puncture test gives better assessment of the combined board strength than the bursting strength and also appears to have better correlation with the package performance against impacts. Puncture resistance tester is used for determine of puncture resistance.

Procedure: Place the sample in clamping jaw, with the outside surface down. Release the pendulum so that the pointer punctures the sample completely. Puncture test result are expressed as inch-ounces inch per tear inch or beach unit.

Water absorptiveness or Cobb's Test : This test is intended to find the penetration of aqueous liquids into paper and paper board. In addition to indicating the extend of sizing in papers, the test is partly useful in assessing the suitability of corrugated and solid fiber boards to be used for shipping containers, which have been the likelihood of being exposed to water spray. The test specifies the amount of water absorbed by a specified area of paper in a given length of time. The Cobbs test apparatus is used for determine the water absorptiveness.

***Procedure* :** The specimen holder consists of a metal cylinder of 11.30 cm inside diameter. This cylinder clamped tightly over the specimen, which in turn is supported underneath by a rubber mat placed over a flat metal plate. With this setup, a water column of 0.6 to 1 cm height (usually 100 ml) is allowed to stand on the specimen for a specific period of time (for paper 1 min and for paper board 30 min). The weight of water absorbed is found out after wiping of the adherent water with blotting paper. From this, the weight of water absorbed by one m^2 of the sample is computed. Printed areas and deforming or cracked surfaces should be avoided for the test. Weight should be performed quickly since evaporation of water at this stage may cause serious error.

Density : Specimen shall be conditioned by submerging it in boiling water for 30 minutes followed by conditioning at 27±2°C for at least 24 h to make it bubble free.

***Procedure* :** Pipette 100 ml dilute alcohol (density 0.8-0.82 g/ml at 27°C) into a clean Drechsel bottle kept immersed in a water bath maintained at 27±0.1°C. After temperature equilibrium has been attained; lower one test specimen carefully into the dilute alcohol avoiding any adhering air bubbles. Add from burette, distilled water, 0.2 ml at a time, with stirring. When the specimen remains just suspended in the solution well away from the glass surface, the density of the solution and the specimen is taken to be the same. Density of the solution may be determined with a pycnometer, or specific gravity bottles at 27±0.1°C.

Tensile Strength and Elongation at Break

Tensile strength has been defined as the force parallel to the plane of the specimen required to produce failure in a specimen of specified width and length under specified conditions of loading. Tensile Strength Machine is used for determining the tensile strength. The machine used should be able to maintain a constant rate of traverse of one grip. The load scale should be accurate to within 1% or 0.1 N whichever is less.

Universal testing machine : Samples should be cut in lengthwise and crosswise direction, five numbers each. Total length should be at least 50mm longer than the gauge length. The thickness should be measured using a micrometer. The conditioned specimen is clamped between the grips of the machine. Machine is the switched on at the preadjusted speed. The load and elongation at break is recorded. The tensile strength at break calculated in kg/cm^2 from the original area of the cross section. The mean of five results each is expressed for the lengthwise and crosswise samples (MD and CD). Elongation at break (ELB) is expressed as percentage of the original length between the reference lines. The mean values of the five results are expressed from MD and CD samples. The ELB and breaking length can be calculated by the following equations.

$$\% \text{ ELB} = \frac{L_2 - L_1 \times 100}{L_1}$$

where L_1 = original length

L_2 = length at the time of break

Tensile strength in kg × length of the strip in m

Breaking length (in meters) = Weight of strip, kg

Usually Tensile Strength is more and Elongation is less in MD.

Gas Transmission Rate (GTR) : The gas transmission rate is normally determined by measuring the change in pressure at constant volume. The quantity of gas flowing across the film is compiled as volume at NTP (Normal Temperature and pressure). GTR is an important property to estimate the efficiency of the packaging material or a package resistance to the flow of gases and helps in selection of barrier materials for oxygen sensitive foods.

Water Vapour Transmission Rate (WVTR) : The WVTR is measured as the quantity of water vapour in grams that will permeate from one side to other side of the film of an area of one square meter in 24 hours, when the relative humidity difference between the two sides is maintained at 90 per cent gradient at 37.8°C. The property is important to estimate the efficiency of the packaging material or a package for resistance to the flow of water vapour and is helpful in considering the selection of barrier materials for hygroscopic foods.

12.5.7 Package Printing

Printing inks for films and papers consist of a dye which is dispersed in a blend of solvents, and a resin which forms a varnish. Solvents must be carefully removed after application of the ink to prevent odour contaminating the product and blocking the film during use. Other considerations include the cost of the ink, and compatibility with the film which is needed to achieve a high bond strength. There are five processes used to print films and papers:

1. *Flexographic printing* (or relief or letterpress) in up to six colours, is high speed and suitable for lines or blocks of colour. A fast-drying ink is applied to the film by a flexible rubber plate with raised characters. The plate is pressed against an inked roller to cover the raised portions with ink and then against the film or paper. It is used, for example, for cartons that do not require high print quality.
2. *Photogravure printing* (or intaglio) is able to produce high-quality detail and realistic pictures and has been more expensive than flexographic printing, although new methods of making gravure cylinders have reduced the cost. It uses an engraved chromium-plated

roller with the printing surfaces recessed in the metal. Ink is applied to the roller and the excess is wiped from all but the recesses. The remaining ink is then transferred to the packaging material.

3. *Offset lithography* (or planographic) is based on the incompatibility of grease and water. A greasy ink is repelled by moistened parts of a printing plate but remains on compatible parts which carry the design. This method produces a print of similar quality to that of rotogravure and is suitable for papers and boards that are too rough for rotogravure printing.
4. *Screen printing* in which ink passes through a porous surface of a printing screen.
5. *Ink-jet printing* in which electrically charged droplets of ink are deflected by charged deflector plates to create the image.

12.5.8 Intelligent Packaging

Intelligent packaging may be defined as (Han et al., 2005). Systems attached as labels, incorporated into, or printed onto a food packaging material offer enhanced possibilities to monitor product quality, trace the critical points, and give more detailed information throughout the supply chain.

It has also been defined by Yam et. al. (2005) as:

A packaging system that is capable of carrying out intelligent functions (such as detecting, sensing, recording, tracing, communicating, and applying scientific logic) to facilitate decision making to extend shelf life, enhance safety, improve quality, provide information and warm about possible problems.

Intelligent Packaging Systems

Intelligent packaging systems can include the following components.

1. Indicators: (*a*) Time–temperature indicators, (*b*) Integrity or gas indicators, (*c*) Freshness indicators (microbial or pathogen spoilage).

2. Barcodes and radiofrequency identification tags (RFID).

3. Sensors: (*a*) Biosensors, (*b*) Gas sensors, (*c*) Fluorescence-based oxygen sensors.

12.6 PACKAGING CONTAINERS

Different types of containers and films used for packaging

Field containers : Picking containers are of many types depending upon the crop, region and availability of materials. Picking bags of canvas, mesh hampers and baskets of woven veneer or bamboo are widely used

Shipping containers : The ideal pack consists of tight fill without a bulge in a lidded container having sufficient stacking strength to protect the contents from all the hazards. In India, baskets and boxes are often used as containers. Fireboard cartons are becoming popular for shipping both tropical and sub-tropical fruits. Their light weight and low cost are advantageous

Primary containers : Primary containers are defined as those containers which come in direct contact with the food.

Secondary containers : Containers that protect primary containers during handling and transportation.

Consumer packages : Use of small sized packages for produce has grown with the increase in large self-service markets for retailing. Bags, plastic films and mesh bags are used as consumer packages

Flexible films : The word flexible film is reserved for non-fibrous materials which are less than 0.25mm thick. In general, they are heat sealable, suitable for high speed filling, suitable for printing and add little weight to the product.

A-Pet films : These films are clear as glass with superior transparency and gloss. They have high mechanical properties and good chemical resistance. Excellent barrier properties, good printability, sealability and good bondability are other advantages of pet films.

Hermetic Closures : Hermetic refers to the container that is sealed completely against the entry of gases and vapours. These are also impervious to bacteria, yeasts, molds and dirt. Hermetic sealing is essential for vacuum and gas packages.

Form Fill and Seal Packages : The package (generally pouches)[of different capacities are preformed from flat rolls of the packaging material (form) then filled with a fixed quantity of food product (fill) and then is sealed air tight (seal) e.g. Kurkure pack, pan masala pack, etc.

Retortable pouches or trays : These are suitable for packing low acid foods which needs to be retorted or heated at high temperatures. These generally consists of 3 layers: polyester. aluminium foil and polypropylene

Aerosol cans : Semi solid foods are generally packed in sealed cans under pressure with inert gas or sterile air mixture. When the nozzle is pressed, food comes out in the form of foam

Coextruded films : These films are formed by coextrusion in 3, 5 or upto 9 layer with materials i.e. nylon, HDPE, metallocene, EVA, LLDPE, LDPE, VLDPE

Resealable Pouches : Some foods now come in a flexible pouch package provided with zipper for sealing the pack again and again after use and produce is safe. It is gaining popularity.

Laminates : Multilayer packages are made from paper, plastic films and metal foils having low permeability to moisture and light, better retention of quality, heat seal ability, etc.

Stretch Films and Shrink Films Wraps

The shrink films are used for individual as well as group packaging of fresh as well as processed products. Shrink film package involves use of thermoplastic films that have been stretched or oriented during manufacturing and have property of shrinking with the application of heat and hold the product in its position.Films such as polypropylene, polystyrene, polyethylene and rubber hydrochloride can be converted into shrink films by molecular orientation methods. After the shrink film is applied to the filled trays in tubular or heat-sealed wrap form, the packages are passed through a heat tunnel to shrink the film cover. This immobilizes the commodity to reduce the possibility of physical damage during handling.

12.7 PACKAGING MATERIALS OF SOME COMMON FOOD SECTORS

12.7.1 Packaging Materials of Fruits and Vegetables

1. ***Raw vegetables and fruits*** : Raw vegetables may be packed loose in bulk or packed in containers for trading and transport. In the latter case, the vegetables should be packed in new loosely woven gunny bags or wooden/plastic crates or in lined or unlined corrugated fibreboard boxes.

2. ***Onion and garlic*** : These should be packed in sound, clean, new loosely woven gunny bags, net bags, bamboo baskets or palm leaf baskets or wooden crates or lined or unlined corrugated fibre board boxes or in any other suitable manner so as to allow proper aeration of the bulbs.

3. *Tomatoes* : Tomatoes should be packed in baskets or wooden boxes or lined or unlined corrugated fibre board boxes. While packing, it should be ensured that the tomatoes are not unduly pressed when the lid is closed.

4. *Chillies* : Fresh chillies should be packed in gunny bags or in bamboo baskets, or in corrugated boxes, lined or unlined. The containers should be so constructed as to allow for proper aeration of the packed material.

5. *Guava, Lime and mandarin*: They should be packed in wooden boxes or lined or unlined corrugated fibre board boxes. The boxes should be made in such a manner as to allow for proper aeration of the fruits. Sufficient quantity of straw should be put in the container to prevent fruits from rubbing against each other. Super grade fruit should be wrapped individually either in tissue paper or in any other suitable material before being packed into the container.

6. *Juices, jams, jellies and marmalades* : They should be packed in glass bottles or open top cans. Tomato juice be packed in glass or tinplate containers and hermetically sealed. The containers may be either plain or lacquered; if lacquered, the lacquer should be of the acid resistant type.

Packaging Material for Fresh Fruits and Vegetables

1. Plastic crates/boxes : used for on farm handling and transportation of fruits and vegetables .now a days some special crates are provided by various companies for transportation of fruits from the field to the cold storage *e.g.* boxes provided by Adani group for apple in himachel Pradesh .Theses plastic crates are very sturdy, water resistant, ventilated and have good staking strength

2. Wooden boxes : earlier these boxes were used for the long transportation of fruits etc. and vegetables (tomato) but now they have become obsolete due to their various disadvantages: environmental problems injury to the fruits etc.

3. CFB cartons : Corrugated fibre board cartons are light in weight easy to handle recyclable, suitable for printing etc. These can also be made water resistant by wax coating or plastic coating. Available in 3 ply or 5 ply.

12.7.2 Packaging Material for Some Spices

Chillies : Chillies should be packed in clean and sound jute bags or in pouches made from PET/ EVA or BOPP/EVA or in suitably lined wooden cases. The material may also be packed in LDPE coated raffia bags.

Black pepper : It should be packed in clean and sound jute bags with or without moisture-proof lining or LDPE coated raffia bags which do not impart any foreign smell to black pepper. The mouth of each bag should be either machine stitched or rolled over or hand stitched.

Cloves : Whole and ground cloves should be packed in clean and sound air-tight containers, made of a material which does not affect the cloves. Packing in PET/LDPE bags may be considered.

12.7.3 Packaging Materials for Grains and their Products

Cereal grains : Cereal gains should be packed in new, clean jute bags or LDPE coated jute bags and raffia bags. The mouth of each bag should be machined stitched.

Cereal flours : The cereal flours should be packed in 1, 2, 10, 20, 40, 65,75, or 90 kg bags. For packages above 65 kg, the material for packaging should be either LDPE coated jute bag/LDPE coated raffia bags or single sound A-twill or B-twill jute bags. The bags used for smaller packs may be polyethylene bags or polyethylene lined jute bags.The mouth of the bag should be either machine stitched or hand stitched. If itis hand stitched, the mouth should be rolled over and then stitched. The stitchesshould be in two rows with at least 14 stitches in each row for jute bags of 65 kg and above.

12.7.4 Packaging Material for Dairy Sector

1. **Pasteurized flavoured milk:** It should be filled in glass bottles and capped. LDPE lined cartons/aseptic cartons or any other suitable containers have also been recommended.
2. **Sterilized flavoured milk:** It should be filled in glass bottles or sanitary cans, properly sterilized. Polypapers or poly-laminated paper packs in tetrahedron, pyramid or other forms may also be used. The containers should be capped or sealed air-tight and placed in a sterilizer where they should be gradually heated to a suitable temperature and cooled to room temperature.
3. **Sterilized milk:** It should be packed in glass bottles or sanitary cans properly sterilized and stocked in such a way as to protect it from contamination. Polypapers or polylaminated paper packs in tetrahedron, pyramid or other forms may also be used.
4. **Condensed milk/Sterilized cream:** These products should be packed in hermetically sealed containers or LDPE lined cartons/aseptic cartons. In case of condensed milk, the side seam of the container may be soldered or cemented. The type of cement used should not impart any odd flavour to the milk and should also be non-toxic.
5. **Fermented milk products and Dahi:** They should be filled in glass bottles or any other suitable container and capped. They should not be exposed to warmer temperature as the products become too sour due to growth of micro-organisms. The fermented milk products should be cooled before dispatch and maintained preferably at a temperature below 10°C; to develop good flavour and texture.
6. **Canned Rasogolla :** For canned rasogolla, the packaging materials suggested are open top sterilized sanitary cans or polystyrene tubs or any other suitable containers with as little air as possible.
7. **Milk powder, Cereal weaning foods :** For the above products, the code has recommended that these products should be packed in hermetically sealed and clean containers in such a way as to protect them from deterioration. These may also be packed in hermetically sealed tinplate containers in N_2 or a mixture of N_2 and CO_2 gas. Other packing material that may be considered is bag-in-box having inner layers made of PET/LDPE which can be gas flushed. Infant milk food and whole milkpowder when manufactured by the spray drying process should be packed in N_2 or a mixture of N_2 and CO_2 gas.

12.7.5 Packaging Material of Meat, Fish and Poultry Products

1. Meat : Meat should be wrapped in polyethylene sheets or bags and delivered in clean, rust free and closed containers. If the time involved in packaging and transport is more than 2 hours, the meat should be covered with ice. If the meat has to be supplied to the distant market, meat should be wrapped in polyethylene sheets and packed in clean, rust free and closed containers which are sufficiently strong to withstand repeated handling. The containers should have an outlet for drinking of water resulting from melting of ice used to chill the meat. When the meat is chilled by using CO_2 or any other more effective chilling medium, the time involved for reaching the destination may be up to 1 hours. This type of packing with ice should be used when the distance involved can be covered in 6 hours from the time of packing to the time of delivery.

2. Cooked meat product : They should be packed in butter paper or any grease proof clean wrapping material. All the sliced cooked meat products shall be wrapped in butter paper and then put in big polyethylene cover. Finally, the polyethylene container should be packed in clean, rust free and closed containers sufficiently strong to prevent any damage to the meat products packed. Alternatively, the meat including whole carcasses and cooked meat products may also be vacuum packed using suitable wrapping materials such as PET/LDPE.

3. Dressed chicken : The drained and dressed birds should be packed into suitable sized polyethylene bags or other suitable packing material. Before final sealing, the packs should be immersed into vats containing water to expel the content of air between the carcass and the bag, taking care that no water is introduced in the pack. Alternatively, vacuum packing or shrink wrapping of the packs may be adopted. After the air inside is expelled, the bag should be sealed on a sealer or should be knotted using rubber bands.

4. Egg powder : Egg powder should be gas packed in nitrogen in suitable tinplate containers or flexible packaging materials. PET/LDPE laminate may be considered for the purpose.

5. Fish : The fresh product should be packed in polyethylene lined insulated containers, made of plywood, country wood or plastic. The thickness of insulation may vary from 15 to 30 mm depending upon the storage period and the mode of transport. Thermocole or fiberglass may be used as insulation material. Adequate drainage of melted ice may be provided.

12.7.6 Packaging Material for Oils and Fats

Oil : The oil should be packed in suitable well closed containers. The packaging material used may be tinplate containers, glass bottles, rigid plastic containers of HDPE, food grade PVC, PET and flexible pouches made of plastic film/foil/laminate. Flexible pouches of biaxially oriented nylon (BON) film/ionomer and coextruded nylon/ionomer may be considered.

Fat, Vanaspati : The material should be packed in suitable sealed packages, such as, flexible packs and well closed tinplate containers. The net mass of oils, fats and Vanaspati to be packed should be 500 g, 1 kg, 2 kg, 5 kg and thereafter in multiples of 5 kg.

12.7.7 Tetrapackaging

These are the packages used extensively for packing various types of products *i.e.* fruit juices, milk, vegetable oils, etc. These packages have 6-7 layers of materials used for their manufacture. They are:

(*a*) *Polyethylene* : innermost layer suitable for sealing

(*b*) *Polyethylene* : adhesion layer

(*c*) *Aluminium foil* : gas and light barrier, aroma retention

(*d*) Polyethylene : adhesion layer

(*e*) Paper : stability, strength and printing

(*f*) Polyethylene : outermost layer makes the package waterproof

12.8 FACTORS INFLUENCING SHELF LIFE OF FOOD PACKAGE

Shelf life is the length of time that foods, beverages, and many other perishable items are given before they are considered unsuitable for sale, use, or consumption. It is the time between the production and packaging of a product and the point at which the product first becomes unacceptable under defined environmental conditions.

Shelf life of a product begins from the time the food is prepared or manufactured. Its length is dependant on many factors including the types of ingredients manufacturing processes, type of packaging and how the food is stored shelf life is indicated by labelling the product with a date mark.

1. Aroma loss as in freshly ground pepper or roasted coffee which results in loss of palatability
2. Pick up of a foreign odour. Ex. Absorption of onion odour by butter when these two items are placed together.
3. Loss of carbonation as in the case of soft drinks or beer
4. Crystallization. Ex. Honey when kept in cold for a long time.
5. Moisture gain as in dry or dehydrated foods such as ready-to-eat breakfast cereals, snack foods which destroys their crisp texture
6. Rancidity of snack items such as potato chips due to the oxidation of the oils absorbed during frying. Browning reactions as in case of freshly cut fruits.

Package : A package is meant to protect the product against an agent which degrades the product. The degree of protection is measured as a water vapour transmission rate (WVTR) and oxygen transmission rate (OTR) for moisture and oxygen sensitive foods respectively. The critical sensitivity of the product to external agents is determined in part by the package. Ex. A product such as snack food which is susceptible to moisture gain and oxygen can be termed as 'moisture sensitive' if texture degrades before rancidity becomes objectionable. The same product, if packed in a sufficient moisture barrier would become oxygen sensitive.

Environment : Product distribution through various network causes stress on the product under a variety of climates, seasons, shipping and warehouse conditions.

12.9 FOOD SAFETY, CONSUMER ACCEPTABILITY AND REGULATORY ISSUES

At least four types of food safety and regulatory issues related to active packaging of foods need to be addressed. First, any need for food contact approval must be established before any form of active packaging is used. Second, it is important to consider environmental regulations covering active packaging materials. Third, there may be a need for labelling in cases where active packaging may give rise to consumer confusion. Fourth, it is pertinent to consider the effects of active packaging on the microbial ecology and safety of foods.

Food contact approval will often be required because active packaging may affect foods in two ways. Active packaging substances may migrate into the food or may be removed from it. Migrants may be intended or unintended. Intended migrants include antioxidants, ethanol and antimicrobial preservatives which would require regulatory approval in terms of their identity, concentration and possible toxicological effects. Unintended migrants include various metal compounds that achieve their active purpose inside packaging materials but do not need to or should not enter foods. Food additive regulations require identification and quantification of any such unintended migration.

Environmental regulations covering reuse, recycling, identification to assist in recycling or the recovery of energy from active packaging materials needs to be addressed on a case by case basis.

Food labelling is currently required to reduce the risk of consumers ingesting the contents of oxygen scavenger sachets or other in-pack active packaging devices. Some active packages may look different from their passive counterparts. Therefore it may be advisable to use appropriate labelling to explain this difference to the consumer even in the absence of regulations.

Finally, it is very important for food manufacturers using certain type of active packaging to consider the effects this will have on the microbial ecology and safety of foods. For example, removing all the oxygen from within packs of high a_w chilled perishable food products may stimulate the growth of anaerobic pathogenic bacteria such as *Clostridium botulinum*. Specific guidance is available to minimize the microbial safety risks of foods packed under reduced oxygen atmospheres. Regarding the use of antimicrobial films, it is important to consider what spectrum of microorganisms will be inhibited. Antimicrobial films that only inhibit spoilage microorganisms without affecting the growth of pathogenic bacteria will raise food safety concerns.

12.10 FOOD STORAGE

As stated in the beginning of the chapter that food items as specially grains need to be stored to prevent them for spoilage and for future use: Here we discuss some general methods of storage.

12.10.1 Losses in Food Grains

Food grains undergo a series of operations such as harvesting, threshing, winnowing. bagging, transportation, storage, and processing before they reach the consumer, and there are appreciable losses in crop output at all these stages. In India, agriculture and its allied sectors are the mainstays for its rural population. 70% of the rural households primarily depend on agriculture as their primary source of income. There are about 82% of the farmers are small & marginal meaning that they own less than 2 acres of farmland. These are mostly fragmented and are involved in growing majorly cereal crops. Smallholder farmers play a significant role in the Indian agricultural value chain as they contribute to over 40 percent of the country's grain production, and over half of its fruits, vegetables, and oilseeds production. The total food grain production as per the 2nd Advances in 2021-22, is estimated at a record 316.06 million tonnes which is higher by 5.32 million tonnes than the production of food grain during 2020-21. Though there has been an increase in production, a significant proportion of the produce is lost or spoiled due to the inadequacy of appropriate farm-to-market logistics. It has been estimated that around INR 92,651 crore per annum is lost due to post-harvest losses out of which INR 63,000 crore per annum is lost due to poor storage facilities.

According to the research conducted by the Indian Council of Agricultural Research on crop losses in India it estimates the loss to be around 3.9% to 6% in the case of cereals, 2.8% to 10.1% for oilseeds, 4.3% to 6.1% for pulses, 5.8% to 18.1% for fruits, and **6.9% to 13% vegetables** were in harvesting and post-harvesting phase. This is attributed to a lack of proper cold storage facilities, inefficient cold-chain network, poor infrastructure, and inaccessibility to small-holder farmers especially in rural areas. This forces farmers to sell their perishable horticultural produce at whatever prices the market offers at the time, which are usually sub-optimal.

Even if cold storages are available, they are majorly used for bulk storage and mainly for a single commodity such as potato, apple, etc. and on a single temperature and for the long term. In addition, a farmer has to travel a substantial distance to avail of this conventional cold storage located away from the village thus adding to the transportation cost and time. The other factor that ails the sector is an unreliable power supply as mostly cold storage run on grid electricity which limits the operations of the system. Further, the volatile fuel prices and dependence on conventional sources of energy pose a hindrance in the scaling of the cold storage industry.

According to a study backed by the government, in 2022 India lost about 5–13% of its fruits and vegetables and 3–7% of other crops including oil seeds and spices between harvesting and consumption.

12.10.2 Storages for the Reduction of Post Harvest Losses

Upon the arrival of grains to the silos, the grains should be analyzed and classified accordingly. These, where condition at reception and mediocre should be directly towards immediate use the either depends on the condition and technologies suitability should be treated and stored appropriately.

The sanitary condition of grain is complex phenomenon and it indicates real state of health of grains. It is appraisal requires the determination of following parameters.

1. Physical state of grain: moisture content, temperature, clear lines
2. Biological state: level of enzymatic activity (particularly amylase)
3. Degree of infestation by insects and micro-organism
4. Milling quality of grains

12.10.3 Purpose of Grain Storage

Grain storage is a component in the grain marketing supply chain that evens out fluctuations in the supply of grain from one season, usually the harvest season to other seasons, and from one year of abundant supply and releasing to lean years. Grain storage may be at farm, trader, and commercial or at government levels.

i. At the farm level, storage is normally inter-seasonal and helps household to ensure food supplies for the farmer and the family, cash or barter exchange and for seed.

ii. At trader level, grain storage is for very limited time – over a period of few days or weeks. The traders buy and sell quickly to make a profit.

iii. Commercial storage, used by millers and co-operatives; the stock is hold for limited periods to meet demands for their needs or for their urban clients

Government involvement in grain storage, through its own special departments, agencies or government grain marketing boards focuses on the intervention in the staple grain market to balance national supply and demand over a time. The purposes being to create a national food reserve especially for the urban population, national food security reserves, stimulation of productivity, price stabilization and for political consideration such as placation of sectional interests.

12.10.3 Storage Requirements

Primary aim of storage is simply to prevent deterioration of quality of grain. This is not done directly, but indirectly through control of moisture and air movements and by preventing attack by micro-organisms, insects, and rodents. The management of objectives during the storage period is to reduce the metabolic activity to such a low level that the grain mass is sufficiently stable with minimal deterioration. The two alternate methods are:

(*i*) Reduction of moisture content to a safe level and cooling of the grain

(*ii*) Modification of atmosphere condition of the storage system

Requirements of grain storage is carried out basically to maintain the quality of grain after harvest for

- retaining the viability of the grain for planting in following reason
- maintaining the supply of grain, and
- taking advantages of higher prices by farmers, governments and industry.

Spoilage of grain

Storability of grains is generally influenced by physiochemical and biological factor. Grains being a biological material themselves and other entities of eco-system determine the health and quântity of the stored product.

We have already discussed about food spoilage in detail in Chapter -11. Here we take some points about food grain spoilage.

(1) Physiochemical spoilage mechanism: Any spoilage mechanism demands the simultaneous fulfillment of two conditions:

(*i*) The presence of agent of spoilage and

(*ii*) The environmental condition associated with spoilage

The physicochemical spoilage may be broadly classified in two categories.

(A) Non enzymatic chemical reaction (degradation): These are five types-

(*i*) **Maillard reaction (non enzymatic browning):** This is basically condensation of carbohydrates and protein giving same intermediate compounds. This reaction requires quite high temperature and occurs principally during drying or as a biological heating.

(*ii*) **Denaturation of protein**: This results in a loss of their functional properties.

(*iii*) **Physico-chemical modification of starch:** This is characterized as high by the bursting of starch grains followed by gelatinization.

(*iv*) **Destruction of vitamins** (especially B_1) due to high temperature.

(*v*) **The Non-enzymatic oxidation:** This reaction starts at low temperature but strongly exotherms and rapidly raises the temperature of grains.

(2) Mechanical and Physical Spoilage: Spoilage of grains may also be due to shock impact which leads to breakage of grain, and thus considerably facilitate other causes of spoilage notably development and inversion of microorganisms.

Environmental Factors Causing Spoilage

(*i*) **Storage time:** The time factor introduces a motion of reaction rate. Knowledge of this is independent in calculating maximum possible storage time. It is sometimes thought that for longer storage period, the moisture content should be lower. The allowable storage time is defined as the maximum time before the germination falls by 5% or visible mould appears.

(*ii*) **Temperature:** It is extremely important for storage. Heat increases the molecular motion and hence kinetic energy of molecule, thus favouring molecular collision and consequently the reaction. Rate constant of a chemical reaction increases exponentially with temperature. From the point of view of grain storage, the spoilage reaction occurs at faster rate at higher temperature, and any small increment in temperature may cause great harmful.

(*iii*) **Humidity:** The moisture factor which is characteristics by water activity is also very important. There are optimum values of relative humidity below or beyond which for a given temperature, the causes of spoilage are initiated.

(*iv*) **Atmospheric conditions:** The O_2 and CO_2 concentration factor (composition inter-granular atmosphere) influences the type of metabolism *i.e.* aerobic and anaerobic of the of microorganism and also of the living cells of the grains. It also affects non-enzymatic oxidation and certain enzymatic reaction.

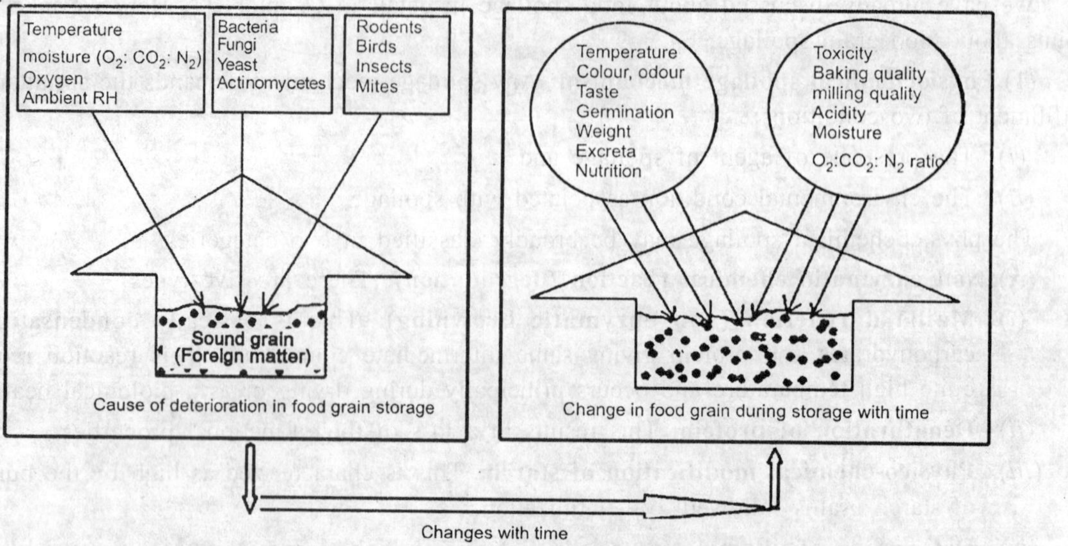

Fig. 1: A diagrammatic representation of interrelation among the grain bulk, organisms and their abiotic environment in the spoilage of stored grain (Singh 1973)

12.10.9 Storage Environment and its Interaction with Stored Product

Grain storage eco-system: A batch of grain stored in bulk or in stacks is an eco-system which is defined as a thermo-dynamic system that includes a group of interacting organisms and their environment. It is also a man-made ecological system *i.e.* artificially created by man in which living organisms and their non living environment interact on each other. In this eco-system, the most important living organism is the grain itself (particularly the germ and aleurone layer). Both the grain and the grain bulk have several attributes which are given below:

Physical: Temperature and humidity of ambient.

Chemical: Moisture and oxygen (O_2:CO_2).

Physiological: respiration and heating.

Biological (Biotic): Insect, fungi, molds, mites, microorganisms and rodents. The abiotic environment of grain includes physical variables (*e.g.* temperature), inorganic chemical variables (CO_2 and O_2) and physico-chemical variables (moisture) and an array of organic compounds which are the by-products of biological activity.

The major biotic variables other than the grain bulk including microorganisms (such as fungi, actinomycetes and bacteria), arthropods (such as insects and mites), and vertebrates (such as rodents and birds), these pests rarely act alone. Their ecological kinship (relationship) develops in time with the grains and amongst themselves, supported by certain other sets of variables in the complex process of deterioration of the quality of the grains. Although, this deterioration is usually slow in the beginning, but as the favourable combination of variables is set and the storage period is prolonged, a very high loss in grain quality and quantity occurs.

Stored product environment interaction: The stored grain bulk is mainly composed of living grains (about 60 % of total volume). The environment factors affect the grain in storage and deterioration in grain quality results from interaction among physical, chemical and biological variables. Some of the variables are temperature, moisture, oxygen, and storage structures, physical, chemical and biological properties of the grain bulks, microorganisms, insects, mites, rodents and birds. These variables interact with the grain and in groups among themselves.

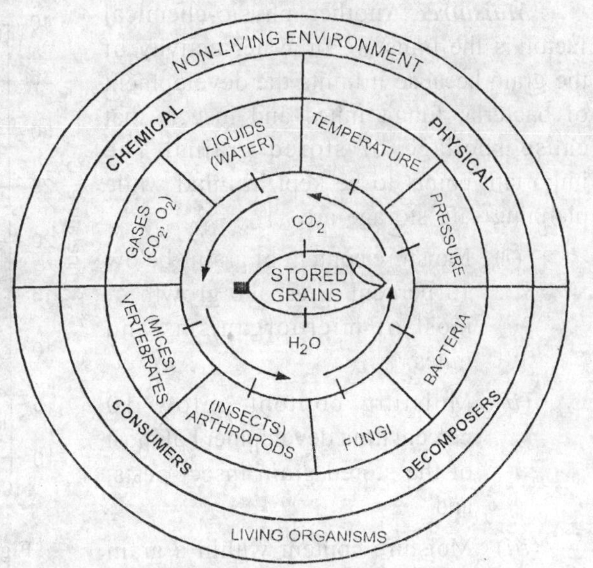

Fig. 2

Physical variables such as temperature and moisture are the most important environmental factors which cause various changes and deterioration in food grains during storage.

Temperature: All living organisms remain alive and flourish only within limits of temperatures. The atmospheric temperature, grain temperature and inter-granular air temperature are all considered to be crucial variable for safer and prolonged storage of grains. The optimum temperatures for the growth and multiplication of insects, fungi and mites in stored grains are

For insects	: 25-32°C
Fungi	: 30-32°C
Mites	: 25°C

The growth rates of insects, fungi and mites decreases with decrease of temperature. The levels of temperature experience during storage in tropic and subtropics are therefore favorable for the attack of grain by these factors.

Therefore, for safe storage system, the following important points are to be kept in mind.

(*i*) Generally, insect do not develop below 15°C neither mites below 5°C.

(*ii*) Most of the storage fungi do not develop below 0°C, and

(*iii*) The effect of temperature on an organism can be correlated with the amount of moisture present because rise in temperature corresponds with decrease in the relative amount of moisture in the atmosphere.

The rate of respiration of grains, the growth of microorganisms and the chemical and enzymatic reactions during storage also accelerate up to a certain temperature. The respiration results in the oxidative break down (*i.e.* deficiency in oxygen quantity) and produce carbon dioxide, moisture and heat energy. The energy liberated during the aerobic respiration is utilized by the cells for metabolic processes resulting in the release of heat. The metabolic heat produced exclusively by dry grains is about 1×10^{-7} cal/sec/cm^3 and by wet (damp) grains is approximately 1.3×10^{-5} cal/sec/cm^3. The amount of heat produced by fungi, insect and other organisms infesting the grain is much higher compared to the above values.

When the grain temperature rises to around 20°C, it starts getting infested easily with insect and microorganisms and at the same time its rate of respiration becomes rapid. The grain temperature is always to be considered along with the grain moisture and equilibrium relative humidity. The relative humidity which is in equilibrium with the grain moisture varies with temperature.

Moisture: Another physic-chemical factor is the moisture or water activity of the grain because it limits the development of bacteria, fungi, mites and insects that cause spoilage of stored grains. The important points to be kept in mind while planning safe storage are

(*i*) Moisture content of grains below 13 percent arrest the growth of most of microorganisms and mites.

(*ii*) Moisture content below 10 percent limit development of most of the stored grain insect pests, and

(*iii*) Moisture content within a grain bulk is seldom uniformly distributed and is changeable from season to season and from one climatic zone to another

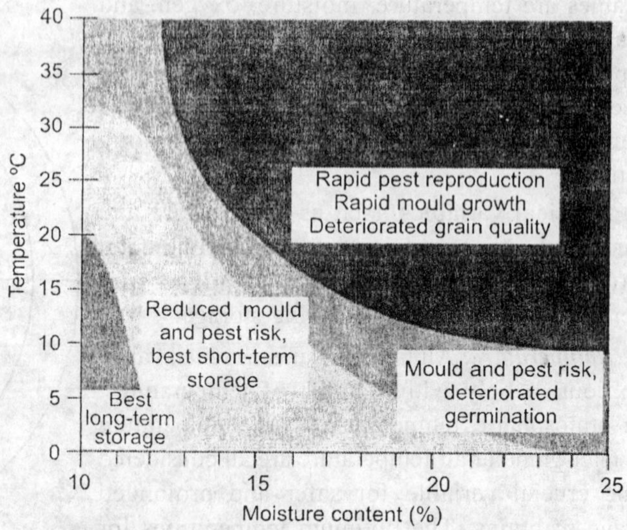

Fig. 3: Effects of Temperature and moisture on stored grain

Table 1: Equilibrium moisture content of the grains

Community	Temperature, °C	Relative humidity			
		30 %	50%	70%	90%
Rice (polished)	28	9.2	10.6	12.5	23.4
Paddy	25	7.9	10.4	13.2	17.6
Wheat	28	8.6	10.5	13.4	20.8
Corn	28	10.5	12.0	14.4	-
Sorghum	28	8.9	11.2	13.6	21.6
Green gram	28	6.2	9.3	11.8	26.3
Groundnut (kernel)	28	3.2	4.8	6.6	18.2

12.11 TEMPERATURE AND MOISTURE MIGRATION

Temperature and moisture are two important physical variables which is given emphasis in the study of deterioration of grain in storage. Even though grain is stored at moisture content generally considered safe, both temperature and moisture content change with both time and position as result of weather changes. Moisture migration in stored grain results from temperature changes and the prediction of the effect due to naturally occurring variations in weather is necessary in order to provide a rational basis for safe storage design.

Moisture changes of stored grain in cylindrical bin: Moisture will move in stored grain if uniform moisture content if temperature gradient exists in the bulk as a result of temperature variations surrounding the grain bin. If the moisture content of the grain is held constant, the equilibrium relative humidity of the air surrounding the grain increases with increasing temperature. Thus, a relative humidity gradient exists parallel to temperature gradient in the stored grain of uniform moisture content. The partial pressure and concentration of water vapour in the air increases as the relative humidity and temperature increases.

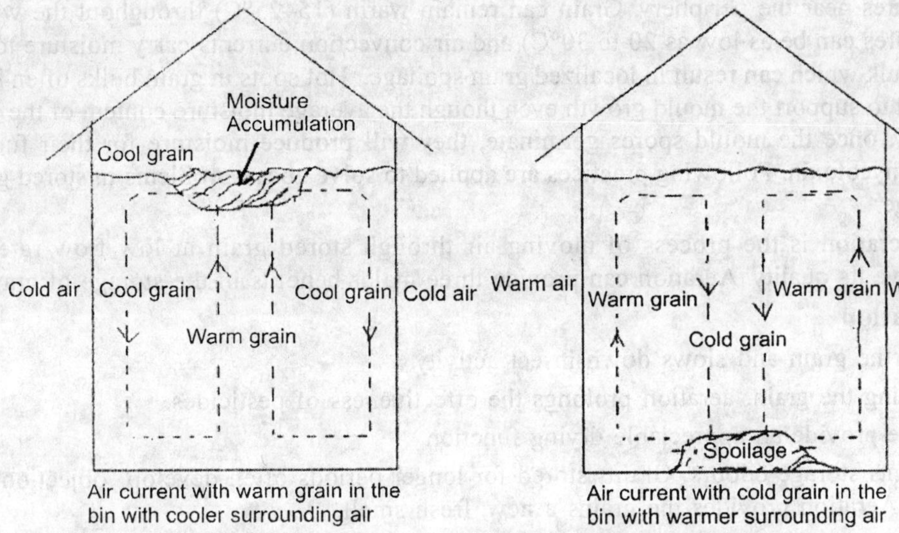

Fig. 4

When warm air moves from warm region to cooler region in the stored grains, the air gives up both moisture and heat. This causes accumulation of moisture due to condensation at the top or bottom of the bin depending upon the direction of natural convection of the air within the air.

During winter season, moisture condenses on the top and during summer season, moisture condenses at cold bottom. Therefore spoilage may occur if counter measures are not taken. Moisture migration is slower in small bin than in larger bin because at most times of the year differences in temperature between the walls and the centre of the bin will be less in smaller bins.

Temperature changes in stored grains: Temperature is one of the crucial factor limiting the distribution and abundance of insects, mites and fungi that contaminate and destroy stored grains. Seasonal changes in atmospheric temperature change the temperature pattern throughout the grain bin. During winter the centre of the bin below the upper surface of the grain remains warmer than the remainder of the bin as convective air current flow upward though the centre of the bin. Conversely, in summer the centre of the bin near bottom remains coldest as the air currents move upward along the warm walls and downward through the centre of the bin. Government policies cold encourage the long-term storage of grain in areas where deterioration is likely to be minimum.

✓ Large bin maintains lower average temperature in stored grain during the summer than small bins. Temperature of small bin rises faster in summer than those in larger bins, which allows for more reproductive cycles of the grain insects in small bins.

✓ During cold winter months, when low grain temperatures are desired in order to reduce the population of insects, small bins cool more rapidly than larger bins. In larger bins pockets of grains remains at high temperatures throughout the winter where insects can accumulate and survive, while in small bins most insects may be killed during winter.

Storage practices

When grains are stored in large bulks without aeration they will be indirectly affected by the weather. The grain bulk will retain the heat it had at harvest in the centre of the bulk and reflect external ambient temperatures near the periphery. Grain can remain warm (15–25°C) throughout the winter (outside temperatures can be as low as 20 to 30°C) and air convection currents carry moisture to the top-centre of the bulk which can result in localized grain spoilage. Hot spots in grain bulks often have moisture sufficient to support the mould growth even though the average moisture content of the bulk is very low or dry, once the mould spores germinate, they will produce moisture for their further development and mycotoxin. Following practices are applied to solve above problems in stored grain during bulk storage.

Aeration: Aeration is the process of moving air through stored grain at low flow rates to maintain or improve its quality. Aeration can provide three major benefits in the storage of grains.

Benefits of Aeration

- It cools the grain and slows down insect activity.
- By cooling the grain, aeration prolongs the effectiveness of pesticides.
- It can be provide an appreciable drying function
- It prevents storage odours. Grains stored for longer periods often develop objectionable odours. Aeration provides the grains a new, fresh smell.
- It reduces moisture accumulation. Moisture condensation by changes in temperature and relative humidity can be reduced by aeration.
- Application of fumigants through an aeration system is an easy and practical method for controlling insects in stored grains.

Purpose of Aeration

- To removal of heat generated in the bulk due to biological activity
- Removal of excess moisture
- Modification of gaseous environment in the bulk
- To facilitate the fumigation
- To removal the of bad odour

Air distribution system: It is of several types. The selection can be done judicially taking care of dimension of bin.

- Single central duct system
- Main with lateral duct system
  - ✓ Central main duct system with lateral
  - ✓ Side main duct with lateral
- Perforated false flour system

Components of Aeration system: Fan is general term which is used for the device to facilitate the movement of air. Air movement is a device however can be classified *i.e.*

(1) Fan (2) Blower, and (3) compressor

1. **Fan:** Air movement device having low static pressure of one psi. But they are capable of moving large volume of air.
2. **Blower:** Blower is that devices, which can be operated against a pressure, head upto 35 psi. But they cannot handle as larger volume as a fan.
3. **Compressor:** A compressor device little smaller air volume of much higher pressure, may be as high as 5000 psi. But volume of air movement is a least.

This is the general criteria of classification of air movement device. However, there is no clear demarcation among them and there is considerable overlapping of pressure for fan, blower and compressor.

Aeration system in a bin: Aeration system can be installed in both horizontal and vertical storages. The following set of basic design parameters are found suitable for cooling of dry grains by aeration.

- ✓ Air flow rate in (Silo) : 0.18 litre /second/tonne
- ✓ Maximum duct velocity : 10 m/s
- ✓ Maximum entry velocity of air into grain : 0.15 m/s

The most common air flow rates for aerating paddy range from 0.07-0.28 m^3/min/tonne of paddy. The above air flow rates for aeration are only a fraction of the air volume needed to dry grains.

Direction of air flow: Air can either be blown or drawn from the bottom of the storage. The following guidelines are helpful in deciding the pattern of storage.

- When air is drawn from top to the bottom, surface of grain is cooled first, whereas when it is blown from bottom to the top the surface is cooled at l last, when the surface inspection is criteria for assessment of performance, drawing air is more effective.
- When surface has become hot downward flow would thrust this hot zone on the bottom grains, blown would move this out to the top. In this situation blowing is advisable.
- In the upward movement of air, the cooling front reaches, the surface, condensation of moisture could occur in this area. There may be appearance of mites due to rise in moisture level of grains at the surface.
- With upward flow air moisture content of grain near the duct will increase and this higher at the surface when fan downward movement of air occurs (when fan mounted at top). The higher moisture level of surface grains is even out during warmer period of the days.
- It is possible that downward flow may draw the grain from the duct when it is not properly designed. This creates problems but upward flow does not create the problem of blockage of duct. In case of grain is having excessive duct downward flow could block the flow in aeration duct.

Fumigation: This is the process of holding the stored grain with a poisonous gas in order to kill any infesting organisms. In India, fumigation with ethylene dibromide or aluminium phosphide is adopted for farm storage and methyl bromide or ethylene dibromide or aluminium phosphide is employed in commercial storage of grains. In addition to fumigation, surface treatment with malathion or pyrethrum is employed in commercial grain storage. Because of low coast of fumigation and convenience the solid fumigant, namely, aluminium phosphide has become popular. Contact insecticides may also be used in combination with fumigation. Fumigation requires sufficient phosphine gas is held with grain for long enough to kill the pests infesting it. Most grain is stored in bags, so to provide a gas-tight enclosure, bag stacks of open-weave bags are placed under gas-proof sheets held down at the edges by flexible, sand-filled tubes called 'sand snakes'. Phosphine gas penetrates easily into a commodity so that a good fumigation will kill 100% of the pests under the gas-proof sheet. It is also important to bear in mind the situations in which grain and grain products should not be fumigated. These are as follows:

- When the enclosure is not sufficiently gas-tight
- When there is human habitation within 100 m

- When there is a danger of liquid water coming into direct contact with the phosphide tablets
- When the temperatures is below 15°C
- When it is very windy
- When the commodity is a flour or in fully sealed bags (special arrangements are required in this case)
- When copper will be exposed to the gas.

Phosphine is most effective as a fumigant when used at low concentrations over long periods. The exposure period is affected by temperature. The minimum temperature for the use of phosphine is about 15°C and at temperatures below 20°C long exposure periods of up to 16 days are recommended.

In addition following some common fumigants are also employed for fumigantion in grain storage system:

- Hydrogen phosphide/phosphine/phostoxin (solid form)
- Methyl bromide/Bromo Methane (gas)
- Ethylene Dichloride (liquid)
- Carbon tetra chloride (liquid)
- Ethylene dibromode (liquid)
- Hydrocynic acid/hydrogen cyanide (gas)
- Carbon disulphide (liquid)

12.12 METHODS OF FOOD STORAGE

Traditional methods: In-situ, Pit storage, clamps, wind breaks, cellar storage, barns, night ventilation, sand and coir, night temperature cooling, natural ice and well water cooling

Advanced methods: Hydro cooling, hypobaric storage, evaporative cooling, forced air cooling, CA storage, MA storage.

1. Storage of non-perishable foods: Cereals, pulses, sugar, salt and also tamarind and some spices are often stored for a year by people in rural areas, generally from one harvest to another. In town and cities where the consumer buys all his food from the markets the trend is different. The limitation of space, facilities, finance to purchase large quantities at one time, and the fairly dependable marketing facilities, encourage most people to go in for just monthly buying. However, even this amount of food items need to be stored adequately to prevent deterioration.

Following precautions while storing non-perishable foods like cereals and pulses:

We should carefully clean them to remove gravel, husk and other foreign matter a (if possible wash), and dry thoroughly in the sun.

We need to store them in clean containers which have tightfitting lids. These containers can be of tin, aluminium, plastic or glass. Clay pots or gunny bags also used in case of large quantities. These containers should be put either in the store room or in the storage cupboard in your kitchen. It is better to have a storage space away from the kitchen because the temperatures in the kitchen are higher than what is ideal for storage.

Storage of semi-perishables: Some of the cereal products, roots and tubers, nuts and oilseeds and fruits come in this category. Let us discuss storage of each one of these.

Cereal products: Cereal products like different flours, semolina, vermicelli, or broker wheat develop an off-flavour, or are infested by insects very easily. They should be sieved and cleaned of all such contamination, exposed to the sun for a few hours, allowed to cool, and then stored in tightly covered bottles or other containers.

Roots and Tubers: Specially onions and potatoes should be stored in a cool, dry and airy place to prevent them from developing moulds or growing shoots. They are best hung up from the ceiling in a wire or plastic-mesh basket, or kept in mesh containers which keep them exposed to air circulation. Do not keep them in the kitchen. They need a cool place.

Nuts: Nuts become rancid and infested with insects very easily, and we should buy them in large quantities only if we can store them, shelled in plastic bags inside a refrigerator. we can also freeze them to make them last for a year or even more.

Fruits: Like apples, oranges and semi-ripe mangoes do last for a few weeks and should be put in a basket lined and covered with paper to prevent them from drying up. Ready-to eat oranges and mangoes are best kept in a plastic bag in the refrigerator. They need a cool environment to last long.

2. Storage of perishables: Low temperatures slow down spoilage in perishable foods - both enzymatic, as well as, that caused by microorganisms. Normally, a domestic refrigerator 1s used at home for storage of perishable foods. The level of. Temperatures prevailing inside a refrigerator keeps these in check only for a short while. A domestic refrigerator is normally maintained at a temperature which varies between 6" C and 10" C.

Meat, fish, poultry: For longer period storage, foods like meat, chicken and fish need to be kept frozen at – 60 °C in a deep freeze. These foods should not be kept at room temperature for more than an hour or two. They should be cooked immediately if you do not have refrigeration facilities. Organ meats like liver, kidney and brain spoil faster than meat. Ground meats also spoil faster because a higher surface area is exposed to contamination, and the opportunities of contamination are also more by way of equipment and handling.

Eggs: should not be kept at room temperature for more than two days or so even in cool weather. They are best kept in a refrigerator.

Milk: The practice of boiling milk destroys the microorganisms as well as the enzymes present in it, and therefore boiled milk can be kept at room temperature for 6 to 12 hours. Giving it a second boil after 6 hours or so during hot weather makes it last longer. It is better to cover it with a netting of some kind to allow for ventilation when kept at room temperature. Inside a refrigerator milk can last 3 to 4 days or even more. The cold temperature of the refrigerator does disturb the emulsified state of the milk allowing the cream to separate and collect at the top.

Vegetables: The keeping quality of a vegetable depends upon its nature. Leafy vegetables wilt and deteriorate within minutes of buying unless they are kept wrapped in a damp cloth or inside a plastic bag in the refrigerator. Even here they do not last for more than a day or two. All other vegetables keep well in a cool place with relatively high humidity - in a basket covered with a damp cloth. They last longer in a refrigerator but must be kept in plastic bags to prevent drying by evaporation. Vegetables do continue to ripen even in the cold environment of a refrigerator. Fresh peas and fresh corn lose their sweetness after a couple of days even inside a refrigerator unless they are properly frozen.

12.12.1 General Tips for Food Handling and Storage

1. **Always choose foods that are at their peak quality.**
   - Select produce that is just ripe and unblemished.
   - Avoid products with signs of spoilage such as mould growth or insect damage.
   - Check dates on product packages you purchase from the store.
   - Check to see that packages are clean, dry and show no signs of product tampering.
   - Check to see that cans are intact, with no bulging, dents, excessive rust or signs of leaking
2. **Handle foods properly in preparation for storage.**
   - Pick up cold foods last at the store and get them home quickly.
   - Immediately refrigerate or freeze cold foods
   - Never leave potentially hazardous foods like meat, poultry, fish, eggs, cut fruits and vegetables, cooked foods and dairy foods at room temperature for more than two hours.
   - Always handle foods with clean hands and clean utensils in clean work areas.
   - Package foods securely for storage.
3. **Make sure storage areas are clean and correct storage temperatures are maintained.**
   - Cupboards or pantries should be clean, cool and dry
   - Refrigerators should be set at 35 to 38 °F so that foods stay at or below 40 °F.
   - Freezers should be set to keep foods at 0 °F or below.
4. **Observe recommended storage times.**
   - Label and date packages of food.
   - Use a system of "first in, first out" when it comes to rotating stored food.

Foods That Need Special Care: Some foods provide good conditions for bacteria to grow if the food is contaminated. Bacteria multiply rapidly in foods that are moist, rich in nutrients and low in acid if these foods are allowed to stay at temperatures between 40 and 140 °F for more than two hours. These foods include meats, poultry, fish and seafood, eggs, cut vegetables and fruits, cooked vegetables, most sauces, and milk. To ensure the safety and quality of these potentially hazardous foods, keep them refrigerated at 40 °F or below or freeze them.

Special Advice for the Pantry: Foods that can be stored safely at room temperature are dry ingredients and food products; foods with low moisture like peanut butter; foods high in sugar like unopened jams and jellies; and, foods that have been commercially canned or properly home-canned. The pantry or cupboard should be clean, free of pests, dry, cool and dark. The temperature should be kept around 50 to 70 °F to maintain the best possible quality for the longest amount of time. Avoid storing foods near ovens, furnaces, water heaters or hot pipes where warm temperatures can hasten a loss of nutrients and cause undesirable changes in the product. Store foods in plastic, glass or metal containers that be tightly sealed. Label foods with the name of the food and the date put in storage. Use foods with the oldest date first.

Special Advice for the Refrigerator: Keep refrigerators clean. Do not allow spills or spoiled foods to remain in your refrigerator. They not only can be a source of contamination, but also can cause undesirable odors that can be absorbed by other foods. Store raw foods like meats separate from foods that are cooked and foods that can be safely eaten without cooking. Do not allow raw juices to drip onto other foods or harmful bacteria may be transferred to the food. Cover foods well with air-tight wraps or put them in air-tight containers before placing them in the refrigerator. This maintains the quality of the foods by keeping them from drying out or absorbing odors from other foods. Use a refrigerator thermometer to be sure your refrigerator keeps food at 40 °F or below

Special Advice for the Freezer: Freezing stops the growth of microorganisms. As long as a food is kept frozen at 0 °F or below, then microorganisms like bacteria, yeasts and moulds will not be increasing in number or "growing." Freezing does not eliminate the need for cooking to destroy bacteria. When exposed to freezing temperatures, some cells may die, but others will survive. If the food is allowed to warm up and thaw, these survivors will begin to multiply again and cause problems. Recommended freezer storage times are for best quality and not for safety. For every degree above 0 °F that the freezer operates, the length of time the product can be stored will decrease. It is important to thaw frozen foods by one of three approved methods:

- By moving it to the refrigerator ahead of time.
- By placing it in cold water and changing the water often – at least every 30 minutes to keep the food cold.
- By using a microwave oven and then follow with immediate cooking either in the microwave or by some other method.

12.12 RURAL AND URBAN STORAGE STRUCTURES

Requirement of Good Storage structure

- It should be adequate protection from rodents, birds, insects, mites etc.
- It should permit aeration and fumigation whenever required.
- It should prevent loss due to moisture and temperature etc.
- It should permit easy inspection and smooth loading and unloading.
- It should facilitate proper cleaning and self cleaning in case of silos.
- It should be economical on unit storage cost basis.

1. Rural storage Structures: These structures are bulk storage structures, made of locally available construction materials. These structures are not moisture proof but they provide protection from rodents, birds, etc. to some extent.

(a) **Bukhari**: Generally used for the storage of wheat, maize, paddy and sorghum and their capacities from about 3.5 to 18 tonnes. This may be made of mud alone or by mud and bamboo. The cylindrical storage structures are raised above the ground by wooden on masonry platform. The floor of the bin is made of either by timber planks or by bamboo splits, plastered over with mud mixed with dung and paddy straw. The walls of the structures are made of timber or bamboo framework and bamboo matting. Over the walls, mud straw plaster is applied on the both sides. An overhanging cone type roof is provided on the cylindrical structures. The roof is generally made of bamboo framework and straw.

(b) **Kothari:** These are used for the storage of paddy, maize, sorghum, wheat and barley and this capacity varies from 9 to 35 tonnes. They are very much like a timber box placed on a raised platform which generally supported on pillars, floor and walls are made of timber planks and roof is either made of thatches or tiles. An overhanging is provided on all four sides to protect it from the rains and sun.

(c) **Morai type structure:** These are used for the storage of paddy, maize, sorghum, in the rural areas of the eastern and southern region of India. Its capacity varies from 3.5 to 18 tonnes. These structures are very similar to inverted truncated cone. They are placed on raised platform supported on wooden or masonry pillars.

2. **Improved Storage Structure:** In order to avoid losses during, it is necessary to use a storage which will help to avoid losses. Storage structures suitable for farm, urban and commercial storage in tropical countries have been described:

1. Farm Storage

a. **Circular steel bin:** This bin has an opening at the top filling and spout at bottom for removing grains. The bottom is made out of plain sheets of mild steel (MS). This is made out of 4 to 6 pieces which can be bolted and assembled on site. The bin has built in arrangement for preventing the development of uneven temperatures that lead to moisture migration and deterioration. It is rendered air-tight by the provision of neoprene washers with bolts. The grain stored in the bin can be fumigated whenever required. Grains such as wheat, paddy, maize, sorghum, millets and legumes can be safely stored in these bins. This bin is recommended for indoor of grain.

b. **Plastic bin:** This is a low cost structure suitable for the indoor storage of grains. It has a tube shaped metal base with a provision for placing bamboo sticks vertically around the inside of the metal drum. A cylindrical rubberized fabric is hung inside, into which the grains are loaded. Grains can be taken out from the top or through a sliding door at the bottom of the metal base. It is a stable and compact structure and can be dismantled when not in use.

c. **Prefabricated steel bin with hopper bottom:** This is a strong and durable outdoor structure with a slopping roof, a manhole for filling, and a hopper bottom with sliding door for discharging grains. A natural aeration arrangement is provided in the bin which prevents the building up of a temperature gradient and the subsequent problems of translocation of moisture and deterioration of grain. The bin stands on firm support creating a clearance of 60 cm at the bottom below the hopper. It is built of 16-gauge curved MS sheet and easily be erected and dismantled. Both manhole and hopper gates have locking arrangements. Metallic ladder and pulley are provided to facilitate filling of the bin.

d. **Aluminium bin:** This outdoor bin consists of a cylindrical body built from aluminium corrugated curved sheets and a conical roof of flat aluminium sheets. This bin is constructed on a 60 cm high platform. There is spout embedded in the platform and a manhole in the roof. Both manhole and spout are provided with locking arrangements.

e. **RCC bin:** An RCC bin is a circular, sturdy, weatherproof structure that can be built according to the requirements for both indoor and outdoor storage. The 6 tonnes structure is conveniently cast at the site, in contrast to other structure made out of 30 cm high rings, the bottom and top having been cast elsewhere the brought to the site and assembled. The joints are sealed with cement. It has a 60 cm diameter manhole on the top and a sliding door/ spout near the bottom for filling and removal of grain.

f. **Cement masonry bin:** This bin is weatherproof and easy to construct. It is built on a 60 cm high platform with a flight of steps along the side which facilitates filling the grain through a 60 cm diameter manhole on the top. The brick- wall sides are 23 cm thick and cement is plastered on both of the sides. A spout at the bottom and a slanting floor makes for the easy discharge of grain. There are locking arrangements for the manhole and spout. The walls can also be made of RCC instead of brick.

g. **Pusa bin:** This is a conventional mud which uses plastic in the form of a p polythene sheet to make the structure moisture and airtight. The bin is a simple design and easy to construct, thus within the reach of the average farmer. A platform is first made with unburnt brick, and then a polythene film of 0.7 mm thickness is spread over it to extend 6 cm beyond the extremities of the base. This is covered with a 7 cm thick layer of unburnt bricks. The walls are raised on the platform with unburnt bricks and the inner side is plastered with mud. A wooden frame is fixed on the top as a support for the top which is constructed with n burnt bricks. A wooden pole is placed inside to serve as a support for same. An outlet for the grain in the form of a pipe with a screw cap is fitted at one side with an adequate slope for the grains to flow out when required. A polythene cover in the form of a bottomless box, which fits in the mud receptacle, is prepared and placed inside to line the side walls and the top. A 50 × 50 cm outlet is left open at the corner. The roof is completed by placing mud slabs on the wooden frame, leaving the manhole uncovered. After grain is placed inside, the manhole is closed with polythene on the outer side tov make the structure airtight. The bin, when filled to capacity and properly closed, becomes an airtight, damp-proof structure which prevents thermal conductivity.

B. Urban Storage: This is a rectangular steel structure, rodent and moisture proof, with an arrangement for controlled aeration as well as fumigation for the household use of consumers in urban areas. The structure is partitioned into 4 to 5 compartments of different sizes and is convenient for the compact storage of cereals and pulse in one place. It has a locking arrangement and is made of galvanized iron sheets with 80-1000 kg capacity.

12.14 GRAIN STORAGE SYSTEM

Grain storage is carried out basically to maintain the quality of grain after harvest for (*i*) retaining the viability of the grain for planning in the following season, (*ii*) maintaining the supply of grain, and (*iii*) taking advantage of higher prices by farmers, government and industry.

The two methods of grain storages are bag storage and loose in bulk storage. The choice between the two depends on the following local factors:

(*i*) Type of grains
(*ii*) Duration of storage
(*iii*) Value of grain
(*iv*) Climate
(*v*) Transport system
(*vi*) Cost and availability of labour
(*vii*) Cost and availability of bags
(*viii*) Incidence of rodents and certain types of insects

In general terms the advantage and disadvantages of bag and bulk storages are:

Bag storage	Bulk storage
• Flexibility of storage	• Inflexible storage
• Partly mechanical	• Mechanical
• Slow handling	• Rapid handling
• Considerable spillage	• Little spillage
• Low capital cost	• High capital cost
• High operating cost	• Low operating cost
• High rodent loss potential	• Low rodent loss potential
• Reinfestation occurs	• Little protection against reinfestation

Sources of Infesting the Stored Grains

There are mainly, the five sources of infestation namely, the field itself, infested gunnies, infested transport, infested godowns and infested stocks.

Field : Insect may attack the crop in the field itself. Grains attacked by these insects when brought to the storage centres will be subject to their continuous attack. The infestation may be visible or invisible. Such stocks should be fumigated immediately on receipt.

Gunny Bags : Even if sound and new gunnies are used for packing the newly harvested grains, the insects hiding in the seams of gunnies will attack the freshly harvested stocks. The gunny bags should be fumigated before packing the freshly harvested grains.

Transport : Transport used for carrying the stocks should invariably be sprayed with DDVP or malathion. If the transport like bullock cart or tractor trolley has been used for carrying infested stocks on the previous occasion, the left over insects may attack the stocks into them.

Godown : Even if the stocks are moved to a freshly taken godown, it is not free with trouble. The insects present in the cracks and crevices of the wall or that hibernate in the structures, may emerge out and attack the grains. Hence, the cracks and crevices should be plugged and empty godowns should thoroughly cleaned and fumigated.

Infested stocks : In case sound stocks are brought to a godown, where infested stocks are in storage, cross infestation takes place.

Modern Storage Systems

The modern storage system may be classified into the following based on the type of storage structure or container, facilities for loading and unloading, and method of controlling the storage atmosphere:

a) Bagged storage system
b) Silo storage system
c) Airtight storage system
d) Aerated storage system
e) Low temperature storage system
f) Controlled or modified atmospheric storage system
g) Damp grain storage system with chemicals

(*a*) **Bagged storage system:** Bagged grains are stored in flat warehouse which are known by the term 'Conventional godown'. Building used for bag storage in the tropic and subtropics have generally not been designed for grain storage. Many are old structures erected for general purposes and have corrugated metal or concrete roofs and mud or bricks walls. The floors are often made of earth or masonry and have inefficient waterproofing. A well-planned bag storage warehouse should have water proof walls, roof, and floor. This structure has a sealable opening for controlled ventilation and complete building fumigation. The opening can be used for both natural and fan controlled aeration. The metal roof should be insulated to minimize temperature buildup. The bags should be placed on wood planking erected above the floor to provide insulation against floor temperature and moisture. The building should be rodent, bird and insect proof.

One of the major disadvantages of the bagged storage system is that the re-adsorption of moisture takes place during humid wet season especially in the outer layers of the bags, and this accelerates biological activity in the food grain and results in deterioration and loss of the product. In hot dry season when the roof and wall surface temperature is extremely high, the food grains stacked within one meter of roof or close to walls become hot. This causes relocation of moisture which results in deterioration of grain during storage.

Table 5: Capacities and dimensions of godowns

No. of bags	Tonnes	Internal dimension	
		Length, m	Width, m
1050	100	12	7.5
2625	250	20	9
5250	500	27	12
10500	1000	33.5	18
21000	2000	50	27

Table 6: Stack height for different food grains

Grains	No. of layers	Stack height, m
Paddy	24	5.64
Wheat, barley, maize, gram, jowar and other millets	20	5.04
Rice and milled pulses	16	3.96
Wheat bran	20	5.04
Milled cereals and pulses	12	2.13
Seed grains	10	2.00

(*b*) Silo storage system: A silo is a storage facility in bin with provision for mechanical loading and unloading of the grains. A silo installation is known as an 'Elevator'. Modern silo facilities are constructed of steel or reinforced concrete and usually consist of battery of adjoining bins with different configuration. Some silos have constructed by FCI at Faridabad with a capacity of 20,000 tonnes consist of 24 circular concrete bin of free standing type. Each bin is 10 m diameter and 22 m high, and has a capacity of 835 tonnes. The grains are loaded into the silo by means of belt conveyors along with steel elevators.

(*c*) Airtight grain storage: This term is used to describe the process whereby grain is held in supposedly airtight silo in which depletion of the oxygen from its normal level of approximately 21 % results in suppression of organisms which would otherwise cause grain deterioration. In general, insect are killed when oxygen in the intergranular air falls to about 2% by the volume. Most fungi on damp grain continue to develop until oxygen level falls to about 0.2%. At higher concentration below 1%, certain microorganisms, particularly yeast can grow and impart a mouldy appearance to the grains. Airtight storage can be used in temperate and cold climates both for the storage of dry grain to prevent and control insect infestations, and of damp grain to be used for animal feed. In tropical conditions, hazards associated with the growth of moulds on damp grain are increased, and airtight storage is not recommended for grain with a moisture content of above 13 percent.

(*d*) Aerated storage system: In aerated storage system, air is moved through stored grain for primary purpose of maintaining a uniform moisture content and or temperature throughout the storage. It also limits the activity of fungi on any damper areas and reduced the rate of auto-deterioration of the grain. Using aeration, safe storage can be provided for grain with 1-2 % moisture above that normally is considered safe for storage. Aeration is used to prevent the accumulation of moisture migration from warm to cold layers. Although about 0.5% moisture is removed in cooling grain from 21 to 4.4°C, the purpose is not to dry the grain. The quantity of air is used for aeration is from 0.021 to 0.104 m^3/min-tonne of grain. Aeration tends to keep the grain mass at temperature and moisture content equivalent to the outside air. Management of aeration system is most critical during the hot humid periods, as fans must not be operated when the humidity is above 70%.

***(e)* Low temperature storage system (Grain chilling by refrigeration):** Cooling of grain with refrigerated air in aeration system provides another method of preserving high moisture grain without using chemicals or holding ahead for the drier. The relationship of grain storage temperature and moisture content to grain deterioration is shown in Fig. 5. From which it can be seen that the lower the temperature of the grain, the higher the moisture content at which it can be successfully stored. This characteristic is shown in Table 4.

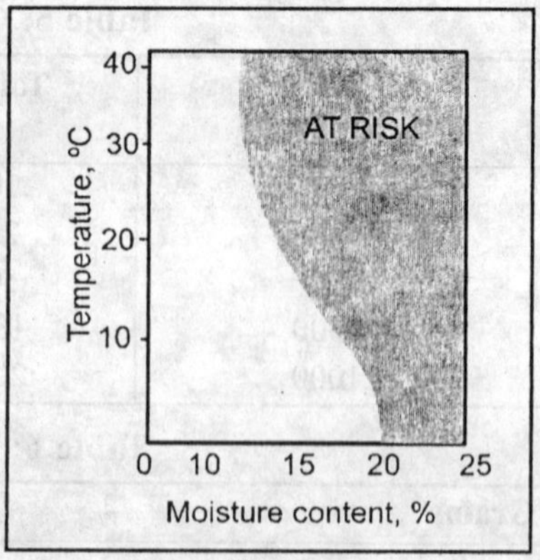

Fig. 5

As the air is cooled its rekative humidity rises, hence, the RH of the air leaving the chiller will be higher than that of the ambient air which enters it. If the RH of air leaving the cooler is not lower than the EMC of the grain, moisture will be deposited in the grain around the duct. The elimination of this problem necessiates warming the air leaving the chiller to such a temperature that its RH is lower than the EMC of the grain. The fan can be operated contnuosely with small flow of 0.052 m^3/min-tonne or less the air is atleast 5.6°C cooler than the grain.

Table 7: Maximum temperature for chilled storage of grain

Grain moisture content (%)	Temperature (°C)	
	Freedom from all deterioration after 8 weeks storage	**Freedom from mould but 5 % loss of germination**
16	13	15
18	7	10
20	4	7
22	2	4

***(f)* Controlled atmosphere storage system:** The technique of controlled atmosphere storage of grain involves alteration of the concentration of normal atmosphere gases present in a storage as to give an artificial atmosphere that is insecticidal and prevent mould growth and quality deterioration of the stored product. The controlled atmosphere (CA) storage is one of the most advanced methods of storage. It reduces nutrient and quality losses, increase the shelf life and best preserves the taste and aroma of products. Extension of storage life under refrigeration storage system is widely in practice despite high losses in quality due to physiological disorders resulting from ill effect of extremely low temperature of storage environment. Low temperature storage is delay ageing by retarding metabolic activity of commodities and suppresses the activity of spoilage agents (biochemical and phytophathogenic). The method of storing commodities (grains or fruits and vegetables) at slightly higher temperature and retarding metabolic process by controlling process by controlling the gaseous composition of storage atmosphere is so called controlled atmosphere storage. Air contains about 20.9% O_2, 78.1% N_2, 0.03% CO_2 and trace amounts of other gases including Ne, He, CH_4 and water vapor. In regular CA storage, oxygen is reduced and CO_2 is increased and ripening and ageing is slowed down. Respiration rates serves as indicator of metabolic activity. Delayed respiration and ageing of food commodities leads to better maintenance of nature resistance against infestation resulting in better storage life.

Benefits of controlled atmosphere: The controlled atmosphere storage offers several advantages as:

- Retardation of senescence and associated biochemical and physiological changes (slowing down respiration and ethylene production).
- Reduction of fruit sensitivity to ethylene action at oxygen (O_2) levels below 8 % and/or carbon dioxide (CO_2) levels above 1 %.
- Useful tool for insect control in some commodities.

Harmful effects of controlled atmosphere:

- Initiation of certain physiological disorders such as blackheart in potatoes, brown stain on lettuce.
- Irregular ripening of fruits such as banana, pear, tomato etc.
- Development of off-flavour and off odours at very low O_2 concentration.

(*g*) Damp grain storage system with chemicals: The main objective of this technique is simple to preserve grain at the optimum moisture content for processing into various rations for livestock. While the most commonly treated crops are barley, the technique has been successfully used for preserving maize, beans, oats and wheat. Formic, acetic and propionic acid etc. have possesses antimicrobial properties. Propionic acid is most effective against microorganisms. The use of propionic acid is not to enhance the nutritional value of the commodity if added. Sometimes common salts and ammonia is used to preserve the damp food grain during storage. The treatment of damp grain with ammonia or ammonium hydroxide in order to inhibit the growth of micro-flora of the grains has currently developed a certain amount of interest.

Value addition: Value addition to agriculture produce is carried out for longer shelf life, maintain/improve quality and enhance form, space and time utility of the produce for food, feed, fibre, fuel and industrial purposes. It includes primary, secondary and tertiary processing operations. The agricultural produces include food crops, horticultural crops, oil seeds, spices and condiments, plantation, medicinal, aromatic, ornamental produce, livestock, poultry and fish produce, mushroom, honey, sugarcane, tobacco, feed, fibre, fuel crops and so on. Value addition is one strategic area that offers an opportunity for shifting from subsistence agriculture to economic development in which it makes intensive use of both human resources and the local agricultural base, with linkage to both agriculture and industries. Thus increasing income and generating off-farm employment at rural level. Value addition may be by way of changing the form colour, texture and others such methods to increase the shelf life of perishable and earn more foreign exchange through export. Value addition operations include on-farm *i.e.* cleaning, grading, drying, moisture conditioning, hulling, waxing, heating, cooling, peeling, dehulling, milling, agglomeration, extraction, extrusion, sizing, freezing, roasting, puffing, flaking, baking, pressure application, cooking, radiation/magnetic application, malting, coagulation, microencapsulation, fermenation, retort processing, canning, packaging, transport and storage.

Value addition can be improved by promoting the production of processed foods like honey, bakery products, dehydrated foods and vegetables, milk starches, neutraceuticals and other health foods and drinks.

In addition, there is a great need for value addition in agricultural products to ensure long term sustainability. "Value addition can be defined as any measure that increase return on investment for farmers". Currently only 2 percent of agricultural commodities are processed. There is a need to increase it to the tune of 10 percent for realizing economic returns through a great role in areas including processing, value addition and transport of agricultural produce from one region of country to the another through an efficient distribution system involving railway, road and shipment transport.

12.15 STORAGE TECHNIQUES OF FRUITS AND VEGETABLES

There are various techniques and methods to increase the storage life of fruit and vegetables, which are discussed below.

1. Air Cooling: When the temperature of the produce is above the desired level, and if the temperature of the outside air is lower, air is circulated through the store by conventional or mechanical means through bottom inlet vents and top outlets fitted with dampers. Fans may be insulated and are controlled manually or automatically with differential thermostat. The air may be humidified, a process that can also be automated. Air cooled stores are cheap to construct and to operate and are still widely used for the storage of potato and sweet potato, both of which need relatively high storage temperature to avoid accumulation of sugar and chilling injury respectively. The efficiency of room cooling can be improved by the use of ceiling jets or fans to increase air velocities. Cabbage and artichokes are primarily cooled with this method, although all vegetables can be room cooled.

2. Hydro Cooling: Hydro cooling, in which water acts as the heat transfer medium, is a rapid method for cooling the produce of the high heat capacity and thermal conductivity of water, which makes it better cooling medium than air. Hydro cooling may also clean the produce but contamination of the produce with spoilage microorganism occurs if soil is not removed from the system regularly and the water must be chlorinated. A further advantage is that the commodities losses little weight during hydro cooling. Its use is limited for packed commodities because the containers must withstand water soaking. The produce must be tolerant of wetting.

3. Vacuum Cooling: Vacuum cooling is a rapid and uniform process, where produce are subjected to very low pressure and water evaporates from the commodities giving off the latent heat of vaporization, thus cooling itself. Cooling is achieved by reducing the atmospheric pressure inside a large, steel chamber containing the product. This reduction in atmospheric pressure causes loss of water vapour from the commodities resulting in cooling. It is used to cool cauliflower, celery, mushrooms, sweet corn, carrots and bell peppers etc. The rate of cooling by this process is largely dependent on the surface to volume ratio of the produce and the ease with which the produce looses water. Fruits, which have a low surface to volume ratio and a waxy cuticle and therefore, loose water slowly and do not benefit by vacuum cooling.

4. Low Temperature Storage (Mechanical Refrigeration): Fruit and vegetables are mostly seasonal crops but they are demanded by consumers throughout the year. They are very highly perishable in nature, which is difficult to preserve for the longer period of time under ambient storage conditions. The low temperature storage retard the activity of various biological and biochemical agents of spoilage and provides longer shelf life to the fruit and vegetables The temperature is brought down by taking out the heat with the help of mechanical refrigeration, This system is based on a liquid absorbing heat as it change to a gas. The more common mechanical refrigeration system use a refrigerant such as (Ammonia, Freon etc.,) takes out the heat from the chamber/ store as it expand. The spoilage agents are microorganism such as (*e.g.* bacteria, yeast and molds etc.) and larva. Optimum storage temperature for most products is kept slightly above the freezing point of the product. Some fruit and vegetables are particularly sensitive to storage temperature are susceptible to called storage disease when stored at temperature below as or above the critical temperature *e.g.*, citrus fruits develop rind pitting when stored at high temperature. On the other hand they are subjected to cold (browning of rind) and watery break down, when stored at temperature below their critical temperature. Banana suffers peel injury when stored below 13°C. Although, onions tends to sprout at temperature above 0°C. Irish potatoes tend to become sweet at storage temperature below 4°C. Squash, green beans and peppers develops pits on their surface when stored at or near 0°C, whereas the best storage temperature for most of the apples varies to –1°C to 0°C. The storage of perishable in their natural state (unpacked) requires close control not only the space temperature but also the space humidity and air movement. One of the main causes of deterioration of unpacked fruit and vegetables is loss of moisture from the surface of the product by evaporation into surrounding air. This process is called dissociation drying or dehydration.

5. Ice Refrigeration: Advances on air cooling storage is the use of natural ice as a refrigerant. The lower temperature obtained enables longer storage of perishable foods *i.e.* horticultural produce. The melting of one kg of ice absorbs 325 kJ, but the considerable bulk of ice needed and disposal of the melt water are the demerits. The introduction of small 'ice box' or ice chest was a great advance in the domestic and commercial preservation of food stuffs.

6. Modified/Controlled Atmospheric Storage: As already discussed A modified atmosphere is the initial alteration of the gaseous environment in the immediate vicinity of the product, permitting the package product interactions to naturally vary their immediate gaseous environment to the desired level. A controlled atmosphere is process by which the gaseous environment is modified to desired level and controlled at this level with strict limits, throughout storage and is usually applied to bulk storage. It reduces losses, increase period of storage and best preserves the taste and aroma of fruit and vegetables. The fashion of storing commodities (fruit and vegetables) at slightly higher temperature and retarding metabolic process by controlling the gaseous composition of storage is so called controlled atmosphere storage (preservation). Usually this is done by increasing the CO_2 concentration and decreasing the O_2 concentration. For some fruits, the best storage atmosphere is one that contains about 3% oxygen and about 2-5% carbon dioxide, the rest being nitrogen. If the air is depleted of much of its oxygen and is enriched in carbon dioxide, respiration of perishable commodities will slow down. These ways to slow down this respiration and physiological changes that accompany it are reducing temperature, reducing eliminating oxygen and increasing the carbon dioxide. The optimum temperature, relative humidities and gas composition of the atmosphere differ for different fruit and vegetables.

7. Individually Quick Frozen (IQF): Term IQF stands for "individually quick frozen" IQF foods are notable for the fact that each individual piece of food is frozen seperately from all the others. For example, a bag of IQF peas doesn't simply contain a solid block of frozen peas rather each of the individually frozen peas is loose inside the bag which makes easier to work with them. Common examples of IQF foods are fruits like blueberries straw berries peaches and plumbs and vegetable like corn, peas, green beans, seafood like shrimp and scallops, or poultry like individual chicken breast. Even whole poultry such as frozen turkey are processed using IQF mehod.

IQF reduces Ice crystallisation. This happens because ice crystals only form between 31-25°F. the longer a food item spends in this range more ice crystals will form.

While in IQF speeding the food through this 31-25°F temperature as quickely as possible. For example in conventional freezing, at home or commercially it take 8-10 hour of time. In IQF it might take only 90 minutes. But cruicially instead of spending a full six hours hours out of 10 hrs, in the 31-25°F range in conventional method it only spends 25 minutes in IQF.

IQF technology allows the freezing on an individual piece of product seperately from the others. Due to this the quality of the finished IQF product is superior to conventional freezing or cold storage freezing. IQF is ideal for freezing smaller products such as fruit cubes, vegetables, cheese, pasta etc.

In IQF texture of nutrients of food will not suffer due to least damage to cell of food product due to smaller ice crystal formation.

IQF is more cost efficient. The benefits are:

1. Better quality products
2. Better Texture
3. Final product has more nutrients.
4. Better apperance
5. Less money loss from the weight loss during dehydration.

Zero Energy Cool Chamber

ICAR, New Delhi (Roy and Pal, 1991) has developed technology for zero energy cool chamber an alternative of common refrigerator. This is an on-farm storage chamber, for fresh fruits, vegetables and flowers to extend their marketability. Storage of fresh horticultural produce after harvest is one of the most pressing problems of a tropical country like India. Due to their high moisture content fruits and vegetables have very short life and are liable to spoil. Moreover, they are living entities and carry out transpiration, respiration and ripening even after harvest. The spoilage of fruits and vegetables can be controlled by reducing the storage temperature. Refrigerated cool storage is not only energy intensive and expensive, but also involves large initial capital investment. Zero energy cool chamber works on evaporative cooling principles that can be used to provide a cool environment.

The zero energy cool chamber can be constructed easily with materials like brick, sand, bamboo, khashkhas/straw, gunny bag etc. The chamber can keep the temperature 10-15°C cooler than the outside temperature and maintain about 90% relative humidity. Multilocational studies at different agroclimatic zones have been found it to be very useful. It is most effective during the dry season.

12.16 COLD CHAIN

Cold chain can be defined as a temperature controlled supply chain cold storage and distribution in which agricultural produce are preserved afresh and their shelf life is extended to a greater period of time. Cold chain is a necessity for not just for the agricultural produce but also for horticulture, floriculture, dairy, confectionary, pharmaceuticals, industrial chemicals, poultry and meat processing. India has seen a significant growth in production of perishable products like fruits, vegetables, meat & poultry products but this was not accompanied by a proportional growth in improved supply chain systems. This disproportional growth has led to widespread price fluctuations and inflation. The existing sub-optimal farm-to-market logistics has contributed to huge losses in perishable foods. Cold chain process has been explained below.

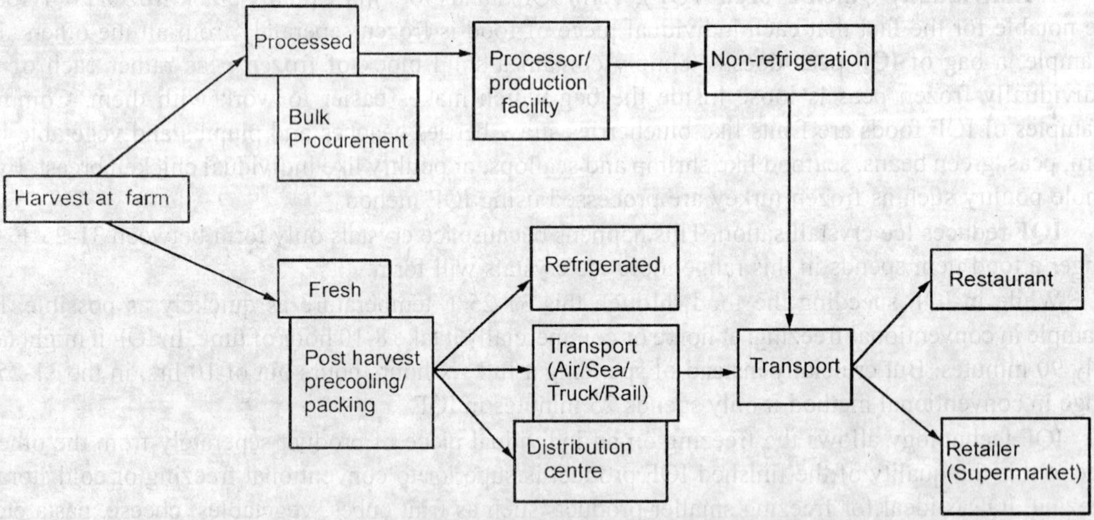

Source: Rodrigue, Dr Jean-Paul and Notteboom, Dr Theo (2014)

Fig 6: Cold chain process

Generally refrigerated trucks with 100 percent GPS, insulated doors which can maintain products in temperature ranging from – 25 degree Celsius to 25 degree Celsius are used. Cold chain serves the important purpose of keeping food fresh for extended periods. Temperature control depends on different kinds of products. Dry ice (Solid carbon dioxide at – 80 degree Celsius) is used to maintain foods at sub-zero temperature. In case of pharmaceuticals & medicinal shipments, large portions are classified as chilled products where a temperature range between 2 degree Celsius and 8 degree Celsius has to be maintained, gel packs are the most preferred in this case.

Ensuring that shipment remains frozen also depends on the type of the container used. The choice of the container depends on duration of transit, size of shipment, external temperatures. Containers used are classified as validated & pre-qualified. Validated packages are specifically tested to transport a certain product under controlled conditions. Pre-qualified containers offer a specific temperature range, but it is not tested for a specific product. The refrigerated trucks are referred to as reefers.

Components of the cold chain

The cold chain has three main components, each of which must combine to ensure safe vaccine transport and storage:

(*i*) Transport and storage equipment (*ii*) Trained personnel

(*iii*) Efficient management procedures.

Any product known to be or labeled "perishable" will likely need cold chain management. This could include foods like meat and seafood, produce, medical supplies and pharmaceuticals.

Elements of cold chain

Cold chain logistics has many moving parts. Some of the elements include:

(*i*) Cold storage – Facilities that store goods and products waiting to be transported.

(*ii*) Cooling systems – Systems that bring food up to and keep it at an appropriate temperature during all aspects of the supply chain, including processing, storing and transporting.

(*iii*) Cold transport – Ensures goods remain at stable temperature and humidity levels.

(*iv*) Cold processing – Facilities that allow for processing goods with sanitation in mind.

(*v*) Cold distribution – Deals with loading boxes or crates and pallets to distribute goods.

Cold Chain Technologies

Cold chain transportation relies on several methods to keep goods at proper temperatures. How long the transport is, the size of the packaged shipment and seasonality are all factors that affect which method is used.

(*i*) Gel packs – Often used for medical and pharmaceutical shipments.

(*ii*) Dry ice – Can keep goods frozen for extended time periods. Used for dangerous goods, pharmaceuticals and food. Sublimates rather than melts when coming in contact with air.

(*iii*) Liquid nitrogen – Used primarily to transport biological cargo (organs, tissues).Extremely cold, keeps items frozen for longer periods.

(*iv*) Eutectic plates – Also called cold plates, similar to gel packs but can be reused.

(*v*) Reefers – A temperature-controlled, insulated van, semi, truck or standard ISO container. Allows for temperature-controlled air circulation.

(*vi*) Quilts – Insulated quilts can be wrapped around or placed over freight and are used to keep temperatures constant, so frozen items will remain frozen for a longer time.

Globally cold chains have now become an integral part of supply chain management for the storage and transportation of temperature-sensitive goods. The focus has now shifted from increasing production to better cold storages and transportation of food produce. The utilisation of cold chain logistics includes both cold storages and refrigerated transportation and is used to increase the shelf life of food produce.

With 35-40% of agricultural produce in India being wasted due to lack of proper cold storage facilities, it is immensely important that a focussed effort is required on part of the government to encourage the use of cold chain among market participants.

12.17 FROZEN FOODS AND COLD STORAGE

The freezing of foods has become very popular and effective method of preserving foods of certain types. The basic principles involved in freezing are to inactivate the living micro-organisms causing decay or to change the liquid water present in foods into crystals of ice rendering the food as if it would have been dried.

Some of the most important applications of refrigeration equipment are found in connection with the preservation of foods by freezing, cold storage of foods (and other materials) and the distribution of foods by refrigerated haulage equipment. Sharp freezing of fish and poultry has been in use since about 1865 A.D.

Sharp Freezing

Sharp freezing consists of placing foods in a cold room with temperatures maintained from – 15 to – 28 °C. No provisions are made for air circulation. This is a relatively slow process and is not as much used today as it once was. It is, however, still used for freezing boxed poultry, fish, packaged meat and some cold-packed fruit.

Quick Freezing

We have already discuss this method under food preservation methods.

Cold Storage

Cold storage refers to a storage facility – usually, a large warehouse that can be temperature-controlled so that perishable goods like dairy, proteins, frozen foods, fresh produce, etc., can be stored in a way that extends their shelf life. Food products that spoil quickly or require refrigeration need temperature control so they can be preserved after manufacturing or harvest, and can be supplied throughout the year even when there is no production output.

Cold storage prevents significant economic losses due to spoilage and allows us to get our favorite food items year-round.

Refrigerated warehouses for cold storage of foods and other products are cooled by a number of different methods:

1. In the direct expansion method, the refrigerant is expanded directly in coils located either in the cold storage room or directly above it.
2. In the brine circulating system, brine is chilled in brine coolers and then circulated through cooling coils in the storage space. This system prevents any danger of food contamination by leaking refrigerant (if ammonia is the refrigerant). Another advantage is the reserve cooling capacity of large amounts of brine if the refrigerating equipment must be shut down.
3. An indirect air circulation system has been more recently developed. Its use permits a more rapid change in temperature and the control of humidity. The cooling of air in such a system is done by blowing air over expansion coils, brine coils or through a spray of brine or water. The air can be dried or wetted, depending on whether low or high humidity is desired. Unit coolers or diffusers, consisting of the cooling coils, air circulating fan and a defrosting arrangement are often used to direct cold air over the desired areas.

A number of different compressor combinations are used in cold storage applications. These are most often designed for ammonia or carbon dioxide service.

1. Two compound reciprocating compressors with clearance pockets (for capacity control), one for low temperature brine and the other for higher temperature brine are used. A third spare unit is usually provided.
2. Smaller plants employ a compound reciprocating compressor with one end on low temperature brine service and the other end on higher temperature brine. A similar unit can be used as a spare.
3. In larger plants, it is often preferable to use several small compressors instead of one large compressor. This will provide more flexibility in handling varying refrigerating loads.

CHAPTER 13

FOOD QUALITY, SAFETY AND HYGIENE

13.1 FOOD QUALITY AND QUALITY ASSURANCE

Quality is a measure of the degree of excellence or degree of acceptability by the consumer. By quality, one can differentiate the individual unit of a product from the other units and can determine the degree of acceptability of the individual unit by the consumer.

According to Code of Federal Regulations "*Quality is the inherent properties of any processed product which determine the relative degree of excellence of such product and includes the effect of preparation and processing and may or may not include the effects of packaging or added ingredients/ additives*".

There are mainly five assurance systems that are mostly adopted to ensure food safety and quality like Good Agricultural Practices (GAP), Euro GAP, Good Manufacturing Practices (GMPs), Good Hygiene Practices (GHP) or Sanitation, Hazard Analysis Critical Control Points (HACCP) and Total Quality Management (TQM). In practical terms GAP, GMP and GHP have been incorporated into the code of practices and protocols for certification under a generic concept of Good Agricultural Practices. GAPs, GMPs, Sanitation (GHP) and HACCP collectively make a food product safer and improve quality and thus, are the basis for implementing Total Quality Management programme. HACCP is not a stand-alone program; GMPs and sanitation procedures are important foundations for a successful HACCP program.

13.2 FOOD SAFETY

Food safety and quality are important at the home level, but are critical in large scale food production and processing, and also where food is freshly prepared and served. The quality of food stuff, raw as well as processed is of public health concern and must be addressed. In the past decade, safety challenges faced globally as well as in India have changed significantly and issues related to food quality and food safety have gained tremendous importance.

Food Safety safety means assurance that food is acceptable for human consumption according to its intended use. An understanding of food safety is improved by defining two other concepts — toxicity and hazard. *Toxicity* is the capacity of a substance to produce harm or injury of any kind under any conditions. *Hazard* is the relative probability that harm or injury will result when substance is not used in a prescribed manner and quantity. Hazards can be physical, chemical and biological causing harmful / adverse effects on the health of consumers.

Food infection /Food Poisoning results from ingestion of live pathogenic organisms which multiply in the body and cause disease. Salmonella is a classic example. This organism exists in the intestinal tract of animals. Raw milk and eggs are also sources. Heat destroys Salmonella, however, inadequate cooking allows some organisms to survive. Often Salmonella is spread through cross-contamination. This could happen when a cook cuts raw meat/poultry on a chopping board and without cleaning uses it for another food which does not involve any cooking, such as salad. Food may become infected by Salmonella if an infected food handler does not wash hands with soap after using bathroom and before touching food. Salmonella can reproduce very quickly and double their number every 20 minutes. The symptoms of Salmonella infection include diarrhea, fever and abdominal cramps.

Food intoxication: Some bacteria produce harmful toxins which are present in food even if pathogen has been killed. Organisms produce toxins when the food has not been hot enough or cold enough. Toxins in food cannot be detected by smell, appearance or taste. Hence foods which smell and appear good are not necessarily safe. One example of such an organism is *Staphylococcus aureus*. Such organisms exist in air, dust, water. They are also present in the nasal passage, throat and on skin, hair of 50 per cent of healthy individuals. People who carry this organism, contaminate food if they touch these places on body while food handling. Diarrhea is also one of the symptoms of this contamination. Parasites can also cause infestation, e.g., worm infestation by tape worm in pork. In addition to this, food can be infested by pests and insects

Among the various hazards, biological hazards are an important cause of food-borne illnesses. In spite of all the efforts in the area of food safety, microbial food-borne pathogens are still a serious concern and new pathogens continue to emerge.

Food should be safe for human consumption and free from hazards that may compromise the health of the consumer

Examples of Food Safety procedures and policies:

- Personal hygiene
- Pest control
- Cleaning and sanitizing
- Food Safety hazard identification
- Personal presentation and preparation
- Waste management
- Temperature control and measurement

Food safety and inspection services of government provides rules and regulation to educate consumers about the safe food handling and storage to reduce risks associated with food borne diseases, illness and hazards.

Food safety is achieved by various avenues and methods.

1. Properly cleaning and sanitizing all surfaces, equipment and utensils.
2. Maintaining a high level of personal hygiene especially hand washing.
3. Storing, chilling and heating food correctly with regards to temperature, environment and equipment.
4. Implementing effective pest control.
5. Comprehending food allergens, food poisoning and intolerance.

Importance of Food Safety

1. Food safety is important as it helps to protect consumer from the risk of food borne illnesses. It also helps to prevent consumers from risks of health –related conditions such as allergy and even death.

2. It gives us the energy and nutrients to grow and develop, be healthy and active, to move, work, play, think and learn. The body needs a variety of the following 5 nutrients - proteins, carbohydrates, fats, vitamins and minerals - from the food we eat to stay healthy and productive.

Principles of Food Safety

Four C's of Food Safety

Four C's - cleaning, cooking, chilling and cross contamination to protect your family against deadly germs.

Four Principles of Food Safety

- Clean — Wash hands and surfaces often.
- Separate — Don't cross-contaminate.
- Cook — Cook to the right temperature.
- Chill — Refrigerate promptly.

Kill step in food safety

Kill-step validation is a preemptive scientific evaluation that provides documentary evidence that a particular process (*e.g.*, cooking, frying, chemical treatment, extrusion, etc.) is capable of consistently delivering a product that meets predetermined specifications.

13.2.1 Food Safety, Quality and Consumer Protection

The terms food safety and food quality can sometimes be confusing. Food safety refers to all those hazards, whether chronic or acute, that may make food injurious to the health of the consumer. It is not negotiable. Quality includes all other attributes that influence a product's value to the consumer. This includes negative attributes such as spoilage, contamination with filth, discoloration, off-odours and positive attributes such as the origin, colour, flavour, texture and processing method of the food. This distinction between safety and quality has implications for public policy and influences the nature and content of the food control system most suited to meet predetermined national objectives.

Food control is defined as:

....a mandatory regulatory activity of enforcement by national or local authorities to provide consumer protection and ensure that all foods during production, handling, storage, processing, and distribution are safe, wholesome and fit for human consumption; conform to safety and quality requirements; and are honestly and accurately labelled as prescribed by law.

The foremost responsibility of food control is to enforce the food law(s) protecting the consumer against unsafe, impure and fraudulently presented food by prohibiting the sale of food not of the nature, substance or quality demanded by the purchaser.

Consumers expect protection from hazards occurring along the entire food chain, from primary producer through consumer (often described as the ***farm-to-table*** continuum). Protection will only occur if all sectors in the chain operate in an integrated way, and food control systems address all stages of this chain.

As no mandatory activity of this nature can achieve its objectives fully without the cooperation and active participation of all stakeholders *e.g.* farmers, industry, and consumers, the term ***Food Control System*** is used in these Guidelines to describe the integration of a mandatory regulatory approach with preventive and educational strategies that protect the whole food chain. Thus an ideal food control system should include effective enforcement of mandatory requirements, along with training and education, community outreach programmes and promotion of voluntary compliance. The introduction of preventive approaches such as the **Hazard Analysis Critical Control Point System (HACCP),** have resulted in industry taking greater responsibility for and control of food safety risks. Such an integrated approach facilitates improved consumer protection, effectively stimulates agriculture and the food processing industry, and promotes domestic and international food trade.

HACCP is designed for use in all segments of the food industry from growing, harvesting, processing, manufacturing, distributing, and merchandising to preparing food for consumption. Prerequisite programs such as current Good Manufacturing Practices (cGMPs) are an essential foundation for the development and implementation of successful HACCP plans. Food safety systems based on the HACCP principles have been successfully applied in food processing plants, retail food stores, and food service operations. The seven principles of HACCP have been universally accepted by government agencies, trade associations and the food industry around the world.

. It is mostly applied in production processes and also in postproduction processes to ensure that no contaminant is present to make the finished products unsafe, and designs measures to reduce the risks of contaminants to safe level at most. HACCP and food safety are inseparable. Proper HACCP application is a requirement to guarantee food safety. Consequently, HACCP aims at avoiding hazards rather than inspecting the finished products for hazards' effects or presence; HACCP is a preventive approach to ensure food safety. HACCP system is employed at all steps in a food chain, from preliminary food preparation to production processes and postproduction handling, including raw materials, production, packaging, storage, distribution, etc.).

Food Safety Needs a Collaborative Approach

While we are adopting global standards, it is important to keep in mind the local, cultural and geographical origin of food items while setting standards. Our country, though agriculturally abundant, is still struggling to provide its large population with the right nutrition. In a few decades, as we continue to grow in numbers and economically, the situation can turn more challenging — if not alarming — if we don't come up with innovative food safety and security solutions now.

A growing economy, higher incomes, rapid urbanization and rising consumer awareness are influencing the Indian palate like never before. While the average Indian consumer is increasingly demanding more variety in food choices and healthier alternatives, she /he is also equally concerned about where the food is coming from, its quality and safety.

13.2.2 Public Health and Food Safety:

Public health has been defined as "the science and art of preventing disease, prolonging life and promoting human health through organized efforts and informed choices of society, organizations, public and private, communities and individuals".

Public health aims to improve the quality of life through prevention and treatment of disease, including mental health. This is done through the surveillance of cases and health indicators, and through the promotion of healthy behaviours. *Common public health initiatives include promotion of handwashing and breastfeeding, delivery of vaccinations, suicide prevention, and distribution of condoms to control the spread of sexually transmitted diseases.*

Modern public health practice requires multidisciplinary teams of public health workers and professionals. Teams might include epidemiologists, biostatisticians, medical assistants, public health nurses, midwives, medical microbiologists, economists, sociologists, geneticists, data managers, and physicians. Depending on the need, environmental health officers or public health inspectors, bioethicists, and even veterinarians, gender experts, or sexual and reproductive health specialists might be called on.

Food Safety and Public Health

Public Health Nutrition (PHN) focuses on the promotion of good health through nutrition and the primary prevention of nutrition related illness in the population

Safe and nutritious food in adequate amounts is required for the sustenance of life and the promotion of good health. However, food provides an environment for microbial growth and, when contaminated, can act as a vector for bacteria, viruses, parasites, and prions, causing food poisoning. Besides, it is often contaminated with toxic chemicals present naturally and/or mixed accidentally or intentionally. which are also potentially harmful. Almost any kind of food can spread disease, and unsafe food is responsible for creating a vicious cycle of disease and malnutrition, affecting all, but particularly infants, young children, and the elderly.

Food safety: a public health priority

Unsafe food poses global health threats, endangering everyone. Infants, young children, pregnant women, the elderly and those with an underlying illness are particularly vulnerable. Every year 220 million children contract diarrhoeal diseases and 96 000 die.

Unsafe food creates a vicious cycle of diarrhoea and malnutrition, threatening the nutritional status of the most vulnerable. Where food supplies are insecure, people tend to shift to less healthy diets and consume more "unsafe foods" – in which chemical, microbiological and other hazards pose health risks.

Everyone can contribute to making food safe. Here are some examples of effective actions:

Policy-makers can:

- build and maintain adequate food systems and infrastructures (*e.g.* laboratories) to respond to and manage food safety risks along the entire food chain, including during emergencies;
- foster multi-sectoral collaboration among public health, animal health, agriculture and other sectors for better communication and joint action;
- integrate food safety into broader food policies and programmes (*e.g.* nutrition and food security);
- think globally and act locally to ensure the food produce domestically be safe internationally.

Food handlers and consumers can:

- know the food they use (read labels on food package, make an informed choice, become familiar with common food hazards);
- handle and prepare food safely, practicing the WHO Five Keys to Safer Food at home, or when selling at restaurants or at local markets;
- grow fruits and vegetables using the WHO Five Keys to Growing Safer Fruits and Vegetables to decrease microbial contamination.

WHO response

WHO aims to facilitate global prevention, detection and response to public health threats associated with unsafe food. Ensuring consumer trust in their authorities, and confidence in the safe food supply, is an outcome that WHO works to achieve.

WHO works closely with FAO, the World Organization for Animal Health (OIE) and other international organizations to ensure food safety along the entire food chain from production to consumption.

Five Keys of WHO to safer Food Programms

(1) Keep clean; (2) Separate raw and cooked; (3) Cook thoroughly; (4) Keep food at safe temperatures; and (5) Use safe water and raw materials.

The Five Keys Practices are:

1. Practice good personal hygiene
2. Use safe water for irrigation
3. Protect fields from faecal contaminantes for animals and birds
4. Use treated manure and treated faecal waste
5. Keep harvest equipment, containers and storage facilities clean and dry

Food Safety Inspection

Routine inspections are required to make sure the food you're eating is safe. ... A Public Health Inspector assesses the risk level of a food premises every year during an inspection. The risk level is given based on the likelihood that a food-borne illness outbreak could occur from the food served at that premises. Some premises might be inspected at least every six months, others much less often. Environmental health officers have the right to enter and inspect food premises at all reasonable hours.

Food Safety Inspection Checklists

Food Safety & Standards Authority of India (FSSAI) has developed inspection checklist for facilitating Food Safety Officers to efficiently inspect the Food Business Operators FBOs. The inspection checklists are used to identify the level of compliance with each requirement that is set out in the regulation These inspection checklists are based on revised Schedule 4 of Food Safety & Standards (Licensing & Registration of Food Businesses) Regulation, 2011 and have been developed for following sectors-

1. General Manufacturing
2. Milk Processing
3. Meat Processing
4. Slaughter house
5. Catering
6. Retail
7. Transport
8. Storage & warehouse
9. Other hygiene factors
10. Personal hygiene staff

13.3 FOOD SAFETY MANAGEMENT SYSTEMS

Over the years, issues related to food safety and quality have gone beyond just the avoidance of food-borne pathogens, chemical toxicants and other hazards. A food hazard can enter/come into the food at any stage of the food chain, therefore, adequate control through out the food chain is essential. Food safety and quality can be ensured through:

- Good Manufacturing Practices (GMP)
- Good Hygiene Practices (GHP)
- Hazard Analysis Critical Control Points (HACCP)

13.3.1 Good Manufacturing Practices (GMP)

Good Manufacturing Practices (GMP) are a part of quality assurance to ensure that manufacturers/processors take proactive steps to ensure that their products are safe. It enables to minimise or eliminate contamination and false labelling, thereby protecting the consumer from being misled and helping in purchasing products that are not harmful. GMP is a good business tool that helps to refine compliance and performance by the manufacturers/producers.

Good Handling Practices indicate a comprehensive approach from the farm to the store or consumer, in order to identify potential sources of risk and indicates what steps and procedures are taken to minimise the risk of contamination. It ensures that all persons who handle food have good hygiene practices.

- A good manufacturing practice (GMP) is a system for ensuring that products are produced and controlled consistently according to quality standards. It is designed to minimize the risks involved in any food, pharmaceutical production that cannot be eliminated through testing the final product. The main risks are: unexpected contamination of products, causing damage to health or even death; incorrect labels on containers, which could mean that receive the wrong medicine; insufficient or too much active ingredient, resulting in ineffective treatment or adverse effects.
- GMP regulations address issues including recordkeeping, personnel qualifications, sanitation, cleanliness, equipment verification, process validation, and complaint handling. Most GMP requirements are very general and open-ended, allowing each manufacturer to decide individually how best to implement the necessary controls. This provides much flexibility, but also requires that the manufacturer interpret the requirements in a manner which makes sense for each individual business.
- All GMP/GHP practices regarding the conditions and measures are necessary to ensure the safety and suitability of food at all stages of the food chain.

13.3.2 Good Hygiene Practices (GHP)

The food safety group promotes the application of preventive food safety management systems by food business operators along the food chain in line with Codex guidelines and recommendations.

- promote the application of Good Hygienic Practices at all stages of the food chain, and the HACCP system as appropriate
- promote sustainable development of capacities and systems by national institutions (private and public) to enable delivery of technical assistance within the country
- develop tools and training materials for adaptation and use in support of national training programmes with the aim to strengthen important value chains and develop sector-specific national codes of practice

Food Business Operators should apply the hygienic practices set out

- Ensure that food is safe and suitable for consumption;
- To ensure that consumers have clear and easily understandable information, through labeling and other appropriate means, to enable them to protect their food from contamination and growth or survival of pathogens to create in food by storage, processing and preparation in an appropriate manner.

13.3.3. Hazard Analysis Critical Control Point (HACCP)

HACCP is a means of providing assurance about safety of food. HACCP is an approach to food manufacture and storage in which raw materials and each individual step in a specific process are considered in detail and evaluated for its potential to contribute to the development of pathogenic micro organisms or other food hazards. It involves identification of hazards, assessment of chances of occurrence of hazards during each step /stage in the food chain — raw material procurement, manufacturing, distribution, usage of food products and defining measures for hazard(s) control.

13.4 INTRODUCTION TO FOOD HYGIENE

Everyone who works with food is responsible for ensuring that consumers are protected from contaminated food and the risk of food poisoning, which causes extreme discomfort, absence from work or school and, in some cases, death.

People get sick from food poisoning because the food they've eaten has contained bacteria, viruses or chemicals. It can take from an hour to a few days to develop food poisoning, depending on the cause, and the best way of preventing food poisoning is to use safe food handling practices.

Bacteria are the biggest problem, because they are so common, and are found in soil, on animals, people and even clothes. In the kitchen, bacteria often come from vegetables and raw meat. Sometimes these bacteria can move from raw ingredients to cooked food, in a process called cross contamination.

The way that these germs can move includes:

- From hands to food.
- From cutting boards, knives and other utensils on to food.
- From one food to another, especially from raw to cooked.

Once bacteria are in a food, they can increase their numbers quickly. They just need the right conditions. This means a temperature of between 5°C and 60°C, (sometimes called the danger zone), time and water.

There are six keys to breaking this chain of food poisoning:

1. Someone who is responsible for every aspect of food preparation and sales.
2. Each person handling or preparing the food must know, about and practise safe food handling.
3. Making sure that everything (utensils) used in preparing the food is clean and germ free
4. Correct and safe food preparation.
5. Correct and safe food storage.
6. Displaying food safely.

Food Hygiene Involves

- preventing the spread of infection by people who handle food
- Protect food from risks of contamination.
- Prevent bacteria from multiplying to levels resulting in ill-health.
- Destroy bacteria in food through adequate cooking or processing.

The Benefits of Food Hygiene

- Return of business through satisfied customers.
- Good reputation.

Compliance with the law.

- High quality food and increased shelf life of food.
- Good working environment for staff, boosting staff morale and job satisfaction.

The Cost of Poor Hygiene

- Food poisoning outbreaks and sometimes death.
- Customer complaints.
- Wastage of goods due to spoilage.
- Pest infection.
- Suspension of trading by local health authorities.
- Fines and cost of legal action by food poisoning sufferers.
- Loss of reputation through word of mouth or media exposure.

Approach to The Problem

- Preventing food being contaminated.
- Killing bacteria.
- Preventing bacteria growth and multiplication.

Prevention

If we are to adopt the main principles of food hygiene we must adhere to the following practices.

- Develop and maintain high standards of personal hygiene
- Avoid cross-contamination of foods
- Establish and maintain correct storage conditions.
- Clean and sanitise all utensils and equipment used in the handling and preparation of food.
- Control pests.

The Food Handler as a Source of Harmful Bacteria

All this focus on the cleanliness of the food handler is because the human body provides a rich environment for microorganisms to live in. Micro-organisms (*e.g.* bacteria) are to be found in and on the body. Most of these bacteria are harmless. Many even have an important role to play in maintaining health. (*e.g.* gut bacteria manufacturing Vitamin K). However some are harmful and can cause food poisoning. Apparently healthy people may be carrying pathogenic bacteria without showing any signs of illness. Everyone has to assume that they may be carrying food poisoning bacteria and so take precautions against spreading the disease. It is estimated that 50% of the population carry Staphylococcus Aureus in their mouths/noses. Staph Aureus may also be present in infected cuts and pimples. This food poisoning bacteria may be spread to food by a food handler coughing or sneezing over food, tasting food using fingers or working with an infected cut. Salmonella and Clostridium perfringens can be present in the intestine of seemingly healthy people. Inadequate washing of hands after going to the toilet may result in faecal material being transferred to the food.

13.4.1 Personal Hygiene

The expression "food hygiene" is often associated to personal hygiene, being many times limited to the care of washing hands. The concept of food hygiene really refers to the general cleanliness state of the food handlers' body and clothes. Man holds bacteria in the mouth, nose, hands and intestines and can contaminate food while handling, coughing or sneezing over it. Although food contamination can result from different sources, from the field to the consumer, one of the main causes for foodborne dissemination is inadequate food handling during processing and distribution. That is why it is of extreme importance for the handler to correctly sanitize everything that is going to come into contact with the food, the handler must also be found in good health condition to avoid any kind of contamination. Microorganisms can easily pass to food and reach the consumer if the handler comes into contact with any pathogenic microorganism by their clothes, hands, hair, nails, rings and then sets out to prepare food. As so, the personal hygiene of whoever contacts with food, as well as behaviours they assume during its processing, constitute an important preoccupation in the food business. The set of rules, conditions and practices that assure adequate personal hygiene make up the good practices for personal hygiene.

All food handlers must be regarded as a potential source of pathogenic organisms, and must therefore be trained in good hygiene practices. The Codex Alimentarius Commission's recommendation on personal hygiene shall be followed. The individual will:

- describe the principles and reasons for effective personal hygiene (*i.e.* hand washing, personal cleanliness, illness, injury, personal behavior, and visitor control).

- explain how to access regulations and customer requirements governing effective personal hygiene (*i.e.*. hand washing, personal cleanliness, illness, injury, personal behavior, and visitor control).
- explain when to apply proper hand washing techniques.
- identify employees with symptoms of illness (*i.e.*. fever, vomiting, diarrhea, sore throat) so they can ensure that ill individuals who might pose a risk to food safety are not allowed to work with food.
- design a system for employees and visitors to notify the organization of any symptoms of illness and injury that may preclude them from working in direct contact with food.
- operate a system for employees and visitors to notify the organization of any symptoms of illness and injury that may preclude them from working in direct contact with food.
- design a system to enforce procedures in relation to illness and injury, personal cleanliness, personal behaviour which could result in the contamination of food and food safety provision for visitors.
- operate a system to enforce procedures in relation to illness and injury, personal cleanliness. personal behaviour which could result in the contamination of food and food safety provision for visitors.

Hands: The hands are often in direct contact with food, making them one of the main routes for contaminating food and transferring food poisoning bacteria (pathogens). Food handlers must wash their hands regularly throughout the day to ensure they avoid food contamination and to avoid picking up any pathogens that could make them sick. Clean fingernails with a nail brush soaked in sanitiser. If handling food, avoid artificial nails or nail polish, which can become food contaminants if they fall off or peel.

Nose, Mouth and Ears: Approximately 40% of all adults carry staphylococci bacteria in their nose or mouth, and coughing or sneezing can spread these bacteria for a surprisingly large distance as fine droplets. To prevent the spread of human pathogens, avoid coughing or sneezing over or around food, or picking or scratching the nose or any other part of the body. If you have to sneeze or cough, move away from food and food preparation surfaces.

Cuts and Sores: If you have any cuts, scrapes, sores, etc, these wounds must be completely covered by waterproof dressings and suitable gloves. Waterproof dressings can also protect cuts from contamination or irritation and prevent them from going septic.

Hair: Keep hair clean and brush it regularly. This should be done before putting on uniform or dress and away from food preparation and handling areas - hair falls out constantly and poses a common food contamination risk. Food preparation workers should wear a suitable head covering, and long hair should be adequately tied back out of the way in food service areas.

Uniform and Protective Clothing: Most food handlers are required to wear uniforms or some kind of protective clothing to avoid food contamination. Normal clothing accumulates dust, pet hairs, human hairs, woollen fibres and other contaminants that consumers don't want in their food.

Jewellery: Jewellery items such as watches, earrings, jewelled rings or brooches, necklaces, etc pose another food contamination hazard. Dirt and bacteria can build up underneath jewellery and inadvertently transferred to food. In addition, damage to jewellery can result in gemstones, small pieces of metal or bits of glass falling into the food, resulting in a customer complaint.

Perfume: Perfumes should not be used when handling food. Any strongly scented substance can taint foods, especially those with a high fat content or strong adsorbent qualities. While this taint may not pose a health hazard, it can result in customer complaints, so it is best to avoid strong fragrances when handling foods.

Smoking: Tobacco products (including cigarettes, pipes or cigars) must not be used in areas, where food is prepared, handled or stored. Not only is there a risk of food contamination from cigarette butts and ashes, but also smoking involves touching the lips, which could result in bacteria being transferred to food. Smoking also increases the risk of food handlers coughing on food, and saliva deposited on cigarette butts can carry human pathogens. It also creates an unpleasant and unhealthy environment for non-smokers.

Worker Health: To prevent spreading illness, workers should only be handling food if they are in good health. Any food worker suffering from respiratory infections, vomiting, diarrhoea or any food-borne infection must not be allowed to work with food until clear of the illness for at least 2 days (or cleared by qualified medical personnel). If symptoms return, they must be excluded from work until clear again. Any food worker with skin infections, sores, heavy cold, eye or ear discharge, runny nose, etc must stay away from work until symptoms have gone.

Rubbish Disposal: Discarded foods can rot quickly become a source of disease. Insects and rodents are attracted to rotting food and bring harmful bacteria that thrive in the rotting rubbish. The smell of rotting food can also become unpleasant. To minimize risk, keep rubbish containers in good condition, and always clean bins after emptying. A tight-fitting lid and use of plastic bin liners will keep unwanted pests out, as well as help to contain unpleasant odors.

13.5 CROSS-CONTAMINATION

The process by which bacteria or other microorganisms are unintentionally transferred from one substance or object to another, with harmful effect. Cross-contamination between raw and cooked food is the cause of most infection.

Cross-contamination prevention

Cross-contamination is the physical transfer of food safety hazards from a contaminated surface to one that is not contaminated. These hazards include all biological, physical or chemical agents in food that are likely to cause illness or injury after the contaminated food is consumed. Food can be contaminated directly or indirectly, from people, work surfaces or equipment, and other foods. Thus, preventing cross-contamination is one of the key factors in preventing foodborne illness.

There are three main routes through which cross-contamination can occur:

1. **"People to food contamination"** is the most common way of food cross-contamination, and it occurs when people working with food do not carefully follow good hygiene practices. Untrained and unaware employees are the main source of cross contamination. For this reason, training employees on good personal hygiene practices and monitoring them on adequate hand washing, hand care, correct glove use, etc., can help spreading hazards and prevent the cross contamination of food.
2. **"Food to food contamination"** involves the transfer of microorganisms directly from other foods. It is especially dangerous if raw foods come into contact with cooked or ready-to-eat foods. Hence, storing foods properly by keeping all foods covered and separating ready-to-eat foods from unwashed or raw foods is the best way to prevent this type of contamination.

3. **"Equipment to food contamination"** occurs when working surfaces and equipment are not properly washed and sanitized between each use. Thus, washing and sanitizing all food contact surfaces, including cutting boards, dishes, counter tops and other utensils, etc., will help preventing this type of contamination.

13.6 HAZARDS

Hazards may be introduced into the food supply any time during harvesting, formulation and processing, packaging and labelling, transportation, storage preparation and serving.

Potential food hazards are responsible for outbreak of food borne illness. Many type of hazards may pose threat to foods, they can be grouped as follows:

(*i*) Microbiological Hazards

Microbiological hazard occurs when food becomes contaminated by microorganisms found in the air, food, water, soil, animals and the human body. Many microorganisms are helpful and necessary for life itself. However, given the right conditions, some microorganisms may cause a foodborne illness. Microorganisms commonly associated with foodborne illnesses include bacteria, viruses and parasites.

(*ii*) Chemical Hazards

Chemical hazards can occur at any point during harvesting, storage, preparation and service. When toxic chemicals used for pest control or for cleaning and sanitizing food contact surfaces and food preparation equipment come into contact with food, the food may be contaminated by those chemicals.

Toxic metals such as copper, brass, cadmium, lead and zinc can be a source of chemical contamination. Zinc, used in galvanized containers (garbage cans) and in gray enamelware containers which may be plated with antimony or cadmium, can make acidic foods such as orange juice or tomato sauce and pickles poisonous. Pottery dishes with lead glazes should not be used to prepare or serve food.

Environmental contaminants are chemicals that accidentally or deliberately enter the environment, often, but not always, as a result of human activities. Some of these contaminants may have been manufactured for industrial use and because they are very stable, they do not break down easily. If released to the environment, these contaminants may enter the food chain. Other environmental contaminants are naturally-occurring chemicals, but industrial activity may increase their mobility or increase the amount available to circulate in the environment, allowing them to enter the food chain at higher levels than would otherwise occur.

Some examples of environmental contaminants include lead, arsenic, bromates, dioxins, furans, mercury and polychlorinated biphenols (PCBs).

Pesticides/Agricultural products.

Pesticides may leave residues on fruits and vegetables. In general, these residues can be removed by scrubbing the surface and washing with water.

Chemical control of pests is a common practice in agriculture. There are more than 1000 pesticides used for minimizing crop losses from various pests. A pesticide is any substance or organism (including organism derived from biotechnology) that are used to control, destroy, repel, or attract pest or mitigate the effects of a pest. Pest is defined as an animal or plant or other organism that is directly or indirectly injurious, noxious or troublesome.

Pesticides are generally consists of insecticides, fungicides and herbicides. Following are the examples.

1. Azoxystobin on peaches
2. Captan on cherries
3. Clethodim on beans
4. Thiocarbamate on apples.

There are 234 pesticides registered in India. Out of these 4 are WHO Class 1a pesticides, 15 are WHO class 1b and 76 are WHO class 11 pesticides. Together constituting 40% of the registered pesticides in India. In terms of consumption too, the greatest volumes consumed in India are of these posions.

24 Pestiides registered and used in India classified as potential Carciogens by the USEPA. Acephate(C), Alachor (B2) Atrazine (C), Benomyl (C), Bifentherin (C), Capten (B2) Chlorothanlovil (B2). Cypermethinim (C), Dichlorvos (C), Diclotp-methyl (C), Dicotel (C), Mancozeb (B2) Methomyl (C). Dicotel (C). Mancozeb (B2), Meyhomyl (C), Metalchor(C), Oxidiazon (C), Oxyflourofen (C),Permethrin (C), Phosphanidon (C), Propicaonazale (C), Triadimefon (C), Thiophenate methyl (C), triadimefon (C), Trifluralin (C).

B - indicates probable human carcinogen

B2- indicates porbable human carcinogen

C - indicates possible human carcinogen (Limited evidence available).

Recently on the advise of expert committee 12(Twelve) peticides are completely banned for use in the country from January 2018 and another 6 from December 2020.

Manufacture, import, registeration, sale, transport, distribution and use of pesticides in India is regulated by the **Insecticides Act**, 1968 and **Insecticides rules**, 1971. As per Insecticides Act pesticides are defined as those substances that are listed on the "schedule" of the insecticides Act 1968.

FSSAI is responsible for recommending tolerance limits of various pesticides in food committees.

Harmful effects of pesticides are now established worldwide. The harm caused may be acute or chronic in nature.

Table 1: Acceptable post-harvest residues of several fungicides for several countries (μg/ml)

Country/fungicides	TBZ	SOPP	2,4-D	Benomyl	Diphenyl
Australia	10	20	5	10x	110
Austria	6	12	-	5	70
FAO/WHO	10	10	2	10	110

TBZ - Thiabendazole, 2-(4′-thiazolyl) benzimidazole (TBZ)

SOPP - Sodium orthophenylphenate

Veterinary Drugs

The use of veterinary drugs such as antimicrobials, growth promoters, NSAIDs, tranquilizers, etc. in food animals, can lead to human health problems. Residues of such drugs may be present in foods of animal origin, including meat and poultry, milk and dairy products, eggs, fish and seafood, and honey

Classification of veterinary medicines

The main authorised veterinary medicines are

a. *Prescription-only Medicine* – Veterinarian; abbreviated to POM-V;
b. *Prescription-only Medicine* – Veterinarian, Pharmacist, Suitably Qualified Person (SQP); abbreviated to POM-VPS;
c. *Non-Food Animal* – Veterinarian, Pharmacist, Suitably Qualified Person; abbreviated to NFA-VPS; and,
d. *Authorised Veterinary Medicine* – General Sales List; abbreviated to AVM-GSL.

(*iii*) Physical Hazards

Physical hazards usually result from accidental contamination and /or poor food handling practices. Examples include, slivers of glass, human hair, nails, false nails, nail polish, pieces of jewelry, metal fragments from worn or chipped utensils and containers, dirt, stones, frilled toothpicks.

Physical material can be considered hazardous due to its hardness, sharpness, size or shape. It may cause lacerations, perforations and wounds or may become a choking hazard.

Physical materials can be differentiated into two categories: unavoidable and avoidable.

Unavoidable physical material may occur in food as a by-product of the processing system or as something inherent to the product itself. Items such as stems in blueberries, microscopic airborne debris, dirt on potatoes, or minute insect fragments in figs are common examples of unavoidable physical matter.

Avoidable physical material is generally less tolerated than unavoidable because it is preventable. It consists of foreign matter which should not be present if proper GMPs are followed. Avoidable physical material may come in many different forms such as small glass fragments, pieces of plastic, chunks of rubber, pieces of jewellery, feather barbules, animal debris or any other unrelated foreign material.

(*iv*) Allergenic Hazards

An allergen is any protein that is capable of producing an abnormal immune response in sensitive segments of the population. Allergic reactions to food usually involve IgE antibodies. Symptoms of an allergic reaction can range in severity from a skin rash or slight itching of the mouth, to migraine headaches, to anaphylactic shock and death. The type and severity of an allergic response is determined by many factors, including dosage, route of administration, frequency of exposure, and genetic factors. This is not to be confused with a food intolerance which is an abnormal physiological response to a specific food. Symptoms of food intolerance may include cramps, diarrhoea and bloating.

Food which represent 95% of allergic reactions are:

- Peanuts
- Tree nuts (almonds, Brazil nuts, cashews, hazelnuts, macadamia nuts, pecans, pine nuts, pistachio nuts, and walnuts)
- Sesame seeds
- Milk
- Eggs
- Seafood (fish, crustaceans, and shellfish)
- Soy
- Wheat
- Sulphites
- Mustard

(*v*) Nutritional Hazards

Nutrients are essential to maintain good health and pertain to a group of substances which includes carbohydrates, proteins, fats, vitamins and minerals. (Details may be seen in chapter-3)

13.7 FORTIFIED FOODS

Food fortification refers to the addition of one or more nutrients (vitamins, minerals, and amino acids) to a food product and plays an important role in ensuring the health. Adding vitamins and minerals to food helps:

- **Protect humans against nutritional deficiencies** - for example, requiring all milk to be fortified with vitamin D virtually eliminated childhood rickets since the 1970s;
- **Maintain and improve the nutritional quality of the food supply** - for example, enriching flour with B vitamins and iron replaces those same nutrients lost in processing;

- **Reduce the risk of diet-related chronic diseases** - for example, fortification contributes to adequate intakes of calcium and vitamin D which help build strong bones and may reduce the risk of osteoporosis.

FSSAI (Food Safety and Standards Authority of India) Guidelines for Fortified Foods

Fortified foods are those foods in which micronutrients are artificially added to increase the nutrition level which contributes to the health benefits of the consumer. Fortified foods have helped to eradicate nutrient deficiency diseases like rickets and pellagra. These foods can be a part of healthy, nutrient diet, but the benefits of the foods depend on the age factor of the consumer. The FSSAI routinely provides guidelines for manufacturing and processing of various food products.

As per FSSAI, fortified foods are foods that help with the following:

- Foods that help prevent the risks of deficiency that are caused by the lack essential nutrients.
- Foods that help reduce the inadequate nutritional level in the foods.
- Foods that help in compensation with the required or recommended nutrients.
- Foods that helps the body maintain and gain health.
- Food that helps improve the nutritional quality of foods.

Under FSSAI, for a food to termed as a fortified food, it should be based on the scientific evidence of the need of the public.

Standards of Micronutrients

One of the major differentiators of fortified foods is the presence or addition of micronutrients and essential nutrients. While manufacturing fortified foods, the manufacturer should ensure that the amount of micronutrients added in the fortified foods is not be lower than the standard minimum level. Also, the manufacturer should ensure that the amount of micronutrients added in the fortified foods does not surpass the standard maximum level.

Quality Assurance

The manufacturer and the packer of the fortified foods should make assurances and evidence to the Food Authority that respective steps have been taken for manufacturing of these foods. The assurances are as follows:

- A certificate stating that the particular fortified food is in agreement with rules of the Food Safety and Standards Authority of India and this certificate should be given by a food laboratory.
- An updated record and inventories of the fortifications including the source from where the nutrients are obtained should be provided.
- The manufacturing and the packing process that happens in different stages are be monitored carefully.
- There are random tests conducted on the fortificants and on the fortified foods.
- Technical equipments and processes are regularly audited.
- The manufacturing processes of the foods given by the Food Authority is always followed.

Packaging and Labelling Requirements for Fortified Foods

While packaging and labelling fortified foods, the manufacturer must ensure that the following standards are followed:

- The packaging of foods should be in such a way that the nature and the effects of the shelf life of the nutrients added should be taken into consideration.

- All packages of the foods should have the words "fortified with (name of the fortificant)" and the logo imprinted on them.
- The food packages with Iron contents in them should have the statement "Not recommended for people with Thalassemia and people of low iron diet" imprinted on them.
- A nutrition claim can be made by the manufacturers and packers in accordance with the provisions of the Act and the rules can be made under the Food Safety and Standard Regulations.

13.8 GENETICALLY MODIFIED (GM) FOODS

A genetically modified food is a food product derived in whole or partially from a genetically modified organism (GMO) through genetic engineering application such as a crop plant, animal or microbe such as yeast. GMOs are genetically modified organisms. These organisms have, in some way, had their genome altered (the 'genome' is the total of all genes in an organisms of a specific species). The creation of GMOs involves using recombinant DNA technology to insert genes from one organism into another of a different species to counter some traits. GM foods were first put on the market in the early 1990s. The most common modified foods are derived from plants: soybean, corn, canola and cotton seed oils.

Potential benefits of GM foods

- Enhanced taste and quality of food material
- Reduced maturation time of foods
- Increased yield and stress tolerance
- Increased nutritional qualities (*e.g.* added vitamins, minerals, iron and nutrients that protect against certain diseases)
- Improved resistance to diseases, pests, herbicide ands environment extremes
- Cold tolerance
- New products and growing techniques (*e.g.* biodegradable plastic)
- Reduced or eliminated natural toxicants (*e.g.* glycoalkaloids in potatoes) or allergens (*e.g.* allergenic proteins in nuts)
- Improved keeping and processing qualities (*e.g.* delayed fruit ripening to extend shelf life)
- Production of pharmaceuticals and edible vaccines

Examples of GM foods with potential health benefits

- Tomatoes with increased amounts of Lycopene, a cancer fighting antioxidant
- Canola or sunflower oil with lower amounts of trans-fatty acids to promote a healthy heart
- Soybeans with reduced amount of saturated fats
- Potatoes with a higher starch content, which absorb less oil during frying

Controversies /risk of GM foods

The genetically modified (GM) food may cause hazard in developing allergenicity, transfer of genes from GM food to cells of the body or to bacteria in the in gastrointestinal tract.

- *Potential human health impact:* allergens, transfer of antibiotic resistance, unknown effect
- *Potential environment impact*: unintended transfer of transgenes through cross pollination, unknown effect on other organisms (*e.g.* soil microbes) and loss of flora and fauna biodiversity

- Unintended introduction of allergens or natural occurring toxins in foods
- Unintended transfer of transgenes beyond GM plants to other species, harming them or making them toxic or allergenic. Recorded deaths from GM and near deaths from allergic reactions
- Increased food allergies
- Increased toxicity, birth defects and lowered nutrition

Table 2: Responsibilities of governmental authorities as regards the regulation of GMOs in India (excluding pharmaceutical applications). Activity Responsible Authority Contained research (laboratory and greenhouse) RCGM (DBT)

Activity	Responsible Authority
Contained research (laboratory and greenhouse)	RCGM (DBT)
Event selection trials/BRL 1 trials	RCGM and GEAC (MoEF)
Food safety assessment of GM foods (viable and processed)	FSSAI
Environmental risk assessment of GM organisms	GEAC
Approval for commercial release of GM foods (processed)	FSSAI
Approval for commercial release of GM foods (viable *i.e.* LMOs)	GEAC
Approval for environmental (commercial) release of GM organisms	GEAC

RCGM : Review Committee on Genetic Manipulation. GEAC : Genetic Engineering Appraisal Committee
MoEF : Ministry of Environment & Forests.

13.9 FOOD HANDLING, STORAGE AND TRANSPORTATION

Safe food handling, storage and preparation methods are key to reducing the risk of food borne illness.

Essentials of Food Handling and Storage

- Date all food when it is received. Make sure that older foods are used up first to maintain nutrition and freshness.
- Seal packages after they are opened and refrigerate uneaten food to avoid spoilage.
- *Keep hot foods hot and cold foods cold.* Hot foods should have an internal temperature of 60°C/140°F. Refrigerate fresh foods (*e.g.*, meat, fish, poultry, milk and milk alternatives, eggs and egg products) right after they are bought or received. Cold foods must be kept at 4°C/40°F or less.
- Place a thermometer in each refrigerator. Check temperatures daily to ensure that foods are kept at a proper temperature of 4°C/40°F or less.
- Keep raw food away from cooked or ready to eat foods.
- Keep toxic and poisonous substances separate from food and out of reach of children and youth.
- Keep re-usable grocery bags clean and wash them regularly (if used).

Always wash your hands before handling food.

Storing food in the fridge

Your fridge temperature should be at 5 °C or below. The freezer temperature should be below –15 °C. Use a thermometer to check the temperature in your fridge.

Freezing food safely

When shopping, buy chilled and frozen foods at the end of your trip and take them home to store as quickly as possible. On hot days or for trips longer than 30 minutes, try to take an insulated cooler bag or icepack to keep frozen foods cold. Keep hot and cold foods separate while you take them home.

When you arrive home, put chilled and frozen foods into the fridge or freezer immediately. Make sure foods stored in the freezer are frozen hard.

Storing cooked food safely

When you have cooked food and want to cool it:

- Put hot food into shallow dishes or smaller portions to help cool the food as quickly as possible.
- Don't put very hot food into the refrigerator. Wait until steam has stopped rising from the food before putting it in the fridge

Storage Food at Restaurants and catering establishment

Any catering organization of food service provider must have adequate storage facility with temperature control equipments to protect food from any kind of spoilage . this includes refrigerated storage, deep freezers and dry food storage.

The ideal and best temperature requirements for various storage systems are :

1, Dry storage systems for non-perishable goods (10 to 21 °C)

2, Refrigerated storage systems for perishables (1 to 4 °C)

3. Deep freezer for perishables (– 6 to – 24 °C)

Storage Temperatures and Procedures

Regardless, there still is a need for storing many types of supplies including dry foods, dairy products, frozen foods, produce, and fresh meats. Storage areas for such items often have design requirements that must be built into the space in order to efficiently handle the specific types of supplies.

Dry Foods

The area should be dry and cool to prevent spoilage and the swelling of canned goods. The ideal temperature range is 10°C to 21°C .

Frozen Foods

Frozen foods should be stored at –18°C (0°F) or lower. If the temperature rises above –18°C, food can become discoloured and lose vitamin content. Lowering the temperature after it has risen does not correct the damage.

Canned Foods

Canned foods should be inspected properly to prevent serious food borne illness like botulism. It must be checked for swelling at top or bottom, any kind of leakage, flowed seals, rust and dent in the container.

Refrigerated Products

Keep foods 4°C (39°F) or colder, the safe temperature for refrigerated storage.

Dairy Products

Dairy products must be stored in the refrigerator at temperatures of 2°C to 4°C (36° to 39°F).

Produce

Most produce is stored in the refrigerator at 2° to 4°C (36° to 39°F) to ensure freshness and to prevent rapid deterioration.

Fresh Meats, Poultry, and Seafood

Keep foods 4°C (39°F) or colder, the safe temperature for refrigerated storage.

Individual meat cuts such as steaks, chops, stewing meat, and ground meat should be kept covered on plastic or stainless steel trays at 2°C to 4°C (36°F to 39°F).

Fresh seafood should be packed in ice, stored at –1°C to 2°C (30°C to 34°F) and used as soon as possible.

All carcass meats should be unwrapped and hung so that air can circulate around them. They should be stored at 1°C to 3°C (34°C to 37°F) in a walk-in refrigerator. Place absorbent paper under the meats for quick cleanup of any unwanted drips.

Handling food

Bacteria cannot move on their own – they are spread from one place to another by poor food handling practices or by contact with pets, flies or other pests. To stop the spread of bacteria:

- Always wash your hands thoroughly with soap and hot water:
  - before handling food, especially cooked food
  - after going to the toilet
  - between handling raw and cooked foods.
- Avoid using bare hands to touch food. Use tongs, forks and spoons whenever possible.
- Always clean and sanitise work surfaces and utensils. Sanitisers kill bacteria, while detergents only remove dirt and grease.
- Wash fruits and vegetables, especially if eaten raw.
- Use safe, treated water when preparing food and cleaning.
- Use separate cutting boards and knives for each type of food, for example raw meat, fish, vegetables and cooked foods.
- Use paper towels whenever possible. Dish cloths and towels can carry bacteria.
- Protect food preparation areas and food from pests, insects and pets.

Transporting food

When potentially hazardous **foods are transported** they should be kept cold (5°C or colder) or hot (60°C or hotter) during the journey. Alternatively, you could use time, rather than temperature, to keep the **food** safe while it is being **transported**. ... If the journey is short, insulated containers may keep the **food** cold.

13.10 GOOD AGRICULTURAL PRACTICES (GAPS)

Concept

Good Agricultural Practices (GAPs) is the new concept and evolved in recent years. The concerns of food production, food security, food safety, quality and environmental sustainability in agriculture among consumers and producers necessitate the concept of good agricultural practices.GAPs apply scientific recommendations and available knowledge to address environmental, economic and social sustainability for on-farm production and post-production processes resulting in safe and healthy food and non-food agricultural products. FAO, 2007 published technical manual on guidelines of "Good Agricultural Practices for Family Agriculture". According to this GAPs and GMPs (Good Manufacturing Practices) are a set of principles, regulations and technical recommendations applicable to production, processing and food transport, addressing human health care, environment protection and improvement of worker conditions and their families (**Fig. 2**). Initially the GAPs are more focused on post-harvest handling, processing, packaging and quality standards. Now the concept of GAPs covers all practices (starting from production level to ultimate consumer) which are environmentally sustainable, economical feasible and socially acceptable. The implementation of GAPs requires active role of farmers, food regulatory authorities, retailers, and consumers in advocating food safety and sustainable food production.

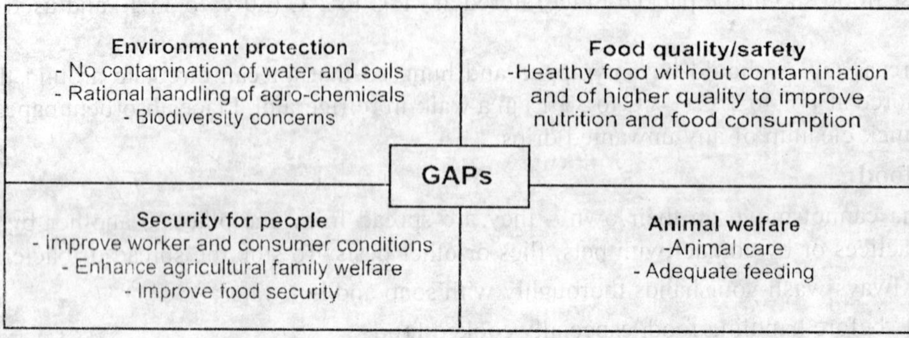

Fig. 2: Good agricultural practices concept

Definition

Food and Agricultural Organization of the United Nations (FAO) defines Good Agricultural Practice as a collection of principles to apply for on-farm production and post-production processes, resulting in safe and healthy food and non-food agricultural products, while taking into account economic, social and environmental sustainability.The pillars of GAPs are economic viability, environmental sustainability, social acceptability and food safety and quality. GAPs may be applied to a wide range of farming systems and at different scales. They are applied through sustainable agricultural methods.

Objectives of GAPS

The major objectives are:

i) To improve sustainable natural resources use, workers' health and working conditions.

ii) To ensures quality and safety of produce in the food chain.

iii) Creating new market opportunities for farmers and exporters

iv) Capturing new market advantages by modifying supply chain mechanism.

Key elements of GAPs

The key elements of GAPs have been enumerated as:

i) Prevention of problems before they occur

ii) Risk assessments

iii) Commitment to food safety at all levels

iv) Communication throughout the production chain

v) Mandatory employee education program at the operational level

vi) Field and equipment sanitation

vii) Integrated pest management

viii) Oversight and enforcement

ix) Verification through independent, third-party audit

Benefits of GAPs

The benefits of GAPs are:

i) Quality and safety of food and other agricultural products are improved with appropriate adoption and monitoring of GAPs

ii) It helps to reduce the risk of non-compliance with national and international regulations, standards and guidelines (in particular of the Codex Alimentarius Commission, World Organization for Animal Health and the International Plant Protection Convention (IPPC) regarding permitted pesticides, maximum levels of contaminants including pesticides, veterinary drugs, radionuclide and mycotoxins in food and non-food agricultural products, as well as other chemical, microbiological and physical contamination hazards.

iii) GAPs help to promote sustainable agriculture and contributes to meeting national and international environment and social development objectives.

Challenges of GAPs

Many challenges are also associated with GAPs as:

i) GAPs implementation and record keeping and certification processes in particular will increases the production costs.

ii) Lack of coordination between existing GAPs-related schemes and availability of affordable certification systems has often led to increased confusion and certification costs for farmers and exporters.

iii) Standards of GAPs can be used to serve competing interests of specific stakeholders in agri-food supply chains by modifying supplier-buyer relations.

iv) Small scale farmers may face high risk of non-availability of export market opportunities unless they are adequately informed, technically prepared, organized and facilitate by governments and public agencies to meet this new challenge.

v) Follow of all GAPs standards does not always promote all the environmental and social benefits, which are claimed.

Quality Council of India (QCI) felt now to be an opportune time to launch Good Agricultural Practices for India - INDGAP as the Governments and the agro-processing industry now acknowledge agriculture to be a growth driver. It would also help in better implementation of the food regulations in India by making available appropriate quality raw material to the food processing industry.

The focus of INDGAP is to address not only the quality and quantity of the produce obtained from a unit area but focuses on various aspects of food safety, pre-and post-harvest practices including workers health and safety ensure sustained supply of produce of the desirable quality.

BAP (Best Aquaculture Practices)

BAP is the world's most trusted, comprehensive and proven third-party **aquaculture** certification program. BAP certification helps in improving the environmental, social and economic performance of the **aquaculture** supply chain and growing the global supply of responsibly farmed seafood since 2002. BAP certification defines the most important elements of responsible aquaculture and provides quantitative guidelines by which to evaluate adherence to those practices for processing plants, farms, hatcheries and feed mills. The number of BAP-certified facilities worldwide grows daily.

13.11 GLP (GOOD LABORATORY PRACTICE)

Analytical capability: There is need for well-equipped, state-of-the-art accredited laboratories to carry out analysis of food. Further, well- trained personnel having knowledge of principles of laboratory management and physical, chemical and microbiological analysis of food, test foods and food products are also required. A broad range of analytical capabilities is required for detecting food contaminants, environmental chemicals, biotoxins, pathogenic bacteria, food-borne viruses and parasites.

Good laboratory practice or GLP is a set of principles intended to assure the quality and integrity of non-clinical laboratory studies that are intended to support research or marketing permits for products regulated by government agencies. The term GLP is most commonly associated with the pharmaceutical industry and the required non-clinical animal testing that must be performed prior to approval of new drug products. However, GLP applies to many other non-pharmaceutical agents such as color additives, food additives, food contamination limits, food packaging, and medical devices.

GLP was first introduced in New Zealand and Denmark in 1972, and later in the US in 1978 in response to the Industrial BioTest Labs scandal. It was followed a few years later by the Organization for Economic Co-operation and Development (OECD) Principles of GLP in 1992; the OECD has since helped promulgate GLP to many countries.

GLP is a quality system concerned with the organizational process and conditions under which non-clinical health and environmental safety studies are planned, performed, monitored, recorded, archived and reported.

1. **GLP principles include**
   - Organization and Personnel
   - Management-Responsibilities
   - Sponsor-Responsibilities
   - Study Director-Responsibilities
   - Principal Investigator-Responsibilities
   - Study Personnel-Responsibilities
2. **Quality assurance program**
   - Quality Assurance Personnel
3. **Facilities**
   - Test System Facilities
   - Facilities for Test and Reference Items
4. **Equipment, reagents and Materials**
5. **Test systems**
   - Physical/Chemical
   - Biological
6. **Test & Reference items**
7. **Standard operating procedures**
8. **Performance of Study**
   - Study Plan
   - Conduct of Study
9. **Reporting of results**
10. **Archival - Storage of Records and Reports**

Food Tolerance/Intolerance

Food intolerance is the term used to describe a range of responses to food, including allergic reactions, adverse reactions resulting from enzyme deficiencies, pharmacological reactions, and responses to toxic or irritant components of food affects as many as 6% of young children and 3% to 4% of adults. Although any food can provoke a reaction, relatively few foods are responsible for the vast majority of significant food-induced allergic reactions: milk, egg, peanuts, tree nuts, fish, and shellfish. One way of distinguishing food intolerance and food poisoning is to consider the former as a defect in the individual and the latter as that of the food. These are abnormal reactions of a person's immune system to foreign but normally harmless substances, such as pollen grains or food constituents.

Food Recall

A food recall is defined as: 'Action taken to remove from sale, distribution and consumption of foods which may pose a safety risk to consumers'.

A food recall may be initiated as a result of a report or complaint from a variety of sources "manufacturers, wholesalers, retailers, government agencies and consumers. It may also occur as a result of a food business's internal testing and/or auditing. Recalls are conducted by food businesses to ensure that potentially hazardous or unsafe foods are not consumed.

A **food recall occurs** when a company removes a **food** product from the market because of the possibility that the **food** may be contaminated or mislabeled.

The Food Safety and Standards Authority of India (FSSAI) has issued Guidelines for Food Recalls on November 28, 2017. This guide provides an overview of how to develop a recall plan and how to implement that plan in the event of a recall.

This guide provides a 10-step procedure for conducting a recall plan:

- Step 1 : Assemble your recall management team
- Step 2 : Inform the authority
- Step 3 : Identify all products to be recalled
- Step 4 : Detain and segregate products to be recalled which are in your firm's control
- Step 5 : Prepare and distribute the information of recall
- Step 6 : Prepare the distribution list
- Step 7 : Verify the effectiveness of the recall
- Step 8 : Control of the recalled product(s)
- Step 9 : Decide what to do with the returned product
- Step 10 : Fix the cause of the recall

This guide aims to assist manufacturers and/or distributors in implementing Food Safety and Standards (Food Recall Procedure) Regulation, 2017.

13.12 QUALITY CONTROL IN FOODS

Food quality control is generally defined as the regulation by law of food manufacture,distribution and sale, in order to prevent health hazards and fraud to customer. Thus it becomes a criminal offence to sell, adulterted, filthy or contaminated food. Food is defined under the law as any article used for food or drink by man or animal. This is interpreted to include substances added to food which may have no nutrittive value what so ever, e.g., artificial coluring, codiments, flavour, spices and preservtives. There are three types of aspects to the application of food quality control: (1) moral, (2) commercial, (3) legal. The application of controls on food quality put a moral responsibility on the food manufacturer towards the consumer. The commercial aspects requires that standard quality products are economically produced. And in increasingly competitive markets, it is important that produces exercise a stringent degree of quality control on what they produce. The legal viewpoint demands that the quality of products conforms to national and international standards. Fruits and vegetable processing industries produce very asrge quantities of products which are intended for consumption, often on a daily basis, by the population at large. The control of food quality by law leads to:

(1) Improved quality of product

(2) Achievementof greater consumer satisfaction

(3) The promotion of quality consciousness

(4) Employment opportunities for scientific and technical personnel
(5) Increases consumption and sales
(6) Avoidance of controversy and litigation in marketing at the national and international level
(7) Promotion of national and international trade.

The sequence of operations in quality control is as follows:

(1) Raw material control.
(2) Process control or the control of the manufacturing process.
(3) Production inspection, including the inspection of the finished product, packaging and storage.
(4) Sensory evaluation or evaluation of the acceptability of the final product.

13.13 TOTAL QUALITY MANAGEMENT (TQM)

TQM was first indroduced by W. E. Deming in 1986 and relied on the concept of continuous improvement.

TQM involves the orgnanisation's long term commitment to the continuous improvement of quality-throughout the organisation, and with the active participation of all members at all levels to meet and exceed participation of all members at all levels to meet and exceed customer's expectations. This top-management driven philosophy is considered a way of organisational life. In a sense, TQM is simply effective management.

When done effectively, TQM should result in greater customer satisfaction, fewer defects and less wastage, increased total productivity, reduced costs and improved profitability and an environment in which quality has high priority.

There are four attributes of TQM such as

(1) customer focus
(2) strategic management and leadership
(3) continuous improvement
(4) empowerment and teamwork.

Deming's 14 Quality Programme

W. Edwards Deming: Edward Deming an early American Guru of management highlighted the following management teachings. These teachings lead a beneficial change in the culture of companies.

Dr. Edward Deming provides a framework of fourteen points as described below:

(*i*) Continual improvement of the product/service.
(*ii*) New philosophy of economic stability in product.
(*iii*) Ban dependence on inspection with a view quality.
(*iv*) Cease practice of awarding business an price tag alone.
(*v*) On the job training.
(*vi*) New and modern methods of training.
(*vii*) Drive out fear.
(*viii*) Remove barriers between departments and individual.
(*ix*) Eliminate the use of slogans and posters.
(*x*) Eliminate work quotas.
(*xi*) Remove barriers that rub the hourly workers.
(*xii*) Implement rigorous programme of training.
(*xiii*) Define permanent commitments of top management.
(*xiv*) Improve system of production.

CHAPTER 14

FOOD STANDARD AND LEGISLATIONS

14.1 FOOD STANDARDS AND REGULATION IN INDIA

Food Safety and Standards Authority of India (FSSAI) is an autonomous body established under the Ministry of Health & Family Welfare, Government of India, responsible for protecting and promoting public health through the regulation and supervision of food safety. FSSAI of India has laid down science based standards for articles of food and to regulate their manufacture, storage, distribution, sale and import, to ensure availability of safe and wholesome food for human consumption. FSSAI has been established under the Food Safety and Standards Act, 2006 which is a consolidating statute related to food safety and regulations in India. This Act replaced all the other food laws existed in the system including Prevention of Food Adulteration (PFA) ACT, 1954, Food Product Order, (FPO), The Vegetable Oil Product Order, 1998 etc. This is an integrated Food Law and has created unified framework for food regulations which has shifted primary responsibility of safety to food businesses and hence assuring food safety across the food chain and ensuring uniform application of standards and practices across the country. Thus, ONE NATION ONE FOOD LAW.

The main goal of FSSAI is to:

- Lay down science-based standards for articles of food
- To regulate manufacture, storage, distribution, sale and import of food
- To facilitate food safety

This nationwide approach is being adopted in India to ensure better transparency, consistency and predictability of food business environment.

In India FSSAI (Food Safety and Standards Authority of India) regulate the food safety and standards Section 92 (1) of Food Safety and Standards (FSS) Act, 2006 empowers the Food Authority to make regulations/standards in consistent with this Act and Rules made there under. After the enactment of the FSS Act, 2006 FSSAI has drafted six principal regulations through extensive consultation and deliberations/meetings with various stakeholders. These regulations have been notified in the gazette of India on 1st August, 2011 and came into force on 5th August, 2011. These regulations/standards are further reviewed and several new regulations are notified taking into account the latest developments in food science, food consumption pattern, new products and additives, advancement in the processing technology and food analytical methods and also with a view to bridge the gap between national and international standards for food products. That formulation and revision of regulations/standards involves several stages. After recommendation by the Scientific Panel, following the due process laid down including validation by the Scientific Committee a regulations/ standards are approved by the Food

Authority. After soliciting comments of stakeholders and their considerations, final notification is issued for implementation. In addition to the Six principal regulations notified on 1st August 2011, following new regulations are notified. These include:

1. Food Safety and Standards (Food or Health Supplements, Nutraceuticals, Foods for Special Dietary Uses, Foods for Special Medical Purpose, Functional Foods and Novel Food) Regulations, 2016.
2. Food Safety and Standards (Food Recall Procedure) Regulation, 2017.
3. Food Safety and Standards (Import) Regulation, 2017.
4. Food Safety and Standards (Approval for Non-Specified Food and Food Ingredients) Regulations, 2017.
5. Food Safety and Standards (Organic Food) Regulation, 2017.
6. Laws and Regulations 1. Food Safety and Standards (Licensing and Registration of Food Businesses) Regulation, 2011.
7. Food Safety and Standards (Food Products Standards & Food Additives) Regulation, 2011.
8. Food Safety and Standards (Prohibition and Restriction of Sales) Regulation, 2011.
9. Food Safety and Standards (Packaging and Labelling) Regulation, 2011.
10. Food Safety and Standards (Contaminants, Toxins and Residues) Regulation, 2011.
11. Food Safety and Standards (Laboratory and Sampling Analysis) Regulation, 2011.
12. Food Safety and Standards (Health Supplements, Nutraceuticals, Food for Special Dietary Use, Food for Special Medical Purpose, Functional Foods & Novel Food) Regulations, 2016
13. Food Safety and Standards (Food Recall Procedure) Regulation, 2017.
14. Food Safety and Standards (Import) Regulation, 2017.
15. Food Safety and Standards (Approval for Non-Specific Food and Food Ingredients) Regulation, 2017.
16. Food Safety and Standards (Organic Food) Regulation, 2017.
17. Food Safety and Standards (Alcoholic Beverages) Regulation, 2016. Food Safety and Standards (Advertising and Claims) Regulation, 2018.
18. Food Safety and Standards (Fortification of Food) Regulation, 2018.
19. Food Safety and Standards (Food Safety Auditing) Regulation, 2018.
20. Food Safety and Standards (Recognition and Notification of Laboratories) Regulation, 2018.
21. Food Safety and Standards (Advertising and Claims) Regulation, 2018.
22. Food Safety and Standards (Packaging) Regulation, 2018.
23. Food Safety and Standards (Recovery and Distribution of Surplus food) Regulation, 2019.
24. Food Safety and Standards Authority of India Business Transaction Regulations, 2010.
25. FSSAI Packaging 2nd Amendment regulation 2022.
26. Food Safety and Standards (Foods for Infant Nutrition) First Amendment Regulations, 2022.
22. Food Safety and Standards (Adversiting and Claims) First Amendment Regulations, 2022.

14.1.1 Food Safety and Standards Act, 2006

The Food Safety and Standards Act received the assent of the President on 23rd August, 2006 and came into effect on 5th August, 2011. The Act officially repeals the regulatory framework established by the previously existing eight food laws by Notification F.No.P15025/41/2011-DFQC, issued by the Ministry of Health and Family Welfare on August 4, 2011, consolidating them into the Food Safety and Standards Rules and Regulations 2011 under a single regulator. The Food Safety and Standards Authority of India. On May 5, 2011, the GOI Ministry of Health and Family Welfare published the final Food Safety and Standards Rules, 2011 vide Notification No.G.S.R.362 (E) in the Indian official gazette.

The implementation of the Food Safety and Standards Act, 2006 formally repeals the following laws:

i) The Prevention of Food Adulteration Act (PFA), 1954.

ii) The Fruit Products Order, 1955.

iii) The Meat Food Products Order, 1973.

iv) The Vegetable Oil Products (Regulation) Order, 1998.

v) The Edible Oils Packaging (Regulation) Order 1988.

vi) The Solvent Extracted Oil, De-Oiled Meal and Edible Flour (Control) Order, 1967.

vii) Milk and Milk Products Order, 1992.

viii) Any other order issued under the Essential Commodities Act, 1955 relating to food.

The following are the statutory powers that the FSS Act, 2006 gives to the Food Safety and Standards Authority of India (FSSAI).

- Framing of regulations to lay down the standards and guidelines for articles of food and system of enforcing various standards.
- Laying down mechanisms and guidelines for accreditation of certification bodies for certification of food safety management system for food businesses and accreditation of laboratories and notification of the accredited laboratories.
- To provide scientific advice and technical support to Central Government and State Governments for framing the policy and rules related to food safety and nutrition.
- Collect and collate data regarding food consumption, incidence and prevalence of biological risk, contaminants in food, residues of various contaminants in food products. identification of emerging risks and introduction of rapid alert system.
- Creating an information network across the country so that the public, consumers, Panchayats, etc., receive rapid, reliable and objective information about food safety and issues of concern.
- Provide training programmes for persons who are involved or intend to get involved in food businesses.
- Contribute to the development of international technical standards for food, sanitary and phyto-sanitary standards.
- Promote general awareness about food safety and food standards.

14.2 SOME PREVIOUS FOOD ACTS

14.2.1 Spice Board Act 1986

The Spices board Act 1986 enforced in the year 1987 vide Govt of India, Ministry of Commerce, Notification No.122(E) dated 26th February 1987 empowers the Board among other functions , the promotion of the export of Spices to evolve suitable quality standards and introduce certification of quality through "Quality Marking" for spices for export and control the quality of Spices.

- To have regulatory system based on science and international standards for the spice industry in India.
- To protect public health
- To ensure fair practices in trade.
- To have an enforceable, transparent food safety and quality assurance system through out the food chain for consistent application by the regulators and the
- FBOs, in Spice processing Industries
- To be in compliance with the national as well as international regulatory Standards, Guidelines and Code of Practices.

14.2.2 Prevention of Food Adulteration Act, 1954

The Act was promulgated by Parliament in 1954 to make provision for the prevention of adulteration of food, along with the Prevention of Food Adulteration Rules, 1955 which was incorporated in 1955 as an extension to the Act. Broadly, the PFA Act covers food standards, general procedures for sampling, analysis of food, powers of authorized officers, nature of penalties and other parameters related to food. It deals with parameters relating to food additives, preservative, colouring matters, packing & labelling of foods, prohibition & regulations of sales etc. Like FPO, amendment in PFA rules are incorporated with the recommendation made by the Central Committee of Food Standards (CCFS) which has been setup by Central Government under the Ministry of Health and Family Welfare comprising members from different regions of the country. The provisions of PFA Act and Rules are implemented by State Government and local bodies as provided in the rules.

14.2.3 Milk & Milk Product Amendment Regulations

2009 (MMPR-09) DIVISION (MMPO, 1992 has been renamed as MMPR, 2009).

Consequent upon de-licensing of Dairy Sector in 1991 under Industrial Development & Regulation Act, the Department of AH, Dairying & Fisheries had promulgated the Milk and Milk Product Order (MMPO) 1992 on 9/6/92 under section 3 of the Essential Commodities Act 1955. The objective of the order is to maintain and increase the supply of liquid milk of desired quality in the interest of the general public and also for regulating the production, processing and distribution of milk and milk products. As per the provisions of this order, any person/dairy plant handling more than 10,000 liters per day of milk or 500 MT of milk solids per annum needs to be registered with the Registering Authority appointed by the Central Government.

14.2.4 Fruit Product Order (FPO), 1955

Fruit Products Order-1955, promulgated under Section 3 of the Essential Commodities Act - 1955, with an objective to manufacture fruit & vegetable products maintaining sanitary and hygienic conditions in the premises and quality standards laid down in the Order. It is mandatory for all manufacturers of fruit and vegetable products including some non fruit products like non fruit vinegar, syrup and sweetened aerated water to obtain a license under this Order.

This order was earlier implemented by Ministry of Food Processing Industries (now by FSSAI) through the Directorate of Fruit & Vegetable Preservation, Headquarter at New Delhi. The Directorate has five regional offices with headquarter located at Delhi, Mumbai, Kolkata, Chennai and Guwahati as well as a sub-office at Lucknow under Northern Region. The field officers of the Regional Offices undertake periodic inspections of the manufacturing units to ensure maintenance of hygienic conditions in the factory and draw random samples of products from the factories as well as from markets which are analyzed in the laboratories to test their conformity according to the specifications laid under FPO.

14.2.5 Meat Food Products Order (MFPO) DIVISION 1973

The main objectives of the MFPO, 1973 are to regulate production and sale of meat food products through licensing of manufacturers, enforce sanitary and hygienic conditions prescribed for production of wholesome meat food products, exercise strict quality control at all stages of production of meat food products, fish products including chilled poultry etc.

14.2.6 Edible Oils Packaging, 1998

In order to ensure availability of safe and quality edible oils in packed form at pre-determined prices to the consumers, the Central Govt. promulgated on 17th September, 1998, an Edible Oils Packaging (Regulation) Order, 1998 under the Essential Commodities Act, 1955 to make packaging of edible oils, sold in retail, compulsory unless specifically exempted by the concerned State Govt.

14.2.7 Vegetable Oil Products Order, 1998

The Vegetable Oil Products industry is regulated by this Order through the Directorate of Vanaspati, Vegetable Oils & Fats, Department of Food, Public Distribution, Ministry of Consumer Affairs, and Food & Public Distribution. The earlier two Orders – Vegetable Oil Products (Control) Order, 1947 and Vegetable Oil Products (Standards of Quality) Order, 1975 have been replaced by a single Order called "Vegetable Oil Products (Regulation) Order, 1998 for proper regulation of manufacture, distribution and sale of Vegetable Oil Products.

14.2.8 Solvent Extracted Oil, De-oiled Meal and Edible Flour (Control) Order, 1967

The Order is basically a quality control order to ensure that the solvent extracted oils in particular are not reached to the consumers for consumption before the same are refined and conformed to the quality standards specified in the Order for the purpose. Standards for the solvent (hexane), which is to be used for extraction of oil from the oil-bearing materials, have also been specified so as to eliminate possible contamination of oil from the solvent used.

14.2.9 The Coffee Act, 1945

It provides rules and regulations curing, assessment of quality and enforcement of quality control measures at different stages of marketing coffee within the country and abroad.

14.2.10 Quality Council of India (QCI)

It was set up in 1997 jointly by the Government of India and the Indian Industry represented by the three premier industry associations *i.e.*, Associated Chambers of Commerce and Industry of India (ASSOCHAM), Confederation of Indian Industry (CII) and Federation of Indian Chambers of Commerce and Industry (FICCI), to establish and operate national accreditation structure and promote quality through National Quality Campaign. The Department of Industrial Policy & Promotion, Ministry of Commerce & Industry, is the nodal ministry for QCI.

The main objectives of QCI are: (*a*) to establish and operate national accreditation structure (*b*) to monitor and administer the National Quality Campaign.

Accreditation is the formal recognition by an accreditation authority to the technical and organisational competence of a conformity assessment body to carry out a specific service in accordance to the standards and technical regulations as described in their scope of accreditation. QCI is the accreditation authority in India.

At its simplest, "conformity assessment" means checking that products, materials, services, systems or people measure up to the specifications of a relevant standard. For example, a customer may want to check that the product he or she ordered from a supplier meets the purpose for which it is required. One of the most efficient ways to do this when the specifications of the product have been defined in an International Standard. That way, both supplier and customer are on the same wavelength, even if they are based in different countries, because they are both using the same references. Conformity assessment is important to suppliers, consumers & regulators. It enables them to demonstrate that the product(s) meet relevant design & safety standards and gives consumer competence when selecting product in market place.

Export Inspection Council: The Export Inspection Council (EIC) is the official export –certification body of India which ensures quality and safety of products exported from India. EIC was set up by the Government of India under Section 3 of the Export (Quality Control and Inspection) Act, 1963 to ensure sound development of export trade of India through quality control and inspection and matters connected therewith. The role of EIC is to ensure that products notified under the Export (Quality Control and Inspection) Act 1963 are meeting the requirements of the importing countries in respect of their quality and safety. Its headquarter is at New Delhi.

14.3 NATIONAL CODEX COMMITTEE (INDIA)

The National Codex Committee has been constituted by the Food Safety and Standards Authority of India for keeping liaison with the CAC.

Core Functions of NCC-INDIA

- To advise government on the implications of various food standardization, food quality and safety issues which have arisen and related to the work undertaken by the CAC so that national economic interest is taken into account, or considered, when international standards are discussed.
- To provide important inputs to the government so as to assist in ensuring quality and safety of food to the consumers, while at the same time maximizing the opportunities for development of industry and expansion of international trade.
- To appoint Shadow Committees on subject matters related to the corresponding Codex Committees to assist in the study or consideration of technical matters; and
- To meet as and when necessary to formulate national position.

Responsibilities of NCC-INDIA

- To cooperate with the Joint FAO/WHO Food Standards Programme and to nominate delegates to attend Codex meetings.
- To formulate national position in consultation with the members of NCC in the matters of Codex and recommend action to government.
- To study Codex documents, collect and review all relevant information relating to technology, economics, health and control systems, so as to give supporting reasons to the government for the acceptance of Codex Standards or otherwise.
- To identify organizations to take action and where necessary commission studies for generation of data base or preparation of base papers projecting the country's interest and for interacting with the CAC; and
- To cooperate with other local/regional or foreign organizations dealing with activities relating to food standardization.

Shadow Committees of NCC-INDIA

The Food Authority has appointed the Shadow Committees of the NCC on subject matters corresponding to the Codex Committees to assist the NCC in the study or consideration of technical matters. Officers in the rank of Joint Secretary or above in the concerned Department/ Ministry / Food Authority who handle the subject at the policy level and also serve as the members of the NCC may be nominated as the Chairpersons of these Shadow Committees. Specialized experts in the relevant field may be nominated as members of these Shadow Committees. These lists of experts may be reviewed from time to time to ensure that they meet the ongoing requirements of the NCC.

Currently, the Shadow Committees assist the National Codex Committee in the following areas:

- Codex Alimentarius Commission
- Executive Committee of the Codex Alimentarius Commission
- Regional Coordinating Committee (including Coordinating Committee for Asia)
- General Principles
- Food labelling
- Pesticides Residues
- Food Hygiene
- Contaminants in Foods
- Nutrition and Foods for Special Dietary Uses
- Fish and Fishery Products
- Fresh Fruits and Vegetables
- Milk and Milk Products
- Methods of Analysis and Sampling
- Veterinary drugs
- Food Additives
- Food Export and Import and Certification Systems
- Fats and Oils
- Processed Fruits and Vegetables
- Spices & Culinary Herbs

Terms of Reference (TOR) of Shadow Committees

- To review and advise on the agenda documents including the Code of Hygienic Practices and Codex Guidelines for the respective Codex Committees;
- To advise on the composition of the Indian Delegation;
- To coordinate with the other Shadow committees and concerned Departments for seeking comments and finalise the India's view point on different agenda items under consideration of the respective Codex Committees;
- To advise the concerned Government Department on all matters relating to Codex procedure and working process for elaboration of Codex Standards, Codex Code of Practices and Codex Guidelines;
- To advise on Capacity Building, food safety, food regulations and technical assistance;
- Any other work assigned by the National Codex Committee and the Chairman, National Codex Committee, from time to time;

Functions of Shadow Committees

- To advise the NCCP / NCC on the implications of various food standardization, food quality and safety issues which have arisen and related to the work undertaken by the relevant Subsidiary Body/Task Force so that national economic interest is taken into account or considered when international standards are deliberated by the relevant committee; and
- To follow the Codex agenda of the relevant Subsidiary Body and provide inputs to the government so as to assist in ensuring quality and safety of food to the consumers while at the same time safeguard national interests and maximize the opportunities for development of industry and expansion of international trade.

Responsibilities of Shadow Committees

- To study Codex documents, collect and revise all relevant information relating to technology, economics, health and control systems so as to give supporting reasons to the government in the acceptance of Codex Standards or otherwise;

- To formulate national position in consultation with the members of the Shadow Committee with respect to the agenda for the forthcoming session / meeting of the Subsidiary Body of the CAC and forward the same to NCCP for sending it to Codex Secretariat after approval by government.
- To finalize the delegation for the meeting of the Codex in consultation with the NCC / NCCP and transmit the names to the host secretariat through the NCCP; and
- To recommend to the NCCP the position to be taken during the Sessions of the Commission with respect to agenda items relevant to the terms of reference of the Shadow Committees.

WHO'S WHO in Composition of the National Codex Committee

The membership of the NCC constituted by the Food Safety and Standards Authority.

Chairperson: Chief Executive Officer, Food Safety and Standards Authority of India, Chairperson of the National Codex Committee, in-charge of Food Safety Regulation/Food Standards in the Food Authority;

14.4 ESSENTIAL COMMODITIES ACT, 1955

The Essential Commodities Ordinance No. 1 of 1955, came into force on 26th January, 1955. This Ordinance was subsequently replaced by the present Act namely, the Essential Commodities Act, 1955 w.e.f 1st April, 1955.

Object and scope of the Act

- It is an Act to provide in the interest of the general public for the control of the production, supply and distribution of, and trade and commerce in, certain commodities.
- The dominant object and intendment of the Act is to secure equitable distribution and availability at fair prices of essential commodities in the interest of the general public.
- The interest of the general public necessarily connotes the interest

Definitions

In this Act, unless the context otherwise requires, -

[3 (ia) "Code" means the Code of Criminal Procedure, 1973 (2 of 1973); 3]

[4 5 (iia) "Collector" includes an Additional Collector and such other officer, not below the rank of Sub-Divisional Officer, as may be authorized by the Collector to perform the functions and exercise the powers of the Collector under this Act; 4]

(a) "essential commodity" means any of the following classes of commodities

(i) cattle fodder, including oilcakes and other concentrates,

(ii) coal, including coke and other derivatives,

(iii) component parts and accessories of automobiles;

(iv) cotton and woolen textiles;

[6 (iv-a) drugs;

Explanation : In this sub-clause, "drug" has the meaning assigned to it in CI.(b) of Sec. 3 of the Drugs and Cosmetics Act, 1940 (23 of 1940); 6]

(v) foodstuffs, including edible oilseeds and oils;

(vi) iron and steel, including manufactured products of iron and steel;

(vii) paper, including newsprint, paperboard and straw board;

(viii) petroleum and petroleum products;

(ix) raw cotton, whether ginned or unginned, and cotton seed;

(x) raw jute;

(xi) any other class of commodity which the Central Government may, by notified order, declare to be an essential commodity for the purposes of this Act, being a commodity with respect to which Parliament has power to make laws by virtue of entry 33 in List III in the Seventh Schedule to the Constitution;

(b) "food-crops" include crops of sugarcane;

(c) "notified order" means an order notified in the Official Gazette;

[7 (cc) "order" includes a direction issued there under; 7]

[8 (d) "State Government", in relation to a Union territory, means the administrator thereof; 8]

[9 (e) "sugar" means, -

(i) any form of sugar containing more than ninety per cent of sucrose, including sugar candy;

(ii) khandsari sugar or bura sugar or crushed sugar or any sugar in crystalline or powdered form; or

(iii) sugar-in-process in vacuum pan sugar factory or raw sugar produced therein; 9]

[10 * * * 10]

[11 (f) Words and expressions used but not defined in this Act and defined in the Code shall have the meanings respectively assigned to them in that Code. 11]

14.5 PACKAGED COMMODITY RULES 2011

The rules called The Legal Metrology (Packged commodities) Rules 2011, came into force on 1.1.2011 in the country.

Declarations are Mandated under the Rules

Rule 6 of the Rules dictate the declarations that must be present in every packaging. They include:–

(*a*) The name and address of the manufacturer/importer/packer, as may be applicable. Note that if the manufacturer and packer are separate entities then their names are to be mentioned separately.

(*b*) Generic name of the commodity being sold.

(*c*) Price at which the product is being sold, inclusive of all taxes. Note that there is a specified format at which the same is to be declared, viz. "Maximum Retail Price .... Inclusive of all taxes" or "MRP .... Inclusive of all taxes". The symbol of the currency is to be mentioned, *i.e.* the Rupee symbol, or Rs. or INR. Price is to be declared up to two decimal places.

(*d*) Date of manufacture/packaging/import, as the case may be, viz. the month and year. If the date of packaging and manufacture differ, separate declarations are to be given.

(*e*) Quantity of the commodity (explained in further detail later on)

(*f*) Name, address, telephone number, e-mail address of the person or office who can be contacted for consumer grievances.

Units to be Used in the Declarations

All units in the packaging material should follow International System of Units (S.I) system. For items sold by number, the qualifying symbol used should be "N" or "U".

For depicting length, if the quantity is less than one meter, it is to be depicted in centimeter. Else, meter.

For depicting mass, if the quantity is less than one kilogram, it is to be depicted in grams. Else, kilogram.

For depicting area, if the quantity is less than one square meter, it is to be depicted in square decimeter. Else, square meter.

For depicting volume, if the quantity is less than one litre/one cubic meter/one cubic decimeter, it is to be depicted in millilitre/cubic centimeter/cubic centimeter respectively. Else, litre/cubic meter respectively.

A schedule to the Rules specifies certain products (*i.e.* their generic name) and in terms of what their quantity is to be declared. For example, curd is to be expressed in terms of weight, but ice cream and other similar frozen products are to be expressed in terms of weight OR volume. The schedule however only specifies twenty six items, and Rule 12 states how other products may be declared, viz.

1. In terms of weight – if the product is solid, semi-solid, viscous or a mixture of liquid and solid.
2. In terms of volume – if the product is sold by cubic measure or is liquid.
3. In terms of number – if the product is sold by numbers.
4. In terms of area – if the product is sold by area measure.
5. In terms of length – if the product is sold by linear measure.

Dimensions of the product may be additionally required to be mentioned in case the same is a pertinent factor for the product in question.

The Second Schedule to the Act also specifies certain commodities (*i.e.* their generic name) and their standard pack sizes, such mentioned products can only be sold in the specified quantities, for example Mineral Water and Drinking Water can only be sold in quantities of 100 ml, 150 ml, 200 ml, 250 ml, 300 ml, 500 ml, 750 ml, 1 litre, 1.5 litres, 2 litres, 3 litres, 4 litres, 5 litres, and subsequently in multiples of 5 litres.

Miscellaneous Provisions

If a product has an outside container or wrapper, the said container/wrapper should also have the relevant declarations. However, this requirement is waived if the container/wrapper is transparent and the declarations are easily readable through such external packaging.

If a product is likely to undergo variations in quantity that are significant owing to environmental or other factors can be qualified by the words "when packed" in its quantity declaration. This allowance is presently restricted to soaps, lotions, creams (other than cream of milk), and camphor.

When stating quantity in terms of weight, the weight of packaging and/or any other object apart from the product is to be excluded.

14.6 CONSUMER PROTECTION ACT, 1986

In order to provide for better protection of the interests of the consumer the Consumer Protection Bill, 1986 was introduced in the Lok Sabha on 5th December, 1986.

Statement of Objects and Reasons

1. The Consumer Protection Bill, 1986 seeks to provide for better protection of the interests of consumers and for the purpose, to make provision for the establishment of Consumer councils and other authorities for the settlement of consumer disputes and for matter connected therewith.
2. It seeks, *inter alia*, to promote and protect the rights of consumers such as-
   a) the right to be protected against marketing of goods which are hazardous to life and property;
   b) the right to be informed about the quality, quantity, potency, purity, standard and price of goods to protect the consumer against unfair trade practices;
   c) the right to be assured, wherever possible, access to an authority of goods at competitive prices;
   d) the right to be heard and to be assured that consumers interests will receive due consideration at appropriate forums;
   e) the right to seek redressal against unfair trade practices or unscrupulous exploitation of consumers; and
   f) right to consumer education.
3. These objects are sought to be promoted and protected by the Consumer Protection Council to be established at the Central and State level.
4. To provide speedy and simple redressal to consumer disputes, a quasi-judicial machinery is sought to be setup at the district, State and Central levels. These quasi-judicial bodies will observe the principles of natural justice and have been empowered to give relief of a specific nature and to award, wherever appropriate, compensation to consumers. Penalties for noncompliance of the orders given by the quasi-judicial bodies have also been provided.
5. The Bill seeks to achieve the above objects.

LIST OF AMENDING ACTS

1. The Consumer Protection (Amendment) Act, 1991 (34 of 1991) (w.r.e.f. 15-6-1991).
2. The Consumer Protection (Amendment) Act, 1993 (50 of 1993) (w.r.e.f. 18-6-1993).
3. The Consumer Protection (Amendment) Act, 2002 (62 of 2002) (w.r.e.f. 15-3-2003).

14.7 VOLUNTARY PRODUCT CERTIFICATION

There are voluntary grading and marking schemes such as ISI mark of BIS and Agmark. The Bureau of Indian Standards (BIS) deals with standardisation of various consumer goods including food products and runs a voluntary certification scheme known as 'ISI' mark for processed foods. Agmark is a voluntary scheme of certification of agricultural products (raw and processed) for safeguarding the health of consumers. Since the government had several regulations and laws, food industry found it cumbersome to adhere to. A need was therefore felt to integrate all such laws for regulating the quality of food. With this in view, Indian Government has passed Food Safety and Standards Act (FSSA), 2006, to bring the different pieces of legislation pertaining to food safety under one umbrella.

14.7.1 Bureau of Indian Standards (BIS)

In the twilight years of British rule in India, when the country was faced with the gigantic task of building up the industrial infrastructure, it was the Institution of Engineers (India), which prepared the first draft of the Constitution of an instruction which could take up the task of formulation of National Standards. This led to the Department of Industries and Supplies issuing a memorandum on 03 September 1946, formally announcing the setting of an organization called the "Indian Standards Institution". The Indian Standards Institution (ISI) came into being on the 06 January 1947 and in June 1947 Dr. Lal C. Verman took over as its first Director.

Bureau of Indian standards (BIS) came into existence, through an act of parliament dated 26 November 1986, on 1 April 1987, with a broadened scope and more powers taking over the staff, assets, liabilities and functions of erstwhile ISI. Through this change over, the government envisaged building a climate for quality culture and consciousness and greater participation of consumers in formulation and implementation of national standards.

The Bureau is a Body Corporate consisting of 25 members representing both Central and State governments, Members of Parliament, industry, scientific and research institutions, consumer organizations and professional bodies; with Union Minister of Consumer Affairs, Food and Public Distribution as its President and with Minister of State for Consumer Affairs, Food and Public Distribution as its Vice-President.

BIS is the National Standard Body of India established under the BIS Act 2016 for the harmonious development of the activities of standardization, marking and quality certification of goods and for matters connected therewith or incidental thereto.BIS has been providing traceability and tangibility benefits to the national economy in a number of ways – providing safe reliable quality goods; minimizing health hazards to consumers; promoting exports and imports substitute; control over proliferation of varieties etc. through standardization, certification and testing.

Vision: The Bureau of Indian Standards (BIS), the National Standards Body of India, resolves to be the leader in all matters concerning Standardization, Certification and Quality.

Mission: BIS Act 1986 provides for the establishment of a Bureau for the harmonious development of the activities of standardization, marking and quality certification of goods and for matters connected therewith or incidental thereto.

मानकः पथप्रदर्शकः
भारतीय मानक ब्यूरो
Bureau of Indian Standrds

The food and agricultural division council (FADs) under BIS formulates National standard in the field of food, feed and agricultural commodities covering of entire food supply chain. In this 2100 Indian standard have been formulated.

The sectional committee and number of proposals for FAD are mentioned in table 1.

Table 1: FAD

S.No.	Sectional Committee	No of Proposals Received
1	FAD 1 (Pesticides)	6
2	FAD 2 (Sugar Industry)	0
3	FAD 3 (Apiary Industry)	0
4	FAD 4 (Tobacco And Tobacco Products)	0
5	FAD 5 (Animal Feeds and Nutrition)	5
6	FAD 6 (Stimulant Foods)	0
7	FAD 7 (Soil Quality And Fertilizers)	1
8	FAD 8 (Food Additives)	2
9	FAD 9 (Spices And Condiments)	0
10	FAD 10 (Fruits, Vegetables, and Allied Products)	0
11	FAD 11 (Agricultural Machinery and Equipment)	4
12	FAD 12 (Fish, Fisheries, and Aquaculture)	0
13	FAD 13 (Oils And Oilseeds)	0
14	FAD 14 (Drinking Water and Carbonated Beverages)	2
15	FAD 15 (Food Hygiene, Safety Management and Other Systems)	2
16	FAD 16 (Foodgrains, Allied products, and other agricultural produce)	2
17	FAD 17 (Farm Irrigation And Drainage Systems)	0
18	FAD 18 (Slaughter House And Meat Industry)	0
19	FAD 19 (Dairy Products And Equipment)	1
20	FAD 20 (Agriculture And Food Processing Equipments)	6
21	FAD 22 (Agricultural Systems And Management)	1
22	FAD 23 (Biotechnology for food and agriculture)	0
23	FAD 24 (Ready-to-eat foods and specialized products)	2
24	FAD 27 (Pesticide Residues analysis)	0
25	FAD 28 (Test methods for food products)	0
26	FAD 29 (Alcoholic Drinks)	0
27	FAD 30 (Water Purification Systems)	1
28	FAD 31 (Food Microbiology Sectional Committee)	0
29	FAD 32 (Animal Husbandry and Equipment Sectional Committee)	0
	Unallocated Proposals	4

Objective and Functions

1. To formulate need based standards and participate in International Standardization.
2. To satisfy the customer's need for quality and safety of goods and services through operation of Certification Schemes (Product Certification, Registration, Management System Certification, Hallmarking) of BIS.
3. To test samples generated through product certification scheme of BIS
4. To organize Training Programmes for Industry to enable & encourage them to produce quality goods.
5. To generate awareness on standards, standard mark, and safety & quality of products through Seminars, Awareness Programmes and Publicity Campaigns.

The major functions of Bureau of Indian Standards are to: establish, publish and promote the Indian Standard, in relation to any article or process;

1. recognize as an Indian Standard, any standard established by any other Institution in India or elsewhere, in relation to any article or process;
2. specify a Standard Mark to be called the Bureau of Indian Standards Certification Mark which shall be of such design and contain such particulars as may be prescribed to represent a particular Indian Standard;
3. grant, renew, suspend or cancel a license for the use of the Standard Mark seek recognition of the Bureau and of the Indian Standards outside India on such terms and conditions as may be mutually agreed upon by the Bureau with any corresponding institution or organization in any country.

Management Systems following the BIS Certification Schemes

(A) Quality Management Systems Certification Scheme (IS/ISO 9001)
(B) Environmental Management Systems Certification Scheme (IS/ISO 14001)
(C) Occupational Health and Safety Management Systems Certification Scheme (IS18001)
(D) Hazard Analysis and Critical Control Point (IS 15000)
(E) Food Safety Management Systems Certification Scheme (IS/ISO 22000)
(F) Service Quality Management Systems Certification Scheme (IS 15700).

Table 2: Items which require compulsory BIS certification.

S.No.	IS No.	Product
1.	IS 15757	Follow-up formula - complementary foods
2.	IS 11536	Processed-cereal based complementary foods
3.	IS 1165	Milk-powder
4.	IS 1166	Condensed milk, partly skimmed and skimmed condensed milk
5.	IS 12176	Sweetened ultra high temperature treated condensed milk
6.	IS 13334 (Part-1)	Skimmed Milk Powder, Standard Grade
7.	IS 13334 (Part-2)	Skimmed milk-powder, extra grade
8.	IS 14543:	Packaged Drinking Water (Other than Packaged Natural Mineral Water)
9.	IS 13428	Packaged Natural Mineral Water
10.	IS 1656	Milk-cereal based weaning foods
11.	IS 3470	Hexane, Food grade.

14.7.2 Agmark (Grading and Marketing Act)

Agmark or agriculture mark is the certification mark to assure the quality of agriculture produce in India. Agmark first introduced in 1937 and later revised in the year 1986. Directorate of Marketing & Inspection (DMI) certifies AGMARK.

The main objective of AGMARK is to provide consumers with quality, unadulterated products. Quality standards for agricultural commodities are framed based on their intrinsic quality. Food safety factors are being incorporated in the standards to compete in world trade. Standards are being harmonized with international standards keeping in view the WTO requirements. Certification of agricultural commodities is carried out for the benefit of produce/manufacturer and consumer. Certification of adulteration prone commodities viz. Butter, Ghee, Vegetable Oils, Ground spices, Honey, Wheat Atta etc. is very popular. Blended Edible vegetable Oils and Fat Spread are compulsorily required to be certified under Agmark (Validity period of AGMARK is 5 years).

14.8 INTERNATIONAL ORGANISATIONS AND AGREEMENTS IN THE AREA OF FOOD STANDARDS, QUALITY, RESEARCH AND TRADE

The major organisations which are playing a key role are:

1. The Codex Alimentarius Commission: It was created in 1963 by the Food Agriculture Organization (FAO) and the World Health Organization (WHO) to develop food standards, guidelines and related texts such as codes of practice under the Joint FAO/WHO Food Standards Programme. The main purposes of this Programme are protecting health of the consumers and ensuring fair trade practices in the food trade, and promoting coordination of all food standards work undertaken by international governmental and non-governmental organizations.

2. International Organisation for Standardisation (ISO): The International Organisation for Standardisation (ISO) is a worldwide, non-governmental federation of national standards bodies (ISO member bodies). The mission of ISO is to promote the development of standardisation and related activities in the world with a view to facilitate the international exchange of goods and services, and to develop cooperation in the spheres of intellectual, scientific, technological and economic activity. The work done by ISO results in international agreements which are published as International Standards. ISO 9000 is an international reference for quality requirements. It is concerned with "Quality Management" of an organisation. Adoption of these standards is voluntary.

3. World Trade Organisation (WTO): WTO was established in 1995. The main objective of WTO is to help trade flow smoothly, freely, fairly and predictably, by administering trade agreements, settling trade disputes, assisting countries in trade policy issues. The WTO Agreement covers goods, services and intellectual property. In order to enforce adoption and implementation of standards, there is a need for a strong Food Control System. An effective food control system must consist of- (*i*) Food Inspection and (*ii*) Analytical capability.

14.8.1. International Standards and Regulations

Quality of the food is major concern worldwide now-a-days. So, each country has formulated its own standards and created agencies for strict quality control measures of the food products. Some of them are internationally accepted standards. International standards may apply to a certain region of the world or any trade between parties of different countries. Setting up of international standard for the purpose of food safety depends upon the following agreements.

- Agreement on Agriculture (AoA)
- Agreement on the Application of Sanitary and Phytosanitary, Measures (SPS Agreement)
- Agreement on Technical Barriers to Trade (TBT Agreement)
- International Health Regulation (2005)

List of main International standards and statutes:

- International Standards Organization (ISO)
- Codex Alimentaires Commission (CAC)
- World Health Organization (WHO)
- Food and Agriculture Organization (FAO)
- World Trade Organization (WTO)
- World Organization for Animal Health (WOAH)
- European Union (EU) Standards
- Food and Drugs Administration (FDA), USA
- International Plant Protection Organization (IPPO)
- Convention on Bio Diversity (CBD)
- International Commission on Microbiological Specifications for Foods (ICMSF)

14.8.2 International Standards Organization (ISO)

ISO is an independent, non-governmental international organization with a membership of 164 national standards bodies. Through its members, it brings together experts to share knowledge and develop voluntary, consensus-based, market relevant International Standards that support innovation and provide solutions to global challenges.

International Standards make things work. They give world-class specifications for products, services and systems, to ensure quality, safety and efficiency. They are instrumental in facilitating international trade.

ISO International Standards ensure that products and services are safe, reliable and of good quality. For business, they are strategic tools that reduce costs by minimizing waste and errors and increasing productivity. They help companies to access new markets, level the playing field for developing countries and facilitate free and fair global trade. ISO has published 22598 International Standards and related documents, covering almost every industry, from technology, to food safety, to agriculture and healthcare. ISO International Standards impact everyone, everywhere.

The ISO story began in 1946 when delegates from 25 countries met at the Institute of Civil Engineers in London and decided to create a new international organization 'to facilitate the international coordination and unification of industrial standards'. On 23 February 1947 the new organization, ISO, officially began operations.

Table 3: The role of International Standards Organisation (ISO) series

ISO series	Role of ISO
ISO 9000 – 1, 2, 3, 4	Quality management and quality assurance
ISO 9004 – 1	Quality management and quality system elements sub contractor
ISO 9004 – 2	Guidelines for services
ISO 9004 – 3	Guidelines for processed materials
ISO 9004 – 4	Guidelines for quality improvement
ISO 9004 – 5	Guidelines for project management
ISO 9004 – 6	Guidelines for quality plans
ISO 9004 – 7	Guidelines for configuration management
ISO 10011 – 1, 2, 3	Guidelines for auditing quality system
ISO 10012 – 1, 2	Quality assurance requirement for measuring equipment
ISO 10013	Guidelines for developing quality manual
ISO 14000-2004	Environmental Management System
ISO 10014	Guidelines for economic effect of quality
ISO 10015	Continuing education and training guidelines
ISO 22000 : 2005	Specifies requirements for a food safety management system where an organisation in food chain needs to demonstrate its ability to control food safety hazards in order to ensure that food is safe at the time of human consumption. It is applicable to all organizations, regardless of size, which are involved in any aspect of the food chain and want to implement systems that consistently provide safe products. The means of meeting any requirements of ISO 22000:2005 can be accomplished through the use of internal and/or external resources.
ISO 22004	Guidelines for application of ISO 22000-2005.
ISO 31000	Risk Management
ISO 27000	International Security Management Systems.
ISO 50001	Energy Management
ISO 18001	Occupational Health and Safety Management Systems
ISO 37001	Anti Bribery Management Systems

ISO 9000: A Quality System: Today consumer is not quantity oriented but quality oriented instead. Hence, for consumer's satisfaction, the manufacturers are focusing on quality products. The quality of a particular product is determined by the ISO, whose certification is of great importance. A 'quality system' is a mechanism by which a company can organize and manage its resources to achieve, sustain and improve quality economically.

ISO 22000:2018 : With a greater focus on risk-based thinking and aligned to ISO's high level structure, the new ISO 22000 Food Safety Management Systems can deliver additional benefits to organizations of all sizes throughout the food chain:

- Improved control over food safety activities
- Customer, statutory and regulatory compliance
- Facilitated market growth
- Increased customer, stakeholder and consumer confidence in products
- Improved risk management
- Integration with other ISO management systems

Organizations currently certified to ISO 22000:2005 will have three years to transition to the new standard.

14.8.3 Codex Alimentarius

The Codex Alimentarius Commission (CAC) commonly referred as "Codex" was created in 1963 by Food and Agriculture Organization (FAO) of the United Nations and World Health Organization (WHO) to develop food standards, guidelines and related texts such as codes of practice under the Joint FAO/WHO Food Standards Programme.

Statutes of the Codex Alimentarius Commission

Article 1- Mandate

The Codex Alimentarius Commission shall, subject to Article 5 below, be responsible for making proposals to, and shall be consulted by, the Directors General of the Food and Agriculture Organization (FAO) and the World Health Organization (WHO) on all matters pertaining to the implementation of the Joint FAO/WHO Food Standards Programme, the purpose of which is:

(*a*) protecting the health of the consumers and ensuring fair practices in the food trade;

(*b*) promoting coordination of all food standards work undertaken by international governmental and non governmental organizations;

(*c*) determining priorities and initiating and guiding the preparation of draft standards through and with the aid of appropriate organizations;

(*d*) finalizing standards elaborated under (*c*) above and publishing them in a Codex Alimentarius either as regional or worldwide standards, together with international standards already finalized by other bodies under (*b*) above, wherever this is practicable;

(*e*) amending published standards, as appropriate, in the light of developments.

Article 2- Membership

Membership of the Commission is open to all Member Nations and Associate Members of FAO and WHO which are interested in international food standards. Membership shall comprise such of these nations as have notified the Director-General of FAO or of WHO of their desire to be considered as Members.

Article 3- Observers (FAO or WHO Member Nations)

Any Member Nation or Associate Member of FAO or WHO which is not a Member of the Commission but has a special interest in the work of the Commission, may, upon request communicated to the Director-General of FAO or WHO, as appropriate, attend sessions of the Commission and of its subsidiary bodies and ad hoc meetings as observers

Article 4- Observers (Other UN Member Nations)

Nations which, while not Member Nations or Associate Members of FAO or WHO, are members of the United Nations, may be invited on their request to attend meetings of the Commission as observers in accordance with the provisions of FAO and WHO relating to the grant of observer status to nations.

Article 5-Reports and Recommendations

The Commission shall report and make recommendations to the Conference of FAO and the appropriate body of WHO through their respective Directors General. Copies of reports, including any conclusions and recommendations, will be circulated to interested Member Nations and international organizations for their information as soon as they become available.

Article 6- Executive Committee

The Commission shall establish an Executive Committee whose composition should ensure an adequate representation of the various geographical areas of the world to which the Members of the Commission belong. Between sessions, the Executive Committee shall act as the Executive organ of the Commission.

Article 7- Other Subsidiary Bodies

The Commission may establish such other subsidiary bodies as it deems necessary for the accomplishment of its task, subject to the availability of the necessary funds.

Article 8- Rules of Procedure

The Commission may adopt and amend its own Rules of Procedure which shall come into force upon approval by the Directors-General of FAO and WHO, subject to such confirmation as may be prescribed by the procedures of these Organizations.

Article 9- Expenses (Commission and Subsidiary Bodies)

The operating expenses of the Commission and of its subsidiary bodies, other than those for which a Member has accepted the Chair, shall be borne by the budget of the Joint FAO/WHO Food Standards Programme which shall be administered by FAO on behalf of the two Organizations in accordance with the financial regulations of FAO. The Directors-General of FAO and WHO shall jointly determine the respective portion of the costs of the Programme to be borne by each Organization and prepare the corresponding annual expenditure estimates for inclusion in the Regular Budgets of the two Organizations for approval by the appropriate governing bodies.

Article 10- Expenses (Preparatory Work)

All expenses (including those relating to meetings, documents and interpretation) involved in preparatory work on draft standards undertaken by Members of the Commission, either independently or upon recommendation of the Commission, shall be defrayed by the government concerned. Within the approved budgetary estimates, the Commission may, however, recommend that a specified part of the costs of the preparatory work undertaken by the government on behalf of the Commission be recognized as operating expenses of the Commission

14.8.4 SPS Agreement

The **Agreement on the Application of Sanitary and Phytosanitary** Measures, also known as the SPS Agreement, is an international treaty of the World Trade Organization (WTO). It was negotiated during the Uruguay Round of the General Agreement on Tariffs and Trade (GATT), and entered into force with the establishment of the WTO at the beginning of 1995. Broadly, the sanitary and phytosanitary ('SPS') measures covered by the agreement are those aimed at the protection of human, animal or plant life or health from certain risks.

Under the SPS agreement, the WTO sets constraints on member-states' policies relating to food safety (bacterial contaminants, pesticides, inspection and labelling) as well as animal and plant health (phytosanitation) with respect to imported pests and diseases. There are 3 standards organizations who set standards that WTO members should base their SPS methodologies on. As provided for in Article 3, they are the Codex Alimentarius Commission (Codex), World Organization for Animal Health (OIE) and the Secretariat of the International Plant Protection Convention (IPPC).

The SPS agreement is closely linked to the Agreement on Technical Barriers to Trade, which was signed in the same year and has similar goals. The TBT emerged from the Tokyo Round of WTO negotiations and was negotiated with the aim of ensuring non-discrimination in the adoption and implementation of technical regulations and standards.

WTO (World Trade Organization) (Headquarter: Geneva, Switzerland) Estd. on 1 Jan., 1995

The World Trade Organization (WTO) is the only global international organization dealing with the rules of trade between nations. At its heart are the WTO agreements, negotiated and signed by the bulk of the world's trading nations and ratified in their parliaments. The goal is to help producers of goods and services, exporters, and importers conduct their business.

The WTO has many roles: It operates a global system of trade rules, it acts as a forum for negotiating trade agreements, it settles trade disputes between its members and it supports the needs of developing countries.

There are a number of ways of looking at the World Trade Organization. It is an organization for trade opening. It is a forum for governments to negotiate trade agreements. It is a place for them to settle trade disputes. It operates a system of trade rules. Essentially, the WTO is a place where member governments try to sort out the trade problems they face with each other.

The WTO agreements are lengthy and complex because they are legal texts covering a wide range of activities. But a number of simple, fundamental principles run throughout all of these documents. These principles are the foundation of the multilateral trading system.

The WTO is run by its member governments. All major decisions are made by the membership as a whole, either by ministers (who usually meet at least once every two years) or by their ambassadors or delegates (who meet regularly in Geneva).

The WTO agreements are lengthy and complex because they are legal texts covering a wide range of activities. But a number of simple, fundamental principles run throughout all of these documents. These principles are the foundation of the multilateral trading system.

14.8.5 Fruit stickers

Fruit stickers are commonly found on fruits bought from the grocery marts than the ones purchased from the local vendors. The sticker has a PLU code printed on it. It's the International Federation for Produce Standards (IFPS) that gives out the stickers all across the world; it enables standardizing of the process

This code does not only consist of a bar code for the ease of billing but also contains important information regarding how the fruit or vegetable was grown. It is known as a "price lookup number". By carefully analyzing the sticker, we are able to make judgments regarding the origin of the fruit. Was it genetically modified? Was it grown organically and in the traditional manner? Was it injected and grown with fungicides and pesticides that pose risk upon consumption?

In case the fruit has a four-digit number such as 4080, then it implies that the fruit has been grown in the conventional manner. The produce was grown traditionally with the use of pesticides and chemicals in nutrient depleted soils. All bananas have 4011 as the code on the sticker.

If it is a five-digit number, beginning with 8, it implies that your fruit was grown with *genetic modification.* This raises an alarm and is often advised to steer away from. Produce grown with genetic modification poses negative effects on the health and could also be carcinogenic.

If the sticker has a five-digit number beginning with 9, it means that your fruit was grown organically and is best for consumption and your fruit or vegetable is *certified organic*.

If your banana or your mango has a "94011" this is a cue for safety of consumption.

Advice for Traders: Stickers without any relevant information such as traceability, grade, price, barcode etc. should not be used. The traders should avoid putting sticker or labels directly on fruits. If stickers are used, the adhesives used on the stickers must be of quality which should not cause any adverse effect on human health. A functional barrier may be used to avoid direct application of stickers on fruits and vegetables. Few fruits may be packed in transparent thin film on which sticker may be applied. The ink used on the stickers should be of food grade. It should not migrate into food.

14.9 HACCP (HAZARD ANALYSIS CRITICAL CONTROL POINT) SYSTEM

The HACCP concept was first developed in the 1960s by the NASA (National Aeronautics and Space Administration) USA working with Pillsbury to ensure crumb and pathogen free food for space travel. In 1980 (WHO/ICMSF) report on HACCP, WHO Europe recommended its use in 1987.

The system is thus designed to control organisms at the point of production and preparation.

- **Control point:** Any point in a specific food system where loss of control does not lead to an unacceptable health risk.
- **Critical control point (CCP):** Any point or procedure in a food system where control can be exercised and a hazard can be minimized or prevented.
- **Critical limit:** One or more prescribed tolerances that must be met to ensure that a CCP effectively controls a microbiological health hazard.
- **CCP decision tree:** A sequence of questions to assist in determining whether a control point is a CCP.
- **Corrective action:** Procedures followed when a deviation occurs.
- **Deviation:** Failure to meet a required critical limit for a CCP.
- **HACCP plan:** The written document that delineates the formal procedures to be followed in accordance with these general principles.
- **Hazard:** Any biological, chemical, or physical property that may cause an unacceptable consumer health risk (unacceptable contamination, toxin levels, growth, and/or survival of undesirable organisms).

- **Monitoring:** A planned sequence of observations or measurements of critical limits designed to produce an accurate record and intended to ensure that the critical limit maintains product safety.
- **Risk category:** One of six categories prioritizing risk based on food hazards.
- **Validation:** That element of verification focused on collecting and evaluating scientific and technical information to determine whether the HACCP plan, when properly implemented, will effectively control the hazards.
- **Verification:** Methods, procedures, and tests used to determine whether the HACCP system is in compliance with the HACCP plan.

HACCP principles: Although interpreted variously, the ICMSF and NACMCF view HACCP as a natural and systematic approach to food safety and as consisting of the following seven principles:

1. Assess the hazards and risks associated with the growing, harvesting, raw materials, ingredients, processing, manufacturing, distribution, marketing, preparation, and consumption of the food in question.
2. Determine the CCP(s) required controlling the identified hazards.
3. Establish the critical limits that must be met at each identified CCP.
4. Establish procedures to monitor the CCP(s).
5. Establish corrective actions to be taken when there is a deviation identified by monitoring a given CCP.
6. Establish procedures for verification that the HACCP system is working correctly.
7. Establish effective record-keeping systems that document the HACCP plan.

Limitations of HACCP:

1. HACCP requires the education of nonprofessional food handlers, especially in the food service industry and in homes; whether this will be achieved remains to be seen. The failure of these individuals to get a proper understanding of HACCP could lead to its failure.
2. To be effective, this concept must be accepted not only by food processors but also by food inspectors and the public. Its ineffective application at any level can be detrimental to its overall success for a product.
3. It is anticipated that experts will differ as to whether a given step is a CCP and how best to monitor such steps. This has the potential of eroding the confidence of others in HACCP.
4. The adoption of HACCP by industry has the potential of giving false assurance to consumers that a product is safe, and, therefore, there is no need to exercise the usual precautions between the purchase and consumption of a product. Consumers need to be informed that most outbreaks of food borne illness are caused by errors in food-handling in homes and food service establishments and that no matter what steps a processor takes, HACCP principles must be observed after foods are purchased for consumption.

14.10 RISK ANALYSIS

Food safety-risk analysis: A food safety-risk analysis is essential not only to produce or manufacture high quality goods and products to ensure safety and protect public health, but also to comply with international and national standards and market regulations.

Risk analysis is defined for the purposes of the Codex Alimentarius Commission as "A process consisting of three components: risk management, risk assessment, and risk communication.

Risk management: Risk management is defined for the purposes of the Codex Alimentarius Commission as "The process, distinct from risk assessment, of weighing policy alternatives, in consultation with all interested parties, considering risk assessment and other factors relevant for the health protection of consumers and for the promotion of fair trade practices, and, if needed, selecting appropriate prevention and control options.

Risk assessment: It forms scientific basis for control actions. It consists of four compartments

(*i*) Hazard identification (*ii*) Hazard characterization
(*iii*) Exposure assessment (*iv*) Risk characterization.

By going through these risk assessment processes, hazards associated with food or food ingredients are evaluated and potential risk to the population is assessed, facilitating formulation of appropriate risk management actions required and risk communication messages to protect public health.

Approaches to food safety risk assessment: There are different approaches which can be adopted:

a) examination of each operation which could create food hazards, *e.g.* sandwich preparation, cleaning procedures;

b) examination of hazards and risks in groups, *e.g.* catering equipment, ingredients, delivery vehicles; and/or

c) examination of specific food production areas, kitchens, serveries.

Principal features of a food safety risk assessment: A food safety risk assessment must:

a) identify all the hazards associated with the food preparation process, equipment or area and evaluate the risks arising from those hazards, taking into account current legal requirements, such as the Food Hygiene (England) Regulations;

b) record the significant findings;

c) identify any part of the process, feature of equipment and part of a premises, as the case may be, where risks could arise;

d) evaluate existing food safety controls, stating whether or not they are satisfactory and, if not, what action should be taken;

e) evaluate the need for the provision of information, instruction, training and supervision of groups of food handlers;

f) judge and record the probability or likelihood of an incident occurring as a result of uncontrolled risk, including the 'worst case' likely outcome;

g) record any circumstances arising from the assessment where significant risks to food safety could arise; and

h) provide an action plan giving information on implementation of additional controls, in order of priority, and with a realistic timescale.

Maintaining the risk assessment: The risk assessment should be maintained. Typical monitoring systems include:

a) preventive maintenance inspections;

b) cleaning efficiency inspections;

c) hygiene audits and inspections;

d) ensuring compliance with food safety specifications to suppliers;

e) inspections to detect the presence of infestation and to monitor the effectiveness of current pest control activities;

f) temperature checks of food commodities;

g) food supplier audits and inspections.

Useful information on checking performance against control standards can also be obtained reactively from the following activities:

a) investigation of food safety incidents;

b) food sampling activities;

c) observation of food handling practices; and

d) health surveillance of food handlers.

Reviewing the risk assessment: The frequency of review depends upon the level of risk in the operation. Further, if a serious food safety incident occurs in the organisation, or elsewhere, but is possible in the organisation, and where a check on the risk assessment shows no assessment or a gap in assessment procedures, then a review is necessary.

Risk communication: Risk communication is defined for the purposes of the Codex Alimentarius Commission as "The interactive exchange of information and opinions throughout the risk analysis process concerning hazards and risks, risk-related factors and risk perceptions, among risk assessors, risk managers, consumers, industry, the academic community and other interested parties, including the explanation of risk assessment findings and the basis of risk management decisions."

Preventing or controlling the risks: A range of controls must be considered, including:

a) well-managed cleaning procedures;

b) temperature monitoring of freezers, display units, cold stores and refrigerators and of frozen foods at time of delivery;

c) planned preventive maintenance systems covering, for instance, structural items, processing equipment, hot water supplies and mechanical ventilation systems;

d) effective structural proofing against various forms of infestation, together with monitoring the performance of pest control contractors;

e) food labelling, dating and stock rotation;

f) measures to protect food from risk of contamination and cross contamination;

g) the provision of information, instruction and training for all staff;

h) health surveillance of food handlers in particular, including the use of health questionnaires for newly-appointed food handlers;

i) hygienic storage and disposal of waste, together with strict control over rejected food;

j) checking the quality and fitness of fresh high risk food supplied from external sources, *e.g.* wholesalers, butchers; and

k) the operation of a formally documented product recall system.

14.10 WORLD HEALTH ORGANIZATION (WHO)

World Health Organization (WHO), the United Nations' specialized agency for Health was founded in 1948.

- Its **headquarters** are situated in **Geneva, Switzerland.**
- There are 194 Member States, 150 country offices, six regional offices.
- It is an inter-governmental organization and works in collaboration with its member states usually through the Ministries of Health.
- The WHO provides leadership on global health matters, shaping the health research agenda, setting norms and standards, articulating evidence-based policy options, providing technical support to countries and monitoring and assessing health trends.
- It began functioning on **April 7**, 1948–a date now being celebrated every year as **World Health Day.**

What are the Objectives?

- To act as the **directing and coordinating authority on international health work.**
- **To establish and maintain effective collaboration with the United Nations,** specialized agencies, governmental health administrations, professional groups and such other organizations as may be deemed appropriate.
- To **provide assistance** to the Governments, upon request, **in strengthening health services.**
- To **promote cooperation among scientific and professional groups** which contribute to the advancement of health.

How is it Governed?

World Health Assembly

- **World Health Assembly (WHA)** is WHO's decision-making body attended by delegations from all of WHO's member states,
- It is held yearly at the headquarters of WHO, *i.e.*, **Geneva, Switzerland.**
- Specific health agenda prepared by the Executive Board remains the focus of this assembly.
- Since the start of the Covid-19 pandemic, 2022's assembly is the first in-person assembly.
- In May 2022, World Health Assembly's 75th session was held at World Health Organization (WHO).

Functions

- The Health Assembly **determines the policies of the Organization.**
- It supervises the financial policies of the Organization and reviews and approves the budget.
- It reports to the **Economic and Social Council** in accordance with any agreement between the Organization and the United Nations.

The Secretariat

The Secretariat comprises of the Director-General and such technical and administrative staff as the Organization may require.

- The **Director-General is appointed by the Health Assembly** on the nomination of the Board on such terms as the Health Assembly may determine.

Membership and Associate Membership

- Members of the United Nations may become Members of the Organization.
- Territories or groups of territories which are not responsible for the conduct of their international relations may be admitted as Associate Members by the Health Assembly.
- The **World Health Organisation (WHO) characterised Covid-19** as a **pandemic** in 2021.

CHAPTER 15

FOOD AUTHORITY AND SAFETY OFFICER

15.1 FOOD AUTHORITY

Any Governmental Entity responsible for the regulation of food products or the enactment, adoption, promulgation or enforcement of Food Safety Laws.

Composition of Food Authority

Food authority consists of (1+22) one chairperson and 22 members.The Chairperson and other Members of the Food Authority shall be appointed in such a manner so as to secure the highest standards of competence, broad range of relevant expertise, and shall represent, the broadest possible geographic distribution within the country.

The Chairperson shall be appointed by the Central Government from amongst thepersons of eminence in the field of food science or from amongst the persons from the administration who have been associated with the subject and is either holding or has held the position of not below the rank of Secretary to the Government of India.

The Food Authority shall consist of a Chairperson and the following twenty-two members out of which one-third shall be women, namely

- Seven Members, not below the rank of a Joint Secretary to the Government of India, to be appointed by the Central Government, to respectively represent the Ministries of agriculture, commerce, consumer affairs, food processing, health, legal affairs and small scale industries.
- Two representatives from food industry, one from small scale.
- Two representatives from consumer organisation.
- Three eminent food technologist or scientist.
- Five members to be appointed by rotation every three years, one each in serial from the Zones as specified in the First Schedule to represent the States and the Union territories.
- Two persons to represent farmer organisation
- One person to represent retail organisation.

Term and Salary of Food Authority

The Chairperson and the members other than *ex officio* Members shall hold office for a term of three years from the date on which they enter upon their offices, and shall be eligible for re-appointment for a further period of three years. Provided that the Chairperson shall not hold office as such after he has attained theage of sixty-five years and in the case of a Member, the age of sixty-two years.

The salary and allowances payable to, and the other terms and conditions of service of the Chairperson and Members other than *ex-officio* Members shall be such as maybe prescribed by the Central Government.

Removal of chairperson or members done if he is adjudged as insolvent, convict any offence, acquired any financial interest, mentally incapable of acting as a member.

Chief Excutive Officer (CEO)

Chief Executive Officer of the Food Authority, not below the rank of Additional Secretary to the Government of India, who shall be the Member-Secretary of the Authority, to be appointed by the Central Government.

CEO looks after day to day administration, drawing up of proposal of work, implementation of work programme, ensuring food authority to carry work according to the requirement of users. Preparation of statement of revenue and expenditure, maintaining contact with the Central government. Every year he submits general report, programme of work, annual account report of previous year and budget for coming year.

CEO have administrative control on officer and other employees, he exercise power of commissioner of food safety, he approves financial expenditure of food safety.

The Central Advisory Committee (CAC) shall consist of two members each to represent the interests of food industry, agriculture, consumers, relevant research bodies and food laboratories and all Commissioners of Food Safety, and the Chairperson of the ScientificCommittee shall be *ex officio* member.

The representatives of the concerned Ministries or Departments of the Central Government in Agriculture, Animal Husbandry and Dairying, Bio-technology, Commerce and Industry, consumer Affairs, Environment and Forests, Food Processing Industries, Health, Panchayati Raj, Small Scale Industries and Food and Public Distribution or14 government institutes organisations and government recognised farmers' shall be invited to the deliberations of the Central Advisory Committee.

Functions of CAC are:

- Cooperation between food authority and enforcement agencies and organisation operating in field of food.
- CAC advises food authority on performance of duties, prioritization of work, identification of risk, pooling of knowledge.
- CAC shall meet at least three times a year.

The frame work of food safety regulators are as follows:

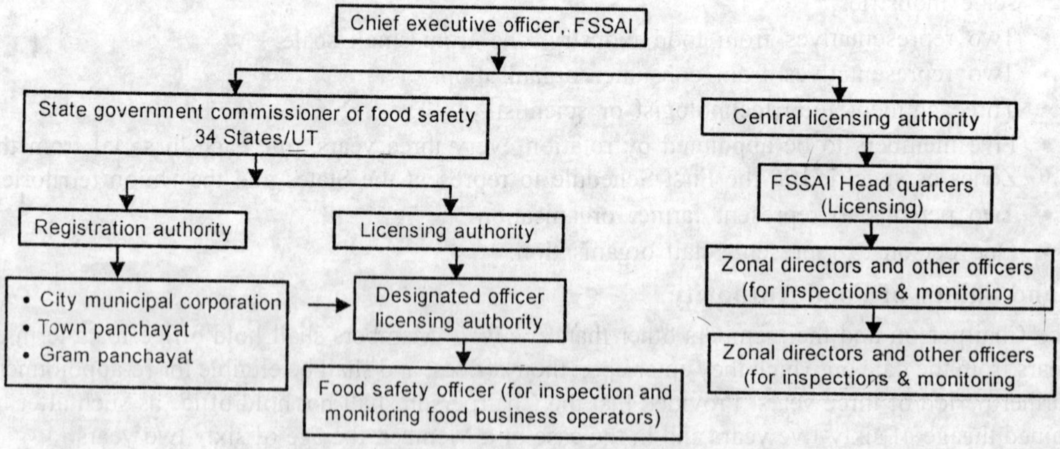

Fig. 1: Framework of Food Safety Regulators

15.1.1 Duties of Food Authority

- It shall be the duty of the Food Authority to regulate and monitor the manufacture, processing, distribution, sale and import of food so as to ensure safe and wholesome food.
- Conduct survey of enforcement and administration of this Act in the country.
- Food labelling standards including claims on health, nutrition, special dietary uses and food category systems for foods and the manner in which and the procedure subject to which risk analysis, risk assessment, risk communication and risk management shall be undertaken.
- The Food Authority Advices to GOI, State Govt. and Individuals.
- Provide scientific advice and technical support to the Central Government and the State Governments in matters of framing the policy and rules in areas which have a direct or indirect bearing on food safety and nutrition. Also for improving co-operation with interorganization.
- Search, collect, collate, analyse and summarise relevant scientific and technical data particularly relating to food consumption and the exposure of individuals to risks related to the consumption of food.
- Promote, co-ordinate and issue guidelines for the development of risk assessment methodologies and monitor and conduct and forward messages on the health and nutritional risks of food to the Central Government, State Governments and Commissioners of Food Safety.
- Provide scientific and technical advice and assistance to the Central Government and the State Governments in implementation of crisis management procedures with regard to food safety and to draw up a general plan for crisis management and work in close co-operation with the crisis unit set up by the Central Government in this regard.
- Establish a system of network of organisations with the aim to facilitate a scientific co operation framework by the co-ordination of activities, the exchange of information, the development and implementation of joint projects, the exchange of expertise and best practices in the fields within the. **Food Authority's responsibility.**
- Provide, whether within or outside their area, training programmes in food safety and standards for persons who are intend to become involved in food businesses, whether as food business operators or employees.
- Undertake any other task assigned to it by the Central Government to carry out the objects of this Act;
- Contribute to the development of international technical standards for food, sanitary and phyto-sanitary standards.
- Contribute, where relevant and appropriate to the development of agreement on recognition of the equivalence of specific food related measures.
- Promote co-ordination of work on food standards undertaken by international governmental and nongovernmental organisations.
- Promote consistency between international technical standards and domestic food standards while ensuring that the level of protection adopted in the country does not reduce.
- Promote general awareness as to Food Safety and Food Standards.
- The Food Authority shall make it public without undue delay–

- The opinions of the Scientific Committee and the Scientific Panel immediately after adoption;
- The annual declarations of interest made by members of the Food Authority, the Chief Executive Officer, members of the Advisory committee and members of the scientific committee and scientific Panel, as well as the declarations of interest if any, made in relation to items on the agenda of meetings.
- The results of its scientific studies; and
- The annual report of its activities.

15.2 FOOD SAFETY OFFICER

Food Safety Officers are the field officers and the backbone of entire food safety compliance structure. Food Safety Officers are appointed by the Commissioner of Food Safety, through notification, for such local areas as he may assign to them for the purpose of performing functions under this Act and the rules and regulations made there under. The State Government may authorise any officer of the State Government having the qualifications prescribed to perform the functions of a Food Safety Officer within a specified jurisdiction. For effective discharge of its functions, the Food Safety Officer is required to have adequate knowledge of the FSS Act, Rule and Regulations and their application in discharge of their duties, proper procedure for inspection and sampling and various other aspects of food safety.

Types of Food Safety Officers

A food safety officer is a specialist who is qualified to examine food samples that have been gathered from various locations. If dangerous foods or crude materials are used in the production of the food item, they can notify the manufacturer, distributor, or vendor.

Below is a list of some of the main categories used by food safety officials.

Food Technologist: A food technologist makes sure that strict hygiene and sanitation standards are maintained when preparing and packaging food. In addition to testing and inspecting food samples, they monitor the use of additives and additional ingredients in food products.

Food researchers: A food scientist examines food trials to take into account how food kinds are handled and how they can get weaker. They examine the food sample to look for any potentially dangerous ingredients or materials. They also discover methods for food preservation and packaging.

Food and Drug Administrator: The role of the Food and Drug Administrator is to protect public health by assuring the safety of food products and, in addition, to decrease the harmful effects of tobacco products that are subject to regulation.

Health Inspector: The Food and Drug Administrator's duties include monitoring the safety of food goods and minimizing the negative impact of regulated tobacco products

Food Safety Officer Qualification

Food Safety Officer shall be a whole time officer and shall, on the date on which he is so appointed possesses the following:

1. a degree in Food Technology or Dairy Technology or Biotechnology or Oil Technology or Agricultural Science or Veterinary Sciences or Bio-Chemistry or Microbiology or Masters Degree in Chemistry or degree in medicine from a recognized University, or
2. any other equivalent/recognized qualification notified by the Central Government, and
3. has successfully completed training as specified by the Food Authority in a recognized institute or Institution approved for the purpose.

Provided that no person who has any financial interest in the manufacture, import or sale of any article of food shall be appointed to be a Food Safety Officer under this rule

1. On the date of commencement of these Rules, a person who has already been appointed as a Food Inspector under the provisions of Prevention of Food Adulteration Act, 1954, may perform the duties of the Food Safety Officer if notified by the state/Central government if

the officer fulfils such other conditions as may be prescribed for the post of Food Safety Officer by the State Government.

2. State Government may, in cases where a Medical Officer of health administration of local area has been performing the function of food Inspector under the Prevention of Food Adulteration Act, 1954, assign the powers and duties of Food Safety Officer to such Medical Officer in charge of health administration of that area.

15.2.1. Powers and Duties of a Food Safety Officer

A food safety officer has a very important role to play as an enforcement officer and in ensuring food safety and quality. The powers and duties of a food safety officer include the following:

(*i*) To issue registration for small and petty food business operators in their capacity as a Registering Authority within the area assigned to him.

(*ii*) To inspect the premises of small and petty food business operators and ensure compliance as per Schedule 4 (Part I) of Food Safety and Standards (Licensing and Registration of Food Businesses), Regulations, 2011, within the area assigned to him.

(*iii*) To inspect, as frequently as may be prescribed by the Designated Officer, all food establishments licensed for manufacturing, handling, packing or selling of an article of food within the area assigned to him.

(*iv*) To satisfy himself that the conditions of licenses are being complied with by each of the Food Business Operators carrying on business within the area assigned to him and report to the Designated Officer.

(*v*) To recommend Designated Officer to issue of improvement notices to the Food Business Operator whenever necessary giving the food business operators an opportunity in order to comply with the conditions of license within a prescribed time limit.

(*vi*) To make such inquiries and inspections as may be necessary to detect the manufacture, storage or sale of articles of food in contravention of the Act or rules framed there under.

(*vii*) To investigate any complaint which may be made to him in writing in respect of any contravention of the provisions of the Act, or rules framed there under.

(*viii*) To stop and inspect any vehicle suspected to contain any unsafe food or food which does not comply with the provisions of this Act and rules, intended for sale or delivery for human consumption.

(*ix*) To recommend to the Designated Officer giving specific grounds, suitable action in regard to licenses issued to any Food Business Operator, if on inspection the Food Safety Officer finds that the Food Business Operator had violated the conditions for grant of license.

(*x*) Take a sample of any food, or any substance, which appears to him to be intended for sale, or to have been sold for human consumption.

(*xi*) Take a sample of any article of food or substance which is found by him on or in any such premises; which he has reason to believe that it may be required as evidence in proceedings under any of the provisions of this Act or of the Regulations or orders made there under.

(*xii*) Take a sample and keep it in the safe custody of the food business operator such article offood after taking a sample; and in both cases send the same for analysis to a Food Analyst for the local area within which such sample has been taken.

(*xiii*) To procure and send for analysis if necessary, samples of any article of food which he has reason to believe or on the basis of information received including from a purchaser are being manufactured, stocked or sold or exhibited for sale in contravention ofthe provisions ofthe Act, or rules and regulations framed there under.

(*xiv*) To draw samples for purposes of surveillance, survey and research, which shall not be used for prosecution.

(xv) Where any sample is taken, its cost calculated at the rate at which the article is usually sold to the public shall be paid to the person from whom it is taken.

(xvi) To carry out food safety surveillance to identify and address the safety hazards.

(xvii) To seize any article of food which appears to the Food Safety Officer to be in contravention of this Act or the regulations made there under.

(xviii) Where any article of food seized is of a perishable nature and the Food Safety Officer is satisfied that such article of food is so deteriorated that it is unfit for human consumption, the Food Safety Officer may, after giving notice in writing to the food business operator, cause the same to be destroyed.

(xix) Any adulterant found in the possession of a manufacturer or distributor of, or dealer in, any article of food or in any of the premises occupied by him.

(xx) Where any books of account or other documents are seized, the Food Safety Officer shall, within a period not exceeding thirty days from the date of seizure, return the same to the person from whom they were seized after copies there of or extracts there from as certified by that person.

(xxi) To respond to incidents of food poisoning in his area and to send report to and assist the Designated Officer to enable him to initiate corrective action.

(xxii) To maintain a data base of all Food Business within the area assigned to him.

(xxiii) To maintain a record of all inspections made and action taken by him in the performance of his duties, including the taking of samples and seizure of stocks, and to submit copies of such records to the Designated Officer as directed in this regard.

(xxiv) When any adulterant is seized under, the burden of proving that such adulterant is not meant for purposes of adulteration shall be on the person from whose possession such adulterant was seized.

(xxv) To facilitate preparation of Food safety plans for Panchayat and Municipalities in accordance with the parameters and guidelines given in schedule IV of Chapter 3 of Regulations.

(xxvi) To detain imported packages which are suspected to contain articles of food, the import or sale of which is prohibited.

(xxvii) To coordinate with the Food Business Operators within his area of operation and facilitate the introduction of food safety systems by the Food Business Operator.

(xxviii) To perform such other duties, as may be entrusted to him by the Designated Officer or Food Safety Commissioner having jurisdiction in the local area concerned.

15.2.2 Liability of Food Safety Officer in Certain Cases

Any Food Safety Officer while exercising powers under this Act or the rules and regulations made there under, seizes any article of food or adulterant without any reasonable ground or with intention to harass or commits any other act to the injury of any person without having reason to believe that such act is necessary for the execution of his duty, will be guilty of an offence under this Act and is liable to a penalty which may extend to one Lac rupees.

However ,in case any false complaint is made against a Food Safety Officer and it is proved so, the complainant will be guilty of an offence under this Act and will be punishable with fine which should not be less than fifty thousand rupees but may extend to one Lac rupees.

Note: The Commissioner of Food Safety and Designated Officer can exercise the same powers as are conferred on the Food Safety Officer and follow the same procedure specified in this Act.

15.2.3 Commissioner of Food Safety of the State

Functions:

- Prohibit the manufacture, storage, distribution or sale of any article of food.
- Survey of the Industrial Units.
- Conduct or organise training programmes.
- Uniform implementation of the standards and other requirements as specified.
- Ensure a high standard of objectivity, accountability, practicability, transparency and credibility.
- Sanction of prosecution for offences punishable with imprisonment under this Act.
- Other functions.

15.2.4 Designated Officer

The Commissioner of Food Safety shall appoint the Designated Officer, who shall not be below the rank of a Sub-Divisional Officer, to be in-charge of food safety administration in such area as may be specified by regulations. There shall be a Designated Officer for each district. The Duties to be performed by the Designated Officer shall be as follows, namely—

- Issue or cancel licence.
- Prohibit the sale of any article of food.
- Receive report and samples of article of foods.
- Recommend to the Commissioner of Food Safety for sanction to launch prosecutions.
- Sanction or launch prosecutions.
- Maintain record of all inspections made by Food Safety Officers and action taken by them in the performance of their duties;
- Investigate any complaint.
- Other duties.

15.2.5 Food Analysist

The Commissioner of Food Safety may, by notification, appoint such persons as he thinks fit, having the qualifications prescribed by the Central Government, to be Food Analysts for such local areas as may be assigned to them by the Commissioner of Food Safety.

Duties of Food Analyst:

- On receipt of a package containing a sample for analysis from a Food Safety Officer or any other person, the Food Analyst shall compare the seal on the container and the outer cover with specimen impression received separately and shall note the conditions of the seal there on.
- Provided that in case a sample container received by the Food Analyst is found to be in broken condition or unfit for analysis, he shall within a period of seven days from the date of receipt of such sample inform the Designated Officer about the same and send requisition to him for sending second part of the sample.
- The Food Analyst shall cause to be analysed such samples of article of food as may be sent to him by Food Safety Officer or by any other person authorized.
- The Food Analyst shall, within a period of fourteen days from the date of receipt of any sample for analysis, send Designated Officer, four copies of the report indicating the method of sampling and analysis.

- Where such sample is received under purchaser, a copy of the report indicating the method of sampling and analysis to the person who had purchased such article of food with a copy to the Designated Officer.
- If in case the sample cannot be analysed within fourteen days of its receipt, the Food Analyst shall inform the Designated Officer and the Commissioner of Food Safety giving reasons and specifying the time to be taken for analysis.
- An appeal against the report of Food Analyst shall lie before the Designated Officer who shall, if he so decides, refer the matter to the referral food laboratory as notified by the Food Authority for opinion.

Proceduce of taking sample by FSO

15.2.5.1 Labeling of the samples

- The label shall bear:
  - Code number of the sample
  - Name of the sender with his official designation
  - Date and place of collection
  - Nature of articles being sent for analysis
  - Nature and quantity of preservative, if any, added to the sample.
- Date and place of collection
  - Grade.
  - Agmark label No./Batch No.
  - Name of packing station.

15.3 VARIOUS IMPORTANT REGULATIONS UNDER THE FSS ACT

The Food Safety Officer should be well acquainted with following Regulations notified by the Food Safety and Standards Authority of India under the FSS Act.

(*i*) Food Safety and Standards (Licensing and Registration of Food Businesses), Regulations 2011

(*ii*) Food Safety and Standards (Food Product Standards and Food Additives), Regulations 2011

(*iii*) Food Safety and Standards (Prohibition and Restriction on Sales), Regulations 2011

(*iv*) Food Safety and Standards (Packaging and Labelling), Regulations 2011

(*v*) Food Safety and Standards (Contaminants, Toxins and Residues), Regulations 2011

(*vi*) Food Safety and Standards (Laboratory and Sampling Analysis), Regulations 2011

(*vii*) Food Safety and Standards (Food or Health Supplements, Nutraceuticals, Food for Special Dietary Uses, Foods for Special Medical Purpose, Functional Foods and Novel Foods), Regulations 2016

(*viii*) Food Safety and Standards (Food Recall Procedure), Regulations 2017

(*ix*) Food Safety and Standards (Import), Regulations 2017

ADDITIONAL NOTES

HYDROCOLLOIDS

Hydrocolloids, also commonly referred to as gums, originate from various sources and most of these are not digested in the human digestive system. Carrageenan, alginate and agar originate from seaweed whilst materials such as guar gum, locust bean gum (LBG), cellulose, starch and pectin are of plant origin. Xanthan gum is produced by fermentation and gelatin is derived from animal collagen. Xanthan and guar gum are cold-swelling materials, whilst carrageenan and LBG are hot-swelling materials.

Gums fulfill several functions in meat products.

- By forming a gel or acting as a thickener (depending on the type of gum) they help to reduce cooking loss and therefore assist in increasing yield
- The formation of gel assists in obtaining texture in a meat product.
- A higher yield results in a more succulent product.
- Gums assist against syneresis in the finished product.
- Gums do not interfere with the activation of protein within meat products.

ALVEOGRAPH

An alveograph is a rheological tool used to assess the baking performance of flours used in baked products (bread, noodles, biscuits etc.) The alveograph test provides results that are common specifications used by flour millers and processors to ensure a more consistent process and product. The alveograph is well suited for measuring the dough characteristics of weak gluten wheats. Weak gluten flour with low *P* value (strength of gluten) and long *L* value (extensibility) is preferred for cakes and other confectionery products. Strong gluten flour will have high *P* values and is preferred for breads.

The alveograph test measures and records the force required to blow and break a bubble of dough. *Parameters measured by the alveograph test are*:

- ***P Value*** is the force required to blow the bubble of dough. It is indicated by the maximum height of the curve and is expressed in millimeters (mm).
- ***L Value*** is the extensibility of the dough before the bubble breaks. It is indicated by the length of the curve and is expressed in millimeters (mm).
- ***P/L Ratio*** is the balance between dough strength and extensibility.
- ***W Value*** is the area under the curve. It is a combination of dough strength (*P* value) and extensibility (*L* value) and is expressed in joules.
- ***Elasticity Index:*** Compares pressure after 200 ml volume of air hs been blown into the dough test piece or bubble versus the maximum pressure (*P*).

Weak gluten flour has lower *P* values than strong gluten flour.

EXTENSOGRAPH

Extensograph test are useful in determining the gluten strength and bread-making characteristics of flour. The effect of fermentation time and additives on dough performance can also be evaluated.

FALLING NUMBER

The level of enzyme activity measured by the falling number test affects product quality. Yeast in bread dough, for example, requires sugars to develop properly and therefore needs some level of enzyme activity in the dough. Too much enzyme activity, however, means that too much sugar and too little starch are present. Since starch provides the supporting structure of bread, too much activity results in sticky dough during processing and poor texture in the finished product. If the falling number is too high, enzymes can be added to the flour in various ways to compensate. If the falling number is too low, enzymes cannot be removed from the flour or wheat, which results in a serious problem that makes the flour unusable.

- A high falling number (for example, above 300 seconds) indicates minimal enzyme activity and sound quality wheat or flour.
- A low falling number (for example, below 250 seconds) indicates substantial enzyme activity and sprout damaged wheat or flour.

FARINOGRAPH

The farinograph test is one of the most commonly used flour quality tests in the world. The results are used as parameters in formulation to estimate the amount of water required to make a dough, to evaluate the effects of ingredients on mixing properties, to evaluate flour blending requirements, and to check flour uniformity. The results are also used to predict processing effects, including mixing requirements for dough development, tolerance to over-mixing, and dough consistency during production. Farinograph results are also useful for predicting finished product texture characteristics. For example, strong dough mixing properties are related to firm product texture.

- The farinograph determines dough and gluten properties of a flour sample by measuring the resistance of dough against the mixing action of paddles (blades).
- Farinograph results include absorption, arrival time, stability time, peak time, departure time, and mixing tolerance index.

MIXOGRAPH

The mixograph determines dough and gluten properties of flour by measuring the resistance of dough against the mixing action. Mixograph results include water absorption, peak time, and mixing tolerance. The mixograph curve indicates gluten strength, optimum dough development time, mixing tolerance (tolerance to over-mixing), and other dough characteristics. The amount of water added (absorption) affects the position of the curve on the graph paper. Less water increases dough consistency and moves the curve upward. The mixograph test quickly analyzes small quantities of flour for dough gluten strength. Wheat breeders use mixograph results to screen early generation lines for dough gluten strength. Flour water absorption measured by the mixograph often serves as bake absorption in bread baking tests.

ACCELERATED FREEZE DRYING

This is a process of food dehydration for certain foods such as peas, prawns and coffee. The process involves placing prepared pieces of quick-frozen food under vacuum and gently heating. As a result, 'sublimation' takes place where crystals of ice turn to water vapour without melting. On completion of the process, the food has a brittle and sponge-like texture. Foods treated in this way have a much longer shelf life providing the packaging is kept intact. When water is added to the product, it enters much faster than with conventional dried products. Furthermore, when reconstituted (or re-hydrated), the food is similar in nature to that of the original food. Re-hydrated foods should be treated in the same way as fresh foods. In AFD, drying time is considerable reduced by hastening heat transfer by heating in a controlled way.

'BEST BEFORE' DATE

This is a system of marking food products with a specific date before which the food will retain its original quality or 'shelf life'. The system is generally applied to low risk foods, some of which have long shelf-lives, such as canned goods, drinks, biscuits and other dry products.

BLAST CHILLING AND FREEZING

Blast chilling is the process of using a fan-assisted refrigeration cabinet or room which lowers the temperature of cooked food very quickly to around 5°C prior to going into refrigerated storage. In order to prevent bacterial multiplication, the process should be completed within 90 minutes. Attention must be paid to the specific size of the food commodities being chilled, particularly in the case of meat joints. Ideally these joints should be no more than 2.5 kg in weight and regularly shaped. Blast freezing takes place in similar manner to blast chilling. Here hot cooked food is quickly reduced to between -18°C and –22°C before being put into refrigerated storage.

CLEANING-IN-PLACE (CIP) SYSTEMS

CIP systems are commonly installed in those premises manufacturing and/or bottling liquid products, such as beer, milk and mineral waters. The system involves extensive pipework connected to all items of equipment which come into contact with the product at various stages of the process. At the completion of the food manufacturing process, or following the completion of a particular batch, the whole of the plant is flushed with a series of detergents and/or detergent/sanitisers followed by hot and cold water rinses. Detergents may be held within the system at a particular temperature for a specified length of time with a view to clearing soiling, food residues and other deposits. Most CIP systems tend to be fully automatic and controlled from a central location. CIP system operate on a combination of four simple principles. Temperature, chemical concentration, mechanical action and time.

CLEANING OUT OF PLACE (COP): Cleaning Out of Place is defined as a method of cleaning equipment items by removing them from their operational area and taking them to a designated cleaning station for cleaning. It requires dismantling an apparatus, washing it in a central washing area using an automated system, and checking it at reassembly.

DEEP FREEZE

This is the process of storing a range of foods at –18°C and below at which the growth of many micro-organisms is virtually reduced and the shelf life greatly increased. However, storage at these temperatures does not necessarily kill pathogenic bacteria and, on thawing, bacteria will commence to multiply. Spoilage enzymes are also inhibited at these temperatures, but long term storage may result in loss of quality. Meat, Fish and Vegetables are preserved by deep freezing.

FREEZER BURN

Freezer burn is a condition that occurs when frozen food has been damaged by dehydration and oxidation due to air reaching the food. It is generally caused by food not being securely wrapped in air-tight packaging. Freezer burn appears as grayish-brown leathery spots on frozen food and occurs when air reaches the food's surface and dries the product. Color changes result from chemical changes in the food's pigment. Freezer burn does not make the food unsafe; it merely causes dry spots in foods. The food remains usable and edible, but removing the freezer burns will improve the flavor. The dehydration of freezer-burned food is caused by water sublimating from the food into the surrounding atmosphere. The lost water may then be deposited elsewhere in the food and packaging as snow-like crystals

ENDOTOXIN

These are hazardous toxic substances which are released from the cells of bacteria and other micro-organisms, including various fungi. They remain within the cell during its normal life and it is only after the death of the cell, damage to the cell wall or during the formation of spores, that they may be released. Endotoxins are associated with *Escherichia coli*, *Salmonellae* and *Clostridium perfringens* and the symptoms of infection include diarrhoea, fever and local tissue shock.

ENTEROTOXIN

These are poisonous waste products which attack the stomach and intestine linings causing diarrhoea and vomiting. Both endotoxins and exotoxins fall within this group. Enterotoxins are particularly poisonous and resistant to heat, being capable of surviving at a temperature of 100°C for 30 minutes. However, the bacteria which produce enterotoxins, such as *Staphylococcus aureus*, are less heat-resistant and the presence of bacteria in a food product is not vital for illness to arise.

EXTRINSIC CONTAMINATION

This is the contamination arising from sources other than the raw food itself, namely external sources of contamination, such as foreign bodies. During manufacturing and catering processes, food can be exposed to extrinsic contamination from items such as glass particles, wood splinters, hairs, small personal items, such as pens, rings and hair grips, rodent droppings, dead insects, cigarette ends, plastic items and metal objects falling from badly-maintained plant and equipment. Contamination may also be associated with poor standards of building maintenance resulting in flaking paintwork, rust from overhead pipes and contaminated water leaking from pipes, all of which could enter the product at some stage of preparation. Food safety management systems should explore the potential for extrinsic contamination at the various stages of processing.

HIGH RISK FOODS

Those foods, typically with a high moisture and protein content, that are at particular risk of contamination by bacterial spoilage or the action of pathogens. High risk foods will, under favourable conditions, support the growth of pathogenic bacteria. High risk foods include:

- meat, fish, eggs and prepared products incorporating these foods, together with smoked or cured meat which has been sliced and cured fish
- soft cheeses ripened with moulds or micro-organisms
- smoked and cured fish
- prepared vegetable salads
- fresh cream and artificial cream cakes
- ice cream and frozen desserts

- milk-based desserts
- cooked cereals, such as rice, beans and vegetables
- sandwiches

Strict temperature control is required with respect to these foods. Such foods should be stored at below 8°C or above 63°C.

HYDROGEN SWELL

The most important chemical spoilage of canned foods is hydrogen swell. The buildup of hydrogen gas in canned goods arising from internal corrosion of the can and resulting in 'blowing' of one or both ends of a can. Hydrogen swell is particularly common with high acidic canned fruits and tomatoes. The can is swelled and the product itself is normal.

LARD

Lard refers to pig fat in both its rendered and unrendered forms. Lard was commonly used as a cooking fat or shortening, or as a spread similar to butter. Its use in contemporary cuisine has diminished because of health concerns posed by its saturated fat content and its often negative image. The culinary qualities of lard vary somewhat depending on the part of the pig from which the fat is taken and how the lard is processed. Lard can be obtained from any part of the pig as long as there is a high concentration of fatty tissue. The highest grade of lard, known as leaf lard, is obtained from the "flare" fat deposit surrounding the kidneys and inside the loin. The next highest grade of lard is obtained from fatback, the hard fat between the back skin and flesh of the pig. The lowest grade (for purposes of rendering into lard) is obtained from the soft caul fat surrounding digestive organs, such as small intestines, though caul fat is often used directly as a wrapping for roasting lean meats or in the manufacture of pates. Industrially produced lard is rendered from a mixture of high and low quality fat sources from throughout the pig. It is typically hydrogenated, and often treated with bleaching and deodorizing agents, emulsifiers, and antioxidants. Such treatments make the lard shelf stable. The fat contains palmitic (20%–32%), stearic (5%–24%), oleic (35%–62%), and linoleic (3%–16%) acids as major components. It is unusual in that 70% of the palmitic acid is in the *sn*-2 position. It also contains cholesterol (0.37%–0.42%).

TALLOW

Tallow is rendered form of beef or mutton fat. Animal edible tallow is normally obtained from beef but also from sheep and goats, processed from suet. Unlike suet, tallow can be stored for extended periods without the need for refrigeration to prevent decomposition, provided it is kept in an airtight container to prevent oxidation. It is used in animal feed, to make soap, for cooking, as bird feed, and was used for making candles. It can be used as a raw material for the production of biodiesel and other oleochemicals. Tallow contains mainly saturated acids (50%): palmitic acid (26%), stearic acid (14%), and myristic acid (3%). It also contains monounsaturated acids (42%), especially oleic acid (47%) and palmitoleic acid (3%), and polyunsaturated acids (4%), especially linoleic acid (3%) and linolenic acid (1%). Also present are odd-chain, branched-chain, and trans-fatty acids, and cholesterol (0.08%–0.14% in beef tallow and 0.23%– 0.31% in mutton tallow). Suet is the raw, hard fat of beef, lamb or mutton found around the loins and kidneys. Suet has a melting point of 45-50°C and congelation between 37-40°C. Its high smoke point makes it ideal for deep frying and pastry production. Primary use of suet is to make tallow.

GELATINIZATION

On heating starch in the presence of water, the crystalline structure of the starch granules is lost irreversibly by a process called gelatinization. It is due to absorption of water by starch granules and turning into a jelly like substance. In this process, amylopectin forms the gel and amylase comes into solution. When heating is continued in excess water, more soluble components of starch come into solution and a paste results. In the food processing, the starch granules are not completely dissolved however, their partial gelatinization is sufficient to allow a good part of the starch to be digested rapidly. In the steaming of food, the process of gelatinization occurs to a small extent whereby a large proportion of slowly digestible starch is preserved.

MICROENCAPSULATION TECHNIQUE

Microencapsulation technology has been defined as the technology of packaging solid, liquid and gaseous materials in small capsules that release their contents at controlled rates over prolonged periods of time. Microencapsulation technology is not only used to produce value added food products but also used to produce entirely new and stable functional food components with desirable properties.

Six significant reasons for applying microencapsulation in Dairy Food Industry:

- To decrease any undesired reaction of core material with environmental factors such as heat, moisture, air, and light
- To reduce or prevent the loss of the core material to outside the environment; to promote easier handling
- To minimize or prevent the release of the core material until encountering the right stimulus
- To mask the taste and odor of the core
- Finally, to dilute the core material when it is intended to use in very small amounts and to separate components in a mixture that would otherwise react with each another.

There are several microencapsulation methods that have been used for microencapsulation of active ingredient. These methods include complex coacervation, spray drying, emulsion followed by spray granulation, fluidized bed drying, freeze drying, electrospraying.

EXOPLYSACCHIRIDES

Polysaccharides is an important content of microbial cell wall, either as storage capsular polysaccharides or as a biofilm called *exopolysaccharides* (EPS) secreted by microbes in the surroundings for the survival in the harsh environments as a protective mechanism. Word EPS is first termed by I.W.Sutherland for high molecular weight marine bacterial carbohydrate polymers in 1972.

In EPSs repeating sugars units, attached with proteins, lipids, organic and inorganic compounds, metal ions, and DNA are found. Bacterial exopolysaccharides (EPS) have possible commercial applications in pharmaceutical industry, food processing, drug detoxification, bioremediation and many more. EPS has shown by scientific experiments, promising application as texture enhancers, gelling agents, emulsifiers, viscosifiers, and also as the newest nanovector for drug delivery systems, resulting in sustained release of drugs. Bacterial EPS owns a varied range of properties which are not found in traditional plant polymers. Although it competes for algal (alginates, carrageenans, and ulvan), crustacean (chitin) or plant polysaccharides. Production level of EPS is low due green house effect, global warming, marine pollution, sea level rise, loss of keystone species, crop failure and overall climate impacts.

RIGOR MORTIS: The term rigor morties is literally, the *stiffness of death.*

Rigor mortis is a post-mortem change resulting in the stiffening of the body muscles due to chemical changes in their myofibrils. Rigor mortis helps in estimating the time since death as well to ascertain if the body had been moved after death. Although the term rigor mortis is common for dead human body. But it is also used in case of animals (*i.e.* in meat processing. It help to know the time of killing of animal. At the time of death, no special signal is conveyed to the body tissues, therefore tissues, including muscle, attempt to respond just as they have in the living animals but with local control. When the oxygen carrying blood supply is cut off with stoppage of circulation at death, the muscle becomes anaerobic and can no longer maintain the level of ATP by oxidative phosphorylation and their is a loss of ATP level.

A major difference of post-mortem change as contrasted to muscle in the living animal is the failure of pyruvic acid to under go the respiration scheme whereby its breakdown products are carbon dioxide and water with concurrent production of ATP. Instead pyruvic acid is converted to lactic acid when subjected to anaerobic glycolysis. Both the ultimate pH and the rate of pH decline have an important bearing on post-mortem muscle characteristic change in the microscopic appearance of muscle.

When microscopic characteristics are considered, sample taken shortly after death of the animal have poorly differentiated fibres that are straight to slightly wavy. As rigor is initiated, same fiber show areas of pronounced contraction, with shortened sarcomeres. At one day post-mortem, the fibres become more distinct. As rigor develops, contraction progress to the formation of rigor nodes, some fibres show areas of pronounced contraction, with shortened sarcomeres. At one day post-mortem, the fibres become more distinct. As rigor develops, contraction progresses to the formation or rigor nodes or contraction nodes and unstimulated are pulled into kinks and waves by the shortening of the activity contracting fibres. Later, breaks begin to occur in the fibres with a loosening the muscles structure so that the passively shortened fibres lose their waxy appearance. Some additional change that occur with development of rigor mortis include exudation of fluid and development of fitness that goes along with the stiffening of the muscles. Muscle colour may change depending on the oxygen partial pressure and rate of post-mortem glycolysis. As the temperature falls, fat solidifies and becomes vulnerable to fat oxidation largely because supply of antioxidants is markedly reduced.

Purple book in FSSAI : The purple Book is a handbook on general recommendations on diets for common medical conditions such as diabetes, hypertension, cancer and so on. It has been developed as a resource for hospitals, clinics and medical centres.

Pink book: The book has nine sections namely, buying food, storing food, preparing and cooking food, serving food, eating healthy food, managing leftover food, packaging food, maintaining hygiene & sanitation in the kitchen and managing waste. It provides useful tips, dos and don'ts, methods and practices that are recommended for Indian kitchens

Golden rules in FSSAI 12 golden rules

Yellow Book in FSSAI : FSSAI launched 'The Yellow Book – your guide to safe and nutritious food at school', that provides age appropriate content which can be adopted across schools through State education machineries as part of their curricular and co-curricular activities.

Green Book: Your Companion on Safe and Nutritious Food @ Home'. This would have useful and practical tips and information about food safety and nutrition that Indian households need on a day-to-day basis.

FSSAI Issues Final Gazette Notification on Healthy Diets for School Kids

The Food Safety and Standards Authority of India (FSSAI) has issued the final Gazette Notification prescribing healthy diets for school children called Food Safety and Standards (Safe Food and Balanced Diets for Children in School) Regulations, 2020.

Apex food regulator review the subject and an Expert Group and later on a HFSS Expert Committee was constituted to give recommendations regarding the food products which are high in saturated fat or trans fats or added sugar or sodium.

Meanwhile, in regulations related to Safe Food and Healthy Diets for School Children, FSSAI has fixed the responsibility of the school authorities to ensure safe food and balanced diets on school premises which earlier was missing in the schools and left only to the canteen contractor or caterer or the in charge of the canteen.

The regulation also has a Schedule attached that lays down detailed guidelines regarding:

(A) which are safe food and balanced diet for children and

(B) also about the selection of foods by the schools for safe food & balanced diet.

General guidance for selection of foods by the schools

Sr.No.	*Inclusion in Menu*	*List of Foods and Beverages*
1.	Always a part of the menu – 75-80% of the foods should belong from this category	Cereals, millets and pulses – Such as whole wheat grain (atta). rice, millets (ragi, bajra, etc.), legumes (all dal and beans) Milk, milk products, egg, meat and fish –milk, curd, yoghurt, lassi, butter milk, paneer, or milk products, lean meat, chicken, fish, egg Fruits and vegetables –vegetables (including green leafy vegetables: other vegetables and roots and tubers) Fresh fruits (Local and seasonal produce) Oils, fats, nuts and oilseeds – walnuts, almonds, pistachios, roasted nuts without salt or sugar, groundnuts, sesame seeds Processed/cooked foods–Freshly made soup, porridge, beverages with no added sugar, stir fried vegetables, snacks - boiled, baked or steamed, cereal or pulses based such as idli, upma, poha, khandvi, dhokla, cheela, namkin daliya, etc.
2.	To be eaten occasionally – in small portion size and reduced frequency (*e.g.*, once in a week)	Desserts – ice creams, milk-based and dairy-based sweet/ desserts Packed foods- cheese, canned and preserved vegetable, packaged meat or fish products, fruits/vegetables/cereal/pulses based snacks, nuts and seeds Bakery products - white breads, biscuits Beverages - Packaged soups and juices cereal or malt based beverages, flavoured soya milk, etc.
3.	Not to be made available in the school, hostel, etc.	Food products high in saturated fat or trans fats or added sugar or sodium

No person shall advertise or market or sell or offer for sale including free sale, or permit sale of, food products high in saturated fat or trans-fat or added sugar or sodium in school campus or to school children in an area within fifty meters from the school gate in any direction.

MERA RATION APP LAUNCHED

The Indian government's launch of the One Nation One Ration Card (ONORC) developed by NIC, plan will help people who migrate to a new place to sustain their livelihood. This initiative makes the state-owned ration services flexible and offers help to the ration cardholders to use a single ration card at their convenience.

The app to get this service is available on android phones on the Google Play Store.

AAHAR KRANTI MISSION

- The Government has launched 'Aahaar Kranti', a **mission dedicated to spread awareness about nutrition.**

Significance:

- It will **help in applying the rich knowledge of Ayurveda-based nutrition** to practice.
- The initiative 'Aahaar Kranti' will focus **on addressing the problem of hunger and diseases in abundance across India and the world.**

UN FOOD SUMMIT

The **United Nations** Secretary General has called for the **first ever UN Food Systems Summit** to held in September 2021 to strategize the actions for positive change in Agri-**food systems** in the World to realize the vision of the 2030 Agenda for Sustainable Development. 15 Apr. 2021. The 2023 UN Food System summit held on 24-26 July, 2023 ast Rome, Lazio, Italy.

YELLOW GOLD 48: YELLOW WATERMELON COMMERCIALLY INTRODUCED June 22, 2021

German agrochemicals major Bayer has commercially launched first-ever yellow watermelon variety called "Yellow Gold 48" in India under Seminis brand.

FSSAI set NEW Trans-fat levels

FSSAI recently announced that all edible refined oils, vegetable fat spreads, vanaspati oils, margarines, bakery shortenings and mixed fat spreads can contain only 3% or less trans-fats.

This is to be implemented by January 2021. By January 2022 this is to be further reduced to 2%. This was done after WHO has called for elimination of trans-fats by 2023.

PROCEDURE FOR LICENSING A FOOD BUSINESS

Any person desirous to commence any food business shall make an application for grant of a licence to the Designated Officer in such manner containing such particulars and fees as may be specified by regulations.

Designated Officer on receipt of an application may either grant the licence or after giving the applicant an opportunity of being heard and for reasons to be recorded in writing, refuse to grant a licence to any applicant, if he is satisfied that it is necessary so to do in the interest of public health and shall make available to the applicant a copy of the order.

Provided that if a licence is not issued within two months from the date of making the application or his application is not rejected, the applicant may start his food business after expiry of the said period and in such a case, the Designated Officer shall not refuse to issue a licence but may, if he considers necessary, issue an improvement notice.

Every licence shall be in such form and subject to such conditions as may be specified by regulations.

A single licence may be issued by the Designated Officer for one or more articles of food and also for different establishments or premises in the same area.

If the articles of food are manufactured, stored, sold or exhibited for sale at different premises situated in more than one area, separate applications shall be made and separate licence shall be issued in respect of such premises not falling within the same area.

An appeal against the order of rejection for the grant of licence shall lie to the Commissioner of Food Safety.

A licence unless suspended or cancelled earlier shall be in force for such period as may be specified by regulations: Provided that if an application for a renewal of licence is made before the expiry of the period of validity of the licence, the licence shall continue to be in force until orders are passed on the application.

The licence shall subsist for the benefit of the deceased's personal representative or any other member of his family, until the expiry of–

(*a*) the period of three months beginning with his death; or

(*b*) such longer period as the Designated Officer may allow.

RESPONSIBILITIES OF FOOD BUSINESS OPERATORS FOR FOOD SAFETY

Every food business operator shall ensure that the articles of food satisfy the requirements of FSSAI Act and the rules and regulations made there under at all stages of production, processing, import, distribution and sale within the businesses under his control. food business operator shall have license in accordance with the Act.

No food business operator shall himself or by any person on his behalf manufacture, store, sell or distribute unsafe, misbranded or substandard food. No food business operator shall employ any person who is suffering from infectious, contagious or loathsome disease. Any food which is unsafe may be destroyed or recalled.

IMPROVEMENT NOTICE

If the Designated Officer has reasonable ground for believing that any foodbusiness operator has failed to comply with any regulations to which this section applies, he may, by a notice served on that food business operator, if he fails to comply the regulation like grounds, measures and matters.

If the food business operator fails to comply with an improvement notice, his licence may be suspended.

If the food business operator still fails to comply with the improvement notice, the Designated Officer may, after giving the licensee an opportunity to show cause, cancel the licence granted to him. Provided that the Designated Officer may suspend any licence forthwith in the interest of public health for reasons to be recorded in writing.

Revocation of licence under this Act, may appeal to the Commissioner of Food Safety whose decision thereon, shall be final. (Appeal period is 15 days from the date of notice)

PROCEDURE FOR TAKING A SAMPLE BY FSO?

When a Food Safety Officer takes a sample of food for analysis, he shall give notice in writing of his intention to have it so analysed to the person from whom he has taken the sample and to the person, if any, whose name,address and other particulars have been disclosed.

The sample is divided into four parts and mark and seal or fasten up each part in such a manner as its nature permits and take the signature or thumb impression of the person from whom the sample has been taken in such place and in such manner as may be prescribed by the Central

Government. Provided that where such person refuses to sign or put his thumb impression, the Food Safety Officer shall call upon one or more witnesses and take his signature or thumb impression, in lieu of the signature or thumb impression of such person.

Send one of the parts for analysis to the Food Analyst under intimation to the Designated Officer. Two parts to the Designated Officer for keeping these in safe custody the remaining part for analysis to an accredited laboratory, if so, requested by the food business operator, under intimation to the Designated Officer:

Provided that if the test reports received under from food analyst and accredited laboratory are found to beat variance, then the Designated Officer shall send one part of the sample kept in his custody,to referral laboratory for analysis, whose decision thereon shall be final.

When a sample of any article of food or adulterant is taken, the Food SafetyOfficer shall, by the immediate succeeding working day, send the sample to the Food Analyst for the area concerned for analysis and report.

Where the part of the sample sent to the Food Analyst is lost or damaged, the Designated Officer shall, on a requisition made to him, by the Food Analyst or the FoodSafety Officer, despatch one of the parts of the sample sent to him, to the Food Analyst for analysis.

An article of food or adulterant seized, shall be produced before the Designated Officer as soon as possible and in any case not later than seven days after the receipt of the report of the Food Analyst:

In case of imported articles of food, the authorised officer of the Food Authority shall take its sample and send to the Food Analyst of notified laboratory for analysis who shall send the report within a period of five days to the authorised officer.

The Designated Officer, the Food Safety Officer, the authorised officer and the Food Analyst shall follow such procedure as may be specified by regulations.

SIZE OF FOOD SAMPLE

A sample unit consists of a minimum of 100 g and usually a consumer size container of product. Take sample unit at random to ensure that the sample is representative of the lot.

Table 1: Quantity of sample to be sent to the Food Analyst for Analysis

S. No.	Article of Food	Approximate Quantity
1.	Milk	500 ml
2.	Sterilized Milk / UHT Milk	500 ml
3.	Malai / Dahi	200 gms
4.	Yoghurt / Sweetened Dahi	500 gms
5.	Chhana / Paneer / Khoya / Shrikhand	250 gms
6.	Cheese / Cheese spread	200 gms
7.	Evaporated Milk / Condensed Milk	200 gms
8.	Ice-Cream / Softy / Kulfi / Icecandy / Icelolly	300 gms
9.	Milk Powder / Skimmed Milk Powder	250 gms
10.	Infant Food / Weaning Food	500 gms
11.	Malt Food / Malted Milk Food	300 gms
12.	Butter / Butter Oil / Ghee / Margarine / Cream / Bakery Shortening	200 gms

13.	Vanaspati, Edible Oils / Fats	400 gms
14.	Carbonated Water	3 litres
15.	Baking Powder	100 gms
16.	Arrow root / Sago	250 gms
17.	Corn flakes / Macaroni Products / Corn Flour / Custard Powder	200 gms
18.	Spices, Condiments and Mixed Masala (Whole)	500 gms
19.	Spices, Condiments and Mixed Masala (Powder)	500 gms
20.	Nutmeg / Mace	250 gms
21.	Asafoetida	100 gms
22.	Compounded Asafoetida	150 gms
23.	Saffron	20 gms
24.	Gur/jaggery, Icing Sugar, Honey, Synthetic Syrup, Bura	250 gms
25.	Cane Sugar / Refined Sugar /Cube Sugar, Dextrose, Misri /Dried Glucose Syrup	200 gms
26.	Artificial Sweetener	100 gm.
27.	Fruit Juice / Fruit Drink / Fruit Squash	1 ltr.
28.	Tomato Sauce / Ketch up / Tomato Paste, Jam / Jelly / Marmalade / Tomato Puree / Vegetable Sauce	300 gms
29.	Non Fruit Jellies	200 gms
30.	Pickles and Chutneys	250 gms
31.	Oilseeds / Nuts / Dry Fruits	250 gms
32.	Tea / Roasted Coffee / Roasted Chicory	500 gms
33.	Instant Tea / Instant Coffee / Instant Coffee-Chicory Mixture	100 gms
34.	Sugar Confectionery / Chewing Gum / Bubble Gum	20 gms
35.	Chocolates	200 gms
36.	Edible Salt	200 gms
37.	Iodised Salt / Iron Fortified Salt	200 gms
38.	Food Grains and Pulses (Whole and Split)	1 kg
39.	Atta / Maida /Suji / Besan/Other Milled Product /Paushtik Fortified Atta /Maida	500 gms
40.	Biscuits and Rusks	200 gms
41.	Bread / Cakes / Pasties	250 gms
42.	Gelatin	150 gms
43.	Catechu	150 gms
44.	Vinegar / Synthetic Vinegar	300 gms
45.	Food Colours	25 gms
46.	Food colour preparation Solid/100 gm (Solid/Liquid) /100 ml liquid	
47.	Natural Mineral Water / Packaged Drinking Water 4000 ml in three minimum original sealed packs.	
48.	Silver Leafs	2 gm
49.	Prepared Food	500 gms
50.	Proprietary Food, (Non Standardized Foods)	500 gms
51.	Canned Foods	6 Sealed cans
52.	Food not specified	500 gms

After test or analysis the certificate thereof shall be supplied forth with to sender in Form B. Fees of certificate of Rs. 1000/- per sample certificate must be signed by Director.

STATE FOOD SAFETY INDEX

FSSAI has **developed it to measure the performance of States on five parameters of food safety** - Human Resources and Institutional Data, Compliance, Food Testing - Infrastructure and Surveillance, Training & Capacity Building and Consumer Empowerment

PARAMETERS OF FOOD SAFETY INDEX : 1) Human Resources and Institutional Data (with 20% weightage): These parameters measure the availability of officers like Food safety and designated officers, facility of adjudications and appellate tribunals, functioning of state/district level Steering Committees, pending of cases and their monitoring participation in Central Advisory Committee meetings of the Foof Authority.

One of the most important parameters, **compliance** (with 30% weightage), which measures overall coverage of food businesses in licensing and registration equivalent with size and population of the State/UT's, special drives, camps organised, yearly increase, promptness and effectiveness in the issue of state licenses/registrations and monitoring of expired licenses

The parameter of **Infrastructure and Surveillance** (with 20% weightage), measures the availability of adequate food testing infrastructure with the trained workforce in the States and UT's for testing food samples.

The parameter of **training and capacity building** (with 10% weightage) focuses on regulatory staff laboratory personnel's training and capacity building.

Consumer empowerment (with 20% weightage), another parameter, measures states-UT's in consumer empowering initiatives FSSAI like Food Fortification, Eat Right Campus, BHOG (Blissful Hygienic Offering to God), Hygiene Rating of Restaurants, RUCO (Repurpose Used Cooking Oil). Clean street food hubs etc., state initiative activities for creating consumer awareness are also considered.

FORTIFIED RICE KERNELS (FRK)

Fortified rice kernels are either **coated rice kernels or extruded rice-shaped kernels prepared with a mix of vitamins and minerals**. Sometimes a powdery blend of nutrients is dusted onto unfortified rice, but this is only useful in countries where consumers do not wash rice before cooking it. **Fortified rice kernels (FRK)** are then produced from this mixture using extruder machines. The kernels is resemble rice grains. FRK is added to non-fortified rice in ratio ranging from 1:50 to 1:200 (ideal being 1:100) resulting in fortified rice nearly identical to traditional rice in aroma, taste, and texture.

FAO (Food and Agriculture Organisation): Established in 1945 as a Specialised Agency of the United Nations to Lead International Efforts to Defeat Hunger, to serve both Developed and Developing Countries. Headquarter at Rome (Italy).

NIN (National Institute of Nutrition). It was founded in 1918 as a beriberi-enquiry unit at Coonor(Kerala), which emerged as full-fledged Nutrition Research Laboratory (NRL) in 1928. NRL was shifted to Hyderabad, in 1958 and was later renamed as National Institute of Nutrition on 1969.

NIN is India's premier nutrition research institute working under the aegis of ICMR (Indian Council of Medical Research, Ministry of Health and Family Welfare, GOI. NIN has attained global recognition for its pioneering studies on various aspects of nutrition research with special reference to protein energy malnutrition (PEM). NIN's mission is to enable, food and nutrition security conductive to good health, growth and development, and increased productivity through dedicated research. so as to achieve the national nutrition goals of GOI in the National Nutrition Policy

FOOD FORTIFICATION RESOURCE CENTRE (Set up by FSSAI with Support from TATA TRUSTS)

A Food Fortification Resource Centre funded by the Tata Trusts and housed at the (Food Safety and Standards Authority of India's) FSSAI headquarters in Delhi, has been set up to scale up fortification across the country. The FFRC is responsible for supporting implementation of Indian food fortification regulations, 2018. The FSSAI-FFRC has also launched a logo for fortification — the + F Logo — which is a mark for fortified products in India. It is also responsible for providing support to the states and union territories and food manufacturers to adopt fortification.

The primary goal of the FFRC is to address the deficiency of vitamins and minerals that are needed for a healthy nation.

Some of the key functions of the FFRC are:

- Providing all information pertaining to fortification of food such as scientific evidence, latest fortification technology, national and international experience, government circulars and orders along with the success stories of various states and the food industry.
- Educating people about the benefits of fortified foods.
- Sensitising states about food fortification and promoting them in the safety net programmes to curb the incidence of micronutrient deficiencies.
- Providing technical support especially to small scale food manufacturers to enable them to produce fortified foods.
- Training and building capacity for large-scale fortification of foods and providing tools to share communication material and lend technical, scientific and financial support to promote large-scale fortification of food.

The FFRC's fortification programme works across India. In the open market, voluntary fortification has begun for five staples, with faster adoption in the oil and milk industries. Currently, 70 of India's top national and regional brands have 113 fortified products available in the retail market. In the government safety net programmes, 17 states and 4 union territories have so far adopted fortification of their chosen commodities at the district level (all districts) in the ICDS, MDM and PDS programmes.

Major Partners:

Line Ministries: Ministry of Women and Child Development (MWCD), Ministry of Human Resource Development (MHRD), Department of Food and Public Distribution, India (DoFPD), NITI Aayog, Ministry of Health and Family Welfare (MoHFW)

Development Partners:

1. Global Alliance for Improved Nutrition (GAIN)
2. PATH (a global team of innovators to accelerate health equity so people of all communities can thrive)
3. World Bank Group
4. Nutrition International
5. World Food Programme
6. The India Nutrition Initiative (TINI)
7. Bill and Melinda Gates Foundation

Premix: means a combination of two or more fortificants in a specific proportion with or without additives packed and meant for use in formulating a product falling under any category as per FSSAI (Fortification of foods) regulations 2018. The FBO (food business operator) licensed or registered under FSSAI act for manufacture, distribution, sale and retail of the above mentioned premix will be defined as premix supplier.

FIVE STAPLES

1. Double Fortified Salt (DFS) is an innovative new fortified food product - delivering small but crucial amounts of iodine and iron to human beings through their diet. In general, DFS formulations are intended to provide 100% of daily dietary iodine requirement, and 30 to 60% of daily dietary iron requirement.

DFS is produced by mixing iodized salt with either/or ferrous sulphate/ encapsulated ferrous fumarate. While producing DFS with ferrous sulphate, sodium hexametaphosphate (SHMP) is used as a stabilizer, ferrous fumarate has been encapsulated with soya stearin to prevent interaction between iodine and iron.

The salt iodization process involves very little technology of using a drip feed equipment to dose potassium iodate (KIO_3) solution to the raw salt to a very sophisticated dewatering, drying and packing system.

Indicative amount of double fortified salt is over 1,53,907.43 MT produced annually in India

It is anticipated that the increase in cost of DFS could be 20-50% higher than iodized salt per kilogram.

Salt shall be fortified with iodine and may also be fortified with iron in combination with iodine, at the level given in the table below:

S. No.	*Component*	*Level of nutrients*	*Source of nutrients*
1.	**Iodine content**		
	(*a*) Manufacture level	20-30 parts per million (on dry weight basis)	Potassium Iodate
	(*b*) Distribution channel including retail level	15-30 parts per million (on dry weight basis)	
2.	**Iron content (as Fe)**	850-1100 parts per million	Ferrous sulphate or Ferrous Fumarate

2. Milk is a rich source of high quality protein, calcium and of fat-soluble vitamins A and D. Vitamins A and D are lost when milk fat is removed during processing. Many countries have a mandatory provision to add back the vitamins removed as it is easily doable. It is called replenishment as the nutrients lost during processing are added back.

1. *Percent share of milk industry*: (*i*) organized -30% (*ii*) unorganized 70%
2. *Percent of milk fortified in the organized sector*: (*i*) private dairies (17.28%) (*ii*) Co-op Dairies (82.72%)

Toned, double toned, skimmed milk or standardized milk shall be fortified with the following micronutrients, at the level given in the table below:

S No.	Nutrients	Level of nutrient per litre of toned/double toned/skimmed milk/standardized milk	Source of nutrient
1.	**Vitamin A**	270 µg RE- 450 µg RE	Retinyl acetate or Retinyl Palmitate
2.	**Vitamin D**	5 µg - 7.5 µg	*Cholecalciferol or *Ergocalciferol (*Only from Plant Source)

Note: Vitamin A (retinol): 1 IU = 0.3 mg RE (Retinol Equivalent); Vitamin D (Cholecalciferol or Ergocalciferol): 1 IU= 0.025 mg.

Since vitamin A and D are fat-soluble vitamins, fortification of edible oils and fats with vitamin A and D is a good strategy to address micronutrient malnutrition and fortified oil is known to provide 25%-30% of the recommended dietary allowances for vitamins A&D.

3. Fortified vegetable oil: Fortified edible oil market size was valued at USD 11.80 Billion in 2022 and is projected to reach USD 17.06 Billion by 2030, growing at a CAGR of 4.37% from 2023 to 2030.

Around 43% (3.01 MMT) of edible oil available in the market today is fortified as per FSSAI standard.

Vegetable oil shall be fortified with the following micronutrients, at the level given in the table below

S No.	Nutrients	Minimum level of nutrient	Source of nutrient
1.	**Vitamin A**	6 μg RE- 9.9 μg RE per gm of oil	Retinyl acetate or Retinyl Palmitate
2.	**Vitamin D**	0.11μg - 0.16 μg per gm of oil	*Cholecalciferol or *Ergocalciferol (*Only from Plant Source)

Note: Vitamin A (retinol): 1 IU = 0.3 μg RE (Retinol Equivalent); Vitamin D (Cholecalciferol or Ergocalciferol): 1 IU = 0.025 μg

The indicative amount of fortified rice is 1000MT produced annually.

4. Rice fortification may be considered as having the highest potential to fill the gap in current staple food fortification programs as it is the staple food of 65 percent of the Indian population and reaches the most vulnerable and poorer section - with the highest uptake in the government safety net programmes.

Rice, when fortified, shall contain added iron, folic acid and Vitamin B-12 at the level, given in the table below:

Sl. No.	*Nutrient*	*Level of fortification per Kg*
1	**Iron-** (*a*) Ferric pyrophosphate	28 mg- 42.5 mg*
	Or	
	(*b*) Sodium Iron (III) Ethylene diamine tetra Acetate Trihydrate (Sodium feredetate, -Na Fe EDTA)	14 mg-2125 mg
2.	**Folic acid-Folic acid**	75 μg- 125 μg
3.	**Vitamin B 12-** Cyanocobalarnine or Hydroxycobalamine	0.75 μg- 1.25 μg

Note: *added at a higher level to account for less bioavailability.

In addition, rice may also be fortified with following micronutrients, singly or in combination, at the level given in the table below:

Sl. No.	Nutrient	Level of fortification per Kg
1.	**Zinc-** Zinc Oxide,	10 mg- 15 mg
2.	**Vitamin A-** Retinyl Palmitate	500 μg RE- 750 μg RE
3.	**Thiamine (Vitamin Bl)-** Thiamine hydrochloride or Thiamine mononitrate	1 mg- 1.5 mg
4.	**Riboflavin (Vitamin B2)-** Riboflavin or Riboflavin 5'-phosphate sodium:	1.25 mg- 1.75 mg
5.	**Niacin (Vitamin B3)-** Nicotinamide or Nicotinic acid	12.5 mg- 20 mg
6.	**Pyridoxine (Vitamin B6)-** Pyridoxine hydrochloride	1.5 mg- 2.5 mg

5. Fortified wheat: The indicative amount of fortified wheat flour is 2.48 million tonnes produced annually

Atta, when fortified, shall contain added iron, folic acid and Vitamin B-12 at the level given in the table below:

Sl.No.	Nutrient	Level of fortification per Kg
1.	**Iron-** Ferrous citrate. or Ferrous lactate or Ferrous sulphate or Ferric pyrophosphate or electrolytic iron or Ferrous fumiarate or Ferrous BisCylycinate; Or Sodium Iron (III) Ethylene diamine tetra acetate Trihydrate (Sodium feredetate-Na Fe EDTA);	28 mg- 42.5 mg* 14 mg- 21.25 mg
2.	**Folic acid**	75 μg- 125μg
3.	**Vitamin B12-** Cyanocobalamine or Hydroxycobalamine.;	0.75 μg- 1.25μg

Note:- * added at a higher level to account for less bioavailability

In addition, atta may also be fortified with following micronutrients, singly or in combination, at the level in the table given below;

Sl.No.	Nutrient	Level of fortification per Kg
1.	**Zinc-** Zinc Sulphate:	10 mg- 1.5 mg
2.	**Vitamin A-** Retinyl acetate or Retinyl Palmitate:	500 μg RE- 750 μg RE
3.	**Thiamine (Vitamin B1)-** Thiamine hydrochloride or Thiamine mononitrate:	1 mg- 1.5 mg
4.	**Riboflavin (Vitamin B2)-** Riboflavin or Riboflavin 5' phosphate sodium	1.25 mg- 1,75 mg
5.	**Niacin (Vitamin B3)-** Nicotinamide or Nicotinic acid;	12.5 mg- 20 mg
6.	**Pyridoxine (Vitamin B6)-** Pyridoxine hydrochloride.	1.5 mg- 2.5 mg

EAT RIGHT INDIA MOVEMENT

- It is an **initiative of FSSAI to transform the country's food system** in order to ensure safe, healthy and sustainable food for all Indians. Its tagline is **'Sahi Bhojan, Behtar Jeevan'.**
- It is aligned to the **National Health Policy 2017** with its focus on preventive and promotive healthcare and flagship programmes like **Ayushman Bharat, POSHAN Abhiyaan, Anaemia Mukt Bharat and Swachh Bharat Mission.**
- Eat Right India **adopts a judicious mix of regulatory, capacity building, collaborative, and empowerment approaches** to ensure that our food is suitable both for the people and the planet.
- The 'Eat Right Station' certification is awarded by **Food Safety and Standards Authority of India (FSSAI)** to railway stations that set benchmarks in providing safe and wholesome food to passengers.
- The station is **awarded a certificate upon a conclusion of an FSSAI**-empanelled third-party audit agency with ratings from 1 to 5.

FSSAI NOTIFIES STANDARDS FOR HONEY AND ITS PRODUCTS TO CURB ADULTERATIONI

The regulator FSSAI has come out with food safety standards for honey and its products, in a bid to curb adulteration. As per the FSSAI notification, honey should comply with 18 parameters like that of sucrose content, glucose ratio, pollen count, foreign oligosaccharides among others. The FSSAI has fixed maximum 5 per cent limit for sucrose content in the honey, while 10 per cent for carviacallosa and Honeydew honey. The moisture percentage should be maximum 20 per cent and pollen count should be 25,000 per gram.

With regard to by-products, the FSSAI has fixed standards for 'Bees wax' and 'royal jelly' also.

Bees wax is obtained from the honeycombs of bees of Apidae family after the honey has been removed by draining or centrifuging. The combs are melted with hot water, steam or solar heat and the melted product is filtered and cast into cakes of yellow bees wax.

White bees wax is obtained by bleaching the yellow bees wax with oxidising agents. Beeswax consists of a mixture of esters of fatty acids and fatty alcohols, hydrocarbons and free fatty acids. Minor amounts of free fatty alcohols are also present.

Royal jelly is the mixture of secretions from hypopharyngeal and mandibular glands of worker bees, free from any additive. It is the food of larval and adult queens.

In the case of 'Monofloral Honey', the regulator said the minimum pollen content of the plant species concerned should not be less than 45 per cent of total pollen content.

In case of 'Multi Floral Honey', the pollen content of any of the plant species should not exceed 45 per cent of the total pollen content.

The government is promoting honey production through the mission for integrated development of horticulture (MIDH) and the National Bee Board has been formed for implementing various activities for development of scientific beekeeping under MIDH.

According to the National Bee Board, India produced over 155,000 tonnes of honey in the financial year 2021-2022.

CARCINOGENIC BY PRODUCTS OF FOOD PROCESSING

Processing, particularly with heat, may lead to undesired changes in food products such as reduction of nutrients or the formation of hazardous substances, such as the carcinogenic polycyclic aromatic hydrocarbons (PAH) or products like acrylamide and 3-monochloropropanediol (MCPD).

1. Polycyclic aromatic hydrocarbons (PAH): Hydrocarbons comprising two or more ring structures, at least one of which is an aromatic (benzene) ring. It is lipophilic pollutants and potential carcinogens. It is found in foods include benzo[*a*]pyrene and phenanthrene; foods afected include cheese, cooked meat and shellfish. It is also called polynuclear aromatic hydrocarbons.

Health **effects** from long-term or chronic exposure to **PAHs** may include decreased immune function, cataracts, kidney and liver damage (*e.g.* jaundice), breathing problems, asthma-like symptoms, and lung function abnormalities

Their presence in surface **water** or groundwater is an indication of a source of pollution. **PAHs** are only slowly biodegradable under aerobic conditions and are stable to hydrolysis. In drinking-**water**, the **PAHs** detected in the highest concentrations are fluoranthene (FA), phenanthrene, pyrene (PY), and anthracene.

Increased incidences of lung, skin, and bladder cancers are associated with occupational exposure to PAHs. These reports, however, provide only qualitative evidence of the carcinogenic potential of PAHs in humans because of the presence of multiple PAH compounds and other suspected carcinogens

Evidence indicates that mixtures of PAHs are carcinogenic to humans. The EPA has classified the following seven PAH compounds: benz(a)anthracene, benzo(a)pyrene, benzo(b)fluoranthene, benzo(k)fluoranthene, chrysene, dibenz(ah)anthracene, and indeno(1,2,3-cd) pyrene as probable human carcinogens.

2. Acrylamide: Acrylamide appears to form when foods, typically plant commodities high in carbohydrates and low in protein, are subjected to high temperature (120 °C) during cooking or other thermal processing. The compound has been reported to cause cancer. Acrylamide is formed from Maillard reaction products, when the amino acid asparagine combines with reducing sugars, producing the highest levels of the carcinogen. Acrylamide formation is non-oxidative in nature and reported reduced formation of acrylamide in high protein material. **Acrylamide** is found mainly in foods made from plants, such as potato products, grain products, or coffee. Acrylamide does not form, or forms at lower levels, in dairy, meat, and fish products. The Joint Expert Committee on Food Additives (JECFA) reported that the major contributing foods to total exposure for most countries were potato chips (16-30%), potato crisps (6-46%), coffee (13-39%), pastry and sweet biscuits (10-20%), and bread rolls/toasts (10-30%) (Anon, 2005). Other food items contributed less than 10% of the total exposure. Recent technological developments in food processing methods could significantly reduce acrylamide levels in some foods.

Acrylamide is a chemical widely used during the manufacturing of paper, dye, and other industrial products. It can also be formed when certain foods are cooked at high temperatures. Frying, baking, or roasting certain foods, such as potatoes or grains, can create acrylamide.

Studies in rodent models have found that acrylamide exposure increases the risk for several types of cancer. In the body, acrylamide is converted to a compound called glycidamide, which causes mutations in and damage to DNA.

3. 3-MCPD: Chlorinated propanols are formed during certain food manufacturing and domestic cooking processes. The compound 3-MCPD and, to a lesser extent 1,3-dichloro-2-propanol (DCP), are the most abundant chloropropanols and they are considered to be carcinogens (Tritscher, 2004). Savory foods containing acid-hydrolyzed vegetable protein were found to be contaminated with the 3-MCPD. The food groups identified as most likely to contain 3-MCPD are bread and biscuits (mainly toasted or roasted), and cooked/cured fish or meat. Although it is toxigenic only at high consumption levels, targeted actions are being taken to reduce the levels of 3-MCPD in soy sauce and related products.

FSSAI, NASSCOM FOUNDATION PARTNERS TO DEVELOP APP TO PREVENT FOOD WASTAGE

- Food regulator FSSAI (Food Safety and Standards Authority of India) and **NASSCOM Foundation**, a trade association of Indian IT and Business Process Outsourcing industry, have signed an Memorandum of Understanding (MoU) to jointly build a technology platform to prevent food wastage and encouraging food donation by developing an app for the purpose.
- The collaboration is a significant step in the direction of leveraging technology for solutions of social problems.

1. FoSTaC: Food Safety Training and Certification for Food Business Operators across the food value chain

FSSAI (Food Safety and Standards Authority of India) has made the following 2 trainings mandatory for Food Handlers

Food Safety Supervisor: For every 25 food **handlers** or less, there should be 1 Food Safety Supervisor [FSSAI] trained under the Food Safety Training and Certification [FoSTaC].

FSSA offer 2 types of FSSAI training :-

1. Advance Manufacturing, 2. Advance Catering

COVID-19 Pandemic: Training: Every Food **handler** needs to undergo this awareness training to understand the extra precautions to be taken during **the COVID.**

2. FSKAN (Food safety Knowledge Assimilation Network): About FSKAN: A system of network of organizations with the aim to facilitate a scientific co-operation framework by the co-ordination of activities, the exchange of information, the development and implementation of joint projects within the Food Authority's responsibility FSSAI has established Food Safety Knowledge assimilation Network (FSKAN).

3. ITCFSAN: International Training Centre for Food Safety and Applied Nutrition, (Ministry of Commerce and World Bank) in partnership with FSSAI imparting training programme in India. ITC-FSAN is an International training centre **for** global food safety & nutrition, located in Mumbai, built in partnership with Food Safety and Standards Authority of India (FSSAI).

4. RUCO: Repurpose used cooking during frying, several properties of oil are altered, Total Polar Compounds(TPC) are formed on repeated **frying. The** toxicity of these compounds is associated with several diseases such as hypertension, atherosclerosis, Alzheimer's disease, liver diseases. Therefore, it is essential to monitor the quality of vegetable oils during frying. In order to safeguard consumer health, FSSAI has fixed a limit **for Total** Polar Compounds at 25 percent beyond which the vegetable oil shall not be used. From 1st July, 2018 onwards, all Food Business Operators (FBOs) are required to monitor the quality of oil during frying by complying with the said regulations. FSSAI is implementing an EEE Strategy (Education, Enforcement and Environment) - to divert Used Cooking Oil from the food value chain and curb current illegal practices. The EEE Strategy approach ensures good health and welfare for all 130-crore citizens, aiding energy security, climate change mitigation, and leading to environmentally sustainable development.

5. Dart Book Detect Adulteration with Rapid Test (DART) booklet is a compilation of common quick tests for detection of food adulterants at household by the citizens themselves so as to induce awareness among the consumers about food safety.

6. Orange book (FSSAI). 'The Orange Book' Safe and Nutritious Food at Workplace' is a nation-wide campaign to help people eat safe and eat right while at work. With the rising incidence of diet-related diseases. This initiative, therefore, educates people on safe and healthy diets.

7. GAMA (Grievances Against Misleading Advertisements): The Department of Consumer Affairs (DoCA) is one of the two Departments under the Ministry of Consumer Affairs, Food & Public Distribution. The mandate of the Department is consumer advocacy. In its endeavour to address the problem of misleading advertisements, the Department of Consumer Affairs has launched this portal for registering online complaints for Grievances Against Misleading Advertisements.

8. FoSCoRIS (Food Safety Compliance through Regular Inspections and Sampling) FSSAI is coming up with an online Food Safety Compliance through Regular Inspections and Sampling (FoSCoRIS) mobile app. The App will capture onsite inspection carried out by FSOs as per the inspection checklist.

FoSCoRIS will require a mobile/tablet with net connectivity. Many States/UTs already have their own Closed User Groups (CUGs) and provide hand held devices to Food Safety Officers for enforcement/ surveillance© 2017 FSSAI - All Rights Reserved. Website Maintained by FSSAI.

9. FoSCOS (Food Safety Compliance System): Wef from 1st Nov. 2020 to replace existing food licensing and registration system. Users of ICRS are now required to visit https:// foscos.fssai.gov.in

10. Food Safety Connect is the Food Safety and Standards Authority of India (FSSAI) initiative to enable citizens to share their concerns regarding food safety violations. It is a online food safety education dedicated to public about food safety and helping them and ensure the health of communities nationwide.

National Institute of Food Technology & Entrepreneurship Management (NIFTEM), an institute of national importance under the aegis of Ministry of Food Processing Industries, Govt. of India has joined hands with GAIN, an international development sector partner and Hexagon Nutrition, a leading food and nutraceutical company. Together, they will be setting up a Centre of Excellence for Food Fortification at NIFTEM to spearhead a food fortification drive aimed at eradicating malnutrition.

The Food Safety and Standards Authority of India (FSSAI) has formulated draft Food Safety and Standards (Vegan Food) Regulations 2021. The draft regulations will define vegan food for the first time in India and introduce safety regulations and labelling rules to identify vegan food products. Vegan food will be defined as "those foods or food ingredients that have not made use of any ingredients, additives and processing aids of animal origin including milk and milk products, fish, poultry and meat, egg or egg products, honey or honey bee products, materials of insect origin like silk, dyes, chitin/chitosan etc or ingredients that are clarified using animal sourced products *e.g.,* bone char used in sugar bleaching, isinglass in clarifying beer etc."

Food safety regulator **FSSAI** h as mandated food business operators to mention FSSAI. licence or registration number on cash receipts or purchase invoice with effect from October 1 2022.

FSSAI tightens vigil against violations related to labelling of coffee chicory mixture products New Delhi, April 1, 2022: FSSAI has recently examined the labels of various centrally licensed FBOs (including both large and mid-sized manufacturers) of Coffee-Chicory mixtures for necessary compliances with the related regulatory provisions. The FSS (Food Products Standards and Food Additives) Regulations, 2011, clearly specifies standards for Coffee and Coffee-Chicory mixtures separately. Every package containing a mixture of coffee and chicory shall declare on its label the percentage content of Coffee and Chicory. FSSAI has also directed the State Food Safety Departments to ensure necessary compliance of regulatory provisions related to coffee and coffee-chicory mixtures.

FSSAI issues FSS (Import) First Amendment Regulations, 2022

On 14th February 2022, FSSAI published a notification on the Food Safety and Standards (Import) First Amendment Regulations, 2022. The amendment is regarding sampling of food imported for captive use or production of value-added products for hundred percent exports and will come into effect from 1st September 2022.

IMPORTANT TABLES FOR FOOD AND MICROBIOLOGY

TABLE -1: Recommended Precooling Methods and Storage conditions for Fruits and Vegetables

Fruits and vegetables	Temperature °F	% Relative humidity	Precooling method	Storage life Days	Ethylene sensitive
Apples	30-40	90-95	R, F, H	90-240	Y
Apricots	32	90-95	R, H	7-14	Y
Asparagus	32-35	95-100	H, I	14-21	Y
Avocados	40-55	85-90		14-28	Y
Bananas	56-58	90-95		7-28	
Beans, snap	40-45	95	R, F, H	10-14	Y
Beans, lima	37-41	95		7-10	
Beets, roots	32	98-100	R	90-150	
Blackberries	31-32	90-95	R, F	2-3	
Blueberries	31-32	90-95	R, F	10-18	
Broccoli	32	95-100	I, F, H	10-14	Y
Brussel sprouts	32	95-100	H, V, I	21-35	Y
Cabbage	32	98-100	R, F	90-180	Y
Cantaloupe	36-41	95	H, F	10-14	Y
Carrots, topped	32	98-100	I, R	28-180	Y
Cauliflower	32	90-98	H, V	20-30	
Celery	32	98-100	I	14-28	Y
Cherries, sweet	30-31	90-95	H, F	14-21	
Corn, sweet	32	95-98	H, I, V	4-6	
Cranberries	36-40	90-95		60-120	
Cucumbers	50-55	95	F, H	10-14	Y
Eggplant	46-54	90-95	R, F	10-14	Y
Endive	32	90-95	H, I	14-21	Y
Garlic	32-34	65-75	N	90-210	
Grapefruit	50-60	85-90		28-42	
Grapes	32	85	F	56-180	
Kiwifruit	32	95-100		28-84	Y
Leeks	32	95-100	H, I	60-90	Y
Lemons	50-55	85-90		30-180	
Lettuce	32	85-90	H, I	14-21	Y
Limes	48-50	85-90		21-35	
Mushrooms	32	95		12-17	
Nectarines	31-32	95	F, H	14-18	Y

Okra	45-50	90-95		7-14	Y
Onions, bulb	32	65-70	N	30-180	
Onions, green	32	95-100	H, I	7-10	
Oranges	32-48	85-90		21-56	
Peaches	31-32	90-95	F, H	14-28	Y
Pears	32	90-95	F, R, H	60-90	Y
Peas, in pods	32	95-98	F, H, I	7-10	Y
Peppers, bell	45-55	90-95	R, F	12-18	Y
Peppers, hot	45-50	60-70	R, F	14-21	Y
Pineapple	45-55	85-90		14-36	
Plums	32	90-95	F, H	14-28	Y
Potatoes, early	50-60	90	R, F	56-140	
Potatoes, late	40-50	90	R, F	56-140	Y
Pumpkins	50-60	50-75	N	84-160	
Radishes	32	95-100	I	21-28	
Raspberries	32	90-95	R, F	2-3	Y
Rutabagas	32	98-100	R	120-180	
Spinach	32	95-100	H, I	10-14	Y
Squash, summer	41-50	95	R, F	7-14	Y
Squash, winter	50-55	50-70	N	84-150	
Strawberries	32	90-95	R, F	5-10	
Sweet potatoes	55-60	85-90	N	120-210	Y
Tangerines	40	90-95		14-28	
Tomatoes	62-68	90-95	R, F	7-28	Y
Turnips	32	95	R, H, V, I	120-150	
Watermelon	50-60	90	N	14-21	

F = forced-air cooling, H = hydrocooling, I = package icing, R = room cooling, V = vacuum cooling, N = no precooling needed. Sources: USDA Agricultural Marketing Service, Kansas State University Cooperative Extension Service

TABLE -2: Potential Chemical Indicators of Food Quality

Ammonia	Indole
Trimethylamine	Ethanol
Dimethylamine	Furfural
Total volatile bases	Hydrogen sulfide
Total volatile acids	Total reducing substances
Free fatty acids	Volatile reducing substances
Water insoluble acids (oleic, palmitic)	Histamine
Organic acids (acetic, lactic, pyruvic, succinic)	Hypoxanthine
	Diacetyl
	Acetylmethylcarbinol

TABLE -3: Approximate Minimum Water Activities for Growth of Microorganisms

Organism	Minimum a_w	Organism	Minimum a_w
Most spoilage bacteria	0.90–0.91	*Staphylococcus albus*	0.88–0.92
Acinetobacter	0.95–0.98	*S. aureus*	0.83–0.92
Aeromonas	0.95–0.98	*Streptococcus*	0.92–0.98
Alcaligenes	0.95–0.98	*Vibrio parohaemolyticus*	0.94–0.98
Arthrobacters	0.95–0.98	Halophilic bacteria	0.75
Bacillus	0.90–0.99	Most yeasts	0.87–0.94
B. cereus	0.92–0.95	Osmophilic yeast	0.60–0.78
Citrobacter	0.95–0.98	Most molds	0.70–0.75
Clostridium botulinum	0.90–0.98	*Xerophilic molds*	0.60–0.70
Type A	0.93–0.95	*Aspergillus*	0.68–0.88
Type B	0.93–0.96	*A. glaucus*	0.70–0.75
Type E	0.94–0.97	*A. flavus*	0.78–0.90
C. perfringens	0.93–0.97	*A. halophilicus*	0.68
Corynebocterium	0.95–0.98	*A. niger*	0.80–0.84
Enterobacter	0.95–0.98	*Botrytis cinerea*	0.93
Escherichia coli	0.94–0.97	*Debaryomyces*	0.87–0.91
Flavobacterium	0.95–0.98	*Fusarium*	0.80–0.92
Klebsiella	0.95–0.98	*Hansenula*	0.89–0.90
Lactobacillus	0.90–0.96	*Mucor*	0.80–0.93
Leuconostoc	0.96–0.98	*Penicillium*	0.78–0.90
Micrococcus	0.90–0.95	*Rhodotorula*	0.89–0.92
M. roseus	0.90–0.93	*Saccharomyces cerevisiae*	0.90–0.94
Pseudomonas aeruginosa	0.96–0.98	*S. rouxii*	0.62–0.81
P. fluorescens	0.94–0.97	*Xeromyces bisporus*	0.60–0.61
Salmonella	0.93–0.96		

SOFTEL - Strengthening of Food Testing Laboratories Information Bank.

Six initiatives of the schemes

1. Support Mobile Food labs.
2. Strengthen referral Food Testing Laboratory.
3. Strengthen State Food Testing Laboratory.
4. Develop Food testing culture in schools/colleges.
5. Capacity building of Food Testing personnel.
6. Incentivize state to use facilities available in FSSAI notified private labs.

TABLE -4: Approximate Water Activities of Selected Foods

Food	a_w	Food	a_w
Fresh fruit or vegetables	0.97-1.00	Jelly	0.82-0.94
Fresh poultry or fish	0.98-1.00	Rice	0.80-0.87
Fresh meats	0.95-1.00	Fruitcake	0.80-0.87
Pudding	0.97-0.99	Flour	0.67-0.87
Eggs	0.97	Cake icing	0.76-0.84
Juices—fruit and vegetable	0.97	Molasses	0.76
Bread	0.95-0.96	Honey	0.54-0.75
White	0.94-0.97	Dried fruits	0.51-0.89
Crust	0.30	Chocolate candy	0.69
Cheese, most types	0.91-1.00	Rolled oats	0.65-0.75
Parmesan	0.68-0.76	Toffee	0.60-0.65
Cured meat	0.87-0.95	Caramels	0.60-0.65
Baked cake	0.90-0.94	Noodles	0.50
Refrigerated biscuit dough	0.94	Dried whole egg	0.40
Maple syrup	0.90	Biscuits	0.30
Salted egg yolk	0.90	Dried vegetables	0.20
Soft, moist pet food	0.83-0.91	Cereals	0.10-0.20
Nuts	0.66-0.84	Crackers	0.10
Jam	0.75-0.80	Sugar	0.10

TABLE -5: Some Typical Microbially Produced Microbial Inhibitors

Inhibitory Organism	Substance Produced	Organism Inhibited	Reference
Serratia marcescens	Prodigiosin	*E. coli, B. subtilis, Enterobacter aerogenes, S. aureus, P. aeruginosa*	Kalesperis, Prahalad, and Lynch (1975)
P. aeruginosa	Amino acid antimetabolite	*Bacillus* sp.	Scannell et. al (1972)
Saccharomyces cerevisiae	Glycoprotein	*Torulopsis glabrata*	Bussey and Skipper (1976)
Lactobacilli	Hydrogen peroxide	*Pseudomonas* sp. *Bacillus* sp. *Proteus* sp.	Price and Lee (1970)
C. perfringens	Unknown	*C. botulinum*	Smith (1975)
S. lactis	Nisin	*C. botulinum*	Scott and Taylor (1981)

TABLE- 6: Food Safety Standards of Milk 2006

Class of Milk	Designation	Milk Fat %	Milk Solid Not Fat %
Cow Milk	Raw Boiled Pasteurized Flavoured and Sterilized	3.5	8.5
Buffalo Milk	Raw, Pasteurized, Boiled, Flavoured, Sterilized	5	9
Goat Milk	Raw, Boiled, Pasteurized, Flavoured and Sterilized	3.5	9
Mixed Milk	Raw, Boiled, Pasteurized, Flavoured and Sterilized	4.5	8.5
Standardized Milk	Pasteurized, Flavoured and Sterilized	4.5	8.5
Toned Milk	Pasteurized, Flavoured and Sterilized	3	8.5
Double Toned Milk	Pasteurized, Flavoured and Sterilized	1.5	9
Skimmed Milk	Raw, Boiled, Pasteurized, Flavoured and Sterilized	Not More Than 0.5	8.7

TABLE -7: Approximate pH Range of Selected Foods

Food	pH Range	Food	pH Range
Egg white	7.6-9.5	Cabbage	5.2-6.3
Shrimp	6.8-8.2	Turnip	5.2-5.6
Crab	6.8-8.0	Spinach	5.1-6.8
Scallops	6.8-7.1	Asparagus	5.0-6.1
Cod. small	6.7-7.1	Cheeses, most	5.0-6.1
Cod. large	6.5-6.9	Camembert	6.1-7.0
Catfish	6.6-7.0	Cottage	4.1-5.4
Soda crackers	6.5-8.5	Gouda	4.7
Staple syrup	6.5-7.0	Bread	5.0-6.0
Milk	6.3-6.8	Carrots	4.9-6.3
Brussels sprouts	6.3-6.6	Beets	4.9-5.8
Whiting	6.2-7.1	Bananas	4.5-5.2
Haddock	6.2-6.7	Dry sausages	4.4-5.6
Cantaloupe	6.2-6.5	Pimientos	4.3-5.2
Dates	6.2-6.4	Tomato juice	3.9-4.7
Herring	6.1-6.6	Mayonnaise	3.8-4.0
Butter	6.1-6.4	Tomatoes	3.7-4.9
Honey	6.0-6.8	jams	3.5-4.0
Mushrooms	6.0-6.5	Apricots	3.5-4.0
Cauliflower	6.0-6.7	Apple sauce	3.4-3.5
Lettuce	6.0-6.4	Pears	3.4-4.7
Egg yolk	6.0-6.3	Grapes	3.3-4.5
Corn, sweet	5.9-6.5	Cherries	3.2-4.7
Oysters	5.9-6.6	Pineapple	3.2-4.1
Celery	5.7-6.0	Peaches	3.1-4.2

Peas	5.6-6.8	Rhubarb	3.1-3.2
Turkey	5.6-6.0	Strawberries	3.0-4.2
Chicken	5.5-6.4	Grapefruit	2.9-4.0
Halibut	5.5-5.8	Raspberries	2.9-3.7
Scans, lima	5.4-6.5	Apples	2.9-3.5
Potatoes, Irish	5.4-6.3	Plums	2.8-4.6
Walnuts	5.4-5.5	Oranges	2.8-4.0
Pork	5.3-6.4	Cranberries	2.5-2.8
Beef	5.3-6.2	Lemons	2.2-2.4
Onions	5.3-5.8	Limes	1.8-2.0
Sweet potatoes	5.3-5.6		

Organism	Temperature (0°C)		
	Minimum	Optimum	Maximum
Cladosporium	–5-8	-	-
Penicillum rubrum	-	25-28	-
Rhizopus stolonijer	5	-	25
Yeasts			
Candida	0	-	29-48
C. lipolytica	5	25	35-40
Hansenula	—	37-42	50
Saccharomyces	0-7	20-35	40
Torulopsis	0	17-25	30-35

TABLE -8: Provitamin A Value of Some Fruits and Vegetables

Product	IU/100 g
Carrots, mature	20,000
Carrots, young	10,000
Spinach	13,000
Sweet potato	6,000
Broccoli	3,500
Apricots	2,000
Lettuce	2,000
Tomato	1,200
Asparagus	1,000
Bean, french	1,000
Cabbage	500
Peach	800
Brussels sprouts	700
Watermelon	550
Banana	400
Orange juice	200

TABLE -9: Development of Pigments in the Ripening Tomato

Pigment	Green (mg/100 g)	Half-ripe (mg/100 g)	Ripe (mg/100 g)
Lycopene	0.11	0.84	7.85
Carotene	0.16	0.43	0.73
Xanthophyll	0.02	0.03	0.06
Xanthophyll ester	0	0.02	0.10

TABLE -10: Some Microbial Defects of Vegetables and Their Products

Food	Defect	Organism
Fresh vegetables	Soft rot, mushy	*Erwinia carotovora, Pseudomonas fluorescens*
	Soft black rot	*Alternaria, Rhizopus nigricans*
	Black mold rot	*Aspergillus niger*
	Blue mold rot	*Penicillium*
Beans, snap	Anthracnose	*Colletotrichum*
	Blight	*Xanthomonas*
Cabbage	Leaf spot	*Alternaria*
	Gray mold	*B. cinerea*
Carrots	Soft rot	*E. carotovora, Rhizopus stolonifer*
	Fungal rot	*Fusarium*
	Decay, wet rot	*Sclerotinia sclerotiorum, Rhizactonia carotae*
Celery	Fungal rot	*Mucor*
	Pink rot	*S. sclerotiorum*
Onions	Neck rot	*Botrytis allii*
	Rot	*Pseudomonas cepacia*
	Brown rot	*P. aeruginosa*
	Black mold	*Aspergillus niger*
Potatoes	Ring rot	*Corynebacterium*
	Dry rot	*Fusarium*
Tomatoes	Ferment	*Candida, Pichia, Hanseniaspora, Kloeckera*
	Fungal rot	*Alternaria, Aspergillus, Botrylis, Col. lelotrichum, Monilia, Penicillium, Rhizopus*
	Bacterial spot	*Xanthomonas*
	Soft rot	*Byssochlamys fulva*
Canned vegetables		
Corn, green beans, peas	Flat-sour	*Bacillus stearothermophilus*
	Sulfide stinker	*Desulfotomaculum nigrificans*
	Putrid swell	*Clostridium sporogenes*
	Hard swell	*Clostridium thermosaccharolyticum*
Tomato	Flat-sour	*Bacillus coagularts*
	Butyric fermentation	*Clostridium pasteurianum,* C. *butyri-cum*
Fermented vegetables		
Brine	Film forming	Yeasts *(Candida, Debaryomyces, Hansenula, Kloeckera, Pichia, Rhodotorula, Saccharomyces) Bacillus*
Pickles	Soft	*Bacillus*
	Black	*Bacillus*
	Soft, mushy, slimy	*B. subtilis*
	Reduced acidity	Yeasts
Sauerkraut	Pink	*Rhodotorula*
Vegetable juice	Sour	*Lactobacillus, Acelobacter*

TABLE -11: Microbial Defects of Red Meats and their Products

Food	Defect	Organism
Fresh, refrigerated (0°-5°C)	Off-odor, slime, discoloration	*Pseudomonas*, *Aeromonas*, *Alcaligenes*, *Acinetobacter*, *Microbacterium*, *Moraxella*, *Proteus*, *Flavobacterium*, *Atteromonas*, *Saccharomyces*
	Lipolysis, pungent odor	*Pseudomonas*, yeasts
	Moldy	*Penicillium*
	Whiskers	*Thamnidium*
	Black spot	*Cladosporium*
	White spot	*Sporotrichum*
Vaccum packaged	Acid, sweet, rancid	*Lactobacillus*, *Microbacterium*, *Fnterobacler*, *Hafnia*
Cured meat		
Bacon	Cheesy, sour, rancid	*Micrococcus*
	Discoloration	Molds
	Slight souring	*Lactobacillus*, *Micrococcus*, *Vibrio*, *Alcaligenes*, *Corynebacterium*
	Putrefaction	*Clostridium sporogenes*
	Vacuum packaged	Cabbage odor *Proleus inconstans*
	Tainted	*Vibrio*
Brines	Turbid	*Debaryomyces*, *Kloeckera*
Hain	Surface slime	*Micrococcus*, *Alicrobacterium*, Yeasts
	Gassy or puffy	*Clostridium*
	Green discoloration	*Lactobacillus*, *Streptococcus*, *Leucon. ostoc*
	Bone and meat "sours"	*Clostridium*
	Surface growth (dry-cured)	Molds
Sausages	Slime on surface	*Micrococcus*, yeasts
	Gas production (vacuum packed)	*Lactobacillus*
	Greenish discoloration	*Lactobacillus viridescens*, *Leuconostoc*
Fermented sausage	Slime	Yeasts
	Spots	Molds Canned
Commercially sterile	Gas, putrefaction	Sporeformers *(Bacillus*, *Clostridium)*
Semi-preserved	Souring, discoloration	*Streptococcus*
	Putrefaction, gas	*Bacillus*, *Clostridium*

BANNED PESTICIDES

TABLE -12 : List of Pesticides Restricted or Banned in the Country

Pesticides restricted for use

	Pesticide	Restriction
1.	Aluminium phosphide	It is to be sold only to government undertakings/ organisations and to be used under strict supervision of government experts or Pest Control Operators.
2.	Captafol	The use of captafol as foliar spray is banned. It shall be used as seed dresser.
3.	Cypermethrin	Cypermethrin 3% Smoke Generator is to be used only through Pest Control Operators and not allowed to be used by General Public.
4.	Dazomet	The use of Dazomet is not permitted on tea.
5.	DDT	Restricted for use in public health only.
6.	Fenitrothion	The use of fenitrothion is banned on Agriculture except for locust control in scheduled desert area and public health
7.	Methyl bromide	Restriction for its sale and use is similar to that of Aluminium phosphide.
8.	Monocrotophos	Banned for use in vegetables.
9.	Trifluralin	Restricted for use in wheat only.

List of pesticides that are banned, refused registration & restricted in use as on 31.10.2019;

1. Pesticides Banned for Manufacture, Import & Usage.

1. Aldicarb	2. Aldrin	3. Benzene Hexachloride
4. Benomyl	5. Calcium Cyanide	6. Carbaryl
7. Chlorbenzilate	8. Chlordane	9. Chlorofenvinphos
10. Copper Acetoarsenite	11. Diazinon	12. Dibromochloropropane
13. Dieldrin	14. Endosulfron	15. Endrin
16. Ethyl Mercury Chloride	17. Ethyl Parathion	18. Ethylene Dibromide
19. Fenarimol	20. Fenthion	21. Heptachlor
21. Lindane	23. Linuron	22. Maleic Hydrazide
25. Menazon	24. Methoxy Ethyl Mercury Chloride	27. Methyl Parathion
26. Metoxuron	29. Nitrofen	28. Paraquat Dimethyl Sulphate
31. Pentachloro Nitrobenzene (PCNB)	30. Pentachlorophenol	33. Phenyl Mercury Acetate
32. Sodium Cyanide	35. Sodium Methane Arsonate	34. Tetradifon
37. Thiometon	36. Toxaphene(Camphechlor)	39. Tridemorph
38. Trichloro acetic acid (TCA)		

2. Pesticide Formulations Banned for Import, Manufacture & Use.

1. Carbofuron 50% SP, 2. Methomyl 12.5% L,
3. Methomyl 24% formulation, 4. Phosphamidon 85% SL

3. Pesticide / Pesticide Formulations Banned for Use but Continued to Manufacture for Export

1. Captafol 80% Powder 2. Nicotin Sulfate

Source: Directorate of Plant Protection, Quarantine & Storage, Ministry of Agriculture and Farmers Welfare.

GLOSSARY

A

Aflatoxins carcinogenic mycotoxins formed by *Aspergillus avus*, *A. parasiticus* and *A. nominus* growing on nuts, cereals, dried fruit and cheese, especially when stored under damp warm conditions.

Absorption: Uptake of moisture by dry foods.

Acid food: A food with a pH of less than 4.6 and a water activity (a_w) equal to or greater than 0.85.

Acidity: It is sourness or tartness in food product.

Actinomycete: An aerobic, gram positive bacterium that forms branching filaments (hyphae) and asexual spores.

Additives: Chemicals added to food to improve their eating quality or shelf life.

Adiabatic process: Processing in which no heat is added or removed from a system.

Adulterants: Chemicals that are intentionally added to food which are forbidden by law. Adulterant means any material which is or could be employed for making the food unsafe or sub-standard or mis-branded or containing extraneous matter;

Advertisement means any audio or visual publicity, representation or pronouncement made by means of any light, sound, smoke, gas, print, electronic media, internet or website and includes through any notice, circular, label, wrapper,, invoice or other documents;

Alkaline phosphatase: An enzyme in raw milk having a similar *D*-value to heat-resistant pathogens, used to test for effectiveness of pasteurization.

Ames test: An *in vitro* test for the ability of chemicals, including potential food additives, to cause mutation in bacteria (the mutagenic potential). Commonly used as a preliminary screening method to detect substances likely to be carcinogenic.

Aseptic processing: Heat sterilization of foods before filling into pre-sterilized (aseptic) containers.

Atomiser: A device to form fine droplets of food (*e.g.* in a spray drier).

Avidin: Protein in white of eggs that binds biotin with very high affinity.

B

Bacteriocins: Naturally produced peptides that inhibit other micro-organisms, similar in effect to antibiotics.

Bacteriophage: The virus which infects bacteria and causes the lysis of bacterial cells.

Basal metabolic rate (BMR): The energy cost of maintaining the metabolic integrity of the body, nerve and muscle tone, respiration and circulation. For children the BMR also includes the energy cost of growth. It depends on the amount of metabolically active body tissue, and hence can be calculated from body weight, height and age.

Biological oxidation demand (BOD): A measure of the oxygen requirement by micro-organisms when breaking down organic matter, used as a measure of the polluting potential of materials in water.

Biological value (BV): A measure of protein quality.

Blancher: Equipment used to blanch foods.

Blanching: Heating foods, especially vegetables, to below 100°C for a short time, to both inactivate enzymes which would cause a loss of quality during storage and to remove air and soften the food.

Blinding: Blocking of a sieve by food particles.

Bloom: A thin layer of unstable forms of cocoa fat that crystallize at the surface of a coating to produce dullness or white specks.

Botulin: An exotoxin produced by *Cl. Botulinum*, able to cause fatal food poisoning.

Breading: The application of pre-prepared breadcrumbs to the surface of a food.

Brine solution: A solution of salt in water.

Brining: The process of soaking vegetables in brine before pickling in vinegar, in order to remove some of the water, and retain a crisp texture.

C

Candy: Sugar confectionery crystallised sugar made by repeated boiling and slow evaporation.

Casson yield value: A measure of the rheological properties (shear stress and viscosity) of chocolate.

Case hardening: Formation of a hard impermeable skin on some foods during drying, which reduces the rate of drying and produces a food with a dry surface and a moist interior.

Cavitation: Production of bubbles in foods by ultrasound and their rapid expansion/ contraction.

Chairperson means the Chairperson of the Food Authority;

Chemical oxidation demand (COD): A chemical method used to measure the polluting potential of materials in water.

Chilling: Reduction in the temperature of a food to between – 1°C and 8°C.

Chilling injury: (1) It is a result from the exposure of susceptible tissues to temperature below 15°C. It is characterized by sunken areas in the skin of vegetable (pitting) discoloration and in tomato failure to ripen. (2) Physiological changes to some types of fruits and vegetables caused by low temperatures which result in loss of eating quality.

Choke: Restriction of the outlet to a mill to retain particles until sufficiently small (or restriction of the outlet in an extruder).

Chromatography : A process in which a chemical mixture carried by a liquid or gas is separated into components as a result of differential distribution of the solutes as they flow around or over a stationary liquid or solid phase.

Claim means any representation which states, suggests, or implies that a food has particular qualities relating to its origin, nutritional properties, nature, processing, composition.

Climacteric: Abrupt increase in respiration rate in some fruits during ripening with in creased ethylene production and cellular respiration.

Climacteric fruits: The **climacteric** is a stage of **fruit** ripening associated with increased ethylene production and a rise in cellular respiration. Apples, bananas, melons, apricots, and tomatoes (among others) are **climacteric fruit.**

Clinching: Partial sealing of can lids.

Collapse temperature: The maximum temperature of a frozen food before solute movement causes a collapse of the food structure and prevents movement of water vapour during freeze drying.

Compressive strength: The maximum compressive stress which a material is capable of sustaining. Compressive strength is calculated from the maximum load during a compression test and the original cross sectional area of the specimen.

Compound coating: A coating material in which cocoa solids and hardened vegetable oils are used to replace cocoa butter.

Computed tomography of foods: A special x-ray examination which provides sectional images of the human body other high technology computer manipulation.

Consumer means persons and families purchasing and receiving food in order to meet their personal needs;

Contaminant means any substance, whether or not added to food, but which is present in such food as a result of the production (including operations carried out in crop husbandry, animal husbandry or veterinary medicine), manufacture, processing, preparation, treatment, packing, packaging, transport or holding of such food or as a result of environmental contamination and does not include insect fragments, rodent hairs and other extraneous matter;

Controlled atmosphere storage (CAS): It refers to decrease oxygen and increased carbon dioxide concentration and implies precise control of these gases.

Cordial: It is also a liquid product similar to squash. It should contain minimum 25 % fruit juice. The sugar and total soluble solids should not be less than 30 percent in a cordial. It can contain 2-2.5 g per litre of potassium metabisulphite as a preservative. One can add citric acid, food colours, preservatives and fruit flavour in a cordial.

Critical control point (CCP): A processing factor of which a loss of control would result in an unacceptable food safety or quality risk.

Critical moisture content: The amount of moisture in a food at the end of the constant- rate period of drying.

Crush: It is also a liquid drink product similar to squash, which should contain fruit juice and pulp. The minimum percentage of fruit juice in crush is about 25 percent. It should contain not less than 55 percent of sugar and total soluble solids in the final product.

Crust: Hard surface layer on baked foods.

Cryogen: A refrigerant that absorbs latent heat and changes phase from solid or liquid to a gas, *e.g.* subliming or evaporating carbon dioxide or liquid nitrogen.

Cryogenic freezers: Equipment that uses subliming or evaporating carbon dioxide or liquid nitrogen directly in contact with food to freeze it.

Cryopreservation: A process where cells or whole tissues are preserved by cooling to low sub-zero temperatures, such as (typically) 77 °K or –196 °C (the boiling point of liquid nitrogen).

Curing: It is process of skin hardening as it reduces the post harvest microbial decay or it is a process which is induced at relatively higher temperature and relative humidity and involves sub-sterilization of outer tissues followed by development of wound periderm which act as effective barriers against infestations and water logged

D

Dead-folding: A crease or fold made in a material that will stay in place.

Degreening: Loss of green colour by the application of ethylene under the controlled condition.

Dehydration: Removal of moisture by application of artificial heat under controlled condition of temperature and humidity.

Dehydro-freezing: In this method freezing is preceded by partial dehydration. In some fruits and vegetables about 50 percent of moisture is removed by dehydration prior to freezing. It can not cause any deterioration and ultimately such types of foods are relatively more stable.

Density: it is the mass per unit volume. $D = M/V$, Where- M is the mass, V is the volume and D is the density.

Designated Officer means the officer appointed under section 36.

Detergents: Chemicals that reduce the surface tension of water and hence assist in the release of soils from equipment or foods.

Detoxication: The metabolism of (potentially) toxic compounds to yield less toxic derivatives that are more soluble in water and can be excreted in the urine or bile.

Development phase: Growth and maturation are often collectively referred to as the development phase.

Dew point: Temperature at which an air–water vapour mixture becomes saturated with moisture, marking the onset of condensation.

Dilatant material: Food in which the consistency increases with shear rate.

Disinfection: It is the killing, inhibition, or removal of microorganisms that may cause diseases.

Dormancy: period of suspended growth.

Dose means quantity in the fields of nutrition, medicine, and toxicology.

Dosimeter: A device that qualitatively or quantitatively measures the dose of irradiation received by a food.

Dry bulb temperature: Temperature measured by a dry thermometer in an air–water vapour mixture.

Dry weight basis (dwb): The composition of a wet food based on the mass of dry solids it contains.

Drying and Dehydration: Drying means removal of water. Fruits and vegetables are dried under the sun to preserve and extend shelf life. Sun is the most abundantly available source of energy. Sun drying has certain limitations such as seasonal variation, exposure to dust, insects, requiring large area for drying.

Drying: Removal of free water (lowering of water activity below 0.7) from fruits and vegetables to the extent where microorganism do not survive and reproduce. Generally this term is used under the influence of non-conventional energy resources.

E

***E. coli* (*Escherichia coli*):** Group of bacteria including both harmless commensals in the human gut and strains that cause food poisoning by production of enterotoxins.

Edible coating: These are continuous matrices prepared from edible materials such as proteins, polysaccharides and lipids and very promising system for preserving fruits and vegetables.

EDTA: Ethylene diamine tetra-acetic acid, a chelating agent that forms stable chelation complexes with metal ions. Also called versene, sequestrol and sequestrene. It can be used both to remove metal ions from a solution (or at least to remove them from activity) and also to add metal ions, for example in plant fertilisers (E-385).

Elastic limit: The greatest stress at which a material is capable of sustaining without any permanent strain remaining upon complete release of the stress. Example: Rubber

Electroporation: Use of high-voltage electric pulses at low-voltage gradients to exchange genetic information between protoplast cells of micro-organisms, plants or animals. At high-voltage gradients (up to 30kV/cm) used to sterilise or pasteurise food by permeabilisation of bacterial cell membranes.

Electrophoresis: It is the migration of charged particles towards opposite poles under the influence of electric field.

Emulsification: Creation of an emulsion by the dispersion of one immiscible liquid (dispersed phase) in the form of small droplets in a second immiscible liquid (continuous phase).

Entrainment: Oil droplets that are carried over in steam produced by vigorously frying foods, leading to loss of oil, or loss of concentrated droplets of product with vapour during evaporation by boiling.

Ergotism: Ergotism is the effect of long-term ergot poisoning, traditionally due to the ingestion of the alkaloids produced by the Claviceps purpurea fungus that infects rye and other cereals, and more recently by the action of a number of ergoline-based drugs.

Eutectic temperature (in freezing): The temperature at which a crystal of an individual solute exists in equilibrium with the unfrozen liquor and ice.

Evaporative Cooling: Evaporative cooling devices are simple and inexpensive ways to keep vegetables fresh without the use of electricity. These devices function according to a basic principle called "evaporative cooling," where the evaporation of water from a surface removes heat, creating a cooling effect.

Expeller: A horizontal barrel, containing a helical screw, used to extract oil from seeds or nuts.

Extractors: Equipment used to extract food components using solvents.

Extraneous matter means any matter contained in an article of food which may be carried from the raw materials, packaging materials or process systems used for its manufacture or which is added to it, but such matter does not render such article of food unsafe;

F

Fehling's reagent: Alkaline cupric tartrate solution used for detection and semi quantitative determination of glucose and other reducing sugars.

Fermentation: Anaerobic metabolism, used generally of alcoholic fermentation of sugars, also production of acetic, lactic, and citric acids by micro-organisms in pickling and manufacture of vinegar.

Filter cake: Solids removed by filtration.

Filtration: The separation of solids from liquids by passing the mixture through a bed of porous material.

Flash point: With reference to frying oils, the temperature at which the decomposition products can be ignited, but will not support combustion; ranges between 290 to 330°C.

Food safety means assurance that food is acceptable for human consumption according to its intended use.

Food safety audit means a systematic and functionally independent examination of food safety measures adopted by manufacturing units to determine whether such measures and related results meet with objectives of food safety and the claims made in that behalf.

Food Safety Officer means an officer appointed under section 37 of the FSS act.

Food Safety Management System" means the adoption of Good manufacturing practices, Good hygienic practices, Hazard Analysis and Critical Control Point (HACCP) and such other practices as may be specified by regulation, for the food business.

Forming: Moulding of doughs and other materials into different shapes.

Fortification: Deliberate addition of one or more micronutrients to particular foods, so as to increase its nutritional quality.

Fouling: Deposits of food or limescale on surfaces of heat exchangers.

Free moisture: Moisture in excess of the equilibrium moisture content at a particular temperature and humidity, and so free to be removed.

Freeze concentration: Concentration of liquid foods by freezing water to ice and removal of ice crystals.

Freeze-drying: In this process food is first frozen at –18 °C on trays in the lower chamber of a freeze drier. Freezing stops microbial activity. Enzyme activity is only retarded at freezing temperature.

Freezing injury: It results from the freezing of the tissue and formation of the ice crystal at the temperature below the freezing point. Fruit is a matured or ripened ovary with or without necessary organs.

Friability: It is the ability of the grains to break down and expose new sharp edges, which will increase the material removal rate with more accurate tolerances

***F*-value:** The time required to destroy a given percentage of micro-organisms at a specified reference temperature and *z* value.

G

Glutelins: Proteins insoluble in water and neutral salt solutions but soluble in dilute acids and alkalis, *e.g.* wheat glutenin.

Goetrichum disease: Geotrichum candidum is an important pathogen on tomato, pointed gourd, watermelon and muskmelon. It is commonly found in foods that contain lactic acid. It is particularly found on pickle forming a white skin. Mycelial hyphae of this fungi break up to into cuboid or cylindrical spores.

Good manufacturing practice (GMP): Part of a food and drink control operations aimed at ensuring that products are consistently manufactured to a quality standard appropriate to their intended use.

Grading: (1) Sorting of produce on the basis of size and color to obtain uniform quality. (2) The assessment of a number of attributes to obtain an indication of overall quality of a food.

Granulation: Processing of a food into small compact particles (granules). Granulators are often used in cane and beet sugar manufacture to remove unbound moisture from the sugar by driers and coolers. Moisture is removed in driers by blowing hot air through a stream of cascading sugar or through a bed of wet sugar.

H

Halphen test: For the presence of cottonseed oil in other oils and fats.

Hardening: It is a treatment given immediately after the harvesting of flowers by using water to restore turgidity.

Harvest maturity: it may be defined as a point in time when a crop can be harvested and it will continue to grow and develop to reach maximum quality if necessary.

Hazard: a danger or risk. It is an agent which has the potential to cause harm to a vulnerable target. The terms "**hazard**" and "risk" are often used interchangeably. Hazard means a biological, chemical or physical agent in food with the potential to cause an adverse health effect.

Hazard analysis: The identification of potentially hazardous ingredients, storage conditions, packaging, critical process points and relevant human factors which may affect product safety or quality.

Headspace: The space in a container between the surface of a food and the underside of the lid.

Heat sterilization: Destruction of the majority of micro-organisms in a food by heating.

Homofermentative micro-organisms: Micro-organisms that produce a single main byproduct.

Hurdle technology: The concept of mild but effective food preservation based on considering all the different factors that inhibit (or act as hurdles to) the growth of spoilage organisms.

Hydrocooling: Immersion of fruits and vegetables in chilled water. It can be used on most commodities that are not sensitive to wetting. Water removes heat about five times faster than air, but is less energy efficient. Mechanical refrigeration is the most efficient method of cooling water. A thermal storage immersion hydro-cooler system can be economically fabricated for various volume needs. Ice in water will also provide a source of coolant.

Hydrophile-lipophile balance (HLB value): The ratio of hydrophilic to hydrophobic groups on the molecules of an emulsifier.

Hydrolyse: To split a complex compound into its constituent parts by the action of water, either enzymically or catalysed by the addition of acid or alkali. Hence hydrolysis.

Hydrophilic: A solute that will dissolve in water and other polar solvents.

Hydrophobic: A solute that will dissolve in non-polar solvents, but not in water.

Hydroponics: The practice of growing plants without soil in a solution of inorganic salts.

Hydrostatic head: The pressure resulting from the weight of a column of liquid.

Hygroscopic foods: Foods in which the partial pressure of water vapour varies with the moisture content.

Hypobaric storage: It is a form of controlled atmospheric storage in which the produce is stored in partial vacuum.

Hypotonic: A solution more dilute than the body ûuids, *See* isotonic.

I

Ion exchange: The selective removal of charged molecules from a liquid by electrostatic adsorption, followed by their transfer to a second liquid using an ion-exchange material.

Ionisation: Breakage of chemical bonds (*e.g.* during irradiation).

Irradiation: It is one of the newer technologies that can be gainfully employed during storage to reduce post-harvest losses and extend storage life of fruits and vegetables. Gamma irradiation helps to extend the shelf life of horticultural produce in the following manner.

Impellers: A driven rotor used to increase the pressure and flow of a fluid.

Ingestion: The process of taking food, drink, or another substance into the body by swallowing or absorbing it.

Instant foods: Dried foods that reconstitute rapidly when water is added *e.g.* Tea, coffee, milk, soups, precooked cereal products, potatoes. The dried powders may be agglomerated to control particle size and improve solubility. 'Instant puddings' are formulated with pre-gelatinised starch and disperse rapidly in cold milk.

Irradiation: Ionising radiation (X-rays, α-rays and γ-rays) kills microorganisms and insects, so is used for sterilisation of foods; also inhibits sprouting of potatoes.

Irritant: A substance that causes slight inflammation or other discomfort to the body.

Isostatic pressure: Uniform pressure throughout a food.

Isoenzymes: Enzymes that have the same catalytic activity, but different structures, properties and/or tissue distribution.

J

Jam: It is a product made by boiling fruit product with sufficient sugar to a reasonably thick consistency, firm enough to the fruit tissues in position.

Jelly: It is a semi solid product prepared by boiling a clear, strained solution of pectin containing fruit extract, free from pulp after the addition of sugar and acid.

Junket: Dessert made from milk by treating with rennet to curdle the protein. flavoured; known in North America as jello.

K

Kelvin: It is the primary unit of temperature measurement in the physical sciences, but is often used in conjunction with the degree Celsius, which has the same magnitude. The definition implies that absolute zero (0 K) is equivalent to –273.15 °C (–459.67 °F).

Karl Fischer method: For determination of the moisture content of dehydrated foods. Water is extracted from the sample into anhydrous methanol, then titrated against the Karl Fischer reagent (sulphur dioxide, pyridine and iodine in anhydrous methanol) with electrometric determination of the end-point

Kimchi: Korean; dish based on fermented cabbage with garlic, red peppers and pimientos, often with the addition of fish and other foods.

Kreis test: It is used to measure rancidity of fat/oil. It is based on the reaction between rancidity product (epihydirin) and phloroglucinol (Kreis reagent) to form red colour complex. The intensity of the red colour is proportional to the extent of oxidation.

L

Label means any tag, brand, mark, pictorial or other descriptive matter, written, printed, stencilled, marked, embossed, graphic, perforated, stamped or impressed on or attached to container, cover, lid or crown of any food package.

Lactobacillus: Genus of bacteria capable of growth in acidic medium, and producing lactic acid by fermentation of carbohydrates. Responsible for souring of milk, and production of flavour in yogurt and other fermented milk products.

Lamination: Bonding together of two or more packaging films, papers or foods.

Lauric acid: A medium-chain length saturated fatty acid (C12:0) in butter, coconut oil and palm oil.

Leaching: Washing out of soluble components from the food.

Lethality: Integrated effect of heating temperature and time on micro-organisms.

Licence means a licence granted under section 31.

Low acid food: A food with a pH greater than 4.6 and a water activity (a_w) equal to or greater than 0.85.

Lyophobic: A solute that has little or no affinity for the solvent medium.When the solvent is water the term hydrophobic is used.

M

Marmalade: it is fruit jelly in which slices of the fruit of its peel are suspended.

Mashing: The process in which cereals are mixed with water and incubated in order to degrade their complex carbohydrates (*e.g.* starch) to more readily usable forms such as simple sugars.

Maturation: It commences before growth ceases and includes different activities in different commodities.

Maturity index: The factors for determining the harvesting of fruits, vegetables and plantation crops according to consumer's purpose, type of commodity, etc. ,and can be judged by visual means (colour, size, shape), physical means (firmness, softness), chemical analysis (sugar content, acid content), computation (heat unit and bloom to harvest period), physiological method(respiration).

Mechanical damage: An alteration in the appearance of commodities in the form of cuts, punctures, cracks, splits *etc.*

Mechanical refrigerators: Equipment which evaporates and compresses a refrigerant in a continuous cycle, using cooled air, cooled liquid or cooled surfaces to freeze foods.

Melting point: The temperature at which a compound melts to a liquid. Often characteristic of a particular chemical and used as a means of identification, and as an index of purity, since impurities lower the melting point.

Methylene blue dye-reduction test: When the dye methylene blue is added to milk, any bacteria present take up oxygen and decolourise the dye.A similar test uses resazurin, which changes from blue-purple to pink. The speed of the change indicates the bacterial content.

Microfiltration: A pressure-driven membrane process using membranes with a pore size of 0.2–2 μm at lower pressures than ultrafiltration.

Mimetics: Low calorie fat substitutes.

Modified atmosphere storage (MAS): The term is used when the composition the storage atmosphere is not closely controlled, *e.g.*, in plastic film packages, where the change in the composition of the atmosphere arises intentionally or unintentionally.

N

Nanofiltration: A membrane process to separate particles with molecular weights from 300–1000Da, using lower pressures than reverse osmosis.

Nectar: It is prepared from fruit juice and the product should contain at least 20percent fruit juice. The total soluble solids in the final product should not be less than 15 percent. It is prepared from mango, apple, orange etc. Tetrapak apple nectar available in the market.

Nip: The gap between rollers in a mill or a moulding/forming machine.

Non-hygroscopic foods: Foods that have a constant water vapour pressure at different moisture contents.

Non-Newtonian liquid: Food in which the viscosity changes with rate of shear.

Nucleoproteins: The complex of proteins and nucleic acids found in the cell nucleus.

Nutrification: The addition of nutrients to foods at such a level as to make a' major contribution to the diet.

O

Ohmic heating: Sterilisation by heat generated by passing an electric current through the food or mixture.

Optimum temperature: It is a particular temperature at which the commodities can be stored for a maximum length of time.

Osmosis: The passage of water through a semi-permeable membrane.

Oxycalorimeter: Instrument for measuring the oxygen consumed and carbon dioxide produced when a food is burned, as distinct from the calorimeter, which measures the heat produced.

P

Panning: The process of building up thin layers of sugar, sweetener or other coatings in a controlled way onto solid cores of nuts, fruit, etc.

Parboiling: A optional hydrothermal treatment given to crop paddy prior to its milling to achieve maximum recovery of head rice and to minimize breakage.

Parts per million (ppm): It means parts of solute (mg) presents in per liter solution

Pasteurisation: A relatively mild heat treatment in which food is heated to below 100°C to preserve it without substantial changes to sensory characteristics or nutritional value. In low acid foods, the main reason for pasteurisation is destruction of pathogens.

Penicillial diseases: Several spp. of penicillum are responsible for rotting in fruits and in some vegetables. The important spp. are *P. expansum* on apple.

Pericarp: The fibrous layers next to the outer husk of cereal grains and outside the testa; of low digestibility and removed from grain during milling. The major constituent of bran.

Perishable: Deterioration quickly after harvest of horticultural and food crops.

Physiological losses: The loss which is caused by changes in Physiological processes and accompanied by decrease in the nutritive value is known as Physiological losses.

Physiological maturity: It refers to the stage in the development of the fruits and vegetables when maximum growth and maturation has occurred. It is usually associated with full ripening in the fruits. The Physiological mature stage is followed by senescence.

Physiological stages: Fruits and vegetables can be conveniently divided into three major physiological stages following initiation and germination. These are – (*i*) Growth (*iv*) Maturation (*iii*) Senescence

Pickling: Preservation of food in common salt or in vinegar is known as pickling. Plant product with aromatic flavour, which are either naturally sweet or normally sweetened before eating,: they are essentially dessert foods (Horticultural).

Plasticiser: Chemicals added to plastic films to make them more flexible.

Polymorphic fat: A fat that can crystallise into more than one form.

Pre-cooling: It is the first post harvest operation and an effective way to remove the field heat from the produce immediately after harvest resulting slowdown deterioration. Fast cooling achieved by pre-cooling rooms or equipments with air (room cooling), iced water (hydro cooler), ice (package icing) or vacuum (vacuum cooler).

Preforms: Small dense pellets made in an extruder from pre-gelatinised cereal dough, which are suitable for extended storage until they are converted to snackfoods by frying, toasting or puffing. (Also known as 'halfproducts'.)

Press cake: Solid residue remaining after extraction of liquid component from foods.

Proportional limit: The greatest stress which a material is capable of sustaining without any deviation from proportionality of stress to strain (Hooke's law).

Pseudoplastic material: Foods in which the viscosity decreases with increasing shear rate.

Psychrometrics: The study of inter-related properties of air–water vapour systems.

Q

Quality assurance: Planned and systematic actions recommended to provide adequate confidence that a product or service will satisfy the given requirements for quality

Quality control: The operational techniques and activities that fulfill quality requirements

Quality system: The organisational structure, responsibilities, procedures and resources for implementing quality management

Quick freezing: Rapid freezing of food by exposure to a blast of air at a very low temperature. Unlike slow freezing, very small crystals of ice are formed, which do not rupture the cells of the food and so the structure is relatively undamaged. A quickfrozen food is commonly defined as one that has been cooled from a temperature of 0 °C to –5° or lower, in a period of not more than 2h and then cooled to –18°C.

Quintal: 1 quintal = 100 kg (220 lb).

Quinine: Bitter alkaloid extracted from bark of the cinchona tree (*Cinchona officinalis*), formerly used to treat or prevent malaria and in apéritif wines, bitters and tonic water.

R

Radurization: Radurization, is a process of food irradiation in which certain packaged and non-packaged foods (such as potatoes and spices) are treated with mild ionizing radiation dose, usually less than 10 kGray, but sufficient to eliminate or to significantly reduce the number of pathogens and to extend the shelf life. The process is intended to sterilize foods by destroying or inactivating microorganisms that contribute to spoilage, including vegetative bacteria. The required dose is in the range of 0.4 – 10 kGy.

Radappertization: Radappertization is a form of food irradiation which applies a dose of ionizing radiation sufficient to reduce the number and activity of viable microorganisms to such an extent that very few, if any, are detectable in the treated food by any recognized method (viruses being excepted). No microbial spoilage or toxicity should become detectable in a food so treated, regardless of the conditions under which it is stored, provided the packaging remains undamaged. The required dose is usually in the range of 25-45 kiloGrays.

Rancidity: Rancidity is the term used to represent the deterioration of fats and oils resulting in an unpleasant taste. Fats containing unsaturated fatty acids are more susceptible to rancidity. Rancidity occurs when fats and oils are exposed to air, moisture, light, bacteria etc. Hydrolytic rancidity occurs due to partial hydrolysis of triacylglycerols by bacterial enzymes. Oxidative rancidity in fats and oil is due to oxidation of unsaturated fatty acids. This results in the formation of unpleasant products such as dicarboxylic acids, aldehydes, ketones etc. Oxygen is required through the formation of intermediate namely, peroxides. Rancid fats and oils are unsuitable for human consumption.

Recrystallisation: Physical changes to ice crystals (changes in shape, size or orientation) which are an important cause of quality loss in some frozen foods.

Redox potential: Oxidation/reduction potential of a food or microbial substrate.

Refractometry: Measurement of refractive index using one of the several types of refractometer.

Refrigerant: A liquid that has a low boiling point and high latent heat of vaporisation so that it can change phase and absorb or lose heat in a refrigerator.

Refrigeration: It is the process of removing the heat from a substance and maintain it at a lower temperature.

Relative humidity: It is the ratio of mass of water vapour actually present in any volume of air at any temperature to the mass of water vapour required to saturate the same volume of air, at the same temperature. It is generally expressed as %.

Rennet: It is a complex set of enzymes produced in the stomachs of ruminant mammals. Chymosin, its key component, is a protease enzyme that curdles the casein in milk. This helps young mammals digest their mothers' milk. **Rennet** can also be used to separate milk into solid curds for cheese making and liquid whey

Resilience: The capacity of material for storage of strain energy in the elastic range (kg/cm^3). Thus the area under the unloading curve is a measure of resilience of the material. As in the case of toughness, when a force deformation curve is used, the size of the specimen and the loaded area should be specified.

Resistance: located 1 cm apart (*i.e.* the resistance of 1 cm^3 of product), having units of ohms cm^{-2} cm^{-1}.

Respiration: It can be described as the oxidative break down of the most complex material normally present in the cell into simpler molecules or Metabolic activity of living animal or plant tissues.

Rice bran: Outer layers of rice seeds. Used as a source of rice bran oils and protein concentrates and as a fibre ingredient in bakery products.

S

Saponification value: No. of milligrams of KOH required to saponify 1 g of fat or oil is the Saponification value. It is the measure of the average molecular weight of the fatty acids. It is also called as *Koettstorfer number.*

Senescence: It may be defined as the period when synthetic biochemical processes give way to degradative processes, leading to ageing and finally death of the tissues.

Sausage: Chopped meat, commonly beef or pork, seasoned with salt and spices, mixed with cereal (usually wheat rusk prepared from crumbed unleavened biscuits) and packed into casings.

Shelf life: It is a period between storage and the use of food product.

Shear strength: The maximum shear stress that a material is capable of sustaining. Shear stress is calculated from the maximum load during a shear or torsion test and is based on the original dimension of the cross section of specimen.

Sorting: Separation of damaged discolored and diseased fruits/ vegetables from the sound ones is called sorting or the process of arbitrarily classifying in to quality groups without following standard(maturity, cleanliness, decay, defects) is called sorting. The separation of foods into categories on the basis of a measurable physical property.

Specific gravity: The relative density of the substance is the ratio of its density to the density of standard substance under ideal conditions of temperature and pressure.

Specific growth rate: The slope of the curve when the natural logarithm of microbial cell concentration is plotted against time.

Specific heat: The amount of heat that accompanies a unit change in temperature by a unit mass of material.

Stabilisers: Hydrocolloids that dissolve in water to form viscous solutions or gels.

Starch Retrogradation: It is a reaction that takes place in gelatinized starch when the amylose and amylopectin chains realign themselves, causing the liquid to gel.

Sterilants: Chemicals that are inactivate micro-organisms.

Sublimation: A change in state of water directly from ice to water vapour without melting.

Substrate: A growth medium for micro-organisms.

Sulphitation: Placing of blanched vegetables 0.5% solution of Potassium metabisulphite for sufficient time.

Supercooling: A phenomenon in which water remains liquid although the temperature is below its freezing point.

Supercritical carbon Dioxide: Liquid CO_2 used to extract food components.

Susceptor: A packaging material that is used to create a localised high temperature in microwave ovens; usually made from lightly metallised polyethylene terephthalate.

T

Tempering: Cooling food to close to its freezing point, or a process of re-heating, stirring and cooling chocolate to remove unstable forms of polymorphic fats.

Tenderometer: Instrument to measure the stage of maturity of peas to determine whether they are ready for cropping or the tenderness of meat. Measures the force required to effect a shearing action.

Tensile strength: The maximum tensile stress that a material is capable of sustaining. Tensile strength is calculated from the maximum load during test carried to rupture and the original cross sectional area of the specimen.

Thermal centre: The point in a food that heats or cools most slowly.

Thermal conductivity: A measure of the heat transfer properties of solid materials. The rate at which heat moves through materials.

Thermal death time (TDT) or *F*-value: The time required to achieve a specified reduction in microbial numbers at a given temperature.

Thermal processing: The basic purpose for the thermal processing of foods is to reduce or destroy microbial activity, reduce or destroy enzyme activity and to produce physical or chemical changes to make the food meet a certain quality standard. *e.g.* gelatenization of starch & denaturation of proteins to produce edible food.

Thermal shock: *Heating:* fracture to a glass container caused by rapid changes in temperature; *freezing:* a rapid reduction in temperature that causes foods to fracture.

Texture: Combination of physical properties perceived by senses of kinaesthesis muscle–nerve endings), touch (including mouthfeel), sight and hearing.

Topping: Trimming of the top portion of the plants.

Toughness: The work required to cause rupture in the material. This can be approximated by the area under the stress strain or force deformation curve upto the point selected as the rupture point (kg/cm^3). If in estimating toughness, a force deformation curve is used, the size of the specimen and loading surface area should be specified.

U

Ultra filtration: (1) A membrane filtration process that removes large organics exceeding 20,000 molecular weight. It is done under high pressure. (2) Unit operation in which solutes having molecular weights in the range of 1–200 kDA are selectively removed using a semi-permeable membrane operating at lower pressure than reverse osmosis.

Ultra high temperature, ultra heat treated something such as milk that has undergone a process of sterilisation at very high temperatures for a very short time. Abbreviation UHT.

Ultrasound: Sound above the normal range of human hearing, commonly above 20kHz.

Ultrasonication: Treatment of foods using ultrasound.

Ultrasonics: The science and application of ultrasonic waves which has a frequency above audible, generally defined as above 20,000 hertz.

Unitised loads: Grouping of packages into larger loads.

Uperization: The sterilisation of milk using pressurised steam to raise temperature to 150°C

V

Vacreation: It is the type of pasteurization of milk or cream under reduced pressure by direct steam

Vacuum drying: Removal of liquid from a solid material while in a vacuum system, to lower the temperature at which evaporation takes place and thus prevent heat damage to the material.

Vanaspati: Grainy hydrogenated vegetable oils used as an alternative to ghee in India and Pakistan. Similar to margarines and often fortified with vitamin A and vitamin D.

Vinegar: A solution of acetic acid (not less than 4%); the product of two fermentations, first with yeast to convert sugars into alcohol; this liquor, called gyle (6–9% alcohol), is then fermented with *Acetobacter* spp. to form acetic acid.

Viscosity: The tendency of a fluid (liquid or gas) by virtue of it suppose to flow is called viscosity. It arises due to opposing forces between layers on account of relative motion.

Viscoelastic material: Food materials which exhibit viscous and elastic properties including stress relaxation, creep and recoil.

Volalility: The vapourzing ability of a fuel at a given temperature. It is measured by the distillation test in the fuel.

Votator a machine used in the manufacture of margarine.

W

Waiting period: Time taken in days to reach the insecticidal residue below the tolerance level.

Water activity: Water activity is denoted by (a_w) ratio between vapour pressure of water in the food and that of pure water at the same temperature.

Water-binding agent salt or sugar used for preserving foods by reducing their water activity.

Whey: The residue from milk after removal of the casein and most of the fat (as in cheese-making) also known as lactoserum.

Winterization: Process involving slow cooling of oils and removal of the precipitated fats with a relatively high melting point, so that the final product remains clear when refrigerated.

Waxing: An application of a thin layer of food grade bags that retards transpiration and add gloss to the fruits and vegetables is called waxing.

X

Xenobiotics: Substances that are foreign to living organisms. Can be synthetic or naturally occurring compounds. Examples include drugs, pesticides and carcinogens.

Xylan: Polysaccharide found in the cell walls of plants, where it forms the bulk of the hemicelluloses component.

Y

Yam: Tubers of perennial climbing plants of a number of species of *Dioscorea*, *D. rotundala* white yam and *D. Cayenensis*. A major food in parts of Africa and also the Far East.

Yeast: Unicellular organisms, sometimes grouped with the fungi; eukaryotic organisms with more complex subcellular organisation than bacteria. Some types are of major importance in the food industry. *Saccharomyces cerevisiae* and *S. carlsbergensis* are used in brewing, wine-making and baking.

Yellowing: It is the result of diminishing rate of chlorophyll synthesis.

Yield value: Relates to the amount of energy required to start a non-Newtonian liquid moving.

Yield: Weight of food after processing compared to weight before processing.

Z

Zeatin: Naturally occurring cytokinin derived from adenine which plays a role in the growth and development of plants.

Zymurgy: the branch of chemistry concerned biochemical process of fermentation an its practical uses in wine making, brewing, prepration of yeasts etc.

ABBREVIATIONS

ACABC : Agri-Clinics and Agri-Business Centres
AICRP : All India Coordinated Research Programmes
AKIS : Agriculture Knowledge Information System
AMFU : Agro -Meteorological Field Units
AMI : Agriculture Marketing Infrastructure
AOAC : Association of the official Analytical Chemists
AOCS : American Oil Chemists Society
APEDA : Agricultural and Processed Food Export Development Authority
ATIF : Agri-Tech Infrastructure Fund
BIS : Bureau of Indian Standards
BOT : Build, operate and transfer
BTT : Block Technology Team
CAC : Codex Alimentarius Commission.
CACP : Commission for Agricultural Costs and Prices
CCCF : Codex Committee on Contaminants in Foods
CCCPL : Codex Committee on Cereals, Pulses and Legumes
CCFA : Codex Committee on Food Additives
CCFAC : Codex Committee for Food Additives and Contaminants
CCFFV : Codex Committee on Fresh Fruits and Vegetables
CCFH : Codex Committee on Food Hygiene
CCFICS : Codex Committee on Food Import and Export Inspection and Certification Systems
CCFL : Codex Committee on Food Labelling
CCFO : Codex Committee on Fats and Oils
CCFSDU : Codex Committee on Nutrition and Foods for Special Dietary Uses
CCGP : Codex Committee on General Principles
CCI : Cotton Corporation of India (Ministry of Textiles)
CCMAS : Codex Committee on Methods of Analysis and Sampling
CCP : Critical Control Point
CCPFV : Codex Committee on Processed Fruits and Vegetables
CCPR : Codex Committee on Pesticide Residues
CCRVDF : Codex Committee on Residues of Veterinary Drugs in Foods
CCSCH : Codex Committee on Spices and Culinary Herbs
CDM : Clean Development Mechanism
CFR : Code of Federal Regulations
CFSAN : Center for Food Safety and Applied Nutrition
CGDM : General Conference on Weights and Measures
CIP : Cleaned in Place
COP : Clean out of Place
CoS : Committee of Secretaries
CPC : Central Processing Centres
CPCB : Central Pollution Control Board
CWC : Central Warehousing Corporation
CWWG : Crop Weather Watch Group

DFPD : Department of Food and Public Distribution

DMC : Direct Microscopic Count

DMI : Directorate of Marketing & Inspection

DSC : Differential Scanning Calorimetry

EAR : Estimated Average Requirement

EDEG : Entrepreneurship Development and Employment Generation

ELISA : Enzyme Linked Immunosorbent Assay

ESR : Electron Spin Resonance

FAO : Food and Agriculture Organization

FASP : Food Additive Safety Profile

FCI : Food Corporation of India

FCN : Food Contact (Substance) Notification

FCS : Food Contact Substance

FDA : Food and Drug Administration

FIFO : First in First Out

FAK : Fortified Rice Kernels

FSSAI : Food Safety and Standards Authority of India

GAP : Good Agricultural Practices

GHP : Good Hygiene Practices

GMP : Good Manufacturing Practices

GRAS : Generally Recognized As Safe

GVA : Gross Value Added

HACCP : Hazard Analysis Critical Control Points

HMF : Hydroxy Methyl Furfural

ICMSF : International Commission on Microbiological Specifications for Foods.

IDDP : Intensive Dairy Development Programme

IINRG : Indian Institute of Natural Resins and Gums, Ranchi

INM : Integrated Nutrient Management

IPPC : The International Plant Protection Convention.

IPPO : International Plant Protection Organization.

ISO : International Organization for Standardization

JECFA : Joint (FAO/WHO) Expert Committee on Food Additives

JEMNU : Joint Expert Meeting on Nutrition.

JEMRA : Joint Expert Meeting on Microbiological Risk Assessment.

JMPR : Joint Meetings on Pesticide Residues.

LAB : Lactic Acid Bacteria

MAP : Modified Atmosphere Packaging

MBRT : Methylene Blue Reduction Test

MIP : Market intervention price

MMPO : Milk and Milk Product Order

MoFPI : Ministry of Food Processing Industries

MPEDA : Marine Products Export Development Agency

MRL : Maximum Residue Limit

MSNF : Milk Solids Not Fat
NARES : National Agricultural Research and Education System
NBS : Nutrient Based Subsidy
NCCF : National Cooperative Consumers' Federation
NDDB : National Dairy Development Board, Hyderabad
NDP : National Dairy Plan Phase
NDRI : National Dairy Research Institute, Karnal
NFDB : National Fisheries Development Board
NFSA : National Food Security Act
NFSM : National Food Security Mission
NIAM : National Institute of Agriculture Marketing
NLM : National Livestock Mission
NMFP : National Mission on Food Processing
NMOOP : National Mission on Oilseeds and Oil Palm
NMPS : National Mission for Protein Supplements
NPDD : National Programme for Dairy Development
OIE : World Organisation for Animal Health.
OIML : International Organization of Legal Metrology
PFA : Prevention of Food Adulteration
PPC : Primary Processing Centres
PPP : Public private partnership
PSS : Price Support Scheme
RDAs : Recommended Dietary Allowances
RNI : Reference Nutrient Intake
RQ : Respiratory Quotient
SCP : Single Cell Protein
SNF : Solids Not Fat
SOP : Standard Operating Procedure
SPS : Sanitary and Phytosanitary Measures.
SSOP : Sanitation Standard Operating Procedure
SWC : State Warehousing Corporations
T.E. : Triennium Ending
TBT : Technical Barriers to Trade.
TPDS : Targeted Public Distribution System
TQC : Total Quality Control
TQM : Total Quality Management
TSS : Total Soluble Solids
UHT : Ultra High Temperature
WDPSCA : Watershed Development Project in Shifting Cultivation Areas
WDRA : Warehousing Development and Regulatory Authority
WHO : World Health Organization
WPC : Whey Protein Concentration
WTO : World Trade Organization.

INSULIN INDEX AND GLYCEMIC INDEX

The insulin index of a food represents the elevation of the insulin concentration in the blood during the 2-h period after the food is ingested. The insulin index represents a comparison of food portions with equal overall caloric content (250 kcal or 1000 kJ).

The insulin index is based on the body's insulin response to white bread, which has a score of 100%. However, there are still foods that may raise insulin more than white bread, which would result in a score that surpasses 100. For example, potatoes tend to have a score of about 121 while oatmeal can have an insulin index of as low as 40. Some foods that have an insulin index lower than 100 include:

- **Vegetables** – tomatoes, broccoli, carrots, cauliflower, peas, pumpkin, sweet potatoes, spinach, etc.
- **Fruit** – apples, avocados, dates, bananas, grapes, oranges, peaches, pears, watermelon, etc.
- **Nuts and Seeds** – walnuts, peanuts, etc.
- **Protein** – eggs, chicken, pork, ham, beef, white fish, tuna, bass, lamb, etc.
- **Bran and Whole Grains** – oats, barley, couscous, bran, brown rice, rice, etc.
- **Beans and Legumes** – baked beans, kidney beans, chickpeas, lentils, etc.
- **Dairy** – brie, cheese, cottage cheese, milk, butter, yogurt, etc.

The glycemic index (GI) is a type of food-related scale that is used to provide information on how fast your body converts carbohydrates into glucose. It's commonly used as a tool when people are trying to manage their blood sugar levels and is particularly beneficial for those living with diabetes.

The rating system goes from zero to 100 and the lower the GI of a food, the less it impacts your blood glucose. Low GI includes foods that are 55 or lower, medium GI incorporates foods between 56 and 69, and high glycemic index foods are those that have a 70 or above. Foods are rated based on how fast they are digested and thus, how much they affect glucose levels.

The insulin index also takes into account food portions and caloric content, but tends to be more effective at diabetes management than the glycemic index. This is because the insulin index takes into consideration how certain foods affect your blood sugar levels, not just their carbohydrate content. Although many foods along the glycemic index and insulin index are correlated, certain high-protein foods can elicit a response regardless of their lack of carbohydrates.

Insulin Index of a food product represents the elevation of the insulin concentration in the blood during the 2–*h* period after the food is ingested. Insulin index represent a comparison of food portion with equal overall calorie content. (250 Kcal or 1000 KJ)

FSSAI has given millets a full group standards as per FSSAI second amendment Regulations 2023. A govt. statement said that the rules would go in to effect on Sep 1, 2022. FSSAI regulations 2011 covers only a few millets, like jowar, ragi, bajra and amaranth crop with their own standards.

FSSAI has now set up comprehensive group standards for **15 types of millets** with 8 quality parameters such as maximum limits for moisture content, uric acid content, extraneous matter, other edible grains, defects, weevilled grains and immature and shrivelled grains so that good quality standardised millets are available in domestic & global markets.

The group standard is applicable to the following millets

1. Amaranthus (Chaulai or Rajgira)
2. Barnyard Millet (Samakechawal or Sanwa or Jhangora)
3. Brown top (Korale)
4. Buckwheat (Kuttu)
6. Finger Millet (Ragi or Mandua)
7. Fonio (Acha)
8. Foxtail Millet (Kangni or Kakun)
9. Job's tears (Adlay)
10. Kodo Millet
11. Little Millet (Kutki)
12. Pearl Millet (Bajra)
13. Proso Millet (Cheena)
14. Sorghum (Jowar)
15. Teff (Lovegrass).

Oct, 22 Restriction of Glyphosate: Ministry of Agriculture and Farmers Welfare have put restriction on the use of glyphosate and no person shall use Glyphosate except pest control operators.

It's Not A Food

S-Adenosyl-L-Methionine (SAMe) Containing Food Products are banned : FSSAI

The FSSAI has made it abundantly clear the ingredient/ product with S-Adenosyl-L-Methionine (SAMe) is not considered as food. Applications for approval of this compound as a 'Health Supplement/ Food for Special Medical Purpose (FSMP)/ Food for Special Dietary Use (FSDU)' have been rejected/ revoked by the FSSAI.

Nutricereals

Millets are nutri cereals comprising of sorgum, pearl millet, finger millet (Major millets) foxtail, little, kodo, proso and barnyard millet (minor millets). These are one of the oldest foods known to humanity.

Millets are hardy crops with very little requirement for the water and nutrients to survive even under extreme weather conditions.

Most of millet crops are native of India and are popularly known as Nutri- cereals as they provide most of the nutrients required for normal functioning of human body. Millets are classified into Major Millets and Minor Millets based on their grain size. **Millets hold great potential in contributing substantially to food and nutritional security**

Storehouses of Nutrition

Crop/Nutrient	Protein (g)	Fiber (g)	Minerals (g)	Iron (mg)	Calcium (mg)
Pearl millet	10.6	1.3	2.3	16.9	38
Finger millet	7.3	3.6	2.7	3.9	344
Foxtail millet	12.3	8	3.3	2.8	31
Proso millet	12.5	2.2	1.9	0.8	14
Kodo millet	8.3	9	2.6	0.5	27
Little millet	7.7	7.6	1.5	9.3	17
Barnyard millet	11.2	10.1		15.2	11
Rice	6.9	0.2	0.6	0.7	10
Wheat	11.8	1.2	1.5	5.3	41

A Sub-Mission on National Food Security Mission – Nutri Cereals comprising sorghum (Jowar), pearl millet (Bajra), finger millet (Ragi/Mandua) and small millets viz; little millet (Kutki), kodo millet (Kodo), barnyard millet (Sawa/Jhangora), foxtail millet (Kangni/Kakun), proso millet (Cheena) is implemented from the year 2018-19 in 212 districts of 14 states. The North Eastern States, Himachal Pradesh and UT of Jammu & Kashmir and Ladakh have been given flexibility to implement programme on nutri- cereals.

Nutricereal help in rendering health benefits like reduction in blood sugar level (diabetes), blood pressure regulation, cardiovascular and celiac diseases.

UN general assembly declares International Year of Millets 2023.

Index